Lecture Notes in Computer Science 10083

Commenced Publication in 1973
Founding and Former Series Editors:
Gerhard Goos, Juris Hartmanis, and Jan van Leeuwen

More information about this series at http://www.springer.com/series/7407

Borzoo Bonakdarpour · Franck Petit (Eds.)

Stabilization, Safety, and Security of Distributed Systems

18th International Symposium, SSS 2016
Lyon, France, November 7–10, 2016
Proceedings

Springer

Editors
Borzoo Bonakdarpour
McMaster University
Hamilton, ON
Canada

Franck Petit
LIP6, INRIA, UPMC Sorbonne Universities
Paris
France

ISSN 0302-9743 ISSN 1611-3349 (electronic)
Lecture Notes in Computer Science
ISBN 978-3-319-49258-2 ISBN 978-3-319-49259-9 (eBook)
DOI 10.1007/978-3-319-49259-9

Library of Congress Control Number: 2015943848

LNCS Sublibrary: SL1 – Theoretical Computer Science and General Issues

Printed on acid-free paper

This Springer imprint is published by Springer Nature
The registered company is Springer International Publishing AG
The registered company address is: Gewerbestrasse 11, 6330 Cham, Switzerland

Preface

The papers in this volume were presented at the 18th International Symposium on Stabilization, Safety, and Security of Distributed Systems (SSS), held November 8–10, 2016, in Lyon, France.

SSS is an international forum for researchers and practitioners in the design and development of distributed systems with self-* properties: self-stabilizing, self-configuring, self-organizing, self-managing, self-healing, self-optimizing, self-adaptive, self-repairing, self-protecting, etc. They mainly aim to tolerate different kinds of undesirable phenomena without human intervention. Research in distributed systems is now at a crucial point in its evolution, marked by the importance of dynamic systems such as peer-to-peer networks, large-scale wireless sensor networks, mobile ad hoc networks, cloud computing, mobile agent computing, opportunistic networks, and robotic networks. Moreover, new applications with self-* requirements are currently coming up in different fields such as grid and Web services, banking and e-commerce, e-health and robotics, aerospace and avionics, automotive, and industrial process control, among others.

SSS started as the Workshop on Self-Stabilizing Systems (WSS), the first two of which were held in Austin in 1989 and in Las Vegas in 1995. Since 1995, the workshop has been held biennially; it was held in Santa Barbara (1997), Austin (1999), and Lisbon (2001). As interest grew and the community expanded, in 2003, the title of the forum was changed to the Symposium on Self-Stabilizing Systems (SSS). SSS was organized in San Francisco in 2003 and in Barcelona in 2005. As SSS broadened its scope and attracted researchers from other communities, significant changes were made in 2006. It became an annual event, and the name of the conference was changed to the International Symposium on Stabilization, Safety, and Security of Distributed Systems (SSS). From then, SSS conferences were held in Dallas (2006), Paris (2007), Detroit (2008), Lyon (2009), New York (2010), Grenoble (2011), Toronto (2012), Osaka (2013), Paderborn (2014), and Edmonton (2015).

This year the Program Committee was organized into three groups reflecting the major trends related to self-* systems: (a) Self-* and Autonomic Computing, (b) Foundations, and (c) Networks, Multi-Agent Systems, and Mobility.

We received 53 submissions from 30 countries. Each submission was reviewed by at least three Program Committee members with the help of external reviewers. Out of the 53 submitted papers, 23 papers were selected for presentation. The symposium also included nine short papers. Selected papers from the symposium will be published in a special issue of *Theory of Computing Systems* (TOCS) journal. This year, we were very fortunate to have three distinguished invited speakers: Hagit Attiya (Technion, Israel), Joseph Halpern (Cornell University, USA), and Maurice Herlihy (Brown University, USA).

We would like to deeply thank the program vice chairs, Stéphane Devismes, Vijay Garg, Manish Parashar, Yvonne-Anne Pignolet, Sergio Rajsbaum, and Roger Wattenhofer. We sincerely acknowledge the tremendous time and effort that the

Program Committee members have put in for the symposium. We are grateful to the external reviewers for their valuable and insightful comments. We also thank the members of the Steering Committee for their invaluable advice. We gratefully acknowledge the publicity chair, Janna Burman, local organization chair, Eddy Caron, and the Organizing Committee members for their time and invaluable effort that greatly contributed to the success of this symposium. Last but not least, on behalf of the Program Committee, we thank all the authors who submitted their work to SSS.

Finally, the process of paper submission, selection, and compilation of the proceedings was greatly simplified thanks to the strong and friendly interface of the EasyChair system (http://www.easychair.org).

November 2016

Borzoo Bonakdarpour
Franck Petit

Organization

General Chair

Franck Petit	UPMC, Sorbonne Universities, France

Program Chair

Borzoo Bonakdarpour	McMaster University, Canada

Vice Chairs

Track 1: Self-* and Autonomic Computing

Stéphane Devismes	University of Grenoble, France
Manish Parashar	Rutgers University, USA

Track 2: Foundations

Vijay Garg	University of Texas Austin, USA
Sergio Rajsbaum	UNAM, Mexico

Track 3: Networks, Multi-Agent Systems, and Mobility

Yvonne Anne Pignolet	ABB Corporate Research, Switzerland
Roger Wattenhofer	ETH-Zurich, Switzerland

Local Arrangements Chairs

Eddy Caron	ENS de Lyon, LIP, France
Sara Bouchenak	INSA Lyon LIRIS, France

Publicity Committee

Janna Burman (Chair)	University of Paris-Sud, France
Anissa Lamani	Kyushu University, Japan
Fahiyeh Faghih	McMaster University, Canada

Webmasters

Daniel Balouek-Thomert	ENS de Lyon/NewGeneration-SR, LIP, France
Violaine Villebonnet	Inria, LIP, Lyon, France

Program Committee

Self-* and Autonomic Computing

Chairs: Stéphane Devismes and Manish Parashar

Eddy Caron	ENS de Lyon, LIP, France
Abhishek Chandra	University of Minnesota, USA
Sylvie Delaet	Université Paris Sud, LRI, France
Simon Dobson	University of St. Andrews, UK
Swan Dubois	Université Pierre et Marie Curie, LIP6, France
Pascal Felber	University of Neuchatel, Switzerland
Salima Hassas	LIRIS, France
Taisuke Izumi	Nagoya Institute of Technology, Japan
Yoonhee Kim	Sookmyung Women's University, South Korea
Adrian Lebre	Inria, France
David Peleg	Weizmann Institute, Israel
Omer Rana	Cardiff University, UK
Elad Schiller	Chalmers University, Sweden
Alexander Schwarzmann	University of Connecticut, USA
Naveen Sharma	Rochester Institute of Technology, USA
Alan Sill	Texas Tech University, USA
Rafael Tolosana	University of Zaragoza, Spain
Volker Turau	Hamburg University of Technology, Germany
Giuseppe Valetto	Fondazione Bruno Kessler, Italy
Vladimir Vlassov	KTH, Sweden
Yukiko Yamauchi	Kyushu University, Japan
Franco Zambonelli	University of Modena and Reggio Emilia, Italy

Foundations

Chairs: Vijay Garg and Sergio Rajsbaum

Costas Busch	Louisiana State University, USA
Fathiyeh Faghih	McMaster University, Canada
Ylies Falcone	University of Grenoble, France
Panagiota Fatourou	University of Ioannina, Greece
Leszek Gasieniec	University of Liverpool, UK
Danny Hendler	Ben-Gurion University, Israel
Ted Herman	University of Iowa, USA
Prasad Jayanti	Dartmouth College, USA
Kishore Kothapalli	IIIT Hyderabad, India
Evangelos Kranakis	Carleton University, Canada
Fabian Kuhn	University of Freiburg, Germany
Petr Kuznetsov	Telecom ParisTech, France
Hammurabi Mendes	University of Rochester, USA
Neeraj Mittal	University of Texas Dallas, USA
Achour Mostefaoui	University of Nantes, France

David Peleg	Weizmann Institute, Israel
Alper Sen	Bogazici University, Turkey
Josef Widder	TU Vienna, Austria
Philipp Woelfel	University of Calgary, Canada

Networks, Multi-Agent Systems, and Mobility

Chairs: Yvonne Anne Pignolet and Roger Wattenhofer

Lelia Blin	LIP6, France
Michael Borokhovich	AT&T, USA
Shiri Chechik	Tel Aviv University, Israel
Yuval Emek	Technion, Israel
Olga Goussevskaia	UFMG, Brazil
Kim Larsen	Aalborg University, Denmark
Stephan Holzer	MIT, USA
Francis Lau	Hong Kong University, SAR China
Erwan Le Merrer	Technicolor, France
Uwe Nestmann	TU Berlin, Germany
Merav Parter	MIT, USA
Paolo Santi	MIT, USA
Christian Scheideler	University of Paderborn, Germany
Gilles Tredan	LAAS CNRS, France
Masafumi Yamashita	Kyushu University, Japan

Steering Committee

Anish Arora	The Ohio State University, USA
Ajoy K. Datta (*Chair*)	University of Nevada, Las Vegas, USA
Shlomi Dolev	Ben-Gurion University of the Negev, Israel
Sukumar Ghosh	University of Iowa, USA
Mohamed Gouda	National Science Foundation, USA
Ted Herman	University of Iowa, USA
Toshimitsu Masuzawa	Osaka University, Japan
Franck Petit	UPMC, Sorbonne Universities, France
Sébastien Tixeuil	UPMC, Sorbonne Universities, France

Additional Reviewers

Andrew Berns
Wyatt Clements
Hardy Corentin
Alain Cournier
Gianlorenzo D'Angelo
Ajoy K. Datta
Klaus-Tycho Förster
Robert Gmyr
Emmanuel Godard
Shreyas Gokhale
Zhenhua Han
Ladislas Jacobe de Naurois
Christina Kolb
Yavuz Koroglu
Hari Krishnan
Ivan Li

K. Alex Mills
Mikhail Nesterenko
Fukuhito Ooshita
Kenneth Platz
Tobias Prehn
Tsvetomira Radeva
Christina Rickmann
Stefan Schmid
Alexander Setzer
Anthony Simonet
Devan Sohier
Thim Strothmann
Hsin-Hao Su
Cesar A. Uribe
Christoph Wagner
Yong Zhang

Contents

Leader Election in Rings with Bounded Multiplicity (Short Paper)

Karine Altisen[1], Ajoy K. Datta[2], Stéphane Devismes[1], Anaïs Durand[1(✉)], and Lawrence L. Larmore[2]

[1] Université Grenoble Alpes, Grenoble, France
{karine.altisen,stephane.devismes,anais.durand}@imag.fr
[2] UNLV, Las Vegas, USA
{ajoy.datta,lawrence.larmore}@unlv.edu

Abstract. We study leader election in unidirectional rings of homonym processes that have no *a priori* knowledge on the number of processes. We show that message-terminating leader election is impossible for any class of rings $\mathcal{K}_k$ with bounded multiplicity $k \geq 2$. However, we show that process-terminating leader election is possible in the sub-class $\mathcal{U}^* \cap \mathcal{K}_k$, where $\mathcal{U}^*$ is the class of rings which contain a process with a unique label.

1 Introduction

We consider *deterministic leader election in unidirectional rings of homonym processes.* The model of homonym processes [1,3] has been introduced as a generalization of the classical fully identified model. Each process has an identifier, called here *label*, which may not be unique. Let $\mathcal{L}$ be the set of labels present in a system of n processes. Then, $|\mathcal{L}| = 1$ (resp., $|\mathcal{L}| = n$) corresponds to the fully anonymous (resp., fully identified) model.

Related Work. Homonyms have been mainly studied for solving the consensus problem in networks where processes are subjected to Byzantine failures [1]. However, Delporte *et al.* [2] have recently considered the leader election problem in *bidirectional rings* of homonym processes. They have given a necessary and sufficient condition on the number of distinct labels needed to design a leader election algorithm. Precisely, they show that there exists a deterministic solution for *message-terminating* (*i.e.*, processes do not terminate but only a finite number of messages are exchanged) leader election on a bidirectional ring if and only if the number of labels is strictly greater than the greatest proper divisor of n. Assuming this condition, they give two algorithms. The first one is message-terminating and does not assume any further extra knowledge. The second one assumes the processes know n, is process-terminating (*i.e.*, every process eventually halts), and is asymptotically optimal in messages. In [3], Dobrev and Pelc investigate a generalization of the process-terminating leader election in both bidirectional

B. Bonakdarpour and F. Petit (Eds.): SSS 2016, LNCS 10083, pp. 1–6, 2016.
DOI: 10.1007/978-3-319-49259-9_1

and unidirectional rings of homonym processes. In their model, processes *a priori* know a lower bound m and an upper bound M on the (unknown) number of processes n. They propose algorithms that decide whether the election is possible and perform it, if so. They give synchronous algorithms for bidirectional and unidirectional rings working in time $O(M)$ using $O(n \log n)$ messages. They also give an asynchronous algorithm for bidirectional rings that uses $O(nM)$ messages, and show that it is optimal; no time complexity is given.

Contribution. We explore the design of *process-terminating* leader election algorithms in unidirectional rings of homonym processes which, contrary to [2,3], know neither the number of processes n, nor any bound on it. We study two different classes of unidirectional rings with homonym processes, denoted by $\mathcal{U}^*$ and $\mathcal{K}_k$. $\mathcal{U}^*$ is the class of all ring networks in which at least one label is unique. $\mathcal{K}_k$ is the class of all ring networks where no label occurs more than k times, so k is an *upper bound on the multiplicity* of the labels. We prove that there are no message-terminating leader elections for any class $\mathcal{K}_k$ with $k \geq 2$ despite processes know k, since $\mathcal{K}_k$ includes symmetric labeled rings. However, we give a process-terminating leader election algorithm for the sub-class $\mathcal{U}^* \cap \mathcal{K}_k$. Interestingly, there are labeled rings (*e.g.*, a ring of three processes with labels 1, 2, and 2) for which we can solve process-terminating leader election, whereas it cannot be solved in the model of [2,3].

2 Preliminaries

Ring Networks. We assume unidirectional rings of $n \geq 2$ processes, $p_1, \ldots, p_n$, operating in asynchronous message-passing model, where links are FIFO and reliable. p_i can only receive messages from its *left* neighbor, p_{i-1}, and can only send messages to its *right* neighbor, p_{i+1}. Subscripts are modulo n.

We assume that each process p has a *label*, $p.id$; labels may not be distinct. For any label ℓ in the ring R, let $mlty[\ell] = |\{p : p.id = \ell\}|$, the *multiplicity* of ℓ in R. Comparison is the only operator permitted on labels.

Leader Election. An algorithm ALG solves the *message-terminating leader election* problem, noted MT-LE, in a ring network R if every execution of ALG on R satisfies the following conditions:

1. The execution is finite.
2. Each process p has a Boolean variable $p.isLeader$ s.t. when the execution terminates, $L.isLeader$ is TRUE for a unique process (*i.e.*, the leader).
3. Every process p has a variable $p.leader$ s.t. when the execution terminates, $p.leader = L.id$, where L satisfies $L.isLeader$.

An algorithm ALG solves the *process-terminating leader election* problem, noted PT-LE, in a ring network R if it solves MT-LE and satisfies the following additional conditions:

4. *p.isLeader* is initially FALSE and never switched from TRUE to FALSE: each decision of being the leader is irrevocable. Consequently, there should be at most one leader in each configuration.
5. Every process $p \in R$ has a Boolean variable *p.done*, initially FALSE, such that *p.done* is eventually TRUE for all p, indicating that p knows that the leader has been elected. More precisely, once *p.done* becomes TRUE, it will never again become FALSE, *L.isLeader* is equal to TRUE for a unique process L, and *p.leader* is permanently set to *L.id*.
6. Every process p eventually *halts* (local termination decision) after *p.done* becomes TRUE.

Ring Network Classes. An algorithm ALG is MT-LE (resp., PT-LE) *for the class of ring network* $\mathcal{R}$ if ALG solves MT-LE (resp., PT-LE) for every network $R \in \mathcal{R}$. It is important to note that, for ALG to be MT-LE (resp., PT-LE) for a class $\mathcal{R}$, ALG cannot be given any specific information about the network (such as its cardinality) unless that information holds for all members of $\mathcal{R}$, since we require that ALG works for every $R \in \mathcal{R}$ without any change in its code.

We consider two main classes of ring networks. $\mathcal{U}^*$ is the class of all ring networks in which at least one label is unique. $\mathcal{K}_k$ is the class of all ring networks such that no label occurs more than k times, where $k \geq 1$.

3 Impossibility Result

A labeled ring network R is *symmetric* if it has a non-trivial rotational symmetry, *i.e.*, there is some integer $0 < d < n$ such that p_{i+d} and p_i have the same label for all i. In our model, it is straightforward to see that there is no solution to the leader election problem for a symmetric ring. Now, for any $k \geq 2$, $\mathcal{K}_k$ contains symmetric rings. Hence, follows.

Theorem 1. *For any $k \geq 2$, there is no algorithm that solves* MT-LE *for $\mathcal{K}_k$.*

4 Leader Election in $\mathcal{U}^* \cap \mathcal{K}_k$

For any $k \geq 2$, we give the algorithm U_k that solves PT-LE for the class $\mathcal{U}^* \cap \mathcal{K}_k$ (see Table 1). U_k always elects the process of minimum unique label to be the leader, namely the process L such that $L.id = \min\{x : mlty[x] = 1\}$. In U_k, each process p has the following variables.

1. *p.id*, constant of unspecified *label type*, the label of p.
2. *p.init*, Boolean, initially TRUE.
3. *p.active*, Boolean, which indicates that p is *active*. If $\neg$*p.active*, we say p is *passive*. Initially, all processes are active, and when U_k is done, the leader is the only active process. A passive process never becomes active.
4. *p.cnt*, an integer in the range $0 \ldots k+1$. Initially, $p.cnt = 0$. *p.cnt* will give to p a rough estimate of the frequency of its label in the ring.
5. *p.leader*, of label type. When U_k is done, $p.leader = L.id$.

6. *p.isLeader*, Boolean, initially FALSE, follows the problem specification. Eventually, *L.isLeader* becomes *true* and remains *true*, while, for all $p \neq L$, *p.isLeader* remains *false* for the entire execution.
7. *p.done*, Boolean, initially FALSE, follows the problem specification.

U_k uses only one kind of message. Each message is the forwarding of a *token* which is generated at the initialization of the algorithm, and is of the form $\langle x, c\rangle$, where x is the label of the originating process, and c is a *counter*, an integer in the range $0 \ldots k+1$, initially zero.

Table 1. Actions of Process p in Algorithm U_k

	Guard		Action
A1	$p.init$	$\rightarrow$	$\mathbf{send}\langle p.id, 0\rangle$ $p.init \leftarrow$ FALSE
A2	$\neg p.init \wedge \neg p.active \wedge \mathbf{rcv}\langle x, c\rangle \wedge x \neq p.id \wedge c \leq k$	$\rightarrow$	$\mathbf{send}\langle x, c\rangle$
A3	$\neg p.init \wedge p.active \wedge \mathbf{rcv}\langle x, c\rangle \wedge x \neq p.id \wedge$ $(p.cnt = 0 \vee c > p.cnt)$	$\rightarrow$	$\mathbf{send}\langle x, c\rangle$
A4	$\neg p.init \wedge p.active \wedge \mathbf{rcv}\langle x, c\rangle \wedge x \neq p.id \wedge c < p.cnt$	$\rightarrow$	$\mathbf{send}\langle x, c\rangle$ $p.active \leftarrow$ FALSE
A5	$\neg p.init \wedge p.active \wedge \mathbf{rcv}\langle x, c\rangle \wedge x > p.id \wedge c = p.cnt \wedge c \geq 1$	$\rightarrow$	$\mathbf{send}\langle x, c\rangle$
A6	$\neg p.init \wedge p.active \wedge \mathbf{rcv}\langle x, c\rangle \wedge x < p.id \wedge c = p.cnt \wedge c \geq 1$	$\rightarrow$	$\mathbf{send}\langle x, c\rangle$ $p.active \leftarrow$ FALSE
A7	$\neg p.init \wedge \neg p.active \wedge \mathbf{rcv}\langle x, c\rangle \wedge x = p.id$	$\rightarrow$	(nothing)
A8	$\neg p.init \wedge p.active \wedge \mathbf{rcv}\langle x, c\rangle \wedge x = p.id \wedge c = p.cnt \wedge$ $c \leq k-1$	$\rightarrow$	$\mathbf{send}\langle x, c+1\rangle$ $p.cnt \leftarrow c+1$
A9	$\neg p.init \wedge p.active \wedge \mathbf{rcv}\langle x, k\rangle \wedge x = p.id \wedge p.cnt = k$	$\rightarrow$	$\mathbf{send}\langle x, k+1\rangle$ $p.isLeader \leftarrow$ TRUE $p.leader \leftarrow p.id$ $p.done \leftarrow$ TRUE $p.cnt \leftarrow k+1$
A10	$\neg p.init \wedge \neg p.active \wedge \mathbf{rcv}\langle x, k+1\rangle$	$\rightarrow$	$\mathbf{send}\langle x, k+1\rangle$ $p.leader \leftarrow x$ $p.done \leftarrow$ TRUE (halt)
A11	$\neg p.init \wedge p.active \wedge \mathbf{rcv}\langle x, k+1\rangle \wedge x = p.id \wedge p.cnt = k+1$	$\rightarrow$	(halt)

Overview of U_k. The explanation below is illustrated by the example in Fig. 1. The fundamental idea of U_k is that a process becomes passive, *i.e.*, is no more candidate for the election, if it receives a message that proves its label is not unique or is not the smallest unique label. Initially, every process initiates a token with its own label and counter zero (see (a)). No tokens are initiated afterwards. The token continually moves around the ring – every time it is forwarded, its counter and the local counter of the process are incremented if the forwarding process has the same label as the token (*e.g.*, Step (a)$\mapsto$(b)). Thus, if the message

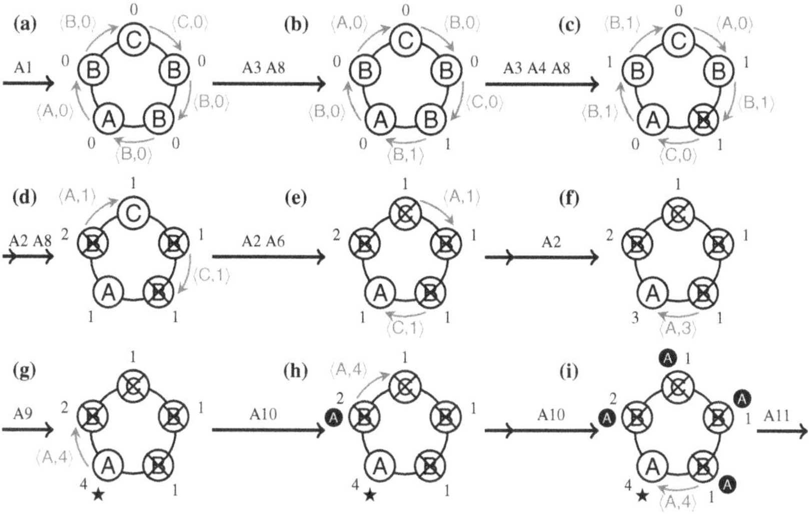

Fig. 1. Extracts from an example of execution of U_k where $k = 3$. The counter of a process is next to the corresponding node. Crossed out nodes are passive. $p.isLeader =$ TRUE if there is a star next to the node. The black bubble contains the elected label.

$\langle x, c \rangle$ is in a channel, that token was initiated by a process whose label is x, and has been forwarded c times by processes whose labels are also x. The token could also have been forwarded any number of times by processes with labels which are not x. Thus, the counter in a message is a rough estimate of the frequency of its label in the ring.

If a process receives a message whose counter is less than $p.cnt$, and $p.cnt \geq 1$, this proves its label is not unique since its counter grows faster than the one of another label. In this case, p executes Action A4 and becomes passive (*e.g.*, Step (b)$\mapsto$(c)). Similarly, if a process p has a unique label but not the smallest one, it will become passive executing Action A6 when p receives a message with the same non-zero counter but a label lower than $p.id$ (*e.g.*, Step (d)$\mapsto$(e)). In both cases, it happens at the latest when the process receives the message $\langle L.id, 1 \rangle$, *i.e.*, before the second time L receives its own token.

So, after the token of L has made two traversals of the ring, it is the only surviving token (the others are consumed by Action A7) and every process but L is passive. The execution continues until the leader L has seen its own label return to it $k + 1$ times, otherwise L cannot be sure that what it has seen is not part of a larger ring instead of several rounds of a small ring. Then, L designates itself as leader by Action A9 (see Step (f)$\mapsto$(g)) and its token does a last traversal of the ring to inform the other processes of its election (*e.g.*, Step (g)$\mapsto$(h)). The execution ends when L receives its token after $k + 2$ traversals (see (i)).

References

1. Delporte-Gallet, C., Fauconnier, H., Guerraoui, R., Kermarrec, A., Ruppert, E., Tran-The, H.: Byzantine agreement with homonyms. Distrib. Comput. **26**(5–6), 321–340 (2013)
2. Delporte-Gallet, C., Fauconnier, H., Tran-The, H.: Leader election in rings with homonyms. In: Networked Systems - 2nd International Conference, NETYS, pp. 9–24 (2014)
3. Dobrev, S., Pelc, A.: Leader election in rings with nonunique labels. Fundam. Inform. **59**(4), 333–347 (2004)

Synchronous Gathering Without Multiplicity Detection: A Certified Algorithm

Thibaut Balabonski[3], Amélie Delga[2,4], Lionel Rieg[1], Sébastien Tixeuil[4,5], and Xavier Urbain[2,3](✉)

[1] Collège de France, 75006 Paris, France
[2] École Nat. Sup. d'Informatique Pour l'Industrie et l'Entreprise (ENSIIE), 91025 Évry, France
[3] LRI, CNRS UMR 8623, Université Paris-Sud, Université Paris-Saclay, Orsay, France
Xavier.Urbain@lri.fr
[4] UPMC Sorbonne Universités, LIP6-CNRS 7606, Paris, France
[5] Institut Universitaire de France, Paris, France

Abstract. In mobile robotic swarms, the gathering problem consists in coordinating all the robots so that in finite time they occupy the same location, not known beforehand. Multiplicity detection refers to the ability to detect that more than one robot can occupy a given position. When the robotic swarm operates synchronously, a well-known result by Cohen and Peleg permits to achieve gathering, provided robots are capable of multiplicity detection.

We present a new algorithm for synchronous gathering, that does *not* assume that robots are capable of multiplicity detection, nor make any other extra assumption. Unlike previous approaches, our proof correctness is certified in the model where the protocol is defined, using the Coq proof assistant.

1 Introduction

Networks of mobile robots have captured the attention of the distributed computing community, as they promise new applications (rescue, exploration, surveillance) in potentially dangerous (and harmful) environments. Since its initial presentation [19], this computing model has grown in popularity[1] and many refinements have been proposed (see [14] for a recent state of the art). From a theoretical point of view, the interest lies in characterising the exact conditions for solving a particular task.

A computing model for mobile robots. In the model we consider, robots operate in Look-Compute-Move cycles. In each cycle a robot "Looks" at its surroundings and obtains (in its own coordinate system) a snapshot containing some information about the locations of all robots. Based on this visual information, the

[1] The 2016 SIROCCO Prize for Innovation in Distributed Computing was awarded to Masafumi Yamashita for this line of work.

B. Bonakdarpour and F. Petit (Eds.): SSS 2016, LNCS 10083, pp. 7–19, 2016.
DOI: 10.1007/978-3-319-49259-9_2

robot "Computes" a destination location (still in its own coordinate system) and then "Moves" towards the computed location. When the robots are oblivious, the computed destination in each cycle depends only on the snapshot obtained in the current cycle (and not on the past history of execution). The snapshots obtained by the robots are not necessarily consistently oriented in any manner.

The execution model significantly impacts the solvability of collaborative tasks. Three different levels of synchronisation have been considered. The strongest model [19] is the fully synchronised (FSYNC) model where each stage of each cycle is performed simultaneously by all robots. On the other hand, the asynchronous model [14] (ASYNC) allows arbitrary delays between the Look, Compute and Move stages and the movement itself may take an arbitrary amount of time, possibly a different amount for each robot. In the semi-synchronous (SSYNC) model [19], which lies somewhere between the two extreme models, time is discretised into rounds and in each round an arbitrary subset of the robots are active. The active robots in a round perform exactly one atomic Look-Compute-Move cycle in that round. It is assumed that the scheduler (seen as an adversary) is fair in the sense that it guarantees that in any configuration, any robot is activated within a finite number of steps.

Furthermore, the scheduler has the ability to stop a robot before it has completed its move, provided the robot has already moved by some positive distance δ. Now, if a robot r wants to move by some distance $d < \delta$, once activated by the scheduler, the scheduler then cannot stop r until it completes its movement. The value of δ is unknown to the robots, and is just meant to prevent the scheduler to make them move by infinitely small distances. These stoppable moves are referred to as *flexible* moves in the remainder of the paper.

The gathering problem. The gathering problem is one of the benchmarking tasks in mobile robot networks, and has received a considerable amount of attention (see [14] and references herein). The gathering task consists in making all robots (considered as dimensionless points in a two dimensional Euclidean space) reach a single point, not known beforehand, in finite time. A foundational result [19] shows that in the SSYNC model, no oblivious deterministic algorithm can solve gathering for two robots[2]. This result can be extended [11] to the bivalent case, that is, when an even number of robots is initially evenly split in exactly two locations. In general, without extra assumptions in the execution model (*e.g.* a common coordinate system, persistent memory, the ability to detect multiple robots at a given location, use of probabilistic variables, etc.), it is impossible to solve gathering [16] for any set of at least two robots in the SSYNC model. As all possible executions in SSYNC are also possible in ASYNC, those impossibilities also hold in ASYNC. Hence, the only possibility to solve gathering without extra assumptions is to consider the FSYNC model.

Cohen and Peleg [9] proposed the *center of gravity* (*a.k.a.* CoG) algorithm (the robots aim for the location that is the barycenter of all observed robot locations) for the purpose of convergence (a weaker requirement than

---

[2] *http://pactole.lri.fr/pub/cffg2d/html/Pactole.Gathering.InR.Impossibility.html.*

gathering, which mandates robots to reach locations that are arbitrarily close to one another) in the SSYNC model. They demonstrate that for the FSYNC model, robots actually solve gathering since they eventually all become closer that δ from the barycenter, and hence all reach it in the next round.

However, the CoG algorithm does not prevent more than one robot to occupy the exact same location before gathering, even if they start from distinct locations. For example, consider two robots r_1 and r_2 aligned toward the barycenter at some round, at distances d_1 and d_2 ($d_1 < d_2$) that are both greater than δ, respectively. Then, the scheduler stops r_1 after δ and r_2 at the same location. Robots r_1 and r_2 now occupy the same location. One immediate consequence of this observation is that in the next round, to compute the barycenter, observing robots must take into account both r_1 and r_2. That is, using the CoG algorithm, robots must make use of *multiplicity detection*, *i.e.* be able to detect how many robots occupy simultaneously a given location.

Overall, the question of gathering feasibility in FSYNC without multiplicity detection (nor any other additional assumption) remained open.

Formal methods for mobile robots. Designing and proving mobile robot protocols is notoriously difficult. Formal methods encompass a long-lasting path of research that is meant to overcome errors of human origin. Not surprisingly, this mechanised approach to protocol correctness was successively used in the context of mobile robots [2,3,5,6,11,13,15,17].

Model-checking proved useful to find bugs in existing literature [3] and assess formally published algorithms [3,13,17], in a simpler setting where robots evolve in a *discrete space* where the number of possible locations is finite. Automatic program synthesis (for the problem of perpetual exclusive exploration in a ring-shaped discrete space) is due to Bonnet *et al.* [5], and can be used to obtain automatically algorithms that are "correct-by-design". The approach was refined by Millet *et al.* [15] for the problem of gathering in a discrete ring network. As all aforementioned approaches are designed for a discrete setting where both the number of locations and the number of robots are known, they cannot be used in the continuous space where the robots locations take values in a set that is not enumerable, and they cannot permit to establish results that are valid for any number of robots.

The use of a mechanical proof assistant like Coq[3] allows for more genericity as this approach is not limited to *particular instances* of algorithms. Recent uses of Coq in Distributed Computing include that of Castéran *et al.* [7], who use Coq and their libray Loco to prove positive and negative results about subclasses of LC systems, and that of Altisen *et al.* [1], who provide a Coq framework to study self-stabilizing algorithms.

Developed for the Coq proof assistant,[4] the Pactole[5] framework enabled the use of high-order logic to certify impossibility results [2] for the problem of

[3] http://coq.inria.fr.

[4] http://coq.inria.fr.

[5] Available at http://pactole.lri.fr.

convergence: for any positive ε, robots are required to reach locations that are at most ε apart. Another classical impossibility result that was certified using the Pactole framework is the impossibility of gathering starting from a bivalent configuration [11]. Recently, positive certified results for SSYNC gathering with multiplicity detection were provided by Courtieu *et al.* [12].

Our contribution. We propose a protocol for oblivious mobile robot gathering in FSYNC that does not require multiplicity detection (nor any other extra assumption). Our protocol, called CoGiL (for Center of Gravity of inhabited Locations), is derived from CoG as follows: robots aim to the barycenter of observed *occupied* locations (that is, without considering how many robots occupy a given location). We also present a proof of correctness for our CoGiL protocol.

Unlike previous approaches, our proof is *certified* in the model where the protocol is defined, using the Coq proof assistant. Throughout this paper, links to the Coq development are italicised in the footnotes. The sources package is available at http://pactole.lri.fr, as well as its online html documentation.

Roadmap. Section 2 describes our formal framework, while our case study is developed in Sect. 3. Section 4 gives some insights about the benefits of our methodology for mobile robot protocol design.

2 A Formal Model to Prove Robot Protocols

To certify results and to guarantee the soundness of theorems, we use Coq, a Curry-Howard-based interactive proof assistant enjoying a trustworthy kernel. The (functional) language of Coq is a very expressive λ-calculus: the *Calculus of Inductive Constructions* (CIC) [10]. In this context, datatypes, objects, algorithms, theorems and proofs can be expressed in a unified way, as terms.

The reader will find in [4] a very comprehensive overview and good practices with reference to Coq. Developing a proof in a proof assistant may nonetheless be tedious, or require expertise from the user. To make this task easier, we are actively developing (under the name Pactole) a formal model, as well as lemmas and theorems, to specify and certify results about networks of autonomous mobile robots. It is designed to be robust and flexible enough to express most of the variety of assumptions in robots network, for example with reference to the considered space: discrete or continuous, bounded or unbounded.

We do not expect the reader to be an expert in Coq but of course the specification of a model for mobile robots in Coq requires some knowledge of the proof assistant. We want to stress that the framework eases the developer's task. The notations and definitions we give hereafter should be simply read as typed functional expressions.

The Pactole model has been sketched in [2,11]; we recall here its main characteristics.

We use two important features of Coq: a formalism of *higher-order* logic to quantify over programs, demons, etc., and the possibility to define *inductive* and *coinductive* types [18] to express inductive and coinductive datatypes and properties. Coinductive types are in particular of invaluable help to express infinite behaviours, infinite datatypes and properties on them, as we shall see with demons.

Robots[6] are anonymous, however we need to identify some of them in the proofs. Thus, we consider given a finite set of *identifiers*, isomorphic to a segment of $\mathbb{N}$. We hereafter omit this set `G` unless it is necessary to characterise the number of robots. Robots are distributed in space, at places called *locations*. We call a *configuration*[7] a *function* from the set of identifiers to the space of locations.

From that definition, there is information about identifiers contained in configurations, notably, equality between configurations does *not* boil down to the equality of the multisets of inhabited locations.

Under the assumption that robots are anonymous and indistinguishable, we have to make sure that the embedded algorithm does not make use of those identifiers.

Spectrum.[8] The computation of any robot's target location is based on the perception they get from their environment, that is, in an FSYNC execution scheme, from a configuration. The result of this observation may be more or less accurate, depending on sensors' capabilities. A robot's perception of a configuration is called a *spectrum*. To allow for different assumptions to be studied, we leave abstract the type *spectrum* (`Spect.t`) and the notion of spectrum of a location. *Robograms*, representing protocols, will then output a location when given a spectrum (instead of a configuration), thus guaranteeing that assumptions over sensors are fulfilled. For instance, the spectrum for anonymous robots with *strong* global multiplicity detection (this capacity refers to the ability to count exactly how many robots occupy any observed location) could be the multiset of inhabited locations. In a setting where robots do not enjoy the detection of multiplicity and just know if a location is inhabited or not, the *set* of inhabited locations is a suitable spectrum.

In the following we will distinguish a *demon* configuration (resp. spectrum), expressed in the global frame of reference, from a *robot* configuration (resp. spectrum), expressed in the robot's own frame of reference. At each step of the distributed protocol the demon configuration and spectrum are transformed (recentered, mirrored, rotated, and scaled) into the considered robots ones before being given as parameters to the robogram. Depending on assumptions, zoom and rotation factors may be constant or chosen by the demon at each step, shared by all robots or not, etc.

Demon for flexible movements. As moves under consideration are *flexible*, robots either reach their goal when it is at most at a certain absolute distance δ, or travel at least δ towards their goal, stopping to an arbitrary location (possibly the computed goal).

---

[6] *http://pactole.lri.fr/pub/cffg2d/html/Pactole.Robots.html#Robots.*

[7] *http://pactole.lri.fr/pub/cffg2d/html/Pactole.Configurations.html#Configuration.*

[8] *http://pactole.lri.fr/pub/cffg2d/html/Pactole.Configurations.html#Spectrum.*

Rounds[9] in this FSYNC setting are thus characterised by each of the oblivious robots getting both its new frame of reference, and the ratio of its actual movement over its computed destination.

We call *demonic action* this operation together with the logical properties ensuring, for example, that new frames of reference make sense, and that the provided ratio belongs to the $[0, 1]$ interval. *Demons* are streams of demonic actions. As such, they are naturally defined in Coq as a coinductive construct. Synchrony constraints (e.g. fairness) may be defined as coinductive properties on demons, as detailed in [2,11].

The Pactole framework provides theorems that state the equivalence between rigid movements models and flexible models when the ratio of actual movement is always 1. Developments in a rigid context may thus be written free of cumbersome irrelevant details.

Robogram. Robograms[10] may be naturally defined in a *completely abstract manner*, without any concrete code, in our Coq model. They consist of an actual algorithm `pgm` that represents the considered protocol and that takes a spectrum as input and returns a location, and a compatibility property `pgm_compat` stating that target locations are the same if equivalent spectra are given (for some equivalence on spectra).

```
Record robogram :=
 {pgm :> Spect.t → Location.t;
 pgm_compat : Proper (Spect.eq ⇒ Location.eq) pgm}.
```

Execution of a round. The actual location of arrival for a robot is determined by the protocol, which computes a local target from the perceived spectrum, and the demon-provided ratio which is applied to the local target to obtain a chosen target. If the distance between the robot's original location and its chosen target is more than δ then the robot stops at the chosen target, otherwise it reaches its protocol-computed destination (local target). This concise way of proceeding ensures that either the protocol-computed destination is reached or at least δ is travelled.

3 Center of Gravity Algorithms

Notations. In the sequel, we denote by: C a configuration, $C(r)$ the location of Robot r in Configuration C, and S_C the global spectrum associated to C.

[9] *http://pactole.lri.fr/pub/cffg2d/html/Pactole.FlexibleFormalism.html.*
[10] *http://pactole.lri.fr/pub/cffg2d/html/Pactole.CommonFormalism.html#Sig.robogram.*

3.1 Center of Gravity Algorithms Variants

Cohen and Peleg [8,9] define the CoG algorithm as depicted in Algorithm 1. A robot simply moves toward the center of gravity of all robots locations. Since robots may occupy the same location in space, the proper calculation of the center of gravity implies that the robots are capable of strong global multiplicity detection: for each inhabited location, the robots can count the number of robots on that location.

Algorithm 1. Protocol CoG (for Robot r in Configuration C)

Move toward the centre of gravity of robot locations $c_{pos} = \frac{1}{|C|} \times \sum_{r \in C} C(r)$

We define the CoGiL algorithm in Algorithm 2. Here, we do not assume that robots are capable of multiplicity detection, so robots simply move toward the center of gravity of inhabited locations. Note that the number of those inhabited locations is not necessarily monotonically decreasing.

Algorithm 2. Protocol CoGiL (for Robot r in Configuration C)

Move toward the centre of gravity of inhabited locations $c_{pos} = \frac{1}{|S_C|} \times \sum_{p \in S_C} p$

Although CoGiL is extremely similar to CoG, proving its correctness is not. For example, Cohen and Peleg [8] first used in the conference version of their paper moments of inertia as a monotonically decreasing measure to prove the convergence of CoG:

$$I(q) = \frac{1}{|C|} \times \sum_{r \in C} ||C(r) - q||^2$$

Expressing this measure with the observed spectrum gives:

$$I(q) = \frac{1}{|S_C|} \times \sum_{p \in S_C} ||p - q||^2$$

Now, without strong global multiplicity detection, it is possible that this measure is *not* monotonically decreasing for c_{pos}. For example, consider four robots in a one-dimension metric space, localised at locations 0; 17; 18; 19.

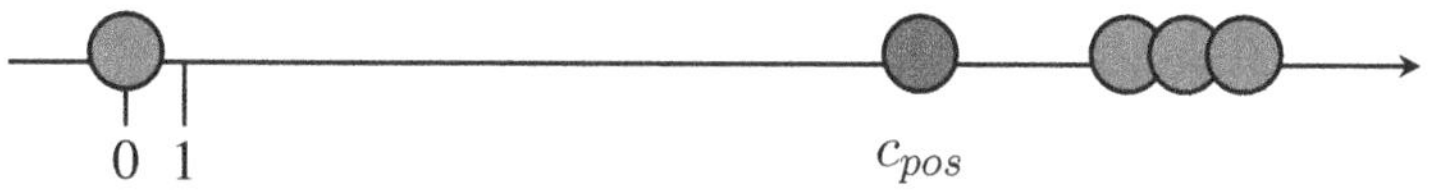

The center of gravity of the inhabited locations c_{pos} is at 13.5 and $I(c_{pos}) =$ 61.25. Now, consider that $\delta = 0.1$. A possible following configuration is that the robot on 0 has moved by δ toward c_{pos} and the others have stopped at location 16.9.

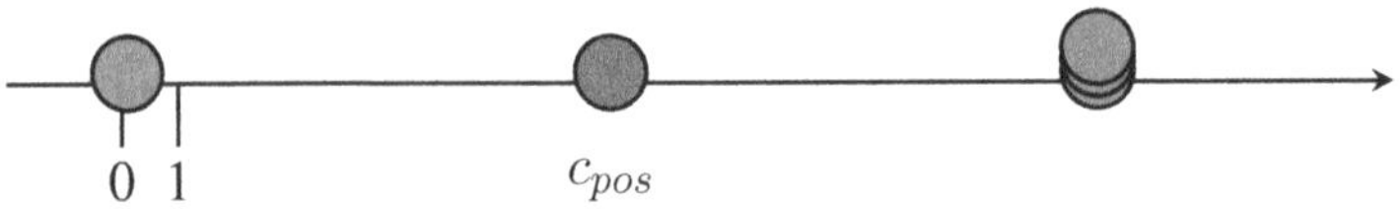

The center of gravity of the inhabited locations c_{pos} is now at 8.5, and $I(c_{pos}) = 70.56$, which is strictly greater than its previous value. So, the proof argument appearing in Cohen and Peleg's conference paper [8] does not extend to the case without global strong multiplicity detection.

Fortunately, the underlying idea of the proof appearing in the journal version of Cohen and Peleg [9] can be extended to the case without multiplicity detection. We thus construct our certified proof along the main arguments of theirs.

3.2 Formalisation, and Key Points to Prove Correctness

Gathering in the context of flexible movements. A way to state Gathering and Convergence has been already described in [2,11]. Those definitions take place in a context where movements are rigid, and thus the specification of what a solution to Gathering is has to be generalised for the case of flexible movements. We name `gathered_at` *pt* the property of a configuration the robots of which are all gathered at[11] the same location *pt*. We say that a location *pt* and an execution enjoy the property `Gather` if all robots are gathered at *pt* for all rounds of the (infinite) execution.

```
Definition Gather (pt: Loc.t) (e : execution) : Prop :=
 Streams.forever (Streams.instant (gathered_at pt)) e.
```

`WillGather` *pt e* means that the (infinite) execution *e* is *eventually* `Gathered` for *pt*. That is: there is a (finitely) reacheable instant in *e* for which *pt* and what remains of *e* fulfils `Gather`.

```
Definition WillGather (pt : Loc.t) (e : execution) : Prop :=
 Streams.eventually (Gather pt) e.
```

We may now characterise that a robogram r is a solution to the Gathering problem for a demon d, in the context of δ-flexible movements.[12] It takes into account the minimal distance of travel δ that is necessary to define the execution.

```
Definition FullSolGathering (r : robogram) (d : demon) δ :=
  ∀ config, ∃ pt : Loc.t, WillGather pt (execute δ r d config).
```

[11] *http://pactole.lri.fr/pub/cffg2d/html/Pactole.Gathering.FlexDefinitions.html#FlexGatheringDefs.gathered_at.*

[12] *http://pactole.lri.fr/pub/cffg2d/html/Pactole.Gathering.FlexDefinitions.html#FlexGatheringDefs.FullSolGathering.*

Expressing the protocol in Pactole. The space of locations is $\mathbb{R}^2$ and its type is `R2.t` in the following. Writing the algorithm is straightforward in our framework, and the Coq implementation is almost exactly an actual robot code. Let `ffgatherR2_pgm` denote the code of the algorithm[13], which takes a spectrum as an input and returns a location, and let `ffgatherR2` denote the robogram, that is the code and its properties (invariance through equivalent spectra).

```
Definition ffgatherR2_pgm (s : Spect.t) : R2.t :=
  let spect := Spect.M.elements s in
    match spect with
      | nil ⇒ (0, 0)                                    (* no robot *)
      | pt :: nil ⇒ pt                                  (* gathered *)
      | _ :: _ :: _ ⇒ barycenter spect
    end.
```

The function computing the barycenter[14] is simply:

```
Definition barycenter (E: list R2.t) : R2.t :=
 1 / (INR (List.length E)) * (List.fold_left R2.add E R2.origin).
```

where `INR` injects a natural number into reals.

The robogram can be expressed in the demon's frame of reference. The input spectrum given to the code above is expressed in the robot's frame of reference (it is a local code). As noticed in [12], we establish explicitly and formally that it is sufficient to reason about the protocol in the frame of reference of the demon. The geometrical concepts in use in the protocol are invariant under the changes of frame that are allowed: scaling, rotation, symmetry and translation, hence we can express the global configuration after one round without making reference to the frames of each robot[15] (Lemma `round_simplify`).

Eventually no-one moves. The main difficulty is to establish that after a finite number of steps, no robot will change its location. This amounts to finding a measure that decreases for a well founded ordering along with the execution.

To this goal, we consider the maximal distance[16] $dm(C)$ between any two robots in a configuration C.

```
Definition measure (conf: Config.t) : ℝ :=
 max_dist_spect (spectrum_of conf).
```

13 *http://pactole.lri.fr/pub/cffg2d/html/Pactole.Gathering.InR2.FSyncFlexNoMultAlgorithm.html#GatheringinR2.ffgatherR2_pgm.*

14 *http://pactole.lri.fr/pub/cffg2d/html/Pactole.Gathering.InR2.R2geometry.html#barycenter.*

15 *http://pactole.lri.fr/pub/cffg2d/html/Pactole.Gathering.InR2.FSyncFlexNoMultAlgorithm.html#GatheringinR2.round_simplify.*

16 *http://pactole.lri.fr/pub/cffg2d/html/Pactole.Gathering.InR2.FSyncFlexNoMultAlgorithm.html#GatheringinR2.max_dist_spect_ex.*

If this distance is less than δ then after one step all robots are gathered and we are done (Theorem round_last_step[17]). If not, we prove that if a configuration C_1 is obtained after one round from a configuration C_0 such that $dm(C_0) > \delta$, then $dm(C_1) \leq dm(C_0) - \delta$. This part is established through Theorem round_lt_config:[18]

```
Theorem round_lt_config: ∀ d conf δ, δ > 0
→ FullySynchronous d
→ δ ≤ measure conf
→ measure (round δ ffgatherR2 (head d) conf) ≤ measure conf - δ.
```

We may then take as a relevant indication for a configuration C the natural number $m(C) = \lceil \frac{dm(C)}{\delta} \rceil$ and define accordingly the ordering we use:

```
Definition lt_config δ x y :=
  (ℤ.to_nat (up(measure x / δ))) < (ℤ.to_nat (up(measure y / δ))).
```

which is well-founded over the naturals.

The crucial step is to prove that for any two inhabited locations p_1 and q_1 in C_1, $\|p_1 - q_1\| \leq dm(C_0) - \delta$. Let us denote by $\mathfrak{b}$ the location of the barycenter of inhabited locations in C_0. As locations p_1 and q_1 are inhabited in C_1, we can assume that some robots P and Q occupying them in C_1 were previously in C_0 at respectively p_0 and q_0. Now let us perform a case analysis on whether $\|p_0 - \mathfrak{b}\|$ and $\|q_0 - \mathfrak{b}\|$ are greater or equal to δ; the only interesting case is the non-degenerate one where both are greater. In this case, P and Q move towards $\mathfrak{b}$, and in particular $p_1 = p_0 + \kappa \times (\mathfrak{b} - p_0)$ and $q_1 = q_0 + \mu \times (\mathfrak{b} - q_0)$ for $\kappa, \mu \in [0, 1]$. Let us suppose $\kappa \leq \mu$ (the other case is symmetrical), then $\|p_1 - q_1\| = \|(p_0 + \kappa \times (\mathfrak{b} - p_0)) - (q_0 + \mu \times (\mathfrak{b} - q_0))\| \leq (1 - \kappa) \times dm(C_0) \leq dm(C_0) - \delta$ by Thales's Basic Proportionality Theorem and since the distance from any robot to $\mathfrak{b}$, the barycenter of locations, is less than or equal to $dm(C_0)$.

This argument can be trusted it as it is formally certified in our mechanical framework.

Robots stay gathered forever. As there is only one phase in the algorithm, the computed target is always the barycenter of the inhabited locations, which is the same for all robots. We need however technical lemmas to complete the final proof. Firstly that when robots are gathered, they will stay forever at the same location, namely:[19]

```
Lemma gathered_at_OK : ∀ δ d conf pt, gathered_at pt conf
 → Gather pt (execute δ ffgatherR2 d conf).
```

[17] *http://pactole.lri.fr/pub/cffg2d/html/Pactole.Gathering.InR2.FSyncFlexNoMultAlgorithm.html#GatheringinR2.round_last_step.*

[18] *http://pactole.lri.fr/pub/cffg2d/html/Pactole.Gathering.InR2.FSyncFlexNoMultAlgorithm.html#GatheringinR2.round_lt_config.*

[19] *http://pactole.lri.fr/pub/cffg2d/html/Pactole.Gathering.InR2.FSyncFlexNoMultAlgorithm.html#GatheringinR2.gathered_at_OK.*

The counterpart is that a robot that is not at the barycenter of inhabited locations will actually move (that is, it will change its location).[20]

```
Lemma not_barycenter_moves: ∀ δ d conf gid, δ > 0
 → FullySynchronous d
 → ¬ R2.eq (conf gid) (barycenter (Spect.M.elements (!! conf)))
 → ¬ R2.eq (round δ ffgatherR2 (Streams.hd d) conf gid)
     (conf gid).
```

We are now ready to tackle the final proof.

The final theorem[21] states that for all positive δ, the robogram `ffgatherR2` is a solution to the gathering problem in FSYNC.

```
Theorem FSGathering_in_R2 : ∀ δ d, δ > 0
 → FullySynchronous d
 → FullSolGathering ffgatherR2 d δ.
```

It is proven via well-founded induction over `lt_config` and by case analysis: if the robots are already gathered or will be gathered at the next step then we are done, else we use `round_lt_config`. That last proof is about 30 lines of Coq.

4 Discussion and Perspectives

We presented the first FSYNC gathering protocol, CoGiL, that does not require robots to be capable of multiplicity detection (nor any other extra assumptions), closing the only remaining open case in Prencipe's set of impossibility results [16]. We advocate that proofs for even small variants of oblivious mobile robot protocols (such a CoGiL, which is a minor variant of Cohen and Peleg's CoG protocol) should be thoroughly checked from the beginning, using mechanised support such as a proof assistant. This methodology enabled the possibility to present a proof for our protocol, whose correctness can be certified.

We want to stress that, even if the actual development of a formal proof remains a difficult task, the *specifications* of properties and protocols in our framework do not require a strong expertise with the Coq proof assistant. As an illustration, many of the specifications appearing in this paper, most notably the specification of the actual protocol, were developed by one of the authors while a M1-level trainee (first year master, Bologna process).

We believe a thorough revision of other results in the context of oblivious mobile robots will lay a solid foundation for further research advances. Thanks to the collaborative effort of the Pactole framework, reuse of previous achievements is facilitated and encouraged.

Acknowledgements. The authors are grateful to the reviewers who provided constructive comments and helped to improve the presentation of this work.

[20] *http://pactole.lri.fr/pub/cffg2d/html/Pactole.Gathering.InR2.FSyncFlexNoMultAlgorithm.html#GatheringinR2.not_barycenter_moves.*

[21] *http://pactole.lri.fr/pub/cffg2d/html/Pactole.Gathering.InR2.FSyncFlexNoMultAlgorithm.html#GatheringinR2.FSGathering_in_R2.*

A Axioms of the Formalisation

In the main file `FSyncFlexNoMultAlgorithm.v`, the last command: `Print Assumptions Gathering_in_R2` shows all the axioms upon which the proof of correctness of our algorithm for gathering in $\mathbb{R}^2$ relies, in total 31 axioms. Here, we break them down. They can be classified in three categories:

- The first category is the axiomatisation of reals numbers from the Coq standard library. It is by far the biggest number of axioms, and they are not listed here.
- The second category is the description of the problem.

```
nG : nat
Hyp_nG : 2 ≤ nG
```

  As one can see, it simply means that our proof is valid for any number `nG` of robots greater than or equal to 2. Notice that with one robot or less, the problem is not interesting (trivially solved).
- The third category contains usual geometric properties that are not part of our library: firstly some properties about barycenters that we think could be provable from its axiomatisation but are currently left as axioms, that the barycenter is unique and the result of the function computing the barycenter is indeed a barycenter:

```
barycenter_n_unique : ∀ (E : list R2.t) (a b : R2.t),
 is_barycenter_n E a→ is_barycenter_n E b→ R2.eq a b

barycenter_n_spec : ∀ E : list R2.t,
 is_barycenter_n E (barycenter E)
```

  Finally that similarities can be expressed with an orthogonal matrix, a zoom factor and a translation. The orthogonal matrix and the scaling factor are combined into two column vectors u and v.

```
similarity_in_R2 : ∀ sim : Sim.t, ∃ u v t : R2.t,
   R2norm u = Sim.zoom sim
 ∧ R2norm v = Sim.zoom sim ∧ perpendicular u v ∧ (∀ pt :
R2.t,
     sim pt = (product u pt * u + product v pt * v + t)ℝ2)
```

References

1. Altisen, K., Corbineau, P., Devismes, S.: A framework for certified self-stabilization. In: Albert, E., Lanese, I. (eds.) FORTE 2016. LNCS, vol. 9688, pp. 36–51. Springer, Heidelberg (2016). doi:10.1007/978-3-319-39570-8_3
2. Auger, C., Bouzid, Z., Courtieu, P., Tixeuil, S., Urbain, X.: Certified impossibility results for byzantine-tolerant mobile robots. In: Higashino, T., Katayama, Y., Masuzawa, T., Potop-Butucaru, M., Yamashita, M. (eds.) SSS 2013. LNCS, vol. 8255, pp. 178–190. Springer, Heidelberg (2013). doi:10.1007/978-3-319-03089-0_13

3. Bérard, B., Lafourcade, P., Millet, L., Potop-Butucaru, M., Thierry-Mieg, Y., Tixeuil, S.: Formal verification of mobile robot protocols. Distributed Computing (2016)
4. Bertot, Y., Castéran, P.: Interactive Theorem Proving and Program Development. Coq'Art: The Calculus of Inductive Constructions. Texts in Theoretical Computer Science. Springer (2004)
5. Bonnet, F., Défago, X., Petit, F., Potop-Butucaru, M., Tixeuil, S.: Discovering and assessing fine-grained metrics in robot networks protocols. In 33rd IEEE International Symposium on Reliable Distributed Systems Workshops, SRDS Workshopps, Nara, Japan, 6–9 October, pp. 50–59. IEEE (2014)
6. Bérard, B., Courtieu, P., Millet, L., Potop-Butucaru, M., Rieg, L., Sznajder, N., Tixeuil, S., Urbain, X.: Formal methods for mobile robots: current results and open problems. Int. J. Inf. Soc. **7**(3), 101–114 (2015). Invited Paper
7. Castéran, P., Filou, V.: Tasks, types and tactics for local computation systems. Stud. Inform. Univ. **9**(1), 39–86 (2011)
8. Cohen, R., Peleg, D.: Robot convergence via center-of-gravity algorithms. In: Královič, R., Sýkora, O. (eds.) SIROCCO 2004. LNCS, vol. 3104, pp. 79–88. Springer, Heidelberg (2004). doi:10.1007/978-3-540-27796-5_8
9. Cohen, R., Peleg, D.: Convergence properties of the gravitational algorithm in asynchronous robot systems. siam j. comput. **34**(6), 1516–1528 (2005)
10. Coquand, T., Paulin, C.: Inductively defined types. In: Martin-Löf, P., Mints, G. (eds.) COLOG 1988. LNCS, vol. 417, pp. 50–66. Springer, Heidelberg (1990). doi:10.1007/3-540-52335-9_47
11. Courtieu, P., Rieg, L., Tixeuil, S., Urbain, X.: Impossibility of gathering, a certification. Inf. Process. Lett. **115**, 447–452 (2015)
12. Courtieu, P., Rieg, L., Tixeuil, S., Urbain, X.: Certified universal gathering in $\mathbb{R}^2$ for oblivious mobile robots. In: Gavoille, C., Ilcinkas, D. (eds.) DISC 2016. LNCS, vol. 9888, pp. 187–200. Springer, Heidelberg (2016). doi:10.1007/978-3-662-53426-7_14
13. Devismes, S., Lamani, A., Petit, F., Raymond, P., Tixeuil, S.: Optimal grid exploration by asynchronous oblivious robots. In: Richa, A.W., Scheideler, C. (eds.) SSS 2012. LNCS, vol. 7596, pp. 64–76. Springer, Heidelberg (2012). doi:10.1007/978-3-642-33536-5_7
14. Flocchini, P., Prencipe, G., Santoro, N.: Distributed Computing by Oblivious Mobile Robots. Synthesis Lectures on Distributed Computing Theory. Morgan & Claypool Publishers (2012)
15. Millet, L., Potop-Butucaru, M., Sznajder, N., Tixeuil, S.: On the synthesis of mobile robots algorithms: the case of ring gatheringD. In: Felber, P., Garg, V. (eds.) SSS 2014. LNCS, vol. 8756, pp. 237–251. Springer, Heidelberg (2014). doi:10.1007/978-3-319-11764-5_17
16. Prencipe, G.: Impossibility of gathering by a set of autonomous mobile robots. Theoret. Comput. Sci. **384**(2–3), 222–231 (2007)
17. Aminof, B., Murano, A., Rubin, S., Zuleger, F.: Verification of asynchronous mobile-robots in partially-known environments. In: Chen, Q., Torroni, P., Villata, S., Hsu, J., Omicini, A. (eds.) PRIMA 2015. LNCS (LNAI), vol. 9387, pp. 185–200. Springer, Heidelberg (2015). doi:10.1007/978-3-319-25524-8_12
18. Sangiorgi, D.: Introduction to Bisimulation and Coinduction. Cambridge University Press (2012)
19. Suzuki, I., Yamashita, M.: Distributed anonymous mobile robots: formation of geometric patterns. SIAM J. Comput. **28**(4), 1347–1363 (1999)

On the Power of Oracle $\Omega?$ for Self-Stabilizing Leader Election in Population Protocols

Joffroy Beauquier[1], Peva Blanchard[2], Janna Burman[1](✉), and Oksana Denysyuk[3]

[1] LRI, Universit Paris-Sud, Orsay, France
{beauquier,burman}@lri.fr
[2] LPD, EPFL, Lausanne, Switzerland
peva.blanchard@epfl.ch
[3] University of Calgary, Calgary, Canada

Abstract. This paper considers the fundamental problem of *self-stabilizing leader election* (*SSLE*) in the model of *population protocols*. In this model an unknown number of asynchronous, anonymous and finite state mobile agents interact in pairs. *SSLE* has been shown to be impossible in this model without additional assumptions. This impossibility can be circumvented for instance by augmenting the system with an *oracle* (an external module providing supplementary information useful to solve a problem). Fischer and Jiang have proposed solutions to *SSLE*, for complete communication graphs and rings, using the oracle $\Omega?$, called the *eventual leader detector*. In this paper, we investigate the power of $\Omega?$ on larger families of graphs. We present two important results.

Our first result states that $\Omega?$ is powerful enough to allow solving *SSLE* over arbitrary communication graphs of bounded degree. Our second result states that, $\Omega?$ is the weakest (in the sense of Chandra, Hadzilacos and Toueg) for solving *SSLE* over rings. We also prove that this result does not extend to all graphs; in particular not to the family of arbitrary graphs of bounded degree.

Keywords: Networks of mobile agents · Population protocols · Self-stabilization · Leader election · Oracles

1 Introduction

There are fundamental problems in distributed computing that are subject to impossibility results. The impossibility can be related to the system asynchrony, limited resources, the presence of failures, their type, or other general conditions. For instance, the consensus problem has been shown to be impossible in asynchronous systems even with only one crash fault [19]. An elegant approach for circumventing the impossibility of consensus is the abstraction known as *failure detectors* introduced by Chandra and Toueg [14]. A failure detector can be viewed as an oracle, which provides to the system nodes a supplementary information about failures allowing to solve a given problem. A fundamental

B. Bonakdarpour and F. Petit (Eds.): SSS 2016, LNCS 10083, pp. 20–35, 2016.
DOI: 10.1007/978-3-319-49259-9_3

issue is to determine the oracle providing the minimum amount of information for solving the problem. Among the different failure detectors proposed to solve consensus in the conventional asynchronous communication model, the *eventual leader elector* Ω, has been proven to be the *weakest* [13]. Informally, that means that it supplies the minimum supplementary information necessary to obtain a solution.

In this work, we consider a very basic communication model called *population protocols*. It has been introduced as a model for large networks of tiny, anonymous and asynchronous mobile agents communicating in pairs [1]. The network has an unbounded but finite population of agents, each with only $O(1)$ states, implying that the size of the population is unknown to the agents. With such minimal assumptions, the impossibility results are not a surprise. For example, consensus is impossible in such a model even without any crash failure [7]. Another impossibility concerns a problem called *self-stabilizing leader election* ($SSLE$), which consists in electing a leader (a distinguishable agent) in a self-stabilizing way. *Self-stabilization* [17] is a framework for dealing with transient state-corrupting faults and can be viewed as allowing the system to start from an arbitrary configuration. In this work, we focus on this fundamental problem $SSLE$ that is shown to be impossible in many different cases [4,5,18].

The eventual leader elector Ω of Chandra and Toueg and other classical failure detectors cannot be used with population protocols, because they assume that the network nodes have unique identifiers, unavailable to anonymous bounded state agents in population protocols. Many other previous oracles, like those proposed for anonymous models (e.g., [10]), cannot be used in population protocols either, e.g., because they assume finite, but unbounded memory depending on the size of the network (see a survey in [7]).

To deal with this issue, Fischer and Jiang introduced a new type of oracle, called the *eventual leader detector* [18] and denoted by $\Omega?$. Instead of electing a leader, like Ω, $\Omega?$ simply reports to each agent an (eventually correct) estimate about whether or not one or more leaders are present in the network (see Sects. 2 and 3.2 for a formal definition). This oracle does not require unique identifiers and has additional drastic differences. One of the important differences is motivated by the self-stabilizing nature of the $SSLE$ problem considered in [18]. While Ω is designed to circumvent impossibility related to crash faults, $\Omega?$ is designed to deal with state-corrupting faults. Thus, while Ω is related to a failure pattern and is independent of the protocol using it, $\Omega?$ interacts with the protocol, providing information related to the system configurations reached during the execution. With $\Omega?$, there is some sort of feedback loop: the outputs of the oracle influence the protocol; and conversely, the protocol influences the outputs of the oracle. Yet, there are some features in common with Ω. Both Ω and $\Omega?$ are unreliable in the sense that $\Omega?$ can make errors, that is, to give false information at some point and at some agents, and is only required to eventually provide correct answers, similarly to Ω. Finally, such weak guarantees allow both Ω and $\Omega?$ to be implemented in practice using timeouts and other features often found in real systems (more details about the implementation of $\Omega?$ can be found in [18]; about Ω, in [14]).

To demonstrate the power of $\Omega?$, [18] gives a *uniform* solution to $SSLE$ using $\Omega?$ in complete communication graphs and rings. Uniform means that the solution is independent of the actual communication graph; the agents only know the graph family to which the graph belongs. Our focus here is on uniform solutions too.[1]

Contribution. In this work, we investigate the power of $\Omega?$. In particular, in Sect. 4, we show that its power exceeds considerably the case of rings and complete graphs (concerned in [18]). In fact, $\Omega?$ is sufficient for solving $SSLE$ on almost all graphs, the only restriction being that the graph must be connected (obvious) and of bounded degree (related to the model requirement of bounded agent states).

In Sect. 5, we show that $SSLE$ allows to implement $\Omega?$ on rings. Coupled with the fact that $\Omega?$ is sufficient for solving $SSLE$ on rings [18], this implies that any oracle strong enough for solving $SSLE$ on rings can be used to implement $\Omega?$ (on rings); i.e. $\Omega?$ is the weakest oracle for solving $SSLE$ on rings.

In contrast with the previous case, we also show that over arbitrary communication graphs of bounded degree (and more generally, over *non-simple* graph families), $SSLE$ is not equivalent to $\Omega?$ (Theorem 2). Intuitively, our results mean that, whereas $SSLE$ and $\Omega?$ are not equivalent over certain families of graphs, this difference disappears on rings due to the strong communication constraints imposed by this topology. Due to the lack of space, some proofs are missing or sketched. All complete proofs appear in [6].

For modeling oracles and problems, and obtaining relations between them, we use the formal framework proposed in [5] and adapted to population protocols (see Sect. 2.2). In this framework, there is no difference between an oracle and a problem, so the relations that we exhibit can equivalently be viewed as relations between oracles or between problems. Note that the framework and our results concern an extremely general class of oracles.

Related Work. Being an important primitive in distributed computing, leader election has been extensively studied in various other models, however much less in population protocols. Because of model differences, previous results do not directly extend to the model considered here. For surveys on these previous results in other models, refer to [4,18]. In the following, we mention only the most relevant works to $SSLE$ in population protocols.

It was shown, e.g. in [2,9], that fast converging population protocols can be designed using an initially provided unique leader. Moreover, many self-stabilizing problems on population protocols become possible given a leader (though together with some additional assumptions, see, e.g., [4,8]). Nevertheless, $SSLE$ is impossible in population protocols over general connected communication graphs [4]. Yet, [4] presents a non-uniform solution for $SSLE$ on rings. A uniform algorithm for rings and complete graphs is proposed in [18], but uses $\Omega?$. Recently, [11] showed that at least n agent states are necessary and

[1] This is in contrast to the non-uniform solutions given to $SSLE$ over rings in [4] that does not use oracles.

sufficient to solve $SSLE$ over a complete communication graph, where n is the population size (unavailable in population protocols). For the enhanced model of *mediated population protocols* (*MPP*) [20], it is shown in [21] that $(2/3)n$ agent states and a single bit memory on every agent pair are sufficient to solve $SSLE$. It is also shown that there is no MPP that solves $SSLE$ with constant agent's state and agent pair's memory size, for arbitrary n. In [12], versions of $SSLE$ are considered assuming $\Omega?$ together with different types of *local fairness* conditions. In the current paper, we consider only *global fairness* (classical for population protocols).

In [5], it is shown that the difficulty in solving $SSLE$ in population protocols comes from the requirement of self-stabilization. Indeed, [5] presents a solution for arbitrary graphs *with a uniform initialization without any oracle*. Then, [5] proposes also a solution for $SSLE$ over arbitrary graphs, but the protocol uses a *much stronger oracle*. This oracle can be viewed as a composition of two copies of $\Omega?$, where one copy is used to control the number of (stationary) leaders and another one to control the number of moving tokens. There, tokens are used for eliminating supplementary leaders. In this paper, we prove that, surprisingly enough, there is no need to control the number of tokens and that a single instance of $\Omega?$ is enough (at least, in the case of bounded degree graphs). Finally, [5] shows that $SSLE$ and $\Omega?$ are not equivalent over *complete* communication graphs. Here, we extend this result to so called *non-simple families* of graphs (Theorem 2).

2 Model and Definitions

2.1 Population Protocol

We use here the definitions of [1,4,18] with some slight adaptations. A *communication graph* is a directed graph $G = (\mathcal{V}, \mathcal{E})$ with n vertices. Each vertex represents a *finite*-state sensing device called an *agent*, and an edge (u, v) indicates the possibility of a communication (interaction) between u and v in which u is the *initiator* and v is the *responder*. The orientation of an edge corresponds to this asymmetry in the communications. In this paper, every graph is weakly connected.

A *population protocol* $\mathcal{A}(\mathcal{Q}, X, Y, Out, \delta)$ consists of a finite state space $\mathcal{Q}$, a finite input alphabet X, a finite output alphabet Y, an output function $Out : \mathcal{Q} \to Y$ and a transition function $\delta : (\mathcal{Q} \times X)^2 \to \mathcal{P}(\mathcal{Q}^2)$ that maps any tuple (q_1, x_1, q_2, x_2) to a non-empty (finite) subset $\delta(q_1, x_1, q_2, x_2)$ in $\mathcal{Q}^2$.[2] A *(transition) rule* of the protocol is a tuple $(q_1, x_1, q_2, x_2, q_1', q_2')$ s.t. $(q_1', q_2') \in \delta(q_1, x_1, q_2, x_2)$ and is denoted by $(q_1, x_1)(q_2, x_2) \to (q_1', q_2')$. The protocol $\mathcal{A}$ is *deterministic* if for every tuple (q_1, x_1, q_2, x_2), the set $\delta(q_1, x_1, q_2, x_2)$ has exactly one element.

[2] The input alphabet can be viewed as the set of possible values given to the agents from the outside environment, like sensed values, output values from another protocol or from an oracle. The output alphabet can be viewed as the set of values that the protocol itself outputs outside. X and Y are both the interface values of the protocol.

A *configuration* is a mapping $C : \mathcal{V} \to \mathcal{Q}$ specifying the states of the agents in the graph, and an *input assignment* is a mapping $\alpha : \mathcal{V} \to X$ specifying the input values of the agents. An *input trace* T is an infinite sequence $T = \alpha_1\alpha_2\ldots$ of input assignments. It is *constant* if $\alpha_1 = \alpha_2 = \ldots$. An input trace can be viewed as the sequence of input values given to the agents from the outside environment.

We now define agents' interactions (called here *actions*) involving the input values. An *action* is a pair $\sigma = (e, r)$ where r is a rule $(q_1, x_1)(q_2, x_2) \to (q'_1, q'_2)$ and $e = (u, v)$ is a directed edge of G, representing a meeting of two interacting agents u and v. Let C, C' be configurations, α be an input assignment, and u, v be distinct agents. We say that σ is *enabled* in (C, α) if $C(u) = q_1, C(v) = q_2$ and $\alpha(u) = x_1, \alpha(v) = x_2$. We say that (C, α) *goes to* C' *via* σ, denoted $(C, \alpha) \xrightarrow{\sigma} C'$, if σ is *enabled* in (C, α), $C'(u) = q'_1, C'(v) = q'_2$ and $C'(w) = C(w)$ for all $w \in \mathcal{V} - \{u, v\}$. In other words, C' is the configuration that results from C by applying the transition rule r to the pair e of two interacting agents. We write $(C, \alpha) \to C'$ when $(C, \alpha) \xrightarrow{\sigma} C'$ for some action σ. Given an input trace $T_{in} = \alpha_0\alpha_1\ldots$, we write $C \xrightarrow{*} C'$ if there is a sequence of configurations $C_0C_1\ldots C_k$ s.t. $C = C_0$, $C' = C_k$ and $(C_i, \alpha_i) \to C_{i+1}$, for all $0 \leq i < k$, and we say that C' is *reachable* from C given the input trace T_{in}.

An *execution* is a sequence of configurations, input assignments and actions $(C_0, \alpha_0, \sigma_0)$ $(C_1, \alpha_1, \sigma_1)\ldots$ such that for each i, $(C_i, \alpha_i) \xrightarrow{\sigma_i} C_{i+1}$. In addition, the sequence satisfies *global fairness* if, for every C, C', α s.t. $(C, \alpha) \to C'$, if $(C, \alpha) = (C_i, \alpha_i)$ for infinitely many i, then $C' = C_j$ for infinitely many j. This definition together with the finite state space assumption, implies that, if in an execution there is an infinitely often reachable configuration, then it is infinitely often reached [3]. Global fairness can be viewed as an attempt to capture the randomization inherent to real systems, without introducing randomization in the model.

The output function $Out : \mathcal{Q} \to Y$ is extended from states to configurations and produces an *output assignment* $Out(C) : \mathcal{V} \to Y$ defined as $Out(C)(v) = Out(C(v))$, given a configuration C. The *output trace* associated to the execution $E = (C_0, \alpha_0, \sigma_0)(C_1, \alpha_1, \sigma_1)\ldots$ is given by the sequence $T_{out} = Out(C_0)Out(C_1)\ldots$. In the sequel, we use the word *trace* for both input and output traces.

2.2 Behaviour, Oracle, Problem and Implementation

The definitions below are adopted from [5] and different from the ones in [4,18]. They are required to obtain a proper framework for defining oracles and establishing relations between them and/or between problems.[3] In particular, this framework is real time independent, which in turn provides self-implementable oracles, in contrast with the traditional failure detectors [15,16]. In short, in this framework, we define a general notion of *behaviour*, which is a relation between input and output traces. A problem and an oracle are defined as behaviours.

[3] In [18], where $\Omega?$ has been introduced, the oracle is defined in a rather informal way.

Then, to compare behaviours, we define a partial order relation using an abstract notion of *implementation* by a population protocol *using* a behaviour.

In the following, a communication graph G is supposed to be fixed and is sometimes implicitly referenced.

A *schedule* is a sequence of edges (representing meetings). An input or an output trace $T = \alpha_0\alpha_1\ldots$ is said to be *compatible* with the schedule $S = (u_0, v_0)(u_1, v_1)\ldots$ if, for every meeting i, for every agent w different from u_i and v_i, $\alpha_i(w) = \alpha_{i+1}(w)$. That is, any two consecutive assignments of a compatible trace can differ only on the values of the two meeting (neighboring) agents. This definition is natural since an agent can only be activated during a meeting, and it makes no sense to allow a change in inputs which cannot be detected by the agents. Note also that the output trace (associated with an execution with a schedule S) is necessarily compatible with S by definition.

A *history* H is a couple (S, T) where S is a schedule and T is a trace compatible with S. Depending on the type of trace, a history can be either an input or an output history. A *behaviour* B over a family of graphs $\mathcal{F}$ is a function that, for a graph $G \in \mathcal{F}$ and a schedule S on G, maps every input history H_{in} with schedule S to a set $B(G, H_{in})$, or simply $B(H_{in})$, of output histories with the same schedule S. The output histories of $B(H_{in})$ are the *legal* output histories of B given H_{in}.

In a natural way, behaviours can be composed in series, parallel, or by self-loop. For instance, in the serial composition, an output trace of a behaviour is the input trace of another one. Formally, consider two behaviours B_1, B_2 over the same family $\mathcal{F}$ of graphs, with input alphabets X_1, X_2 (for the input traces), and output alphabets Y_1, Y_2 (for the output traces). In the following, T_Z denotes a trace with values in Z.

Let S be a schedule on $G \in \mathcal{F}$. If $Y_1 = X_2 = Z$, the *serial composition* $B = B_2 \circ B_1$ is the behaviour over $\mathcal{F}$, with alphabets X_1, Y_2 s.t. $(S, T_{Y_2}) \in B(S, T_{X_1})$ iff there exists a trace T_Z compatible with S, s.t. $(S, T_Z) \in B_1(S, T_{X_1})$ and $(S, T_{Y_2}) \in B_2(S, T_Z)$.

The *parallel composition* $B = B_1 \otimes B_2$ is the behaviour over $\mathcal{F}$, with alphabets $X_1 \times X_2$, $Y_1 \times Y_2$ s.t. $(S, T_{Y_1}, T_{Y_2}) \in B(S, T_{X_1}, T_{X_2})$ iff $(S, T_{Y_1}) \in B_1(S, T_{X_1})$ and $(S, T_{Y_2}) \in B_2(S, T_{X_2})$.

If $X_1 = U \times V$ and $Y_1 = U \times W$, the *self-loop composition* $B = Self_U(B_1)$ *on* U is the behaviour over $\mathcal{F}$, with alphabets V, W, s.t. $(S, T_W) \in B(S, T_V)$ iff there exists a trace T_U compatible with S s.t. $(S, T_U, T_W) \in B_1(S, T_U, T_V)$. As already mentioned, the self-loop composition is necessary to describe the interactions between a protocol and an oracle.

Given a (possibly infinite) set $\mathcal{U}$ of behaviours, a *composition of behaviours in* $\mathcal{U}$ is defined inductively as either a behaviour in the family $\mathcal{U}$, or the parallel, serial or self-loop composition of compositions of behaviours in $\mathcal{U}$.

The behaviour B_2 is called a *sub-behaviour of* B_1 if they are defined over the same family of graphs $\mathcal{F}$, and for every graph $G \in \mathcal{F}$, for every history H on G, $B_2(G, H) \subseteq B_1(G, H)$.

Given a population protocol $\mathcal{A}$ with input alphabet X and output alphabet Y, the *behaviour* $Beh(\mathcal{A})$ *associated to the protocol* $\mathcal{A}$ is the behaviour with input alphabet X, output alphabet Y s.t. $(S, T_Y) \in Beh(\mathcal{A})(S, T_X)$ iff there exists an execution of $\mathcal{A}$ with schedule S, input trace T_X and output trace T_Y.

A *problem* and an *oracle* are simply defined as behaviours. Now, we are ready to define what it means for a protocol $\mathcal{A}$ to implement a behaviour (or solve the problem) B using an oracle O. The population protocol $\mathcal{A}$ *implements the behaviour* B (or *solves the problem* B) using the behaviour O if there exists a composition B^* involving the behaviours O and $Beh(\mathcal{A})$, s.t. B^* is a sub-behaviour of B.

We say that a behaviour B_1 is *weaker* than a behaviour B_2 over a graph family $\mathcal{F}$, denoted by $B_1 \preccurlyeq_{\mathcal{F}} B_2$, if there exists a self-stabilizing[4] population protocol that implements B_1 using B_2 over $\mathcal{F}$. The two behaviours are *equivalent* over $\mathcal{F}$, denoted $B_1 \simeq_{\mathcal{F}} B_2$, if $B_1 \preccurlyeq_{\mathcal{F}} B_2$ and $B_2 \preccurlyeq_{\mathcal{F}} B_1$. In the case where B_2 is a problem and B_1 is an oracle, B_1 is *the weakest* oracle for implementing B_2 over $\mathcal{F}$. The reason is that, because $B_1 \preccurlyeq_{\mathcal{F}} B_2$, *any* oracle that can be used to implement B_2, can be used to implement B_1, and thus, B_1 is weaker than any such oracle.

3 Specific Behaviours

3.1 Eventual Leader Election Behaviour $\mathcal{ELE}$

$\mathcal{ELE}$ is defined with the input alphabet $\{\perp\}$ (i.e., no input) and the output alphabet $\{0, 1\}$ such that, given a graph G and a schedule S on G, a history $(S, T) \in \mathcal{ELE}(S)$ if and only if the output trace T has a constant suffix $T' = \alpha\alpha\alpha\ldots$ and there exists an agent λ such that $\alpha(\lambda) = 1$ and $\alpha(u) = 0$ for every $u \neq \lambda$. In other words, λ is the unique leader. Notice that for all our protocols, there is an implicit output map that maps a state to 1 if it is a leader state, and to 0 otherwise.

In our framework, the problem of Self-Stabilizing Leader Election ($SSLE$) consists in defining a population protocol that solves $\mathcal{ELE}$ using another behaviour (if necessary) and starting from arbitrary initial configurations.

3.2 Oracle $\Omega?$

Informally, $\Omega?$ (introduced in [18]) reports to agents whether or not one or more leaders are present. Thus, it does not distinguish between the presence of one or more leaders in a configuration (of a protocol composed with $\Omega?$).

Formally, $\Omega?$ is simply a relation between input and output traces with binary values. The input and output alphabets are $\{0, 1\}$. Given an assignment α, we denote by $l(\alpha)$ the number of agents that are assigned the value 1 by α. Given a graph G and a schedule S on G, $(S, T_{out}) \in \Omega?(S, T_{in})$ if and only if the

[4] In this paper, we are only interested in comparing oracles as far as self-stabilization is concerned.

following conditions hold for input and output traces T_{in} and T_{out}. If T_{in} has a suffix $\alpha_0\alpha_1\ldots$ such that $\forall i, l(\alpha_i) = 0$, then T_{out} has a suffix during which at each output assignment at least one agent is assigned 0. If T_{in} has a suffix $\alpha_0\alpha_1\ldots$ such that $\forall s, l(\alpha_s) \geq 1$, then T_{out} has a suffix equal to the constant trace where each agent is permanently assigned the value 1. Otherwise, any T_{out} is in $\Omega?(S, T_{in})$.

$\Omega?$ is easy to implement in practice, provided that timeouts are available. Each leader periodically broadcasts a "leader signal". Each agent resets the timer when it receives the signal. If the timeout expires, the agent sets a flag to false, signaling the absence of leader. The flag is reset to true when a "leader signal" is received. In a chaotic environment in which communications are bad or nodes are malfunctioning, the implemented oracle can give incorrect answers, making the system unstable. But, eventually, after the environment has regain its consistency, $\Omega?$ will give a correct information and the system will stabilize.

4 *SSLE* Using $\Omega?$ over Graphs with Bounded Degree

In this section, we show that, for any given integer d, the behaviour $\mathcal{ELE}$ can be implemented in a self-stabilizing way using $\Omega?$ over the family of weakly connected graphs with a degree bounded above by d. Precisely, we present a population protocol $\mathcal{A}_d$ and prove that the behaviour given by the composition $Self(Beh(\mathcal{A}_d) \circ \Omega?)$ is a sub-behaviour of $\mathcal{ELE}$. We first give a solution over the family of *strongly connected* graphs with bounded degree. The transformation of this solution into one over *weakly connected* graphs with bounded degree is formally presented in [6].

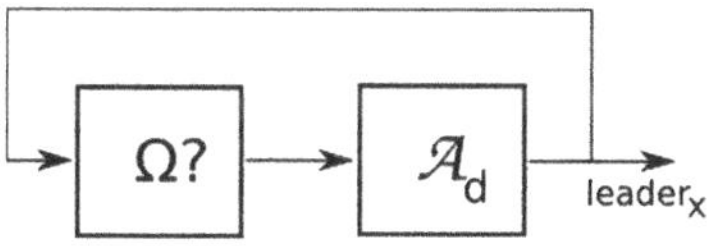

Fig. 1. Serial composition $Beh(\mathcal{A}_d) \circ \Omega?$ followed by a self-loop composition.

We first briefly recall how the Fischer and Jiang's protocol for rings [18] works. As said before, the information given by $\Omega?$ does not allow to distinguish between the presence of a single or more leaders. Thus, a leader should try to eliminate other leaders, while avoiding a scenario where all leaders are eliminated infinitely often (without any help from the oracle). On a ring, a strategy performing this goal is relatively simple to install. Leaders send tokens, circulating on the ring in one direction and send also shields, circulating in the opposite direction. Shields absorb tokens when they meet, but a leader that receives a token is eliminated. When there remains a single leader, it sends a token and a shield (in opposite directions) and the ring structure ensures that the token cannot avoid the shield, so that a unique leader cannot eliminate itself.

The situation is completely different on arbitrary graphs, since tokens and shields can take different routes. This requires a completely different management for a single leader not eliminating itself. As the agents are finite-state, a bounded degree is needed for implementing such a management.

For distinguishing between the different possible routes, each agent has to give different (local) names to its neighbors. For that, we use the 2-hop coloring self-stabilizing population protocol, denoted by $2HC$, proposed in [4]. A 2-hop coloring is a coloring such that all neighbours of the same agent have distinct colors. We denote by $Colors$ the corresponding set (of size $O(d^2)$) of possible colors.

The input variables (read-only) of our protocol $\mathcal{A}_d$ at each agent x are: the *oracle output* $\Omega?_x$ (values in $\{0,1\}$); and the *agent color* c_x (values in $Colors$), which stores the output of $2HC$. The working variables are: the *leader bit* $leader_x$ (values $\{0,1\}$); the *token vector* $token_x$ (vector with values in $\{0,1\}$ indexed by $Colors$); and the *shield vector* $shield_x$ (vector with values in $\{0,1\}$ indexed by $Colors$).

The idea of the protocol is the following. An agent may hold several shields (resp. tokens), each of them waiting to be forwarded to an out-neighbour, from initiator to responder, with associated color, lines 14–18 (resp. in-neighbour, from responder to initiator, lines 7–12). The information required for implementing this is encoded in the shield and token vectors. The purpose of the tokens is to eliminate leaders (line 10), whereas the purpose of the shields is to protect them by absorbing tokens (line 17). A leader is created when the oracle reports that there are no leaders in the system (lines 2, 3). When a leader is created, it comes with (loads) a shield for every color (line 5), and thus is protected from any token that could come from one of its out-neighbors. To maintain the protection, each time an agent receives a shield from its in-neighbor, it reloads shields for every color (line 16). Dually, any time an agent receives a token, it reloads tokens for every color (line 11). In addition, whenever a leader interacts as an initiator, it loads tokens for every color (line 22).

Algorithm 1. Protocol $\mathcal{A}_d$ - initiator x, responder y

1 (Create a leader at x, if needed)
2 **if** $\Omega?_x = 0$ **then**
3     $leader_x \leftarrow 1$
4     $\forall c \in Colors, token_x[c] \leftarrow 1$
5     $\forall c \in Colors, shield_x[c] \leftarrow 1$
6 **end**
7 (Move token from y to x, if any)
8 **if** $token_y[c_x] = 1$ **then**
9   **if** $shield_x[c_y] = 0$ **then**
10         $leader_x \leftarrow 0$
11         $\forall c \in Colors, token_x[c] \leftarrow 1$
12     $token_y[c_x] \leftarrow 0$
13 **end**
14 (Move shield from x to y, if any)
15 **if** $shield_x[c_y] = 1$ **then**
16     $\forall c \in Colors, shield_y[c] \leftarrow 1$
17     $token_y[c_x] \leftarrow 0$
18     $shield_x[c_y] \leftarrow 0$
19 **end**
20 (Load tokens if x is a leader)
21 **if** $leader_x = 1$ **then**
22     $\forall c \in Colors, token_x[c] \leftarrow 1$

Before proving the correctness of the algorithm, we introduce some definitions. A *path* in G is a sequence of agents $\pi = x_0 \ldots x_r$ such that (x_i, x_{i+1}) is a directed edge of G. If $x_0 = x_r$, π is a *loop at* x_0. If u is an agent that appears in π, we denote it by $u \in \pi$, and by $ind_\pi(u)$ the index of the first occurrence of u in π, i.e. the minimum i such that $x_i = u$. If (x, y) is an edge of G, we say that x *has a shield against* y if $shield_x[c_y] = 1$. Similarly, we say that y *has a token against* x if $token_y[c_x] = 1$.

The crucial idea of the proof relies on the notion of *protected leader*. Intuitively, a leader λ is protected if, in any loop at λ, some agent (the protector) protects λ thanks to a shield against its successor, and no agent between λ and the protector has a token against its predecessor.

Definition 1 (Protected Leader). *Consider a loop* $\pi = x_0 \ldots x_{r+1}$ *at a leader* λ $(= x_0 = x_{r+1})$. *We say that* λ *is a* leader protected in π *if there exists* $i \in \{0, \ldots, r\}$ *such that* x_i *has a shield against* x_{i+1} *and, if* $i \geq 1$, x_i *is not a leader and has no token against* x_{i-1}. *In addition, for every* $j \in \{1, \ldots, i-1\}$, x_j *is not a leader, has no shield against* x_{j+1} *and no token against* x_{j-1}. *The agent* x_i *is the* protector of λ in π*; the path* $x_0 \ldots x_i$ *is the* protected zone in π. *The agent* λ *is a* protected leader *if it is protected in every loop at* λ.

Note that a new leader or a leader that receives a shield becomes protected by loading shields for every color.

Given an execution E, S_E denotes the maximum (infinite) suffix of E such that each couple (C, α) (C being a configuration, and α an input assignment) in S_E occurs infinitely often. IRC_E denotes the (finite) set of configurations occurring in S_E, i.e., the set of configurations that occur infinitely often in E. The following lemma constitutes the core of our argument. We give a detailed proof.

Lemma 1. *If* $C \in IRC_E$ *has a protected leader, then every configuration in* IRC_E *has a protected leader.*

Proof. Consider a couple (C, α) that occurs in S_E, C being a configuration (in IRC_E) and α an input assignment. The assumption on the protocol $2HC$ states that α yields a correct 2-hop coloring. Consider a configuration C' that follows the occurrence of (C, α) in S_E. In particular, $(C, \alpha) \to C'$. We note (x, y) be the pair of edges involved (initiator x, responder y).

When a leader is created, it is already protected by itself since it has a shield against every of its out-neighbors. We thus focus on transition rules that do not involve the creation of a leader. Hence, such a transition may eliminate a leader, or move or create shields and tokens.

Let λ be a protected leader in γ and π be any loop at λ. Let μ be the protector of λ in π. If x and y do not appear in the protected zone in π, then after the transition, the states of the agents in the protected zone have not changed and λ is still protected in π. Then, assume that x or y appear in the protected zone. Let $z \in \{x, y\}$ be the agent with the lowest index $ind_\pi(z)$. The previous assumption implies $ind_\pi(z) \leq ind_\pi(\mu)$.

Consider first the case $ind_\pi(z) < ind_\pi(\mu)$. If $z = x$, then z cannot receive a token (from y), i.e., either x has a shield against y or y has no token against x. Otherwise, the path that goes from λ to (the first occurrence of) $z = x$ followed by any path that goes from y to λ yields a loop within which λ is not in protected in C; hence a contradiction. Hence, if $z = x$, after the transition, λ is still protected by μ in π. Now, if $z = y$, y may only receive a shield, and thus, after the transition, λ is still protected in π (by μ or y).

Now, assume that $ind_\pi(z) = ind_\pi(\mu)$. This implies that $z = \mu \in \{x, y\}$, and that every agent in the protected zone, except μ, is different from x and y. If $\mu = y$, then during the transition, μ may only receive a shield (which merges with its shield); hence, λ is still protected by μ in π after the transition. We now focus on the case $\mu = x$. First consider the subcase where y is not the agent that follows the first occurrence of μ in π. Then μ cannot receive a token during the transition, otherwise, the same argument as above shows the existence of a loop at λ within which λ is not protected in C. After the transition, (the first occurrence of) μ still has a shield against the agent right after it, which proves that λ is still protected in π. Consider now the subcase where y is the agent that follows the first occurrence of μ in π. If y is not a leader, then after the transition, y becomes the new protector of λ in π. If y is a leader, then after the transition, λ is no longer protected, but y is protected since the reception of a shield produces shields for every color. In both cases, after the transition, there is a protected leader in C'.

We thus have shown that, in every case, C' contains a protected leader. Given any configuration $C'' \in IRC_E$, there must be a sequence of actions from (C, α) to (C'', α'') during S_E, for some input assignment α''. Since C has a protected leader, the previous argument shows that every configuration in this sequence has a protected leader, in particular C''. Therefore, any configuration in IRC_E has a protected leader. □

Lemma 2. *All configurations in IRC_E have the same number $l \geq 1$ of leaders. In addition, no configuration in IRC_E contains an unprotected leader.*

Proof (Sketch). Full details are presented in [6]. If there is either no leader, then at some point, $\Omega?$ will force the creation of a (protected) leader. If there is always at least one leader, but they are all unprotected, then it means that infinitely often there is a possibility to kill a leader. Global fairness ensures that all the unprotected leaders will eventually be eliminated, which is a contradiction. In all cases, it means that every configuration in IRC_E contains at least one protected leader. In particular, $\Omega?$ will not create new leaders. This implies that, once all unprotected leaders have been killed, there is a constant number of protected leaders. □

Theorem 1. *The protocol $\mathcal{A}_d$ solves the problem $\mathcal{ELE}$ using $\Omega?$ (i.e., $\Omega? \succcurlyeq \mathcal{ELE}$) over strongly connected graphs with degree less than or equal to d.*

Proof (Sketch). See [6] for full details. Any configuration in IRC_E has the same number $l \geq 1$ of (protected) leaders. Assume that $l \geq 2$, consider two protected leaders λ_1, λ_2 and the loop π built from the shortest path from λ_1 to λ_2 followed by the one from λ_2 to λ_1. By moving the protector of λ_1 behind λ_2, and making λ_2 fires a token, it is possible to eliminate λ_1. The global fairness ensures that this eventually happens, which reduces the number l; hence a contradiction. Thus, there is eventually a unique leader. □

5 Is $\Omega?$ the Weakest Oracle for Solving $SSLE$?

Now, we come to the second important result of this paper. The search for weakest oracles, since the weakest failure detector of Chandra and Toueg, has been a constant quest in distributed computing. The weakest oracle, for solving a problem elsewhere impossible, represents the minimum supplementary information needed. As this supplementary information can be provided naturally by the environment, its determination is of great interest for implementing a solution. Our approach here is different from the approach of failure detectors, in the sense that the oracles we consider are in a larger class. Indeed, failure detectors only observe a pattern of failures, whereas oracles like $\Omega?$ are able to react to the output of the protocol. We would like to emphasize the fact that, for dealing with transient failures (state corruptions) an oracle must have access to the states of the agents. It is not a choice that we make, but a necessity. In such a general setting, the issue of the weakest oracle is reduced to the issue of the equivalence of such an oracle with the problem itself. In consequence, we have to prove that $SSLE$ allows to implement this oracle. We answer this issue relatively to different communication topologies.

5.1 An Impossibility Result for Non-Simple Families of Graphs

It turns out that for some graph families, a negative answer (Theorem 2) holds. A somewhat similar result, for the case of complete graphs, has been presented in our previous work [5]. Here we present a more general result that applies to infinite families of graphs, called here *non-simple* (like in [4]). A family $\mathcal{F}$ is non-simple if there exists a graph $G \in \mathcal{F}$, and two disjoint subgraphs G_1, G_2 of G such that $G_1, G_2 \in \mathcal{F}$. Complete and arbitrary graphs of bounded degree are some examples of non-simple families of graphs. In contrast, notable *simple* families of graphs include rings, or, more generally, connected d-regular graphs.

The following theorem states the impossibility of a self-stabilizing implementation of $\Omega?$ using $\mathcal{ELE}$ over any non-simple family of graphs. Coupled with the result of Sect. 4, i.e. $\Omega? \not\succeq \mathcal{ELE}$ over connected arbitrary graphs of bounded degree, we have $\Omega? \succ \mathcal{ELE}$ over the same graph family. Similarly, $\Omega?$ is not the weakest oracle for $SSLE$ over complete graphs, and, by the $SSLE$ protocol of [18], we have $\Omega? \succ \mathcal{ELE}$ over complete graphs. The proof of Theorem 2 uses a classical *partitioning argument* and appears in [6].

Theorem 2. *For any non-simple family of graphs $\mathcal{F}$, there is no self-stabilizing population protocol A implementing $\Omega?$ over $\mathcal{F}$ using the behaviour $\mathcal{ELE}$ (i.e., there is no composition $B = Beh(A) \circ \mathcal{ELE} \subseteq \Omega?$). In particular, $\Omega? \succ \mathcal{ELE}$ over complete graphs and over arbitrary connected graphs of bounded degree.*

5.2 $\Omega?$ Is the Weakest Oracle for *SSLE* over Rings

Now, we show that $\Omega?$ can be implemented in a self-stabilizing way given the behaviour $\mathcal{ELE}$ over *oriented* rings. Note that this is not about detecting the agent selected by $\mathcal{ELE}$ (which would be trivial). Instead, we define a protocol which uses the eventual presence of a distinguishable agent (guaranteed by $\mathcal{ELE}$), hereafter called the *master*, to detect the presence or absence of leaders in the input trace. This implementation is given by the *RingDetector* protocol presented below (see Algorithm 2). This result is straightforward to extend to non-oriented rings thanks to the self-stabilizing ring orientation protocol presented in [4]. The meaning of this result, coupled with the result of Sect. 4, is that $\Omega? \simeq_{rings} \mathcal{ELE}$, when self-stabilization is concerned; i.e., $\Omega?$ is the weakest oracle for solving *SSLE* over rings.

Implementing $\Omega?$ by the *RingDetector* protocol using $\mathcal{ELE}$ (Algorithm 2). The input variables (read-only) at each agent x are: the *master bit* $master_x$ (values in $\{0, 1\}$) that keeps the output of $\mathcal{ELE}$; and the *leader bit* $leader_x$ (values in $\{0, 1\}$), which represents the input of $\Omega?$. The working variables are: the *probe field* $probe_x$ (with values: $\perp$ - no probe, or 0 - white probe, or 1 - black probe); the *token field* (with values: $\perp$ - no token, or 0 - white token, or 1 - black token); the *flag bit* $flag_x$ (with values: 0 - cleared, 1 - raised); and the *output bit* (values in $\{0, 1\}$), which represents the corresponding output of $\Omega?$.

Each time an agent has its leader bit set to 1, it raises its flag (and the flag of the other agent in the interaction) – line 5. A token moves clockwise, and its purpose is to detect a leader (actually, a raised flag) and to report it to the master (lines 18–26). A probe moves counter-clockwise, and its purpose is to report to the master the lack of tokens (lines 7–13). The master loads a white probe each time it is the responder of an interaction (line 2). When a probe meets a token, the probe becomes black (line 10). When two probes meet, they merge into a black probe if one of them was black, and into a white probe otherwise (line 12). The master loads a token colored with its flag only when it receives a white probe (line 17). Each time a token meets an agent with its flag raised, the token becomes black (line 21) and the flag is cleared (line 25). Two meeting tokens merge into a black token if one of them is black, and into a white token otherwise (line 23). When the master receives a token, it whitens the token, and it outputs 0 if the token is white, and 1 otherwise (lines 28–31). In any interaction, the responder copies the output of the initiator, unless the responder is the master (line 33).

Correctness. We use the same notations S_E and IRC_E as in the previous section. By the definition of $\mathcal{ELE}$, a unique agent eventually becomes the master permanently. We focus on the corresponding suffix of the execution (S_E is included in this suffix). Furthermore, we denote by $C(x).token$ (resp. $C(x).probe$, etc.) the value of the variable *token* (*probe*, etc.) in the configuration C at agent x. Similarly, we denote by $\alpha(x).leader$ (resp. $\alpha(x).master$) the value of

Algorithm 2. Protocol $RingDetector$ - initiator x, responder y

1 (if the master is the responder, it creates a white probe)

2 **if** $master_y = 1$ **then** $probe_y \leftarrow 0$

3

4 (raise flags if needed)

5 **if** $leader_x \vee leader_y$ **then** $flag_x \leftarrow flag_y \leftarrow 1$

6

7 (move probe from y to x)

8 **if** $probe_y \neq \bot$ **then**

9 (the probe becomes black when meeting a token)

10 **if** $token_x \neq \bot$ **then** $probe_x \leftarrow 1$

11 otherwise, keeps the same color or merges)

12 **else if** $probe_x \in \{\bot, 0\}$ **then** $probe_x \leftarrow probe_y$

13 $probe_y \leftarrow \bot$

14 **end**

15

16 (if the master receives a white probe, it loads a token)

17 **if** $master_x = 1$ **and** $probe_x = 0$ **then** $token_x \leftarrow flag_x$

18 (move token from x to y)

19 **if** $token_x \neq \bot$ **then**

20 (the token becomes black when meeting a flag)

21 **if** $flag_y = 1$ **then** $token_y \leftarrow 1$

22 (otherwise, keeps the same color or merges)

23 **else if** $token_y \in \{\bot, 0\}$ **then** $token_y \leftarrow token_x$

24 (the flag is cleared)

25 $flag_y \leftarrow 0$

26 $token_x \leftarrow \bot$

27 **end**

28 (if the master receives a token, it changes its output and whitens the token)

29 **if** $master_y = 1$ **and** $token_y \neq \bot$ **then**

30 $out_y \leftarrow token_y$

31 $token_y \leftarrow 0$

32 (a non-master responder copies the output of the initiator)

33 **if** $master_y = 0$ **then** $out_y \leftarrow out_x$

the variable $leader$ (resp. $master$) in the input assignment α at x. The following lemma states that, eventually, a unique token circulates in the ring.

Lemma 3. *In any configuration $C \in IRC_E$, there is exactly one token (white or black) in C, i.e., there exists a unique agent x such that $C(x).token \neq \bot$.*

Proof (Sketch). If there are no tokens, some probe sent by the master will return to the master with the color white (recall that the probes and tokens move in opposite directions). This causes the master to fire a token. Two colliding tokens merge into one. This implies that there will always be at least one token. In particular, all the probes sent by the master will return to the master with the color black; thus no more tokens are created. Moreover, thanks to the global fairness, if there are several tokens, they eventually all merge into a unique token. □

This unique circulating token (from the lemma above) allows to divide the execution into *rounds*. We define a *round* to be a segment of S_E that begins with the token loaded at the master, and ends up right before the token returns to the master. The following lemma describes the output of the master at the end of each round.

Lemma 4. *Consider a round R in S_E. We denote by $(C_0, \alpha_0) \ldots (C_r, \alpha_r)$ the corresponding sequence of configurations and input assignments. Case (a) If there* *are no leaders during R, i.e., for every* $0 \leq i \leq r$, *and every agent* x, *we have* $\alpha_i(x).leader = 0$, *then after the last action of the round, all the agents have their flags cleared (set to zero). Case (b) If there are no leaders during R, and if all the agents have their flags cleared at the beginning of the round, then after the last action of the round, the master outputs* 0 *and all the agents have their flags cleared. Case (c) If there is at least one leader in each assignment during R, i.e., for every* $0 \leq i \leq r$, *there is some agent* x_i *such that* $\alpha_i(x_i).leader = 1$, *then after the last action of the round, the master outputs* 1.

Proof (Sketch). We only prove here the case (c). Full proof details are presented in [6]. Assume that there is a leader in each input assignment. Let μ be an agent that holds a leader in assignment α_0, i.e., $\alpha_0(\mu).leader = 1$. During the round, there must be some i, such that $\mu = v_i$ is the responder and the initiator u_i holds the token. If μ holds a leader in assignment α_i, then after the transition, the token must have turned black. If μ does not hold a leader in assignment α_i, since μ did hold a leader in assignment α_0, there must be some $j < i$ such that $\alpha_j(\mu).leader = 1$ and $\alpha_{j+1}(\mu).leader = 0$. Now, since the input trace is compatible with the schedule, μ must be the initiator u_j or the responder v_j in the transition $(C_j, \alpha_j) \rightarrow C_{j+1}$. Hence, μ must raise its flag, i.e., we have $C_{j+1}(\mu).flag = 1$ $(j + 1 \leq i)$. Recall that there is a unique token, so the flag cannot be cleared during the remaining actions until i. Hence, at i, the token turns black when the token moves from the initiator u_i to the responder $v_i = \mu$. In all cases, the master receives a black token at the end of the round, and thus outputs 1. □

Theorem 3. *The protocol RingDetector is a self-stabilizing implementation of* $\Omega?$ *using* $\mathcal{ELE}$ *(i.e.,* $\mathcal{ELE} \succcurlyeq \Omega?$*) over oriented rings. Moreover,* $\Omega? \simeq_{rings} \mathcal{ELE}$ *(by [18]), and thus* $\Omega?$ *is the weakest oracle for solving* $\mathcal{ELE}$ *over rings.*

Proof (Sketch). Full proof details are presented in [6]. We divide the execution in rounds as defined above. If there are no leader forever, then Lemma 4 ensures that after a finite number of rounds, the master permanently outputs 0. If there is a leader in each input assignment, then Lemma 4 ensures that after a finite number of rounds, the master permanently outputs 1. In both cases, the propagation of the master's output ensures that the output trace of the protocol satisfies the oracle $\Omega?$ conditions (see Sect. 3.2 for its definition). □

References

1. Angluin, D., Aspnes, J., Diamadi, Z., Fischer, M.J., Peralta, R.: Computation in networks of passively mobile finite-state sensors. Distrib. Comput. **18**(4), 235–253 (2006)
2. Angluin, D., Aspnes, J., Eisenstat, D.: Fast computation by population protocols with a leader. Distrib. Comput. **21**(3), 183–199 (2008)
3. Angluin, D., Aspnes, J., Eisenstat, D., Ruppert, E.: The computational power of population protocols. Distrib. Comput. **20**(4), 279–304 (2007)

4. Angluin, D., Aspnes, J., Fischer, M.J., Jiang, H.: Self-stabilizing population protocols. ACM Trans. Auton. Adapt. Syst. **3**(4), 13 (2008). Kindly check and confirm whether the inserted page range for Ref. [4] is correct. Amend if necessary.
5. Beauquier, J., Blanchard, P., Burman, J.: Self-stabilizing leader election in population protocols over arbitrary communication graphs. In: Baldoni, R., Nisse, N., Steen, M. (eds.) OPODIS 2013. LNCS, vol. 8304, pp. 38–52. Springer, Heidelberg (2013). doi:10.1007/978-3-319-03850-6_4
6. Beauquier, J., Blanchard, P., Burman, J., Denysyuk, O.: On the power of oracle omega? for self-stabilizing leader election in population protocols. Technical report, INRIA (2016). http://hal.archives-ouvertes.fr/hal-00839759
7. Beauquier, J., Blanchard, P., Burman, J., Kutten, S.: The weakest Oracle for symmetric consensus in population protocols. In: Bose, P., Gąsieniec, L.A., Römer, K., Wattenhofer, R. (eds.) ALGOSENSORS 2015. LNCS, vol. 9536, pp. 41–56. Springer, Heidelberg (2015). doi:10.1007/978-3-319-28472-9_4
8. Beauquier, J., Burman, J.: Self-stabilizing synchronization in mobile sensor networks with covering. In: Rajaraman, R., Moscibroda, T., Dunkels, A., Scaglione, A. (eds.) DCOSS 2010. LNCS, vol. 6131, pp. 362–378. Springer, Heidelberg (2010). doi:10.1007/978-3-642-13651-1_26
9. Beauquier, J., Burman, J., Clement, J., Kutten, S.: On utilizing speed in networks of mobile agents. In: PODC, pp. 305–314. ACM (2010)
10. Bonnet, F., Raynal, M.: Anonymous asynchronous systems: the case of failure detectors. In: DISC, pp. 206–220 (2010)
11. Cai, S., Izumi, T., Wada, K.: How to prove impossibility under global fairness: on space complexity of self-stabilizing leader election on a population protocol model. Theory Comput. Syst. **50**(3), 433–445 (2012)
12. Canepa, D., Potop-Butucaru, M.G.: Self-stabilizing tiny interaction protocols. In: WRAS, pp. 10:1–10:6 (2010)
13. Chandra, T.D., Hadzilacos, V., Toueg, S.: The weakest failure detector for solving consensus. J. ACM **43**(4), 685–722 (1996)
14. Chandra, T.D., Toueg, S.: Unreliable failure detectors for reliable distributed systems. J. ACM **43**(2), 225–267 (1996)
15. Charron-Bost, B., Hutle, M., Widder, J.: In search of lost time. Inf. Process. Lett. **110**(21), 928–933 (2010)
16. Cornejo, A., Lynch, N.A., Sastry, S.: Asynchronous failure detectors. In: PODC, pp. 243–252 (2012)
17. Dijkstra, E.W.: Self-stabilizing systems in spite of distributed control. Commun. ACM **17**(11), 643–644 (1974)
18. Fischer, M., Jiang, H.: Self-stabilizing leader election in networks of finite-state anonymous agents. In: Shvartsman, M.M.A.A. (ed.) OPODIS 2006. LNCS, vol. 4305, pp. 395–409. Springer, Heidelberg (2006). doi:10.1007/11945529_28
19. Fischer, M.H., Lynch, N.A., Paterson, M.S.: Impossibility of consensus with one faulty process. J. ACM **32**(2), 374–382 (1985)
20. Michail, O., Chatzigiannakis, I., Spirakis, P.G.: Mediated population protocols. Theor. Comput. Sci. **412**(22), 2434–2450 (2011)
21. Mizoguchi, R., Ono, H., Kijima, S., Yamashita, M.: On space complexity of self-stabilizing leader election in mediated population protocol. Distrib. Comput. **25**(6), 451–460 (2012)

Self-stabilizing Byzantine-Tolerant Distributed Replicated State Machine

Alexander Binun[1(✉)], Thierry Coupaye[2], Shlomi Dolev[1(✉)], Mohammed Kassi-Lahlou[2], Marc Lacoste[2], Alex Palesandro[2], Reuven Yagel[1,3], and Leonid Yankulin[4]

[1] Department of Computer Science, Ben-Gurion University of the Negev, Beersheba, Israel
{binun,dolev}@cs.bgu.ac.il
[2] Orange Labs, Lannion, France
[3] Azrieli - Jerusalem College of Engineering, Jerusalem, Israel
[4] Open University of Israel, Ra'anana, Israel

Abstract. Replicated state machine is a fundamental concept used for obtaining fault tolerant distributed computation. Legacy distributed computational architectures (such as Hadoop or Zookeeper) are designed to tolerate crashes of individual machines. Later, Byzantine fault-tolerant Paxos as well as self-stabilizing Paxos were introduced. Here we present for the first time the self-stabilizing Byzantine fault-tolerant version of a distributed replicated machine. It can cope with any adversarial takeover on less than one third of the participating replicas. It also ensures automatic recovery following any transient violation of the system state, in particular after periods in which more than one third of the participants are Byzantine. A prototype of self-stabilizing Byzantine-tolerant replicated Hadoop master node has been implemented. Experiments show that fully distributed recovery of cloud infrastructures against Byzantine faults can be made practical when relying on self-stabilization in local nodes. Thus automated cloud protection against a wide variety of faults and attacks is possible.

1 Introduction

Computing and communication systems are in transition to become a commodity just like electricity, where clients are served by companies that supply state-of-the-art commuting services. Availability and security are the most important aspects in such modern computing systems, i.e., systems that should always be up and operating while protecting the clients' (privacy and) security. Self-stabilization [13] fosters availability and security, capturing the ability of systems to automatically recover following a temporary violation of the assumptions made for the system to work properly. Self-stabilization is a property that every ongoing system should have, as self-stabilizing systems automatically recover from unanticipated states. For example, states that have been reached due to insufficient error detection in messages, changes of bit values in memory [17]

B. Bonakdarpour and F. Petit (Eds.): SSS 2016, LNCS 10083, pp. 36–53, 2016.
DOI: 10.1007/978-3-319-49259-9_4

or any temporary violation in the assumptions made for the system to operate correctly. The approach is comprehensive, rather than the one addressing specific fault scenarios (thus risking missing a scenario that will appear later). In the self-stabilization paradigm the designer considers every arbitrary system state (not necessarily desired or even consistent). Thereafter the designer must prove that from every arbitrary configuration the system execution converges to exhibit the desired behavior.

Thus, self-stabilizing systems do not rely on the consistency of an initial configuration and on the application of correct steps thereafter. In contrast, self-stabilizing systems assume that the consistency can be broken initially or along the execution and the system will need to recover automatically thereafter. The designers assume an arbitrary configuration and prove convergence not because they would like the system to be started in an arbitrary configuration. The reason is that consistency preservation relying on the safety of initial configuration and on the inductive arguments that are based on applying only predefined allowed steps is usually broken. The system must eventually and automatically regain consistency, even if it is lost in the middle of the recovery process. This exhibits safer behavior than that of non-stabilizing systems, namely, initially safe and eventually safe [12].

Security and privacy are the concerns that should be integrated into self-stabilizing systems to mitigate cyber attacks, e.g., [35].

The focus of the paper is self-stabilizing Byzantine fault-tolerant tolerant replicated service which responds to requests from clients. Such services are state-based and therefore will be referred to as *replicated state machines*.

State of the art. Self-stabilizing systems should be constructed over self-stabilizing hardware, otherwise the stabilization of the system may be blocked by, e.g., the fact that the microprocessor is in a halt state [17]. Fortunately, self-stabilizing components can be build by composition. Once the underlying hardware stabilizes a self-stabilizing operating system [28] and a self-stabilizing hypervisor (that copes with attacks of malicious agents) [2,29] yield the self-stabilizing infrastructure.

Despite recent significant advances in applying self-stabilization techniques and concepts to system design (e.g., [7]), industrial prototypes and products incorporating self-stabilization still do not exist. Recently proposed techniques include self-stabilizing hardware and boot programs [18], stabilization preserving compilers [19,34] and high-level approaches facilitating development like the application recovery tool [8], the recovery-oriented computing paradigm [5], and the automatic creation of (stabilizing) programs [6]. A self-stabilizing distributed file system has been implemented [20].

An important aspect that needs to be integrated into self-stabilizing systems is security. One approach in addressing security attacks is to assume that some computing devices (usually the minority) are controlled by an adversary that has taken over their actions. The term *Byzantine*, or *malicious* (device, processor, process, etc.) is used for such components. The design of self-stabilizing systems that copes with Byzantine processes has been investigated in, e.g., [3,21,23–27,29]. In particular, Ostrovsky and Yung [36] introduced the notion of a mobile virus attack (see also [1,14]) where recovering components are attacked again; still, at any given time the number of Byzantine components is restricted by a certain threshold.

Repeated consensus for implementing replicated state machines is one of the core research fields in distributed computing and distributed systems, as it has proven a great abstraction for practical implementations of distributed systems. The capability to tolerate crashes in distributed systems allows us to utilize the redundancy in the system; otherwise, a single crash can block the entire system functionality. Thus, asynchronous consensus, which is always safe and in practice terminates (by the use of failure detector heuristics), has been investigated for decades and serves the industry in implementing robust, highly available replicated state machines based, for example, on Paxos [4,38]. Unfortunately systems are still not robust enough, and companies suffer service breaks due to unavoidable faults, sometimes called *transient faults*. For example, single event upsets cause bits to be changed in memory and may drive the system to an unpredicted state, possibly changing the consensus version counter to its maximal value at once. Thus, there is a great need for automatic recovery from any arbitrary initial state. Such automatic recovery can be achieved by designing the system to be self-stabilizing. Once transient faults cease and the system state is left in an arbitrary state the system converges to the desired behavior by regular execution of the distributed system components of their (hardwired) programs. Another important facet of fault tolerance, beyond crashes and cooperative automatic recovery (where all components execute their code to ensure convergence) is the never stopping (not only passive) malicious behavior of Byzantine components. Byzantine components can be attributed to unpredictable never stopping faults or a compromised component controlled by an adversary. Obviously, the design of a distributed system that copes with Byzantine components controlled by the most powerful malicious adversary will withstand any behavior of these components including non-sophisticated crashes. Thus, when a system tolerates Byzantine faults there is no risk in neglecting a fault that can happen in practice. Clearly only a portion of the system can be constantly Byzantine, otherwise any system behavior is possible. Thus, we are interested in a self-stabilizing replicated state machine that withstands a portion of the components being Byzantine (including those that crashed). In a system that is designed to cope only with Byzantine faults, there is a risk of losing consistency when the non-Byzantine portions experience short-time transient faults (say due to an electricity spike). The consistency of self-stabilizing systems is not built on the consistency of the initial state and induction over the execution of the (long sequence of) allowed steps. In the (possibly years of) execution, a self-stabilizing system rebuilds the consistency while executing seamless consistency maintenance steps. They are considered as a (fortune) side effect of steps executed during regular execution. This occurs while exhibiting the desired behavior when no transient fault occurs and after convergence from an illegal state.

We present the first self-stabilizing Byzantine replicated state machine for semi-synchronous settings [11,27].

For any system, especially a distributed one, anti-attack protection measures have been viewed as endless series of steps where each new counter-measure is introduced to mitigate an upcoming attack or failure, until the next unexpected event occurs. This is particularly the case for dependability of cloud systems which are becoming the infrastructure used by many mission critical software systems. Security and safety concerns impact core cloud features. For example, the expectations from resource sharing, elasticity, or virtualization can grow deeper and broader to an initially unsuspecting researcher or engineer. What if threats and failures were evolving faster than defense mechanisms? What if stacking so many counter-measures mechanisms was simply not fast enough? We take the approach to admit that faults or attacks will occur no matter what. Instead, emphasis should be placed on a combination of attack mitigation and graceful automatic recover. These measures should follow overwhelming (possibly zero-day) attacks that derive the system to inconsistent state.

The combination of self-stabilization with Byzantine fault tolerance should become the standard property for cloud infrastructures, especially for the cloud management replicated state machine (e.g., Chubby, Zookeeper, Hadoop). Such a robust design is enabled by the algorithms and architecture presented here. How to build such clouds? We leverage on the previous research addressing the single host layer, in the hypervisor [2]. The stabilization of a single machine in the distributed system is based on the hardware watchdog (see [18] and the references therein) that bootstrap larger and larger tiers of monitors and consistency establishments. Thus, when a single participant loses its consistency the participant will automatically regain the consistency. Still one would like to avoid using the self-stabilization property as the sole mean for mitigating attacks. This is because self-stabilization requires (sometimes expensive) recovery period in which the system is not operating as it should. Moreover, allowing the attackers to drive the machine into an arbitrary inconsistent state may imply the loss of the memorized state and a transition to a consistent state (even default or initial consistent state) that may not be correlated to the operations done in the past. Thus, we advocate the use of any known mitigation tool to obtain *super-secure-stabilization* design (as in [2]), where only zero-day or overwhelming attacks as well as transient faults, imply the need for the self-stabilization convergence fall-back. This is similar to the case when super-stabilizing Byzantine fault-tolerant algorithms do not ignore communication graph dynamic changes but try to address them to avoid stabilization convergence.

Once participants are designed to be super-secure-stabilizing we turn to the core coordination entity of data-centers and clouds that is based on implementing replicated state machine. Replicated state machine exploit the distributed architecture to overcome the possibility of a single point of failure in the critical mission entity of the system. Variants of Paxos [32,33] are used in practice to implement the replicated state machine. We present for the first time a self-stabilizing Byzantine tolerant replicated state machine. The design allows less than one third of the participants to be malicious (Byzantine). Thus, even if at any given time less than one third participants are in an inconsistent state or are recovering the system continues to operate as required.

Elaboration on the self-stabilizing techniques. The local state of each node or host is periodically monitored and updated by the *stabilization manager* instance running at the host, partly at the bios level. It enforces self-stabilization on the local hypervisor. In [2] we presented the architecture for a self-stabilizing hypervisor which is able to recover itself in the presence of Byzantine faults regardless of the state it is currently in.

Active monitoring. We assume that consistency may be lost due to overwhelming zero-day attacks or transient faults as in [40]. Thus, the state of each machine in the system should always be refreshed to reflect the reality. For example, assume the replicated state machine managing the data-center maintains the list of the active (slave) machines and the jobs they were assigned to. It is possible, that after an overwhelming attack or transient fault the replicated state machine will converge to an internally consistent state of the replicated state machine, with a totally different data on the slaves and their assigned jobs with relation to the actual situation of the slaves. Thus, replicated state machines are always suspicious concerning their records and actively check with the slaves the actual situation and refresh their memory accordingly. In other words, periodically verifying the state held by each participant by repeatedly querying and examining the source for the data, refreshing the data to gain global consistency by distributed independent updates. In the worst case scenarios in which update synchronization races are possible, the need for active monitoring may imply the need to use global distributed snapshots and assignment of a consistent distributed state.

Super-Secure-Stabilization. The obvious advantage of the self-stabilization approach is that the details of an attack (e.g. who attacks, the attack surface) are completely ignored. Self-stabilization ensures a system always converges to a consistent state from an inconsistent one, no matter how the latter was reached or looks like. Thus, self-stabilizing systems do not risk ignoring a scenario or coping with a yet unknown possible scenario, while addressing all scenarios in an holistic fashion. The convergence procedure might be very inefficient and sometimes disastrous: for example a system moves towards the entire reboot, discarding very sensitive data that was accumulated so far (and could be still saved). If we knew some attack details, we could offer a more efficient rescue plan and save our data. To put it another way, as a first step a system tries to mitigate attacks and perform local state modifications, fixing the damage caused by a known kind of attack. The "local repair" approach is the cornerstone of the super-stabilization approach as in [22]. This approach requires that the repair process meets some weak minimal security requirement (expressed by the so-called "safe passage predicate") should still be met during the repair process. In our case the passage predicate incorporates security requirements so we developed the super-secure-stabilization approach. It employs known attack mitigation tools (e.g., anti-virus) to avoid the need for the self-stabilization fallback. If a passage predicate is not satisfied (in a certain number of computation steps) we resort to the classic self-stabilization approach.

Agreement in the presence of Byzantine behavior. Individual nodes might be conquered by malware and then deliberately obstruct the distributed system functionality. Thus the latter exposes Byzantine behavior - at least for a while, before recovering. Loopholes in the cloud software may ease the process of conquering nodes. For example, an OpenStack controller node may be taken over by malware and expose Byzantine behavior, obstructing the entire Hadoop master node behavior; the latter becomes a single point of failure. To address the problem we replicate every service that runs at the controller node. Then we deploy a Byzantine fault-tolerant self-stabilizing replicated state machine algorithm to ensure that the service state is consistent. The system state is periodically agreed upon and updated according to the (agreed upon) arriving inputs following the previous clock pulse. The clock pulse is generated by a self-stabilizing and Byzantine fault-tolerant clock synchronization algorithm. In our implementation we used the first such algorithm suggested in [27][1].

The rest of the paper is organized as follows, Sect. 2 discusses briefly related works. Section 3 contains system settings, Sect. 4 details the BFT Consensus algorithm and a sketch of proof, Sect. 5 discusses various aspects of the prototype, and Sect. 6 concludes.

2 Related Work

The basic Byzantine consensus protocol was presented by [38], where it was shown that in a synchronous system with maximum f Byzantine processes, $3f+1$ processes are needed to solve the Byzantine consensus problem. The celebrated classic example of practical Byzantine agreement appears in [11]. Recently, BFT-SMaRT [10] uses authenticated Byzantine agreement (through signatures based on private/public-key) to avoid a Byzantine participant claiming this is the vote of another participant as a participant cannot sign the vote on behalf of the another participant. We note that any replica might become Byzantine at any time. In practice we assume that the set of Byzantine replicas is fixed between two consecutive pulses generated by the self-stabilizing and BFT-tolerant clock synchronization algorithm [27]. The set of Byzantine replicas can be seamlessly changed if the new non-Byzantine replicas participate in a consensus where they

[1] The number of participants in the replicated state machine is typically small $n = 3f + 1 = 4$, allowing quarter of the system to expose Byzantine behavior as the benefit of a larger system is bounded by tolerating one third of the participants being Byzantine (when approaching infinite number of participants). Moreover, the algorithm already proved itself in real practical systems. See [30] where it is stated that: "I used the entire paper a few years ago to design some middleware", "The article is 19 pages long, very readable, and, as mentioned above, was used to create real software". Subsequently, more complicated solutions to implement can be found in [16] and the references therein.

are updated with the previous agreed upon state before non-Byzantine replicas become Byzantine. In [10] the replica that becomes Byzantine holds a private key that may be used for future malicious purposes or even be passed to an outside adversary, nullifying the benefit of the encryption.

In our solution every clock pulse repeatedly trigers a totally new instance of Byzantine agreement. We use Exponential Information Gathering (EIG) [31] to obtain Byzantine agreement.

Paxos [32,33] is commonly used in replicated state machine infrastructures. One legacy implementation is Zookeeper [37] which tolerates crashes of participating machines. Recently, Byzantine tolerant Paxos as well as self-stabilizing Paxos and replicated state machine implementations were presented [4,15].

While implementing our algorithms we used OpenStack [45] which is an open source platform for cloud computing. We also used Hadoop [44] which is a platform for carrying out distributed computations. Some of our implementations used an open source container platform Docker [42] that is capable to simulate the cloud settings through its lightweight virtual machines.

3 System Settings

We use the standard settings of semi-synchronous distributed system [27] (Sects. 2 and 4). The state of a *processor* (node or machine) is the content of the CPU memory including the program counter. Processors communicate by exchanging messages. A *configuration* c is a vector of the states of the n processors in the system and a FIFO-queue of messages between any two (connected) processors. The queue consists an ordered set of messages that were sent from one processor to its neighbor and not yet received, the order reflects the time at which the messages were sent. An *execution* is an alternating sequence of configurations and events $c_0, e_1, c_1, e_2 \cdots$. In a semi-synchronous execution, events happen in real time, taking one configuration to the next by the execution of input output operations (including inputs from the independent local physical clock) and local state transition (local computation). There are two types of events, one is a tick from some processor's physical clock, which happen every 1 to $1 + \epsilon$ time units as assumed in [27]. In the state transition, the processor may or may not receive a message. There are globally known lower and upper bounds on the time delivery of a message. A message sent at a given time will be received within the time range between the lower bound of message delivery and the upper bound of message delivery. There is a set of f, $n > 3f$, Byzantine processors. We allow Byzantine processors to send spontaneously any message at any given time. A state transition of a non-Byzantine processor obeys its transition function.

We assume that a typical cloud system is composed of a set of processors connected by an eventually reliable network. Each processor runs a stack consisting of a BIOS and of an operating system (that possibly includes a virtualization layer and user mode programs, as in the local case [2]). Each node contains the stabilization manager that ensures its own correctness.

Malicious and transient faults can lead to corruption of all node memory including code and data, except from the read only memory chips. An example is a faulty or compromised machine that tries to attack the rest of the system or to affect a proper resource allocation, e.g., by sending malicious request allocation messages.

4 Self-Stabilizing Byzantine Tolerant Replicated State Machine

In our settings a *client* process sends requests to a *master* process which runs the replicated state machine algorithm. The replicated state machine implemented in a distributed fashion acts as a (coordinated) single master entity that assigns the task of processing requests to *slaves* in the data-center. The agreed state is sent to the slave processes conducting certain computation accordingly. Slaves report on the result to the replicated state machine, which in turn sends the outcome to the requesting client (after updating the replicated state machine that contains a map of the tasks assigned to slaves). See more details in Sect. 5 and the figures within, detailing the Hadoop prototype. The BFT Consensus algorithm is operated by replicated master processes on $n = 3f + 1$ replicas $\langle r_1, r_2 \ldots r_n \rangle$ where f is the maximum number of Byzantine replicas. Each replica maintains its own copy of the state machine and the history of messages that were received from client and slave processes. We say that replicas are *in consensus* when:

- All non-Byzantine replicas agree on the same state S of the replicated state machine, and
- Histories of all non-Byzantine replicas contain the messages recently sent by each active client/slave where "active client" is the one that runs an infinite message sending loop. The history may also include arbitrary messages of inactive clients/slaves.

Replicas use a self-stabilizing BFT clock [27] to synchronously start executing the consensus algorithm. Upon receiving a pulse from a BFT clock each replica begins exchanging the (recent) message history of the replica with all other replicas. Then it collects histories sent by other replicas until all histories received or timeout happens. This exchange may yield a subset of the histories because some of the sent histories may be lost, may not arrive in a predefined time or may not be sent at all due to Byzantine behavior. Eventually each replica has a set of messages that includes the messages from its own history and the messages it received from other replicas. Next we use the Exponential Information Gathering (EIG) that implements a Leader-Less Byzantine Fault Tolerant algorithm (LLBFT) (see a similar use of EIG in the implementation in [9]) over the state S of the replicated state machine. Then another n instances of the LLBFT algorithm are invoked, one instance for a history of every of the n participants. These n LLBFT invocations are used to obtain an identical vector of histories, one for each replica, held by all non-Byzantine participants. To put it another way, every non-Byzantine replica holds a vector of message histories that is the same among all non-Byzantine replicas. Note that this vector may include duplicated messages. We will address this issue in the next paragraph. The algorithm denotes by H_i the history of messages maintained in replica r_i before the start of the algorithm. S_i denotes the state S of the replicated state machine maintained by replica i. We use $\mathcal{H}$ to denote a vector of all messages from histories of all replicas that were collected during the recent execution of the algorithm.

---

1 **upon a clock pulse**
2 $\quad \mathcal{H} \leftarrow \emptyset$
3 $\quad$ send H_i to all replicas
4 $\quad$ **while** {*not timeout*} **do**
5 $\quad\quad \mathcal{H}[j] \leftarrow$ **receive** H_j where $j \in [1..n]$
6 $\quad S_i \leftarrow$ **execute *LLBFT*** on S_i
7 $\quad$ **foreach** $\{j \in [1..n]\}$ **do**
8 $\quad\quad \mathcal{H}[j] \leftarrow$ **execute *LLBFT*** on $\mathcal{H}[j]$
9 $\quad$ **apply** $\mathcal{H}$ over S_i
10 $\quad$ renew accumulating additional inputs to H_i

Fig. 1. BFT consensus pseudocode for replica i

Sketch of proof. By the self-stabilizing property of the BFT clock synchronization algorithm, all non-Byzantine participants start the algorithm in Fig. 1 every Δ time, and finish the execution prior to the trigger of the next pulse in any non-Byzantine participants. After Line 5, $\mathcal{H}[j]$ stores the same message history H_j of any non-Byzantine replica j. At Line 6 consensus on current state S is reached among all valid replicas as a property of the LLBFT algorithm, meaning at least $2f+1$ replicas share the same state. For the same reason consensus is reached in Lines 7–8 regarding $\mathcal{H}$, whether the messages in it belong to Byzantine replica or not. Thus, when the last non-Byzantine participants executes Line 8 (prior to the next pulse trigger at any non-Byzantine replica) it holds that all non-Byzantine replicas have the same value for the agreed upon state S of the replicated state machine. Moreover, after executing Lines 7–8, they also have an identical vector of histories $\mathcal{H}$ - no matter if the history belongs to a non-Byzantine participant or to a Byzantine participant. In the first case, when the history belongs to a non-Byzantine participant NP the agreed history is identical to the history NP broadcasts in the proceeding execution of Line 3 of its code. In the second case, if the history belongs to a Byzantine participant then the agreed history is an arbitrary but *identical* value taken from the history vectors of all non-Byzantine participants. Thus, the deterministic application of the **Apply** procedure executed by every non-Byzantine participants has the same outcome. One should note that after the first pulse the agreed upon replica state is kept identical, as all non-Byzantine participants agree on the state in Line 6 and modify the state in an identical fashion in Line 9, prior to the next pulse state agreement. Note that whereas the algorithm is executed inputs may still arrive; these are accumulated in the incoming buffers. Once the algorithm finalizes the **Apply** procedure the inputs in the incoming buffers of each of the participants are continuously appended (Line 10) to the history of the participant until the subsequent clock pulse.

```
1  map ← ∅
2  foreach {m ∈ 𝓗} do
3      if (|H_k : m ∈ H_k ∧ k ∈ [1..n]| ≥ 2f + 1) then
4          execute m over S_i
5          if (m.timestamp > map[m.source].timestamp) then
6              map[m.source].timestamp ← m.timestamp
7          drop all copies of m from 𝓗
8  foreach {m ∈ 𝓗} do
9      if (m.timestamp < map[m.source].timestamp) then
10         drop all copies of m from 𝓗
```

Fig. 2. apply($S_i, \mathcal{H}$) algorithm for replica i

Apply in the scope of Hadoop management. We now apply the generic replicated state machine algorithm to the case of the Hadoop management. The part of the **apply** processing is interpreting messages based on the majority rule: if there are at least $2f + 1$ identical messages then the message will be processed. It is due to the fact that after executing the Algorithm in Fig. 1, $\mathcal{H}$ stores at least $2f+1$ appearances of any messages sent by client/slave and already arrived to all non-Byzantine replicas. We assume that each client/slave maintains a local time-stamp (or local counter) used in the messages the client/slave sends to the replicated state machine. This time stamp is used by the replicated state machine to eliminate old messages arrived from the same client/slave. We denote by $m.source$ an identity of the message m sender and by $m.timestamp$ a time when a sender dispatched m. The timestamp may be just a local counter maintained by each client/slave used to order the messages of this client/slave. Active monitoring initiated by the replicated state machine maybe used to eliminate messages with future timestamps from the histories.

Sketch of proof. In Line 1 of the algorithm in Fig. 2, the map of the message sources to the dispatch time is initialized. The map stores a time of the last messages sent by a given to replicas (regardless whether a source is a client or a slave). After executing Lines 2–7 all messages in $\mathcal{H}$ that appear in at least $2f+1$ copies are executed by forwarding to correct destination. Two such messages that arrive from the same client/slave are executed according to the time stamp these messages possess: first arrived, first executed. It means that after execution of Line 7 the $\mathcal{H}$ contains only messages that have less than $2f+1$ copies. A part of the processing (Lines 5–6) is to update the map with information of the executed messages. This process is identical in all non-Byzantine replicas as a property of the agreement over $\mathcal{H}$ as it was shown in the algorithm in Fig. 1. The loop in Lines 8–10 of Fig. 2 uses the updated map to distinguish between malicious/corrupted messages from messages that yet to be received by more replicas. Given a message m was dispatched earlier than the most recently executed message from the same source, all copies of m are dropped from $\mathcal{H}$. Otherwise, m is kept in the history H_i and will be passed to next iteration. Eventually, after the last non-Byzantine replica executes **Apply** all valid messages are sent to client or slave processes.

5 Implementation

This section outlines the implementation details of the prototype whose concepts are provided in the previous sections. The idea is to extend the local self-stabilizing hypervisor infrastructure from [2] to the distributed scenario. The local self-stabilizing infrastructure is used to guarantee safe crash recovery *of an individual host*. However, if the state machine algorithm at a Master (Dispatcher) host is Byzantine, it may mislead the entire system in an intelligent way, without crashes. Therefore we replicate the master host, making its state machine distributed. Its state is then brought to the consensus using the Byzantine fault-tolerant algorithm that is fired upon a pulse from the distributed self-stabilizing Byzantine fault-tolerant clock synchronization algorithm (and not by hardware clock of an individual host).

Overview of the Local Stabilization manager. The local self-stabilizing infrastructure is three layered, including the *Stabilization Manager (SM)* that employs security policies to avoid, when possible, using (only) the self-stabilization fallback, the *Software Watchdog* that verifies the SM integrity upon a software clock pulse integrity and the hardware *Integrity Checker* that enforces the integrity of the above layers when a pulse from hardware (therefore unmaskable) clock arrives. By virtue of residing in ROM the hardware Integrity Checker is protected from tampering and guarantees the return to the clean initial state in the worst case scenario.

The Stabilization Manager acts upon a software timer interrupt, sending an *IAmAlive* message to the software watchdog. This serves as the next line of defence, verifying the system integrity and possibly causing a system reboot. However, an intelligent adversary may corrupt any software piece, including the kernel and the Software Watchdog. Then the Hardware Watchdog comes to the rescue. We put the integrity checking code into a separate ROM region which is write-protected by hardware means. Integrity checking will be un-tampered. It will ultimately occur because a hardware timer signal that triggers the watchdog is out of the control of the CPU and thus cannot be influenced by an adversary. Any Byzantine behavior at the software level cannot affect the watchdog. Our prototype runs on Intel architecture machines so we use the memory associated with System Management Mode (SMM) to provide the hardware-based write-protection of the Integrity Checker code. Most of the modern hardware support hardware-based memory protection.

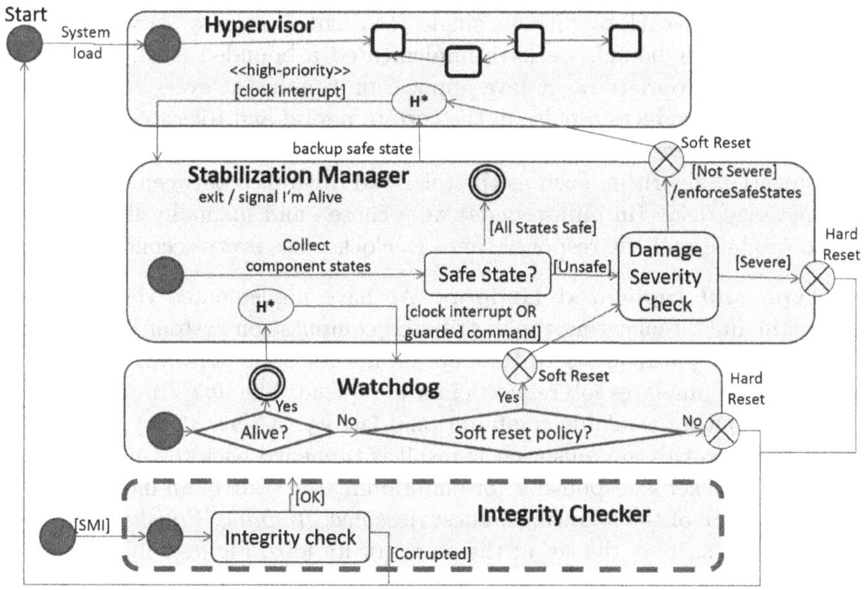

Fig. 3. The self-stabilizing hypervisor (Figure taken from [2]) (Color figure online)

Figure 3 summarizes the entire life cycle of the Stabilization Manager using three state machines.

- The Integrity Checker is wrapped by the thick red dashed line; showing that we put it into the hardware-protected memory zone.
- The History pseudo-node serves either as the target node (as in the UML standard, denoting the current execution context) or as the source node (denoting an arbitrary state in a given state machine). A History node illustrates that a timer interrupt causes the execution to leave the current context at any possible state.
- State transition priority. The stereotype "high-priority" near the interrupt transition means that the latter occurs as soon as possible. To check whether the system state is stable, the Stabilization Manager may scan system logs, internal kernel structures and any other state component.

The Stabilization Manager runs as a system daemon, scanning the repository of security policies and applying them in the order they appear in the repository. A security policy is formulated in the form $\langle condition, action \rangle$. When the condition is satisfied, the action is fired. The Stabilization Manager may consult various modules [39] to carry out security policies. For example, in case of malicious/corrupt inter-VM communication an application at a virtual machine sends malware; it attacks the target host, breaching the hypervisor defense. The attack can be revealed by inspecting the network traffic and can be prevented, e.g., by isolating suspicious guests or hosts.

Clock Synchronization. Since a single transient fault may cause the clock to reach the upper bound, we have implemented a bounded clock that wraps around when appropriate (as a Java application running at every replica). Our implementation produces a pulse in the certain period and tolerates the Byzantine behavior of less than one third of replicas. The parameters of the clock synchronization algorithm such as the tolerated difference between clock pulses or the message delay (in milliseconds) were chosen and manually fine-tuned in order to produce realistic response times (a clock pulse every second).

Prototype and replicated Hadoop. We have implemented the prototype as a Java module, replicating the distributed computation system Hadoop [44]. The client sends job requests to Hadoop; its master node performs dispatching functions. It accumulates job requests in a job queue. The *Job Tracker* agent at Master finds out an available computational facility (a *slave node*) and assigns a job to it. When this job finishes, the result is tunnelled back to Client through Master. Job Tracker is responsible for maintaining the state of an individual job, which can be one of the following values: *Accepted*, *Running*, *Finished* or *Failed*. The dispatcher state is the set of the states of its jobs. Figure 4 illustrates the Hadoop scenario.

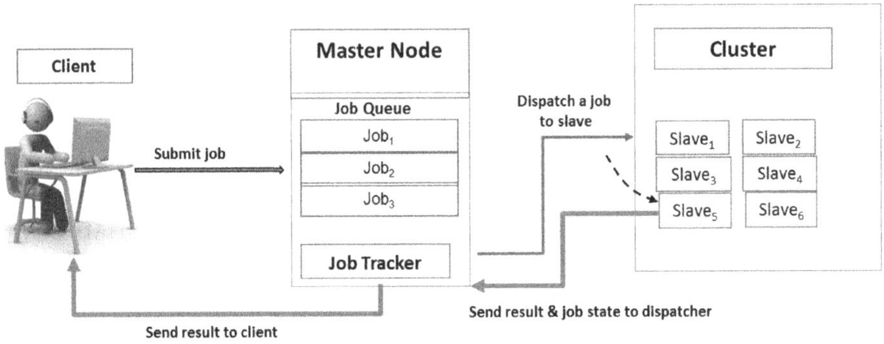

Fig. 4. Hadoop Scenario

To stage replicas, we use Docker [42] virtual machines instead of physical hosts to reduce the expenses. A Docker machine has its own IP, disk and memory space but the host kernel is shared among all virtual machines. In such lightweighted and efficient virtual machine we can reproduce most of the scenarios occurring in real life. The only implementation issue that is relevant for this situation is that we launch the Stabilization Manager as a system service, not as a Linux Kernel Module (LKM). This is because injecting LKMs into a Docker machine applies to the host kernel; therefore only the first attempt will succeed.

In the replicated Hadoop a job request is sent asynchronously to every replica. Then a cluster find an available slave and assigns it to this request. At this moment the recently arrived job enters the Accepted state. The job actually

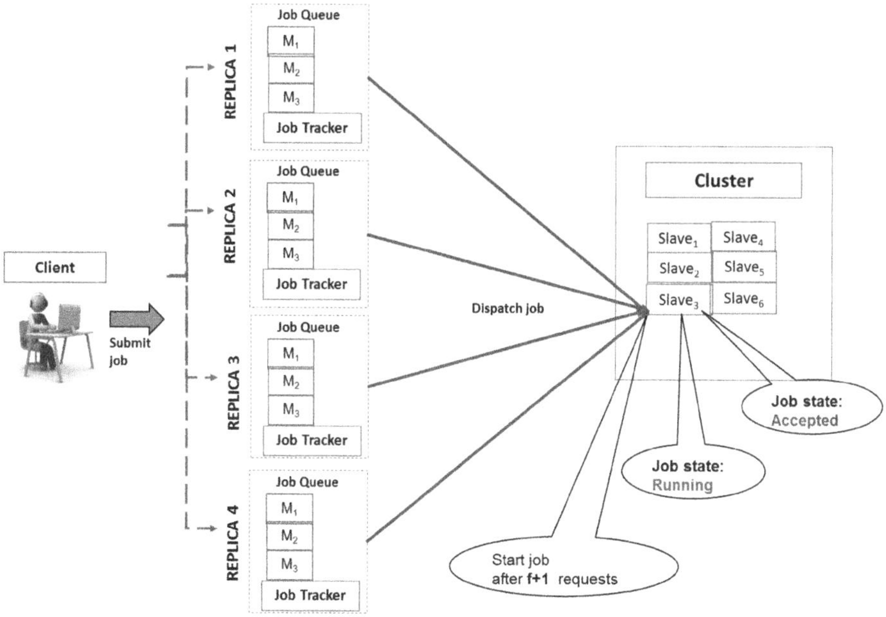

Fig. 5. Submitting a job to the replicated Hadoop

starts running after *f+1* identical requests are obtained (where *f* is the upper bound on the number of faulty replicas). This is the necessary in order to verify that at least one proper replica joined the "run job" bid. At this moment the job enters the Running state. Figure 5 illustrates the process of job launching and running.

After a job is done the result is tunnelled back to every replica which, in turn, processes it by executing the **Apply** procedure. Every non-Byzantine replica sends the (common) response to the client. The client decides that a job is completed if at least *f+1* identical responses are arrived. The job enters the Finished state. This is illustrated in Fig. 6.

We simulate infecting of replicas with a simple virus signature EICAR [43] in order to illustrate the super-secure-stabilization approach. This signature contains a typical payload sequence that is recognized by many antiviruses as dangerous. The simulator uploads EICAR onto replicas at random time; the Clam antivirus [41] periodically scans the replica disk spaces and cleans them, avoiding a corruption of the state and the invocation of self-stabilization convergence.

Unlike in other implementations of Byzantine fault-tolerant consensus like BFT-SMaRT [10] we do not use private or public keys. Instead we implement the leaderless consensus algorithm, setting in turn every replica as a leader, which guarantees the BFT consensus without using cryptography. The algorithm is implemented using the Extended Information Gathering tree data structure as in [9].

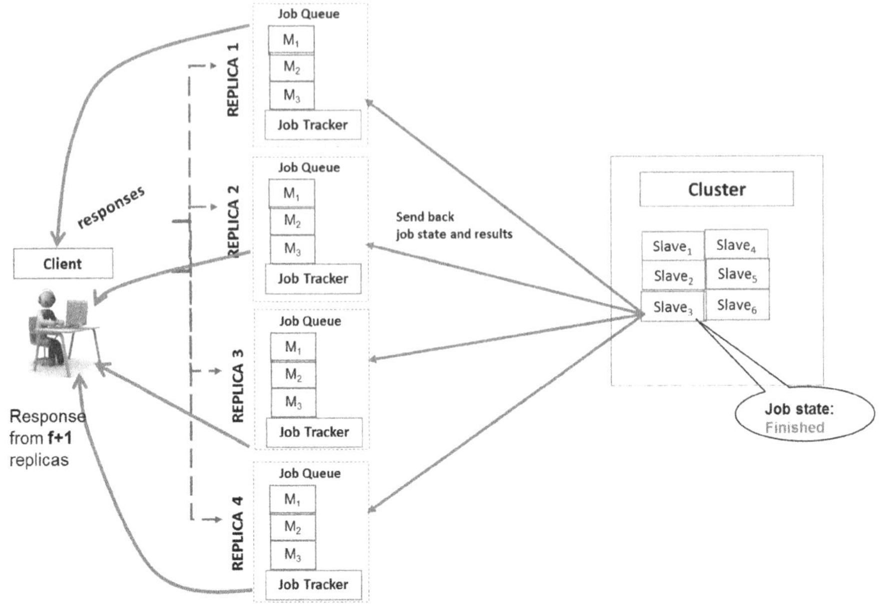

Fig. 6. Collecting responses from Hadoop replicas

The parameters of the simulator such as the delay between subsequent messages or the GUI update frequency were chosen and manually fine-tuned in order to demonstrate realistic response times. The simple prototype implemented by us is already interactive and useful. A sample Hadoop job used in it moves from the Accepted to the Finished state in approximately one minute.

6 Conclusions

This work is the first to present distributed algorithms that obtain a self-stabilizing Byzantine tolerant replicated state machine. Moreover, the resulting design has been implemented and has been proven to be practical. The design concept, in which each replica is self-stabilizing by itself, ensures automatic recovery of the faulty or even Byzantine individual participants, and the self-stabilizing Byzantine tolerant distributed algorithm ensures the convergence to a legal behavior after catastrophic events. Events that no system can withstand (e.g., all replicas are Byzantine for a while). The system protects its consistency (after convergence), tolerating less than one third Byzantine replicas (e.g., replicas overtaken by an adversary for a while, prior to reestablishing its individual consistency by its own stabilization manager). The system mitigates known attacks to avoid state corruptions as much as possible, and therefore avoids the need for individual and/or global convergence. We view the obtained system as a first step of improving the replicated state machines used by leading companies to obtain reliability, robustness and serviceability.

Acknowledgments. The research was partially supported by the Rita Altura Trust Chair in Computer Sciences, Orange Labs under external research contract number 0050012310-C04021, grant of the Ministry of Science, Technology and Space, Israel, and the National Science Council (NSC) of Taiwan, and a grant of the Ministry of Science, Technology and Space, Israel, the Ministry of Foreign Affairs, Italy.

References

1. Baron, J., El Defrawy, K., Lampkins, J., Ostrovsky, R.: How to withstand mobile virus attacks, revisited. In: PODC, pp. 293–302 (2014)
2. Binun, A., Bloch, M., Dolev, S., Kahil, M., Menuhin, B., Yagel, R., Coupaye, T., Lacoste, M., Wailly, A.: Self-stabilizing virtual machine hypervisor architecture for resilient cloud. In: IEEE International Workshop on Dependable and Secure Services (DSS) (2014)
3. Bonomi, S., Dolev, S., Potop-Butucaru, M., Raynal, M.: Stabilizing server-based storage in Byzantine asynchronous message-passing systems. In: PODC, pp. 471–479 (2015)
4. Blanchard, P., Dolev, S., Beauquier, J., Delaët, S.: Practically self-stabilizing paxos replicated state-machine. In: Noubir, G., Raynal, M. (eds.) NETYS 2014. LNCS, vol. 8593, pp. 99–121. Springer, Heidelberg (2014). doi:10.1007/978-3-319-09581-3_8
5. Brukman, O., Dolev, S.: Recovery oriented programming: runtime monitoring of safety and liveness. STTT **13**(4), 377–395 (2011)
6. Brukman, O., Dolev, S., Weinstock, M., Weiss, G.: Self-∗ Programming: run-time parallel control search for reflection box, Evolving Systems. Also in SASO 2008, pp. 481–482 (2013)
7. Brukman, O., Dolev, S., Haviv, Y., Lahiani, L., Kat, R., Schiller, E.M., Tzachar, N., Yagel, R.: Self-stabilization from theory to practice. Bulletin EATCS **94**, 130–150 (2008)
8. Brukman, O., Dolev, S., Kolodner, E.K.: A self-stabilizing autonomic recoverer for eventual Byzantine software. J. Syst. Softw. **81**(12), 2315–2327 (2008)
9. Borran, F., Schiper, A.: A leader-free Byzantine consensus algorithm. In: Kant, K., Pemmaraju, S.V., Sivalingam, K.M., Wu, J. (eds.) ICDCN 2010. LNCS, vol. 5935, pp. 67–78. Springer, Heidelberg (2010). doi:10.1007/978-3-642-11322-2_11
10. Bessani, A., Sousa, J., Alchieri, E.E.: State machine replication for the masses with BFT-SMART. In: Proceedings of the 44th Annual IEEE/IFIP International Conference on Dependable Systems and Networks, Atlanta, GA 23–26 June 2014
11. Castro, M., Liskov, B.: Practical Byzantine fault tolerance and proactive recovery. ACM Trans. Comput. Syst. **20**(4), 398–461 (2002)
12. Delaët, S., Dolev, S., Peres, O.: Safe and Eventually Safe: comparing self-stabilizing and non-stabilizing algorithms on a common ground. In: Abdelzaher, T., Raynal, M., Santoro, N. (eds.) OPODIS 2009. LNCS, vol. 5923, pp. 315–329. Springer, Heidelberg (2009). doi:10.1007/978-3-642-10877-8_25. Also, "Safer Than Safe: on the initial state of self-stabilizing systems". In: SSS 2009, pp. 775–776 (2009)
13. Dolev, S.: Self-Stabilization. MIT Press, Cambridge (2000)
14. Dolev, S., El Defrawy, K., Lampkins, J., Ostrovesky, R., Yung, M.: Proactive secret sharing with a dishonest majority. In: 10th International Conference, Security and Cryptography for Networks (SCN), brief announcment in PODC (2016)
15. Dolev, S., Georgiou, C., Marcoullis, I., Schiller, E.M.: Self-stabilizing Virtual Synchrony. In: SSS, pp. 248–264 (2015)

16. Dolev, D., Fuegger, M., Lenzen, C., Posch, M., Schmid, U., Steininger, A.: Rigorously modeling self-stabilizing fault-tolerant circuits: an ultra-robust clocking scheme for systems-on-chip. J. Comput. Syst. Sci. **80**(4), 860–900 (2014)
17. Dolev, S., Haviv, Y.A.: Self-stabilizing microprocessor: analyzing and overcoming soft errors. IEEE Trans. Comput. **55**(4), 385–399 (2006)
18. Dolev, S., Haviv, Y.A.: Stabilization enabling technology. IEEE Trans. Dependable Sec. Comput. **9**(2), 275–288 (2012)
19. Dolev, S., Haviv, Y.A., Sagiv, M.: Self-stabilization preserving compiler. ACM Trans. Program. Lang. Syst. **31**(6) (2009)
20. Dolev, S., Kat, R.I.: Self-stabilizing distributed file system. J. High Speed Networks **14**(2), 135–153 (2005)
21. Dolev, S., Liba, O., Schiller, E.M.: Self-stabilizing Byzantine resilient topology discovery and message delivery, CoRR abs/1208.5620 (2012)
22. Dolev, S., Hermann, T.: SuperStabilizing protocols for dynamic distributed systems. In: PODC (1995)
23. Dolev, S., Rajsbaum, S.: Stability of long-lived consensus. J. Comput. Syst. Sci. **67**(1), 26–45 (2003)
24. Dolev, S., Schiller, E.M., Spirakis, P.G., Tsigas, P.: Robust and scalable middleware for selfish-computer systems. Comput. Sci. Rev. **5**(1), 69–84 (2011)
25. Dolev, S., Schiller, E.M., Spirakis, P.G., Tsigas, P.: Strategies for repeated games with subsystem takeovers implementable by deterministic, self-stabilizing automata. IJAACS **4**(1), 4–38 (2011)
26. Dolev, S., Tzachar, N.: Randomization adaptive self-stabilization. Acta Inf. **47**(5–6), 313–323 (2010)
27. Dolev, S., Welch, J.L.: Self-stabilizing clock synchronization in the presence of Byzantine faults. J. ACM **51**(5), 780–799 (2004)
28. Dolev, S., Yagel, R.: Towards self-stabilizing operating systems. IEEE Trans. Softw. Eng. **34**(4), 564–576 (2008)
29. Dolev, S., Yagel, R.: Stabilizing trust and reputation for self-stabilizing efficient hosts in spite of Byzantine guests. Operating Syst. Rev. **44**(3), 65–74 (2010)
30. Dolev, S., Welch, J.: Bayard Kohlhepp Review #: CR130437 (0504-0452) on Self-stabilizing clock synchronization in the presence of Byzantine faults. J. ACM **51**(5), 780–799 (2004). ACM Computing Review
31. Lynch, N.A.: Distributed Algorithms. Morgan Kaufmann, San Francisco (1996)
32. Lamport, L.: The part-time parliament. ACM Trans. Comput. Syst. **16**(2), 133–169 (1998)
33. Lamport, L., Paxos made simple, fast, and Byzantine. In: OPODIS, pp. 7–9 (2002)
34. Tommy, M., McGuire, T.M., Gouda, M.G.: The Austin Protocol Compiler. Advances in Information Security. Springer, New York (2005)
35. Neumann, P.G.: Risks to the Public. ACM SIGSOFT Softw. Eng. Notes **37**(1), 21–26 (2012)
36. Ostrovsky, R., Yung, M.: How to withstand mobile virus attacks. In: PODC, pp. 51–59 (1991)
37. Hunt, P., Konar, M., Junqueira, F.P., Reed, B.: ZooKeeper: wait-free coordination for internet-scale systems. In: Proceedings of the USENIX Annual Technical Conference, p. 11, 23–25 June 2010, Boston, MA (2010)
38. Pease, M., Shostak, R., Lamport, L.: Reaching agreement in the presence of faults. J. ACM **27**(2), 228–234 (1980)
39. Wailly, A., Lacoste, M., Debar, H.: Vespa: multi-layered self-protection for cloud resources. In: Proceedings of the 9th Inter-national Conference on Autonomic Computing (ICAC) 2012, pp. 155–160, New York (2012)

40. Yagel, R., Dolev, S., Binun, A., Yankulin, L., Lacoste, M., Coupaye, T., Kassi-Lahlou, M., Palesandro, A., Wailly, A.: Data stabilization enforcement via active monitoring the cloud infrastructure consistency case. In: SSS (2015)
41. Clam Anti-Virus. https://www.clamav.net/
42. Docker. https://www.docker.com/
43. European Expert Group For IT-Security. www.eicar.org/download/eicar.com.txt
44. Apache Hadoop. http://hadoop.apache.org/
45. OpenStack. https://www.openstack.org/

Self-stabilizing Robots in Highly Dynamic Environments

Marjorie Bournat[1(✉)], Ajoy K. Datta[2], and Swan Dubois[1]

[1] UPMC Sorbonne Universités, CNRS, Inria, LIP6 UMR 7606, Paris, France
marjorie.bournat@lip6.fr

[2] University of Nevada Las Vegas, Las Vegas, USA

Abstract. This paper deals with the classical problem of exploring a ring by a cohort of synchronous robots. We focus on the perpetual version of this problem in which it is required that each node of the ring is visited by a robot infinitely often.

The challenge in this paper is twofold. First, we assume that the robots evolve in a highly dynamic ring, *i.e.*, edges may appear and disappear unpredictably without any recurrence nor periodicity assumption. The only assumption we made is that each node is infinitely often reachable from any other node. Second, we aim at providing a self-stabilizing algorithm to the robots, *i.e.*, the algorithm must guarantee an eventual correct behavior regardless of the initial state and positions of the robots. Our main contribution is to show that this problem is deterministically solvable in this harsh environment by providing a self-stabilizing algorithm for three robots.

1 Introduction

We consider a cohort of autonomous and synchronous robots that are equipped with motion actuators and sensors, but that are otherwise unable to communicate [1]. They evolve in a *discrete environment*, where the space is partitioned into a finite number of locations, represented by a graph, where the nodes represent the possible locations of robots and the edges the possibility for a robot to move from one location to another. Refer to [2] for a survey of results in this model. One fundamental problem is the *exploration* of graphs by robots. Basically, each node of the graph has to be visited by at least one robot. There exist several variants of this problem depending on whether the robots are required to stop once they completed the exploration of the graph or not.

Typically, the environment of the robots is modeled by a *static* undirected connected graph where vertices are possible locations of robots and edges represent the moving abilities of the robots. Clearly, such modeling is not suitable for dynamic environments that we use in this paper. Numerous models dealing with topological changes over time have been proposed in the past few decades.

This work has been partially supported by the ANR project ESTATE and was initiated while the second author was visiting UPMC Sorbonne Universités.

B. Bonakdarpour and F. Petit (Eds.): SSS 2016, LNCS 10083, pp. 54–69, 2016.
DOI: 10.1007/978-3-319-49259-9_5

There have been some attempts to unifying them as well. The *evolving graphs* were introduced in [3]. They proposed modeling the time as a sequence of discrete time instants and the dynamicity of the system by a sequence of static graphs, one for each instant of time. More recently, another graph model, called *Time-Varying Graphs* (TVG), has been introduced in [4]. In contrast with evolving graphs, TVGs allow systems evolving in continuous time. Also in [4], TVGs are ordered into classes based on mainly two features: the quality of connectivity of the graph and the possibility/impossibility to perform tasks.

As in other distributed systems, *fault-tolerance* is a central issue in robot networks. Indeed, it is desirable that the misbehavior of some robots does not prevent the whole system to reach its objective. *Self-stabilization* [5–7] is a versatile technique to tolerate *transient* (*i.e.*, of finite duration) faults. After the occurrence of a catastrophic failure that may take the system to some arbitrary global state, self-stabilization guarantees recovery to a correct behavior in finite time without external (*i.e.*, human) intervention. In the context of robot networks, that implies that the algorithm must guarantee an eventual correct behavior regardless of the initial state and positions of the robots.

Our objective in this paper is to study the feasibility of the exploration of a highly dynamic graph by a cohort of self-stabilizing deterministic robots.

Related Work. Since the seminal work of Shannon [8], exploration of graphs by a cohort of robots has been extensively studied. There exist mainly three variants of the problem: (*i*) *exploration with stop*, where robots are required to detect the end of the exploration, then stop moving (*e.g.*, [9]); (*ii*) *exploration with return*, where robots must come back to their initial location once the exploration completed (*e.g.*, [10]); and (*iii*) *perpetual exploration*, where each node has to be infinitely often visited by some robots (*e.g.*, [11]). Even if we restrict ourselves to deterministic approaches, there exist numerous solutions to these problems depending on the topology of the graphs to explore (*e.g.*, ring-shaped [9], line-shaped [12], tree-shaped [13], or arbitrary network [14]), and the assumptions made on robots (*e.g.*, limited range of visibility [15], common sense of orientation [16], *etc.*). But, most of the above work considered only static graphs.

Recently, some work dealt with the exploration of dynamic graphs. The first two papers [17,18] focused on the exploration (with stop) of so-called periodically varying graphs (*i.e.*, the presence of each edge of the graph is totally periodic). The papers [19–21] considered another restriction on dynamicity by considering T-interval-connected graphs (*i.e.*, the graph is always connected and there exists a stability of this connectivity in any interval of time of length T [22]). However, there exist no exploration algorithms for highly dynamic graphs, *i.e.*, graphs where edges may appear and disappear unpredictably without any recurrence, periodicity, or stability assumption and where the only assumption made is that each node is infinitely often reachable from any other node.

To the best of our knowledge, there exist no self-stabilizing algorithm for exploration either in a static or a dynamic environment. Note that there exist solutions in static graphs to other problems (*e.g.*, naming and leader election [23]).

Our Contribution. The main contribution of this paper is to give a positive answer to the open question whether self-stabilizing deterministic exploration of highly dynamic graphs is possible or not. We answer that question by providing a self-stabilizing algorithm to perpetually explore any highly dynamic ring with three deterministic synchronous robots. This is the first exploration algorithm that deals with highly dynamic graphs. This is also the first self-stabilizing algorithm for exploration.

Organization of the paper. This paper is organized as follows. In Sect. 2, we present the formal model and state the assumptions made. In Sect. 3, we describe our algorithm. Section 4 contains the proof sketch of our algorithm.

2 Model

In this section, we propose an extension of the classical model of robot networks in static graphs introduced by [24] to the context of dynamic graphs.

Dynamic graphs. In this paper, we consider the model of *evolving graphs* introduced in [3]. We hence consider the time as discretized and mapped to $\mathbb{N}$. An evolving graph $\mathcal{G}$ is an ordered sequence $\{G_1, G_2, \ldots\}$ of subgraphs of a given static graph $G = (V, E)$. In the following, we restrict ourselves to bidirectional graphs. For any $i \geq 0$, we have $G_i = (V, E_i)$ and we say that the edges of E_i are *present* in $\mathcal{G}$ at time i. The *underlying graph* of $\mathcal{G}$, denoted $U_\mathcal{G}$, is the static graph gathering all edges that are present at least once in $\mathcal{G}$ (*i.e.*, $U_\mathcal{G} = (V, E_\mathcal{G})$ with $E_\mathcal{G} = \bigcup_{i=0}^{\infty} E_i$). An *eventual missing edge* is an edge of $E_\mathcal{G}$ such that there exists a time after which this edge is never present in $\mathcal{G}$. A *recurrent edge* is an edge of $E_\mathcal{G}$ that is not eventually missing. The *eventual underlying graph* of $\mathcal{G}$, denoted $U_\mathcal{G}^\omega$, is the static graph gathering all recurrent edges of $\mathcal{G}$ (*i.e.*, $U_\mathcal{G}^\omega = (V, E_\mathcal{G}^\omega)$ where $E_\mathcal{G}^\omega$ is the set of recurrent edges of $\mathcal{G}$). In this paper, we chose to make minimal assumptions on the dynamicity of our graph since we restrict ourselves on *connected-over-time* evolving graphs. The only constraint we impose on evolving graphs of this class is that their eventual underlying graph is connected [25] (intuitively, that means that any node is infinitely often reachable from any other one). For the sake of the proof, we also consider the weaker class of *edge-recurrent* evolving graphs where the eventual underlying graph is connected and matches to the underlying graph. In the following, we consider only connected-over-time evolving graphs whose underlying graph is an anonymous and unoriented ring of arbitrary size. Although the ring is unoriented, to simplify the presentation and discussion, in this paper, we, as external observers, distinguish between the clockwise and the counter-clockwise (global) direction in the ring.

Robots. We consider systems of autonomous mobile entities called robots moving in a discrete and dynamic environment modeled by an evolving graph $\mathcal{G} = \{(V, E_1), (V, E_2) \ldots\}$, V being a set of nodes representing the set of locations where robots may be, E_i being the set of bidirectional edges representing connections through which robots may move from a location to another one at time i. Robots are uniform (they execute the same algorithm), identified (each of them has a distinct identifier), have a persistent memory but are unable to directly communicate with one another by any means. Robots are endowed with local strong multiplicity detection (*i.e.*, they are able to detect the exact number of robots located on their current node). They have no a priori knowledge about the ring they explore (size, diameter, dynamicity...). Finally, each robot has its own stable chirality (*i.e.*, each robot is able to locally label the two ports of its current node with *left* and *right* consistently over the ring and time but two different robots may not agree on this labeling). We assume that each robot has a variable *dir* that stores a direction (either *left* or *right*). At any time, we say that a robot points to *left* (resp. *right*) if its *dir* variable is equal to this (local) direction. We say that a robot considers the clockwise (resp., counter-clockwise) direction if the (local) direction pointed to by this robot corresponds to the (global) direction seen by an external observer.

Execution. A configuration γ of the system captures the position (*i.e.*, the node where the robot is currently located) and the state (*i.e.*, the value of every variable of the robot) of each robot at a given time. Given an evolving graph $\mathcal{G} = \{G_1, G_2, \ldots\}$, an algorithm $\mathcal{A}$, and an initial configuration γ_0, the execution $\mathcal{E}$ of $\mathcal{A}$ on $\mathcal{G}$ starting from γ_0 is the infinite sequence $(G_0, \gamma_0), (G_1, \gamma_1), (G_2, \gamma_2), \ldots$ where, for any $i \geq 0$, the configuration γ_{i+1} is the result of the execution of a synchronous round by all robots from (G_i, γ_i) as explained below.

The round that transitions the system from (G_i, γ_i) to (G_{i+1}, γ_{i+1}) is composed of three atomic and synchronous phases: Look, Compute, Move. During the Look phase, each robot gathers information about its environment in G_i. More precisely, each robot updates the value of the following local predicates: (*i*) $NumberOfRobotsOnNode()$ returns the exact number of robots present at the node of the robot; (*ii*) *ExistsEdgeOnCurrentDirection*() returns true if an edge is present at the direction currently pointed by the robot, false otherwise; (*iii*) *ExistsEdgeOnOppositeDirection*() returns true if an edge is present in the direction opposite to the one currently pointed by the robot, false otherwise; (*iv*) *ExistsAdjacentEdge*() returns true if an edge adjacent to the current node of the robot is present, false otherwise. During the Compute phase, each robot executes the algorithm $\mathcal{A}$ that may modify some of its variables (in particular *dir*) depending on of its current state and the values of the predicates updated during the Look phase. Finally, the Move phase consists of moving each robot trough one edge in the direction it points to if there exists an edge in that direction, otherwise, *i.e.*, if the edge is missing at that time, the robot remains at its current node. Note that the ith round is entirely executed on G_i and that the transition from G_i to G_{i+1} occurs only at the end of this round. We say that a robot is *edge-activated* during a round if there exists at least one edge adjacent to its location during that round.

Self-stabilization. Intuitively, a self-stabilizing algorithm is able to recover in a finite time a correct behavior from any arbitrary initial configuration (that captures the effect of an arbitrary transient fault in the system). More formally, an algorithm $\mathcal{A}$ is *self-stabilizing* for a problem on a class of evolving graphs $\mathcal{C}$ if and only if it ensures that, for any configuration γ_0, the execution of $\mathcal{A}$ on any $\mathcal{G} \in \mathcal{C}$ starting from γ_0 contains a configuration γ_i such that the execution of $\mathcal{A}$ on $\mathcal{G}$ starting from γ_i satisfies the specification of the problem. Note that, in the context of robot networks, this definition implies that robots must tolerate both arbitrary initialization of their variables and arbitrary initial positions (in particular, robots may be stacked in the initial configuration).

Perpetual Exploration. Given an evolving graph $\mathcal{G}$, a perpetual exploration algorithm guarantees that every node of $\mathcal{G}$ is infinitely often visited by at least one robot (*i.e.*, a robot is infinitely often located at every node of $\mathcal{G}$). Note that this specification does not require that every robot visits infinitely often every node of $\mathcal{G}$.

3 Exploring a Highly Dynamic Ring with Three Robots

In this section, we present our self-stabilizing deterministic algorithm for the perpetual exploration of any connected-over-time ring with three robots. In this context, the difficulty to complete the exploration is twofold. First, in connected-over-time graphs, robots must deal with the possible existence of some eventual missing edge (without the guarantee that such edge always exists). Note that, in the case of a ring, there is at most one eventual missing edge in any execution (otherwise, we have a contradiction with the connected-over-time property). Second, robots have to handle the arbitrary initialization of the system (corruption of variables and arbitrary position of robots).

Principle of the algorithm. The main idea behind our algorithm is that a robot does not change its direction (arbitrarily initialized) while it is isolated. This allows robots to perpetually explore connected-over-time rings with no eventual missing edge regardless of the initial direction of the robots.

Obviously, this idea is no longer sufficient when there exists an eventual missing edge since, in this case, at least two robots will eventually be stuck (*i.e.*, they point to an eventual missing edge that they are never able to cross) forever at one end of the eventual missing edge. When two (or more) robots are located at the same node, we say that they form a tower. In this case, our algorithm succeed (as we explain below) to ensure that at least one robot leaves the tower in a finite time. In this way, we obtain that, in a finite time, a robot is stuck at each end of the eventual missing edge. These two robots located at two ends of the eventual missing edge play the role of "sentinels" while the third one (we call it a "visitor") visits other nodes of the ring in the following way. The "visitor" keeps its direction until it meets one of these "sentinels", they then switch their roles: After the meeting, the "visitor" still maintains the same direction (becoming thus a "sentinel") while the "sentinel" robot changes its direction (becoming thus a "visitor" until reaching the other "sentinel").

In fact, robots are never aware if they are actually stuck at an eventual missing edge or are just temporarily stuck on an edge that will reappear in a finite time. That is why it is important that the robots keep consider their directions and try to move forward while there is no meeting in order to track a possible eventual missing edge. Our algorithm only guarantees a convergence in a finite time towards a configuration where a robot plays the role of "sentinel" at each end of the eventual missing edge if such an edge exists. Note that, in the case where there is no eventual missing edge, this mechanism does not prevent the correct exploration of the ring since it is impossible for a robot to be stuck forever.

Our algorithm easily deals with the initial corruption of its variables. Indeed, we use variables only to save some information about the environment of the robots in the previous rounds and we update them at each round. Thus, their arbitrary initial value is erased in a finite time. The main difficulty to achieve self-stabilization is to deal with the arbitrary initial position of robots. In particular, the robots may initially form towers. In the worst case, all robots of a tower may be stuck at an eventual missing edge and be in the same state. They are then unable to start the "sentinels"/"visitor" scheme explained above. Our algorithm needs to "break" such a tower in a finite time (*i.e.*, one robot must leave the node where the tower is located). In other words, we tackle a classical problem of symmetry breaking. We succeed by providing each robot with a function that returns, in a finite number of invocations, different global directions to two robots of the tower based on the private identifier of the robot and without any communication among the robots. More precisely, this is done thanks to a transformation of the robot identifier: each bit of the binary representation of the identifier is duplicated and we add the bits "01" at the end of the sequence of these duplicated bits. Then, at each invocation of the function, a robot reads the next bit of this transformed identifier. If the robot reads zero, it try to move to its left. Otherwise, it try to move to its right. Doing so, in a finite number of invocation of this function, at least one robot leaves the tower. If necessary, we repeat this "tower breaking" scheme until we are able to start the "sentinels"/"visitor" scheme.

The main difficulty in designing this algorithm is to ensure that these two mechanisms ("sentinels"/"visitor" and "tower breaking") do not interfere with each other and prevent the correct exploration. We solve this problem by adding some waiting at good time, especially before starting the procedure of tower breaking by identifier to ensure that robots do not prematurely turn back and "forget" to explore some parts of the ring.

Formal presentation of the algorithm. Before presenting formally our algorithm, we need to introduce the set of constants (*i.e.*, variables assumed to be not corruptible) and the set of variables of each robot. We also introduce three auxiliary functions.

As stated in the model, each robot has an unique identifier. We denote it by *id* and represent it in binary as $b_0 b_1 \dots b_{|id|-1}$. We define, for the purpose of the "breaking tower" scheme, the constant $TransformedIdentifier$ by its binary representation $b_0 b_0 b_1 b_1 \dots b_{|id|-1} b_{|id|-1} 01$ (each bit of *id* is duplicated and we add the two bits 01 at the end). We store the length of the binary representation of $TransformedIdentifier$ in the constant ℓ and we denote its ith bit by $TransformedIdentifier[i]$ for any $0 \leq i \leq \ell - 1$.

In addition to the variable *dir* defined in the model, each robot has the following three variables: (*i*) the variable $i \in \mathbb{N}$ corresponds to an index to store the position of the last bit read from $TransformedIdentifier$; (*ii*) the variable $NumberRobotsPreviousEdgeActivation \in \mathbb{N}$ stores the number of robots that were present at the node of the robot during the look step of the last round where it was edge-activated; and (*iii*) the variable $HasMovedPrevious$-$EdgeActivation \in \{true, false\}$ indicates if the robot has crossed an edge during its last edge-activation.

Our algorithm makes use of a function UPDATE that updates the value of the two last variables according to the current environment of the robot each time it is edge-activated. We provide the pseudo-code of this function in Algorithm 1. Note that this function also allows us to deal with the initial corruption of the two last variables since it resets them in the first round where the robot is edge-activated.

We already stated that, whenever robots are stuck forming a tower, they make use of a function to "break" the tower in a finite time. The pseudo-code of this function GIVEDIRECTION appears in Algorithm 2. It assigns the value $left$ or $right$ to the variable *dir* of the robot depending on the the ith bit of the value of $TransformedIdentifier$. The variable i is incremented modulo ℓ (that implicitly resets this variable when it is corrupted) to ensure that successive calls to GIVEDIRECTION will consider each bit of $TransformedIdentifier$ in a round-robin way. As shown in the next section, this function guarantees that, if two robots are stuck together in a tower and invoke repeatedly their own function GIVEDIRECTION, then two distinct global directions are given in finite time to the two robots regardless of their chirality. This property allows the algorithm to "break" the tower since at least one robot is then able to leave the node where the tower is located.

Algorithm 1. Function Update

```
function UPDATE
    if ExistsAdjacentEdge() then
        NumberRobotsPreviousEdgeActivation ← NumberOfRobotsOnNode()
        HasMovedPreviousEdgeActivation ← ExistsEdgeOnCurrentDirection()
    end if
end function
```

Finally, we define the function OPPOSITEDIRECTION that simply affects the value $left$ (resp. $right$) to the variable dir when $dir = right$ (resp. $dir = left$).

There are two types of configurations in which the robots may change the direction they consider. So, our algorithm needs to identify them. We do so by defining a predicate that characterizes each of these configurations.

The first one, called $WeAreStuckInTheSameDirection()$, is dedicated to the detection of configurations in which the robot must invoke the "tower breaking" mechanism. Namely, the robot is stuck since at least one edge-activation with at least another robot and the edge in the direction opposite to the one considered by the robot is present. More formally, this predicate is defined as follows:

$$\begin{aligned}
&WeAreStuckInTheSameDirection() \equiv \\
&\quad (NumberOfRobotsOnNode() > 1) \\
&\wedge\ (NumberOfRobotsOnNode() = NumberRobotsPreviousEdgeActivation) \\
&\wedge\ \neg ExistsEdgeOnCurrentDirection() \\
&\wedge\ ExistsEdgeOnOppositeDirection() \\
&\wedge\ \neg HasMovedPreviousEdgeActivation
\end{aligned}$$

The second predicate, called $IWasStuckOnMyNodeAndNowWeAreMoreRobots()$, is designed to detect configurations in which the robot must transition from the "sentinel" to the "visitor" role in the "sentinel"/"visitor" scheme. More precisely, such configuration is characterized by the fact that the robot is edge-activated, stuck during its previous edge-activation, and there are strictly more robots located at its node than at its previous edge-activation. More formally, this predicate is defined as follows:

$$\begin{aligned}
&IWasStuckOnMyNodeAndNowWeAreMoreRobots() \equiv \\
&\quad (NumberOfRobotsOnNode() > NumberRobotsPreviousEdgeActivation) \\
&\wedge\ \neg HasMovedPreviousEdgeActivation \\
&\wedge\ ExistsAdjacentEdge()
\end{aligned}$$

Algorithm 2. Function GiveDirection

```
function GIVEDIRECTION
    i ← i + 1 (mod ℓ)
    if TransformedIdentifier[i] = 0 then
        dir ← left
    else
        dir ← right
    end if
end function
```

Now, we are ready to present the pseudo-code of the core of our algorithm (see Algorithm 3). The basic idea of the algorithm is the following. The function GIVEDIRECTION is invoked when $WeAreStuckInTheSameDirection()$ is true (to try to "break" the tower after the appropriate waiting), while the function OPPOSITEDIRECTION is called when $IWasStuckOnMyNodeAndNowWeAre$-

MoreRobots() is true (to implement the "sentinel"/"visitor" scheme). Afterwards, the function UPDATE is called (to update the state of the robot according to its environment).

Algorithm 3. Self-stabilizing perpetual exploration

if *WeAreStuckInTheSameDirection*() **then**
    GIVEDIRECTION
end if
if *IWasStuckOnMyNodeAndNowWeAreMoreRobots*() **then**
    OPPOSITEDIRECTION
end if
UPDATE

4 Proof Sketch

Due to the lack of space, we present only a sketch of the proof of our algorithm in this paper. This section captures the main ideas behind the proof and summarizes its main steps. The detailed proof of our algorithm is available in a companion technical report [26].

Preliminaries. First, we introduce some definitions and preliminary results that are extensively used in the proof.

We saw previously that the notion of tower is central in our algorithm. Intuitively, a tower captures the simultaneous presence of all robots of a given set on a node at each time of a given interval. We require either the set of robots or the time interval of each tower to be maximal. Note that the tower is not required to be on the same node at each time of the interval (robots of the tower may move together without leaving the tower).

We distinguish two kinds of towers according to the agreement of their robots on the global direction to consider at each time there exists an adjacent edge to their current location (excluded the last one). If they agreed, the robots form a long-lived tower while they form a short-lived tower in the contrary case. This implies that a short-lived tower is broken as soon as the robots forming the tower are edge-activated, while the robots of a long-lived tower move together at each edge activation of the tower (excluded the last one).

Definition 1 (Tower). *A tower T is a couple (S, θ), where S is a set of robots ($|S| > 1$) and $\theta = [t_s, t_e]$ is an interval of $\mathbb{N}$, such that all the robots of S are located at a same node at each instant of time t in θ and S or θ are maximal for this property. Moreover, if the robots of S move during a round $t \in [t_s, t_e[$, they are required to traverse the same edge.*

Definition 2 (Long-lived tower). *A long-lived tower $T = (S, [t_s, t_e])$ is a tower such that there is at least one edge-activation of all robots of S in the time interval $[t_s, t_e[$.*

Definition 3 (Short-lived tower). *A short-lived tower T is a tower that is not a long-lived tower.*

For $k > 1$, a long-lived (resp., a short-lived) tower $T = (S, \theta)$ with $|S| = k$ is called a k-long-lived (resp., a k-short-lived) tower.

In the remainder of this section, we consider an execution $\mathcal{E}$ of Algorithm 3 executed by three robots r_1, r_2, and r_3 on a connected-over-time ring $\mathcal{G}$ of size $n \in \mathbb{N}^*$ starting from an arbitrary configuration.

For the sake of clarity, the value of a variable or a predicate *name* of a given robot r at the end of the Look phase of a given round t is denoted by the notation $name(r, t)$.

We say that a robot r has a coherent state at time t, if during the Look phase of round t, the value of its variable $NumberRobots$-$PreviousEdgeActivation(r, t)$ corresponds to the value of its predicate $NumberOfRobotsOnNode()$ at its previous edge-activation and the value of its variable $HasMovedPreviousEdgeActivation(r, t)$ corresponds to the value of its predicate $ExistsEdgeOnCurrentDirection()$ at its previous edge-activation. The following lemma states that, for each robot, there exists a suffix of the execution in which the robot is coherent.

Lemma 1. *For any robot, there exists a time from which its state is always coherent.*

Let t_1, t_2, and t_3 be respectively the time at which the robot r_1, r_2, and r_3, respectively are in a coherent state. Let $t_{max} = max\{t_1, t_2, t_3\}$. From Lemma 1, the three robots are in a coherent state from t_{max}. In the remaining of the proof, we focus on the suffix of the execution after t_{max}.

The two following lemmas show that, regardless of the chirality of the robots and the initial values of their variables i, a finite number of synchronous invocations of the function GiveDirection by two robots of a tower returns them a distinct global direction. To prove that, we need to take a close look at properties granted by the transformed identifiers of the robots.

Lemma 2. *Let tl_1 and tl_2 be two transformed identifiers, such that $tl_1 \neq tl_2$. Let i and j be two integers such that $i \in [0, |tl_1| - 1]$ and $j \in [0, |tl_2| - 1]$. If $tl_1[i] = tl_2[j]$, then there exists an integer k such that $tl_1[(i + k) \pmod{|tl_1|}] \neq tl_2[(j + k) \pmod{|tl_2|}]$.*

Lemma 3. *Let tl_1 and tl_2 be two transformed identifiers, such that $tl_1 \neq tl_2$. Let i and j be two integers such that $i \in [0, |tl_1| - 1]$ and $j \in [0, |tl_2| - 1]$. If $tl_1[i] \neq tl_2[j]$, then there exists an integer k such that $tl_1[(i + k) \pmod{|tl_1|}] = tl_2[(j + k) \pmod{|tl_2|}]$.*

Technical lemmas on towers. We are now able to state a set of lemmas that show some interesting technical properties of towers under specific assumptions during the execution of our algorithm. These properties are extensively used in the main proof of our algorithm. Their proofs are very technical, hence omitted due to lack of space.

Lemma 4. *The robots of a long-lived tower* $T = (S, [t_s, t_e])$ *consider a same global direction at each time between the Look phase of round* t_s *and the Look phase of round* t_e *included.*

Lemma 5. *If there exists an eventual missing edge, then all long-lived towers have a finite duration.*

Lemma 6. *Every execution containing only configurations without any long-lived tower cannot reach a configuration with a 3-short-lived tower.*

Lemma 7. *Every execution starting from a configuration without a 3-long-lived tower cannot reach a configuration with a 3-long-lived tower.*

Lemma 8. *Let* γ *be a configuration such that all but one robots consider the same global direction. Then starting from* γ, *no execution without any long-lived towers can reach a configuration where all robots consider the same global direction.*

Lemma 9. *Consider an execution containing no 3-long-lived towers. If a 2-long-lived tower* $T = (S, [t_s, t_e])$ *is located at a node* u *at round* t_e, *then the robot that does not belong to* S *cannot be located at node* u *during the Look phase of round* t_e. *Moreover during the Look phase of round* $t_e + 1$, *one robot of* S *located at* u *considers a global direction opposite to the one considered by the other robot of* S *(which is not on* u*).*

The following lemma is used to prove, in combination with Lemmas 2 and 3, the "tower breaking" mechanism since it proves that robots of a long-lived tower synchronously invoke their GIVEDIRECTION function after their first edge-activation.

Lemma 10. *For any long-lived tower* $T = (S, [t_s, t_e])$, *any* (r_i, r_j) *in* S^2, *and any* t *less or equal to* t_e, *we have* $WeAreStuckInTheSameDirection()(r_i, t) = WeAreStuckInTheSameDirection()(r_j, t)$ *if all robots of* S *have been edge-activated between* t_s *(included) and* t *(not included).*

The next two lemmas show that the whole ring is visited between two consecutive 2-long-lived towers if these two towers satisfy some properties. They are used in the proof of the "sentinels"/"visitor" scheme.

Lemma 11. *Consider an execution* $\mathcal{E}$ *without any 3-long-lived tower but containing a 2-long-lived tower* $T = (S, [t_s, t_e])$. *If there exists another 2-long-lived tower* $T' = (S', [t'_s, t'_e])$ *after* T *in* $\mathcal{E}$ *and if* T' *is the first 2-long-lived tower in* $\mathcal{E}$ *such that* $t'_s > t_e + 1$, *then all the edges of* $\mathcal{G}$ *have been crossed by at least one robot between time* t_e *and time* t'_s.

Lemma 12. *Consider that there are no 3-long-lived towers in* $\mathcal{E}$, *and let* $T_i = (S_i, [t_{s\_i}, t_{e\_i}])$ *be the* i^{th} *2-long-lived tower of* $\mathcal{E}$ *(with* $i \geq 2$*). If* $T_{i+1} = (S_{i+1}, [t_{s\_i+1}, t_{e\_i+1}])$ *exists such that* $t_{s\_i+1} = t_{e\_i} + 1$, *then all the edges of* $\mathcal{G}$ *have been crossed by at least one robot between time* $t_{s\_i} - 1$ *and time* t_{s_i+1}.

Main lemmas. Upon establishing all the above properties of towers, we are now ready to state the main lemmas of our proof. Each of these three lemmas below shows that our algorithm performs the perpetual exploration in a self-stabilizing way for a specific subclass of connected-over-time rings. We only sketch the proof of these lemmas due to space constraints.

Lemma 13. *Algorithm 3 is a self-stabilizing perpetual exploration algorithm for the class of static rings of arbitrary size using three robots.*

Sketch of proof. Assume that $\mathcal{G}$ is a static ring. The robots executing our algorithm consider a direction in each round. Moreover, in our algorithm, the robots do not change the direction they consider if there exists an adjacent edge to their current location in the direction they consider. As $\mathcal{G}$ is static, this implies that in each round all the edges of $\mathcal{G}$ are present. Thus, the robots never change their directions.

As (i) the robots have a stable direction, (ii) they always consider the same global direction, and (iii) there always exists an adjacent edge to their current locations in the global direction they consider, the robots move infinitely often in the same global direction. Moreover, as $\mathcal{G}$ has a finite size, this implies that all the robots visit infinitely often all the nodes of $\mathcal{G}$. □

Lemma 14. *Algorithm 3 is a self-stabilizing perpetual exploration algorithm for the class of edge-recurrent but non static rings of arbitrary size using three robots.*

Sketch of proof. Assume that $\mathcal{G}$ is an edge-recurrent but non static ring. Let us study the following cases.

Case 1: There exists at least one 3-long-lived tower in $\mathcal{E}$.

Case 1.1: One of the 3-long-lived towers of $\mathcal{E}$ has an infinite duration.
Denote by T the 3-long-lived tower of $\mathcal{E}$ that has an infinite duration. According to the definition of the predicate $WeAreStuckInTheSameDirection()$, Lemmas 2, 3 and 10, T is eventually not stuck during two consecutive edge-activations. Thus, after the formation of T, the robots see infinitely often an adjacent edge in the direction they consider. Moreover, as there are three robots in the system, the predicate $IWasStuckOnMyNodeAndNowWeAreMoreRobots()$ is not true for these robots. Thus, the three robots eventually consider the same global direction. This implies that the three robots are able to move infinitely often in the same global direction. Moreover, as $\mathcal{G}$ has a finite size, all the robots visit infinitely often all the nodes of $\mathcal{G}$.

Case 1.2: Any 3-long-lived tower of $\mathcal{E}$ has a finite duration.
By Lemma 7, once a 3-long-lived tower is broken, it is impossible to have another 3-long-lived tower in $\mathcal{E}$. Then, $\mathcal{E}$ admits an infinite suffix that matches either case 2 or 3.

Case 2: There exists at least one 2-long-lived tower in $\mathcal{E}$.

Case 2.1: There exists a finite number of 2-long-lived towers in $\mathcal{E}$.
If the last 2-long-lived tower of $\mathcal{E}$ has a finite duration, then $\mathcal{E}$ admits an infinite suffix with no long-lived towers thus matching Case 3.

Otherwise, (*i.e.*, the last 2-long-lived tower T of $\mathcal{E}$ has an infinite duration), as in Case 1.1, the robots of the 2-long-lived tower eventually see infinitely often an adjacent edge in the direction they consider since they are eventually not stuck. The only case when the robots of the 2-long-lived tower change their direction is when they meet the third robot of the system.

Case 2.1.1: The robots of T meet the third robot finitely often.
After the last meeting with the third robot in the system, the robots of T have their predicates $IWasStuckOnMyNodeAndNowWeAre$-$MoreRobots()$ always false. Thus, after the last meeting, the robots of T always consider the same global direction. This implies that they are able to move infinitely often in the same global direction. Moreover, as $\mathcal{G}$ has a finite size, this implies that all the robots visit infinitely often all the nodes of $\mathcal{G}$.

Case 2.1.2: The robots of T meet the third robot infinitely often.
The third robot does not change its direction while it is isolated. Similarly, the robots of T maintain their directions until they meet the third robot. Moreover, we can prove that, after a meeting, the third robot and the robots of T consider two opposite global directions. Then, we can deduce that all the nodes of $\mathcal{G}$ are visited between two consecutive meetings of T and the third robot. As T and the third robot infinitely often meet, the nodes of $\mathcal{G}$ are infinitely often visited.

Case 2.2: There exist an infinite number of 2-long-lived towers in $\mathcal{E}$.
By Lemmas 11 and 12, we know that between two consecutive 2-long-lived towers (from the second one), all the edges, and thus all the nodes of $\mathcal{G}$ are visited. As there is an infinite number of 2-long-lived towers, the nodes of $\mathcal{G}$ are infinitely often visited.

Case 3: There exist no long-lived towers in $\mathcal{E}$.
Then, we know, by Lemma 6, that $\mathcal{E}$ contains only configurations with either three isolated robots or one 2-short-lived tower and one isolated robot. The robots can then start the "sentinels"/"visiting" scheme which permits the perpetual exploration of $\mathcal{G}$ even when there is no eventual missing edge. Note that, as there is no eventual missing edge, it is possible that no 2-short-lived towers are formed. In this case, all the robots maintain their directions.

Thus, we obtain the desired result in every cases. □

Lemma 15. *Algorithm 3 is a self-stabilizing perpetual exploration algorithm for the class of connected-over-time but not edge-recurrent rings of arbitrary size using three robots.*

Sketch of proof. Consider a connected-over-time but not edge-recurrent ring. This implies that there exists exactly one eventual missing edge in $\mathcal{E}$. Denote by $\mathcal{E}^1$ the suffix of $\mathcal{E}$ in which the eventual missing edge never appears.

Assume that there exists a 3-long-lived tower in $\mathcal{E}^1$. According to Lemma 5, this 3-long-liver tower is broken in finite time. Moreover, once this tower is broken, according to Lemma 7, it is impossible to have a configuration containing a 3-long-lived tower. Then, $\mathcal{E}^1$ admits an infinite suffix $\mathcal{E}^2$ without a 3-long-lived tower.

Assume that there exists a 2-long-lived tower in $\mathcal{E}^2$. According to Lemma 5, this 2-long-lived tower is broken in finite time. Once this tower is broken, in the remainder of $\mathcal{E}^2$, there exists at most one 2-long-lived tower T_{second}. Indeed, according to Lemma 5, if T_{second} exists, it is broken in finite time. Moreover, T_{second} cannot be the first 2-long-lived tower of the execution. Then, by Lemmas 11 and 12, $\mathcal{E}^2$ admits an infinite suffix $\mathcal{E}^3$ without a 2-long-lived tower.

In other words, there are no long-lived towers in $\mathcal{E}^3$. By Lemma 6, all configurations in $\mathcal{E}^3$ contain either three isolated robots or one 2-short-lived tower and one isolated robot. The robots can then start the "sentinels" / "visiting" scheme which permits the perpetual exploration of $\mathcal{G}$ and proves the result. □

The end of the road. To conclude the proof, it is sufficient to observe that a connected-over-time ring is by definition either static, edge-recurrent but non static, or connected-over-time but not edge-recurrent. As we prove the self-stabilization of our algorithm in these three cases in Lemmas 13, 14, and 15, we can claim the following final result.

Theorem 1. *Algorithm 3 is a self-stabilizing perpetual exploration algorithm for the class of connected-over-time rings of arbitrary size using three robots.*

5 Conclusion

In this paper, we addressed the open question: "Is it possible to achieve self-stabilization for swarm of robots evolving in highly dynamic graphs?". We answered positively to this question by providing a self-stabilizing algorithm for three synchronous robots that perpetually explore any connected-over-time ring, *i.e.*, any dynamic ring with very weak assumption on connectivity: every node is infinitely often reachable from any another one without any recurrence, periodicity, nor stability assumption.

In addition to the above contributions, our algorithm overcomes the robot networks state-of-the-art in a couple of ways. First, it is the first algorithm dealing with highly dynamic graphs. All previous solutions made some assumptions on periodicity or on all-time connectivity of the graph. Second, it is the first self-stabilizing algorithm for the problem of exploration, either for static or for dynamic graphs.

This work opens an interesting field of research with numerous open questions. First, we should investigate the necessity of every assumption made in this paper. For example, we assumed that robots are synchronous. Is this problem solvable with asynchronous robots? Second, we can investigate the issue of the number of robots. What are the minimal/maximal number of robots to solve the problem? It would be worthwhile to explore other problems in this rather complicated environment, *e.g.*, gathering, leader election, *etc.*It may also be interesting to consider other classes of dynamic graphs and other classes of faults, *e.g.*, crashes of robots, Byzantine failures, *etc.*

References

1. Suzuki, I., Yamashita, M.: Distributed anonymous mobile robots: formation of geometric patterns. SIAM J. Comput. **28**(4), 1347–1363 (1999)
2. Potop-Butucaru, M., Raynal, M., Tixeuil, S.: Distributed computing with mobile robots: an introductory survey. In: International Conference on Network-Based Information Systems (NBiS), pp. 318–324 (2011)
3. Xuan, B., Ferreira, A., Jarry, A.: Computing shortest, fastest, and foremost journeys in dynamic networks. Int. J. Found. Comput. Sci. **14**(02), 267–285 (2003)
4. Casteigts, A., Flocchini, P., Quattrociocchi, W., Santoro, N.: Time-varying graphs and dynamic networks. Int. J. Parallel Emergent Distrib. Syst. **27**(5), 387–408 (2012)
5. Dijkstra, E.: Self-stabilizing systems in spite of distributed control. Commun. ACM **17**(11), 643–644 (1974)
6. Dolev, S.: Self-Stabilization. MIT Press, Cambridge (2000)
7. Tixeuil, S.: Self-stabilizing Algorithms, Chapman & Hall. In: Algorithms and Theory of Computation Handbook, pp. 26.1-26.45. CRC Press, Taylor & Francis Group (2009)
8. Shannon, C.: Presentation of a maze-solving machine. In: 8th Conference of the Josiah Macy, Jr. Foundation, pp. 173–180 (1951)
9. Flocchini, P., Ilcinkas, D., Pelc, A., Santoro, N.: Computing without communicating: ring exploration by asynchronous oblivious robots. In: Tovar, E., Tsigas, P., Fouchal, H. (eds.) OPODIS 2007. LNCS, vol. 4878, pp. 105–118. Springer, Heidelberg (2007). doi:10.1007/978-3-540-77096-1_8
10. Diks, K., Fraigniaud, P., Kranakis, E., Pelc, A.: Tree exploration with little memory. J. Algorithms **51**(1), 38–63 (2004)
11. Baldoni, R., Bonnet, F., Milani, A., Raynal, M.: On the solvability of anonymous partial grids exploration by mobile robots. In: Baker, T.P., Bui, A., Tixeuil, S. (eds.) OPODIS 2008. LNCS, vol. 5401, pp. 428–445. Springer, Heidelberg (2008). doi:10.1007/978-3-540-92221-6_27
12. Flocchini, P., Ilcinkas, D., Pelc, A., Santoro, N.: How many oblivious robots can explore a line. Inf. Process. Lett. **111**(20), 1027–1031 (2011)
13. Flocchini, P., Ilcinkas, D., Pelc, A., Santoro, N.: Remembering without memory: tree exploration by asynchronous oblivious robots. Theor. Comput. Sci. **411**(14–15), 1583–1598 (2010)
14. Chalopin, J., Flocchini, P., Mans, B., Santoro, N.: Network exploration by silent and oblivious robots. In: Thilikos, D.M. (ed.) WG 2010. LNCS, vol. 6410, pp. 208–219. Springer, Heidelberg (2010). doi:10.1007/978-3-642-16926-7_20
15. Datta, A., Lamani, A., Larmore, L., Petit, F.: Ring exploration by oblivious agents with local vision. In: IEEE International Conference on Distributed Computing Systems (ICDCS), pp. 347–356 (2013)
16. Blin, L., Milani, A., Potop-Butucaru, M., Tixeuil, S.: Exclusive perpetual ring exploration without chirality. In: Lynch, N.A., Shvartsman, A.A. (eds.) DISC 2010. LNCS, vol. 6343, pp. 312–327. Springer, Heidelberg (2010). doi:10.1007/978-3-642-15763-9_29
17. Flocchini, P., Mans, B., Santoro, N.: Exploration of periodically varying graphs. In: Dong, Y., Du, D.-Z., Ibarra, O. (eds.) ISAAC 2009. LNCS, vol. 5878, pp. 534–543. Springer, Heidelberg (2009). doi:10.1007/978-3-642-10631-6_55

18. Ilcinkas, D., Wade, A.M.: On the power of waiting when exploring public transportation systems. In: Fernàndez Anta, A., Lipari, G., Roy, M. (eds.) OPODIS 2011. LNCS, vol. 7109, pp. 451–464. Springer, Heidelberg (2011). doi:10.1007/978-3-642-25873-2_31
19. Ilcinkas, D., Wade, A.M.: Exploration of the T-interval-connected dynamic graphs: the case of the ring. In: Moscibroda, T., Rescigno, A.A. (eds.) SIROCCO 2013. LNCS, vol. 8179, pp. 13–23. Springer, Heidelberg (2013). doi:10.1007/978-3-319-03578-9_2
20. Ilcinkas, D., Klasing, R., Wade, A.M.: Exploration of constantly connected dynamic graphs based on cactuses. In: Halldórsson, M.M. (ed.) SIROCCO 2014. LNCS, vol. 8576, pp. 250–262. Springer, Heidelberg (2014). doi:10.1007/978-3-319-09620-9_20
21. Di Luna, G., Dobrev, S., Flocchini, P., Santoro, N.: Live exploration of dynamic rings. In: IEEE International Conference on Distributed Computing Systems (ICDCS), pp. 570–579 (2016)
22. Kuhn, F., Lynch, N., Oshman, R.: Distributed computation in dynamic networks. In: Symposium on the Theory of Computing (STOC), pp. 513–522 (2010)
23. Blin, L., Gradinariu Potop-Butucaru, M., Tixeuil, S.: On the self-stabilization of mobile robots in graphs. In: Tovar, E., Tsigas, P., Fouchal, H. (eds.) OPODIS 2007. LNCS, vol. 4878, pp. 301–314. Springer, Heidelberg (2007). doi:10.1007/978-3-540-77096-1_22
24. Klasing, R., Markou, E., Pelc, A.: Gathering asynchronous oblivious mobile robots in a ring. In: Asano, T. (ed.) ISAAC 2006. LNCS, vol. 4288, pp. 744–753. Springer, Heidelberg (2006). doi:10.1007/11940128_74
25. Dubois, S., Kaaouachi, M.-H., Petit, F.: Enabling minimal dominating set in highly dynamic distributed systems. In: Pelc, A., Schwarzmann, A.A. (eds.) SSS 2015. LNCS, vol. 9212, pp. 51–66. Springer, Heidelberg (2015). doi:10.1007/978-3-319-21741-3_4
26. Bournat, M., Datta, A.K., Dubois, S.: Self-stabilizing robots in highly dynamic environments. Technical report (2016). arXiv:1609.06161

Packet Efficient Implementation of the Omega Failure Detector

Quentin Bramas[1], Dianne Foreback[2], Mikhail Nesterenko[2](✉), and Sébastien Tixeuil[1]

[1] UPMC Sorbonne Universités & IUF, Paris, France
[2] Kent State University, Kent, OH, USA
mikhail@cs.kent.edu

Abstract. We assume that a message may be delivered by packets through multiple hops and investigate the feasibility and efficiency of an Omega Failure Detector implementation. We prove the existence and sustainability of a leader is exponentially more probable in a multi-hop than in a single-hop implementation.

An implementation is: *message efficient* if all but finitely many messages are sent by a single process; *packet efficient* if the number of packets used to transmit a message in all but finitely many messages is linear w.r.t. the number of processes; *super packet efficient* if the number of channels used by packets to transmit all but finitely many messages is linear.

Our results for deterministic algorithms implementing Omega follow. If reliability and timeliness of messages do not correlate, packet efficiency is impossible. We establish necessary and sufficient conditions for the existence of message and packet efficiency and prove correct our deterministic implementation. We prove the eventuality of channels' timeliness makes super packet efficiency impossible.

1 Introduction

The asynchronous system model places no assumptions on message propagation delay or relative process speeds. This makes the model attractive for distributed algorithm research as the results obtained in the model are applicable to an arbitrary network and computer architecture. However, the fully asynchronous system model is not well suited for fault tolerance studies. An elementary problem of consensus, where processes have to agree on a single value, is unsolvable even if only one process may crash [11]: the asynchrony of the model precludes processes from differentiating a crashed and a slow process.

A failure detector [7] is a construct that enables the solution to consensus or related problems in the asynchronous system model. Potentially, a failure detector may be very powerful and, therefore, hide the solution to the problem within its specification. Conversely, the weakest failure detector specifies the least

B. Bonakdarpour and F. Petit (Eds.): SSS 2016, LNCS 10083, pp. 70–87, 2016.
DOI: 10.1007/978-3-319-49259-9_6

amount of synchrony required to implement consensus [6]. One such detector is Omega[1].

Naturally, a failure detector may not be implemented in the asynchronous model itself. Hence, a lot of research is focused on providing the implementation of a detector, especially Omega, in the least restrictive communication model. These restrictions deal with timeliness and reliability of message delivery. Aguilera et al. [1] provide a remarkable Omega implementation which requires only a single process to have eventually timely channels to the other processes and a single process to have so called fair-lossy channels to and from all other processes. Aguilera et al. present what they call an efficient implementation where only a single process sends infinitely many messages. In their work, Aguilera et al. consider a direct channel as the sole means of message delivery from one process to another. In this paper, we consider a more general setting where a message may arrive to a particular process through several intermediate processes. Otherwise, we preserve model assumptions of Aguilera et al.

Our contribution. We study Omega implementation under the assumption that a message may come to its destination through other processes.

To motivate this multi-hop Omega implementation approach, we consider a fixed probability of channel timeliness and study the probability of leader existence in a classic single-hop and in multi-hop implementations. We prove that the probability of leader existence tends to zero for single-hop implementations and to one for multi-hop ones as network size grows. Moreover, the probability of leader persisting while the timeliness of channel changes tends to zero for single-hop and to infinity for multi-hop implementations.

We then consider deterministic algorithms and study three classes of Omega implementations: message efficient, packet efficient and super packet efficient. In a message efficient implementation all but finitely many messages are sent by a single process. In a packet efficient implementation, the number of packets in all but finitely many transmitted messages is linear w.r.t. the number of processes in the network. However, in a (simple) packet efficient implementation, packets of different messages may use different channels such that potentially all channels in the system are periodically used. In a super packet efficient implementation, the number of channels used in all but finitely many messages is also linear w.r.t. to the number of processes.

Our major results are as follows. If timeliness of one message does not correlate with the timeliness of another, i.e., there are no timely channels, we prove that any implementation of Omega has to send infinitely many messages whose number of packets is quadratic w.r.t. the number of processes in the network. This precludes a packet efficient implementation of Omega. If eventually timely and fair-lossy channels are allowed, we establish the necessary and sufficient conditions for the existence of a packet efficient implementation of Omega. We then prove that this eventuality of timely and channels precludes the existence

[1] In literature, the detector is usually denoted by the Greek letter. However, we use the letter to denote the complexity lower bound. To avoid confusion, we spell out the name of the failure detector in English.

of a super packet efficient implementation of Omega. We present an algorithm that uses these necessary conditions and provides a message and packet efficient implementation of Omega.

Related work. The implementation of failure detectors is a well-researched area [2,3,9,13–19]. Refer to [1,2] for detailed comparisons of work related to the kind of Omega implementation we are proposing. We are limiting our literature review to the most recent and closest to our studies.

Delporte-Gallet et al. [9] describe algorithms for recognizing timely channel graphs. Their algorithms are super packet efficient and may potentially be used to implement Omega. However, their solutions assume non-constant size messages and perpetually reliable channels. That is, Delporte-Gallet et al. deviate from the model of Aguilera et al. and the algorithms of Delporte-Gallet et al. do not operate correctly under fair-lossy and eventually timely channel assumptions.

A number of papers consider an Omega implementation under various modifications of Aguilera et al. model. Hutle et al. [13] implement Omega assuming a send-to-all message transmission primitive where f processes are guaranteed to receive the message timely. Fernandez and Raynal [2] assume a process that is able to timely deliver its message to a quorum of processes over direct channels. This quorum and channels may change with each message. A similar rotating set of timely channels is used by Malkhi et al. [16]. Larrea et al. [15] give an efficient implementation of Omega but assume that all channels are eventually timely. In their Omega implementation, Mostefaoui et al. [17] rely on a particular order of message interleaving rather than on timeliness of messages. Biely and Widder [3] consider message-driven (i.e., non-timer based) model and provide an efficient Omega implementation.

There are several recent papers on timely solutions to problems related to Omega implementation. Charron-Bost et al. [8] use a timely spanning tree to solve approximate consensus. Lafuente et al. [14] implement the eventually perfect failure detector using a timely cycle of processes.

2 Notation and Definitions

Model specifics. To simplify the presentation, we use an even more general model than what is used in Aguilera et al. [1]. The major differences are as follows. We use infinite capacity non-FIFO channels rather than single packet capacity channels. Our channel construct makes us explicitly state the packet fairness propagation assumptions that are somewhat obscured by the single capacity channels.

In addition, we do not differentiate between a slow process and a slow channel since slow channels may simulate both. Omega implementation code is expressed in terms of guarded commands, rather than the usual more procedural description. The operation of the algorithm is a computation which is a sequence of these command executions. We express timeouts directly in terms of computation steps rather than abstract or concrete time. This simplifies reasoning about them.

Despite the differences, the models are close enough such that all of the results in this paper are immediately applicable to the traditional Omega implementation model.

Processes and computations. A computer network consists of a set N of processes. The cardinality of this set is n. Each process has a unique identifier from 0 to $n-1$. Processes interact by passing messages through non-FIFO unbounded communication channels. Each process has a channel to all other processes. That is, the network is fully connected. A message is *constant size* if the data it carries is in $O(\log n)$. For example, a constant size message may carry several process identifiers but not a complete network spanning tree.

Each process has variables and actions. The action has a *guard*: a predicate over the local variables and incoming channels of the process. An action is enabled if its guard evaluates to **true**. A *computation* is a potentially infinite sequence of global network states such that each subsequent state is obtained by executing an action enabled in the previous state. This execution is a computation *step*. Processes may crash. *Crashed* process stops executing its actions. *Correct* process does not crash.

Messages and packets. We distinguish between a packet and a message. *Message* is particular content to be distributed to processes in the network. *Origin* is the process that initiates the message. The identifier of the origin is included in the message. Messages are sent via packets. *Packet* is a portion of data transmitted over a particular channel. A message is the payload of a packet. A process may receive a packet and either forward the message it contains or not. A process may not modify it: if a process needs to send additional information, the process may send a separate message. A process may forward the same message at most once. In effect, a message is transmitted to processes of the network using packets. A particular process may receive a message either directly from the origin, or indirectly possibly through multiple hops.

Scheduling and fairness. We express process synchronization in terms of an adversarial scheduler. The scheduler restrictions are as follows. We do not distinguish slow processes and slow packet propagation. A scheduler may express these phenomena through scheduling process action execution in a particular way. A packet transmission immediately enables the packet receipt action in the recipient process. A packet is lost if the receipt action is never executed. A packet is not lost if it is eventually received.

Timers. Timer is a construct with the following properties. A timer can be reset, stopped and increased. It can also be checked whether the timer is on or off. It has a *timeout integer* value and a *timeout action* associated with it. A timer is either a receiver timer or a sender timer. If a *sender timer* is on, the timeout action is executed once the computation has at most the timeout integer steps without executing the timer reset. If a *receiver timer* is on, the timeout action is executed once the computation has at least the timeout integer steps without executing the timer reset. Increasing the timer adds an arbitrary positive integer value to the timeout integer. An off timer can be set to on by resetting it.

Reliable and timely messages and packets. A packet is *reliable* if it is received. A message is reliable if it is received by every correct process; i.e. one that does not crash. A channel is reliable if every packet transmitted over this channel is reliable.

A channel is *fair-lossy* if it has the following properties. If there is an infinite number of packet transmissions over a particular fair-lossy channel of a particular message type and origin, then infinitely many are received. We assume that a fair-lossy channel is not type discriminating. That is, if it is fair-lossy for one type and origin, it is also fair-lossy for every pair of message type and origin.

Observe that if there is an infinite number of message transmissions of a particular message type and origin over a path that is fair-lossy, then infinitely many succeed. There converse is true as well: if there is an infinite number of successful message transmissions, there must be a fair-lossy path between the origin an the destination.

A packet is *timely* if it is received within a bounded number of computation steps. Specifically, there is a finite integer B such that the packet is received within B steps. Naturally, a timely packet is a reliable packet. A message is timely if it is received by every process via a path of timely packets. A channel is timely if every packet transmitted over this channel is timely. A channel is eventually timely if the number of non-timely packets it transmits is finite. Note that a channel that transmits a finite number of packets is always eventually timely.

The timely channel definition is relatively clear. The opposite, non-timely channel, is a bit more involved. A channel that occasionally delays or misses a few packets is not non-timely as the algorithm may just ignore the missed packets with a large enough timeout. Hence, the following definition.

A channel is *strongly non-timely* if the following holds. If there is an infinite number of packet transmissions of a particular type and origin over a particular non-timely channel, then, for any fixed integer, there are infinitely many computation segments of this length such that none of the packets are delivered inside any of the segments.

Similarly, the non-timeliness has to be preserved across multiple channels, a message may not gain timeliness by finding a parallel timely path, then, for example, the two paths may alternate delivering timely messages. Therefore, we add an additional condition for non-timeliness.

All paths between a pair of processes x and y are *strongly non-timely* if x sends an infinite number of messages to y, yet regardless of how the message is forwarded or what path it takes, for any fixed integer, there are infinitely many computation segments of this length such that none of the messages are delivered inside any of the segments. Unless otherwise noted, when we discuss non-timely channels and paths, we mean strongly non-timely channels and paths.

Communication models. To make it easier to address the variety of possible communication restrictions, we define several models. *The dependable (channel) model* allows eventually or perpetually reliable timely or fair-lossy channels. In the dependable model, an algorithm may potentially discover the dependable channels by observing packet propagation. *The general propagation model* does not allow either reliable or timely channels. Thus, one message propagation is not related to another message propagation.

Message propagation graph. *Message propagation graph* is a directed graph over network processes and channels that determines whether packet propagation over a particular channel would be successful. This graph is connected and has a single source: the origin process. This concept is a way to reason about scheduling of the packets of a particular message.

Each message has two propagation graphs. In *reliable propagation graph* R, each edge indicates whether the packet is received if transmitted over this channel. In *timely propagation graph* T each edge indicates whether the packet is timely if transmitted over this channel. Since a timely packet is a reliable packet, for the same message, the timely propagation graph is a subgraph of the reliable propagation graph. In general, a propagation graph for each message is unique. That is, even for the same source process, the graphs for two messages may differ. This indicates that different messages may take divergent routes.

If a channel from process x to process y is reliable, then edge (x, y) is present in the reliable propagation graph for every message where process x is present. In other words, if the message reaches x and x sends it to y, then y receives it. A similar discussion applies to a timely channel and corresponding edges in timely propagation graphs.

Propagation graphs are determined by the scheduler in advance of the message transmission. That is, the recipient process, depending on the algorithm, may or may not forward the received message along a particular outgoing channel. However, if the process forwards the message, the presence of an edge in the propagation graph determines the success of the message transmission. Note that the process forwards a particular message at most once. Hence, the propagation graph captures the complete possible message propagation pattern. A process may crash during message transmission. This crash does not alter propagation graphs.

Proposition 1. *A message is reliable only if its reliable propagation graph* R *is such that every correct process is reachable from the origin through non-crashed processes.*

Proposition 2. *A message is timely only if its timely propagation graph* T *is such that every correct process is reachable from the origin through non-crashed processes.*

Omega implementation and its efficiency. An algorithm that implements the Omega Failure Detector (or just Omega) is such that in a suffix of every computation, each correct process outputs the identifier of the same correct process. This process is the *leader*.

An implementation of Omega is *message efficient* if the origin of all but finitely many messages is a single correct process and all but finitely many messages are constant size. An implementation of Omega is *packet efficient* if all but finitely many messages are transmitted using $O(n)$ packets.

An Omega implementation is *super packet efficient* if it is packet efficient and the packets of all but finitely many messages are using the same channels. In other words, if a packet of message m_1 is forwarded over some channel, then a packet of another message m_2 is also forwarded over this channel. The intent of a super packet efficient algorithm is to only use a limited number of channels infinitely often. Since a packet efficient algorithm uses $O(n)$ packets infinitely often, a super packet efficient algorithm uses $O(n)$ channels infinitely often.

3 Probabilistic Properties

In this section, we contrast a multi-hop implementation of Omega and a classic single-hop, also called direct channel, implementation. We assume each network channel is timely with probability p. The timeliness probability of one channel is independent of this probability of any other channel.

Leader existence probability. We assume that the leader may exist only if there is a process that has timely paths to all processes in the network. In case of direct channel implementation, the length of each such path must be exactly one.

As n grows, Omega implementations behave radically differently. Theorems 1 and 2 state the necessary conditions for leader existence and indicate that the probability of leader existence for direct channel implementation approaches zero exponentially quickly, while this probability for multi-hop implementation approaches one exponentially quickly. In practical terms, a multi-hop omega implementation is far more likely to succeed in establishing the leader.

Theorem 1. *If the probability of each channel to be timely is $p < 1$, then the probability of leader existence in any direct channel Omega implementation approaches zero exponentially fast as n grows.*

Proof. Let D_x be the probability that some process x does not have direct timely channels to all processes in the network. This probability is $\mathbb{P}(D_x) = 1 - p^{n-1}$. For two distinct processes x and y, D_x and D_y are disjoint since channels are oriented. Thus, if $p < 1$, the probability that no leader exists is $\mathbb{P}(\bigcap_{x \in V} D_x) = (1 - p^{n-1})^n \overset{n \to +\infty}{\rightarrow} 1$. □

Theorem 2. *If the probability of each channel to be timely is $p < 1$, then the probability of leader existence in any multi-hop Omega implementation approaches* 1 *exponentially fast as n grows.*

Proof. A channel is *bitimely* if it is timely in both directions. The probability that there exists at least one process such that there exist timely paths from this process to all other processes is greater than the probability to reach them through bitimely paths. We use the probability of the latter as a lower bound for our result. If p is the probability of a channel to be timely, $\tilde{p} = p^2$ is the probability that it is bitimely. Consider graph G where the edges represent bitimely channels. It is an Erdos-Renyi graph where an edge exists with probability $\tilde{p}$. It was shown (see [12]) that $\mathbb{P}(G \text{ is connected}) \sim 1 - n(1 - \tilde{p})^{n-1} \overset{n \to +\infty}{\rightarrow} 1$. □

Leader stability. As in the previous subsection, we assume the leader has timely paths to all other processes in the network. If channel timeliness changes, this process may not have timely paths to all other processes anymore. *Leader stability time* is the expected number of rounds of such channel timeliness change where a particular process remains the leader.

Again, direct channel and multi-hop implementations of Omega behave differently. Direct channel leader stability time approaches zero as n increases and cannot be limited from below by fixing a particular value of channel timeliness probability. Multi-hop leader stability goes to infinity exponentially quickly. In a practical setting, a leader is significantly more stable in a multi-hop Omega implementation than in a direct channel one.

Theorem 3. *In any direct channel Omega implementation, if the probability of each channel to be timely is $p < 1$, leader stability time goes exponentially fast to 0 as n grows. If leader stability time is to remain above a fixed constant $E > 0$, then the channel timeliness probability p must converge to 1 exponentially fast as n grows.*

Proof. At a given time, a given process has timely channels to all other processes with probability p^{n-1}. The number of rounds X a given process retains timely paths to all other processes follows a geometric distribution $\mathcal{P}(X = r) = q^r(1-q)$, where $q = p^{n-1}$. Thus, the expected number of rounds a process retains timely channels to all other processes is $\frac{q}{1-q} = \frac{p^{n-1}}{1-p^{n-1}} \sim p^{n-1}$, which tends exponentially fast toward 0 if p is a constant less than 1.

Assume $\mathbb{E}(X)$ converges towards a given fixed number E as n tends towards infinity. That is, we need $\lim_{n\to\infty} \mathbb{P}(G \text{ is connected}) = \frac{1}{E+1}$. Then, p^{n-1} tends to $\frac{1}{E+2}$, which implies that p converges towards 1 exponentially fast. □

Theorem 4. *In any multi-hop Omega implementation, if the probability of each channel to be timely is $p < 1$, leader stability time goes to infinity exponentially fast as n grows. If leader stability time is to remain above a fixed constant $E > 0$, then channel timeliness probability may converge to 0 exponentially fast as n grows.*

Proof. If we fix $\tilde{p}$, $0 < \tilde{p} < 1$, we have $\mathbb{P}(G \text{ is connected}) \sim 1 - n(1-\tilde{p})^{n-1}$ (see [10,12]). Then, the expected number of rounds a given process retains timely paths to all other processes is asymptotically $n^{-1}\left(\frac{1}{1-\tilde{p}}\right)^n$, which increases exponentially fast.

Assume $\mathbb{E}(X)$ converges towards a given fixed number E as n tends to infinity. This means that

$$\lim_{n\to\infty} \mathbb{P}(G \text{ is connected}) = \frac{1}{E+1} = e^{-e^{-c}}$$

Using well-known results of random graph theory [4], we can take

$$\tilde{p}(n) = \frac{\ln n}{n} + \frac{c}{n} = \frac{\ln n}{n} - \frac{\ln\ln(1+E)}{n}$$ □

4 Necessity and Sufficiency Properties

We now explore the properties of a deterministic Omega implementation.

Model independent properties. The below Omega implementation properties are applicable to both general propagation and dependable channel model. Intuitively, Theorem 5 states that the leader needs to periodically inform other processes of its correctness or they will not be able to detect its crash.

Theorem 5. *In an implementation of Omega, at least one correct process needs to send infinitely many timely messages.*

Proof. Assume $\mathcal{A}$ is an implementation of Omega where every correct process sends a finite number of timely messages. Start with a network where all but two processes x and y crash, wait till all timely messages are sent. Since $\mathcal{A}$ is an implementation of Omega, eventually x and y need to agree on the leader. Let it be x. Since all timely messages are sent, the remaining messages may be delayed arbitrarily. If x now crashes, process y must eventually elect itself the leader. Instead, we delay messages from x to y. The crash and the delay are indistinguishable to y so it elects itself the leader. We now deliver messages in an arbitrary manner. Again, since $\mathcal{A}$ implements Omega, x and y should agree on the leader. Let it be y. The argument for x is similar. We then delay messages from y to x forcing x to select itself the leader. We continue this procedure indefinitely. The resultant sequence is a computation of $\mathcal{A}$. However at least one process, either x or y, oscillates in its leader selection infinitely many times. To put another way, this process never elects the leader. This means that, contrary to the initial assumption, $\mathcal{A}$ is not an implementation of Omega. This proves the theorem. □

If single process sends an infinite number of messages in a message efficient implementation of Omega, this process must be the leader. Otherwise processes are not able to recognize the crash of the leader. Hence, the corollary of Theorem 5.

Corollary 1. *In a message efficient implementation of Omega, the leader must send infinitely many timely messages.*

General propagation model properties. The intuition for the results in this subsection is as follows. Since there are no channel dependability properties in the general propagation model, for timely delivery a message needs to be sent across every channel. Indeed, in case some channel is skipped, this may be the channel that contains the only timely path leading to some process. Skipping this channel precludes timely message delivery. It follows that $\Omega(n^2)$ packets are required to timely deliver a message in the general propagation model. Therefore, there does not exist a message and packet efficient implementation of Omega in this model.

Lemma 1. *To timely deliver a message in the general propagation model, each recipient process needs to send it across every outgoing channel, except for possibly the channels leading to the origin and the sender.*

Proof. Assume the opposite. There exists an algorithm $\mathcal{A}$ that timely delivers message m from the origin x to all processes in the network such that some process y receives it timely yet does not forward it to some process $z \neq x$.

Consider the propagation graph T for m to be as follows.

$$x \rightarrow y \rightarrow z \rightarrow \text{rest of the processes}$$

That is, the timely paths to all processes lead from x to y then to z. If $\mathcal{A}$ is such that x sends m to y, then, by assumption, y does not forward m to z. Therefore, no process except for y gets m through timely packets. By definition of the timely message, m is not timely received by these processes. If x does not send m to y, then none of the processes receive a timely message. In either case, contrary to the initial assumption, $\mathcal{A}$ does not timely deliver m to all processes in the network. □

The below corollary follows from Lemma 1.

Corollary 2. *It requires $\Omega(n^2)$ packets to timely deliver a message in the general propagation model.*

Combining Corollary 2 and Theorem 5 we obtain Corollary 3.

Corollary 3. *In the general propagation model, there does not exist a message and packet efficient implementation of Omega.*

Proposition 3. *There exists a message efficient implementation of Omega in the general propagation model where each correct process can send reliable messages to the leader.*

The algorithm that proves the above proposition is a straightforward extension of the second algorithm in Aguilera et al. [1] where every process re-sends received messages to every outgoing channel.

Dependable channel model properties. Unlike the general propagation model where dependability properties of a channel cannot be established, if timely and reliable channels are allowed, packet and message efficient implementation of Omega is possible. However, the super-packet efficiency is not.

Lemma 2. *In any message efficient implementation of Omega, each correct process must have a fair-lossy path to the leader.*

Proof. Assume there is a message-efficient implementation $\mathcal{A}$ of Omega where there is a correct process x that does not have a fair-lossy path to the leader. According to Corollary 1, x itself may not be elected the leader. Assume there is a computation σ_1 of $\mathcal{A}$ where process $y \neq x$ is elected the leader. Note that fair-lossy channels are not type discriminating. That is, if x does not have a fair-lossy path to y, but has a fair lossy path to some other process z, then z does not have a fair-lossy path to y either. Thus, there must be a set of processes $S \subset N$ such that $x \in S$ and $y \notin S$ that do not have fair-lossy paths to processes outside S.

Since $\mathcal{A}$ is message efficient, processes of S only send a finite number of messages to y. Consider another computation σ_2 which shares prefix with σ_2 up to the point were the last message from processes of S is received outside of S. After that, all messages from y to processes in S and all messages from S to outside are lost. That is in σ_2, y does not have timely, or every fair-lossy, paths to processes of S. It is possible that some other process w is capable of timely communication to all processes in the network. However, since $\mathcal{A}$ is efficient, no other processes but y is supposed to send infinitely many messages.

Since all messages from S are lost, σ_1 and σ_2 are indistinguishable for the correct processes outside S. Therefore, they elect y as the leader. However, processes in S receive no messages from y. Therefore, they have to elect some other process u to be the leader. This means that $\mathcal{A}$ allows correct processes to output different leaders. That is, $\mathcal{A}$ is not an implementation of Omega. □

We define a *source* to be a process that does not have incoming timely channels.

Lemma 3. *To timely deliver a message in the dependable channel model, each recipient needs to send it across every outgoing channel to a source, except for possibly the channels leading to the origin and the sender.*

The proof of the above lemma is similar to the proof of Lemma 1. Observe that Lemma 3 states that the timely delivery of a packet requires n messages per source. If the number of sources is proportional to the number of processes in the network, we obtain the following corollary.

Corollary 4. *It requires $\Omega(n^2)$ packets to timely deliver a message in the dependable channel model where the number of sources is proportional to n.*

Theorem 6. *In the dependable channel model, the following conditions are necessary and sufficient for the existence of a packet and message efficient implementation of Omega: (i) there is at least one process l that has an eventually timely path to every correct process (ii) every correct process has a fair-lossy path to l.*

Proof. We demonstrate sufficiency by presenting, in the next section, an algorithm that implements Omega in the dependable channel model with the conditions of the theorem.

We now focus on proving necessity. Let us address the first condition of the theorem. Assume there is a message and packet efficient implementation $\mathcal{A}$ of Omega in the dependable channel model even though no process has eventually timely paths to every correct process. Let there be a computation of $\mathcal{A}$ where some process x is elected the leader even though x does not have a timely path to each correct process. According to Corollary 1, x needs to send infinitely many timely messages. According to Corollary 4, each such message requires $\Omega(n^2)$

packets. That is, $\mathcal{A}$ may not be message and packet efficient. This proves the first condition of the theorem. The second condition immediately follows from Lemma 2. □

The below theorem shows that (plain) efficiency is all that can be achieved with the necessary conditions of Theorem 6. That is, even if these conditions are satisfied, super packet efficiency is not possible.

Theorem 7. *There does not exist a message and super packet efficient implementation of Omega in the dependable communication model even if there is a process l with an eventually timely path to every correct process and every correct process has a fair-lossy path to l.*

Proof. Assume the opposite. Suppose there exists a super packet efficient algorithm $\mathcal{A}$ that implements Omega in the network where some process l has an eventually timely path to all correct processes and every correct process has fair-lossy paths to l.

Without loss of generality, assume the number of processes in the network is even. Divide the processes into two sets S_1 and S_2 such that the cardinality of both sets is $n/2$. Refer to Fig. 1 for illustration. S_1 is completely connected by timely channels. Similarly, S_2 is also completely connected by timely channels. The dependability of channels between S_1 and S_2 is immaterial at this point.

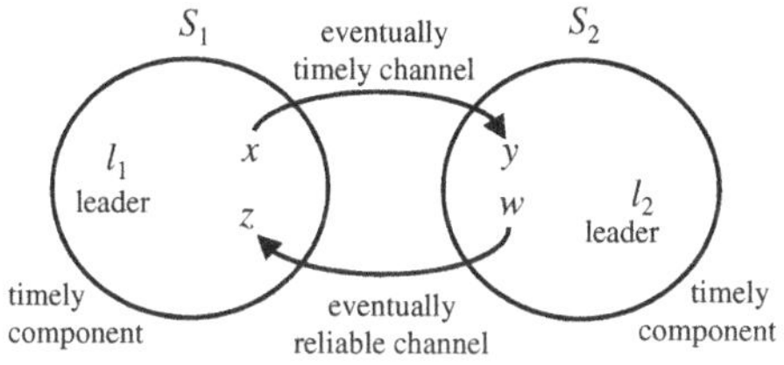

Fig. 1. Network for σ_3 computation of Theorem 7.

Consider a computation σ_1 of $\mathcal{A}$ on this network where all processes in S_1 are correct and all processes in S_2 crashed in the beginning of the computation. Since $\mathcal{A}$ is an implementation of Omega, one process $l_1 \in S_1$ is elected the leader. Since $\mathcal{A}$ is message efficient, only l_1 sends messages infinitely often. Since $\mathcal{A}$ is super packet efficient, only $O(n)$ channels carry theses messages infinitely often. Since the network is completely connected, there are $(n/2)^2$ channels leading from S_1 to S_2. This is in $O(n^2)$. Thus, there is least one channel (x, y) such that $x \in S_1$ and $y \in S_2$ that does not carry messages from l_1 infinitely often.

Let us consider a computation σ_2 of $\mathcal{A}$ where all processes S_2 are correct and all processes in S_1 crash in the beginning of the computation. Similar to σ_1, there is a process $l_2 \in S_2$ that is elected the leader in σ_2, and there is a channel (z, w) such that $z \in S_2$ and $w \in S_1$ that carries only finitely many messages of l_2.

We construct a computation σ_3 of $\mathcal{A}$ as follows. All processes are correct. Channel dependability inside S_1 and S_2 is as described above. All channels between S_1 and S_2 are completely lossy, i.e., they lose every transmitted message. An exception is channel (x, y) that becomes timely as soon as it loses the last message it is supposed to transmit. Similarly, channel (z, w) becomes reliable as soon as it loses the last message.

To construct σ_3, we interleave the actions of σ_1 and σ_2 in an arbitrary manner. Observe that to processes in S_1 computations σ_1 and σ_3 are indistinguishable. Similarly, to processes in S_2, the computations σ_2 and σ_3 are indistinguishable.

Let us examine the constructed computation closely. Sets S_1 and S_2 are completely connected by timely channels, and (x, y), connecting S_1 and S_2 is eventually timely. This means that l_1 has an eventually timely path to every correct process in the network. Moreover, due to channel (z, w), every process has a fair-lossy path to l_1. That is, the conditions of the theorem are satisfied. However, the processes of S_1 elect l_1 as their leader while the processes of S_2 elect l_2. This means that the processes do not agree on the single leader. That is, contrary to the initial assumption, $\mathcal{A}$ is not an implementation of Omega. The theorem follows. □

5 $\mathcal{MPO}$: Message and Packet Efficient Implementation of Omega

In this section we present an algorithm we call $\mathcal{MPO}$ that implements Omega in the fair-lossy channel communication model. As per Theorem 6, we assume that there is at least one process that has an eventually timely path to every correct process in the network and every correct process has a fair-lossy path to this process. The code of the algorithm is shown in Fig. 2. The main idea of $\mathcal{MPO}$ is for processes to attempt to claim the leadership of the network while discovering the reliability of its channels. Each process weighs each channel by the number of messages that fail to come across it. The lighter channel is considered more reliable. If a process determines that it has the lightest paths to all processes in the network, the process tries to claim leadership of the network.

The leadership is obtained in phases. First, the leader candidate sends *startPhase* message. Then, the candidate periodically sends *alive* message. In case an *alive* fails to reach one of the processes on time, the recipient replies with *failed*. The size of *startPhase* depends on the network size. The size of the other message types is constant.

The routes of the messages vary. Messages that are only sent finitely many times are *broadcast*: sent across every channel in the network. Once one process receives such a message for the first time, the process re-sends it along all of its outgoing channels. Specifically, *startPhase*, *stopPhase* and *failed* are broadcast. The leader sends *alive* infinitely often. Hence, for the algorithm to be packet efficient, *alive* has to be sent only along selected channels. Message *alive* is routed through the channels that the origin believes to be the most reliable.

```
constants
    p // process identifier
    N // set of network process identifiers, cardinality is n
    timers[p] length is TO, i.e. initially an arbitrary integer
variables
    leader, initially ⊥ // local leader
    phases[n], initially zero // current phase number
    edges[n][n], initially zero // edge fault weights
    arbs[n], initially arbitrary // arborescences
    timers[n], initially timers[p] on, others off
        length of timers[x] : x ≠ p is arbitrary // timer to send/receive a message
    shout, initially zero // process id to send alive to all neighbors
actions
    timeout(timers[q]) ⟶
        if p = q then // own/sender timeout
            // compute arb rooted in p based on edges
            newArb = arborescence(edges, p)
            newLeader := minWeight((arbs[r] : r ≠ p : on(timers[r])), newArb))
            if leader ≠ newLeader then // leadership changes
                if newLeader = p then // p gains leadership
                    arbs[p] := newArb
                    send startPhase(p, phases[p], arbs[p]) to N/p
                if leader = p then // p loses leadership
                    phases[p] := phases[p] + 1
                    send stopPhase(p, phases[p]) to N/p
                leader := newLeader

            else // leadership persists
                if leader = p then
                    shout := shout + 1 mod n
                    if shout ≠ p then
                        send alive(p, phases[p], shout) to arbs[p](p.children)
                    else // my turn to shout
                        send alive(p, phases[p], shout) to N/p
            reset(timers[p]) // own timer never off

        // neighbor timeout/receiver timeout, assume failed, increase, do not reset
        else
            send failed(q, p, arbs[q](p.parent)) to N/p
            increase(timers[q])

    receive startPhase(q, phase, arb) for the first time ⟶
        // if new phase, propagate message, reset timer
        if p ≠ q ∧ phases[q] ≤ phase then
            arbs[q] := arb
            phases[q] := phase
            send startPhase(q, phase, arb) to N/p
            reset(timers[q])

    receive stopPhase(q, phase) for the first time ⟶
        if p ≠ q ∧ phase[q] < phase then
            phases[q] := phase
            send stopPhase(q, phase) to N/p
            stop(timers[q])

    receive alive(q, phase, sh) for the first time from r ⟶
        if p ≠ q ∧ phase[q] = phase then
            if r = arbs[q](p.parent) then // received through arborescence
                if sh ≠ p then
                    send alive(q, phase, sh) to arbs[q](p.children)
                else // my turn to shout
                    send alive(q, phase, sh) to N/p
                reset(timers[q])
            else // received from elsewhere
                if off(timers[q]) then
                    reset(timers[q])

    receive failed(q, r, s) for the first time ⟶
        if p = q then // if p's alive failed
            edges[s][r] := edges[s][r] + 1 // increase weight of edge from parent
        else
            send failed(q, r, s) to N/p
```

Fig. 2. Message and packet efficient implementation of Omega $\mathcal{MPO}$.

Specifically, *alive* is routed along the channels of a minimum weight *arborescence*: a directed tree rooted in the origin reaching all other processes. The arborescence is computed by the origin once it claims leadership. It is sent in the *startPhase* that starts a phase. Once each process receives the arborescence, the process stores it in the *arbs* array element for the corresponding origin. After receiving *alive* from a particular origin, the recipient consults the respective arborescence and forwards the message to the channels stated there.

In addition to routing *alive* along the arborescence, each process takes turns sending the leader's *alive* to all its neighbors. The reason for this is rather subtle: see Theorem 7 for details. Due to crashes and message losses, *arbs* for the leader at various processes may not reach every correct process. For example, it may lead to a crashed process. Thus, some processes may potentially not receive *alive* and, therefore, not send *failed*. Since *failed* are not sent, the leader may not be able to distinguish such a state from a state with correct *arbs*.

To ensure that every process receives *alive*, each process, in turn, sends *alive* to its every neighbor rather than along most reliable channels. Since only a single process sends to all neighbors a particular *alive* message, the packet complexity remains $O(n)$.

Message *failed* is sent if a process does not receive a timely *alive*. This message carries the parent of the process which was supposed to send the *alive*. That is, the sender of *failed* blames the immediate ancestor in the arborescence. Once the origin of the missing *alive*, receives *failed*, it increments the weight of the appropriate edge in *edges* that stores the weights of all channels. If a process has timely outgoing paths to all processes in the network, its arborescence in *edges* convergences to these paths.

Action specifics. The algorithm is organized in five actions. The first is a timeout action, the other four are message-receipt actions.

The timeout action handles two types of timers: sender and receiver. Process p's own timer ($q = p$) is a sender timer. It is rather involved. This timer is always on since the process resets it after processing. First, the process computes the minimum weight of the arborescence for each leader candidate. A process is considered a leader candidate if its timer is on. Note that since p's own timer is always on, it is always considered.

The process with the minimum weight arborescence is the new leader. If the leadership changes ($leader \neq newLeader$), further selection is made. If p gains leadership ($newLeader = p$), then p starts a new phase by updating its own minimum-weight arborescence and broadcasting *startPhase*. If p loses leadership, it increments its phase and broadcasts *stopPhase* bearing the new phase number.

If the leadership persists ($leader = newLeader$) and p is the leader, it sends *alive*. Process p keeps track of whose turn it is to send *alive* to all its neighbors in the *shout* variable. The variable's value rotates among the ids of all processes in the network.

The neighbor timer ($q \neq p$) is a receiver timer. If the process does not get *alive* on time from q, then p sends *failed*. In case the process sends *failed*, it also increases the timeout value for the timer of q thus attempting to estimate the channel delay.

For our algorithm, the timer integers are as follows. The sender timer is an arbitrary constant integer value TO. This value controls how often *alive* is sent. It does not affect the correctness of the algorithm. Receiver timers initially hold an arbitrary value. The timer integer is increased every time there is a timeout. Thus, for an eventually timely channel, the process is able to estimate the propagation delay and set the timer integer large enough that the timeout does not occur. For untimely channels, the timeout value may increase without bound.

The next four actions are message receipt handling. Note that a single process may receive packets carrying the same message multiple times across different paths. However, every process handles the message at most once: when it encounters it for the first time. Later duplicate packets are discarded.

The second action is *startPhase* handling. The process copies the arborescence and phase carried by the message, rebroadcasts it and then resets the *alive* receiver timer associated with the origin process. The third action is the receipt of *stopPhase* which causes the recipient to stop the appropriate timer.

The forth action is *alive* handling. If *alive* is the matching phase, it is further considered. If *alive* comes through the origin's arborescence, the receiver sends *alive* to its children in the origin's arborescence or broadcasts it. The process then resets the timer to wait for the next *alive*. If *alive* comes from elsewhere, that is, it was the sender's turn to send *alive* to all its neighbors, then p just resets the timeout and waits for an *alive* to arrive from the proper channel. This forces the process to send *failed* if *alive* does not arrive from the channel of the arborescence.

The last action is *failed* handling. If *failed* is in response to an *alive* originated by this process ($p = q$) then the origin process increments the weight of the edge from the parent of the reporting process to the process itself according to the message arborescence. If *failed* is not destined to this process, p rebroadcasts it.

The algorithm's correctness is summarized by the below theorem. Its detailed proof can be found here [5].

Theorem 8. *Algorithm $\mathcal{MPO}$ is a message and packet efficient implementation of Omega in the fair-lossy channel model.*

6 Algorithm Extensions

We conclude the paper with several observations about $\mathcal{MPO}$. The algorithm trivially works in a non-completely connected network provided that the rest of the assumptions used in the algorithm design, such as eventually timely paths from the leader to all correct processes, are satisfied. Similarly, the algorithm works correctly if the channel reliability and timeliness is origin-related. That is, a channel may be timely for some, not necessarily incident, process x, but not for another process y. Algorithm $\mathcal{MPO}$ may be modified to use only constant-size messages. The only non-constant size message is *startPhase*. However, the message type is supposed to be timely. So, instead of sending a single large message, the modified $\mathcal{MPO}$ may instead send a sequence of fixed-size messages with the content to be re-assembled by the receivers. If one of the constituent messages does not arrive on time, the whole large message is considered lost.

References

1. Aguilera, M.K., Delporte-Gallet, C., Fauconnier, H., Toueg, S.: On implementing omega in systems with weak reliability and synchrony assumptions. Distrib. Comput. **21**(4), 285–314 (2008)
2. Anta, A.F., Raynal, M.: From an asynchronous intermittent rotating star to an eventual leader. IEEE Trans. Parallel Distrib. Syst. **21**(9), 1290–1303 (2010)
3. Biely, M., Widder, J.: Optimal message-driven implementations of omega with mute processes. ACM Trans. Auton. Adapt. Syst. (TAAS) **4**(1), 4 (2009)
4. Bollobás, B.: Random Graphs, 2nd edn. Cambridge University Press, Cambridge (2001)
5. Bramas, Q., Foreback, D., Nesterenko, M., Tixeuil, S.: Packet efficient implementation of the omega failure detector, Research Report. UPMC Université Paris VI; Kent State University, February 2016. arXiv:1505.05025
6. Chandra, T.D., Hadzilacos, V., Toueg, S.: The weakest failure detector for solving consensus. J. ACM **43**(4), 685–722 (1996)
7. Chandra, T.D., Toueg, S.: Unreliable failure detectors for reliable distributed systems. J. ACM **43**(2), 225–267 (1996)
8. Charron-Bost, B., Függer, M., Nowak, T.: Approximate consensus in highly dynamic networks. arXiv preprint arXiv:1408.0620 (2014)
9. Delporte-Gallet, C., Devismes, S., Fauconnier, H., Larrea, M.: Algorithms for extracting timeliness graphs. In: Patt-Shamir, B., Ekim, T. (eds.) SIROCCO 2010. LNCS, vol. 6058, pp. 127–141. Springer, Heidelberg (2010). doi:10.1007/978-3-642-13284-1_11
10. Erdös, P., Rényi, A.: On random graphs I. Publ. Math. Debrecen **6**, 290–297 (1959)
11. Fischer, M.J., Lynch, N.A., Paterson, M.S.: Impossibility of distributed consensus with one faulty process. J. ACM **32**(2), 374–382 (1985)
12. Gilbert, E.N.: Random graphs. Ann. Math. Stat. **30**(4), 1141–1144 (1959)
13. Hutle, M., Malkhi, D., Schmid, U., Zhou, L.: Chasing the weakest system model for implementing ω and consensus. IEEE Trans. Dependable Secur. Comput. **6**(4), 269–281 (2009)
14. Lafuente, A., Larrea, M., Soraluze, I., Cortiñas, R.: Communication-optimal eventually perfect failure detection in partially synchronous systems. J. Comput. Syst. Sci. **81**(2), 383–397 (2015)
15. Larrea, M., Fernández, A., Arévalo, S.: On the implementation of unreliable failure detectors in partially synchronous systems. IEEE Trans. Comput. **53**(7), 815–828 (2004)
16. Malkhi, D., Oprea, F., Zhou, L.: ω meets paxos: leader election and stability without eventual timely links. In: Fraigniaud, P. (ed.) DISC 2005. LNCS, vol. 3724, pp. 199–213. Springer, Heidelberg (2005). doi:10.1007/11561927_16

17. Mostefaoui, A., Mourgaya, E., Raynal, M.: Asynchronous implementation of failure detectors. In: 43rd Annual IEEE/IFIP International Conference on Dependable Systems and Networks (DSN), pp. 351–351. IEEE Computer Society (2013)
18. Mostéfaoui, A., Raynal, M., Travers, C.: Time-free and timer-based assumptions can be combined to obtain eventual leadership. IEEE Trans. Parallel Distrib. Syst. **17**(7), 656–666 (2006)
19. De Prisco, R., Lampson, B.W., Lynch, N.A.: Revisiting the PAXOS algorithm. Theor. Comput. Sci. **243**(1–2), 35–91 (2000)

Probabilistic Asynchronous Arbitrary Pattern Formation (Short Paper)

Quentin Bramas(✉) and Sébastien Tixeuil

Sorbonne Universités, UPMC Univ Paris 06, CNRS, LIP6 UMR 7606, 4 Place Jussieu, 75005 Paris, France
quentin.bramas@lip6.fr

Abstract. We propose a new probabilistic pattern formation algorithm for oblivious mobile robots that operates in the ASYNC model. Unlike previous work, our algorithm makes no assumptions about the local coordinate systems of robots (the robots do *not* share a common "North" nor a common "Right"), yet it preserves the ability from any initial configuration that contains at least 5 robots to form any general pattern (and not just patterns that satisfy symmetricity predicates). Our proposal also gets rid of the previous assumption (in the same model) that robots do not pause while moving (so, our robots really are fully asynchronous), and the amount of randomness is kept low – a single random bit per robot per Look-Compute-Move cycle is used. Our protocol consists in the combination of two phases, a probabilistic leader election phase, and a deterministic pattern formation one. As the deterministic phase does not use chirality, it may be of independent interest in the deterministic context. A noteworthy feature of our algorithm is the ability to form patterns with multiplicity points (except the gathering case due to impossibility results), a new feature in the context of pattern formation that we believe is an important asset of our approach.

1 Introduction

We consider a set of mobile robots that move freely in a continuous 2-dimensional Euclidian space. Each robot repeats asynchronously Look-Compute-Move (LCM) cycles [5]. First, it *Looks* at its surroundings to obtain a snapshot containing the locations of all robots as points in the plane, with respect to its ego-centered coordinate system. Based on this visual information, the robot *Computes* a destination and then *Moves* towards the destination. The robots are identical, anonymous and oblivious et al., the computed destination in each cycle depends only on the snapshot obtained in the current cycle (and not on

This work was performed within the Labex SMART supported by French state funds managed by the ANR within the Investissements d'Avenir programme under reference ANR-11-IDEX-0004-02. A preliminary version of this work appears as a brief announcement in PODC'16.

B. Bonakdarpour and F. Petit (Eds.): SSS 2016, LNCS 10083, pp. 88–93, 2016.
DOI: 10.1007/978-3-319-49259-9_7

the past history of execution). The snapshots obtained by the robots are not consistently oriented in any manner.

In this particularly weak model it is interesting to characterize which additional assumptions are needed for the robots to cooperatively perform a given task. In this paper, we consider the pattern formation problem in the most general asynchronous (ASYNC) model. The robots start in an arbitrary initial configuration where no two robots occupy the same position, and are given the pattern to be formed as a set of coordinates in their own local coordinate system. An algorithm solves the pattern formation problem if within finite time the robots form the input pattern and remain stationary thereafter.

Related Work. The pattern formation problem has been extensively studied in the deterministic setting [1–3,5].

The best deterministic algorithm so far in the ASYNC model without a common coordinate system [3] proves the following: If ρ denotes the geometric symmetricity of a robot configuration (i.e., the maximum integer ρ such that the rotation by $2\pi/\rho$ is invariant for the configuration), and I and P denote the initial and target configurations, respectively, then P can be formed if and only if $\rho(I)$ divides $\rho(F)$.

To circumvent the impossibility to form any general pattern, the probabilistic path was taken by Yamauchi and Yamashita [6]. However, their approach makes use of three hypotheses that are not proved to be necessary: *(i)* all robots share a common chirality, *(ii)* a robot may not make an arbitrary long pause while moving (more precisely, it cannot be observed twice at the same position by the same robot in two different Look-Compute-Move cycles while it is moving), and *(iii)* infinitely many random bits are required (a robot requests a point chosen uniformly at random in a continuous segment) anytime access to a random source is performed. While the latter two are of more theoretical interest, the first one is intriguing, as a common chirality was also used extensively in the deterministic case.

Our Contribution. In this paper, we propose a new probabilistic pattern formation algorithm for oblivious mobile robots that operate in the ASYNC model. Unlike previous work, our algorithm makes no assumptions about the local coordinate systems of robots (they do *not* share a common "North" nor a common "Right"), yet it preserves the ability from any initial configuration that contains at least 5 robots to form any general pattern (and not just patterns such that $\rho(I)$ divides $\rho(F)$). Besides relieving the chirality assumption, our proposal also gets rid of the previous assumption [6] that robots do not pause while moving (so, they really are fully asynchronous), and the amount of randomness is kept low – a single random bit per robot is used per use of the random source – (*vs.* infinitely many previously [6]). Our protocol consists in the combination of several phases, including a deterministic pattern formation one. As the deterministic phase does not use chirality, it may be of independent interest in the deterministic context.

A noteworthy property of our algorithm is that it permits to form patterns with multiplicity points (*without* assuming robots are endowed with multiplicity detection), a new feature in the context of pattern formation that we believe is an important asset of our approach. Of course, the case of gathering (a special pattern defined by a unique point of multiplicity n) remains impossible to solve in our settings [4].

2 Model

Robots operate in a 2-dimensional Euclidian space. Each robot has its own local coordinate system. For simplicity, we assume the existence (unknown from the robots) of a global coordinate system. Whenever it is clear from the context, we manipulate points in this global coordinate system, but each robot only sees the points in its local system. Two set of points A and B are *similar*, denoted $A \approx B$, if B can be obtained from A by translation, scaling, rotation, or symmetry. A *configuration* P is a set of positions of robots at a given time. Each robot that looks at this configuration may see different (but similar) set of points.

Each time a robot is activated it starts a Look/Compute/Move cycle. After the *look* phase, a robot obtains a configuration P representing the positions of the robots in its local coordinate system. After an arbitrary delay, the robot *computes* a path to a destination. Then, it *moves* toward the destination following the previously computed path. The duration of the move phase, and the delay between two phases, are chosen by an adversary and can be arbitrary long. The adversary decides when robots are activated assuming a *fair* scheduling et al., in any configuration, all robots are activated within finite time. The adversary also controls the robots movement along their target path and can stop a robot before reaching its destination, but not before traveling at least a distance $\delta > 0$ (δ being unknown to the robots).

An execution of an algorithm is an infinite sequence $P(0), P(1), \ldots$ of configurations. An algorithm ψ forms a pattern F if, for any execution $P(0), P(1), \ldots$, there exists a time t such that $P(t) \approx F$ and $P(t') = P(t)$ for all $t' \geq t$. In the sequel, the set of points F denotes the pattern to form. The coordinates of the points in F are given to the robots in an arbitrary coordinate system so that each robot may receive different, but equivalent, pattern F. If the pattern contains points of multiplicity, the robots receives a multiset, which is a set where each element is associated with its multiplicity. Even if the robots are not endowed with multiplicity detection, they know from the pattern what are the points of multiplicity to form. In particular, then can deduce from the pattern, the number n of robots, even if they do not see n robots.

3 Algorithm Overview

Our algorithm is divided into four phases. Since robots are oblivious and the scheduling is asynchronous, we cannot explicitly concatenate several phases to be executed in a specific order. However, one can simulate the effect of concatenation of two (or more) phases by inferring from the current configuration which phase to execute. Implementing this technique is feasible if phases are associated with disjoint sets of configurations where they are executed. Also, in order to simplify the proof of correctness, robots should not switch phases when placed in a configuration containing moving robots *i.e.*, a phase has to ensure that if the configuration resulting from a movement is associated with another phase, then all the robots are static (that is, none of them is moving). When this property holds, the first time a phase is executed, we can suppose that the configuration is static.

Our algorithm can form an arbitrary pattern. In particular, the pattern F can contain points of multiplicity (but cannot be a single point). If this is the case, the robots create a new pattern $\tilde{F}$ from F where they remove the multiplicity, and add around each point p of multiplicity m, $m-1$ points really close to p, and located at the same distance to the center of the smallest circle enclosing F. The algorithm then proceed as usual with $\tilde{F}$ instead of F. The initial pattern F is formed by the termination phase, when $\tilde{F}$ is almost formed. So from now, we suppose that the pattern does not contains points of multiplicity.

In the following we define the phases of our algorithm and the set of associated configurations, starting from the more precise one (the phase we intuitively execute at the end to complete the pattern formation). Unless otherwise stated, the *center* of a configuration refers to the center of the smallest enclosing circle of this configuration.

Termination. The termination phase occurs when all robots, except the closest to the center, forms the target pattern (from which we remove one of the point closest to the center). The phase consists in moving the last robot towards its destination. While moving, the robot remains the closest to the center, so that the resulting configuration is associated to the same phase.

Almost Pattern Formation. Among the remaining configurations, we associate the guided ones to this phase. A configuration is *guided* when a unique robot is sufficiently close to the center and induces by its position a global sense of direction and orientation to every robot. In particular, when executing this phase, robots are totally ordered and have a unique destination assigned. The phase consists first in moving all the robots (except the one that is closest to the center), one by one, so that they are at the same distance to the center as their destination in the pattern. Secondly, the robots moves toward their destination, keeping their distance to the center and the ordering unchanged. The configuration has to remain guided until each robot, except the closest to the center, reaches its destination. A configuration obtained after executing this phase is either associated to the same phase, or to the termination phase (Figs. 1, 2 and 3).

Formation of a Guided Configuration 1 (FBC1). Among the remaining configurations, we associate the ones that contain a *centered equiangular or biangular* (CEB) set to this phase. A CEB-set is a subset of robots that exists when the configuration is symmetric or has a non-trivial symmetricity. Moreover it is constructed independently from the coordinate system (so it is unique when it exists), and is invariant when the robots in this set move toward (or away

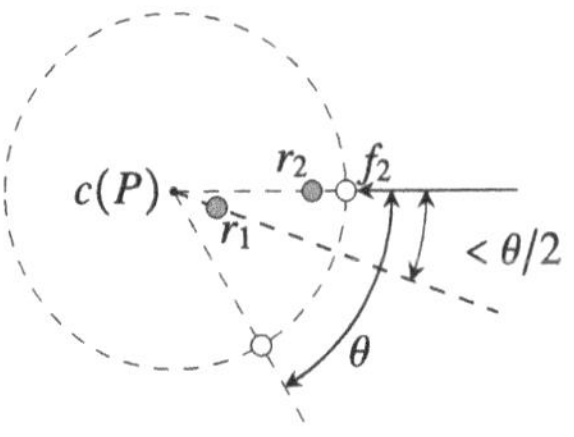

Fig. 1. Positioning r_1 and r_2 to define a guided configuration.

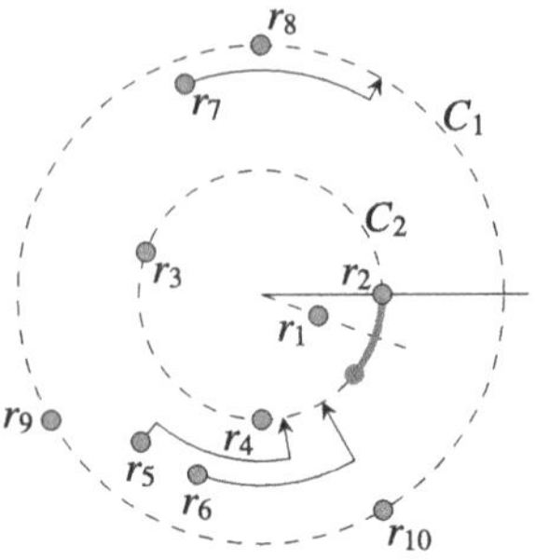

Fig. 2. Moving robots to a correct distance from the center.

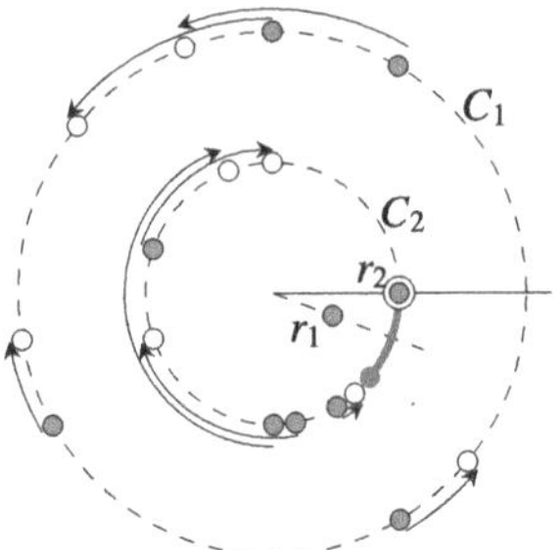

Fig. 3. Robots move toward their final destination.

from) the center of the configuration. When the configuration contains a CEB-set, our algorithm consists in moving the robots in this set to obtain a guided configuration. The invariance property of the CEB-set is important to ensure that resulting configurations are still associated with this phase.

In more details, when this phase is executed, the robots in the CEB-set Q moves either toward or away from the center with probability 1/2. We show that, with probability 1, a unique robot is elected after a finite number of activations. Then, the elected robot performs a special move to force the other robots in Q to terminate their movement. Once each robot is static, the elected robot moves toward the center to create a guided configuration. During the execution of this phase, it is possible that the configuration is associated with the termination phase. If this happens, our algorithm makes sure that all robots are static.

Formation of a Guided Configuration 2 (FBC2). We associate all remaining configurations to this phase. When executing this phase, the configuration does not have a CEB-set. This implies that the configuration is not symmetric, so the robots are totally ordered. Therefore, the smallest robot moves toward the center to create a guided configuration (it remains the smallest robot while doing so). Before the movement, the robot checks if there exists a point in its path that creates a configuration containing a CEB-set. If it is the case, the robot chooses this point as its destination so that, when the configuration contains a CEB-set (and the robots switch to the FBC1 phase), all the robots are static.

References

1. Bouzid, Z., Lamani, A.: Robot networks with homonyms: the case of patterns formation. In: Défago, X., Petit, F., Villain, V. (eds.) SSS 2011. LNCS, vol. 6976, pp. 92–107. Springer, Heidelberg (2011). doi:10.1007/978-3-642-24550-3_9
2. Flocchini, P., Prencipe, G., Santoro, N., Widmayer, P.: Arbitrary pattern formation by asynchronous, anonymous, oblivious robots. Theor. Comput. Sci. **407**(1–3), 412–447 (2008)

3. Fujinaga, N., Yamauchi, Y., Kijima, S., Yamashita, M.: Asynchronous pattern formation by anonymous oblivious mobile robots. In: Aguilera, M.K. (ed.) DISC 2012. LNCS, vol. 7611, pp. 312–325. Springer, Heidelberg (2012). doi:10.1007/978-3-642-33651-5_22
4. Prencipe, G.: Impossibility of gathering by a set of autonomous mobile robots. Theor. Comput. Sci. **384**(2), 222–231 (2007)
5. Suzuki, I., Yamashita, M.: Distributed anonymous mobile robots: formation of geometric patterns. SIAM J. Comput. **28**(4), 1347–1363 (1999)
6. Yamauchi, Y., Yamashita, M.: Randomized pattern formation algorithm for asynchronous oblivious mobile robots. In: Kuhn, F. (ed.) DISC 2014. LNCS, vol. 8784, pp. 137–151. Springer, Heidelberg (2014). doi:10.1007/978-3-662-45174-8_10

Flocking with Oblivious Robots

Davide Canepa[1], Xavier Defago[2], Taisuke Izumi[3], and Maria Potop-Butucaru[1](✉)

[1] LIP6, Univ. Pierre & Marie Curie - Paris 6, LIP6-CNRS UMR 7606, Paris, France
maria.potop-butucaru@lip6.fr
[2] School of Information Science, Japan Advanced Institute in Science and Technology (JAIST), Nomi, Japan
[3] Graduate School of Engineering, Nagoya Institute of Technology, Nagoya, Japan

Abstract. We propose a new self-stabilizing flocking algorithm for oblivious robot networks, and prove its correctness. With this algorithm, a flock head emerges from a *uniform* flock of robots, and the algorithm allows those robots to follow the head, whatever its direction on the plane. Robots are *oblivious* in that they do not recall the result of their previous computations and do not share a common coordinate system.

The novelty of our approach consists in identifying the sufficient conditions to set on the flock pattern placement and the velocity of the flock-head (rotation, translation or speed), such that the flock head and the flock pattern are both preserved while the flock moves (following the head). Additionally, our system is both *self-healing* and *self-stabilizing*. In case the head leaves (e.g., disappears or is damaged) the flock agrees on a new head and follows its trajectory. Also, robots keep no record of their previous computations and we make no assumption on their initial position. The step complexity of our solution is $O(n)$.

1 Introduction

Robot networks is an area that received in the last ten years an increasing attention from the distributing computing community. The first model and the first distributed algorithms where proposed by Suzuky and Yamashita in '94. Since then the model spreads with success both in the distributed computing comunity and the roboticians comunity[1]. The model introduced by Suzuki and Yamashita, SYm, [21–23] states that robots are oblivious and perform a cycle of elementary actions as follows: *observation* (the robot observes the environment), *computation* (the robot computes its next position based on the information collected in the observation phase), and *motion* (the rogresses toward the newly computed position). In this model, a robot cannot be interrupted during the execution of a cycle. Several problems have been studied in the SYm model. An important place, as for the case of traditional distributed computing, is occupied by the agreement problems. Two types of agreement problems have been studied

[1] The curent work is supported by the ANR project R-DISCOVER that brings together roboticians and computer scientiests.

B. Bonakdarpour and F. Petit (Eds.): SSS 2016, LNCS 10083, pp. 94–108, 2016.
DOI: 10.1007/978-3-319-49259-9_8

so far: pattern agreement, that further divides inpoint agreement and shape agreement, and flocking. *Point agreement* (gathering or convergence), [22] aims at instructing robots to reach an exact or approximate common point not known *a priori*. The dual is the scattering problem, [22], where robots are instructed to reach different positions in the plane. Furthermore, shape agreement, [6,9,22], deals with instructing robots to eventually arrange themselves into a predefined shape (i.e., circle, rectangle, etc.).

Flocking refers to the ability of robots to coordinate and move in a space without any external intervention. This coordinated motion has several civil and military applications ranging from zone exploration to spacecraft self-organization. Flocking is also gaining increasing attention in diverse areas such as biology, economy, language study or agent/sensor networks. In biology, flocking refers to the cooperative behavior of a group of birds or animals when they sense an imminent threat, migration, or food foraging. In economy, the emergent behavior that regulates stock markets can be seen as a form of flocking. And so is the emergence of a common language in primitive societies.

The *flocking problem*, although largely discussed for real robots [13,17,19], was studied from the distributed algorithms point of view mainly by Gervasi and Prencipe [10,11]. The literature agrees on two different strategies to implement flocking. The first strategy is based on a predefined hierarchy [13,17,19]. That is, there is an *a priori leader* clearly identified in the group that will lead the group and each group member will follow the leader trajectory. Obviously, the leader is a single point of failure, and thus the flock comes to a permanent halt should the leader fail. An alternative is to obtain an emergent coordination of the group without a predefined leader. That is, all the robots in the system execute the same algorithm. The system is called in this case *uniform*. The difficulty of this approach comes from the permanent stress to keep the same leader throughout the whole computation. That is, if the flock splits (following two different leaders) then it may never converge back to a single flock. Extending the results of Flocchini *et al.* [8], Canepa *et al.* [3] propose a uniform probabilistic flocking architecture. However, this approach is based on the assumption that the leader, and consequently the flock, do not change their direction and trajectory. The main stress in the curent work is to identify the conditions that the uniform flock should satisfy in order to maintain and follow the same leader even if this leader change its direction in the plane. Also in our approach, differently from [13,17,19], the flock-head is not known a priori but will emerge during the computation. When the current flock-head disappears or is damaged and not recognized as a correct robot, the remaining robots agree on a new head and the flock can finish its task.

Fault-tolerant (but not self-stabilizing) flocking has been addressed in [20,25], both in the SYm model. Souissi *et al.* [20] proposes a fault tolerant flocking algorithm in the SYm model using a leader oracle that gives to the robots the current head and a failure detector. In our solution the head of the flock emerges during the computation and robots' decisions are solely based on their current observations (no oracle is needed). Yang *et al.* [25] also proposes a fault tolerant flocking. The algorithm relies on the SYm model with a k-bounded scheduler (no robot executes more than k actions between two consecutive actions of any non failed robot). The bounded scheduler, together with the assumption that robots are non-oblivious, is used to implement a failure detector. The solution requires a common agreement on one axis, on chirality (i.e., agreement on clockwise order). In contrast, our solution does not need any a priori agreement on axis or chirality. Moreover, we assume oblivious robots.

Several works from robotics recently proposed heuristics for flocking (e.g., [16,18]). Lee and Chong [16], for example, proposes a solution for non-uniform flocking. In their proposal the leader has to execute a different strategy than the rest of the flock. Hence, the system is not uniform. The focus of the study is on maintaining a geometric structure for the flock, while handling separation/joining of the flock in response to obstacles. Other recent works [12,14,15,24] address the pure flocking where the flock has to follow a leader or a set of leaders issued from the flock or an external target. In these papers it is assumed either a wifi communication between robots in order to maintain the flock connectivity or an a priori knowledge of the speed of the other robots in the system in order to locally compute the differential equations that characterize the system trajectory. Also it is implicitly assumed that robots are synchronized during the whole run of the system. Our work does not assume any knowledge on the speed of the other robots in the system, neither the memory of their state nor the explicit communication in order to synchronize their motion.

Our contribution. In this paper, we propose and prove the correctness of a new flocking algorithm in systems with oblivious and *uniform* robots. Differently from the above discussed works and in particular [25] our solution does not need any memory on the previous computations nor some agreement between robots in the system. Also, we make no assumption on the initial configuration of the robots. Therefore, our solution is *self-stabilizing.*

Additionally, we identify the sufficient conditions on the flock pattern placement and the flock head velocity (rotation, translation, speed) so that the flock preserves the emerged leader, an agreed common coordinate system, and the motion pattern. Our solution consists of one probabilistic preprocessing phase and two deterministic ones. First, robots agree on a common coordinate system and the head of the flock. Second, the robots form a flocking pattern, and third, they move while preserving the agreed head and the coordinate system. Only the preprocessing phase (agreement on the common coordinate system) uses a probabilistic ingredient and a partial synchronization of robots. The other two phases are deterministic and asynchronous. Moreover, if the head fails (it disappears or is damaged and cannot be recognized by other robots) the flock agrees on another head and follows the trajectory of the new head. The complexity of our flocking solution is $O(n)$ steps.

Paper organization. The paper is organized as follows: Sect. 2 defines the model of the system, Sect. 3 specifies the problem based on the flocking informal definitions in different areas ranging from biological systems to space navigation.

In this section we also proposes a brief description of our system architecture. Section 4 sets up the common coordinate system. Section 5 details the formation of the flocking pattern and the sufficient conditions on the flock placement, Sect. 6 proposes the rules for moving the flock and identifies the necessary conditions on the flock head velocity.

2 Model

We consider a system of autonomous mobile robots that works in the SYm model [23].

Each robot is capable of observing its surroundings, computing a destination based on what it observed, and moving towards the computed destination: hence it performs an (endless) cycle of observing, computing, and moving. Each robot has its own local view of the world. This view includes a local Cartesian coordinate system having an origin, a unit of length, and the directions of two coordinate axes (which we will refer to as the x and y axis), together with their orientations, identified as the positive and negative sides of the axes.

The robots are modeled as units with computational capabilities that are capable of moving freely in the plane. They are equipped with sensors that let them observe the positions of the other robots with respect to their own local coordinate system. Each robot is viewed as a point, and can observe all other robots in the flock.

The robots act in phases, and do not rely on any centralized directive. Furthermore, they are oblivious, meaning that they do not remember any previous observations or computations performed in the previous steps. Note that this feature combined with no assumptions on the initial positions of the robots gives to the algorithms designed in this model the nice property of *self-stabilization* [7]. That is, every decision taken by a robot does not depend on what happened previously in the system and robots do not use potentially corrupted data stored in their local memory.

Robots in the flock are anonymous (i.e., they are a priori indistinguishable by their appearance and they do not have any kind of identifiers that can be used during the computation). Moreover, there are no explicit direct means of communication; hence, the only way they can interact or acquire information from their fellow robots is through the environment, by observing their positions. They execute the same algorithm (the system is uniform), which takes as input the observed positions of the fellow robots, and returns a destination point towards which they target their move.

3 The Flocking Problem

Reynolds proposed in the mid-80's three rules that have to be respected by any algorithm that simulates a flock-like behavior. He successfully applied these rules in designing several animations. At that time, the flock entities were called boids and the model was as follows: each boid has the ability to sense its local neighbors; each boid can sense the whole environment; all boids recalculate their current state simultaneously once each time unit during the simulation.

In this model, according to Reynolds, the flocking rules are as follows. *Separation*: steer to avoid crowding local flock-mates; *Alignment*: steer towards the average heading of local flock-mates; *Cohesion*: steer to move toward the average position of local flock mates.

Interestingly, the model proposed by Reynolds is similar to the SYm model described previously. Robots can sense the environment (the other robots in the system) and they periodically and simultaneously recalculate their state. Nevertheless, the most important difference with respect to Reynolds' assumptions is the impossibility to use the history of the computation in order to implement the flocking rules. Note that the second rule of Reynolds indirectly uses this information. Therefore, in the case of robot networks these rules should be adapted.

In distributed robot networks acceptance, flocking allows a group or a formation of robots to change their position either by following a pre-designated or an emergent leader. In this case, the flocking is referred to as being *uniform*. Intuitively, a flock is a group of robots that move in the plane in order to execute a task while maintaining a specific formation. This informal definition implicitly assumes (a) the existence of a unique head of the flock that will lead the group during the task execution, and (b) the existence of a flocking pattern. Also it is assumed that a virtual link exists between the head and the rest of the group. Therefore, three elements seem to be essential in the definition of flocking: (1) the head of the group, (2) the pattern, and (3) the orientation of the pattern with respect to the head. Based on these elements, flocking can be seen as the motion of the virtual rigid shape formed by the flock and its head following a trajectory (predefined or defined on-the-fly). It follows that both the flock and its head periodically synchronize their velocity in order to maintain the flock. In the following, we specify the uniform flocking problem (i.e., the leader emerges during the computation). We first recall the definition of leader election and pattern formation. According to a recent study, [6,9], pattern formation and leader election are related problems. Our specification naturally extends this observation to the flocking problem.

Definition 1 (Leader Election). *[9] Given the positions of n robots in the plane, the n robots are able to deterministically agree on the same robot called the leader.*

Definition 2 (Pattern Formation). *[9] The robots have in input the same pattern, called the target pattern $\mathcal{F}$, described as a set of positions in the plane given in lexicographic order (each robot sees the same pattern according to the direction and orientation of its local coordinate system). They are required to form the pattern: at the end of the computation, the positions of the robots coincide, in everybody's local view, with the positions of $\mathcal{F}$, where $\mathcal{F}$ may be translated, rotated, and scaled in each local coordinate system.*

Definition 3 (Uniform Flocking). *Given a set of n robots and $\mathcal{F}$ a target pattern (called in the following flocking pattern), the set of robots satisfies the flocking specification if the following properties hold:*

- **head emergence** *eventually robots agree on a unique head;*
- **pattern emergence** *eventually robots but the head, form the pattern $\mathcal{F}$;*
- **velocity agreement** *after any modification of the position of the head, robots in the pattern rotate and translate $\mathcal{F}$ in order to converge to the same relative position and orientation between the head and $\mathcal{F}$ as it was before the modification.*
- **no collision** *any robot motion is collision free.*

Note the common flavor between Reynolds' rules and the above properties. The property called "*No collision*" corresponds to the separation rule. "*Velocity agreement*" corresponds to the alignment rule, and finally "*head and pattern emergence*" properties are similar to the cohesion property.

In the following, we combine three different tasks to solve uniform flocking. First, we design a novel strategy for equipping a set of robots with a common coordinate systems. To this end, we proposes a probabilistic strategy that creates two singularity points. Then, we combine this module with existing probabilistic election strategies [3,5] in order to create the third singularity point. The motion of this third point eventually designates the head of the flock and the orientation of the common coordinate system. Then, the emergent common coordinate system is further used by all the robots but the head to arrange themselves in a flocking pattern, $\mathcal{F}$, that will further follow the head. During the pattern motion, both the head and the common coordinate system are preserved.

4 Common Coordinate System and Flock Head Emergence

The construction of a common coordinate system is as follows. First, robots agree on one axis, then they agree on the second axis and the orientation of the axes. Finally, robots agree on the head of the flock. The detailed code and the correctness proof of these algorithms are proposed in the technical report [2].

Agreement on the first axis. Note that one axis is defined by two distinct points. The key idea of the algorithm is very simple: robots compute the barycenter of their convex hull. The furtherest pairs of robots with respect to the barycenter (if their number is greater than one) move randomly further away from the barycenter, along the line defined by their current position and the barycenter. Two robots R_i and R_j belong to the set of the *Far Robots* if $\text{dist}(i, j) \geq \text{dist}(w, k)$ for every pair of robots w, k in the system. It is easy to prove that with probability 1, the above strategy converges to a configuration where the set *Far Robots* contains a unique pair of robots. It is possible that once the set *Far Robots* contains exactly two robots one or both of them are not on the SEC (the smallest enclosing circle). Then, robots in *Far Robots* move to the SEC.

Agreement on the second axis. The construction of the second axis is conditioned by the existence of two unique nodes. We choose these two nodes as follows: one is the center of the smallest enclosing circle (also called SEC), while the second one is given by the probabilistic leader election we previously proposed in [3]).

Axis orientation and flock head emergence. In order to orient the axis, we first align the two *Far Robots*: R_A and R_B, and the leader (see Fig. 1). Once the alignment is performed, the first is oriented instructing the leader to create a dissymmetry between the two points and one of them becomes the head of the flock.

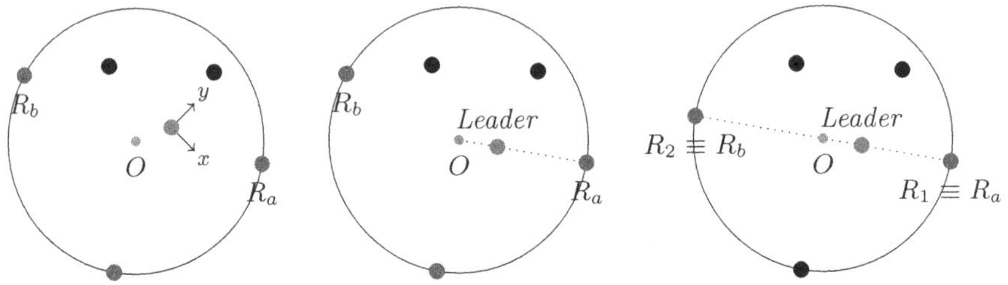

Fig. 1. Alignment of *Far Robots* and *Leader.*

The alignment strategy is as follows. If the leader is not aligned with the other two robots, then it will choose among the two robots belonging to the *Far Robots*, the one with a larger value of x. In case of symmetry, a larger value of y. Then, it will move toward the intersection of the radius corresponding to that robot and the circumference of the circle centered in O (the center of the SEC) and the radius equal to dist(O, *Leader*). Finally, the robot not chosen by the Leader (denoted R_B) will align with the other two robots. R_B moves only when the Leader is aligned with R_A. That is, when one of the two *Far Robots* sees that the Leader is aligned with the other robot in *Far Robots* and O, then it moves following the SEC until it forms a line together with the Leader, the center of the SEC and the other robot in *Far Robots*. Note that the two robots in *Far Robots* are on the *SEC*.

From now on, the robot in *Far Robots* nearest to the Leader will be referred to as $R1$, and the other one as $R2$. Robot $R1$ will play the role of *flock head.* The robot called Leader will just play a regulation role in the flocking process.

The next section presents the pattern emergence, then we proposes the details and the correctness proof of the flocking strategy briefly described above together with the necessary conditions to preserve the head and the pattern.

5 Pattern Emergence

In this section we address the formation of the flocking pattern. Note that we work in a system where robots do not have a common coordinate system. The previous section proposes strategies to uniquely identify 3 robots that together with the center of the SEC define a common coordinate system. In the following, we assume that over the initial set of n robots 3 robots (referred in the previous section Leader, R1 and R2) are reserved for maintaining the coordinate system while the other $n - 3$ can be placed in any shape that will be further reffered to as the flocking pattern. However, we impose a condition on the placement of the shape with respect to the position of the robots that define the references (Leader, R1 and R2) in order to preserve both the uniqueness of the references and the common coordinate system.

Lemma 1. *The area where the pattern is placed has to satisfy the following three conditions in order to preserve the common coordinate system defined by Leader, R1 and R2.*

1. *All robots must be inside the circumference having* $\overline{R1R2}$ *as diameter.*
2. *All the robots must be in the side of the SEC with R2 and* y *negative.*
3. *The circle with radius* $dist(Leader, O)$ *and center in* O *must be empty.*

Proof. If a robot moves outside the SEC, at the next round[2] the SEC will change and consequently the references. It follows the necessity of condition one. If there exist robots in symmetrical positions with respect to the x axis, then the system loses the capability to distinguish $R1$ and $R2$. This proves the necessity of point two. Point three is motivated by the need of a unique leader. If a robot goes closer to the center of the SEC than the leader then it becomes *Leader* and so the references will change.

In order to realize the flocking additional constraints on the shape of the area where the pattern is deployed are needed. These conditions will be discussed in the next section.

The flocking pattern is obtained in two steps. A first step called bootstrapping and a second step that is basically a collision free strategy to move to the pattern positions. In between these two phases the Leader will move perpendiculary to the segment $R1R2$ in order to orient the second axis. This orientation will be used by the robots in defining a total order among them.

Pattern bootstrapping. The bootstrapping process takes two phases. In the first phase, all robots but the leader are placed on the smallest enclosing circle (SEC). First, the robots closest to the boundaries of the SEC are placed, then recursively the other robots. The algorithm avoids collisions and ensures that robots preserve the references (e.g., Leader, R1 and R2) computed in the previous section. In the second phase, the robots on the SEC but R1 will be placed on the semi-circle not occupied by the R1 as follows. $R1$ is in the position $SEC \cap [O, Leader)$ and $R2$ is on the opposite side of the SEC ([O, Leader) denotes the open segment starting in O and passing through *Leader*). The other robots are disposed on the quarter of circle around $R2$. During this process the references are used to

[2] A round is a fragment of execution where each robot in the system executes its actions.

help the deployment of the others robots. Also, the movement of robots is done such a way that the semantic of the references is preserved. The detailed code of the algorithms and their analysis are proposed in [2].

Flocking Pattern Formation. In the following we define the flocking pattern robots can form in order to maintain the common coordinate system and the references defined in the previous section.

The flocking pattern $\mathcal{F} = \{p_1, p_2, \cdots, p_{n-3}, p_o, p_{R2}\}$ is the set of points given in input to the robots. It has two distinguished points p_o and p_{R2}. We call the two distinguished points the *Anchor Bolts* of the pattern, which will correspond to the position of robots $R2$ and to the point $(0, dist(Leader, O))$ of the common coordinate system. Note that robots start this phase in the following configuration: the segment $OLeader$ is perpendicular to the segment $R1R2$ (where O is the center of the SEC) and all the other robots are disposed on the quarter of circle around $R2$. In order to form the flocking pattern in a collision free manner robots adopt the following strategy. First, all robots but the references hook the pattern, eventually scale and rotate it to $R2$ and to the point (0, $dist(Leader, O)$). Then they totally order the set of robots based on their coordinates in the common coordinate system and associate to each robot a position in the pattern. Since the order is based on the common coordinate system, all robots will define the exact same order. Then robots move following their order, hence collisions are avoided. In Fig. 2 robot $R2$ has a trajectory that intersects the trajectory of both robots $R1$ and $R3$. However collisions are avoided since following the total order $R1$ moves first, then $R2$ and finally $R3$. The detailed code of the algorithm and its analysis are proposed in [2].

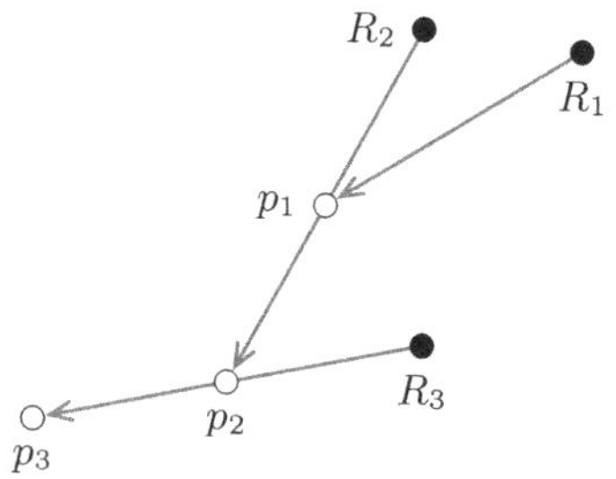

Fig. 2. No trajectory deadlock

Once the flocking pattern is formed, the Leader moves to the center of the *SEC*. This last movement brings the robots in what will be called later **Flocking Formation**. The motion of this formation will be studied in the next section.

6 Flocking

In this section we proposes a strategy to synchronize the *Flocking Formation* and the head of the flock. The idea of our flocking is as follows. $R1$ (the head of the flock) and $R2$ act as two ends of a virtual spring. The other robots, arranged in a flocking pattern, will be "pulled" by $R1$ and "pushed" by $R2$. Both the SEC and the flocking pattern will be deformed by this motion. Then, using the position of the Leader with respect to the center of the SEC, the motion of $R1$ and $R2$ is blocked until the flocking pattern is reformed. Furthermore, the Leader moves to the center of the SEC which unblocks the motion of robots $R1$ and $R2$ and implicitly the flocking pattern.

In the following we characterize two safe regions $\mathcal{M}$ and $\mathcal{K}$. $\mathcal{M}$ is the zone where $R1$ is allowed to move and $\mathcal{K}$ is the area where the pattern can be disposed. In the following we proposes a generic definition of $\mathcal{M}$ and $\mathcal{K}$; the specific characterization of these areas will be proposed in the sequel.

Definition 4. *Let k, h and h' be positive constants. Let $\mathcal{M}$ be the area with $y \geq |kx| + R1$. Let $\mathcal{K}$ be the area between the lines $y = \pm h'x$ for $y < 0$ and $y = \pm hx + R2$ for $y < 0$.*

We additionally define two particular angles, α and β between the lines that border $\mathcal{M}$ and $\mathcal{K}$. later, we prove that α and β should be greater than 90° in order to verify the conditions stated in Lemma 1.

Definition 5. *Let α be the angle between $y = hx + R2$ and $y = -kx + R1$. Let us denote by A the intersection of these two lines. Let β be the angle between $y = h'x$ and $y = -kx$ (see Fig. 3).*

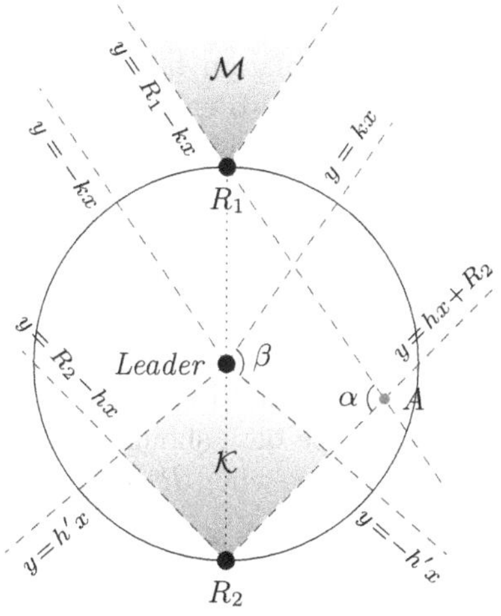

Fig. 3. Angles α and β, and safe areas $\mathcal{M}$ and $\mathcal{K}$.

The flocking algorithm, Algorithm 6.1 is executed only when the *Flocking Formation* is reached (see Sect. 5). The algorithm begins with the movement of robots $R1$, $R2$ and the *Leader*. $R1$ is the robot that imposes the direction of the movement so it can move to any point in the $\mathcal{M}$ area. When it moves, thanks to the constraints we imposed, the references hold steady and so, at the next observation, all the robots can recognize the references: Leader, R1 and R2. Additionally, all the other robots will be inside the SEC (on the $R2$ side). Then, all the other robots but $R2$ execute the flocking pattern formation algorithm (presented in Sect. 5) to align the pattern to the new direction (defined by the axis $R2R1$). Once the *Flocking Formation* is recreated the robots $R1$ or $R2$ can move again. When the distance between $R1$ and $R2$ is greater than some parameter d_{Rmax}, then $R2$ moves inside the $\mathcal{K}$ area (along the $R2R1$ segment) within distance d. Following Lemma 3 below, this distance should be less or equal than $(\frac{dist(R1,R2)}{2} - \frac{dist(R1,B)}{2\cos\delta})$ where B is the first robot hit by a SEC as $R2$ approaches $R1$ and δ is the angle $\angle R2R1B$.

Algorithm 6.1. The motion of the Flocking Formation with parameters d and d_{Rmax}.

1) **if** (Robots form the **Flocking Formation**)
   if ($dist(R1, R2) < d_{Rmax}$) **then** R1 moves to a point $\in \mathcal{M}$;
2) **else if** ($dist(R1, R2) \geq d_{Rmax}$) **then**
   R2 moves within distance d along the segment $R2R1$;
3) **else** the Leader moves to the line perpendicular to $R1R2$
   that passes through the center of the SEC;
   then robots execute Flocking Formation algorithm (Section 5).

In the sequel we determine the relation between the lines that define the areas $\mathcal{M}$ and $\mathcal{K}$ (i.e., angles α and β) so that after each movement of $R1$ or $R2$ all the references are preserved. Firstly, we must guarantee that the SEC will change coherently with the movement of $R1$ and $R2$. At each step the SEC corresponds to the circumference having $R1$ and $R2$ as diameter. That is, we should prove that the new SEC contains all the robots. Lemma 2 proves that the circle having as diameter $R1'R2$ contains all the robots if the angle α is at least 90° where $R1'$ is the new position of $R1$ after its move. Lemma 3 exhibits the condition on $R2$ movement in order to maintain all robots inside the new SEC. Lemma 4 proves that the angle beta should be at least of 90° in order to preserve the Leader and the references when $R1$ or $R2$ move.

Lemma 2. *Let $R1'$ be the point where robot $R1$ moves (inside the $\mathcal{M}$ area). The circle having as diameter $R1'R2$ contains all the robots if the angle α is at least* 90°.

Proof. Consider the worst case: $R1'$ belongs to $y = \pm kx + R1$ and there exists a robot $B \neq R2$ on the border of the $\mathcal{K}$ areas: $y = \pm hx + R2$. Without restraining the generality consider the case where $R1'$ moves on the segment $y = -kx + R1$ and B is on the line $y = hx + R2$. When $R1'$ diverges from $R1$ the circumference of the new SEC defined by the point $R1'$ and $R2$ intersects the line $R1B$ at a point T. When $\alpha < 90°$ and $R1'$ diverges from $R1$, T moves inside the segment $R1B$ towards $R1$. Hence, at least one robot in the formation (robot B) will be outside the new position of the SEC. When $\alpha \geq 90°$ and $R1'$ diverges from $R1$ then T never crosses the line passing through R2 and the intersection of SEC and the line $y = -kx + R1$ hence every robot in the formation will be inside the new SEC.

Lemma 3. *After the movement of* $R2$, *the circle having as diameter* $R1R2'$, *contains all the robots if* $d \leq (\frac{dist(R1,R2)}{2} - \frac{dist(R1,B)}{2\cos\delta})$ *where* B *is the first robot hit by a SEC as* $R2$ *approaches* $R1$ *and* δ *is the angle* $\angle R2R1B$.

Proof. According to Algorithm 6.1, $R2$ will move on the y axis within distance d from its current position. Let this position be $R2'$. Now we will find a value of d such that any robot inside the $\mathcal{K}$ zone, is always inside (or at least on) the circumference having $R1R2'$ as diameter. Consider the robot B such that after $R2$ moves, B is on the border of the new SEC and no other robot is outside the new SEC. Let δ be the angle between $R2, R1$ and B. Using simple geometrical constructions it follows that d, the maximal distance $R2$ can move, should be less or equal than $(\frac{dist(R1,R2)}{2} - \frac{dist(R1,B)}{2\cos\delta})$.

Note that after the movement of $R1$ or $R2$ they are still in the set *Far Robots*.

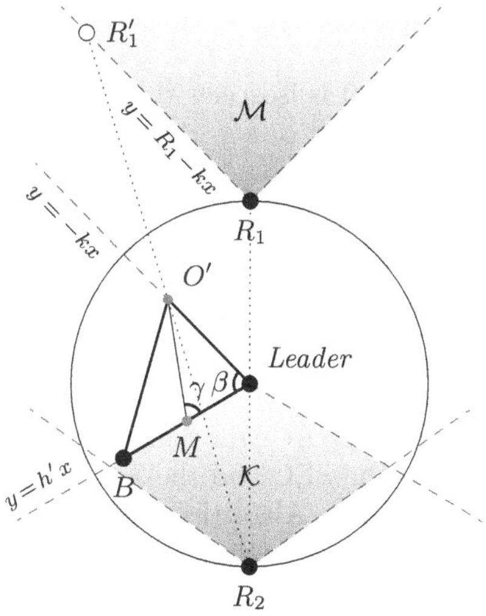

Fig. 4. Angle β.

In the following we identify a second relation between the lines defining the areas $\mathcal{M}$ and $\mathcal{K}$ in order to verify the conditions of Lemma 1.

Lemma 4. *After the movement of* $R1$ *or* $R2$, *the Leader is preserved and also the references, if* $\beta \geq 90°$ *(Fig. 4).*

Proof. Now we will find the smallest value of β such that the *Leader* is preserved. First, note that the pattern formation algorithm described in the previous sections starts only if the *Leader* is perpendicular to the $R1R2$ axis, with respect to the center of the SEC. So, if one of $R1$ or $R2$ moves, the only one that can move after them is the *Leader*. Then, all the other robots must wait until it reaches its final position. After the Leader moves, it is still the Leader since it is the closest to the SEC center.

Note also that if $R2$ moves, the Leader is always preserved independently of the value of β. In this case the new center O' of the SEC will ever be on the $R1R2$ axis, between the *Leader* and $R1$. Once again the *Leader* is preserved since it is the closest robot to O'.

Consider the case $R1$ moves. In the worst case $R1$ moves on the border of $\mathcal{M}$. Let $R1'$ be the next position of $R1$. To each point $R1'$ corresponds a new point O' (the middle point of the segment $\overline{R1'R2}$) which is the center of the new SEC. If $R1'$ moves on the lines $y = \pm kx + R1$, then O' moves on the parallel lines $y = \pm kx$ and if $R1'$ goes to infinity, then O' also goes to infinity.

Let B be a robot on one of the borders of $\mathcal{K}$, $y = \pm h'x$ for $y < 0$. In the following we determin the value of β in order to preserve the *Leader*. That is, there is no robot closer to O' than the *Leader*. Assume robot B and *Leader* are equidistant with respect to O'. Let M be the middle point of the segment $BLeader$. Notice that:

(1) if *Leader* and B are equidistant to O' then the triangle $(B, O', Leader)$ is isosceles.
(2) if the triangle $(B, O', Leader)$ is isosceles then the angle γ between *Leader*, M, O' is right. It follows that $\beta < 90°$.

So, in order to never have $\overline{O'Leader} \leq \overline{O'B}$, $\beta \geq 90°$.

Lemma 5. *Starting in any configuration or after any movement of robot $R1$ or robot $R2$ the system converges to the flocking specification in $O(n)$ steps.*

Proof. Starting in a configuration that is not a $Flocking\ Formation$ the system converges in $O(n)$ to a $Flocking\ Formation$ (see [2]). After the movement of either $R1$ or $R2$, the center of the SEC will change. It follows that the *Leader* is not anymore on the center of the SEC and the $Flocking\ Formation$ is invalid. Now, due to the first condition in Algorithm 6.1 any movement of $R1$ or $R2$ is impossible. Then the flocking formation algorithm is executed until a new $Flocking\ Formation$, consistent with the new references, is reached. Following the analysis provided in [2] this process takes $O(n)$ robot moves. Then, $R1$ and $R2$ are again free to move.

7 Conclusions

The current work studies the flocking problem in the following settings: semi-synchronous robot networks (SY model), oblivious robots, arbitrary initial positions. We proposed a self-stabilizing solution that uses a probabilistic ingredient in order to break symmetry. The self-stabilization of our solution comes from the fact that robots can start in any configuration and in the event of the head leaving the flock agrees on another head. Moreover, robots are oblivious, can start in any initial configuration and do not share any common knowledge. Additionally, the flock follows the head whatever its trajectory in plane is. Also, the algorithm makes sure that the flock will follow the same head (once emerged) and the system of coordinates will not change during the execution. To this end we identified the necessary conditions that both the pattern and the head velocity have to satisfy in order to maintain the flock pattern, the same unique head and the same coordinate system. A nice extension of this problem would be to use energy constraints similar to biological systems. There, in order to conserve the energy of the group, the head is replaced from time to time. Including energy considerations in the model is a challenge in itself. Also, when the head of the group changes in order to conserve the energy of the group, some common knowledge has to be shared by the members of the group. This common knowledge may help in bypassing the impossibility results related to symmetric configurations. Another interesting extension would be the volumic model. The current solution cannot work in these settings since it is based essentially on alignment properties. Furthermore, it would be interesting to investigate the minimal requirements in order to implement flocking in systems where robots have a local view.

Acknowledgements. The last author would like to thank Ted Herman for helpful discussions related to flocking in biological systems that inspired the current specification and also the potential use of the energy constraints in order to conserve the head energy. We also would like to thank Shlomi Dolev for pointing us [1] and [4] that investigate the problem in a different model.

References

1. Ben-Shahar, O., Dolev, S., Dolgin, A., Michael, S.: Direction election in flocking swarms. Ad Hoc Netw. **12**, 250–258 (2014)
2. Canepa, D., Défago, X., Izumi, T., Potop-Butucaru, M.: Emergent velocity agreement in robot networks. CoRR, abs/1105.4082 (2011)
3. Canepa, D., Potop-Butucaru, M.G.: Stabilizing flocking via leader election in robot networks. In: Masuzawa, T., Tixeuil, S. (eds.) SSS 2007. LNCS, vol. 4838, pp. 52–66. Springer, Heidelberg (2007). doi:10.1007/978-3-540-76627-8_7
4. Chazelle, B.: The convergence of bird flocking. J. ACM **61**(4), 21:1–21:35 (2014)
5. Dieudonné, Y., Petit, F.: Circle formation of weak robots and lyndon words. Inf. Process. Lett. **101**(4), 156–162 (2007)
6. Dieudonné, Y., Petit, F., Villain, V.: Leader election problem versus pattern formation problem. In: Lynch, N.A., Shvartsman, A.A. (eds.) DISC 2010. LNCS, vol. 6343, pp. 267–281. Springer, Heidelberg (2010)
7. Dolev, S.: Self-stabilization. MIT Press (2000)
8. Flocchini, P., Prencipe, G., Santoro, N., Widmayer, P.: Pattern formation by anonymous robots without chirality. In: Proceedings of the SIROCCO, pp. 147–162 (2001)

9. Flocchini, P., Prencipe, G., Santoro, N., Widmayer, P.: Arbitrary pattern formation by asynchronous, anonymous, oblivious robots. Theor. Comput. Sci. **407**(1–3), 412–447 (2008)
10. Gervasi, V., Prencipe, G.: Flocking by a set of autonomous mobile robots. Technical report TR-01-24, Universitat di Pisa (2001)
11. Gervasi, V., Prencipe, G.: Coordination without communication: the case of the flocking problem. Discrete Appl. Math. **144**(3), 324–344 (2004)
12. Gu, D., Wang, Z.: Leader-follower flocking: algorithms and experiments. IEEE Trans. Control Syst. Technol. **17**(5), 1211–1219 (2009)
13. Huang, A.Q.J., Farritor, S.M., Goddard, S.: Localization, follow-the-leader control of a heterogeneous group of mobile robots. IEEE ASME Trans. Mechatron. **11**, 205–215 (2006)
14. La, H.M., Sheng, W.: Flocking control of a mobile sensor network to track and observe a moving target. In: Proceedings of the ICRA, pp. 3129–3134, May 2009
15. La, H.M., Sheng, W.: Flocking control of multiple agents in noisy environments. In: Proceedings of the ICRA, pp. 4964–4969, May 2010
16. Lee, G., Chong, N.-Y.: Adaptive flocking of robot swarms: algorithms and properties IEICE Trans. **91-B**(9), 2848–2855 (2008)
17. Lindhe, M.: A flocking and obstacle avoidance algorithm for mobile robots. Ph.D. thesis, KTH Stockholm (2004)
18. Moeslinger, C., Schmickl, T., Crailsheim, K.: Emergent flocking with low-end swarm robots. In: Dorigo, M., et al. (eds.) ANTS 2010. LNCS, vol. 6234, pp. 424–431. Springer, Heidelberg (2010). doi:10.1007/978-3-642-15461-4_40
19. Renaud, P., Cervera, E., Martiner, P.: Towards a reliable vision-based mobile robot formation control. IEEE/ASME Trans. Mechatron. **4**, 3176–3181 (2004)
20. Souissi, S., Izumi, T., Wada, K.: Oracle-based flocking of mobile robots in crash-recovery model. In: Guerraoui, R., Petit, F. (eds.) SSS 2009. LNCS, vol. 5873, pp. 683–697. Springer, Heidelberg (2009). doi:10.1007/978-3-642-05118-0_47
21. Suzuki, I., Yamashita, M.: A theory of distributed anonymous mobile robots formation and agreement problems. Technical report, Wisconsin Univ. Milwaukee Dept. of Electrical Engineering and Computer Science 6 (1994)
22. Suzuki, I., Yamashita, M.: Distributed anonymous mobile robots–formation and agreement problems. In: Proceedings of the 3rd International Colloquium on Structural Information and Communication Complexity (SIROCCO 1996), Siena, Italy, June 1996
23. Suzuki, I., Yamashita, M.: Distributed anonymous mobile robots: formation of geometric patterns. SIAM J. Comput. **28**(4), 1347–1363 (1999)
24. Wang, Z., Gu, D.: A local sensor based leader-follower flocking system. In: Proceedings of the ICRA, pp. 3790–3795, May 2008
25. Yang, Y., Souissi, S., Défago, X., Takizawa, M.: Fault-tolerant flocking for a group of autonomous mobile robots. J. Syst. Softw. **84**(1), 29–36 (2011)

Making Local Algorithms Wait-Free: The Case of Ring Coloring

Armando Castañeda[3], Carole Delporte[1], Hugues Fauconnier[1], Sergio Rajsbaum[3], and Michel Raynal[2(✉)]

[1] IRIF, Université Paris Diderot, Paris, France
[2] IUF & IRISA (Université de Rennes), Rennes, France
raynal@irisa.fr
[3] Instituto de Matemáticas, UNAM, 04510 Mexico D.F., Mexico

Abstract. When considering distributed computing, reliable message-passing synchronous systems on the one side, and asynchronous failure-prone shared-memory systems on tyhe other side, remain two quite independently studied ends of the reliability/asynchrony spectrum. The concept of *locality* of a computation is central to the first one, while the concept of *wait-freedom* is central to the second one. The paper proposes a new $\mathcal{DECOUPLED}$ model in an attempt to reconcile these two worlds. It consists of a synchronous and reliable communication graph of n *nodes*, and on top a set of asynchronous crash-prone *processes*, each attached to a communication node.

To illustrate the $\mathcal{DECOUPLED}$ model, the paper presents an asynchronous 3-coloring algorithm for the processes of a ring. From the processes point of view, the algorithm is wait-free. From a locality point of view, each process uses information only from processes at distance $O(\log^* n)$ from it. This local wait-free algorithm is based on an extension of the classical Cole and Vishkin vertex coloring algorithm in which the processes are not required to start simultaneously.

1 Introduction

Locality in synchronous distributed computing. The standard synchronous message passing model (e.g. see [19,20]) consists of a graph, whose vertices represent computational processes and whose edges represent bidirectional communication links. In each synchronous round, a process sends messages to its neighbors, then receives messages from them, and finally performs arbitrary computations. Failures are not considered: each message is received in the same round in which it was sent, and processes do not fail. The time complexity of a distributed algorithm in this model is the maximum number of rounds any process requires to terminate.

In sequential computing only the most trivial tasks can be solved in constant time. In contrast, there are many synchronous distributed algorithms that run in a number of rounds d which is constant (or nearly constant), independently of the number of vertices of the graph [23]. In such an algorithm, a process is

B. Bonakdarpour and F. Petit (Eds.): SSS 2016, LNCS 10083, pp. 109–125, 2016.
DOI: 10.1007/978-3-319-49259-9_9

able to collect information from others at most d links away, and hence we can think of the algorithm as a function that maps the d-neighborhood of a node to a local output, for each node. In synchronous distributed computing the focus is on *locality*, or to what extent a global property about the graph can be obtained from locally available data [16].

The study of the $\mathcal{LOCAL}$ synchronous model was initiated at the very early days of distributed computing [19], with problems such as coloring the vertices of a ring with 3 colors. This is a problem that depends globally on the ring, yet it can be solved locally. Cole and Vishkin [7] designed an algorithm that finds a 3-coloring of the vertices of a ring in $O(\log^* n)$ rounds. Soon after, Linial proved that $\Omega(\log^* n)$ rounds are needed for 3-coloring a ring. For general graphs, only recently it was shown that $(\Delta+1)$-coloring can be done in time $O(\Delta)+\frac{1}{2}\log^* n$, where Δ is the largest degree in the graph [6]. Developments on what can or cannot be locally computed can be found in many papers (e.g., [4,15,16,18] to cite a few; more references can be found in the survey [23]). This part of distributed computing is mainly complexity-oriented [11,19], as every problem can be solved in d rounds, where d equal to the diameter of the graph.

Fault-tolerance in asynchronous distributed computing. At the same time that the $\mathcal{LOCAL}$ model began to be studied, ignoring asynchrony and failures, an orthogonal branch of distributed computing was beginning to focus on fault-tolerance, and disregarding the communication network topology [9,13]. In an asynchronous crash-prone distributed computing model [21,22], (i) there are communication links between every pair of processes, (ii) there are no bounds on message transfer delays and each process runs at its own arbitrary speed, which can vary along with time, and (iii) processes can fail by crashing. In this area, consensus is a fundamental problem, because, roughly speaking, it allows processes to agree on a function of their inputs, which can then be used by each process to individually perform a consistent computation. However, it was proved early on that there is no deterministic distributed asynchronous message-passing consensus algorithm even if only one process may crash [9]. Hence, computability questions are central in this part of distributed computing. Given assumptions about how many processes may fail, how severe the failures can be, and other assumptions about communication, one tries to identify the distributed problems that are solvable in a specific model.

Reliable message-passing synchronous systems and asynchronous failure-prone systems remain two quite independently studied poles of distributed computing.

Aim and content of the paper. In a distributed system failures and asynchrony are rarely coming from the hardware, but much more often from the software. Hence, it is natural to consider a model composed of two distinct layers, with distinct reliability and synchrony features, namely:

- A synchronous and reliable communication graph G with n nodes, and
- n asynchronous crash-prone processes, each one attached to a distinct node.

At each vertex of G there are two components: a failure-free synchronous *node* in charge of communicating with the nodes of its neighbors, and a failure-prone asynchronous *process* in charge of performing the actual computation. Notice that, in contrast to the $\mathcal{LOCAL}$ model, in the $\mathcal{DECOUPLED}$ model after d rounds of communication, a process can collect the local inputs of only a subgraph of its d-neighborhood, since processes can start at distinct times and run at different speeds. Thus, the new model is in principle more challenging than the $\mathcal{LOCAL}$ model.

To illustrate the $\mathcal{DECOUPLED}$ model approach, the paper considers a fundamental problem of failure-free synchronous distributed computing. It presents a 3-coloring algorithm for a ring, denoted WLC (for Wait-free Local Coloring), suited to the $\mathcal{DECOUPLED}$ model. This algorithm is based on the time-optimal Cole and Vishkin's vertex coloring algorithm, which is denoted CV86 in the following [7][1]. The CV86 algorithm runs in $\log^* n + 3$ rounds[2] while the new algorithm runs in $\log^* n + 6$ rounds. From the processes point of view, the algorithm is fully asynchronous, wait-free, i.e., a process never waits for an event in another process. Yet the algorithm is local, in the sense that each process uses information only from processes at distance $O(\log^* n)$ from it. Moreover, this amount of information is optimal due to Linial's lower bound [16] and because in the absence of failures and asynchrony, the $\mathcal{DECOUPLED}$ model boils down to the $\mathcal{LOCAL}$ model.

The WLC algorithm for the $\mathcal{DECOUPLED}$ model is built in two stages. First an extension of CV86 is presented that may be interesting in itself. This extension, denoted AST-CV, is an implementation of CV86 in a synchronous system where reliable processes need not start at the very same round. The main idea of the first stage is to run CV86 within each segment of the ring that happens to wake up at precisely the same time. Then, adjacent endpoints of such segments fix their colors by giving priority to the segment that began earlier. Somewhat surprisingly this approach works even when *all* segments happen to consist of a single process. In the second stage it is shown how to derive the wait-free algorithm WLC from AST-CV. When a process starts (asynchronously with respect to other processes), it obtains information on the "current state" of the processes at distance at most $O(\log^* n)$ from it; then, using the information obtained, the process executes alone a purely local simulation of AST-CV, at the end of which it obtains its final color.

The new algorithm shows how it is possible to extend the scope of a synchronous failure-free algorithm to run on asynchronous and crash-prone processes, without losing its fundamental locality properties, and at the cost of only a small constant number of rounds. Up to the best of our knowledge this is the first time the design of fault-tolerant asynchronous algorithms on top of a synchronous

[1] CV86 was designed for trees in the PRAM model. It can be easily adapted to failure-free message-passing synchronous systems, for a ring, or a chain of processes.

[2] Assuming $n \geq 2$, $\log^* n$ is the number of times the function "$\log_2$" needs to be applied in the invocation $\log_2(\log_2(\log_2 ...(\log_2 n)....))$ to obtain value 1. Let us remember that $\log^*$(approx. number of atoms in the universe) = 5.

communication network is considered from the locality perspective. However this is certainly not the first work that relates synchronous and asynchronous systems, a few examples follow. From very early on the performance of asynchronous processes with access to a global clock has been considered [1]. The performance of wait-free algorithms running on top of partially synchronous, fully-connected systems has been of interest for some time, e.g. [10,14]. The opposite problem, of running a synchronous algorithm in an asynchronous (failure-free) network was introduced in [2], and there are extensions even to the case where links are assumed to crash and recover dynamically [3]. In globally asynchronous locally-synchronous (GALS) design for microprocessor networks, the system is partitioned into synchronous blocks of logic which communicate with each other asynchronously [17]. An example of a reliable network infrastructure is provided by the highly popular Synchronous Optical Networking (SONET), which provides synchronous transport signals for fiber-optic based transmissions on top of which asynchronous algorithms may be deployed.

Roadmap. The remaining of the paper is organized as follows. Section 2 presents the first contribution, namely the $\mathcal{DECOUPLED}$ model. Section 3 presents first the distributed graph coloring problem and then a version of CV86 tailored for a ring. Section 4 presents the extension of CV86 which does not require simultaneous starting times, and Sect. 5 derives the algorithm WLC. Finally, Sect. 6 concludes the paper. Due to page limitations, the missing proofs can be found in [8].

2 The Two-Component-Based Model

Here the $\mathcal{DECOUPLED}$ model is presented, where asynchronous crash-prone processes running a wait-free algorithm are mounted on top of a reliable, synchronous network.

Communication component. The communication component is modelled by a connected graph G of n vertices. Its vertices represent *nodes,* nd_1, ..., nd_n. Each node nd_i is a communication device connected with two types of entities. It is connected with its neighbor nodes in G, and to its local process p_i, in charge of running the wait-free algorithm. A node is connected to each of these entities through an *input port* and an *output port.* Moreover, a node nd_i is a device in charge only of transmitting messages (the actual computation of the wait-free algorithm is performed by the process p_i).

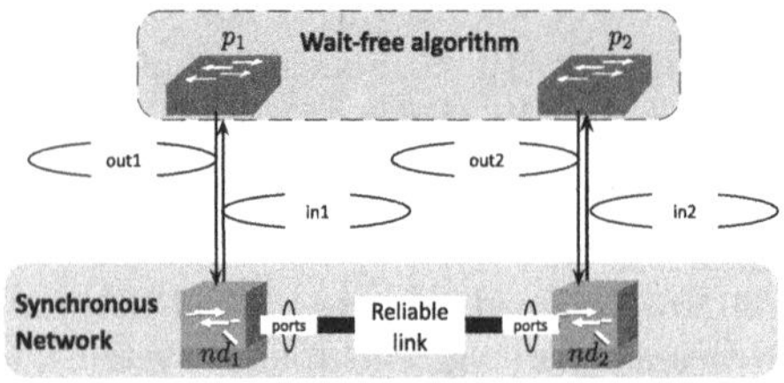

$\mathcal{DECOUPLED}$ model

Each edge of G represents a reliable *communication link*, which does not corrupt, lose, create, nor duplicate messages. Similarly, nodes do not fail in any way. The communication component is synchronous. All its entities and message exchanges proceed in a lock-step manner. More precisely, there is a global clock which governs the progress of the communication component: at every clock tick[3], each node nd_i reads its input ports (from its neighbor nodes, and from its process p_i), composes a message from what it has read, and sends this message on all its output ports (to its neighbor nodes, and to p_i). Every message is received in the same clock tick as the one in which it was sent. Recall that the communication component is always active: at every clock tick, each node nd_i sends and receives messages, independently of the behaviour of its associated process p_i.

Computing component. Each communication node nd_i has an associated sequential *process* p_i. A process p_i can communicate only with its node nd_i. A process is asynchronous, which means that it proceeds at its own speed, which can vary along with time, and is independent of the sped of other processes. Moreover, processes may crash, and when a process crashes it never recovers. As processes are asynchronous, they can wake up at arbitrary times to participate in an algorithm. Therefore, when a process wakes up, it may find messages from its input port waiting to be read, which were sent by its neighbors that started the algorithm before it, as described below.

Interaction between the components. The input and output ports connecting a process p_i with its node nd_i have two buffers (in our algorithms they are bounded). The one denoted out_i is from p_i to nd_i, while the one denoted in_i is from nd_i to p_i, initially empty. When a process starts, it writes in out_i some value, which may depend on the problem being solved. At every communication step, node nd_i first receives a message from each of its neighbors, and reads the local buffer out_i. Then, it packs the content of these messages and the current value of out_i into a single message, sends it to its neighbors, and writes it in in_i. Notice that a process p_i, D time units after it started, can have information from processes in the graph at distance up to D from it.

The global ticks of the communication component govern when each communication step happens. In addition, each tick is associated to a global time. Given a process p_i, ts_i is the global time at which p_i wakes up and starts executing. Thanks to the underlying messages exchanged by the communication nodes at every clock tick (communication step), a process p_i which started participating in the algorithm can know (a) which of its neighbors (until some predefined distance D) started the algorithm, and (b) at which time they started[4]. More precisely, considering a process p_i that starts at time st_i, after D time units, p_i can have information from processes in the graph at distance up to D from it.

[3] We use the "*time*" and "*clock tick*" terminology for the communication component, to prevent confusion with the "*round*" terminology used in the description of the CV86 and AST-CV algorithms.

[4] The assumption that processes know the global time is made only to simplify the description of our algorithms. All that a process p_i needs to know is the relative order of wake up with respect to its neighbors, which can be deduced from the content of the buffers at wake up time st_i.

Initial knowledge. Each of the n pairs made up of a communication node (nd_i) and a process (p_i) has a unique identity id_i. It is assumed that each identity can be encoded in $\log n$ bits. Initially, a process knows its identity, the value of n, and possibly the graph G. Moreover, while a process knows that no two processes have the same identity, it does not know the identities of the other processes.

Power of the model. The $\mathcal{DECOUPLED}$ model behaves exactly like the $\mathcal{LOCAL}$ model, in the absence of failures and presence of synchrony: all processes run in lock-step manner until decisions are made. Thus, if there is an algorithm solving a given problem in $\mathcal{DECOUPLED}$, then one can easily obtain an algorithm solving the corresponding problem in $\mathcal{LOCAL}$. The rest of the paper presents WLC, a 3-vertex coloring algorithm for a ring, showing that, in principle, the other direction is possible as well.

3 Distributed Graph Coloring and a Look at Cole and Vishkin's Algorithm

In the 3-*coloring* problem, each vertex of a graph is assigned a color from a set of three possible colors, in such a way that no two adjacent vertices have the same color. In sequential computing, deciding if a graph can be 3-colored is a famous NP-complete problem [12].

3.1 Graph Coloring

In the context of synchronous systems, there is an $\Omega(\log^* n)$ rounds lower bound on the number communication rounds needed to 3-color the nodes of a ring [16], and the CV86 algorithm solves the problem in $\log^* n+3$ rounds [7]. A monograph entirely devoted to distributed graph coloring can be found in [5].

The structure of Cole and Vishkin's algorithm. This algorithm assumes that the underlying bi-directional communication graph has a logical orientation, such that each process has at most a single predecessor. It assumes that the processes have distinct identities, each consisting of $O(\log n)$ bits. The algorithm can be decomposed in two phases.

- Phase 1. From n colors to six colors. An original and clever bit-level technique is first used (see below), which allows the processes to be properly colored with six colors. Starting with colors encoded with $\log n$ bits (node identities), a sequence of synchronous communication steps is executed, such that in each step a process computes a new proper color whose size in bits is exponentially smaller than the previous one. This is repeated until attaining at most six colors, which requires $\log^* n$ communication rounds.
- Phase 2. From six colors to three colors. The algorithm uses then a simple reduction technique to reduce the number of colors from six to three. This requires three additional rounds (each one eliminating a color).

Features of CV86. Those are the following: it is *local*, it's time complexity is $\log^* n + 3$, *time optimal* [16], and *deterministic*. Combining the locality and determinism properties, it follows that the final color of a process depends only on the $\log^* n + 3$ identities of the processes on its predecessor path.

3.2 A Version of Cole and Vishkin's Algorithm Suited to a Ring

A version of CV86 suited to a ring in Fig. 1. The two neighbors of a process p_i are denoted $pred_i$ and $next_i$. The local variable $color_i$ contains initially the identity of p_i, using $\log n$ bits. Let $m = \lceil \log n \rceil - 1$. The initial value of $color_i$ is a sequence of $(m+1)$ bits $b_m, b_{m-1}, \cdots, b_1, b_0$, and no two processes have the same initial sequence of bits. We say that "b_y is at position y", i.e., the position of a bit in a color is defined by starting from position 0 and going from right to left.

Underlying principle. The aim is, from round to round, to compress as much as possible the size of the colors of the processes, while keeping invariant the property that no two neighbors have the same color. Basically, a process compares its current color with the one of its predecessor, to define its new color (using the logical orientation of the ring).

The two issues that have then to be solved are (i) how to compare current colors and how to compute a new shorter color (while maintaining adjacent processes with different colors), and (ii) how many iterations have to be executed to get to at most three colors.

```
color_i ← bit string representing p_i's identity;
when r = 1, 2, ..., log* n do % Part 1: reduction from n colors to 6 colors %
begin synchronous round
  send COLOR(color_i) to next_i;
  receive COLOR(color_p) from pred_i;
  x = position (starting at 0 from the right) where color_i and color_p differ;
  color_i ← bit string encoding the binary value of x followed at its right
                 by b_x (first bit of color_i where color_i and color_p differ)
end synchronous round;
% Here color_i ∈ {0, 1, ···, 5}; Part 2: reduction from 6 to 3 colors %
when r = log* n + 1, log* n + 2, log* n + 3 do
begin synchronous round
  send COLOR(color_i) to pred_i and next_i;
  receive COLOR(color_p) from pred_i and COLOR(color_n) from next_i;
  let k be r − log* n + 2; % k ∈ {3, 4, 5} %
  if (color_i = k) then color_i ← min({0, 1, 2} \ {color_p, color_n}) end if
end synchronous round;
% Here color_i ∈ {0, 1, 2} %
return(color_i).
```

Fig. 1. Cole and Vishkin's synchronous algorithm for a ring (code for p_i)

Description of the algorithm. Let r denote the current round number. Initialized to 1, it takes then the successive values 2, 3, etc. It is a global variable provided by the synchronous system, which can be read by all processes. Each process p_i first defines its current color as the bit string representing its identity (line 01). As already indicated, it is assumed that each identity can be coded in $\log n$ bits. Then p_i executes synchronous rounds until it obtains its final color (line 16). The total number of rounds that are executed is $\log^* n + 3$, which decompose into two parts.

The first $\log^* n$ rounds (lines 03–08) allow each process p_i to compute a color in the set $\{0, 1, \cdots, 5\}$. Considering a round r, let k be an upper bound on the number of different colors at the beginning of round k, and m be the smallest integer such that $k \leq 2^m$. Hence, at round r, the color of a process is coded on m bits. After a send/receive communication step (lines 04–05), a process p_i compares its color with the one it has received from its predecessor ($color\_p$), and computes (starting at 0 from the right), the rightmost bit position x where they differ (line 06). Then (line 07), p_i defines its new color as the bit sequence whose prefix is the binary encoding of x in $\log m$ bits and suffix is the first bit of its current color where both colors differ, namely b_x.

Consider two neighbor processes during a round r. If they have the same value for x, due to the bit suffix they use to obtain their new color, they necessarily obtain different new colors. If they have different values for x, they trivially have different new colors. It is easy to see that the round r reduces the number of colors from k to at most $2\lceil \log k \rceil \leq 2m$. It is shown in [7] that, after at most $\log^* n$ rounds, the binary encoding of a color requires only three bits, where the suffix b_x is 0 or 1, and the prefix is 00, 10, or 01. Hence, only six color values are possible.

The second part of the algorithm consists of three additional rounds, each round eliminating one of the colors in $\{3, 4, 5\}$ (lines 10–15). Each process first exchanges its color with its two neighbors. Due to the previous $\log^* n$ rounds, these three colors are different. Hence, if its color is 3, p_i selects any color in $\{0, 1, 2\}$ not owned by its neighbors. This is then repeated twice to eliminate the colors 4 and 5.

Proofs of the algorithm correctness and its time complexity can be found in [7]. A simple way to go from a ring to a chain is described in [8].

4 Extending Cole and Vishkin's Algorithm to Asynchronous Starting Times

This section presents an extension of CV86 for synchronous systems, where reliable processes may start at different rounds.

4.1 Asynchronous Starting Times and Unit-Segment

Asynchronous starting times. Let st_i denote the round number at which process p_i wakes up and starts participating in the algorithm. A process may start at any time, but when it starts, it does so at the beginning of a round, and then runs synchronously.

Notion of a unit-segment. A *unit-segment* is a maximal sequence of consecutive processes in the ring, p_a, p_{next_a}, $\cdots$, p_{pred_z}, p_z, that start the algorithm in the same round.

A unit-segment is identified by a starting time (round number), and any two contiguous unit-segments are necessarily associated with distinct starting times. It follows that, from an omniscient observer's point of view, and at any time, the ring can be decomposed into a set of unit-segments, some of these unit-segments being contiguous, while others are separated by processes that have not yet started (or will never start, due to an initial crash). In the particular case where all processes start simultaneously, the ring is composed of a single unit-segment, and if all start at different times, it is composed of n unit-segments.

4.2 A Coloring Algorithm with Asynchronous Starting Times

This section presents the local algorithm AST-CV, which allows processes to start at different Each process executes $\Delta = \log^* n + 6$ rounds. The algorithm is decomposed into four parts.

Starting round of the algorithm. The underlying synchronous system defines the first round ($r = 1$) as being the round at which the first process(es) starts the algorithm. Hence, when such a process p_i starts the algorithm, we have $st_i = 1$. Then, the progress of r is managed by the system synchrony.

Part 1 and Part 2. These parts are described in Fig. 2. Considering a unit-segment (identified by a starting time st) they are a simple adaptation of CV86, which considers the behavior of any process p_i belonging to this unit-segment.

A process p_i executes first $\log^* n$ synchronous rounds. During each round, it sends its current color to its neighbors, and receives their current colors. $msg\_pred = \bot$ if there is no message from $pred_i$ (line 04).

In line 05, p_i can tell if its predecessor belongs to the same unit-segment from the st value received. If so, p_i executes CV86. If its predecessor belongs to a different unit-segment or has not yet started the algorithm, p_i considers a fictitious predecessor whose identity is the same as its own identity, except for the first bit, starting from the right (see the last paragraph of Annex Sect. 3.2). Lines 06–10 constitute the core of CV86, which exponentially fast reduces the bit size representation of $color_i$ at every round, to end up with a color in the set $\{0, 1, \cdots, 5\}$ after $\log^* n$ rounds.

Part 2 of AST-CV (lines 13–21) is the same as the part in CV86 that reduces the set of colors in each unit-segment from at most six to at most three [7], and hence, at the end of this part, the processes of the unit-segment identified by st_i have obtained a proper color within their unit-segment. Moreover, if the process is internal to its unit-segment, it will have obtained its final color (after $\log^* n+3$ rounds).

init: $color_i$: bit string initialized to p_i's identity; st_i: starting round of p_i;
when p_i starts, there are three cases for each of its neighbors $pred_i$ and $next_i$:
(a) it already started the algorithm;
(b) it starts the algorithm at the very same round;
(c) it will start the algorithm at a later round.
In the first case, the messages sent in previous rounds by the corresponding neighbor are in p_i's input buffer, and can be consequently read by p_i.
In the last case, to simplify the presentation, we consider that p_i receives a dummy message.
$fict\_pred_i$: fictitious process whose identity is the same as p_i's identity except for its first bit (starting from the right); used as predecessor in case p_i discovers it is a left end of a unit-segment.

================ Part 1 : reduction from n colors to 6 colors =====

(01)**when** $r = st_i, st_i + 1, ..., (st_i - 1) + \log^* n$ **do**
(02)**begin synchronous round**
(03) send COLOR$(0, st_i, color_i)$ to $next_i$ and $pred_i$;
(04) receive msg_pred_i from $pred_i$;
(05) **if** $(msg\_pred_i$ = COLOR$(0, st_i, col))$
(06) **then** x= first position (starting right at 0) where $color_i$ and col differ;
(07) $color_i \leftarrow$ bit string encoding the binary value of x followed at
(08) its right by b_x (first bit of $color_i$ where $color_i$ and col differ)
(09) **else** p_i has no predecessor (it is an end process of its unit segment) it
(10) considers $fict\_pred_i$ as its predecessor and executes lines 06-08
(11) **end if**;
(12)**end synchronous round**;
% Here $color_i \in \{0, 1, \cdots, 5\}$

================== Part 2 : reduction from 6 to 3 colors ======

(13)**when** $r = (st_i - 1) + \log^* n + 1, (st_i - 1) + \log^* n + 2, (st_i - 1) + \log^* n + 3$ **do**
(14)**begin synchronous round**
(15) send COLOR$(0, st_i, color_i)$ to $pred_i$ and $next_i$;
(16) $color\_set \leftarrow \emptyset$;
(17) **if** COLOR$(0, st_i, color_p)$ received from $pred_i$
then $color\_set \leftarrow color\_set \cup color\_p$ **end if**;
(18) **if** COLOR$(0, st_i, color_n)$ received from $next_i$
then $color\_set \leftarrow color\_set \cup color\_n$ **end if**;
(19) **let** k **be** $r - (st_i - 1 + \log^* n) + 2$; % $k \in \{3, 4, 5\}$ %
(20) **if** $(color_i = k)$ **then** $color_i \leftarrow$ any color from $\{0, 1, 2\} \setminus color\_set$ **end if**
(21)**end synchronous round**;

=======================================

% Here $color_i \in \{0, 1, 2\}$, and the unit segment including p_i is properly colored but
% two end processes of two consecutive unit segments may have the same color

Fig. 2. Initialization, Part 1, and Part 2, of AST-CV (code for p_i)

Message management. Let us observe that, as not all processes start at the same round, it is possible that, while executing a round of the synchronous algorithm of Fig. 2, a process p_i receives a message COLOR$(0, st, -)$ with $st \neq st_i$ from its predecessor, or messages COLOR$(j, -)$ (where $j \in \{1, 2, 3\}$, sent in Parts 3 or 4)

In the following parts of the algorithm, each process p_i uses local variables denoted $color_i[j, nbg]$, where $j \in \{1, 2, 3\}$ and $nbg \in \{pred_i, next_i\}$.
These variables are initialized to -1 (no color) and updated when p_i receives a message COLOR$(j, -)$ from $pred_i$ or $next_i$. Due to the fact that the processes do not start the algorithm at the same round, process p_i may have received messages COLOR$(j, -)$ during previous synchronous rounds.

== Part 3: $color_i$ can be changed only if p_i is the left end of its unit-segment
(22)**when** $r = (st_i - 1) + \log^* n + 4$ **do**
(23)**begin synchronous round**
(24) send COLOR$(1, color_i)$ to $pred_i$ and $next_i$;
(25) **for each** $j \in \{1, 2, 3\}$ **do**
(26) **if** (COLOR$(j, color)$ received from $pred_i$ in a round $\leq r$)
then $color_i[j, pred_i] \leftarrow color$ **end if**;
(27) **if** (COLOR$(j, color)$ received from $next_i$ in a round $\leq r$)
then $color_i[j, next_i] \leftarrow color$ **end if**
(28) **end for**;
(29) **if** $(st_i > st_i[pred_i])$ **then** % p_i has not priority
(30) **case** $(st_i = st_i[next_i])$ **then**
$color_i \leftarrow$ a color in $\{0, 1, 2\} \setminus \{color_i[2, pred_i], color_i[1, next_i]\}$
(31) $(st_i > st_i[next_i])$ **then**
$color_i \leftarrow$ a color in $\{0, 1, 2\} \setminus \{color_i[2, pred_i], color_i[2, next_i]\}$
(32) $(st_i < st_i[next_i])$ **then** $color_i \leftarrow$ a color in $\{0, 1, 2\} \setminus \{color_i[2, pred_i]\}$
(33) **end case**
(34) **end if**
(35)**end synchronous round**;

== Part 4: $color_i$ can be changed only if p_i is the right end of its unit-segment
(36)**when** $r = (st_i - 1) + \log^* n + 5$ **do**
(37)**begin synchronous round**
(38) send COLOR$(2, color_i)$ to $pred_i$ and $next_i$;
(39) same statements as in lines 25-28;
(40) **if** $(st_i > st_i[next_i])$ **then** % p_i has not priority
(41) **case** $(st_i = st_i[pred_i])$ **then**
$color_i \leftarrow$ a color in $\{0, 1, 2\} \setminus \{color_i[2, pred_i], color_i[3, next_i]\}$
(42) $(st_i > st_i[pred_i])$ **then**
$color_i \leftarrow$ a color in $\{0, 1, 2\} \setminus \{color_i[3, pred_i], color_i[3, next_i]\}$
(43) $(st_i < st_i[pred_i])$ **then** $color_i \leftarrow$ a color in $\{0, 1, 2\} \setminus \{color_i[3, next_i]\}$
(44) **end case**
(45) **end if**
(46)**end synchronous round**;

== Additional round to inform the neighbors that will start later
(47)**when** $r = (st_i - 1) + \log^* n + 6$ **do** send COLOR$(3, color_i)$ to $pred_i$ and $next_i$;
(48)return$(color_i)$.

Fig. 3. Part 3 and Part 4 of AST-CV (code for p_i)

from one or both of its neighbors. To simplify and make clearer the presentation, the reception of these messages is not indicated in Fig. 2. It is implicitly assumed that, when they are received during a synchronous round, these messages are saved in the local memory of p_i (so that they can be processed later, if needed, at lines 25–28 and line 39 of Fig. 3).

Moreover, a process p_i learns the starting round of $pred_i$ (resp., $next_i$) when it receives for the first time a message COLOR$(0, st, -)$ from $pred_i$ (resp. $next_i$). To not overload the presentation, this is left implicit in the description of the algorithm.

Part 3 and Part 4. These parts are described in Fig. 3. If p_i is a left end, or a right end, or both, of a unit-segment[5], its color at the end of Part 2 is not necessarily its final color, because Part 1 and Part 2 color different unit-segments independently from each other. Hence, it is possible for two contiguous unit-segments to be such that the left end of one, say p_i, and the right end of the other, say p_j, have $color_i = color_j$.

The aim of Part 3 and Part 4 is to resolve these coloring conflicts. To this end, each process p_i manages six local variables, denoted $color_i[j, nbg]$, where $j \in \{1, 2, 3\}$ and $nbg \in \{pred_i, next_i\}$. They are initialized to -1 (no color).

Solving the conflict between neighbors belonging to contiguous unit-segments. A natural idea to solve a coloring conflict between two neighbor processes belonging to different unit-segments, consists in giving "priority" to the unit-segment whose starting time is the first.

Let $st_i[pred_i]$ (resp., $st_i[next_i]$) be the knowledge of p_i on the starting time of its left (resp., right) neighbor. If $pred_i$ has not yet started let $st_i[pred_i] = +\infty$ (and similarly for $next_i$). Thanks to this information, p_i knows if it is at the left (resp., right) end of a unit-segment: this is the case if $st_i \neq st_i[pred_i]$ (resp., if $st_i \neq st_i[next_i]$). Moreover, if p_i is a left (resp., right) end of a unit-segment, it knows that it has not priority if $st_i > st_i[pred_i]$ (resp., $st_i > st_i[next_i]$). If such cases, p_i may be required to change its color to ensure it differs from the color of its neighbor belonging to the priority contiguous unit-segment.

The tricky cases are the ones of the unit-segments composed of either a single process p or two processes p_a and p_b. This is because, in these cases, it can be required that p (possibly twice, once as right end, and once as left end of its unit-segment), or once p_a and once p_b (in the case of a 2-process unit-segment), be forced to change the color they obtained at the end of Part 2, to obtain a final color consistent with respect to their neighbors in contiguous unit-segments. To prevent inconsistencies from occurring, it is required that (in addition to the previous priority rule) (a) first a left end process of a unit-segment modifies its color with respect to its predecessor neighbor (which belongs to its left unit-segment), and (b) only then a right end process of a unit-segment modifies its color if needed (this specific order is immaterial; the other order –first right, then left– would be equally fine).

Conflict resolutions rules summary. Let us consider a process p_i.

[5] If p_i is both a left end and a right end of a unit-segment, it forms its own unit-segment.

- If p_i is inside a unit-segment (i.e., $st_i = st_i[pred_i] = st_i[next_i]$), or is the left end of a unit-segment and $pred_i$ began after it (i.e., $st_i < st_i[pred_i]$), or is the right end of a unit-segment and $next_i$ began after it (i.e., $st_i < st_i[next_i]$), then the color it obtained at the end of Part 2 is its final color.
- If p_i is the left end of a unit-segment and $pred_i$ began before p_i (i.e., $st_i > st_i[pred_i]$), then p_i may be forced to change its color. This is done in Part 3. The color p_i obtains at the end of Part 3 will be its final color, if it is not also the right end of its unit-segment and $next_i$ began before it (i.e., $st_i > st_i[next_i]$).
- This case is similar to the previous one. If p_i is the right end of a unit-segment and $next_i$ began before it (i.e., $st_i > st_i[next_i]$), p_i may be forced to change its color to have a final color different from the one of $next_i$. This is done in Part 4.

Recall that a process that is neither the left end, nor the right end of a unit-segment obtains its final color in Part 2. It follows that, during Part 3 and Part 4, such a process only needs to execute the sending of messages COLOR$(j, -)$, $j \in \{1, 2, 3\}$ it lines 24,38, and 47 (the other statements cannot change its color).

Part 3. This part is composed of a single round (lines 22–35). A process p_i sends first to its neighbors a message COLOR$(1, c)$ carrying the color c it has obtained at the end of Part 2. Then, according to the messages it received from them up to the current round, p_i updates its local variables $color_i[j, pred_i]$ and $color_i[j, next_i]$ (lines 25–28).

Part 4. This part, composed of a single round (lines 36–46), is similar to the previous one. Due to the predicate of line 40, the lines 41–44 are executed only if p_i is the right end of its unit segment. Their meaning is similar to the one of lines 30–33. Finally, p_i sends (line 47) to its two neighbors the message COLOR$(3, color_i)$ to inform them of its last color, in case it was modified in Part 4.

An execution of AST-CV and a proof of the following theorem are given in [8].

Theorem 1. *If p_i and p_j wake up and are neighbors, their final colors are different and in the set $\{0, 1, 2\}$.*

4.3 Properties of the Algorithm

AST-CV inherits the two most important properties from CV86: locality and determinism. A proof of the algorithm is given in [8].

- The locality property of CV86 states that a process obtains its final color by $\log^* n + 3$ rounds. In AST-CV, it obtains it $\log^* n + 6$ rounds after its starting round.
- In CV86, the determinism property states that the final color of a process depends only of the identities of the consecutive processes which are its $\log^* n + 3$ predecessors on the ring. In AST-CV, its final color depends only of the starting times and the identities of the consecutive processes which are its $\log^* n + 6$ predecessors on the ring.

5 From Asynchronous Starting Times to Wait-Freedom

This section presents the WLC (Wait-free Local Coloring) algorithm for the $\mathcal{DECOUPLED}$ model described in Sect. 2, which 3-colors the processes of a ring. This algorithm consists of two consecutive stages executed independently by each process p_i. The first stage is a communication stage during which p_i, whatever its starting time, obtains enough information to execute its second stage, which consists of a communication-free computation.

The following solvability notion incorporates asynchrony and failures, as needed by the $\mathcal{DECOUPLED}$ model. An algorithm *wait-free* solves m-coloring if for each of its executions: (1) Validity. The final color of any process is in $\{0, ..., m-1\}$. (2) Agreement. The final colors of any two neighbor nodes in the graph are different. (3) Termination. All processes that take an infinite number of steps decide a final color.

5.1 On the Communication Side

A ring structure for the synchronous communication network. The neighbors of a node nd_i (or process p_i with a slight abuse of language) are denoted as before, $pred_i$ and $next_i$.

On the side of the communication nodes. While each input buffer in_i is initially empty, each output buffer out_i is initialized to $\langle i, +\infty, \bot \rangle$. When a process starts its participation in the algorithm, it writes the pair $\langle i, st_i, id_i \rangle$ in out_i, where st_i is its starting time (as defined by the current tick of the clock governing the progress of the underlying communication component), and id_i is its identity.

As already described, at every clock tick (underlying communication step), nd_i first receives two messages (one from each neighbor), and reads the local buffer out_i. Then, it packs the content of these two messages and the content of out_i (which can be $\langle i, +\infty, \bot \rangle$ if p_i has not yet started) into a single message, sends it to its two neighbors, and writes it in in_i (full-information behavior of a node).

5.2 Wait-Free Algorithm: First a Communication Stage

Let p_i be a process that starts the algorithm at time $st_i = t$. As previously indicated, this means that, at time t (clock tick defined by the communication component), p_i writes $\langle i, t, id_i \rangle$ in its output buffer out_i. Then p_i waits until time $t + \Delta$ where $\Delta = \log^* n + 5$. ([6]). At the end of this waiting period, and as far p_i is concerned, the "dices are cast". No more physical communication will be necessary. As we are about to see, p_i obtained enough information to compute alone its color: the rest of the algorithm executed by p_i is purely local (see below). This feature, and the fact that the starting time of a process depends only on it, makes the algorithm wait-free.

[6] Being asynchronous, the waiting of p_i during an arbitrary long (but finite) period does not modify its allowed behavior.

It follows from the underlying communication component that, at time $t+\Delta$, p_i has received information (i.e., a triplet $\langle j, st, id_j \rangle$) from all the processes at distance at most Δ of it. If $st = t$, p_i knows that p_j started the algorithm at the same time as itself. If $st < t$ (resp., $st > t$), p_i knows that p_j started the algorithm before (resp., after) it. (If $st = +\infty$ –we have then $id_j = \perp$– and p_j is at distance d from it, p_i knows that p_j did not start the algorithm before the clock tick $t + \Delta - d$.)

5.3 Wait-Free Algorithm: Then a Local Simulation Stage of AST-CV

At the end of its waiting period, p_i has information (triplets composed of an index, a starting time –possibly $+\infty$–, and a process identity –possibly $\perp$–) of all the processes at distance $\Delta = \log^* n + 5$ from it, and also from the processes at distance k that started before $st_i + \Delta - k$ (each triplet from process p_j at distance k was propagated from it to a process p_ℓ at distance Δ from p_i, and then from p_ℓ to p_i). More precisely, for each of these processes p_j, p_i knows whether p_j started before it ($st_j < st_i$), at the same time as it ($st_j = st_i$), or after it ($st_j > st_i$).

Simulation of AST-CV. It follows from the previous observation that, after its waiting period, p_i has all the inputs (starting times and process identities) needed to simulate AST-CV and compute its final color, be it inside a unit-segment, the left end of a unit-segment, the right end of a unit-segment, or both ends of a unit-segment (a maximal sequence of consecutive processes that start the algorithm at the same time).

More precisely, the purely local simulation by a process p_i is a follows. Starting from round 0, p_i simulates $st_i + \Delta$ rounds of AST-CV, this simulation involving the processes from which it has the initial information $\langle j, st_j, id_j \rangle$ and are s.t. $st_j \leq st_i$.

Notice that the crash of a process p_j has no impact on the termination and the correctness of the coloring of other processes. This follows from the locality property of AST-CV, and the fact that as soon as a process has obtained a triplet $\langle j, st_j, id_j \rangle$ (where $st_j \leq st_i$), it considers p_j as competing for a color, whatever is its behavior after it started participating in the algorithm.

Optimality of WLC. When it executes WLC, each process waits during $O(\log^* n)$ time units, which occurs during the communication phase. This duration is asymptotically optimal as (1) $\Omega(\log^* n)$ is a lower bound on the number of time units needed to color the nodes of a ring with at most three colors [16] in $\mathcal{LOCAL}$, and (2) when there is neither asynchrony nor failures, $\mathcal{DECOUPLED}$ behaves like $\mathcal{LOCAL}$.

6 Conclusion

The paper proposed a model where communication and processing are decoupled, consisting of asynchronous crash-prone processes that run on top of a reliable synchronous network. This $\mathcal{DECOUPLED}$ model is weaker than the synchronous model (on the process side) and stronger than the asynchronous crash-prone model (on the communication side), while encompassing in a single framework two fundamental issues of distributed computing, locality [16] and wait-freedom [13].

A 3-coloring algorithm for a ring was derived for the $\mathcal{DECOUPLED}$ model. This algorithm uses as a subroutine a generalization of Cole and Vishkin's algorithm [7]. A process needs to obtain initial information from processes at distance at most $O(\log^* n)$ of it. As far as we know, this is the first wait-free local coloring algorithm, which colors a ring with at most three colors.

In contrast to $\mathcal{LOCAL}$, in the $\mathcal{DECOUPLED}$ model, after d rounds of communication, a process collects the initial inputs of only a subgraph of its d-neighborhood. The paper has shown that, despite this uncertainty, it is possible to combine locality and wait-freedom, as far as 3-coloring is concerned. The keys to this marriage were (a) the decoupling of communication and processing, and (b) the design of a synchronous coloring algorithm (AST-CV), where the processes are reliable, proceed synchronously, but are not required to start at the very same round, which introduces a first type of asynchrony among the processes. As we have seen, the heart of this algorithm lies in the consistent coloring of the border vertices of subgraphs which started at different times (unit segments).

It would be interesting if this methodology applies to other coloring algorithms, or even to other distributed graph problems which are solvable in the $\mathcal{LOCAL}$ model.

Acknowledgments. This work has been partially supported by the French ANR project DESCARTES, devoted to abstraction layers in distributed computing. The first author was supported in part by UNAM PAPIIT-DGAPA project IA101015. The fourth author is currently on leave at CSAIL-MIT and was supported in part by UNAM PAPIIT-DGAPA project IN107714.

References

1. Arjomandi, E., Fischer, M., Lynch, N.: Efficiency of synchronous versus asynchronous distributed systems. J. ACM **30**(3), 449–456 (1983)
2. Awerbuch, B.: Complexity of network synchronization. JACM **32**(4), 804–823 (1985)
3. Awerbuch B., Patt-Shamir B., Peleg D., Saks M.: Adapting to asynchronous dynamic networks (extended abstract). In: Proceedings of the 24th ACM Symposium on Theory of Computing (STOC 1992), pp. 557–570 (1992)
4. Barenboim, L., Elkin, M.: Deterministic distributed vertex coloring in polylogarithmic time. J. ACM **58**(5), 23 (2011)
5. Barenboim, L., Elkin, M.: Distributed Graph Coloring, Fundamental and Recent Developments, 155 p. Morgan & Claypool Publishers (2014)
6. Barenboim, L., Elkin, M., Kuhn, F.: Distributed (Delta+1)-coloring in linear (in Delta) time. SIAM J. Comput. **43**(1), 72–95 (2014)

7. Cole, R., Vishkin, U.: Deterministic coin tossing with applications to optimal parallel list ranking. Inf. Control **70**(1), 32–53 (1986)
8. Castañeda, A., Delporte, C., Fauconnier, H., Rajsbaum, S., Raynal, M.: Wait-freedom and locality are not incompatible (with distributed ring coloring as an example). Technical report #2033, 19 p., IRISA, University of Rennes, France (2016)
9. Fischer, M.J., Lynch, N.A., Paterson, M.S.: Impossibility of distributed consensus with one faulty process. J. ACM **32**(2), 374–382 (1985)
10. Fraigniaud, P., Gafni, E., Rajsbaum, S., Roy, M.: Automatically adjusting concurrency to the level of synchrony. In: Kuhn, F. (ed.) DISC 2014. LNCS, vol. 8784, pp. 1–15. Springer, Heidelberg (2014)
11. Fraigniaud, P., Korman, A., Peleg, D.: Towards a complexity theory for local distributed computing. J. ACM **60**(5), 16 (2013). Article 35
12. Garey, M.R., Johnson, D.S.: Computers, Intractability: A Guide to the Theory of NP-Completeness, 340 p. W.H. Freeman, New York (1979)
13. Herlihy, M.P.: Wait-free synchronization. ACM Trans. Program. Lang. Syst. **13**(1), 124–149 (1991)
14. Keidar, I., Rajsbaum, S.: On the cost of fault-tolerant consensus when there are no faults: preliminary version. ACM SIGACT News **32**(2), 45–63 (2001)
15. Kuhn, F., Moscibroda, T., Wattenhofer, R.: What cannot be computed locally! In: Proceedings of the 23rd ACM Symposium on Principles of Distributed Computing, pp. 300–309. ACM Press (2004)
16. Linial, N.: Locality in distributed graph algorithms. SIAM JC **21**(1), 193–201 (1992)
17. Meincke, T., et al.: Globally asynchronous locally synchronous architecture for large high-performance ASICs. In: Proceedings of the IEEE International Symposium on Circuits and Systems (ISCAS 1999), vol. 2, pp. 512–515 (1999)
18. Naor, M., Stockmeyer, L.: What can be computed locally? SIAM J. Comput. **24**(6), 1259–1277 (1995)
19. Peleg, D.: Distributed computing, a locally sensitive approach. SIAM Monographs on Discrete Mathematics and Applications, 343 p. (2000). ISBN 0-89871-464-8
20. Raynal, M.: Fault-Tolerant Agreement in Synchronous Message-Passing Systems, 165 p. Morgan & Claypool Publishers (2010). ISBN 978-1-60845-525-6
21. Raynal, M.: Communication and Agreement Abstractions for Fault-Tolerant Asynchronous Distributed Systems,251 p. Morgan & Claypool Publishers (2010). ISBN 978-1-60845-293-4
22. Raynal, M.: Concurrent Programming: Algorithms, Principles, and Foundations, 530 p. Springer (2013). ISBN 978-3-642-32026-2
23. Suomela, J.: Survey of local algorithms. ACM Comput. Surv. **45**(2), 40 (2013). Art. 24

Meta-algorithm to Choose a Good On-Line Prediction (Short Paper)

Alexandre Dambreville[1(✉)], Joanna Tomasik[2], and Johanne Cohen[3]

[1] LRI, CentraleSupélec, Université Paris-Sud, Université Paris-Saclay, Orsay, France
Alexandre.Dambreville@lri.fr

[2] LRI, CentraleSupélec, Université Paris-Saclay, Orsay, France
Joanna.Tomasik@lri.fr

[3] LRI, CNRS, Université Paris-Saclay, Orsay, France
Johanne.Cohen@lri.fr

Abstract. Numerous problems require an on-line treatment. The variation of the problem instance makes it harder to solve: an algorithm used may be very efficient for a long period but suddenly its performance deteriorates due to a change in the environment. It could be judicious to switch to another algorithm in order to adapt to the environment changes.

In this paper, we focus on the prediction on-the-fly. We have several on-line prediction algorithms at our disposal, each of them may have a different behaviour than the others depending on the situation. First, we address a meta-algorithm named *SEA* developed for experts algorithms. Next, we propose a modified version of it to improve its performance in the context of the on-line prediction.

We confirm the efficiency gain we obtained through this modification in experimental manner.

1 Introduction

Let us assume that we have several algorithms at our disposal to solve a given problem. One of them may perform very well for a situation but badly for another situation whereas for another algorithm it is the opposite. If we were in an off-line scenario, we could determine in which situation we are and select the best algorithm once for all. In this paper, we address an on-line scenario, i.e. the environment may change with time and evolve from one situation to another. Our goal is to use a meta-algorithm that dynamically switches among the available algorithms.

First, we analyse a meta-algorithm named *Strategic Expert meta-Algorithm* (*SEA*) [3] and discuss its advantages and drawbacks in Sect. 2. Next, we modifie it (Sect. 3) to make it fit the environment quicker. We evaluate the performance of our meta-algorithm through numerical experiments in Sect. 4.

B. Bonakdarpour and F. Petit (Eds.): SSS 2016, LNCS 10083, pp. 126–130, 2016.
DOI: 10.1007/978-3-319-49259-9_10

2 Existing Meta-algorithm, *SEA*

Let us assume that we have n algorithms at our disposal. We denote M_i the average payoff of algorithm i since we used it, and N_i the number of steps on which we use algorithm i when it is selected. *SEA* (Strategic Expert meta-Algorithm [3]) alternates the exploration and exploitation phases as described in Algorithm 1:

Algorithm 1. SEA

For each $i \in [\![1;n]\!]$, $M_i \leftarrow 0$, $N_i \leftarrow 0$, iter $\leftarrow 1$
procedure SEA
    loop
        $U \leftarrow \text{Random}(0,1)$
        if $U < 1/\text{iter}$ **then** $i \leftarrow \text{Random}([\![1;n]\!])$ ▷ *Exploration phase*;
        else $i \leftarrow \underset{i \in [\![1;n]\!]}{\text{argmax}}\, M_i$ ▷ *Exploitation phase*;
        $N_i \leftarrow N_i + 1$.
        Execute algorithm i for N_i steps;
        $R \leftarrow$ average payoff of i during these N_i steps;
        $M_i \leftarrow M_i + \frac{2}{N_i+1}(R - M_i)$;
        iter $\leftarrow$ iter + 1;
    end loop
end procedure

The analysis of the *SEA* algorithm leads us to formulate a list of its advantages and a list of its drawbacks. Its strengths are:

1. If the environment does not change, *SEA* is able to find the best algorithm which fits the situation.
2. If the environment does change, the average reward of *SEA* is at least as good as the average reward of the best algorithm when it was played in infinite time (see Theorem 3.1 of [3]).

Its weaknesses are:

1. It is proved that, in the long run, all of the algorithms will be used countless times by *SEA*. However, if there are many algorithms available, some of them might not be tried before a long time. Indeed, the more the time passes, the smaller the probability of an exploration is (Lemma 3.1 of [3]).
2. *SEA* computes the mean M_i since the first iteration that is why M_i suffers from inertia when the number of iterations increases. Even a drastic change for the average payoff R may be impossible to be detected what slows down the switching between algorithms. In certain situations, it would have been advantageous to switch to a very efficient algorithm, but *SEA* is not reactive enough to do it (see Figs. 2a and b).

3 Our *Dynamic SEA*

We modify *SEA*, trying to overcome its weaknesses mentioned above. For the second point, to make the mean be more reactive, instead of a long run mean, for M_i, we use the average payoff during the last N_i steps, i.e. at line 10 of Algorithm 1, we put $M_i \leftarrow R$. It allows *SEA* to have a good overview of the recent performance of an algorithm. Now, to switch to another algorithm, *SEA* just has to wait for a new exploration. This brings us to the first point of the drawbacks: an exploration may take a long time to come and it will take even much more time to try each algorithm.

In order to ensure more frequent explorations, we reset our meta-algorithm occasionally. During the exploitation of an algorithm i (line 6 of Algorithm 1), if the payoff is smaller compared to the previous iteration, we set $\forall i' \neq i, M_{i'} = \infty$ (after line 9). With this mechanism, the next exploitations will try each algorithm (different than i) at least once and then determine the best of them for the actual situation. Likewise, we use this mechanism to overcome the first weakness listed and we make our version of *SEA* try each algorithm at least once. Thereby we avoid having an untested algorithm for too long time.

4 Experiments

We start this section by explaining the experimental setup used. We evaluate our meta-algorithm for the following prediction problem. Let (D_i) be a positive integer sequence. This sequence is disturbed by a noise (N_i), which give us a jammed sequence $(J_i) = (D_i + N_i)$. At time i we receive the real data D_i and the jammed data for the next step J_{i+1}. Our goal at each time i is to recover D_{i+1} from J_{i+1}. We denote (R_{i+1}) the result of our recovering. To measure the performance of the result at time i, we propose to use a reward $\delta_i = \exp\left(-\left|\frac{R_i - D_i}{D_i}\right|\right)$, whose value always is in $(0; 1]$. If we obtain $R_i = D_i$ (the optimal result), the reward reaches the maximal value and $\delta_i = 1$. Moreover, the farther from D_i our result R_i is, the closer to 0 the reward δ_i is.

Our proposition consists in using multi-armed bandit algorithms [1]. A bandit is a method that offers us several strategies, represented by its arms, to play. Each arm has a certain reward attributed. At each time, a player choses a bandit arm and expects to win, i.e. to maximize the mean of the rewards obtained. In our problem, each arm corresponds to a modification of J_i, expressed in terms of a percentage ($x\%$) of J_i. We denote $(Arm)(J_i) = J_i + x\%(J_i) = R_i$ the effect of an arm on the jammed value J_i.

-5%	-4%	-3%	-2%	-1%	0%	1%	2%	3%	4%	5%

(a) Bandit adapted for $\mathcal{N}(0\%, 3\%)$

-25%	-24%	-23%	-22%	-21%	-20%	-19%	-18%	-17%	-16%	-15%

(b) Bandit adapted for $\mathcal{N}(-20\%, 3\%)$

15%	16%	17%	18%	19%	20%	21%	22%	23%	24%	25%

(c) Bandit adapted for $\mathcal{N}(+20\%, 3\%)$

Fig. 1. Three bandits

In our experiments, we use the trace of the 1998 World Cup Web site [2], which gives the number of requests by hour on the site as (D_i) (this trace is commonly used in the context of evaluation of scheduling algorithms). We generate different kind of noise on this trace in order to pinpoint the effect of our modifications and validate the dynamic version of *SEA*. We use a Gaussian noise for (N_i): at each time i, we set the mean and the variance as percentages of D_i: $N_i = \mathcal{N}(D_i\mu\%, D_i\sigma\%)$. More precisely, we divide (D_i) into three equal parts and we add a different noise on each of them. We denote $n_1 \to n_2 \to n_3$ the sequence of noise used. The four types of noise we use are: $n_{+20,\pm3} = \mathcal{N}(+20\,\%, 3\,\%)$, $n_{-20,\pm3} = \mathcal{N}(-20\,\%, 3\,\%)$, $n_{0,\pm3} = \mathcal{N}(0\,\%, 3\,\%)$ and $n_{0,\pm30} = \mathcal{N}(0\,\%, 30\,\%)$.

For the first three noise variants, we have three bandit algorithms, one specialized for each environment as illustrated in Fig. 1. The last noise variant has a great variability that makes it unpredictable for any of our bandit algorithms. We consider three scenarii: $n_{-20,\pm3} \to n_{20,\pm3} \to n_{0,\pm3}$, $n_{0,\pm3} \to n_{-20,\pm3} \to n_{20,\pm3}$ and $n_{0,\pm30} \to n_{0,\pm30} \to n_{0,\pm30}$.

We show our results in Fig. 2 which represent the evolution of the average reward of our algorithms. Each curve is the mean of one hundred different runs of the algorithm.

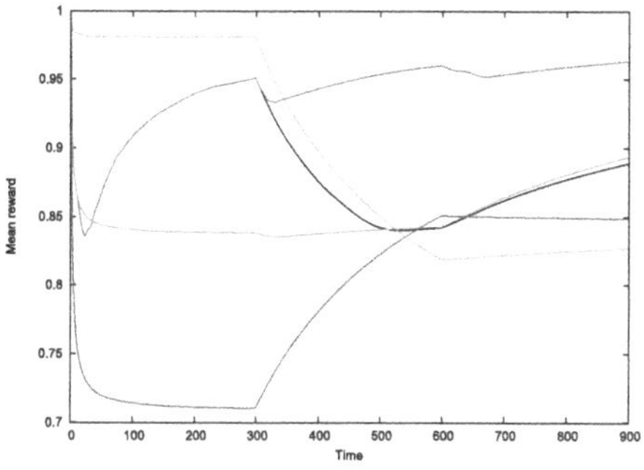

(a) $n_{-20,\pm3} \to n_{20,\pm3} \to n_{0,\pm3}$

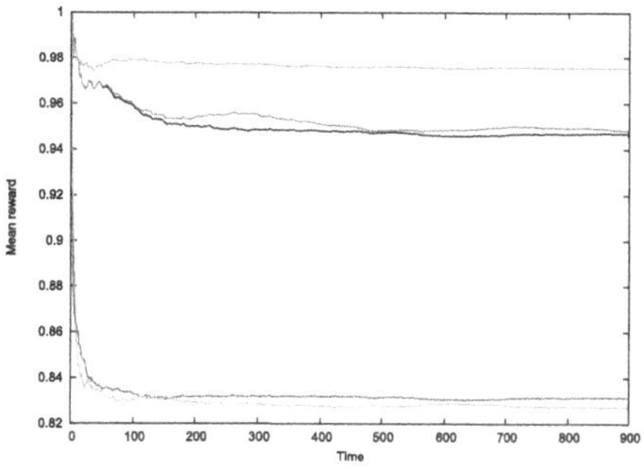

(c) $n_{0,\pm30} \to n_{0,\pm30} \to n_{0,\pm30}$

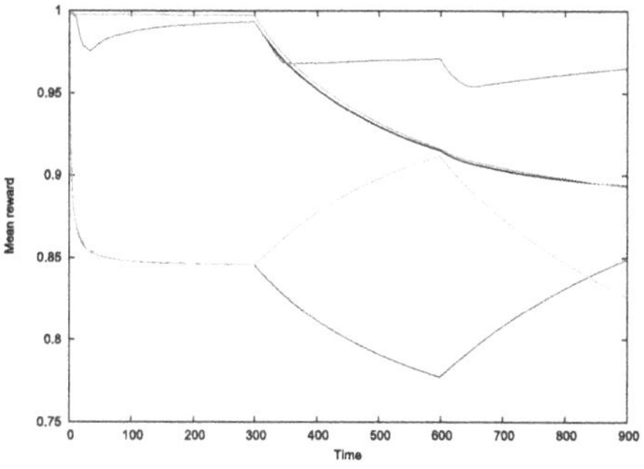

(b) $n_{0,\pm3} \to n_{-20,\pm3} \to n_{20,\pm3}$

Dynamic SEA
SEA
Bandit 1 (Fig. 1a)
Bandit 2 (Fig. 1b)
Bandit 3 (Fig. 1c)

(d) Legend

Fig. 2. Mean rewards of our algorithms

The half-width of confidential intervals computed at confidence level $\alpha = 0.05$ never exceeds 1.5 % of the corresponding mean. We do not thus incorporate them in the figures.

We discuss the results of our experiments for $n_{-20,\pm3} \rightarrow n_{20,\pm3} \rightarrow n_{0,\pm3}$ and for $n_{0,\pm3} \rightarrow n_{-20,\pm3} \rightarrow n_{20,\pm3}$ depicted in Figs. 2a and b respectively.

We build N_i in such a way that each bandit algorithm outperforms the others for a third of the time, and indeed, it is what we note in Figs. 2a and b. We observe that the *SEA* algorithm follows the best algorithm in average as time grows. Nevertheless, due to the inertia of the mean, *SEA* is very slow to switch from an algorithm to another. At the opposite, the *Dynamic SEA* can fit the environment very quickly.

For the last experiment in which the prediction is characterized by an excessive variability of the noise (Fig. 2c), both *SEA* and *Dynamic SEA* follow the first bandit (Fig. 1a) which has the best reward in average. Whatever the situation, *Dynamic SEA* is at least as good as *SEA*.

5 Conclusion

At first, we tested the *SEA* algorithm to dynamically choose an algorithm among those available. We observed the deterioration of *SEA* performance with time. The modification we brought to *SEA* improved its reactivity and its overall performance.

Acknowledgment. The PhD thesis of Alexandre Dambreville is financed by Labex Digicosme within the project E-CloViS (Energy-aware resource allocation for Cloud Virtual Services).

References

1. Bubeck, S., Cesa-Bianchi, N.: Regret analysis of stochastic and nonstochastic multi-armed bandit problems. Found. Trends Mach. Learn. **5**, 1–122 (2012)
2. http://ita.ee.lbl.gov/html/contrib/WorldCup.html
3. Farias, D.P.D., Megiddo, N.: Combining Expert Advice in Reactive Environments. J. ACM **53**, 762–799 (2006)

On-Line Path Computation and Function Placement in SDNs

Guy Even[1], Moti Medina[2(✉)], and Boaz Patt-Shamir[1]

[1] School of Electrical Engineering, Tel Aviv University, Tel Aviv, Israel
{guy,boaz}@eng.tau.ac.il
[2] MPI for Informatics, Saarbrücken, Germany
mmedina@mpi-inf.mpg.de

Abstract. We consider service requests that arrive in an online fashion in Software-Defined Networks (SDNs) with network function virtualization (NFV). Each request is a flow with a high-level specification of routing and processing (by network functions) requirements. Each network function can be performed by a specified subset of servers in the system. The algorithm needs to decide whether to reject the request, or accept it and with a specific routing and processing assignment, under given capacity constraints (solving the *path computation* and *function placement* problems). Each served request is assumed to "pay" a prespecified benefit and the goal is to maximize the total benefit accrued.

In this paper we first formalize the problem, and propose a new service model that allows us to cope with requests with *unknown duration* without preemption. The new service model augments the traditional accept/reject schemes with a new possible response of "stand by." We also present a new expressive model to describe requests abstractly using a "plan" represented by a directed graph. Our algorithmic result is an online algorithm for path computation and function placement that guarantees, *in each time step*, throughput of at least a logarithmic fraction of a (very permissive) upper bound on the maximal possible benefit.

1 Introduction

Conventional wisdom has it that in networking, models are reinvented every twenty years or so. A deeper look into the evolution of networks shows that there is always a tension between ease of computation, which favors collecting all data and performing processing centrally, and ease of communication, which favors distributing the computation over nodes along communication paths. It seems that recently the pendulum has moved toward the centralized computation side once again, with the emergence of software-defined networks (SDNs), in which one of the main underlying abstractions is of a centrally managed network. Network Function Virtualization (NFV) is another key abstraction: roughly speaking, the idea is that instead of having functions implemented by special-purpose

This work was supported in part by the Neptune Consortium, Israel.
The full version of this paper can be found in http://arxiv.org/abs/1602.06169.

B. Bonakdarpour and F. Petit (Eds.): SSS 2016, LNCS 10083, pp. 131–147, 2016.
DOI: 10.1007/978-3-319-49259-9_11

expensive hardware, functions can be virtualized and implemented by virtual machines running on cheap general-purpose boxes.

Among the key conceptual components of such networks are *path computation* and *function placement* [12], which allows potentially complex requests to be routed over the network. Informally, each request specifies a "processing plan" for a flow, that includes a source-destination pair as well as a description of a few processing stages that the flow needs to go through. The task is to find a route in the network starting at the source to the destination that includes the requested processing. The main difficulty, of course, is the bounded processing capacity of servers and links, so not all requests can be served.

Our Contribution. Our contribution is both conceptual and technical. From the conceptual viewpoint, we introduce a new service model that is both natural from the user's perspective and, from the operator's perspective, allows for on-line algorithms with strong performance guarantees, even when dealing with requests that do not specify their duration upon arrival, and without resorting to preemption (i.e., once a request is admitted, it has the resources secured until it leaves). The main idea in the new service model is to place a non-admitted request in a "standby" mode, until (due to other requests leaving the system) there is room to accept it. Once a request is accepted, it is guaranteed to receive service until it ends (i.e., until the user issues a "leave" signal). We also present a new powerful model for describing requests. In a nutshell, a request specifies and abstract directed graph whose nodes represent the required functions, and the system is required to implement that abstraction by a physical route that includes the requested processing, in order.

Our algorithmic contribution consists of a deterministic algorithm that receives requests in an on-line fashion, and determines when each request starts receiving service (if at all), and how is this service provided (i.e., how to route the request and where to process it). We note that in this, our algorithm solves path computation and function placement *combined*, which is different from the common approach that separates the problems (separation may result in performance penalties). Quantitatively, in our model each request specifies a benefit per time unit it pays when it is served, and the algorithm is guaranteed to obtain $\Omega(1/\log(nk))$ of the *best possible* benefit, where n is the system size and k is the maximum number of processing stages of a request.[1] More precisely, in every time step t, the total benefit collected by the algorithm is at least an $\Omega(1/\log(nk))$-fraction of the largest possible total benefit that can be obtained at time t (i.e., from all requests that have arrived and did not leave by time t) while respecting the capacity constraints. The above performance guarantee of the algorithm holds under the conditions that no processing stage of a request requires more than an $O\big(1/(k\log(nk))\big)$ fraction of the capacity of any component (server or link) in the system, and assuming that the ratio of the highest-to-lowest benefits of requests is bounded by a polynomial in n. (We

[1] Typically, k is constant because the number of processing stages does not grow as a function of the size n of the network.

provide precise statements below.) We also prove a lower bound on the competitive ratio of $\Omega(\log n)$ for every online algorithm in our new model. Hence, so long as k, the number of processing stages in a request, is bounded by a polynomial in n, our algorithm is asymptotically optimal (see Sect. 6).

1.1 Previous Work

Abstractions via High Level SDN Programming Languages. Merlin [14,15] is a language for provisioning network resources in conjunction with SDNs. In Merlin, requests are specified as a regular expression with additional annotation, and the main task is path computation. The system works in an off-line fashion: given the set of all requests and a system description, an algorithm computes feasible routes for (some of) the requests. The algorithm suffers from two weaknesses: first, as mentioned above, it is *off-line*, i.e., it requires knowing all requests ahead of time; and second, the algorithm is not polynomial, as it is based on employing a solver for integer linear programs (ILP). For more information on SDN languages (and SDN in general) we refer the reader to [12].

Function placement. Cohen et al. [6] present a model and an offline bi-criteria approximation algorithm for the NFV placement of functions. In their model, routes are already determined, and the question is where to place the requested functions: if a required function is not placed on the given route of some flow, then a detour must be taken by that flow. The goal is to minimize the cost, which consists of a setup cost for each function placed, and a penalty for each detour from the prescribed routes. This algorithm is also off-line, and it has another serious handicap in that it supports only requests in which the functions are unordered: there is no way to require that a flow first undergoes processing of some function f and only then it is handled by another function g.

Path Computation and Function Placement in SDNs. Recently, Even et al. [9] followed our model for describing SDN requests. They designed an *offline* randomized algorithm. The algorithm serves at least a $(1-\varepsilon)$ fraction of the requests the optimal solution can serve provided that the SDN requests have small demands (i.e., $\max_j d_j \leq \min_e c_e \cdot \varepsilon^2/(k \cdot O(\log n))$).

Online Routing Algorithms. Our work leverages the seminal algorithm of Awerbuch et al. [2], which is an on-line algorithm for routing requests with given benefits and *known durations.* The algorithm of [2] decides whether to admit or reject each request when it arrives; the algorithm also computes routes for the admitted requests. The goal of the algorithm in [2] is to maximize the sum of benefits of accepted requests.

From the algorithmic point of view, one should note that the throughput-maximization algorithm of [2] resembles the load-minimization algorithm presented in [1], both dealing with on-line routing. In [1], each request has a specified non-negative load. All requests *must* be served, and the goal is to minimize the maximal ratio, over all links, between the load on the link and its capacity (link load is the sum of the loads of the requests it serves).

Buchbinder and Naor [4,5] analyze the algorithm of [2] using the primal-dual method. This allows them to bound the benefit of the computed solution as a function of the benefit of an optimal fractional solution (see also [11]).

As mentioned, the above algorithms assume that each request specifies the duration of the service it needs when it arrives. The only on-line algorithm for unknown durations we know of in this context is for the problem of minimizing the maximal load [3]. The algorithm in [3] is $O(\log n)$-competitive, but it requires rerouting of admitted requests (each request may be rerouted $O(\log n)$ times). Our algorithm is for benefit maximization, and it handles unknown durations by allowing the "standby" mode, without ever rerouting an accepted request.

1.2 Advocacy of the Service Model

In the classical non-preemptive model with guaranteed bandwidth, requests must specify in advance what is the exact duration of the connection (which may be infinite), and the system must give an immediate response, which may be either "reject" or "admit." While immediate responses are preferable in general, the requirement that duration is specified in advance is unrealistic in many cases (say, because the length of the connection may depend on yet-unavailable inputs). However, requests with unknown durations seem to thwart the possibility for a competitive algorithm due to the following reasoning. Consider any system, and suppose that there are infinitely many requests available at time 0, all with unit benefit per time step. Clearly there exists a request, say r^*, that is rejected due to the finite capacity of the system. Now, the following adversarial scenario may unfold: all admitted requests leave the system at time 1 (accruing some finite benefit), and request r^* persists forever (i.e., can produce any desired benefit). Clearly, this means that no deterministic algorithm can guarantee a non-trivial competitive ratio in the worst case.

We therefore argue that if unknown durations are to be tolerated, then the requirement for an immediate reject/admit response must be relaxed. One relaxation is to allow preemption, but if preemption is allowed then the connection is never certain until it terminates. Our service model suggests to commit upon accept, but not to commit to rejection. In other words, we never reject with certainty because we may accept later, but when we accept, the request is certain to have the required resources for as long it wishes. This type of service is quite common in many daily activities (e.g., waiting in line for a restaurant seat), and is actually implicitly present even in some admit/reject situations: in many cases, if a request is rejected, the resourceful user may try to re-submit it or abandon.

Finally, from a more philosophical point of view, the "standby" service model seems fair for unknown durations: on one hand, a request does not commit ahead of time to when it will leave the system, and on the other hand, the algorithm does not commit ahead of time to when the request will *enter* the system.

2 Request Model and Service Model

In this section we formalize the problem of path computation and function mapping in SDNs. The main new concept in the way the input is specified is called PR-*graphs*. The nodes of a PR-graph represent servers and the edges represent communication paths, so that a PR-graph is an abstract representation of a request.[2] The main novelty of our output model is in allowing the system to put arriving requests in a "standby" mode instead of immediately rejecting them. Details are provided in the remainder of this section.

2.1 The Physical Network

The network is a fixed network of servers and communication links. The network is represented by a graph $N = (V, E)$, where V is the set of *nodes* and E is the set of *edges*. Nodes and edges have *capacities*. The capacity of an edge e is denoted by c_e, and the capacity of a node $v \in V$ is denoted by c_v. All capacities are positive integers. We note that the network is static and undirected (namely each edge represents a bidirectional communication link), but may contain parallel edges.

2.2 Request Model and the Concept of PR-Graphs

Each request is a tuple $r_j = (G_j, d_j, b_j, U_j)$ with the following interpretation.

- $G_j = (X_j, Y_j)$ is a directed graph called the PR-graph, where X_j is the set of PR-vertices, and Y_j is the set of PR-edges. We elaborate on the PR-graph below.
- $d_j : X_j \cup Y_j \to \mathbb{N}$ is the *demand* of the request from each PR-graph component (i.e., bandwidth for links, processing for nodes).
- $b_j \in \mathbb{N}$ is the *benefit* paid by the request for each time step it is served.
- $U_j : X_j \cup Y_j \to 2^V \cup 2^E$ maps each node in the PR-graph to a set of nodes of N, and each edge in the PR-graph is mapped to a set of edges of N. We elaborate below.

The Processing and Routing Graph (PR-graph). We refer to edges and vertices in G_j as PR-edges and PR-vertices, respectively. There are three types of vertices in the PR-graph G_j:

- A single *source* vertex $s_j \in X_j$ (i.e., vertex with in-degree zero) that represents the location from which the packets arrive.
- A single *sink* vertex $t_j \in X_j$ (i.e., vertex with out-degree zero) that represents the location to which the packets are destined.
- *Action vertices*, which represent transformations to be applied to the flow (such as encryption/decryption, deep packet inspection, trans-coding etc.)

[2] Our PR-graphs are similar to Merlin's regular expressions [15], but are more expressive and, in our humble opinion, are more natural to design.

Realization of PR-paths *and the U function.* The semantics of a PR-graph is that the request can be served by any source-sink path in the PR-graph. However, these paths are abstract. To interpret them in the network, we map PR-nodes to physical network nodes and PR-edges to physical network paths. To facilitate this mapping, each request r_j also includes the U_j function, which, intuitively, says which physical nodes (in V) can implement each PR-node, and which physical links (in E) can implement each PR-edge. Formally, we define the following concepts.

Definition 1 (valid realization of PR-edge). *A simple path $p = (v_0, \ldots, v_k)$ in the network N is a* valid realization *of a* PR*-edge e if for all $0 < i \leq k$ we have that $(v_{i-1}, v_i) \in U_j(e)$.*

Note that the empty path in N is a valid realization of any PR-edge.

Definition 2 (valid realizations of PR-path). *A path $p = (v_0, \ldots, v_k)$ in N is a* valid realization *of a path $\tilde{p} = (x_0, \ldots, x_\ell)$ in G_j under* segmentation *$f : \{0, \ldots, \ell\} \to \{0, \ldots, k\}$ if*

- *for all $0 \leq i \leq \ell$, $v_{f(i)} \in U_j(x_i)$, and*
- *for all $0 < i \leq \ell$, the sub-path $(v_{f(i-1)}, \ldots, v_{f(i)})$ of p is a valid realization of (x_{i-1}, x_i).*

The interpretation of mapping a PR-node x to a network node v is that the service represented by x is implemented by v. $U_j(x)$ in this case represents all physical nodes in which that service can be performed. Given a PR-edge e, $U_j(e)$ is the set of links that may be used to realize e. By default, $U_j(e) = E$, but $U_j(e)$ allows the request designer to specify a set of edges to be avoided due to any consideration (e.g., security). Regarding processing, consider the segmentation of the path in N induced by a valid realization. The endpoint of each subpath is a network node in which the corresponding action takes place. Moreover, the same network node may be used for serving multiple actions for the same request.

We are now ready to define the set of valid routings and processing for request r_j.

Definition 3 (valid realizations of request). *A path p in N is a valid realization of a request r_j if there exists a simple path $\tilde{p}$ in the* PR*-graph G_j from s_j to t_j such that p is a realization of $\tilde{p}$.*

Examples. Let us illustrate the utility of PR-graphs with a few examples.

Simple Routing. A request r_j to route a connection from node v to node v' is modeled by a single-edge PR-graph $s \xrightarrow{e} t$ with mappings $U_j(s) = \{v\}$, $U_j(t) = \{v'\}$, and $U_j(e) = E$. The demand from e is the requested connection bandwidth.

Serial Processing. A stream that needs to pass k transformations $a_1, \ldots, a_k$ in series is modeled by a path of $k+1$ edges $s_j \to a_1 \to \cdots \to a_k \to t_j$, where $U_j(a_i)$ is the set of network nodes that can perform transformation a_i, for $i = 1, \ldots, k$. Note that we can model bandwidth changes (e.g., if one of the transformations is compression) by setting different demands to different PR-edges.

Regular Expressions. Given any regular expression of processing we can construct a PR-graph by constructing the NFA corresponding to the given expression [10].

We note that our request model is more expressive than the regular-expression model proposed by Merlin [15]. For example, we can model changing loads.[3]

Capacity constraints and feasible realizations. Let $\tilde{p} = (s_j \xrightarrow{e_1} a_1, \ldots, a_k \xrightarrow{e_{k+1}} t_j)$ denote a path in the PR-graph G_j. Let $p = p_1 \circ \cdots \circ p_{k+1}$ denote a valid realization of $\tilde{p}$, where p_i is a valid realization of e_i. Let v_i denote the endpoint of subpath p_i for $1 \leq i \leq k$ (v_i is where action a_i takes place). The load incurred by serving request r_j with demand d_j by p on each node and edge in p is defined as follows (the load incurred on edges and nodes not in p is zero):

$$\mathit{load}(v,p) \triangleq \sum_{i:v=v_i} \frac{d_j(a_i)}{c_v} \text{ for all } v \in \{v_1, \ldots, v_k\}$$

$$\mathit{load}(e,p) \triangleq \sum_{i:e \in p_i} \frac{d_j(e_i)}{c_e} \text{ for all } e \in p\ .$$

Informally, $\mathit{load}(v,p)$ is the relative capacity of v consumed by p, and similarly $\mathit{load}(v,e)$.

Definition 4 (capacity constraints). *Given a sequence of requests $\{r_j\}_{j \in I}$, a sequence of realizations $\{p^j\}_{j \in I}$ satisfies the capacity constraints if*

$$\forall v \in V : \sum_{j \in I} \mathit{load}(v, p^j) \leq 1 \text{ and } \forall e \in E : \sum_{j \in I} \mathit{load}(e, p^j) \leq 1\ .$$

Given loads for nodes and edges, we say that a path p from s_j to t_j is a *feasible realization* of request r_j if p is a valid realization of an s-t path of r_j, and if p satisfies the capacity constraints.

2.3 The Acc/Stdby Service Model

We now describe the service model, i.e., the user-system interface and guarantees.

[3] In Merlin, the input may also contain a "policing" function of capping the maximal bandwidth of a connection. We focus on resource allocation only. Policing may be enforced by an orthogonal entity.

Input. The input to the algorithm is the fixed network $N = (V, E)$ and a sequence of events $\sigma = \{\sigma_t\}_{t \in \mathbb{N}}$ which arrive one at a time. An event is either an arrival of a new request, or the departure of a request that arrived earlier. The attributes of an arriving request r_j are as described in Sect. 2.2, along with the *arrival time* of the request $\alpha_j \in \mathbb{N}$. We use s_j and t_j to denote the source and the destination of the jth request. A departure event specifies which request is departing and the current time.

Output. The algorithm must generate a response to each arrival event, and may generate any number of responses after a departure event. There are two types of responses.

• *Accept*: A request that has already arrived is accepted to the system; the response also includes a feasible realization of the request. The request will be served continuously from the time it is accepted until its departure event (i.e., no preemption). An "accept" response may follow any event; moreover, multiple accepts (of multiple requests) are possible after a single event (typically after a departure).

• *Standby:* In this case an arriving request is not accepted immediately, but may be accepted later. When a request arrives, the system must respond immediately by either accept or standby.

Performance Measure. We evaluate algorithms by their *competitive ratio* [13]. Formally, given an algorithm ALG and a finite input sequence σ, let $\text{ALG}(\sigma)$ denote the total benefit ALG receives on input σ, where the system receives the benefit b_j of request r_j for each time unit in which r_j is served. The competitive ratio of an online algorithm ALG for σ is $\rho(\text{ALG}(\sigma)) \triangleq \text{ALG}(\sigma)/\text{OPT}(\sigma)$, where $\text{OPT}(\sigma)$ denotes the maximal possible benefit from σ by any allocation that respects the capacity constraints. The competitive ratio of ALG is $\rho(\text{ALG}) \triangleq \inf_\sigma \rho(\text{ALG}(\sigma))$.

3 Computation of Light Valid Realizations

The algorithm presented in Sect. 4 uses an "oracle" (subroutine) that finds a feasible realization of requests. In this section we explain how to implement this oracle.

3.1 Construction of Product Network and Product Request

Input. We are given a weighted (physical) network $N = (V, E, w)$ with weights $w : V \cup E \to \mathbb{R}^{\geq 0}$ over nodes and edges, and a request $r_j = (G_j, d_j, b_j, U_j)$, where $G_j = (X_j, Y_j)$ is the PR-graph with PR-nodes X_j and PR-edges Y_j (cf. Sect. 2.2). We are also given, for every PR-node x and PR-edge e, the set of allowed nodes $U_j(x) \subseteq V$ and edges $U_j(e) \subseteq E$, respectively.

Output: The product network. We construct the *product network*, denoted $\text{pn}(N, r_j)$, which is a weighted directed graph, with weights over nodes only. The nodes of $\text{pn}(N, r_j)$, denoted V', are $V' = V \times Y_j$. The edges of $\text{pn}(N, r_j)$, denoted $E' = E_1 \cup E_2$, are of two categories, E_1 and E_2, defined as follows (we use w to denote the weight function in the product network too).

- $E_1 = \{((v, y), (v', y)) \mid y \in Y_j,\ (v, v') \in U_j(y)\}$ *(routing edges)*.
  The weight of a routing edge is defined by $w((v, y), (v', y)) \triangleq w(v, v')$, i.e., the weight of the corresponding edge in N.
- $E_2 = \{((v, y), (v, y')) \mid y, y' \in Y_j$ s.t. y, y' share a node x and $v \in U_j(x)\}$ *(processing edges)*.
  The weight of a processing edge is defined by $w((v, y), (v, y')) = w(v)$, i.e., the weight of the corresponding node in N.

Output: The product request. The *product request* $\text{pr}(N, r_j)$ is a pair of sets (S_j, T_j), called the *source* and *sink* sets, respectively. The source set S_j is the set of all (v, e) pairs such that $v \in U(s_j)$ (i.e., v is a physical node that can be a source of the request r_j) and e is incident to v in G_j (i.e., e is a PR-edge that can be the first edge in a source-sink path in the PR-graph). Similarly, the sink set T_j is defined by $T_j \triangleq \{(v, e) \mid v \in U(t_j),\ e \text{ is incident to } t_j \text{ in } G_j\}$.

Recall that a realization of a request is a path in N. Given a realization and weights w over nodes and edges of N, we define the *weight of a realization* p of r_j is defined to be $w(p) \triangleq \sum_{x \in p} d_j \cdot m_p(x)$, where $m_p(x)$ denotes the number of times node or edge x appears in p. The weight of a path q in $\text{pn}(N, r_j)$ is simply the sum of the edge weights in q.

The following lemma states the main property of the construction of $\text{pn}(N, r)$. The proof contains definitions of the functions *fold* and *expand* that convert between paths in N and $\text{pr}(N, r_j)$.

Lemma 1. *Let $N = (V, E, w)$ be a physical weighted network and let r_j be a request. There is a one-to-one weight preserving correspondence between valid realizations of r_j in N and simple paths in* $\text{pn}(N, r_j)$ *that start in a vertex of S_j and end in a vertex of T_j.*

Proof sketch: Define a function *fold* to map a path p'_j in the product graph to a realization $p = \mathit{fold}(p'_j)$ by the following local transformation: a processing edge $((v, y), (v, y'))$ is contracted to the node $v \in V$; each routing edge $((v, e), (v', e))$ of p'_j is replaced by the edge $(v, v') \in E$. Clearly, p_j is a valid realization of r_j under the segmentation that segments p_j at the nodes representing both ends of a contracted processing edge.

Conversely, assume that a valid realization is given, where $p_j = (v_0, \ldots, v_k)$ is the path with segmentation $p_j = p_j^1 \circ p_j^2 \circ \cdots \circ p_j^\ell$. We define $p'_j = \mathit{expand}(p_j)$ as follows. By assumption, each subpath p_j^i is a valid realization of some PR-edge $e_j^i = (x_{i-1}, x_i)$, and such that the endpoint of subpath p_j^i is in $U_j(x_i)$. To obtain $p'_j = \mathit{expand}(p_j)$, apply the following mapping. Map each edge (v, v'), say in the ith subpath of p_j, to the routing edge $((v, e_j^i), (v', e_j^i)) \in E'$, and map each endpoint v of subpath $i < \ell$ to the processing edge $\big((v, e_j^i), (v, e_j^{i+1})\big) \in E'$. Clearly, p'_j is a path in N', and it connects a node in S_j with a node in T_j because p'_j starts with a node (s'_j, e) for some $s'_j \in U_j(s_j), e \in Y_j$ and ends with a node (t'_j, e') for some $t'_j \in U_j(t_j), e' \in Y_j$.

It is straightforward to verify that *fold* and *expand* preserve weights. □

We note that an edge or a node of N might be mapped to at most k times by *fold*, where k is the length of the longest simple s-t path in the PR-graph G_j.

3.2 The Oracle

We refer to the algorithm which computes the realization as an *oracle*. The oracle's description is as follows.

We are given a request $r_j = (G_j, d_j, b_j, U_j)$ and a weighted physical network N. We then apply the following procedure to find a valid realization of r_j in N.

1. $N' \leftarrow \mathrm{pn}(N, r_j)$.
2. Let P_j denote the set of simple paths in N' that (1) start in a node in $\{(v, e) \mid v \in U_j(s_j)\}$, (2) end in a node in $\{(v, e) \mid v \in U_j(t_j)\}$, and (3) have weight at most b_j.
3. Let $\Gamma_j \leftarrow \{fold(p') \mid p' \in P_j\}$.
4. Return an arbitrary path $p_j \in \Gamma_j$, or "FAIL" if $\Gamma_j = \emptyset$.

Step 2 can be implemented by any shortest-paths algorithm, e.g., Dijkstra's. Note that the oracle ignores the demand d_j (and thus does not verify that the returned path p_j satisfies the capacity constraints; feasibility will follow from the weight assignment and the assumption on the maximal demand).

4 The Algorithm

In this section we describe our algorithm. We analyze our algorithm in Sect. 5.

To solve the problem described in Sect. 2.3, we employ the resource allocation algorithm of [7,8] (which extends [2,4]). The general idea is as follows. We assign weights to nodes and edges according to their current load. For each incoming request, a realization in the network is found as described in Sect. 3.2, and submitted to the resource allocation algorithm. If that algorithm decides to accept the request, our algorithm algorithm accepts; otherwise the request is put in the standby mode, and it will be tried again when any accepted request leaves.

We assume for now that (1) the allocations of resources to requests are simple paths, and that (2) the demand function is defined only over edges and that all demands in a given request are equal. We lift these restrictions in Sect. 5.1.

Terminology. Let k denote an upper bound on the length of a longest simple path in the PR-graphs. Let $p_{\max}$ denote an upper bound on the length of valid realizations (clearly, $p_{\max} < |V|k$). Let $b_{\max}$ denote an upper bound on the benefit per time unit offered by any request. Define

$$\Phi \triangleq \log(3p_{\max}b_{\max} + 1) \tag{1}$$

Note that $\Phi = O(\log n + \log b_{\max} + \log k)$.

A *feasible path* p for request r_j is a path which is a valid realization of r_j with minimum edge capacity at least $d_j \cdot (3k\Phi)$. We denote the set of feasible paths for request r_j by Γ_j.

We say that a request r is *active* at time t if it has arrived before time t and has not departed by time t. Given time t in the run of the algorithm and an edge e of N, $f(e)$ denotes the sum of demands of accepted active requests that are routed over e. Recall that the *load* of an edge e is defined by $load(e) \triangleq \frac{f(e)}{c_e}$. The *exp-load* of e is defined by

$$x_e \triangleq \frac{1}{p_{\max}} \cdot \left(2^{load(e)\cdot\Phi} - 1\right). \tag{2}$$

4.1 Algorithm Operation

Pseudo-code for the algorithm, called ALG, is provided in Fig. 1. The algorithm maintains a set L of the requests in standby mode: these are all active requests currently not served. The set A contains all active requests currently served. The path allocated for an active request r_j is denoted by p_j. When a request arrives, the algorithm tries to route it by calling ROUTE. If it fails, r_j is inserted into L (line 4). A departure of an active request is handled by invoking the UNROUTE procedure (line 8), and then the algorithm tries to serve every request in L by invoking ROUTE (line 9). Any order can be used to try the standby requests, thus allowing for using arbitrary dynamic priority policies. The ROUTE procedure calls ALLOCATE, which is an online procedure for a generalization of the path-packing problem (see below). If ALLOCATE allocates a path p_j in N, then r_j is accepted. Otherwise r_j is inserted to the standby list L. Procedure ALLOCATE first searches for a path in N which is a realization of the request. The weight of a path is defined as the sum of the exp-loads of the edges along it. If a path whose weight is less than the benefit b_j is found, then the request is allocated. The task of finding such a path is done via the oracle described in Sect. 3. The UNROUTE procedure removes a request from A or L; if the request was receiving service, the load of its edges is adjusted (line 23).

5 Analysis

We compare the performance of ALG with an offline fractional optimal solution, denoted by OPT_f. More precisely, we compare the benefit produced by ALG with the benefit and load of *any* allocation that respects the capacity constraints. Such

State:
- L: a set, contains all unserved active requests (in standby mode)
- A: a set, contains all served active requests. Each request $r_j \in A$ is routed over a path p_j.

Actions:

```
Upon arrival of request $r_k$:
Begin
    ROUTE($r_k$)
    if $r_k \notin A$ then                                        ▷ request not accepted now
        $L \leftarrow L \cup \{r_k\}$ ; output "$r_k$: standby"
    end if
End
Upon departure of request $r_k$:
Begin
    UNROUTE($r_k$)
    for all $r_j \in L$ do ROUTE($r_j$).                          ▷ all orders allowed
End
procedure ROUTE($r_j$)
    Invoke ALLOCATE($r_j$)
    if ALLOCATE returned a path $p_j \neq \perp$ then
        $A \leftarrow A \cup \{r_j\}$; $L \leftarrow L \setminus \{r_j\}$
        output "$r_j$ accepted, path $p_j$"
    end if
end procedure
procedure UNROUTE($r_k$)
    if $r_k \in A$ then
        $A \leftarrow A \setminus \{r_k\}$
        for all $e \in p_k$ do
            let $m(e)$ be the multiplicity of $e$ in $p_k$
            $f(e) \leftarrow f(e) - m(e) \cdot d_k$                ▷ Free the path $p_k$
        end for
    else
        $L \leftarrow L \setminus \{r_k\}$
    end if
end procedure
procedure ALLOCATE($r_k$) where $r_k = (G_k, d_k, b_k)$
    Assign to each edge $e$ in $N$ weight $x_e$                 ▷ $x_e$ defined in Eq. 2
    Let $C_k$ be a subset of $\Gamma_k$ whose weight is at most $b_k$
    Pick an arbitrary path $p_k \in C_k$       ▷ Invocation of the oracle. See Sec. 3.2
    for all $e \in p_k$ do
        let $m(e)$ be the multiplicity of $e$ in $p_k$
        $f(e) \leftarrow f(e) + m(e) \cdot d_k$                    ▷ update loads
    end for
    return $p \in C_k$, or $\perp$ if $C_k = \emptyset$
end procedure
```

Fig. 1. ALG - an online algorithm for the SDN problem.

allocations may serve a request partially and obtain the prorated benefit, and may also split the flow of one request over multiple paths. Among these allocations, OPT_f denotes the allocation that achieves the maximal benefit. Moreover, in each time step, OPT_f induces a new multicommodity flow (independent of the flow of OPT_f at any other time step). Implicitly, this means that OPT_f may also arbitrarily preempt and resume requests, partially or wholly.

Given time step t, let $\textit{benefit}_t(\text{ALG})$ denote the benefit to ALG due to step t, and analogously, let $\textit{benefit}_t(\text{OPT}_f)$ denote the benefit gained by OPT_f in time step t. The competitiveness of ALG is stated in the following theorem.

Theorem 1. *Let z range over nodes and edges of N. If $\max_j d_j \leq \min_z c_z/(3k\Phi)$ for each request r_j, then $benefit_t(\text{ALG}) \geq \frac{1}{3\Phi} \cdot benefit_t(\text{OPT}_f)$ in each time step t.*

The proof of Theorem 1 is based on an analysis of the online algorithm RA-PERSIST for the resource allocation problem with persistent requests, in each time step (which is analogous to an analysis with respect to persistent requests). This analysis appears in Sect. 5.1. The proof of Theorem 1 appears in Sect. 5.2.

5.1 Online Resource Allocation with Persistent Requests

We now present another key ingredient in our solution, namely the *online resource allocation* problem with respect to persistent requests (and the classical accept/reject service model). The algorithm to solve it is a generalization of [2].

By online resource allocation we mean the following setting. Consider a set E of m *resources*, where each resource $e \in E$ has a capacity c_e. Requests $\{r_j\}_j$ arrive in an online fashion. Each request r_j specifies a set of possible *allocations* denoted $\Gamma_j \subseteq 2^E$. Let $p_{\max}$ be an upper bound on the number of resources in every feasible allocation. i.e., $|p| \leq p_{\max}$ for all $p \in \bigcup_j \Gamma_j$. We allow a general setting in which the demand requirement depends on the request, the allocation, and the resource. Formally, the demand of the jth request with respect to allocation p is a function $d_{j,p} : p \rightarrow \mathbb{N}$. Each request r_j has a benefit b_j that it pays if served. Let $b_{\max}$ denote an upper bound on $\max_j b_j$, and $\Phi \triangleq \log(1 + 3p_{\max}b_{\max})$. Small demands mean that $d_{j,p}(e)/c_e \leq 1/(3\Phi)$ for every $e \in p$.

Resource allocation generalizes allocations in circuit switching networks and SDNs:

- In the virtual circuits problem, Γ_j is simply the set of feasible paths from the source to the destination.
- For an SDN request $r_j = (G_j, d_j, b_j, U_j)$, the set of allocations Γ_j is simply the set of valid realizations, each of which is a subset of network edges and nodes. Since a realization p may contain cycle, resources may be used more than once by p. Therefore, the load on a resource $e \in p$ incurred by a realization p of request r_j is $d_j \cdot m_p(e)$, where $m_p(e)$ denotes the number of times e appears in p.

In the general resource allocation problem, Γ_j does not need to have any particular structure, but an algorithm to solve it must have an *oracle*. The task of the oracle is as follows. Assume that every resource e has a *weight* x_e. The weight of an allocation $p \subseteq E$ is simply $x_p \triangleq \sum_{e \in p} x_e$. Given a request r_j with benefit b_j, the oracle returns either an allocation $p \in \Gamma_j$ such that $x_p < b_j$, or returns "FAIL" if no such allocation exists.

The online algorithm RA-PERSIST for the resource allocation problem with persistent requests uses a modified variant of Procedure ALLOCATE for each request. The modifications of ALLOCATE are as follows. First, the term "path" is interpreted as a feasible allocation. Second, lines 31–32 are replaced by an invocation of the oracle. If a feasible allocation of weight at most b_j is found, then the flow is updated accordingly (as in Line 35).

An online resource allocation algorithm for persistent requests appears in [7, 8] (this algorithm extends the path packing algorithm for persistent requests of [2] using the analysis in [4]). Since Algorithm RA-PERSIST is a special case of this extension, we obtain the following theorem.

Theorem 2 ([7,8] based on [2,4]). *Let N be a given network and let $\sigma = \{r_j\}$ be a sequence of persistent requests. If $d_{j,p}(e) \leq c_e/(3 \cdot \Phi)$, for every request r_j, every allocation $p \in \Gamma_j$, and every resource e, then* RA-PERSIST$(\sigma) \geq$ OPT$^f(\sigma)/(3 \cdot \Phi)$.

Application to SDN requests. The oracle for finding light-weight feasible realizations for SDN requests finds a lightest path in the weighted product network (see Sect. 3.2). Folding such a path may result in a realization with cycles in the SDN network. Multiple occurrences of an edge or node z in a realization p means that the load on z is multiplied by the number $m_p(z)$ of occurrences of z in p. Hence the demand from $z \in E \cup V$ induced by a realization p for request r_j satisfies $d_{j,p}(z) = d_j \cdot m_p(z)$. Let k denote an upper bound on the number of processing stages in realizations (i.e., k equals the length of a longest simple source-sink path in the PR-graphs). Then $m_p(z) \leq k$. Since Procedure ALLOCATE considers unfolded paths for its decisions, the requirement that $\max_j d_j \leq \min_z c_z/(3k\Phi)$ allows us to apply Theorem 2 to procedure ALLOCATE in the context of SDN persistent requests.

Regarding persistence, observe that the benefit in a single time step where each request pays b_j per served time step is identical to the benefit with respect to persistent requests (where each request pays b_j if served).

5.2 Proof of Theorem 1

Proof (Proof of Theorem 1). The proof proceeds by a simulation argument. Specifically, we interpret the execution of ALG as a repeated execution of the ALLOCATE algorithm in each time step with respect to the active requests. For the purpose of the simulation, assume that in the ALLOCATE algorithm, each request r_k may be accompanied by a preferred feasible path p'_k. If the weight of p'_k is less than b_k (i.e., $p'_k \in C_k$), then the ALLOCATE algorithm allocates the preferred path p'_k to r_k.

We prove the theorem by induction on t. The base case $t = 1$ follows from Theorem 2. For the induction step, let A_t and L_t denote the sets A (served requests) and L (pending requests) at time t, respectively. The event σ_{t+1} that occurs in step $t + 1$ is either an arrival of a new request or the departure of an active request.

Suppose first that σ_t is an arrival of a new request r_k. In this case, we simulate the ALLOCATE algorithm by feeding it first with the requests in A_t according to the order in which they were served (this order may be different than the order in which they arrived). Each request $r_j \in A_t$ is accompanied by a preferred path p'_j, where p'_j is the path that was allocated to r_j in time step t. The flow along each edge when a request is introduced to the ALLOCATE algorithm is not greater than the flow along the edge just before ALG first served the same request. Hence, the weight of p'_j during this simulation of step $t+1$ does not exceed its weight when it was first allocated to r_j, and hence $p'_j \in C_j$ also in time step $t+1$. This implies that the ALLOCATE algorithm accepts all the requests in A_t and routes each one along the same path allocated to it in the previous time step. Next we feed r_k to the ALLOCATE algorithm (without a preferred path). The result of this simulation is identical to the execution of ALG in time step $t+1$. By Theorem 2, the theorem holds for step $t+1$ in this case.

We now consider the case that σ_t is a departure of an active request r_k. In this case we may simulate the ALLOCATE algorithm by feeding it first with the served requests in $A_t \setminus \{r_k\}$ according to the order in which they were served, each request accompanied with its preferred path. Again, all these requests will be served by their preferred paths. After that, the pending requests in L_t are input to the ALLOCATE algorithm in the same order that they are processed by ALG in step $t+1$; each pending request that is served by ALG in step $t+1$ is accompanied by a preferred path that equals the path that is allocated to it by ALG. As the states of ALG and the simulated ALLOCATE algorithm are identical, the ALLOCATE algorithm accepts the same pending requests and serves them along their preferred paths. By Theorem 2, the theorem holds for step $t+1$ in this case as well.

Note that the proof easily extends to the case that multiple events occur in each time step.

6 Lower Bound

In this section we state a lower bound which implies that the competitive ratio of ALG is asymptotically optimal, up to an additive $O(\log k)$, where k is the maximal length of a source-sink path in any PR-graph. We note that with current technology, k is typically a small constant.

We note that our lower bound is based on the arguments used in [2]. However, that lower bound cannot be directly used in our case, because of the different service model.

Theorem 3. *Every online algorithm in the Acc/Stdby service model is $\Omega(\log(n \cdot b_{\max}))$-competitive.*

The idea of the proof is to reduce the bad scenarios for the persistent request model [2] to bad scenarios in the Acc/Stdby model. To do that, consider requests arriving one per time unit, followed by some T time units in which no event occurs, after which all the requests leave. Observe that since all requests leave together, there is no advantage in placing a request at standby: we might as well reject it immediately. Hence, the $\Omega(\log n)$ lower bound of [2, Lemma 4.1] applies in this case. Using similar techniques as in [2] it can be showed that every online algorithm is also $\Omega(\log b_{\max})$ competitive.

7 Discussion

In this paper we have proposed a blueprint of a certain view of routing for software-defined networks with network function virtualization. Specifically, we have presented the following.

- A new model for requests that may involve both routing and processing. The model allows for representing sophisticated plans using fairly intuitive graph concepts.
- A new twist to the admit/reject non-preemptive service model, that allows for a "standby" response to requests.
- An online algorithm that demonstrates the viability of our approach from a theoretical viewpoint: it proves that meaningful worst-case performance guarantees are possible for the proposed models.

We view our proposal as first step, or possibly a basis for a rigorous discussion of algorithmic approaches to SDN/NFV. Let us point out some immediate gaps we wish to be filled.

For example, it seems very interesting to test the performance of our algorithm using typical data of large instances (which are hard to come by). We conjecture that the typical performance of the algorithm is far better than what its theoretical-worst case analysis indicates.

Another algorithmic issue is the computational complexity of the implementation: while it is straightforward to implement the algorithm with polynomial running time, this may not be good enough for practical implementations. It is interesting to look for very frugal variants, possibly at the price of weaker worst-case guarantees.

Regarding the request model, we note that our graphical approach makes it hard to specify unordered processing: the size of such a representation in our model is exponential in the number of unordered processing stages involved. However we believe that having many unordered processing stages is quite rare: in most cases the processing stages are at least partially ordered, and when there are alternative functions, their number tends to be very small. Once again, it is important to understand what are the useful patterns in such an environment.

In conclusion, we hope that this work will encourage and contribute to the discussion of issues related to modeling of requests and service, optimization goals, and efficient algorithms. In particular we believe that the validity of new models should be supported by an algorithmic "proof of concept."

References

1. Aspnes, J., Azar, Y., Fiat, A., Plotkin, S., Waarts, O.: On-line routing of virtual circuits with applications to load balancing, machine scheduling. J. ACM **44**(3), 486–504 (1997)
2. Awerbuch, B., Azar, Y., Plotkin, S.: Throughput-competitive on-line routing. In: Proceedings of the 34th IEEE Annual Symposium on Foundations of Computer Science, pp. 32–40 (1993)

3. Awerbuch, B., Azar, Y., Plotkin, S., Waarts, O.: Competitive routing of virtual circuits with unknown duration. J. Comput. Syst. Sci. **62**(3), 385–397 (2001)
4. Buchbinder, N., Naor, J.S.: Improved bounds for online routing and packing via a primal-dual approach. In: 47th Annual IEEE Symposium on Foundations of Computer Science, pp. 293–304 (2006)
5. Buchbinder, N., Naor, J.S.: Online primal-dual algorithms for covering and packing. Math. Oper. Res. **34**(2), 270–286 (2009)
6. Cohen, R., Lewin-Eytan, L., Naor, J.S., Raz, D.: Near optimal placement of virtual network functions. In: 2015 IEEE Conference on Computer Communications (INFOCOM), pp. 1346–1354, April 2015
7. Even, G., Medina, M.: Online multi-commodity flow with high demands. In: Erlebach, T., Persiano, G. (eds.) WAOA 2012. LNCS, vol. 7846, pp. 16–29. Springer, Heidelberg (2013). doi:10.1007/978-3-642-38016-7_3
8. Even, G., Medina, M., Schaffrath, G., Schmid, S.: Competitive, deterministic embeddings of virtual networks. Theoret. Comput. Sci. **496**, 184–194 (2013). Distributed Computing and Networking (ICDCN 2012)
9. Even, G., Rost, M., Schmid, S.: An approximation algorithm for path computation and function placement in sdns. Appeared in SIROCCO (2016)
10. Hopcroft, J.E., Motwani, R., Ullman, J.D.: Introduction to Automata Theory, Languages, and Computation, 3rd edn. Pearson, Boston (2006)
11. Kleinberg, J.M.: Approximation algorithms for disjoint paths problems. Ph.D. thesis, Massachusetts Institute of Technology (1996)
12. Kreutz, D., Ramos, F., Verissimo, E.P., Rothenberg, C.E., Azodolmolky, S., Uhlig, S.: Software-defined networking: a comprehensive survey. Proc. IEEE **103**(1), 14–76 (2015)
13. Sleator, D.D., Tarjan, R.E.: Amortized efficiency of list update and paging rules. Commun. ACM **28**(2), 202–208 (1985)
14. Soulé, R., Basu, S., Kleinberg, R., Sirer, E.G., Foster, N.: Managing the network with merlin. In: Proceedings of the 12th ACM Workshop on Hot Topics in Networks, p. 24. ACM (2013)
15. Soulé, R., Basu, S., Marandi, P.J., Pedone, F., Kleinberg, R., Sirer, E.G., Foster, N.: Merlin: a language for provisioning network resources. In: Proceedings of the 10th ACM International Conference on emerging Networking Experiments and Technologies, pp. 213–226. ACM (2014)

Infinite Unlimited Churn (Short Paper)

Dianne Foreback[1(✉)], Mikhail Nesterenko[1], and Sébastien Tixeuil[2]

[1] Kent State University, Kent, OH, USA
dforebac@kent.edu
[2] UPMC Sorbonne Universités and IUF, Paris, France

Abstract. We study unlimited infinite churn in peer-to-peer overlay networks. Under this churn, arbitrary many peers may concurrently request to join or leave the overlay network; moreover these requests may never stop coming. We prove that unlimited adversarial churn, where processes may just exit the overlay network, is unsolvable. We focus on cooperative churn where exiting processes participate in the churn handling algorithm. We define the problem of unlimited infinite churn in this setting. We distinguish the fair version of the problem, where each request is eventually satisfied, from the unfair version that just guarantees progress. We focus on local solutions to the problem, and prove that a local solution to the Fair Infinite Unlimited Churn is impossible. We then present our algorithm $\mathcal{UIUC}$ that solves the Unfair Infinite Unlimited Churn Problem for a linearized peer-to-peer overlay network. We extend this solution to skip lists and skip graphs.

1 Our Contribution

We study the problem of churn in (structured) peer-to-peer overlay networks in the asynchronous message passing system model. Peers in the overlay network maintain the identifiers of its overlay neighbors in memory; message routing is left to the underlay. Specifically, we consider cooperative churn as opposed to adversarial when processes just exit. We prove that there does not exist an algorithm that can handle unlimited adversarial churn.

We define infinite unlimited churn in peer-to-peer overlay networks. *Infinite churn* handles an unbounded number of churn requests under which the overlay network has to maintain services (e.g. content retrieval) while handling it. This is opposed to *finite* churn, where services are either considered suspended or they are disregarded altogether [2]. We consider *unlimited churn* where there is no bound on the number of concurrently joining or leaving processes; potentially all processes presently in the overlay network may request to leave concurrently. Note that the infinite and unlimited churn properties are orthogonal. For example, churn may be finite but unlimited: all processes may request to leave but no more join or leave requests are forthcoming. Alternatively, in infinite limited churn, there may be an infinite total number of join or leave requests but only, for example, five of them in any given state. To the best of our knowledge, this paper is the first systematic study of unlimited infinite churn.

B. Bonakdarpour and F. Petit (Eds.): SSS 2016, LNCS 10083, pp. 148–153, 2016.
DOI: 10.1007/978-3-319-49259-9_12

2 The Infinite Unlimited Churn Problem

We distinguish fair and unfair types of the problem. A request to join and, in cooperative churn, leave the overlay network is submitted to the overlay by the *churning process*. A churn handling algorithm is *fair* if it eventually satisfies every request. By contrast, a churn algorithm that allows the possibility, under infinite churn, to bypass indefinitely some requests (still guaranteeing progress, i.e., satisfying some churn requests indefinitely), is *unfair*. Unfair algorithms are possibly more efficient.

A *link* is the state of channels between a pair of neighbor processes. As a churn algorithm services requests, it may temporarily violate the overlay network topology that is being maintained. A *transitional link* violates the overlay network topology while a *stable link* conforms to it. An algorithm that solves the infinite churn problem conforms to a combination of the following properties: **request progress:** if there is a churn request in the overlay network, some churn request is eventually satisfied; **fair request:** if there is a churn request in the overlay network, this churn request is eventually satisfied; **terminating transition:** every transitional link eventually becomes stable; **message progress:** a message in a stable link is either delivered or forwarded closer to the destination; **message safety:** a message in a transitional link is not lost. Note that the fair request property implies the request progress property. The converse is not necessarily true.

We define two variants of the problem. *The Unfair Infinite Unlimited Churn Problem* is the combination of request progress, terminating transition, message progress and message safety properties. *The Fair Infinite Unlimited Churn Problem* is the combination of fair request, terminating transition, message progress and message safety properties. In other words, Fair Infinite Unlimited Churn guarantees that every churn request is eventually satisfied while Unfair Infinite Unlimited Churn does not.

3 Impossibilities

A network topology is *expansive* if there exists a constant m independent of the network size such that for every pair of processes x and y where the distance between x and y is greater than m, a finite number of processes may be added m hops away from x to increase the distance between x and y by at least one. This constant m is the *expansion vicinity* of the topology. Note that a completely connected topology is not expansive since the distance between any pair of processes is always one. However, a lot of practical peer-to-peer overlay network topologies are expansive. For example, a linear topology is expansive with expansion vicinity of 1 since the distance between any pair of processes at least two hops away may be increased by one if a process is added outside the neighborhood of one member of the pair.

A churn request may potentially be far away, i.e. a large number of hops, from the place where the topology maintenance operation needs to occur. We will consider an overlay network that maintains a linear topology, i.e., a topological sort. *Place of join* for a join request of process x, is the pair of processes y and z that already joined the overlay network, such that y has the greatest identifier less than x and z has the smallest identifier greater than x. In every particular state of the overlay network, for any join request, there is a unique place of join. Note that as the algorithm progresses and other processes join or leave the overlay network, the place of join may change. *Place of leave* for a leave request of process x is defined similarly. *Place of churn* is a place of join or leave.

A churn algorithm is *local* if there exists a constant l independent of the overlay network size, such that only processes within l hops from the place of churn need to take steps to satisfy this churn request. The minimum such constant l is the *locality* of the algorithm. Note that a local algorithm may maintain only an expansive topology, and that the expansive vicinity of this topology must be greater than the locality of the algorithm.

Theorem 1. *There does not exist a solution for unlimited adversarial churn if the maintained topology is not fully connected*[1].

Theorem 2. *There does not exist a local solution to the Fair Infinite Unlimited Churn Problem for an expansive overlay network topology.*

```
constant p // process identifier
variables
          left, right: ids of left and right neighbors,
                  ⊥ if undefined
          leaving: boolean, initially false, read only,
                  application request
          busy: boolean, initially false; true when
                servicing a join/leave request
                or when joining
          C: incoming channel

actions
joinRequest:  join ∈ C ⟶
                 receive join (reqId)
                 if (p < reqId < right) and not leaving
                 and not busy then
                     send sua(right) to reqId
                     busy := true
                 else
                     if reqId < p then
                         send join(reqId) to left
                     else
                         send join(reqId) to right

leaveRequest: leave ∈ C ⟶
                 receive leave(reqId, q)
                 if reqId = right and not leaving
                 and not busy then
                     send sua(⊥) to q
                     busy := true
                 else
                     if p <= reqId then
                         send leave(reqId, q) to left
                     else
                         send leave(reqId, q) to right

setUpA:       sua ∈ C ⟶
                 receive sua(reqId) from q
                 if reqId ≠ ⊥ then // Join 1.1 received
                     right := reqId
                     left := q
                     send sua(⊥) to right
                 else // Join 1.2 or Leave 1 received
                     left := q
                     send sub to left

setUpB:       sub ∈ C ⟶
                 receive sub from q
                 if q ≠ right then // Join 2.2 or Leave 2 received
                     send tda to right
                     right := q
                 else // Join 2.1 received
                     send sub to left

tearDownA:    tda ∈ C ⟶
                 receive tda from q
                 if q ≠ left then // Join 3 or Leave 3.2 received
                     send tdb to q
                 else // Leave 3.1 received
                     send tda to right

tearDownB:    tdb ∈ C ⟶
                 receive tdb from q
                 if q ≠ right then // Join 4 or Leave 4.2 received
                     send ftd to q
                     busy := false
                 else // Leave 4.1 received
                     send tdb to left

tranDone:     ftd ∈ C ⟶
                 receive ftd from q
                 if leaving then // Leave 5 received, p may exit
                     right = ⊥
                     left = ⊥
                 else
                     busy := false // Join 5 received
```

Fig. 1. Algorithm $\mathcal{UIUC}$ for process p.

[1] Proofs and referenes are in the full version of the paper [3].

4 Local Unfair Infinite Unlimited Churn ($\mathcal{UIUC}$)

We present a local algorithm *Unfair Infinite Unlimited Churn* ($\mathcal{UIUC}$) in Fig. 1 that satisfies the four properties of the Unfair Infinite Unlimited Churn Problem while maintaining a linear topology. The basic idea of the $\mathcal{UIUC}$ algorithm is to have the *handler* process with the smaller identifier coordinate churn requests to its immediate right. This handler considers one such request at a time. This serializes request processing and guarantees the accepted request's eventual completion. The request is sent in the form of a single *join* or *leave* message. Each process p maintains two identifiers: *left*, where it stores the largest identifier greater than p and *right*, where it stores the smallest identifier less than p. Read-only variable *leaving* is set to **true** by the environment once the joined process wishes to leave the overlay network. Variable *busy* is used by the handler process to indicate whether it currently coordinates a churn request, or it is initialized to **true** for a joining process. The incoming channel for process p is variable C. Communication channels are FIFO with unlimited message capacity. We refer to processes and their identifiers interchangeably. Process p is a *neighbor* of process q if q stores the identifier of p. Note that q is not necessarily a neighbor of p. A process may send a message to any of its neighbors. A process may send a message only to the receiver with a specific id, i.e., we do not consider broadcasts or multicasts. The processes have unique identifiers. The largest process stores positive infinity in its *right* variable; the smallest process stores negative infinity in *left*. A *left end* of a link is the smaller-id neighbor process. A *right end* is the greater-id process. As a process joins or leaves the overlay network it may change the values of its own or its neighbors variables thus transitioning the link from one state to another. In a linear topology, a link is *transitional* if its left end is not a neighbor of its right end or vice versa. The link is *stable* otherwise. The largest and smallest processes may not leave. The links to the right of the largest process and to the left of the smallest processes are always stable. A process may leave the overlay network only after it has joined. We assume that in the initial state of the overlay network, all links are stable.

We assume that a *join* and, for symmetry, a *leave* message is inserted into an incoming channel of an arbitrary joined process in the overlay network. Message *join* carries the identifier of the process wishing to join the overlay network. Message *leave* carries the identifier of the leaving process as well as the identifier of the process immediately to its right. If the receiver realizes that it is to the immediate right of the place of join or leave, and the receiver is not currently handling another request, i.e., $busy \neq$ **true**, and it does not want to leave, it starts handling the arrived request. Otherwise, the recipient process forwards the request to its left or right.

Request handling is accomplished by the order messages are sent and received to setup stable links and tear down transitional links to maintain the linear topology. It is similar for join and leave and is divided into five stages. The first two stages are *setup* stages: they set up the channels for the links of the joining process or for the processes that are the neighbors of the leaving process. The third and forth stages are *teardown stages*: they remove the channels of the links being replaced. The last stage informs either the leaving process that it may exit, or the joining process that it may start coordinating its own churn requests. In the case of join, two links need to be set up, hence the setup stages are divided into two substages 1.1, 1.2, 2.1 and 2.2, followed by the teardown stages 3 and 4, then stage 5; these join substage numbers are included in the comments of Fig. 1. Similarly, in the case of leave, links setup stages 1 and 2 are followed by the teardown stages that are divided into substages 3.1, 3.2, 4.1, 4.2 because two links need to be torn down, then stage 5. The messages transmitted during corresponding stages are 1. set up A **sua**, 2. set up B **sub**, 3. tear down A **tda**, 4. tear down B **tdb** and 5. finish teardown **ftd**.

Theorem 3. *Algorithm $\mathcal{UIUC}$ is local and it solves the Unfair Infinite Unlimited Churn Problem.*

5 $\mathcal{UIUC}$ Extensions to Skip List and Skip Graph and Further Work

Churn algorithm $\mathcal{UIUC}$ extends to more complicated topologies such as skip lists and skip graphs In these topologies, the processes have links on multiple levels. The processes are linearized in the lowest level. In the higher levels, the processes have links to progressively more distant peers. These higher level links accelerate overlay network searches and other operations. To extend $\mathcal{UIUC}$ to such a structure a separate version of $\mathcal{UIUC}$ should be run at each level. The churn request should bear the level number to differentiate which level $\mathcal{UIUC}$ they belong to. The churning process should proceed up and down the levels as follows. A joining process first joins the first, linear, level, then the next and so on until it joins all the levels appropriate to the particular structure. The leaving process should proceed in reverse: the leaving process requests to leave the levels in decreasing order.

As further research it is interesting to consider extensions of $\mathcal{UIUC}$ to ring structures such as Chord [4] or Hyperring [1]. Another important area of inquiry is addition of limited adversarial churn. This problem is difficult to address in the asynchronous message passing model where the exited process may not be differentiated from a slow one. Oracles determining a process exit [2] may have to be used.

References

1. Awerbuch, B., Scheideler, C.: The hyperring: a low-congestion deterministic data structure for distributed environments. In: SODA, pp. 318–327. Society for Industrial and Applied Mathematics, Philadelphia (2004)
2. Foreback, D., Koutsopoulos, A., Nesterenko, M., Scheideler, C., Strothmann, T.: On stabilizing departures in overlay networks. In: Felber, P., Garg, V. (eds.) SSS 2014. LNCS, vol. 8756, pp. 48–62. Springer, Heidelberg (2014). doi:10.1007/978-3-319-11764-5_4

3. Foreback, D., Nesterenko, M., Tixeuil, S.: Infinite unlimited churn. Technical report 1608.00726, arXiv (2016)
4. Stoica, I., Morris, R., Liben-Nowell, D., Karger, D.R., Frans Kaashoek, M., Dabek, F., Balakrishnan, H.: Chord: a scalable peer-to-peer lookup protocol for Internet applications. IEEE/ACM Trans. Netw. **11**(1), 17–32 (2003)

Perfect Failure Detection with Very Few Bits

Pierre Fraigniaud[1], Sergio Rajsbaum[2], Corentin Travers[3(✉)], Petr Kuznetsov[4], and Thibault Rieutord[4]

[1] IRIF and U. Paris Diderot, Paris, France
[2] Instituto de Matemáticas, UNAM, Mexico City, Mexico
[3] LaBRI, U. Bordeaux, Bordeaux, France
travers@labri.fr
[4] Télécom ParisTech, Paris, France

Abstract. A *failure detector* is a distributed oracle that provides each process with a module that continuously outputs an estimate of which processes in the system have failed. The *perfect* failure detector provides accurate and eventually complete information about process failures. We show that, in asynchronous failure-prone message-passing systems, perfect failure detection can be achieved by an oracle that outputs at most $\lceil \log \alpha(n) \rceil + 1$ bits per process in n-process systems, where α denotes the inverse-Ackermann function. This result is essentially optimal, as we also show that, in the same environment, no failure detector outputting a constant number of bits per process can achieve perfect failure detection.

Keywords: Failure detectors · Well-quasi-order · Higman's lemma

1 Introduction

Failure detectors have influenced research and development of fault-tolerant distributed systems for over 20 years, since their introduction in two seminal papers [2,3]. A *failure detector* is an abstraction layer that provides each process with information about which other processes have crashed. The concept of failure detector provides a modular approach of distributed computing and an elegant framework which yields two orthogonal but interacting working projects: developing portable algorithms on top of failure detectors, and developing efficient failure detector implementations in various message passing and shared memory settings. This concept has been very successful in a wide variety of settings, including network communication protocols, group membership protocols, and algorithms for solving consensus, atomic commit, broadcast, mutual

This research has been carried out within the framework of ECOS Nord (Project M12M01).
S. Rajsbaum—Additional support from PAPIIT-UNAM grant IN107714.
C. Travers—Additional support from the French State, managed by the French National Research Agency (ANR) in the frame of the "Investments for the future" Programme IdEx Bordeaux - CPU (ANR-10-IDEX-03-02).

B. Bonakdarpour and F. Petit (Eds.): SSS 2016, LNCS 10083, pp. 154–169, 2016.
DOI: 10.1007/978-3-319-49259-9_13

exclusion, leader election, as well as several other services (see Sect. 1.2). More generally, the failure detector abstraction has fostered the theoretical understanding of failures, and of their effects in distributed computing. Indeed, failure detectors abstract away details of the system (e.g., the message delivery times on each link, the process speeds, etc.), by focussing only on extracting process failure information. Given a failure detector, one can then investigate what are the distributed computing tasks that are solvable with the information provided by this failure detector layer (irrespective of the underlying network on top of which the failure detector is implemented).

In a nutshell, failure detectors provide a formal framework to tackle questions such as: How much, and what kind of information about failures is necessary to solve a given distributed computing task?

At the one end of the spectrum, the concern is the *minimum information about failures* needed to solve a given task, e.g., notably, the *consensus* problem. Various *weakest* failure detectors for consensus have been identified, that show that the question of *how much* information about failures is needed to solve a problem is subtle. The weakest failure detectors enabling to solve consensus are all equivalent, that is, given any of these failure detectors, one can build any other such failure detector. Yet, they seem to provide very different kind of information, presented in very different forms. For instance, the failure detector Ω outputs the identity of a single process at each process [2]. This identity is such that, eventually, all the correct processes are provided with the same identity, which is the identity of a correct process. In contrast, the failure detector $\Diamond S$ outputs a set of process identities at each process [3]. These identities are the ones of suspected processes, and are such that, eventually, they include all the processes that have crashed, and there is a correct process whose identity is included in none of the sets. These two failure detectors are equivalent (they both are weakest failure detectors enabling to solve consensus in an asynchronous message-passing system where a majority of processes are correct).

At the other end of the spectrum, the concern is failure detectors that provide *perfectly accurate information about failures*. Remarkably, also at this end of the spectrum, there are failure detectors that provide "the same information" about failures, but they do so in a very different way. This is raising the question of what is the *amount* of information provided by failure detectors. Consider for example the failure detector classes $\mathcal{P}$ and ψ^t. A failure detector $\mathcal{P}$ provides each process with a set of identities of processes that are suspected to have failed [3]. These sets are such that non-faulty processes are never suspected, and all faulty processes are eventually suspected by each process. In a system where at most t processes can crash, a failure detector ψ^t outputs an integer at each process [17]. These integers are such that they are at most the number of processes that have crashed, and, eventually, they are all equal to the number of processes that have actually crashed. While $\mathcal{P}$ and ψ^t are quite similar qualitatively as they both provide perfectly accurate information about failures, they are quantitatively quite different: one provides sets of identities, while the other provides integers in a bounded range of values.

In this paper, we initiate the study of how many bits should be provided to each process by a failure detector to ensure specific knowledge about the failure pattern, or to solve a given task. We start our investigation by tackling this question at the latter end of the spectrum, namely, the case of a failure detector that guarantees perfectly accurate information about failures. Specifically, in this paper, we tackle the following question: *how many bits should be provided to each process by a failure detector that guarantees perfectly accurate information about failures?*

1.1 Contributions

We describe a new failure detector, called *micro-perfect*, denoted μP, which outputs at most $\lceil \log \alpha(n) \rceil + 1$ bits at each process, in asynchronous failure-prone message-passing systems with n processes, where α denotes the inverse-Ackermann function. We show that μP is equivalent to the perfect failure detector. This result is essentially optimal, as we also show that, in asynchronous failure-prone message-passing systems, no failure detector outputting a constant number of bits at each process can achieve perfect failure detection.

For establishing both our lower and upper bounds, we use techniques from well-quasi-ordering theory [13]. This important tool in logic and computability has a wide variety of applications [15]. Here we proceed to explore the depth of the connection of well-quasi-orderings with distributed computing, stemming from an essential difficulty when dealing with processes that may crash. In fault-tolerant computing, when a process considers a list L of local states of other processes, it may well be the case that its view is incomplete, e.g., the actual global state is L' with $L \subset L'$, because it is possible that processes in $L' \setminus L$ are delayed. This bares resemblance to well-quasi-ordering theory, which studies words over alphabets, and the sub-words that can be obtained by deleting some symbols of each word. We show that fault-tolerant computing does not only bare resemblance to well-quasi-ordering theory, but that well-quasi-ordering theory is inherently present in some aspects of fault-tolerant computing.

More specifically, for the lower bound, a key ingredient is Higman's lemma [11], which essentially says that if $w^{(1)}, w^{(2)}, \ldots$ is an infinite sequence of words over some *finite* alphabet Σ, then there exist indices $i < j$ such that $w^{(i)}$ can be obtained from $w^{(j)}$ by deleting some of its letters. We show how to use Higman's lemma to prove that no failure detector outputting a constant number of bits at each process can achieve perfect failure detection.

For the upper bound, i.e., for the design of the micro-perfect failure detector μP, we use a combination of failure detector techniques, with the notion of *distributed encoding* of the integers recently introduced in [6]. A distributed encoding of the integers is a distributed structure that encodes each positive integer n by a word $w^{(n)} = w_1^{(n)}, \ldots, w_n^{(n)}$ over some (non-necessarily finite) alphabet Σ, such that no proper sub-words of $w^{(n)}$ can be interpreted as the distributed encoding of n' with $n' < n$. In [6], using well-quasi-ordering theory, it is proved that the first n integers can be distributedly encoded using words on an alphabet with letters on $\lceil \log \alpha(n) \rceil + 1$ bits, where α is a function growing at least as slowly as the inverse-Ackerman function. We explain how to use this encoding to prove that there exists a failure detector μP outputting $\lceil \log \alpha(n) \rceil + 1$ bits at each process, which achieves perfect failure detection. A companion technical report [7] contains the proofs and some additional material.

1.2 Related Work

We refer to [8] for a recent survey on the failure detector abstraction. In this section, we just survey work closely related to our paper.

In [17], two failure detectors are introduced, which output an integer that approximates the number of crashed processes. More precisely, a query to a failure detector of the class ψ^y returns an integer that is always between $t - y$ and the number of processes that crashed during the execution (where t is the maximum of processes that can crash, and $0 \leq y \leq t$). More precisely, for any time τ, the output returned by a query issued at time τ is at most $\max(t-y, f^\tau)$ where f^τ is the number of processes that have crashed at time τ. Furthermore, there is a time τ' from which the output returned by any query issued at any time τ'' after time τ' is equal to $\max(t - y, f^{\tau''})$. The class $\Diamond\psi^y$ relaxes ψ^y by allowing the properties defining ψ^y to be satisfied only eventually. It is proved that the classes ψ^y and $\Diamond\psi^y$ are respectively equivalent[1] to the classes ϕ^y and $\Diamond\phi^y$ of [16]. A failure detector of the class ϕ^y provides the processes with a query primitive which has a set X of processes as parameter, and which returns a boolean answer. When $|X|$ is too small (or too big), the invocation of the query for X by a process returns systematically *true* (resp., *false*). Otherwise, namely, when $t - y < |X| \leq t$, $0 \leq y \leq t$, the query returns *true* only if all the processes in X have crashed. Moreover, if all the processes of X have crashed, and a process repeatedly issues the query, then it eventually obtains the answer *true*. Notice that ϕ^0 provides no information about failures, while ϕ^t is equivalent to a perfect failure detector. In the follow-up paper [17], the relation of the failure detector Ω_z to set agreement is studied, including relations with respect to the failure detector $\Diamond S_x$.

A failure detector class whose output is binary has been introduced in [9] to solve non-blocking atomic commit. This class, called *anonymously perfect failure detectors*, and denoted by $?\mathcal{P}$, is defined as follows. Each process has a flag (initially equal to *false*) that is eventually set to *true* if and only if a process has crashed (the identity of the crashed process is not necessarily known, hence the name "anonymous"). The definition of $?\mathcal{P}$ has been extended in [17] to take into account the fact that k processes have crashed (instead of just one). This class, denoted $?\mathcal{P}k$, provides each process with a flag that is eventually set to *true* if and only if at least k processes have crashed (observe that $?\mathcal{P}$ is $?\mathcal{P}1$). An interesting question raised in [17] is the issue of additivity of failure detectors. It is known that combining two failure detectors may enable solving consensus,

[1] We stress that, in the literature, by "equivalent" it is meant that, given any failure detector of one class, it is possible to build a failure detector of the other class, and it is understood that "both provide the same information on failures" (see, e.g., [17]).

while none of them is individually strong enough to enable solving consensus. In this paper, we aim at quantifying such phenomenon, by considering the number of bits provided to each process by the failure detector.

The notion of *well-quasi-ordering* (wqo) is a "frequently discovered concept", as already pointed out by Kruskal [13] in 1972. One important application of wqo is providing *termination arguments* in decidability results [1]. Indeed, thirteen years after publishing his undecidability result, Turing [21] proposed the now classic method of proving program termination using so-called "bad sequences", with respect to a wqo. In the setting of wqo, the problem of *bounding* the length of bad sequences is of utmost interest as it yields upper bounds on terminating program executions. Hence, the interest in *algorithmic aspects* of wqos has grown recently as witnessed by the amount of work collected in [19]. For more applications and related work on wqos, including rewriting systems, tree embeddings, lossy channel systems, and graph minors, see recent works [10,19]. The notion of distributed encoding of the integers was proposed in [6] to show that every one-shot system specification can be wait-free runtime monitored non-deterministically using only three opinions.

2 The Model

Our results are stated in the classical model used for investigating failure detectors. Specifically, we consider an asynchronous crash-prone message-passing system consisting of n processes denoted by $p_1, \ldots, p_n$. Each process p_i has a unique identity $i = \mathsf{id}(p_i)$, and the total number n of processes is known to each of the processes. Each pair of processes $\{p_i, p_j\}$ is connected by a reliable, yet asynchronous channel. That is, any message sent by p_i to p_j is eventually received by p_j but there are no upper bounds on the time to transfer that message. Channels are reliable in the sense that they do not alter, duplicate or create messages. An arbitrary large number of processes can fail, by crashing, as long as at least one process remains correct. When a process crashes, it permanently stops functioning, that is, it does not execute any more steps of computation (including sending and receiving messages).

2.1 Failure Detectors

For modeling failure detectors, we assume the existence of a global clock, with non-negative integer values. This clock is however not accessible to the processes. Let $\Pi = \{p_1, \ldots, p_n\}$. A *failure pattern* is a function $\mathcal{F} : \mathbb{N} \to 2^{\Pi}$ that specifies which are the processes that have crashed by time $\tau \in \mathbb{N}$. Let $\mathsf{faulty}(\mathcal{F}) = \bigcup_{\tau \in \mathbb{N}} \mathcal{F}(\tau)$ be the set of processes that fail in the failure pattern $\mathcal{F}$. The set of processes that do not fail is $\mathsf{correct}(\mathcal{F}) = \Pi \setminus \mathsf{faulty}(\mathcal{F})$. When there is no ambiguity on the underlying failure pattern $\mathcal{F}$, we say that a process p_i is *correct* if $p_i \in \mathsf{correct}(\mathcal{F})$ and *faulty* if $p_i \in \mathsf{faulty}(\mathcal{F})$. An *environment* is a set of failure patterns. In this paper, as specified before, all failure patterns in which at least one process is correct can occur.

A failure detector [3] is a distributed device that provides each process with some information on the failure pattern. Each process can *query* the failure detector, and each query returns a value in some (potentially infinite) range $\mathcal{R}$ that depends on the failure detector. The outputs of a failure detector during an execution is described by a failure detector *history*, which is a function $H : \Pi \times \mathbb{N} \rightarrow \mathcal{R}$ that maps each pair process-time to a value in $\mathcal{R}$. The value returned by the failure detector to process p_i at time τ is $H(p_i, \tau)$. A failure detector D with range $\mathcal{R}$ associates a non-empty set of histories with range $\mathcal{R}$ to every failure pattern. The set of histories corresponding to a failure pattern $\mathcal{F}$ is denoted by $D(\mathcal{F})$. That is, $D(\mathcal{F})$ is a collection of functions of the form $H : \Pi \times \mathbb{N} \rightarrow \mathcal{R}$, and when the failure pattern is $\mathcal{F}$, the behavior of the failure detector coincides with some history $H \in D(\mathcal{F})$. For instance, the failure detector Ω [2] has range $\{0, 1\}$, and guarantees that it eventually outputs 1 at a single correct process, and 0 at every other processes. That is, for every failure pattern $\mathcal{F}$, the history $H : \Pi \times \mathbb{N} \rightarrow \{0, 1\} \in \Omega(\mathcal{F})$ if and only if there exists $p_i \in \mathsf{correct}(\mathcal{F})$, and $\tau \in \mathbb{N}$ such that, for every $\tau' \geq \tau$, $H(p_i, \tau') = 1$ and $H(p_j, \tau') = 0$ for every $j \neq i$.

The so-called *perfect* failure detector P [3] provides a list of processes that have crashed to each process. The failure detector P does not make any mistake, in the sense that no process is declared crashed before it has failed. Moreover, it is eventually complete, in the sense that its output at every process eventually matches the set of faulty processes. More formally, the range of P is 2^{Π}, and, for every failure pattern $\mathcal{F}$, the history $H : \Pi \times \mathbb{N} \rightarrow 2^{\Pi}$ belongs to $P(\mathcal{F})$ if and only if the following two properties are satisfied: (Accuracy) for every time τ and process p_i, $H(p_i, \tau) \subseteq \mathcal{F}(\tau)$; and (Completeness) there exists a time τ such that, for every $\tau' \geq \tau$ and process p_i, $H(p_i, \tau') = \mathcal{F}(\tau')$.

Similarly, the *eventual perfect* failure detector $\Diamond P$ [3] is identical to the failure detector P except that the accuracy property only holds eventually. Formally, for every failure pattern $\mathcal{F}$, $H : \Pi \times \mathbb{N} \rightarrow 2^{\Pi}$ belongs to $\Diamond P(\mathcal{F})$ if and only if there exists $\tau \in \mathbb{N}$ such that, for every $\tau' \geq \tau$ and every process p_i, $H(p_i, \tau') = \mathcal{F}(\tau')$.

2.2 Protocols and Executions

A *distributed protocol* $\mathcal{A}$ consists of n local algorithms $\mathcal{A}(p_1), \ldots, \mathcal{A}(p_n)$, one per process. An *execution* is a sequence of *steps*. During a step, every process p_i acts according to its local algorithm. First, it performs some local computation, and then it performs one of the following five actions: (1) sending a message to some process, (2) receiving a (possibly empty) set of messages, (3) querying the failure detector, (4) receiving an external input or, (5) sending an external output. In a reception step performed by process p_i, since the communication channels are asynchronous, the set of messages might be empty even if a message has been previously send to p_i and not yet received by it. Receiving an external input (resp., sending an external output) are actions enabling to specify protocols that implement, or emulate failure detectors. External inputs correspond to queries to the emulated failure detector. As a result of such a query, an external output is eventually sends, which corresponds to the result of the query.

An *execution* of a protocol $\mathcal{A}$ using failure detector D in environment $\mathcal{E}$ is a tuple $exec = (\mathcal{F}, H, S, T)$ where $\mathcal{F}$ is a failure pattern in $\mathcal{E}$, H is a failure detector history in $D(\mathcal{F})$, S is a sequence of steps of $\mathcal{A}$, and T is a strictly increasing sequence of clock ticks in $\mathbb{N}$. S is called a *schedule*, and the ith step $S[i]$ in S is taken at time $T[i]$. A tuple $exec = (\mathcal{F}, H, S, T)$ defines an execution of $\mathcal{A}$ if and only if the following conditions are satisfied: (1) every correct process takes infinitely many steps in S, (2) no processes take a step after they have crashed, (3) the sequence T and S are either both finite with the same length, or are both infinite, (4) no messages are loss, i.e., if a process performs infinitely many receive step, it eventually receives all messages that were sent to it, (5) if the ith step $S[i]$ is a failure detector query by process p_j that returns d, then $d = H(p_j, T[i])$, i.e., the failure detector queries return values that are consistent with the history H, and (6) the steps taken in S are consistent with the protocol $\mathcal{A}$. Formalizing the above conditions is straightforward but requires care and heavy notation. We refer to [4,12] for such a formalization.

2.3 Comparing Failure Detectors

A protocol $\mathcal{A}$ that implements a failure detector D receives queries as external inputs, and produces responses in the range of D. Since computing a response may entail sending/receiving messages as well as local computations, there might be some delay between the time τ at which $\mathcal{A}$ receives a query, and the time τ' at which $\mathcal{A}$ produces a response d to that query. The correctness condition taken from [12] requires that d must be a legal output for D at some point in time between τ and τ'. Hence the implementation $\mathcal{A}$ of D behaves as an atomic failure detector, for which responses to queries are given instantaneously. More precisely, a protocol $\mathcal{A}$ implements a failure detector D using a failure detector D', or, for short, *emulates* D using D', in environment $\mathcal{E}$ if, for every failure pattern $\mathcal{F} \in \mathcal{E}$, and for every execution $exec = (\mathcal{F}, H', S, T)$ of $\mathcal{A}$ where $H' \in D'(\mathcal{F})$ the following hold. Let H_Q and H_R be the histories of external inputs (queries) and outputs (responses to queries) in execution $exec$. A query occurs at process p_i at time τ if $H_Q(p_i, \tau) = query$. Similarly, a response occurs at time τ at process p_i if $H_R(p_i, \tau) = d$, where d is a value in the range of D. The following three properties must be fulfilled: (1) for every correct process p_i, and every integer $i \geq 1$, if the ith query at process p_i occurs at time τ, then a response occurs at p_i at some time $\tau' > \tau$ (the ith query and the ith response occurring at the same process p_i are said to be *matching*); (2) for every process p_i, and every integer $i \geq 1$, if the ith response occurs at time τ, then the ith query occurs at p_i at some time $\tau' < \tau$; (3) there exists a failure detector history $H \in D(\mathcal{F})$ such that, for every process p_i, and every times τ_1, τ_2, if $H_Q(p_i, \tau_1) = query$, $H_R(p_i, \tau_2) = d$, and this query/response pair is matching, then $d = H(p_i, \tau)$ for some time $\tau \in [\tau_1, \tau_2]$.

We are now ready to describe how to compare failure detectors. Let D and D' be two failure detectors. We say that D *is at least as weak as* D' in environment $\mathcal{E}$, denoted by $D \leq_{\mathcal{E}} D'$, if there is a protocol that implements D using D' in environment $\mathcal{E}$. Then D and D' are said *equivalent* in environment $\mathcal{E}$ if $D \leq_{\mathcal{E}} D'$

and $D' \leq_{\mathcal{E}} D$. These notions are motivated by the fact that if a failure detector D can be used to solve some task T in some environment $\mathcal{E}$ then every failure detector D' such that $D \leq_{\mathcal{E}} D'$ can be used as well to solve the task T. For example, consensus can be solved using Ω [18]. If $\Omega \leq_{\mathcal{E}} D$, then, in $\mathcal{E}$, one can compose a protocol $\mathcal{B}$ that implements Ω using D with a protocol $\mathcal{A}$ solving consensus using Ω. Finally, a failure detector D is said to be a *weakest* failure detector for a task T in environment $\mathcal{E}$ if and only if (1) there is a protocol that solves T using D in environment $\mathcal{E}$ and, (2) for every failure detector D' that can be used to solve T in $\mathcal{E}$, we have $D \leq_{\mathcal{E}} D'$. For example, it has been shown [2] that Ω is a weakest failure detector for consensus in the *majority* environment, i.e., the environment in which every failure pattern $\mathcal{F}$ satisfies $|\mathsf{faulty}(\mathcal{F})| < \frac{n}{2}$. Also, Ω is the weakest failure detector to implement eventual consistency [5].

3 Perfect Failure Detection Requires $\omega(1)$ Bits per Process

In this section, we show that any failure detector emulating the perfect failure detector P must output values whose range depends on the size n of the system.

Theorem 1. *A failure detector that outputs a constant number of bits at each process cannot emulate the perfect failure detector P.*

Preliminaries. Key ingredients in the proof of Theorem 1 are *Ramsey's Theorem* and some elements of the *well-quasi-order* theory.

Ramsey's Theorem might be seen as a generalization of the pigeonhole principle. The statement of its finite version, which we are going to use in the proof is recalled below. An n-subset is a subset of size n and coloring α is a function that maps each n-subset to some element of a set of size c.

Theorem 2 (Ramsey's Theorem). *For all natural numebrs n, m, and c, there exists a natural number $g(n, m, c)$ with the following property. For every set S of size at least $g(n, m, c)$, and any coloring of the n-subsets of S with at most c colors, there is some subset C of S of size m that has all of its n-subsets colored the same color.*

We recall next some basic notions of well-quasi order theory. Let A be a (finite or infinite) set, and let $\preceq$ be a binary relation over A. A (finite or infinite) sequence $a_1, a_2, \ldots, a_\ell$ of elements of A is *good* if there exists two indices $i < j$ such that $a_i \preceq a_j$. Otherwise, if for every $i < j$, $a_i \not\preceq a_j$, the sequence is said to be *bad*. The pair $(A, \preceq)$ is a *well-quasi-order* (*wqo* for short), if (1) $\preceq$ is transitive and reflexive, and (2) every infinite sequence of elements of A is good.

A finite sequence $a_1, a_2, \ldots, a_k$ of elements of A is called a *word*. Let A^* denote the set of words, and let $\preceq_*$ be the sub-word relation over A^* induced by the relation $\preceq$. That is, $a = a_1, \ldots, a_k \preceq_* b = b_1, \ldots, b_\ell$ if and only if $k \leq \ell$ and there exists a strictly increasing mapping $m : [1, k] \rightarrow [1, \ell]$ such that $a_i \preceq b_{m(i)}$, for every i, $1 \leq i \leq k$. Higman's lemma essentially states that every bad sequence of words in $(A^*, \preceq_*)$ is finite whenever $(A, \preceq)$ is a wqo:

Lemma 1 (Higman's lemma [11]). *If* $(A, \preceq)$ *is a well-quasi-order, then so is* $(A^*, \preceq_*)$.

For the purpose of establishing Theorem 1, we are interested in $(\Sigma^*, =^*)$ where Σ is a *finite* set, and $=^*$ denotes the sub-word relation based on the equality relation. That is, for any two words $a = a_1, \ldots, a_k, b = b_1, \ldots, b_\ell$, $a =^* b \in \Sigma^*$ if and only if there exists a strictly increasing map $m : [1, k] \to [1, \ell]$ such that $a_i = b_{m(i)}$, for every $i, 1 \leq i \leq k$.

Since Σ is finite, $(\Sigma, =)$ is a wqo. It thus follows from Higman's lemma that $(\Sigma^*, =^*)$ is also a wqo. Hence, every bad sequence over $(\Sigma^*, =^*)$ is finite. We are interested in the maximal length of such bad sequences. Of course, if no further assumption is made, bad sequences of arbitrary lengths can be constructed. However, in the case of *controlled* bad sequences, (coarse) upper bounds on the length of bad sequence have been established:

Theorem 3 (Length function Theorem [20]). *For a finite set* Σ *and a given* $d \in \mathbb{N}$, *let* $L_{\Sigma^*}(d)$ *be the maximal length of bad sequences* $x_0, x_1, x_2, \ldots$ *over* $(\Sigma^*, =^*)$ *such that* $|x_i| \leq f^i(d) = f(f(\ldots f(d)))$ *for* $i = 0, 1, 2, \ldots$. *If the* control function f *is primitive-recursive, then the* length function $L_{\Sigma^*}(d)$ *is bounded by a function in* $\mathcal{F}_{\omega^{|\Sigma|-1}}$.[2]

In the proof below, we will construct a sequences $x = x_1, x_2, \ldots$ over $(\Sigma^*, =^*)$ where $|x_i| = i$, for every $i = 1, 2, \ldots$, i.e., we will restrict our attention to sequences controlled by the successor function $f : n \to n + 1$, whose initial element has length 1. By the Length function Theorem, there is a bound on the length of every such sequence that is bad, depending solely on the cardinality of Σ:

Corollary 1. *Let* Σ *be a finite set. There exists an integer* L_{Σ^*} *with the following property: Every bad sequence* $x = x_1, x_2, \ldots$ *over* $(\Sigma^*, =^*)$ *such that* $|x_i| = i$ *for every* $i = 1, 2, \ldots$ *has length at most* L_{Σ^*}.

Overview of the Proof of Theorem 1. Let Σ be a finite set. We are going to show that there exists an integer N such that no failure detector with range Σ can emulate the perfect failure detector P in a N-process system.

For the sake of contradiction, let us assume that there is a failure detector X whose range is Σ and an algorithm $T_{X \to P}$ that emulates P in a system $\Pi = \{p_1, \ldots, p_N\}$ consisting of N processes. We aim at constructing two executions $exec_1$ and $exec_2$ that are indistinguishable to a subset of the processes up to a certain point in time. However, the executions have different failure patterns and, by leveraging the indistinguishably of $exec_1$ and $exec_2$ from the perspective of some processes, we show that in one of these executions, a correct process is erroneously suspected by the emulated perfect failure detector.

[2] The function classes $\mathcal{F}_\alpha$ are the elementary-recursive closure of the functions F_α, which are the ordinal-indexed levels of the Fast-Growing Hierarchy [14]. Multiply-recursive complexity starts at level $\alpha = \omega$, i.e., Ackermannian complexity, and stops just before level $\alpha = \omega^\omega$, i.e., Hyper-Ackermannian complexity.

For a process p not to be able to distinguish between $exec_1$ and $exec_2$, it must in particular receive the same sequence of outputs from the underlying failure detector X in the two executions. Let $\mathcal{F}$ be a failure pattern in which p is correct. Since the range of X is finite, in any valid history $H \in X(\mathcal{F})$, there exists a symbol in the range Σ of X that is output infinitely often at process p. Hence, by appropriately scheduling the queries to the failure detector X, we can concentrate on executions in which the failure detector output is constant at each process. Furthermore, we only consider failure patterns in which all faulty processes fail initially, e.g., before taking any step in the emulation algorithm.

Each such execution $exec$ can be associated with a word $x_{exec} \in \Sigma^*$, namely the word formed by the failure detector constant outputs at each correct process. More precisely, the rth symbol of x_{exec} is the (constant) output of the failure detector X at the rth correct process, where processes are ordered by increasing ids. By considering executions with increasing sets of correct processes, we obtain a sequence $x = x_1, x_2, \ldots$ of words of Σ^*. If the system is sufficiently large and, thus, the induced sequence x of words in Σ^* is sufficiently long, x is good by The Length function Theorem. Hence, we are able to exhibit two words $x_{i_1}, x_{i_2}, i_1 < i_2$ where x_{i_1} is a sub-word of x_{i_2}. By construction, these words represent in fact the outputs of X at the correct processes in two executions $exec_1$ and $exec_2$ respectively with two different sets of correct processes.

Hence, in $exec_1$ and $exec_2$, two sets of correct processes of the same size (i_1) get the same output of X, although the failure patterns differ. This is, however, insufficient to conclude that $exec_1$ and $exec_2$ are indistinguishable from the perspective of some processes. Indeed, a common symbol in x_1 and x_2 may be output in $exec_1$ and $exec_2$ by processes with distinct ids. We resolve this issue by leveraging Ramsey's Theorem. We show that in a sufficiently large system, there is a subset S of processes of size strictly larger than L_{Σ^*} for which the outputs of X are essentially id-oblivious: sets of correct processes in S of the same size are provided with the same failure-detector outputs.

In more detail, for any set of processes C, let $\mathcal{F}_C$ denote the failure pattern in which the set of correct processes is C and every faulty process crashes at time 0. Let $L = L_{\Sigma^*} + 1$, where L_{Σ^*} is the bound in Corollary 1. Provided that the total number of processes is large enough, we show that there exists a sequence $x = x_1, \ldots, x_L$ of words of Σ^* such that $|x_i| = i$ for every $i, 1 \leq i \leq L$ with the following property. For every i-subset $C \subseteq S$, $1 \leq i \leq L$, there is a failure detector history in $X(\mathcal{F}_C)$ in which for each r, $1 \leq r \leq i$ the failure detector outputs infinitely often the rth symbol of x_i to the rth process (where the processes are ordered by increasing ids).

By construction, sequence x is good and, thus, in some executions $exex_1$ and $exec_2$ with failure patterns $\mathcal{F}_{C_1}$ and $\mathcal{F}_{C_2}$, respectively, where $C_1 \subsetneq C_2$, processes in C_1 obtain the same information about failures. But the given emulation of P in $exec_1$ should indicate eventually, at some time τ, that some process in $C_2 \setminus C_1$ is faulty. Now by delaying all messages of processes in $C_2 \setminus C_1$ in execution $exec_2$ until after τ, we get that $exec_1$ and $exec_2$ are indistinguishable to C_1 up to time τ and, thus, in $exec_2$, some correct process is suspected—a contradiction.

4 Perfect Failure Detection with Quasi-constant #bits per Process

In this section, we show that there exists a failure detector emulating the perfect failure detector P that outputs values whose range depends on the size of the system, but increases extremely slowly with that size.

Theorem 4. *There exists a failure detector equivalent to P that, in any n-process system, outputs $\lceil \log \alpha(n) \rceil + 1$ bits at each process, where $\alpha : \mathbb{N} \rightarrow \mathbb{N}$ is a function that grows as least as slowly as the inverse Ackermann function.*

The rest of the section is dedicated to the proof of Theorem 4. A key ingredient to achieve failure detection with such a small amount of output values at each process is the notion of *distributed encoding of the integers*, recently introduced in [6]. Let Σ denote a finite or infinite alphabet of symbols. Recall from Sect. 3 that a word w over Σ is a finite sequence of symbols of Σ, and the length of w, i.e., the number of symbols in w, is denoted by $|w|$. Σ^* denotes the set of words of Σ, and a word $u = u_1, \ldots, u_k$ is a sub-word of word $v = v_1, \ldots, v_\ell$, denoted by $u =_* v$ if and only if $k \leq \ell$ and there exists a strictly increasing mapping $m : [1, k] \rightarrow [1, \ell]$ such that $u_i = v_{m(i)}$, for every i, $1 \leq i \leq k$. u is said to be a *strict sub-word* of v if $u =_* v$ and $|u| < |v|$.

Definition 1 ([6]). A *distributed encoding of the integers* is a pair (Σ, f) where Σ is a possibly infinite alphabet and $f : \Sigma^* \rightarrow \{\text{true}, \text{false}\}$ is a function such that, for every integer $n \geq 1$, there exists a word $w = w_1, \ldots, w_n \in \Sigma^n$ satisfying $f(w) = \text{true}$ and $f(w') = \text{false}$ for every strict sub-word $w' \in \Sigma^*$ of w. The word w is called the *code* of n, denoted by $\mathsf{code}(n)$.

A trivial example of a distributed encoding consists in setting $\Sigma = \mathbb{N}$, and encoding every integer n with the word $n, \ldots, n$ of length n. For any $s \in \mathbb{N}^*$, the function f returns true on input s if $s = |s|, \ldots, |s|$, and false otherwise. To encode the first n integers, this encoding uses words in an alphabet of n symbols, each symbols being encoded on $O(\log n)$ bits. We are interested in parsimonious distributed encodings of the integers, i.e., encodings that use fewer than $\log n$ bits to encode the first n integers. Given a distributed encoding $E = (\Sigma, f)$, and $n \geq 1$, let $\Sigma_n \subseteq \Sigma$ denote the set of all symbols used in the code of at least one integer in $[1, n]$. More precisely, for every $u \in \Sigma$, $u \in \Sigma_n$ if and only if u is a symbol appearing in $\mathsf{code}(k)$ for some $1 \leq k \leq n$. We get that E uses symbols encoded on $O(\log |\Sigma_n|)$ bits to encode the first n integers.

Theorem 5 ([6]). *There exists a distributed encoding of the integers (Σ, f) such that, for every integer $n \geq 1$, $|\Sigma_n| \leq \alpha(n)$ where $\alpha : \mathbb{N} \rightarrow \mathbb{N}$ grows as least as slowly as the inverse-Ackermann function.*

We now show how to use distributed encoding of the integer to encode a perfect failure detector. Let (Σ, f) be a distributed encoding of the integers. We define a failure detector, called *micro-perfect*, and denoted by μP, induced by (Σ, f). We then show that μP is equivalent to the perfect failure detector P.

That is, for any distributed encoding (Σ, f), there is a protocol that emulates P in any environment whenever the failure detector μP induced by (Σ, f) is available, and, conversely, there is a protocol that emulates μP in any environment whenever the failure detector P is available. Combining these two results with Theorem 5 yields Theorem 4.

The failure detector μP. Let (Σ, f) be a distributed encoding of the integers. An instance of the failure detector μP is built on top of each such encoding. Given (Σ, f), the range of μP is Σ. We denote by w_i^τ the output $H(p_i, \tau)$ of a failure detector history for μP at time τ at process p_i. Let w^τ denotes the output sequence of the failure detector at time τ at the processes that have not crashed by time τ, ordered by processes IDs. More formally, $w^\tau = w_{j_1}^\tau, w_{j_2}^\tau, \ldots, w_{j_k}^\tau$ where $\{p_{j_1}, \ldots, p_{j_k}\} = \Pi \setminus \mathcal{F}(\tau)$, and $\mathsf{id}(p_{j_1}) < \ldots < \mathsf{id}(p_{j_k})$. For every failure pattern $\mathcal{F}$, a failure detector history H belongs to $\mu P(\mathcal{F})$ if and only if there exists $\ell \in [1, n]$ (recall that n is the number of processes) for which

- there exist $a_i \in \mathbb{N}$ for $i = 1, \ldots, \ell$, with $1 \leq a_\ell < a_{\ell-1} < \ldots < a_2 < a_1 \leq n$;
- there exist $\tau_i \in \mathbb{N}$ for $i = 0, \ldots, \ell$, with $0 = \tau_0 < \tau_1 < \ldots < \tau_\ell = +\infty$

such that, for every i with $1 \leq i \leq \ell$, and for every τ, τ' with $\tau_{i-1} \leq \tau, \tau' < \tau_i$, the four following conditions hold:

(C1) $w_j^\tau = w_j^{\tau'}$ for every p_j, i.e., the output of the failure detector does not change between τ_{i-1} and τ_i;
(C2) $w^\tau =_* \mathsf{code}(a_i)$, i.e., the word formed by the outputs of the failure detector at each process that has not crashed by time τ is a sub-word of the code of a_i;
(C3) $a_i \geq n - |\mathcal{F}(\tau)|$, i.e., a_i is an upper bound on the number of non-faulty processes during $[\tau_{i-1}, \tau_i)$;
(C4) $a_\ell = |\mathsf{correct}(\mathcal{F})|$, i.e., a_ℓ is the number of correct processes.

Let us consider some time τ, and let $k = |\Pi \setminus \mathcal{F}(\tau)|$ denote the number of processes that have not crashed by time τ. By concatenating the failure detector outputs of the non-crashed processes (ordered by process IDs), we obtain a word $w^\tau \in \Sigma^k$. The failure detector μP guarantees that this word is either the distributed code of the current number k of non-crashed processes, or a sub-word of the distributed code of some integer $k' > k$. Moreover, eventually, μP outputs the distributed code of the number of correct processes.

Failure detector μP *can emulate the perfect failure detector* P. Protocol 1 emulates the perfect failure detector P using μP, in any environment.

Each time a query to P occurs, the protocol strives to identify a set of processes that (1) contains every correct process and (2) does not contain the processes that have failed prior to the beginning of the query. Given such a set S, $\Pi \setminus S$ is a valid output for P (line 4), as it does not contain any correct process (Accuracy), and, if the query starts after every faulty process has failed, $\Pi \setminus S$ is exactly the set of faulty processes (Completeness).

Protocol 1. Emulation of P using μP induced by (Σ, f). Code of Process p_i.

1: **function** P-QUERY()
2: **for all** $S \subseteq \Pi : p_i \in S$ **do** launch thread th_S computing CHECK(S) **end for**
3: **wait until** $\exists S$: th_S terminates; **stop** all other threads $\mathsf{th}_{S'}$ for $S' \neq S$
4: **return** $\Pi \setminus S$
5: **function** CHECK(S)
6: $r \leftarrow 0$; $count \leftarrow 0$
7: **repeat**
8: $r \leftarrow r + 1$; **send** $query(S, r)$ **to** every $p_j \in S$
9: **wait until** $resp((S, r), w_j)$ has been received from every $p_j \in S$
10: $w \leftarrow w_{j_1}, \ldots, w_{j_s}$ where $S = \{p_{j_1}, \ldots, p_{j_s}\}$ and $\mathsf{id}(p_{j_1}) < \ldots < \mathsf{id}(p_{j_s})$
11: **if** $f(w) =$ true **then** $count \leftarrow count + 1$ **end if**
12: **until** $count = n$
13: **when** $query(S, r)$ **is received from** p_j **do**
14: $w_i \leftarrow \mu P$-QUERY(); **send** $resp((S, r), w_i)$ to p_j

When P-QUERY() is invoked by some process p_i, 2^{n-1} threads are launched (line 2), one for each subset of Π containing p_i. Thread th_S associated to set S consists in a **repeat** loop (lines 7–12), each iteration of which aiming at collecting the outputs of the underlying failure detector μP at the processes of S. Each iteration is identified by a round number r[3]. In iteration r, *query* messages are first sent to every process in S (line 8), and then p_i waits for a matching *response* message[4] from each process in S (line 9). Iteration r may never ends if some processes of S fail. Nevertheless, for at least one set S, namely the set of correct processes, every iteration of the associated thread th_S terminates.

Each of the *response* messages received by p_i contains the output w_j of μP at its sender p_j when the message is sent (line 14). Assuming that *response* have been received from each process $p_j \in S$, let w be the word obtained by concatenating the outputs of μP in these messages, ordered by process id (line 10). Recall that a valid history of failure detector μP can be divided into ℓ *epochs* $e_1 = [0, \tau_1), e_2 = [\tau_1, \tau_2), \ldots, e_\ell = [\tau_{\ell-1}, +\infty)$, for some $\ell \leq n$. In each epoch $e_k, 1 \leq k \leq \ell$, the output of μP at each process does not change (cf. **(C1)**) and satisfy conditions **(C1)**–**(C4)** of the definition.

Let us assume that iteration r entirely fits within epoch e_k for some $k, 1 \leq k \leq \ell$. That is, every message *query* or *response* of that iteration is sent during e_k. Thus, by condition **(C2)**, w is a sub-word of $\mathsf{code}(a_k)$, i.e., the encoding of the integer a_k associated with epoch e_k by the distributed code (Σ, f). By using the function f, it can be determined whether $w = \mathsf{code}(a_k)$ or not. Indeed, for every proper sub-word w' of $\mathsf{code}(a_k)$, $f(w') =$ false and $f(\mathsf{code}(a_k)) =$ true (cf. Definition 1). Moreover, integer a_k is an upper bound on the number of alive processes in epoch e_k (cf. **(C3)**). Therefore, if $f(w) =$ true, then $w = \mathsf{code}(a_k)$, and, since $|w| = |S|$, we get $|S| = a_k$. Since all processes in S have not failed

[3] Round numbers may be omitted, we keep them to simplify the proof of the protocol.

[4] *query* and *response* messages are implicitly tagged in order not to confuse messages sent during different invocations of P-QUERY().

at the beginning of e_k (as each of them has sent a *response* in that interval), it follows that every process not in S has failed. Furthermore, if $k = \ell$, then a_ℓ is the number of correct processes (cf. **(C4)**), and thus in that case $\Pi \setminus S$ is the complete set of faulty processes. To summarize, if the word w collecting during iteration r satisfies $f(w) =$ true, and iteration r entirely fits within an epoch, then $\Pi \setminus S$ is a valid output of P.

Unfortunately, it may be the case that an iteration terminates while not fitting entirely within an epoch. The word w collected during that iteration may contain values output by the failure detector μP in distinct epochs. It is thus no longer guarantied that w is a sub-word of a valid code, and, from the fact that $f(w) =$ true, it can no longer be concluded that $\Pi \setminus S$ is a valid output of P. Recall however that the ℓ epochs are consecutive, they span the whole time range (last epoch e_ℓ never ends), and there are at most n of them. Hence, if n iterations terminate, at least one of these iterations fits entirely in an epoch. In thread th_S, the variable *count* enumerate the number of iterations that terminate with an associated word w such that $f(w) =$ true (cf. line 11). When this counter reaches the value n, at least one successful iteration fitting entirely in an epoch has occurred, and $\Pi \setminus S$ can therefore be returned as a valid result of a query to P (cf. lines 3–4).

Failure detector P can emulate the failure detector μP. Failure detectors P and μP are in fact equivalent. Protocol 2 emulates μP using the perfect failure detector P, in any environment.

Protocol 2. Emulation of μP induced by (Σ, f) using P. Code of Process p_i.

1: **init** $\mathsf{alive} \leftarrow \{p_1, \ldots, p_n\}$; $r \leftarrow 0$
2: **function** μP-QUERY()
3:     **repeat**
4:         $r \leftarrow r + 1$; $S \leftarrow P$-QUERY(); $\mathsf{alive} \leftarrow \mathsf{alive} \setminus S$
5:         **send** *query*(r, alive) **to** all other processes
6:         **repeat** $S \leftarrow P$-QUERY()
7:         **until** *response*(r, a_j) has been received from every $p_j \in \Pi \setminus S$
8:         $\mathsf{rec} \leftarrow$ set of all received sets a_j
9:     **until** there exists $a \subseteq \Pi$ such that $\mathsf{rec} = \{a\}$
10:     $k \leftarrow$ rank of $\mathsf{id}(p_i)$ in a; $w_i \leftarrow k$th symbol of $\mathsf{code}(|a|)$
11:     **return** w_i
12: **when** *query*(r, a) **is received from** p_j **do**
13:     $S \leftarrow P$-QUERY(); $\mathsf{alive} \leftarrow (\mathsf{alive} \cap a) \setminus S$; **send** *response*$(r, \mathsf{alive})$ **to** p_j

Proof of Theorem 4. By Theorem 5 there exists a distributed encoding of the integers (Σ, f) where $|\Sigma_n| \leq \alpha(n)$, for some $\alpha : \mathbb{N} \to \mathbb{N}$ growing at least as slowly as the inverse Ackermann function. That is, for any n, each symbol in the code of n is encoded on $\lceil \log \alpha(n) \rceil + 1$ bits. Consider failure detector μP induced by the distributed encoding (Σ, f). In an n-process system, any output of this failure detector is a symbol in Σ that is part of the code of some integer

$n' \leq n$. Hence, the output of μP can be encoded on $\lceil \log \alpha(n) \rceil + 1$ bits at each process. Moreover it follows from the correctness of Protocols 1 and 2 that μP is equivalent to the perfect failure detector P. □

References

1. Byron Cook, A.R., Podelski, A.: Proving program termination. Commun. ACM **54**(5), 88–98 (2011)
2. Chandra, T.D., Hadzilacos, V., Toueg, S.: The weakest failure detector for solving consensus. J. ACM **43**(4), 685–722 (1996)
3. Chandra, T.D., Toueg, S.: Unreliable failure detectors for reliable distributed systems. J. ACM **43**(2), 225–267 (1996)
4. Delporte-Gallet, C., Fauconnier, H., Toueg, S.: The minimum information about failures for solving non-local tasks in message-passing systems. Distrib. Comput. **24**(5), 255–269 (2011)
5. Dubois, S., Guerraoui, R., Kuznetsov, P., Petit, F., Sens, P.: The weakest failure detector for eventual consistency. In: ACM Symposium on Principles of Distributed Computing (PODC), pp. 375–384 (2015)
6. Fraigniaud, P., Rajsbaum, S., Travers, C.: Minimizing the number of opinions for fault-tolerant distributed decision using well-quasi orderings. In: Kranakis, E., Navarro, G., Chávez, E. (eds.) LATIN 2016. LNCS, vol. 9644, pp. 497–508. Springer, Heidelberg (2016). doi:10.1007/978-3-662-49529-2_37
7. Fraigniaud, P., Rajsbaum, S., Travers, C., Kuznetsov, P., Rieutord, T.: Perfect failure detection with very few bits. Technical report Hal-01365304, LaBRI (2016). https://hal.inria.fr/hal-01365304
8. Freiling, F.C., Guerraoui, R., Kuznetsov, P.: The failure detector abstraction. ACM Comput. Surv. **43**(2), 9 (2011)
9. Guerraoui, R.: Non-blocking atomic commit in asynchronous distributed systems with failure detectors. Distrib. Comput. **15**(1), 17–25 (2002)
10. Haase, C., Schmitz, S., Schnoebelen, P.: The power of priority channel systems. Logical Meth. Comput. Sci. **10**(4) (2014)
11. Higman, G.: Ordering by divisibility in abstract algebras. In: Proceedings of the London Mathematical Society, vol. 3(2), pp. 326–336 (1952)
12. Jayanti, P., Toueg, S.: Every problem has a weakest failure detector. In: 27th ACM Symposium on Principles of Distributed Computing (PODC), pp. 75–84 (2008)
13. Kruskal, J.B.: The theory of well-quasi-ordering: a frequently discovered concept. J. Comb. Theory Ser. A **13**(3), 297–305 (1972)
14. Löb, M.H., Wainer, S.S.: Hierarchies of number theoretic functions. I Arch. Math. Logic **13**, 39–51 (1970)
15. Milner, E.: Basic WQO- and BQO-theory. In: Graphs and Order, The Role of Graphs in the Theory of Ordered Sets and Its Applications. NATO ASI Series, pp. 487–502 (1985)
16. Mostéfaoui, A., Rajsbaum, S., Raynal, M., Travers, C.: The combined power of conditions and information on failures to solve asynchronous set agreement. SIAM J. Comput. **38**(4), 1574–1601 (2008)
17. Mostéfaoui, A., Rajsbaum, S., Raynal, M., Travers, C.: On the computability power and the robustness of set agreement-oriented failure detector classes. Distrib. Comput. **21**(3), 201–222 (2008)

18. Mostéfaoui, A., Raynal, M.: Leader-based consensus. Parallel Process. Lett. **11**(1), 95–107 (2001)
19. Schmitz, S., Schnoebelen, P.: Algorithmic aspects of WQO theory. Technical report Hal-00727025, HAL (2013). https://cel.archives-ouvertes.fr/cel-00727025
20. Schmitz, S., Schnoebelen, P.: Multiply-recursive upper bounds with Higman's lemma. In: Aceto, L., Henzinger, M., Sgall, J. (eds.) ICALP 2011. LNCS, vol. 6756, pp. 441–452. Springer, Heidelberg (2011). doi:10.1007/978-3-642-22012-8_35
21. Turing, A.: Checking a large routine. In: Conference on High Speed Automatic Calculating Machines, pp. 67–69 (1949)

Snap-Stabilizing Tasks in Anonymous Networks

Emmanuel Godard(✉)

Aix-Marseille Université, CNRS, Centrale Marseille, LIF, Marseille, France
emmanuel.godard@lif.univ-mrs.fr

Abstract. We consider snap-stabilizing algorithms in anonymous networks. Self-stabilizing algorithms are well known fault tolerant algorithms: a self-stabilizing algorithm will eventually recover from arbitrary transient faults. On the other hand, an algorithm is snap-stabilizing if it can withstand arbitrary initial values and immediately satisfy its safety requirement. It is a subset of self-stabilizing algorithms. Distributed tasks that are solvable with self-stabilizing algorithms in anonymous networks have already been characterized by Boldi and Vigna in [BV02b].

In this paper, we show how the more demanding snap-stabilizing algorithms can be handled with standard tools for (not stabilizing) algorithms in anonymous networks. We give a characterization of which tasks are sovable by snap-stabilizing algorithms in anonymous networks. We also present a snap-stabilizing version of Mazurkiewicz' enumeration algorithm.

This work exposes, from a task-equivalence point of view, the complete correspondence between self or snap-stabilizing tasks and distributed tasks with various termination detection requirements.

1 Introduction

In the world of fault-tolerance, dsitributed tasks that admits self-stabilizing solutions have been long studied [Dol00]. An algorithm is self-stabilizing if, starting from arbitrary initial values in the registers used by the algorithm, it can eventually stabilize to a correct final value. In particular, when looking at some computed values, the algorithm can output incorrect values as long as it eventually outputs correct ones.

In contrast, an algorithm is snap-stabilizing if it can withstand arbitrary initial values and output only correct values [BDPV99]. Snap-stabilizing tasks form a subset of self-stabilizing tasks where the algorithm is required to retain computed values until it is "sure" that they are correct. Snap-stabilizing algorithms have really interesting properties, they can withstand arbitrary transient failures, while at the same time, improving on self-stabilizing algorithms about a key point: the stabilization moment is not unknown: when a response is given, it is correct.

We present here the first characterization of snap-stabilizing tasks on anonymous networks. Not only we are reusing techniques borrowed from the study of the non-stabilizing tasks in anonymous networks and show they apply also

B. Bonakdarpour and F. Petit (Eds.): SSS 2016, LNCS 10083, pp. 170–184, 2016.
DOI: 10.1007/978-3-319-49259-9_14

here, but we complete the correspondence between self/snap-stabilizing tasks and termination detection.

How does snap-stabilizing tasks differs from self-stabilizing tasks has not been considered so far to the best of our knowledge. Here we show that, on anonymous networks, there are tasks that admits self-stabilizing solutions but that have no snap-stabilizing ones. We show that the difference between self and snap stabilization is actually the same one gets with non-stabilizing tasks when considering implicit vs explicit termination.

1.1 Our Result

We give the first characterization of the computability of snap-stabilization. In order to show that it complements known results about self-stabilizing and non self-stabilizing tasks in anonymous networks, we recall the previous equivalence established by Boldi and Vigna. Solving a task means solving a given specification linking inputs labels to output labels for a given set of graphs. Informally an algorithm has implicit termination if it is possible to write numerous time a (tentative) solution in the dedicated OUT register. An algorithm has explicit termination when it is possible to write in OUT only once. Whenever the OUT register is defined, this means that (locally) the algorithm has terminated its computation.

Theorem 1 (Boldi and Vigna [BV01,BV02b]**).** *A task is solvable on a family of anonymous networks by a self-stabilizing algorithm if and only if it is solvable with implicit termination.*

The "only if" part being obvious, the merit of [BV02b] is to show that there is a universal algorithm to solve tasks (that are at all solvable) by a self-stabilizing algorithm on anonymous networks, and that the condition for solvability (informally speaking: stability of the specification by lifting) is exactly the one required by implicit termination. In other words, once a problem is solvable with implicit termination, it admits a reliable self-stabilizing solution without any additional condition.

Theorem 2 (this paper). *A task is solvable on a family of anonymous networks by a snap-stabilizing algorithm if and only if it is solvable with explicit termination.*

As in the Boldi and Vigna result, the "only if" part is immediate. We therefore focus on establishing the "if" part. So the main contribution of this paper is a universal snap-stabilizing algorithm that solves the task at hand if this task satisfies the condition for being solvable by an algorithm with explicit termination.

This condition was first given by [BV01]. In the presentation we will use here, it was also presented in [CGM08]. We first prove our results for terminating tasks in the asynchronous model, then we show how to extend the technique for long lived tasks in the synchronous model (for simplicity of exposition).

The presentation follow the order of [BV02b]. Instead of the view algorithm, we use Mazurkiewicz' algorithm. A variation of this algorithm was proved to be self-stabilizing in [God02], in Mazurkiewicz' model, a model that offers strong synchronization between neighbours. We present here a version for the state model.

1.2 Related Work

Snap-stabilizing algorithms were introduced in [BDPV99]. Since this definition is very general, we choose here to formally distinguish, as in the non-stabilizing case, snap-stabilization from self-stabilization: we consider only specification where the OUT register has to be readily correct when defined. In [CDV09], a general transformation technique is given to obtain simple snap-stabilizing algorithms. In [CDV09], the authors expose a sufficient condition for snap-stabilizing algorithm equivalence. In this paper, we prove the task equivalence between snap-stabilization and explicit termination. The complexity of the respective solutions might not be equivalent.

In [AD14], a probabilistic correction condition is proposed for snap-stabilizing algorithms. This condition has the interest that it defines, in a sound way, what is a Las Vegas self-stabilizing algorithm.

On the distributed computability side, the first complete characterization of tasks that admits self-stabilizing algorithms has been given in [BV02b]. Here, we use a mix of different techniques, some of which were first introduced in [CGM08].

There is an unpublished version of Mazurkiewicz' algorithm in the communication model of this paper but without transient faults in [Cha06, chap. 4], where the model is coined the "cellular model". One of the main advantage of Mazurkiewicz' algorithm is that it is always stabilizing, contrary to the view algorithm of [BV02b] where it is necessary to know or derive an estimate of the size to make it stabilizing.

2 Definitions and Notations

2.1 Basic Definition for Computability

A network is represented by a graph or digraph where vertices corresponds to nodes and edges or arcs corresponds to (possibly asymmetric) communication links. We consider a set of labels Λ. Labels are used to represent the local states of parts of the communication network.

So we consider labelled graphs in the general sense. Nodes can be labelled (internal state of the nodes), arcs can be labelled (messages in transit, port numbering). We will use $\mathbf{G}$ to denote a (di)graph with all its associated labels. Since the input labels can be encoded in the labels, we consider all labelled graphs as the possible inputs for distributed algorithms. The set of all labelled graphs is denoted $\mathcal{G}$.

Given a network $\mathbf{G} \in \mathcal{G}$ and a vertex v in $\mathbf{G}$, we assume that the state of v during the execution of any algorithm is of the form $(\text{MEM}(v), \text{OUT}(v))$: $\text{MEM}(v)$ is the memory of v, $\text{OUT}(v)$ will contain its output value, i.e. the result of the computation at v. When OUT is not defined, it contains the value $\perp$.

A distributed algorithm is an algorithm that is replicated on every node and operates on the local state of the node v by way of communication with the neighbours of v. The communication here is done in the *shared variables* model, that is also called the *state* model. A distributed algorithm is a set of rules (a pair of precondition and command) that describe how a processor has to change its current state (the command) according to the state of *all its neighbors* (the precondition or guard). We say that a rule R is activable at a processor v if the neighborhood of v satisfies the precondition of R. In this case, the vertex v is also said to be activable. If a rule R is activable in v, an atomic move for v consists of reading the states of all its neighbors, computing a new value of its state according to the command of R, and writing this value to the local memory MEM. An execution is a sequence of such moves. If more than one rule is activable at a node, one is chosen non-deterministically. Of course, it is possible to have priorities for rules, and to discard this non-determinism. If only one such move can occur at a time, this is a *central daemon* execution. If any combination of such moves can occur, this is an *asynchronous daemon* execution. If all possible moves occur, this is the *synchronous daemon* execution. We consider here the asynchronous daemon (which contains the synchronous daemon).

A vertex-relabelling relation is a relation between labelled graphs where the underlying graphs are identical. The evolution of the global system can be seen as a sequence of relabelling steps where only local part of the labels of the graphs are modified, according to rules prescribe by the algorithm and the kind of daemon that is considered. Under a given execution ρ, the global configuration of the system is described by the sequence of labelled graphs $(\mathbf{G}, \text{MEM}_1), (\mathbf{G}, \text{MEM}_2), \cdots$; this is abbreviated in $(\mathbf{G}_1, \mathbf{G}_2, \cdots)$ for convenience. Such a sequence is an execution of algorithm ALGO. If the sequence is finite, that is if there is a step where no rule is applicable, we say that the execution has terminated and denote by $\mathbf{G}_f$ the labelled graph with component OUT, $\mathbf{G}_f = (\mathbf{G}, \text{OUT})$, it is the *terminal state* of the execution.

We formally define now what is a terminating distributed problem.

Definition 3. *A* terminating distributed task *is a couple* $(\mathcal{F}, S)$ *where* $\mathcal{F} \subset \mathcal{G}$ *is a family of labelled graphs and* S *is a vertex-relabelling relation.*

The *specification* S is a general way to describe our distributed problem in terms of relation between inputs and outputs. This description is independent of the domain $\mathcal{F}$ where we want to solve our problem.

Definition 4. *Given* $\mathbf{G} \in \mathcal{G}$*, an algorithm* ALGO *solves* S *on* $\mathbf{G}$ *if for any execution:*

stabilization *there is a terminal state* $\mathbf{G}_f$*;*
decision OUT_v *is written exactly once for any vertex* v*;*
correction $\mathbf{G} S \mathbf{G}_f$*.*

Definition 5. *The task* $(S, \mathcal{F})$ *is solvable if there exists an algorithm* ALGO *such that* ALGO *solves* S *for all* $\mathbf{G} \in \mathcal{F}$.

When, besides **correction**, the **stabilization** property is the only property, we talk about *implicit termination* (or message termination [Tel00]). When we have both **stabilization** and **decision**, we talk about *explicit termination.* Those are the main termination mode that are classically considered in distributed algorithms. See also [CGM08, GMT10] for other types of termination.

2.2 Self- and Snap-Stabilization

Informally, a distributed algorithm is said to be self-stabilizing if an execution starting from any arbitrary global state has a suffix belonging to the set of legitimate states. A distributed algorithm is snap-stabilizing if an execution starting from any arbitrary global state has *all its causal suffixes* belonging to the set of legitimate states. Note that when we consider terminating tasks, the set of legitimate states corresponds simply to the set of $S-$admissible outputs for the given input graph, that is the set $\{\mathbf{G}' \mid \mathbf{G}S\mathbf{G}'\}$.

In anonymous networks, self-stabilization, on the task level, relates to implicit termination whereas snap-stabilization relates to explicit termination. To emphasize this relation, we first define snap-stabilization for terminating tasks. Then we will proceed to long lived ones.

Given the registers can be corrupted in any way, there would be no way to compute snap-stabilizing task if there weren't a restriction on the outputs to be considered. Formally, the output values are to be correct only when they have been causally influenced by a special "request" event. This event is an event exterior to the algorithm and occurs *after* the end of the faults that led to arbitrary incorrect values.

The setting is the following, given an arbitrary state of the system, one or more external actions, *the requests*, are applied at some nodes $U \subset V$. Then the system evolves according to the daemon and the algorithm: at one step, some nodes (or only one in the central daemon case) are activable and activated (their actions are processed). Given a sequence $A_1, A_2, \cdots$ of activated nodes, an execution ρ is the sequence $\mathbf{G} = \mathbf{G}_0, \mathbf{G}_1, \mathbf{G}_2...$ of labelled obtained by applying to $\mathbf{G}_{i-1}$ the actions for the nodes of A_i.

A node v is *causally influenced* by U if there exists a path $u_0, u_1, \cdots, u_k$ such that $u_0 \in U$, and there exists a strictly increasing function $\sigma : \mathbb{N} \longrightarrow \mathbb{N}$ $\forall i \geq 1, u_i \in A_{\sigma(i)}$ and $u_k = v$. Given $i \in \mathbb{N}$, we define V_i to be the set of vertices that have been causally influenced at step i, that is if $\sigma(k) \leq i$. Given a set U of requested processes, $\mathcal{C}(U)$ is the set of causally influenced processed by processes of U. We define $\mathcal{C}_i(\mathbf{G}) = \mathbf{G}_{|V_i}$ to be the subgraph of $\mathbf{G}_i$ that is induced by V_i.

Definition 6. *An algorithm* ALGO *is snap-stabilizing to the terminating task* $(S, \mathcal{F})$ *on* $\mathbf{G} \in \mathcal{F}$ *if, starting from any global configuration,*

stabilization *there is a terminal state* G_f*;*
causal decision OUT_v *is written exactly once when* v *has been causally influenced;*
$S-$**correction** GSG_f.

Synchronous Daemon for Long Lived Tasks. The specification of a long lived tasks is given by a set of infinite sequences $\mathcal{S} = \{(S_1, S_2, \cdots)\}$, where the S_i are relabelling relations as in the terminating case. Given a set P of requested processes, $\mathcal{C}^{sync}(P)$ is the set of causally influenced processed by processes of P.

Definition 7. *Given a set* U *of requested processes, an algorithm* ALGO snap-stabilizes *to* $\mathcal{S}$ *against the synchronous daemon if* $\mathbf{G}_{\mathrm{OUT}|\mathcal{C}^{sync}(P)} \in \mathcal{S}$.

3 Terminating Tasks

We start by considering snap-stabilizing terminating tasks. This is where it is easier to show how the general techniques from explicitly terminating non-stabilizing tasks can be extended to the snap-stabilizing case as well.

3.1 Digraphs and Fibrations

Definitions. In the following, we give the definitions for the tools introduced by Boldi and Vigna, and extensively studied in [BV02a], to characterize self-stabilizing tasks in [BV02b]. To introduce the main tool, that is *fibrations*, we need to consider directed graphs (or digraphs) with multiple arcs and self-loops. A *digraph* $D = (V(D), A(D))$ is defined by a set $V(D)$ of vertices and a set $A(D)$ of arcs. Given an arc a, we say that a is adjacent to the vertices $s(a)$ and $t(a)$, the source and target of the arc. An undirected graph G corresponds to the digraph $Dir(G)$ obtained by replacing all edges of G by the two corresponding arcs. In the following, we will not distinguish G and $Dir(G)$ when the context permits. The family of all digraphs with multiple arcs and self-loops is denoted $\mathcal{D}$.

A dipath π of length p from u to v in D is a sequence of arcs $a_1, a_2, \cdots, a_p$ such that $s(a_1) = u, t(a_p) = v$ and for all i, $s(a_{i+1}) = t(a_i)$. A digraph is strongly connected if there is a path between all pairs of vertices. We assume all digraphs to be strongly connected. Note that $\mathcal{G}$ is embedded in $\mathcal{D}$ via dir. Moreover we only consider undirected networks, i.e. symmetric digraphs, however, the reader shall note that they can be fibrations of general digraphs. Labelled digraphs will be designated by bold letters like $\mathbf{D}$, $\mathbf{G}$, $\mathbf{H}$...

A *homomorphism* γ between the digraphs D and D' is a mapping $\gamma : V(D) \cup A(D) \longrightarrow V(D') \cup A(D')$ such that for each $a \in A(D)$, $\gamma(s(a)) = s(\gamma(a))$ and $\gamma(t(a)) = t(\gamma(a))$. A homomorphism $\gamma : V(D) \cup A(D) \longrightarrow V(D') \cup A(D')$ is an *isomorphism* if γ is bijective. Homomorphisms will also preserve labelling.

In a digraph $\mathbf{G}$, given $v_0 \in V(\mathbf{G})$ and $r \in \mathbb{N}$, we denote by $B^-_{\mathbf{G}}(v_0, r)$ the in-ball of center v_0 and radius r, that is the set of vertices v and arcs a such that there is a dipath of length at most r from v to v_0.

Fibrations and Quasi-Fibrations. The notion of fibrations have been proved fundamental for the study of distributed tasks in anonymous networks in the work of Boldi and Vigna [BV02b], definitions and main properties are presented in [BV02a]. This notion enables to express the "similarity" between two anonymous networks in the state model.

A digraph $\mathbf{D}$ is a fibration of a digraph $\mathbf{D}'$ via ϕ if ϕ is a homomorphism from $\mathbf{D}$ to $\mathbf{D}'$ such that each arc $a' \in A(\mathbf{D}')$ and for each vertex $v \in \phi^{-1}(t(a'))$ (resp. $v \in \phi^{-1}(s(a'))$), there exists a unique arc $a \in \phi^{-1}(a')$ such that $t(a) = v$ (resp. $s(a) = v$).

The following lemma shows the importance of fibrations when we deal with anonymous networks. This is the counterpart of the lifting lemma that Angluin gives for coverings of simple graphs [Ang80] and the proof can be found in [BCG+96,BV02b,CM07].

Lemma 8 (Lifting Lemma [BCG+96]). *If $\mathbf{D}$ is a fibration of $\mathbf{D}'$ via ϕ, then any execution of an algorithm* ALGO *on $\mathbf{D}$ can be lifted up to an execution on $\mathbf{D}$, such that at the end of the execution, for any $v \in V(\mathbf{D})$, v is in the same state* (MEM, OUT) *as $\phi(v)$.*

In the following, one also needs to express similarity between two digraphs up to a certain distance. The notion of quasi-coverings was introduced as a formal tool in [MMW97,GM02] for this purpose. The next definition is an adaptation of this tool to fibrations.

Definition 9. *Given digraphs $\mathbf{K}$ and $\mathbf{H}$, and integer r and $v \in V(\mathbf{K})$ and an homomorphism γ from $B^-_{\mathbf{K}}(v,r)$ to $\mathbf{H}$, $\mathbf{K}$ is a quasi-fibration of $\mathbf{H}$ of center v and radius r via γ if there exists a finite or infinite digraph $\mathbf{G}$ such that $\mathbf{G}$ is a fibration of $\mathbf{H}$ via a homomorphism ϕ and there exists $w \in V(\mathbf{G})$ and an isomorphism δ from $B^-_{\mathbf{K}}(v,r)$ to $B^-_{\mathbf{G}}(w,r)$ such that for any $x \in V(B^-_{\mathbf{K}}(v,r)) \cup A(B^-_{\mathbf{K}}(v,r)), \gamma(x) = \phi(\delta(x))$*

If a digraph $\mathbf{G}$ is a fibration of $\mathbf{H}$, then for any $v \in V(\mathbf{G})$ and for any $r \in \mathbb{N}$, $\mathbf{G}$ is a quasi-fibration of $\mathbf{H}$, of center v and of radius r. Reversely, if $\mathbf{K}$ is a quasi-fibration of $\mathbf{H}$ of radius r strictly greater than the diameter of $\mathbf{K}$, then $\mathbf{K}$ is a fibration of $\mathbf{H}$. The following lemma is the counterpart of the lifting lemma for quasi-fibrations.

Lemma 10 (Quasi-Lifting Lemma). *Consider a digraph $\mathbf{K}$ that is a quasi-fibration of $\mathbf{H}$ of center v and of radius r via γ. For any algorithm* ALGO, *after r rounds of the synchronous execution of an algorithm* ALGO *on $\mathbf{K}$, v is in the same state as $\gamma(v)$ after r rounds of the synchronous execution of* ALGO *on $\mathbf{H}$.*

3.2 Necessary Condition

It is obvious that the necessary condition of [CGM08] applies here, as well as its proof. We present the result briefly to make the paper self-contained.

We denote $\mathcal{D}_\bullet$ the disjoint union $\{(\mathbf{G}, v) \mid \mathbf{G} \in \mathcal{D}, v \in V(\mathbf{G})\}$. Given a family $\mathcal{F} \subset \mathcal{G}$, we denote by $\mathcal{F}_\bullet$ the set $\{(\mathbf{G}, v) \mid \mathbf{G} \in \mathcal{F}, v \in V(\mathbf{G})\}$. A function $f : \mathcal{D} \longrightarrow \cup\{\perp\}$ is an *output function* for a task $(S, \mathcal{F})$ if for each network $\mathbf{G} \in \mathcal{F}$ the labelling obtained by applying f on each node $v \in V(\mathbf{G})$ satisfies the specification S, that is $\mathbf{G}S(\mathbf{G}, \lambda)$ where $\forall v \in V(\mathbf{G})$, $\lambda(v) = f(\mathbf{G}, v)$.

In order to give our characterization, we need to formalize the following idea. When the neighbourhood at distance k of two processes v_1, v_2 in two digraphs $\mathbf{D}_1, \mathbf{D}_2$ cannot be distinguished (this is captured by the notion of quasi-fibrations and Lemma 10), and if v_1 computes its final value in k rounds, then v_2 computes the same final value in the same number of rounds.

Definition 11. *Given a function $r : \mathcal{D}_\bullet \longrightarrow \mathbb{N} \cup \{\infty\}$ and a function $f : \mathcal{D}_\bullet \longrightarrow \Lambda$, the function f is $r-$lifting closed if for all $\mathbf{K}, \mathbf{H} \in \mathcal{D}$ such that $\mathbf{K}$ is a quasi-fibration of $\mathbf{H}$, of center $v \in V(\mathbf{G})$ and of radius k via γ with $k \geq \min\{r(\mathbf{G}, v), r(\mathbf{H}, \gamma(v))\}$, then $f(\mathbf{G}, v) = f(\mathbf{H}, \gamma(v))$.*

In the previous definition, the value of $r(\mathbf{G}, v)$ can be understood as the number of rounds needed by v to compute *in the synchronous execution* its final value in $\mathbf{G}$.

We give now the characterization of terminating snap-stabilizing tasks. We give the proof of the necessary condition. The converse will be proved in the following section, by introducing a snap-stabilizing version of Mazurkiewicz' algorithm.

Theorem 12. *Let $t \in \mathbb{N} \cup \{\infty\}$. A terminating task $(S, \mathcal{F})$ is computable by a terminating snap-stabilizing algorithm if and only if there exists a function $r : \mathcal{D}_\bullet \longrightarrow \mathbb{N} \cup \{\infty\}$ and a function $f : \mathcal{D}_\bullet \longrightarrow \Lambda \cup \{\perp\}$ such that,*

12.i for all $(\mathbf{G}, v) \in \mathcal{D}_\bullet$, $r(\mathbf{G}, v) \neq \infty$ if and only if $f(\mathbf{G}, v) \neq \perp$;
12.ii f and r are $r - lifting$-closed;

Proof (of the necessary condition). Consider ALGO a distributed algorithm that snap-stabilizes to S on $\mathcal{F}$ in t rounds.

We construct r and f by considering a subset of the possible executions of ALGO. We consider the synchronous execution of ALGO on any digraph $\mathbf{G} \in \mathcal{D}$ with initial values *init*. For any $v \in V(\mathbf{G})$, if $\text{OUT}(v) = \perp$ during the whole execution, then we set $f(\mathbf{G}, v) = \perp$ and $r(\mathbf{G}, v) = \infty$. This is possible since it could be that $\mathcal{F} \subsetneq \mathcal{D}$. Let r_v be the first causal round after which $\text{OUT}(v) \neq \perp$; in this case, if $r_v \leq t$, we set $f(\mathbf{G}, v) = \text{OUT}(v)$ and $r(\mathbf{G}, v) = r_v$. If $t < r_v$, then we set $f(\mathbf{G}, v) = \perp$ and $r(\mathbf{G}, v) = \infty$. By construction 12.i is satisfied.

We also show that f is an output function and that f and r satisfy 12.ii. Consider two digraphs $\mathbf{K}$ and $\mathbf{H}$ such that $\mathbf{K}$ is a quasi-fibration of $\mathbf{H}$, of center $v_0 \in V(\mathbf{K})$ and of radius k via γ with $k \geq r_0 = \min\{r(\mathbf{G}, v_0), r(\mathbf{H}, \gamma(v_0))\}$. If $r_0 = \infty$, then $r(\mathbf{K}, v_0) = r(\mathbf{H}, \gamma(v_0)) = \infty$ and $f(\mathbf{G}, v_0) = f(\mathbf{H}, \gamma(v_0)) = \perp$.

Otherwise, from Lemma 10 (the initial labelling *init* is liftable), we know that after r_0 rounds, $\text{OUT}(v_0) = \text{OUT}(\gamma(v0))$. Thus $r_0 = r(\mathbf{G}, v_0) = r(\mathbf{H}, \gamma(v0))$ and $f(\mathbf{G}, v_0) = f(\mathbf{H}, \gamma(v_0))$. Consequently, f and r are $r-$lifting closed.

4 Main Algorithm

In this section, we present a general algorithm for which we use as parameter elements from the terminating task $(S, \mathcal{F})$ we are interested in, in order to obtain our sufficient condition. This algorithm is a combination of a snap-stabilizing enumeration algorithm, adapted from [God02] and a generalization of an algorithm of Szymanski, Shy and Prywes (the SSP algorithm for short) [SSP85].

The algorithm in [God02] is described in a different model, where each computation step involves some strong synchronization between adjacent processes. It is a self-stabilizing adaptation of an enumeration algorithm presented by Mazurkiewicz' in [Maz88]. The SSP algorithm enables to detect the global termination of an algorithm provided the processes know a bound on the diameter of the graph. The Mazurkiewicz-like algorithm always stabilizes on any network $\mathbf{G}$ and during its execution, each process v can reconstruct at some computation step i a digraph $\mathbf{G}_i(v)$ such that $\mathbf{G}$ is a quasi-fibration of $\mathbf{G}_i(v)$. However, this algorithm does not enable v to compute effectively the radius of this quasi-fibration. We use a generalization of the SSP algorithm to compute a lower bound on this radius, as it has already been done in Mazurkiewicz's model [GMT10] and in the message passing model [CGM08].

4.1 Modifying Mazurkiewicz' Enumeration Algorithm

An enumeration algorithm on a network $\mathbf{G}$ is a distributed algorithm such that the result of any computation is a labelling of the vertices that is a bijection from $V(\mathbf{G})$ to $\{1, 2, \cdots, |V(\mathbf{G})|\}$.

We give first a general description of the algorithm. Every vertex attempts to get its own name(which shall be an integer between 1 and $|V(\mathbf{G})|$, however here we would need more work to enforce this, however since this is not need for oour purpose, these technicalities will be skipped, see [God02]). A vertex chooses a name and broadcasts it together with its neighborhood all over the network. If a vertex u discovers the existence of another vertex v with the same name, then it compares its *local view*, i.e., the labelled in-ball of center u, with the *local view* of its rival v. If the local view of v is "stronger", then u chooses another name. Node u also chooses another name if its appears twice in the view of some other vertex as a result of a corrupted initial state. Each new name is broadcast again over the network. At the end of the computation it is not guaranteed that every node has a unique name, unless the graph is fibration minimal. However, all nodes with the same name will have the same local view, i.e., isomorphic labelled neighborhoods.

The crucial property of the algorithm is based on a total order on local views such that the "strength" of the local view of any vertex cannot decrease during the computation. To describe the local view we use the following notation: if v has degree d and its in-neighbors have names $n_1, \cdots, n_d$, with $n_1, \cdots, n_d$, then $\overline{N}(v)$, the local view, is the $d-$tuple $(n1, \cdots, n_d)$. Let T be the set of such ordered tuples. The alphabetic order defines a total order, $\prec$, on T. Vertices v are labelled by triples of the form $(n, \overline{N}, M)$ representing during the computation:

- $n(v) \in \mathbb{N}$ is the name of the vertex v,
- $\overline{N}(v) \in T$ is the latest view of v,
- $M(v) \subset \mathbb{N} \times T$ is the mailbox of v and contains all information received at this step of the computation.

We introduce other notations. We want to count the number of times a given name appear in a local view. For a local view $\overline{N}$, and $n \in \mathbb{N}$, we define $\delta_{\overline{N}}(n)$ to be the cardinality of n in the tuple $\overline{N}$. For a given view $\overline{N}$, we denote by $sub(\overline{N}, n, n')$ the copy of $\overline{N}$ where any occurrence of n is replaced by n'.

The algorithm is given in Fig. 1. The rules are given in the *priority order.*

The labeling function obtained at the end of a run ρ of Mazurkiewicz' algorithm is noted π_ρ. If v is a vertex of **G**, the couple $\pi_\rho(v)$ associated with v is denoted $(n_\rho(v), M_\rho(v))$. We also note the final local view of v by $N_\rho(v)$. For a given mailbox M and a given $n \in \mathbb{N}$, we note $\text{STRONG}_M(n)$ the local view

Enum1 : **Initialization**

Guard :
- $Request(v_0)$

Action :
- $n(v_0) := 0$,
- $\overline{N}(v_0) := N(v_0)$,
- $M(v_0) := \emptyset$,
- $a(v_0) := -1$.

Enum2 : **Diffusion rule**

Guard :
- There exists $v \in B(v_0)$ such that $M(v) \neq M(v_0)$.

or $(n(v_0), N(v_0)) \notin M(v_0)$,

or $\overline{N}(v_0) \neq N(v_0)$.

Action :
- $M(v_0) := \bigcup_{w \in B(v_0)} M(w) \cup \{(n(v_0), N(v_0))\}$.
- $\overline{N}(v_0) := N(v_0)$.
- $a(v_0) := -1$.

Enum3 : **Renaming rule**

Guard :
- For all $v \in B(v_0), M(v) = M(v_0)$.
- $(n(v_0) = 0)$ or $(n(v_0) > 0$ and there exists $(n(v_0), N) \in M(v_0)$ such that $((N(v_0) \prec N)))$.
- $n(v_0) > 0$ and $\exists (n_1, N_1) \in M(v_0)$ such that $\delta_{N_1}(n(v_0)) \geq 2$.

Action :
- $n(v_0) = 1 + \max\{n \in \mathbb{N} \mid (l, n, N) \in M(v_0)$ for some $l, N\}$.
- $M(v_0) = M(v_0) \cup \{(n(w), N(w)) | w \in B(v_0)\}$,
- $a(v_0) = -1$.

gSSPfix : **Fix gSSP counter**

Guard :
- If there exists $v \in B(v_0)$, $|a(v) - a(v_0)| \geq 2$ or $(M(v) \neq M(v_0)$ and $a(v_0) \neq -1)$

Action :
- $a(v_0) := -1$.

gSSP : **gSSP rule**

Guard :
- $\forall v \in B(v_0)$, $M(v) = M(v_0)$, $|a(v) - a(v_0)| \leq 1$ and $\neg\mathbb{P}(v_0)$

Action :
- $a(v_0) := 1 + \min\{a(v) \mid v \in B(v_0)\}$.

Decision : **Output rule**

Guard :
- For all $v \in B(v_0)$, $M(v) = M(v_0)$ and $\mathbb{P}(v_0)$

Action :
- $\text{OUT}(v_0) = f(\mathbf{K}(v_0), w(v_0))$

Fig. 1. Snap-stabilizing Mazurkiewicz' algorithm $\mathcal{M}_\mathbb{P}$, the parameter is the predicate $\mathbb{P}$

that dominates all $\overline{N}, (n, \overline{N}) \in M$ (i.e. $\overline{N} \prec \textsc{Strong}_M(n)$. Except for the first corrupted stages, $\textsc{Strong}_{M(v)}(n)$ is actually the "strongest local" view of n.

Theorem 13. *A run ρ of Mazurkiewicz' Enumeration Algorithm on $\mathbf{G}$ with any initial values finishes and computes a final labeling π_ρ verifying the following conditions for all vertices v, v' of $V(\mathbf{G})$:*

13.i $M_\rho(v) = M_\rho(v')$.
13.ii $\textsc{Strong}_{M_\rho(v')}(n_\rho(v)) = \overline{N}(v) = N_\rho(v)$.
13.iii $n_\rho(v) = n_\rho(v')$ *if and only if* $N_\rho(v) = N_\rho(v')$.

Proof. This is similar to the one in [God02].

First we explain how it is possible to extract the map of the minimum base. This is usually done by considering the graphs induced by the numbers and associated local views that have maximal views. However, here, due to the arbitrary initial failures, the mailbox should be cleaned up before use. It is possible to have some maximal $(n, \overline{N})$ but n does not actually exists on any v.

Now, each vertex shall compute locally the set of actual final names from the final mailbox M_ρ. We note $\mathbf{G}_\rho$ the graph defined by

$$V_\rho = \{n_\rho(v) | v \in V(\mathbf{G})\},$$
$$A_\rho = \{(n_\rho(v_1), n_\rho(v_2)) | (v_1, v_2) \in A(G)\}.$$

For a mailbox M and an integer n, we define the set $V^M(n)$ by induction.

$$V_0^M = \{n\},$$
$$V_{i+1}^M = V_i^M \cup \{t | \exists s\ V_i^M, \delta_{\textsc{Strong}_M(s)}(t) = 1\}.$$

If i_0 is such that $V_{i_0}^M = V_{i_0+1}^M$ then we define $V^M(n) = V_{i_0}^M$. Finally, we have,

Lemma 14 ([God02]). *For all $v \in V(\mathbf{G})$, $V^{M_\rho}(n_\rho(v)) = V_\rho$.*

By defining A^M by $\{(n_1, n_2) | n_1, n_2 \in V^M(n)$ and $\delta_{\textsc{Strong}_M(n_1)}(n_2) = 1\}$, we obtain a graph $\mathbf{G}_{M(v)} = (V^{M(v)}, A^{M(v)})$. We can not readily use $\mathbf{G}_{M(v)}$ since it could be that it is not in $\mathcal{F}$. We denote by $\mathbf{K}(v)$ the digraph that is in $\mathcal{F}$ and that is a quasi-fibration of $\mathbf{G}_{M(v)}$ of radius $a(v)$ and of center $w(v)$. This can be found by enumerating (locally) all graphs and vertices of $\mathcal{F}_\bullet$ until one is found. This semi-algorithm will terminate because of the following property.

Proposition 15. *Let P be the set of requesting processes. Let v that has been causally influenced by P, and such that $a(v) \geq 0$. The graph $\mathbf{G}$ is a quasi-fibration of $\mathbf{G}_{M(v)}$ of center v and radius $a(v)$.*

Proof. We add that every $w \in B(v, a(v))$ has been influenced to the statement and prove this new statement by induction on i, the number of rounds since P has received the requests.

At round 0, no request has been yet processed by Enum1, i.e. the set of influenced nodes is empty and the property holds trivially.

Assume the property holds at round i and consider v_0 a vertex that is activated at round $i+1$. We have to consider two cases, either v_0 was already influenced at round i or it is a newly influenced node.

If v_0 is a newly influenced node. The only rule of interest is gSSP because other rules are setting $a(v_0)$ to -1. But we show that v_0 cannot apply this rule. Indeed, assume $M(v_0) \neq \emptyset$, then, the causality path to v_0 starts in a root whose variables have been reset, and from which the causality chain of applications will propagate its new name. So $M(v_0)$ has to be updated to, at least, this name before beeing able to apply gSSP.

If v_0 has already been influenced then the induction statement applies at the previous round. Denote $a(v_0)$ the value of the counter at the end of round i and assume that for all $v \in N(v_0), a(v) = a(v_0)$. We prove that the statement holds for $a(v_0)+1$ at round $i+1$.

If $a(v_0) = 0$ then, by the same argument as in the previous case, the neighbours of v_0 have all been influenced and the statement holds with a radius 1.

If $a(v_0) > 0$ then the neighbours have been influenced by induction assumption. Moreover, every $v \in N(v_0)$ is the center of a quasi-fibration of radius $a(v_0)$. Therefore, v_0 is the center of a quasi-fibration of radius $a(v_0)+1$. Similarly, every $w \in B(v, a(v_0))$ has been influenced and the ball $B(v_0, a(v_0)+1)$ is totally influenced. The statement holds at round $i+1$.

The algorithm from Fig. 1 uses a special parameter $\mathbb{P}$. This predicate will be formally defined below. It needs to make the counter a increase when what can be extracted from the mailboxes (that is the minimum base of $\mathbf{G}$)) is the same locally. But it must also make the algorithm stop when there is enough information to conclude. This information is enough when the value r for the reconstructed base match the counter of stability a.

Theorem 16. *With* $\mathbb{P}(v) := (a(v) < r(\mathbf{K}(v), n(v)))$*, the algorithm* $\mathcal{M}_{\mathbb{P}}$ *snap-stabilizes to* S*.*

Proof. Consider a node v just after it has applied rule Decision, we have $\text{STRONG}(M(v))$ that is stable, $r(\mathbf{K}(v), n(v)) \leq a(v)$ and $out(v) = f(\mathbf{K}(v), w(v))$. Since, by construction, $\mathbf{K}(v)$ is a quasi-fibration of $\mathbf{G}_{M(v)}$ of radius $a(v) \geq r(\mathbf{K}(v), n(v))$ and of center $n(v)$, and since f and r are $r-$lifting closed, $\text{OUT}(v) = f(\mathbf{K}(v), w(v)) = f(\mathbf{G}_{M(v)}, n(v))$, and $r(\mathbf{K}(v), w(v)) = r(\mathbf{G}_{M(v)}, n(v))$. From Proposition 15, since $a(v) \geq r(\mathbf{G}_{M(v)}, n(v)$ and since f is $r-$lifting closed, $\text{OUT}(v) = f(\mathbf{G}_M(v), n(v)) = f(\mathbf{G}, v)$.

5 Long Lived Tasks

From the results of the previous section, it is quite easy to derive a characterization for long lived tasks, that is tasks that do not terminate but evolve in a prescribe way. We mainly have to extend our previous techniques to sequences of labelled graphs. This can be done using the self-stabilizing clock uses in [BV02b]. For lack of space, we omit the proof and refer the interested reader to [BV02b].

Theorem 17. *A task $(\mathcal{S}, \mathcal{F})$ admits a snap-stabilizing synchronous solution if and only if there exists a function $r : \overline{\mathcal{F}}_{\bullet} \longrightarrow \mathbb{N} \cup \{\infty\}$ and a sequence of output functions $(f_1, f_2, \cdots)$, $\forall i, f_i : \overline{\mathcal{F}}_{\bullet} \longrightarrow L \cup \{\bot\}$.*

17.i $\forall \mathbf{G} \in \mathcal{F}, (f_1(\mathbf{G}), f_2(\mathbf{G}), \cdots) \in \mathcal{S}$,
17.ii r *is* $r-lifting$*-closed;*
17.iii $\forall i \in \mathbb{N}$, f_i *is* $r-lifting$*-closed.*

6 Application

In this section, we show how the previous characterizations can be applied to characterize the families of homonymous rings where it is possible to solve the MUTUAL EXCLUSION problem. This is a long lived task that is defined by:

Safety: At every moment, there is at most one node with OUT $= CriticalSection$.
Liveness: There is no infinite suffix with requesting nodes and no nodes with OUT $= CriticalSection$.

As in the Election case in [CGM12, Sect. 6.4], we consider $\Lambda = \mathbb{N}$ and the set of homonymous rings $\mathcal{R}$. Let $k \in \mathbb{N}$ and $\mathbf{G} \in \mathcal{R}$, we denote $\mu_{\mathbf{G}}(k)$ the number of vertices with initial label equal to k in $\mathbf{G}$. More precisely, we consider the set of homonymous rings $\mathcal{R}_*$ with a least one distinguished node, that is if $\mathbf{G} \in \mathcal{R}_*$ then there is at least one integer k such that $\mu_{\mathbf{G}}(k) = 1$. All graphs of $\mathcal{R}_*$ are fibrations minimal, i.e. it is possible to solve MUTUAL EXCLUSION on any graph of $\mathcal{R}_*$. Indeed, for a given $\mathbf{G}$, it is possible to design a sequence of output functions that simulate a token circulation by using the node u with unique name as leader. It is then possible to have a self-stabilizing solution to Mutual Exclusion on $\mathcal{R}_*$ (see [BV02b]).

However, it is not possible to solve the Mutual Exclusion problem with a snap-stabilizing algorithm on $\mathcal{R}_*$. Indeed, for any $n \in \mathbb{N}$, there exists a quasi-fibration $\mathbf{K} \in \mathcal{R}_*$ of radius n via γ such that u has more than one pre-image. This remark prohibits the existence of $r-$lifting closed functions on $\mathcal{R}_*$ satisfying the unicity implied by the Safety condition. The subfamilies $\mathcal{F} \subset \mathcal{R}_*$ that admit a snap-stabilizing solution to the mutual exclusion problem are therefore the families for which the radius of quasi-fibrations is bounded. This bound can be a bound on the size of the ring network, or, more generally, on the number of repetitions that a "name patterns" (a sequence of consecutive names on the ring) can have in $\mathcal{F}$.

7 Conclusion

We have shown that for anonymous networks, the terminating tasks that can be solved by a snap-stabilizing algorithms are exactly the ones that can be solved by a distributed algorithm with explicit termination. This complements the already known task-equivalence between self-stabilizing terminating tasks and distributed tasks computed with implicit termination. The important consequence is that the partial knowledge (like bound on the size, diameter etc. ...) that could be used to get explicit termination in the non-stabilizing case are also the ones that can be used to have snap-stabilizing solutions.

For lack of space, we do not discuss probabilistic snap-stabilization [AD14]. It is not difficult to see that the techniques presented here enable to prove that a task has a probabilistic snap-stabilizing solution if and only it has a (non-stabilizing) Las Vegas solution.

An interesting open question, as in the self-stabilizing case, would be to find a *direct* way to transform any given anonymous algorithm into a snap-stabilizing one. Such transformation might have benefits regarding the complexity.

The author wishes to thank Jérémie Chalopin for sharing ideas and fruitful discussions about distributed computability in various settings, including some closely related to this paper.

References

[AD14] Altisen, K., Devismes, S.: On probabilistic snap-stabilization. In: Chatterjee, M., Cao, J., Kothapalli, K., Rajsbaum, S. (eds.) ICDCN 2014. LNCS, vol. 8314, pp. 272–286. Springer, Heidelberg (2014). doi:10.1007/978-3-642-45249-9_18

[Ang80] Angluin, D.: Local and global properties in networks of processors. In: Proceedings of the 12th Symposium on Theory of Computing, pp. 82–93 (1980)

[BCG+96] Boldi, P., Codenotti, B., Gemmell, P., Shammah, S., Simon, J., Vigna, S.: Symmetry breaking in anonymous networks: Characterizations. In: Proceedings 4th Israeli Symposium on Theory of Computing and Systems, pp. 16–26. IEEE Press (1996)

[BDPV99] Bui, A., Datta, A.K., Petit, F., Villain, V.: State-optimal snap-stabilizing pif in tree networks. In Workshop on Self-stabilizing Systems, ICDCS 1999, pp. 78–85. IEEE Computer Society (1999)

[BV01] Boldi, P., Vigna, S.: An effective characterization of computability in anonymous networks. In: Welch, J. (ed.) DISC 2001. LNCS, vol. 2180, pp. 33–47. Springer, Heidelberg (2001). doi:10.1007/3-540-45414-4_3

[BV02a] Boldi, P., Vigna, S.: Fibrations of graphs. Discrete Math. **243**(243), 21–66 (2002)

[BV02b] Boldi, P., Vigna, S.: Universal dynamic synchronous self-stabilization. Distr. Comput. **15**, 137–153 (2002)

[CDV09] Cournier, A., Devismes, S., Villain, V.: Light enabling snap-stabilization of fundamental protocols. ACM Trans. Auton. Adapt. Syst. **4**(1), 6:1–6:27 (2009)

[CGM08] Chalopin, J., Godard, E., Métivier, Y.: Local terminations and distributed computability in anonymous networks. In: Taubenfeld, G. (ed.) DISC 2008. LNCS, vol. 5218, pp. 47–62. Springer, Heidelberg (2008). doi:10.1007/978-3-540-87779-0_4

[CGM12] Chalopin, J., Godard, E., Métivier, Y.: Election in partially anonymous networks with arbitrary knowledge in message passing systems. Distrib. Comput. **25**(4), 297–311 (2012)

[Cha06] Chalopin, J.: Algorithmique distribuée, calculs locaux et homomorphismes de graphes. Ph.D. thesis, Université de Bordeaux I (2006)

[CM07] Chalopin, J., Métivier, Y.: An efficient message passing election algorithm based on mazurkiewicz's algorithm. Fundam. Inform. **80**(1–3), 221–246 (2007)

[Dol00] Dolev, S.: Self-Stabilization. MIT Press, Cambridge (2000)

[GM02] Godard, E., Métivier, Y.: A characterization of families of graphs in which election is possible. In: Nielsen, M., Engberg, U. (eds.) FoSSaCS 2002. LNCS, vol. 2303, pp. 159–171. Springer, Heidelberg (2002). doi:10.1007/3-540-45931-6_12

[GMT10] Godard, E., Métivier, Y., Tel, G.: Termination detection of local computations. Technical Report. arXiv:1001.2785v2, January 2010

[God02] Godard, E.: A self-stabilizing enumeration algorithm. Inf. Process. Lett. **82**(6), 299–305 (2002)

[Maz88] Mazurkiewicz, A.: Solvability of the asynchronous ranking problem. Inf. Process. Lett. **28**, 221–224 (1988)

[MMW97] Métivier, Y., Muscholl, A., Wacrenier, P.-A.: About the local detection of termination of local computations in graphs. In: Krizanc, D., Widmayer, P. (eds.), SIROCCO 97–4th International Colloquium on Structural Information & Communication Complexity, Proceedings in Informatics, pp. 188–200. Carleton Scientific (1997)

[SSP85] Szymanski, B., Shy, Y., Prywes, N.: Terminating iterative solutions of simultaneous equations in distributed message passing systems. In: Proceedings of the 4th Symposium of Distributed Computing, pp. 287–292 (1985)

[Tel00] Tel, G.: Introduction to distributed algorithms. Cambridge University Press, New York (2000)

Polynomial Silent Self-Stabilizing p-Star Decomposition (Short Paper)

Mohammed Haddad[1], Colette Johnen[2], and Sven Köhler[3(✉)]

[1] Université Claude Bernard Lyon 1, Villeurbanne, France
mohammed.haddad@univ-lyon1.fr
[2] University of Bordeaux, Talence Cedex, France
johnen@labri.fr
[3] University of Freiburg, Freiburg, Germany
koehlers@informatik.uni-freiburg.de

Abstract. We present a silent self-stabilizing distributed algorithm computing a maximal p-star decomposition of the underlying communication network. Under the unfair distributed scheduler, the most general scheduler model, the algorithm converges in at most $12\Delta m + \mathcal{O}(m+n)$ moves, where m is the number of edges, n is the number of nodes, and Δ is the maximum node degree. Regarding the move complexity, our algorithm outperforms the previously known best algorithm by a factor of Δ. While the round complexity for the previous algorithm was unknown, we show a $5\left\lfloor \frac{n}{p+1} \right\rfloor + 5$ bound for our algorithm.

1 Introduction

Fault-tolerance is among the most important requirements for distributed systems. Self-stabilization is a fault-tolerance technique that deals with transient faults. It was first introduced by Dijkstra [5]. Starting in an arbitrary configuration, a self-stabilizing distributed system converges to a legitimate configuration in finite time without any external intervention. This makes self-stabilization an elegant approach for non-masking fault-tolerance [6].

An H-decomposition of a graph G subdivides a graph into disjoint components which which are isomorphic to H. A p-star is a complete bipartite graph $K_{1,p}$ with one center node and p leaves.

One of the famous and well studied graph decompositions in literature is star decomposition [4,7,9]. A decomposition of a graph into stars is a way of expressing the graph as the union of disjoint stars [3]. The problem of star decomposition

This study has been carried out with financial support from the French State, managed by the French National Research Agency (ANR) in the frame of the "Investments for the future" Programme IdEx Bordeaux - CPU (ANR-10-IDEX-03-02) and by the Sustainability Center Freiburg, Germany.

B. Bonakdarpour and F. Petit (Eds.): SSS 2016, LNCS 10083, pp. 185–189, 2016.
DOI: 10.1007/978-3-319-49259-9_15

has several applications including scientific computing, scheduling, load balancing, parallel computing [1], and important nodes detection in social networks [8]. Decomposing a graph into stars is also used in parallel computing and programming. This decomposition offers similar feature as Master-Slave paradigm, used in grids [10] and P2P infrastructures [2].

The first self-stabilizing algorithm for the p-star decomposition problem was proposed in [12]. It finds a maximal decomposition into node-disjoint p-stars. The decomposition is maximal in the sense that the nodes not part of any p-star cannot form a p-star. However, the algorithm proposed in [12] always converges to a unique legitimate configuration according to the input graph and does not guarantee a polynomial move complexity. An improvement was proposed in [11] where authors dealt with the uniqueness of legitimate state and proved their algorithm to converge within $O(\Delta^2 m)$ moves under the unfair distributed scheduler where m is the number of edges and Δ is maximum node degree in the graph. A bound on the round complexity of the algorithm was not given.

Our Results. In this paper, we improve the move complexity of the previous algorithm to $12\Delta m + \mathcal{O}(m + n)$ and prove an $\mathcal{O}(n)$ bound on the round complexity. The algorithm does not converge to a unique legitimate configuration. In fact, there is a legitimate configuration for any valid maximal p-star decomposition. The above results hold with respect to the unfair distributed scheduler, the most powerful adversary. For the definition of the computational model we direct the reader at [11].

2 The p-Star Decomposition Algorithm

The implementation of the p-Star decomposition is algorithm is given in Algorithms 1 and 2. The algorithm is given as a set of rules, each of the form *guard*$(v) \to$ *action*. In this section we give a rough overview of how the algorithm works. Assume that some nodes are already a *member* of a star, while others are not. Each node v indicates to their neighbors whether they are a member of a star or not via the Boolean variable *inStar*(v). In addition, each node indicates whether it may be a *viable center* of a new star using the Boolean variable *viableCenter*(v). That is the case only if the node itself and p of its neighbors are not a member of a star, yet.

Each node v keeps track of the viable centers within its closed neighborhood $N[v] = N(v) \cup \{v\}$. Unless v is a member of a star, it invites the viable center having the minimum identifier (c.f. the macro *bestCenter*(v)) to form new p-star by setting *center*(v) to the viable center's identifier (rule RI). The invitation is updated as needed if the set of viable centers within the closed neighborhood changes. Directing the invitation at the viable center with the minimum identifier makes sure that no deadlocks occur. Eventually, some viable center u is invited by itself and at least p neighbors. Then u picks p neighbors as the leaves of the star and assigns them to the set *leaves*(u) (rule RA). This creates a new p-star

Algorithm 1. Shared Variables, Predicates, Macros and Guard predicates

Shared variables of each node $v \in V$

- $center(v)$ — a node identifier or $\perp$
  The center of the p-star that v belongs to or the viable center that v invites to form new p-star. The value $\perp$ is used if v is not a member of a p-star and is not inviting any node.
- $leaves(v)$ — a set of up to p node identifiers
  The set is empty if v is not the center of a p-star.
  Otherwise it contains the leaves of the p-star.
- $inStar(v) \in Boolean$
  Indicates whether v is a member of a p-star.
- $viableCenter(v) \in Boolean$
  Indicates whether v is a viable center for a new p-star.
- $lockedCenter(v) \in Boolean$
  Indicates whether the value of $center(v)$ is locked or not.

Predicates

- $isCenter(v) \equiv |leaves(v)| = p$
- $incorrectCenter(v) \equiv (leaves(v) \neq \emptyset) \wedge ((center(v) \neq v) \vee (\exists u \in leaves(v) : center(u) \neq v) \vee \neg isCenter(v) \vee (leaves(v) \not\subseteq N(v)))$
- $correctLeaf(v) \equiv (center(v) \in N(v)) \wedge isCenter(center(v)) \wedge (v \in leaves(center(v))$
- $correctCenter(v) \equiv isCenter(v) \wedge \neg incorrectCenter(v)$
- $isInStar(v) \equiv correctLeaf(v) \vee correctCenter(v)$
- $isViableCenter(v) \equiv \neg isInStar(v) \wedge (|\{ u \in N(v) \mid \neg inStar(u) \}| \geq p)$

Macros

- $bestCenter(v)$ is the element of $\{u \in N[v] \mid viableCenter(u) \wedge leaves(u) = \emptyset\}$ having the smallest identifier or $\perp$ if the set is empty
- $potentialLeaves(v)$ is the set $\{u \in N(v) \mid center(u) = v \wedge lockedCenter(u)\}$

Guard Predicates

- $starToUpdate(v) \equiv \neg isInStar(v) \wedge (|potentialLeaves(v)| \geq p) \wedge (v = center(v))$
- $centerToUpdate(v) \equiv \neg isInStar(v) \wedge (center(v) \neq bestCenter(v) \vee \neg lockedCenter(v))$
- $variablesToUpdate(v) \equiv (inStar(v) \neq isInStar(v)) \vee (viableCenter(v) \neq isViableCenter(v)) \vee incorrectCenter(v)$

---

centered at u. Note that at this point, every node v that is member of the star satisfies $center(v) = u$.

Algorithm 2. Rules of each node $v \in V$

Procedures

- $updateBooleans(v)$: $inStar(v) := isInStar(v);$
  $viableCenter(v) := isViableCenter(v);$
- $updateVariables(v)$: if $incorrectCenter(v)$ then $leaves(v) := \emptyset;$
  $updateBooleans(v);$

Rules

RA(v) : $starToUpdate(v) \longrightarrow$
 $leaves(v) :=$ subset of $potentialLeaves(v)$ with exactly p elements;
 $updateBooleans(v);$

RI(v) : $\neg starToUpdate(v) \wedge centerToUpdate(v) \wedge \neg lockedCenter(v) \longrightarrow$
 $lockedCenter(v) :=$ true;
 $center(v) := bestCenter(v);$
 $updateVariables(v);$

RGI(v) : $\neg starToUpdate(v) \wedge centerToUpdate(v) \wedge lockedCenter(v) \longrightarrow$
 $lockedCenter(v) :=$ false;
 $updateVariables(v);$

RU(v) : $\neg starToUpdate(v) \wedge \neg centerToUpdate(v) \wedge variablesToUpdate(v)$
 $\longrightarrow updateVariables(v);$

To mitigate the potential issue that an invitation is withdrawn concurrently to the execution of rule RA, the Boolean variable $lockedCenter(v)$ is used. If $lockedCenter(v)$ is true, then node v is guaranteed to not change $center(v)$ during the next step. Before $center(v)$ can be changed by rule RI, rule RGI must be executed to set $lockedCenter(v)$ to false.

The variables $inStar(v)$ and $viableCenter(v)$ are regularly updated by rule RU. This rule is also responsible for correcting other inconsistencies such as invalid identifiers in $leaves(v)$.

The algorithm is silent, i.e., it eventually reaches a terminal configuration in which the guards of all rules evaluate to false for every node. It can be shown that in such a configuration, no viable centers exist and thus the decomposition is maximal.

We conclude with the following result:

Theorem 1. *The algorithm terminates after at most* $12\Delta m + \mathcal{O}(m+n)$ *moves under the unfair distributed scheduler. These moves happen within at most* $5\left\lfloor \frac{n}{p+1} \right\rfloor + 5$ *(asynchronous) rounds.*

The proofs are omitted and will appear in the full version of the paper.

3 Conclusion

We revisited the problem of decomposing a graph into node-disjoint p-stars from a self-stabilization point of view. This problem is a generalization of maximal matching. The proposed algorithm performs better than both previously proposed algorithms. In fact, we improved the move complexity while also solving the uniqueness legitimate configuration problem that [12] suffered from, without losing linearity of round complexity. As future work, we aim to generalize the proposed algorithm to the weighted p-star decomposition problem.

References

1. Andreev, K., Räcke, H.: Balanced graph partitioning. In: 16th Annual ACM Symposium on Parallelism in Algorithms and Architectures, pp. 120–124 (2004)
2. Bendjoudi, A., Melab, N., Talbi, E.G.: P2p design and implementation of a parallel branch and bound algorithm for grids. Int. J. Grid Util. Comput. **1**(2), 159–168 (2009)
3. Bryant, D.E., El-Zanati, S.I., Eynden, C.V.: Star factorizations of graph products. J. Graph Theor. **36**(2), 59–66 (2001)
4. Cain, P.: Decomposition of complete graphs into stars. Bull. Austral. Math. Soc. **10**, 23–30 (1974)
5. Dijkstra, E.W.: Self-stabilizing systems in spite of distributed control. Commun. ACM **17**(11), 643–644 (1974)
6. Dolev, S.: Self-stabilization. MIT Press, Cambridge (2000)
7. Lee, H.C., Lin, C.: Balanced star decompositions of regular multigraphs and lambda-fold complete bipartite graphs. Discrete Math. **301**(2–3), 195–206 (2005)
8. Lemmouchi, S., Haddad, M., Kheddouci, H.: Robustness study of emerged communities from exchanges in peer-to-peer networks. Comput. Commun. **36**(10–11), 1145–1158 (2013)
9. Merly, E.E.R., Gnanadhas, N.: Linear star decomposition of lobster. Int. J. Contemp. Math. Sci. **7**(6), 251–261 (2012)
10. Mezmaz, M., Melab, N., Talbi, E.G.: A grid-based parallel approach of the multi-objective branch and bound. In: 15th Euromicro International Conference on PDP, pp. 23–30 (2007)
11. Neggazi, B., Haddad, M., Kheddouci, H.: A new self-stabilizing algorithm for maximal p-star decomposition of general graphs. Inf. Process. Lett. **115**(11), 892–898 (2015)
12. Neggazi, B., Turau, V., Haddad, M., Kheddouci, H.: A self-stabilizing algorithm for maximal p-star decomposition of general graphs. In: Higashino, T., Katayama, Y., Masuzawa, T., Potop-Butucaru, M., Yamashita, M. (eds.) SSS 2013. LNCS, vol. 8255, pp. 74–85. Springer, Heidelberg (2013). doi:10.1007/978-3-319-03089-0_6

Analysis of Computing Policies Using SAT Solvers (Short Paper)

Marijn J.H. Heule(✉), Rezwana Reaz, H.B. Acharya, and Mohamed G. Gouda

The University of Texas at Austin, Austin, USA
{marijn,rezwana,acharya,gouda}@cs.utexas.edu

Abstract. A computing policy is a sequence of rules, where each rule consists of a predicate and a decision, and where each decision is either "accept" or "reject". A policy P is said to accept (or reject, respectively) a request iif the decision of the first rule in P, that matches the request is "accept" (or "reject", respectively). Examples of computing policies are firewalls, routing policies and software-defined networks in the Internet, and access control policies. A policy P is called *adequate* iff P accepts at least one request. It has been shown earlier that the problem of determining whether a given policy is adequate (called the policy adequacy problem) is NP-hard. In this paper, we present an efficient algorithm that use SAT solvers to solve the policy adequacy problem. Experimental results show that our algorithm can determine whether a given policy with 90 K rules is adequate in about 3 min.

Keywords: Policies · Firewalls · Access control · Routing policies · SAT

1 Introduction

A computing policy is a filter that is placed at the entry point of some resource. Each request to access the resource needs to be examined against the policy to determine whether to accept or reject the request.

Examples of computing policies are firewalls in the Internet, routing policies and software-defined networks in the Internet, and access control policies. Early methods for the logical analysis of computing policies have been reported in [4–6].

The decision of a policy to accept or reject a request depends on two factors:

1. The values of some attributes that are specified in the request and
2. The sequence of rules in the policy that are specified by the policy designer.

A policy is a sequence of rules where a rule in a policy consists of a predicate and a decision, which is either "accept" or "reject". To examine a request against a policy, the rules in the policy are considered one by one until the first rule, whose predicate matches the values of the attributes in the request, is identified.

B. Bonakdarpour and F. Petit (Eds.): SSS 2016, LNCS 10083, pp. 190–194, 2016.
DOI: 10.1007/978-3-319-49259-9_16

Then the decision of the identified rule, whether "accept" or "reject", is applied to the request.

A rule in a policy is defined as a pair, one predicate and one decision, written as follows:

$$\langle \text{predicate} \rangle \rightarrow \langle \text{decision} \rangle$$

A rule whose decision is "accept" is called an accept rule, and a rule whose decision is "reject" is called a reject rule.

A predicate is of the form: $\big((u_1 \in X_1) \wedge \cdots \wedge (u_t \in X_t)\big)$, where each u_i is an attribute whose value is taken from an integer interval denoted $D(u_i)$, each X_i is an integer interval that is contained in $D(u_i)$, and each $\wedge$ denotes the logical AND or conjunction operation.

A request is a tuple $(b_1, \ldots, b_t)$ of t integers, where t is the number of attributes and each integer b_i is taken from the domain $D(u_i)$ of attribute u_i. A request $(b_1, \ldots, b_t)$ is said to match a predicate $\big((u_1 \in X_1) \wedge \cdots \wedge (u_t \in X_t)\big)$ iff each integer b_i in the request is an element in the corresponding integer interval X_i in the predicate.

A request is said to match a rule in a policy iff the request matches the predicate of the rule. A policy P is said to accept (or reject, respectively) a request rq iff P has an accept (or reject, respectively) rule r such that request rq matches rule r and does not match any rule that precedes rule r in P.

2 The Policy Adequacy Problem

A policy P is said to be adequate iff there is a request rq that is accepted by P. The policy adequacy problem is to design an efficient algorithm that can take as input any policy P and determine whether P is adequate.

It has been shown in [2] that the time complexity of the policy adequacy problem is NP-hard. In [7], the authors present an algorithm that uses SAT solvers, for example `Glucose` [1], to solve the policy adequacy problem. Unfortunately, the algorithm in [7] is based on rule predicates of a form that is different from the form of the rule predicates described in the current paper. Therefore, the presented algorithm in [7] cannot be applied efficiently to solve the policy adequacy problem described in the current paper.

3 Solving the Policy Adequacy Problem Using SAT Solvers

In this paper, we present an algorithm, named Algorithm 1, that uses any SAT solver to solve the policy adequacy problem that is described in this paper. Because of space limitation, our presentation of Algorithm 1 is restricted to the case where Algorithm 1 is applied to the following example policy P:

$$\big((u \in [3,5]) \wedge (v \in [4,4])\big) \rightarrow \text{accept}$$
$$\big((u \in [2,4]) \wedge (v \in [4,4])\big) \rightarrow \text{reject}$$
$$\big((u \in [2,5]) \wedge (v \in [4,4])\big) \rightarrow \text{accept}$$

This example policy has 2 attributes u and v whose value domains are as follows: $D(u) = [1, 4]$ and $D(v) = [1, 4]$. Note that this example policy has 2 accept rules and 1 reject rule.

Our Algorithm 1 consists of the following 4 steps:

Step 1. In the first step of Algorithm 1, P is encoded into the following Boolean formula FP such that a request rq is accepted by P iff rq makes the value of FP true:

$$FP = \big(\mathrm{ac}(1) \vee \mathrm{ac}(2)\big) \wedge \mathrm{ar}(1) \wedge \mathrm{ar}(2) \wedge \mathrm{rr}(1) \wedge LP$$

Each $\mathrm{ac}(i)$, where $i \in \{1, 2\}$, is a Boolean variable denoting that the i-th accept rule in P is matched by rq. Each $\mathrm{ar}(i)$, where $i \in \{1, 2\}$, is a predicate whose value is true iff $\mathrm{ac}(i)$ is false or request rq matches the i-th accept rule in policy P. Each $\mathrm{rr}(j)$, where $j \in \{1\}$, is a predicate whose value is true iff the j-th reject rule in policy P is preceded by some i-th accept rule where $\mathrm{ac}(i)$ is true or request rq does not match the j-th reject rule in policy P. Predicate LP is discussed below.

Step 2. In the second step of Algorithm 1, we introduce into formula FP Boolean variables that we will use in the third step of the algorithm to encode the predicates $\mathrm{ar}(1)$, $\mathrm{ar}(2)$, $\mathrm{rr}(1)$ and LP.

For each interval $[y, z]$, of an attribute w, that occurs in any rule in policy P, introduce into FP two Boolean variables named $\mathrm{le}(w, y - 1)$ and $\mathrm{le}(w, z)$. Therefore, we end-up introducing the following six Boolean variables in this case: $\mathrm{le}(u, 2)$, $\mathrm{le}(u, 5)$, $\mathrm{le}(u, 1)$, $\mathrm{le}(u, 4)$, $\mathrm{le}(v, 3)$, and $\mathrm{le}(v, 4)$.

Step 3. In the third step of Algorithm 1, we use the introduced "le" Boolean variables to encode the predicates $\mathrm{ar}(i)$, $\mathrm{rr}(j)$, and LP as follows.

Let the i-th accept rule in policy P be of the form:

$$u_1 \in [y_1, z_1] \wedge \cdots \wedge u_t \in [y_t, z_t] \to \text{accept}$$

In this case, predicate $\mathrm{ar}(i)$ can be encoded as follows:

$$\big(\overline{\mathrm{ac}}(i) \vee \overline{\mathrm{le}}(u_1, y_1 - 1)\big) \wedge \big(\overline{\mathrm{ac}}(i) \vee \mathrm{le}(u_1, z_1)\big) \wedge$$
$$\cdots$$
$$\big(\overline{\mathrm{ac}}(i) \vee \overline{\mathrm{le}}(u_t, y_t - 1)\big) \wedge \big(\overline{\mathrm{ac}}(i) \vee \mathrm{le}(u_t, z_t)\big)$$

Let the j-the reject rule in policy P be of the form:

$$u_1 \in [y_1, z_1] \wedge \cdots \wedge u_t \in [y_t, z_t] \to \text{reject}$$

and assume that there are k (note that k can be 0) accept rules that precede the j-th reject rule in P. In this case, predicate $\mathrm{rr}(j)$ can be encoded as follows:

$$\big(\mathrm{ac}(1) \vee \cdots \vee \mathrm{ac}(k) \vee \mathrm{le}(u_1, y_1 - 1) \vee \overline{\mathrm{le}}(u_1, z_1) \vee \cdots \vee \mathrm{le}(u_t, y_t - 1) \vee \overline{\mathrm{le}}(u_t, z_t)\big)$$

Predicate LP in formula FP describes some expected restrictions on the values of the "le" Boolean variables introduced into FP. For example, for the two Boolean variables $\text{le}(u, 2)$ and $\text{le}(u, 5)$ that are introduced into FP, predicate LP should include the clause $(\overline{\text{le}}(u, 2) \vee \text{le}(u, 5))$.

Therefore, we encode the predicates $\text{ar}(1)$, $\text{ar}(2)$, $\text{rr}(1)$, and LP as follows:

$$\begin{aligned}
\text{ar}(1) &= (\overline{\text{ac}}(1) \vee \overline{\text{le}}(u, 2)) \wedge (\overline{\text{ac}}(1) \vee \text{le}(u, 5)) \wedge (\overline{\text{ac}}(1) \vee \overline{\text{le}}(v, 3)) \wedge (\overline{\text{ac}}(1) \vee \text{le}(v, 4)) \\
\text{ar}(2) &= (\overline{\text{ac}}(2) \vee \text{le}(u, 1)) \wedge (\overline{\text{ac}}(2) \vee \text{le}(u, 5)) \wedge (\overline{\text{ac}}(2) \vee \overline{\text{le}}(v, 3)) \wedge (\overline{\text{ac}}(2) \vee \text{le}(v, 4)) \\
\text{rr}(1) &= (\text{ac}(1) \vee \text{le}(u, 1) \vee \overline{\text{le}}(u, 4) \vee \text{le}(v, 3) \vee \overline{\text{le}}(v, 4)) \\
LP &= (\overline{\text{le}}(u, 1) \vee \text{le}(u, 2)) \wedge (\overline{\text{le}}(u, 2) \vee \text{le}(u, 4)) \wedge \\
&\quad (\overline{\text{le}}(u, 4) \vee \text{le}(u, 5)) \wedge (\overline{\text{le}}(v, 3) \vee \text{le}(v, 4))
\end{aligned}$$

Step 4. In the fourth step of Algorithm 1, we use any SAT solver, for example `Glucose` [1], to determine whether the above formula FP is satisfiable. The above policy P is adequate iff formula FP is satisfiable.

Complexity. The complexity of Algorithm 1 to determine whether a given policy P is adequate is measured by the number of Boolean variables introduced into formula FP in Algorithm 1.

Note that if the given policy P has n rules and t attributes, then formula FP in Algorithm 1 has $\mathcal{O}(nt)$ Boolean variables and the complexity of Algorithm 1 does not depend on the range of values of the different attributes in policy P.

We performed some experiments to evaluate the effectiveness of Algorithm 1. In each experiment, we applied Algorithm 1 to determine whether a given firewall P selected at random, is adequate. The given firewall P is a policy with

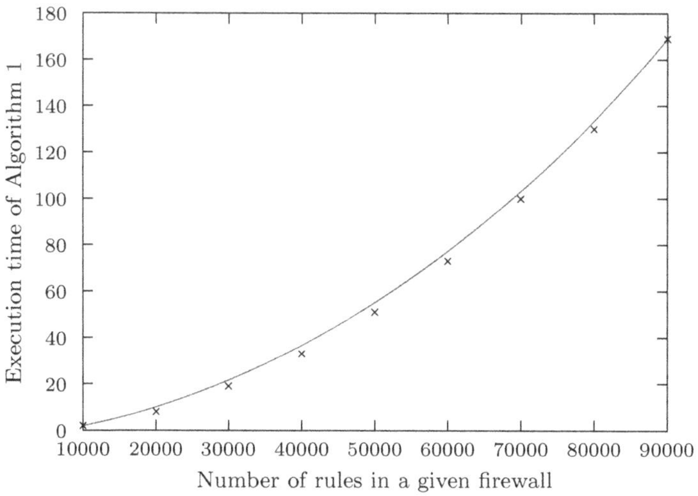

Fig. 1. Execution time (in seconds) of Algorithm 1 to determine whether a given firewall is adequate.

5 attributes and between 10 K and 90K rules. The value domain of each attribute in firewall P is the integer interval $[0, 2^{16} - 1]$. The state-of-the-art SAT solver `Glucose` version 3.0 [1] was used to check whether the generated Boolean formula FP is satisfiable[1].

Figure 1 shows the relationship between the number of rules in a given firewall P and the execution time of Algorithm 1 when this algorithm is applied to firewall P to determine whether P is adequate. From Fig. 1, the execution time of Algorithm 1 is less than 3 min when the given firewall P has up to 90,000 rules.

4 Concluding Remarks

In the full version of this paper [3], we show how to extend Algorithm 1 to solve other policy problems beyond policy adequacy. In particular, we show how to solve the problems of policy completeness, policy implication, policy equivalence, and redundancy checking in policies.

Acknowledgements. Research of M. J. H. Heule is supported by DARPA Contract FA8750-15-2-0096 and NSF Award CCF-1526760. Research of M. G. Gouda is supported by NSF Award 1440035.

References

1. Audemard, G., Simon, L.: Predicting learnt clauses quality in modern SAT solvers. In: Boutilier, C. (ed.) IJCAI 2009, pp. 399–404 (2009)
2. Elmallah, E.S., Gouda, M.G.: Hardness of firewall analysis. In: Noubir, G., Raynal, M. (eds.) NETYS 2014. LNCS, vol. 8593, pp. 153–168. Springer, Heidelberg (2014). doi:10.1007/978-3-319-09581-3_11
3. Heule, M.J.H., Reaz, R., Acharya, H.B., Gouda, M.G.: Analysis of computing policies using sat solvers. In: Technical Report No. TR-16-14, Department of Computer Science, The Universisty of Texas at Austin (2016)
4. Hoffman, D., Yoo, K.: Blowtorch: a framework for firewall test automation. In: Proceedings of the 20th IEEE/ACM International Conference on Automated Software Engineering (ASE), pp. 96–103. ACM (2005)
5. Kamara, S., Fahmy, S., Schultz, E., Kerschbaum, F., Frantzen, M.: Analysis of vulnerabilities in internet firewalls. Comput. Secur. **22**(3), 214–232 (2003)
6. Mayer, A., Wool, A., Ziskind, E.: Fang: A firewall analysis engine. In: IEEE Symposium on Security and Privacy, pp. 177–187. IEEE (2000)
7. Zhang, S., Mahmoud, A., Malik, S., Narain, S.: Verification and synthesis of firewalls using SAT and QBF. In: Proceedings of the 20th IEEE International Conference on Network Protocols (ICNP), pp. 1–6. IEEE (2012)

[1] Files are available at http://www.cs.utexas.edu/~marijn/firewall.

An Efficient Silent Self-stabilizing 1-Maximal Matching Algorithm Under Distributed Daemon Without Global Identifiers

Michiko Inoue[1(✉)], Fukuhito Ooshita[1], and Sébastien Tixeuil[2]

[1] Nara Institute of Science and Technology, Ikoma, Japan
kounoe@is.naist.jp
[2] UPMC Sorbonne Universités, LIP6 - CNRS 7606, IUF, Paris, France

Abstract. We propose a new self-stabilizing 1-maximal matching algorithm that works under the distributed unfair daemon for arbitrarily shaped networks without cycle whose length is a multiple of three. The *1-maximal* matching is a $\frac{2}{3}$-approximation of a maximum matching, a significant improvement over the $\frac{1}{2}$-approximation that is guaranteed by a maximal matching.

Our algorithm is as efficient (its stabilization time is $O(e)$ moves, where e denotes the number of edges in the network) as the best known algorithm operating under the weaker central daemon. It significantly outperforms the only known algorithm for the distributed daemon (with $O(e)$ moves vs. $O(2^n \delta n)$ moves, where δ denotes the maximum degree of the network, and n its number of nodes), while retaining its silence property (after stabilization, its output remains fixed).

1 Introduction

Self-Stabilization [7] is a versatile technique to withstand any kind of transient failure that may occur in computer networks, *e.g.*, caused by memory corruption, erroneous initialization, or topology change. A self-stabilizing distributed system is able to recover from any inconsistent system configuration, and stabilize to a configuration that satisfies its specification, without the need of any external (that is, human) help.

Maximal and *maximum matchings* are thoroughly studied problems in computer networks. A matching is a set of pairs of adjacent nodes in a network such that any node belongs to at most one pair. A matching is maximal if no proper superset of it is a matching as well, and it is maximum if its cardinality is the largest among all matchings. Matchings are typically used in distributed applications where pairs of nodes are required. For example, when each server gives some service to one client, a matching algorithm can pair a server and a client. Another application is communication scheduling in wireless

This work was supported by JSPS KAKENHI Grant Numbers 26330084 and 15H00816. Part of this work was carried out while the third author was visiting NAIST thanks to Erasmus Mundus TEAM program.

B. Bonakdarpour and F. Petit (Eds.): SSS 2016, LNCS 10083, pp. 195–212, 2016.
DOI: 10.1007/978-3-319-49259-9_17

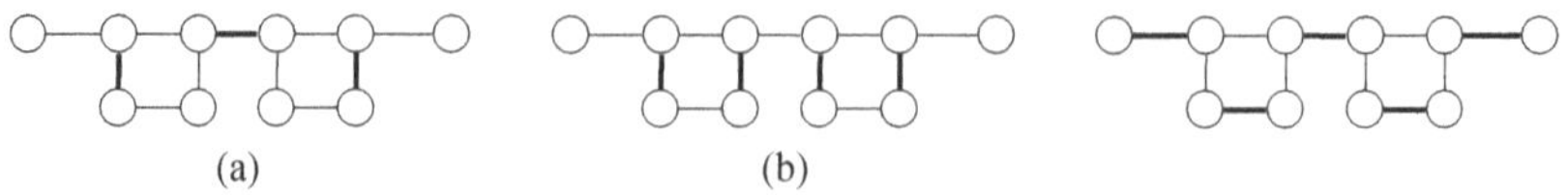

Fig. 1. (a) Maximal matching, (b) 1-maximal matching and (c) maximum matching.

networks where collisions (inducing conflicts) can occur. Since a matching can represent non-conflicting sender-receiver pairs, many communication scheduling algorithms make use of matchings. The higher the cardinality of the matching, the better the usage of the resources in the target application, so matchings of higher cardinality are most sought after.

This paper proposes an efficient self-stabilizing algorithm for *1-maximal matching*. A matching M is 1-maximal if, for any $e \in M$, no matching can be produced by removing e from M and adding two edges to $M - \{e\}$ (See Fig. 1). A 1-maximal matching is a $\frac{2}{3}$-approximation of the maximum matching[1]. Hence, a 1-maximal matching is expected to produce more matching pairs than a *maximal matching*, which only guarantees a $\frac{1}{2}$-approximation of the maximum matching.

Related Works. Self-stabilizing algorithms for the maximum and maximal matching problems have been well studied [11]. Table 1 summarizes the results, where n and e denote the numbers of nodes and edges, respectively.

For maximum, maximal, and 1-maximal matching problems, several self-stabilizing algorithms have been proposed with various assumptions.

Most algorithms use a "pointer to a neighbor" variable, that is meant to designate unambiguously a particular neighbor v of a node u, in such a way that v is aware that u points to it. Using global unique identifiers, u can simply use the global ID of v to designate it unambiguously, but this requires $O(\log n)$ bits for each pointer variable. When global identifiers are not available, one can use edge coloring, or distance 2 node coloring, to implement pointer to neighbors. So, without global identifiers, the memory cost decreases to $O(\log \delta)$ bits per pointer variable, where δ denotes the degree of the network. The algorithms that do not use global identifiers are often called "anonymous" in the literature.

Another important notion to classify algorithms is the notion of daemon [8], which decides the particular times an algorithm is executed at each node. Most algorithms assume a *central daemon*, or a *distributed daemon*. A central daemon may only select one node to execute its code at the same time, while a distributed daemon may select any number of nodes simultaneously. Of course, an algorithm that can run with a distributed daemon will also run under a central daemon, but the converse is not true.

The time complexity can be measured in *moves*, or in *rounds*. A move is the execution of one algorithm action by one node, while a round is a minimal sub-sequence of an execution in which every node has at least once the

[1] We say matching M is an α-approximation of the maximum matching if $|M| \geq \alpha|M_{max}|$ holds, where M_{max} is a maximum matching.

opportunity to execute an action. That is, when a node may execute an action at the beginning of a round, either it executes at least one action, or it becomes unable to execute any action due to the move(s) of neighboring nodes. In some sense, round complexity refers to the global time to achieve stabilization when all nodes run in parallel, while move complexity refers to the total amount of work that is required to stabilize. The move complexity is an upper bound on the round complexity, but the converse is not true (*e.g.*, some self-stabilizing algorithm have polynomial round complexity but exponential move complexity). Considering move complexity has another advantage: the daemon can be *unfair*, that is, it may prevent some enabled node from being executed, as it only need to provide progress (some enabled node is executed). By contrast, algorithms whose complexity is only measured in rounds often make the hypothesis that the daemon is *fair* (if a node is continuously enabled, it is eventually scheduled for execution).

Table 1. Self-stabilizing matching algorithms. n denotes the number of nodes, e denotes the number of edges, δ denotes the maximum degree, and *diam* denotes a diameter of the network.

Reference	Matching	Topology	Global IDs	Daemon	Complexity
[3]	maximum	tree	no*	distributed	$O(n^2)$ moves
[2]	maximum	tree	yes	distributed	$O(n^2)$ moves
[14]	maximum	tree	no	central	$O(n^4)$ moves
[5]	maximum	tree	no	distributed	$O(n \cdot diam)$ moves
[4]	maximum	bipartite**	no	central	$O(n^2)$ rounds
[13]	maximal	arbitrary	no	central	$O(e)$ moves
[16]	maximal	arbitrary	no	distributed	$O(e)$ moves
[6]	maximal	arbitrary	no	distributed	$O(\delta n)$ rounds
[9]	maximal	arbitrary	no	central	finite moves
[10]	1-maximal	tree, ring***	no	central	$O(n^4)$ moves
[17]	1-maximal	arbitrary	yes	distributed	$O(2^n \delta n)$ moves
[1]	1-maximal	arbitrary***	no	central	$O(e)$ moves
This paper	1-maximal	arbitrary***	no	distributed	$O(e)$ moves

* The tree is rooted, that is, there is a unique distinguished node.
** Each node knows its bipartition.
*** A network does not contain a cycle of length of a multiple of 3.

Self-stabilizing optimal solutions to the matching problem (solutions that produce a maximum matching) are known for restricted classes of networks. Blair *et al.* [3] and Blair and Manne [2] proposed algorithms with $O(n^2)$ moves using structural information (distinguished nodes, global identifiers) under a distributed daemon, and Karaata *et al.* [14] proposed an algorithm that runs in $O(n^4)$ moves without using global identifiers under a central daemon. Recently,

Datta *et al.* [5] proposed an algorithm for trees that outperforms the previous algorithms. The proposed algorithm does not use global identifiers, and runs in $O(n \cdot diam)$ moves under an unfair distributed daemon, where *diam* is a diameter of the network. For bipartite networks where nodes know their bipartition, Chattopadhyay *et al.* [4] proposed an algorithm stabilizing in $O(n^2)$ rounds under a distributed fair daemon. No evidence is given that this algorithm stabilizes in a finite number of moves under an unfair daemon.

The case of maximal matching (that is, $\frac{1}{2}$-approximations) considered arbitrary shaped networks. The seminal work of Hsu and Huang [13] proposed an algorithm that does not require global identifiers and performs under the central daemon. They initially demonstrated a time complexity of $O(n^3)$ moves, this bound was refined to $O(n^2)$ moves [15,18], and finally to $O(e)$ moves by Hedetniemi et al. [12]. Manne *et al.* [16] proposed a *maximal* matching algorithm for the more general distributed daemon, still preserving this $O(e)$ move complexity. Self-stabilizing *maximal* matching algorithms with additional properties were also proposed in the literature. Devismes *et al.* [6] proposed a communication-efficient maximal matching algorithm. While its stabilization time complexity of $O(\delta n)$ rounds is not an improvement, only a subset of the nodes must execute forever after stabilization (while in general, all nodes must execute forever in a self-stabilizing algorithm). Dubois *et al.* [9] proposed a Byzantine-tolerant maximal matching algorithm under a central daemon. This algorithm guarantees that, even if Byzantine-faulty nodes continue to change their states arbitrarily, correct nodes that are sufficiently distant from Byzantine-faulty nodes are able to construct a maximal matching in finite moves.

The case of 1-maximal matching (that is, $\frac{2}{3}$-approximations) remains intriguing. Goddard *et al.* [10] proposed a *1-maximal* matching with $O(n^4)$ moves for trees and rings whose length is *not* a multiple of 3, under a central daemon. They also showed that there is no self-stabilizing 1-maximal matching algorithm for rings with length of a multiple of 3 when there is no access to structural information such as global identifiers or a distinguished unique node. Using global unique identifiers, Manne *et al.* [17] managed to produce a 1-maximal matching for arbitrary networks under a distributed unfair daemon, but the move complexity is $O(2^n \delta n)$ moves. By contrast, the recent work of Asada *et al.* [1] is efficient (only $O(e)$ moves are required to stabilize) but considers the more restricted central daemon.

Table 1 summarizes our observations. Overall, for 1-matchings, the following question remains open: does versatility (tolerating a distributed daemon) come at the cost of complexity (with respect to the number of moves that are necessary to stabilize in the worst case)?

Our contribution. In this paper, we answer negatively to the aforementioned open question. Our response is constructive, as we propose a new self-stabilizing 1-maximal matching algorithm that retains both efficiency (its move complexity is $O(e)$) and versatility (it performs under the unfair distributed daemon). Still, our algorithm does not require unique identifiers, and is silent, meaning that after stabilization, its output remains fixed.

The remaining of the paper is organized as follows. In Sect. 2, we define distributed systems and the 1-maximal matching problem. A 1-maximal matching algorithm is proposed in Sect. 3, and proofs for its correctness and performance are given in Sect. 4. Finally Sect. 5 concludes this paper.

2 Preliminaries

A distributed system consists of multiple asynchronous processes. Its topology is represented by an undirected connected graph $G = (V, E)$ where a node in V represents a process, and an edge in E represents the interconnection between the processes. In this paper, we assume no global structural information such as global identifiers, however in order to implement "pointer to neighbor" variables, we assume that nodes have colors that are unique within distance two. A node is a state machine which changes its state by actions. Each node has a set of actions, and a collection of actions of nodes is called a *distributed algorithm.*

In this paper, we consider *state-reading model* as a communication model where each node can directly read the state of its neighboring nodes. An action of a node is expressed $\langle label \rangle :: \langle guard \rangle \mapsto \langle statement \rangle$. A guard is a Boolean function of all the states of the node and its neighboring nodes, and a statement updates its local state. We say a node is privileged if it has an action with a true guard. Only privileged node can *move* by selecting one action with a true guard and executing its statement.

Moves of nodes are scheduled by a *daemon.* We consider an *unfair distributed daemon* in this paper. A distributed daemon chooses one or more privileged nodes at one time, and the selected nodes move simultaneously. A daemon is unfair if it can choose any non empty set of nodes among privileged nodes.

A problem $\mathcal{P}$ is specified by its legitimate configurations where configuration is a collection of states of all the nodes. We say a distributed algorithm $\mathcal{A}$ is *self-stabilizing* if $\mathcal{A}$ satisfies the following properties. (1) **convergence**: The system eventually reaches to a legitimate configuration from any initial state, and (2) **closure**: The system once reaches to a legitimate configuration, all the succeeding moves keep the system configuration legitimate. A self-stabilizing algorithm is *silent* if, from any arbitrary initial configuration, the system reaches a terminal configuration where no node can move.

A *matching* in an undirected graph $G = (V, E)$ is a subset M of E such that each node in V is incident to at most one edge in M. We say a matching is *maximal* if no proper superset of M is a matching as well. A maximal matching M is *1-maximal* if, for any $e \in M$, any matching cannot be produced by removing e from M and adding two edges to $M - \{e\}$. In this paper, we propose a silent self-stabilizing algorithm to construct a 1-maximal matching for graphs without a cycle whose length is a multiple of 3. This last assumption is mandatory when no global structural information is available [10].

3 Algorithm MM1D

First, we show an overview of a proposed algorithm MM1D. The pseudo code of MM1D is shown in Figs. 6 and 7. There are ten stages of a node; `single`, `proposing`, `discouraged`, `approved`, `faithful`, `curious`, `open`, `promise`, `confirmed` and `ready`. Stages `single`, `proposing`, `discouraged` and `approved` mean that the node is not matched with any node. We say a node is *free* if the node is in these four stages, otherwise it is said *non-free*. A stage `faithful` means the node is faithfully matched with its partner. In stages `curious`, `open`, `promise`, `confirmed` and `ready`, two matched nodes are trying to increase matches by breaking their match and making new matches with new partners. To avoid unnecessary moves, nodes make progress step by step. A node i has three variables; $\texttt{stage}_i$, $\texttt{m-ptr}_i$, $\texttt{i-ptr}_i$. The variable $\texttt{m-ptr}_i$ means a matching pointer that points to its partner, while the variable $\texttt{i-ptr}_i$ means an invitation pointer that is used to invite a neighboring node to make a new match.

single** and **proposing: Figure 2 shows how free nodes make a match. Consider two `single` nodes i and j (Fig. 2(a)). When the free node i finds the free neighboring node j, i invites j by $\texttt{i-ptr}_i$ in Fig. 2(b) (i becomes `proposing`). Then the invited node j makes a match with i by $\texttt{m-ptr}_j$ in Fig. 2(c) (j becomes `faithful`). Finally i makes a match with j by $\texttt{m-ptr}_i$ in Fig. 2(d) (i becomes `faithful`). If two adjacent nodes i and j point to each other by `m-ptr`, we consider they are matching, that is $(i, j) \in M$.

In MM1D, `single` node also can invite a `proposing` node and a `proposing` node can accept the invitation. However, an unexpected scenario might occur under the distributed daemon. Consider a situation where a node k is inviting a node i and i is inviting another node j (Fig. 3(a)). If both i and j accept the invitations simultaneously, i can make a match with k but j's `m-ptr` becomes pending. To avoid such a scenario, a `proposing` node i is allowed to accept an invitation from a node k when it is inviting another node j ($j \neq k$) if i's color is the minimum among these three nodes i, j, k (Fig. 3(b)).

While a `proposing` node is inviting its neighboring node, the invited node may make a match with another node. In this case, the `proposing` node cancels its invitation and goes back to `single`.

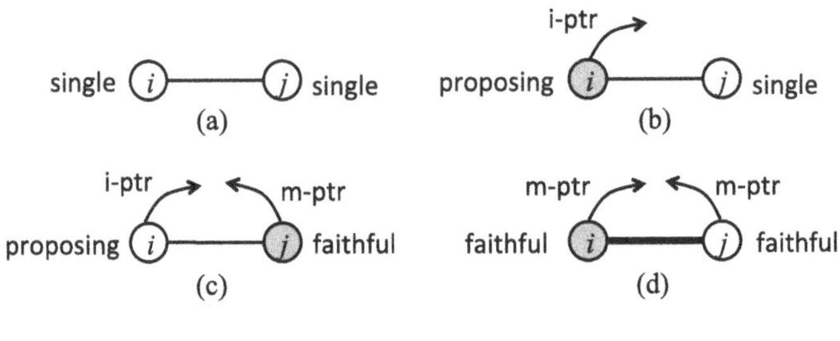

Fig. 2. Making a match between free nodes

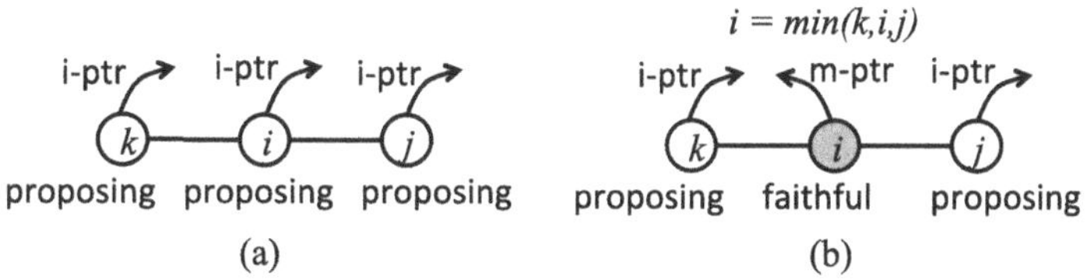

Fig. 3. Chain of proposing nodes

faithful, *curious*, *open*, *confirmed*, *ready and approved*: Matching nodes try to increase the number of matches if they have free neighboring nodes. Figure 4 shows how to increase matches, where matches are increased by breaking a match between i and j, and creating new matches between i and k, and j and l. We now explain the behaviors of i and k, and nodes j and l behave similarly. In Fig. 4(a), a `faithful` node i invites its free neighbor k and i becomes `curious` (Fig. 4(b)). When i notices that j is also `curious`, i becomes `open` to indicate that k is ready to approve the invitation (Fig. 4(c)). Then k approves the invitation by `i-ptr` (k becomes `approved`)(Fig. 4(d)). Node i becomes `confirmed` if it notices k's approval (Fig. 4(e)), and becomes `ready` when it notices that j is also `confirmed`(Fig. 4(f)). This indicates that i is ready to break a match. Then k excutes `match` and becomes `faithful` (Fig. 4(g)) and then i executes `migrate` and becomes `faithful` (Fig. 4(h)).

The above series of actions are not always executed successfully. An invited node may make a match with another node. In such a case, nodes that are trying to break a match (i and j in the above case) cancels the progress and go back to `faithful` and invited nodes go back to `single`.

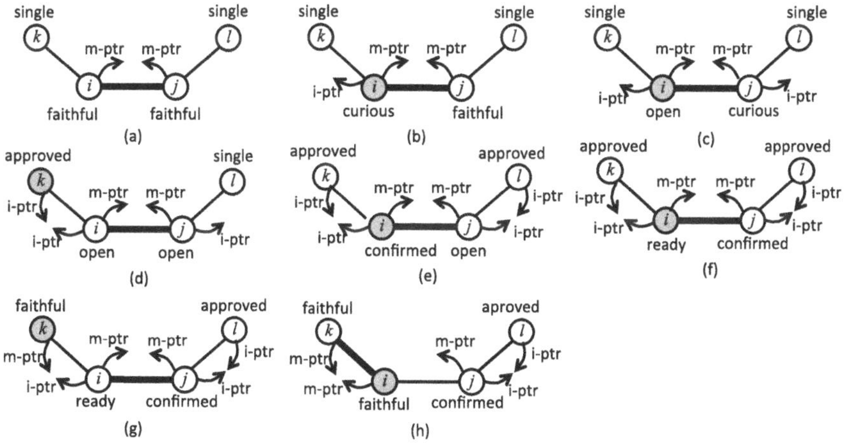

Fig. 4. Increasing matches

`promise`, *`discouraged`*: To increase the number of matches, four nodes cooperatively moves. Note that the above matching nodes i and j do not need to synchronize exactly. It may possible that one node is already `confirmed` while the other node is still `open`. In this case, the `confirmed` node is waiting for the `open` node to become `confirmed` and the `open` node is waiting for its inviting node to approve its invitation. However, if the invited node (k in Fig. 5(a)) is `proposing` and it is also waiting for some node to accept its invitation, these waiting chain may form a deadlock. To break such a deadlock, two stages `promise` and `discouraged` are used.

In case of Fig. 5(b), a node i becomes `promise` to promise k to make a match with k. Then k becomes `discouraged` if its invited node (x in Fig. 5) is `proposing` or `approved` to another node. That indicates that k will cancel the invitation (Fig. 5(c)). The node x does not accept the invitation from a `discouraged` node and k can approve the invitation from i (Fig. 5(d)). Then, i can become `confirmed` (Fig. 5(e)). However, under a distributed daemon, x may accept k's invitation simultaneously when k becomes `discouraged` (Fig. 5(f)). In such a case, k makes a match with x (Fig. 5(g)), and i cancels its invitation to k (Fig. 5(h)).

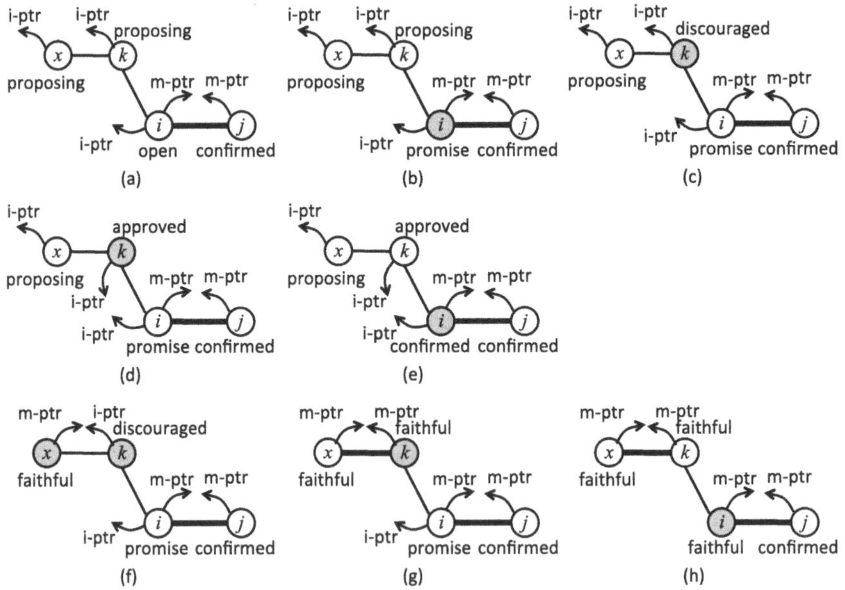

Fig. 5. Promise and discouraged

Reset to `single`: Each node always checks its validity, and resets to `single` if it is invalid. We consider two kinds of validities, *one node validity* and *multi nodes validity*. The one node validity means that the combination of three variables represents some stage. For example, if a stage is `proposing` but `m-ptr` points to some neighboring node, the state is one node invalid. The multi nodes validity means that a relation with neighboring nodes is consistent. For example, if a `faithful` node i points to a node j by `m-ptr`, and j is also `faithful` but points to another node k ($\neq i$) by `m-ptr`, i is multi nodes invalid. The full definitions of one node validity and multi nodes validity of i are given as $valid1(i)$ and $valid(i)$ in Fig. 6, respectively. A node does not move while some neighboring node is one node invalid.

A code of MM1D is shown in Figs. 6 and 7. In the algorithm, $N(i)$ represents a set of neighboring nodes of a node i. This is a set of colors (local IDs) for each node and the algorithm does not use any global IDs. We only assume the local IDs are unique at distance two.

4 Correctness

First, we show that 1-maximal matching is constructed in a terminal configuration where the topology is required to exclude any cycle of length of a multiple of 3.

We can observe that a `ready` node can execute either of `reset`, `match` or `migrate`, and a `discouraged` node can execute either of `reset`, `match` or `approve`. These lead Lemmas 1 and 2.

Lemma 1. *There are no* `ready` *nodes in any terminal configuration.*

Lemma 2. *There are no* `discouraged` *node in any terminal configuration.*

Lemma 3. *In any terminal configuration, if* $\texttt{m-ptr}_i = j$ *for nodes* i *and* j, $\texttt{m-ptr}_j = i$ *also holds.*

Proof. By contradiction. There is no `discouraged` or `ready` node and all nodes are valid in any terminal configuration. Assume that $\texttt{m-ptr}_i = j \wedge \texttt{m-ptr}_j \neq i$. A node i is `faithful` since validity $curious(i)$, $open(i)$, $promise(i)$ or $confirmed(i)$ does not hold. A node j is `proposing` and $\texttt{i-ptr}_j = i$ from $faithful(i)$. In this case, j can execute `match`. A contradiction.

Lemma 4. *There are no two nodes* i *and* j *such that* i *is* `approved` *and* $\texttt{i-ptr}_i = j$, *and* j *is* `open`, `promise` *or* `confirmed` *and* $\texttt{i-ptr}_j = i$ *in any termination configuration for any graphs without a cycle of length of a multiple of 3.*

Proof. By contradiction. There is no `ready` or `discouraged` node and all nodes are valid in any terminal configuration. Assume that there are adjacent nodes i and j such that i is `approved`, j is `open`, `promise` or `confirmed`, $\texttt{i-ptr}_i = j$, and $\texttt{i-ptr}_j = i$. If j is `open` or `promise`, j can execute `confirm`.

Therefore, j is `confirmed`. In the following observation, we show there is a chain of nodes as in Fig. 8. From validity $confirm(j)$, there is a node $k \in N(j)$ such that k is `faithful`, `curious`, `open`, `promise` or `confirmed`, $\texttt{m-ptr}_j = k$ and $\texttt{m-ptr}_k = j$. Node j can execute `cancel_migration` if k is `faithful`, k can

Variables
$\texttt{stage}_i \in \{\texttt{single}, \texttt{proposing}, \texttt{discouraged}, \texttt{approved}, \texttt{faithful}, \texttt{curious}, \texttt{open}, \texttt{promise}, \texttt{confirmed}, \texttt{ready}\}$
$\texttt{m-ptr}_i \in N(i) \cup \{\bot\}$
$\texttt{i-ptr}_i \in N(i) \cup \{\bot\}$

Predicates
single(i): $\texttt{stage}_i = \texttt{single} \wedge \texttt{m-ptr}_i = \bot \wedge \texttt{i-ptr}_i = \bot$
proposing(i,j): $\texttt{stage}_i = \texttt{proposing} \wedge \texttt{m-ptr}_i = \bot \wedge \texttt{i-ptr}_i = j$
discouraged(i,j): $\texttt{stage}_i = \texttt{discouraged} \wedge \texttt{m-ptr}_i = \bot \wedge \texttt{i-ptr}_i = j$
approved(i,j): $\texttt{stage}_i = \texttt{approved} \wedge \texttt{m-ptr}_i = \bot \wedge \texttt{i-ptr}_i = j$
faithful(i,j): $\texttt{stage}_i = \texttt{faithful} \wedge \texttt{m-ptr}_i = j \wedge \texttt{i-ptr}_i = \bot$
curious(i,j,k): $\texttt{stage}_i = \texttt{curious} \wedge \texttt{m-ptr}_i = j \wedge \texttt{i-ptr}_i = k \wedge j \neq k$
open(i,j,k): $\texttt{stage}_i = \texttt{open} \wedge \texttt{m-ptr}_i = j \wedge \texttt{i-ptr}_i = k \wedge j \neq k$
promise(i,j,k): $\texttt{stage}_i = \texttt{promise} \wedge \texttt{m-ptr}_i = j \wedge \texttt{i-ptr}_i = k \wedge j \neq k$
confirmed(i,j,k): $\texttt{stage}_i = \texttt{confirmed} \wedge \texttt{m-ptr}_i = j \wedge \texttt{i-ptr}_i = k \wedge j \neq k$
ready(i,j,k): $\texttt{stage}_i = \texttt{ready} \wedge \texttt{m-ptr}_i = j \wedge \texttt{i-ptr}_i = k \wedge j \neq k$

proposing(i): $\exists j \in N(i) proposing(i,j)$
discouraged(i): $\exists j \in N(i)(discouraged(i,j) \wedge ((\texttt{stage}_j = \texttt{faithful} \wedge \texttt{m-ptr}_j = i) \vee \exists k \in N(i)(k \neq j \wedge \texttt{stage}_k = \texttt{promise} \wedge \texttt{i-ptr}_k = i)))$
approved(i): $\exists j \in N(i)(approved(i,j)$
$\wedge\ (\texttt{stage}_j = \texttt{faithful}, \texttt{curious}, \texttt{oepn}, \texttt{promise}, \texttt{confirmed}\ or\ \texttt{ready}))$
faithful(i): $\exists j \in N(i)(faithful(i,j)$
$\wedge\ (((\texttt{stage}_j = \texttt{faithful}, \texttt{curious}, \texttt{open}\ or\ \texttt{confirmed}) \wedge \texttt{m-ptr}_j = i)$
$\vee\ ((\texttt{stage}_j = \texttt{proposing}, \texttt{discouraged}\ or\ \texttt{ready}) \wedge \texttt{i-ptr}_j = i)))$
curious(i): $\exists j, k \in N(i)(curious(i,j,k)$
$\wedge\ (\texttt{stage}_j = \texttt{faithful}, \texttt{curious}, \texttt{open}\ or\ \texttt{confirmed}) \wedge \texttt{m-ptr}_j = i)$
open(i): $\exists j, k \in N(i)(open(i,j,k)$
$\wedge\ (\texttt{stage}_j = \texttt{faithful}, \texttt{curious}, \texttt{cpen}\ or\ \texttt{confirmed}) \wedge \texttt{m-ptr}_j = i)$
promise(i): $\exists j, k \in N(i)(promise(i,j,k) \wedge \texttt{stage}_j = \texttt{confirmed} \wedge \texttt{m-ptr}_j = i)$
confirmed(i): $\exists j, k \in N(i)(confirmed(i,j,k)$
$\wedge\ (\texttt{stage}_j = \texttt{faithful}, \texttt{curious}, \texttt{open}, \texttt{promise}, \texttt{confirmed}\ or\ \texttt{ready})$
$\wedge\ \texttt{m-ptr}_j = i \wedge \texttt{stage}_k = \texttt{approved} \wedge \texttt{i-ptr}_k = i)$
ready(i): $\exists j, k \in N(i)(ready(i,j,k) \wedge ((\texttt{stage}_k = \texttt{approved} \wedge \texttt{i-ptr}_k = i) \vee (\texttt{stage}_k = \texttt{faithful} \wedge \texttt{m-ptr}_k = i)))$

valid1(i): $single(i) \vee \exists j \in N(i)(proposing(i,j) \vee discouraged(i,j) \vee approved(i,j) \vee faithful(i,j))$
$\vee\ \exists j, k \in N(i)(curious(i,j,k) \vee open(i,j,k) \vee promise(i,j,k)$
$\vee\ confirmed(i,j,k) \vee ready(i,j,k))$
no_invalid1_neighbor(i): $\forall x \in N(i)\ valid1(x)$
valid(i): $single(i) \vee proposing(i) \vee discouraged(i) \vee approved(i) \vee faithful(i) \vee curious(i) \vee open(i) \vee promise(i) \vee confirmed(i) \vee ready(i)$

Actions
$\texttt{reset} :: \neg valid1(i) \vee (\neg valid(i) \wedge no\_invalid1\_neighbor(i))$
$\mapsto \texttt{stage}_i = \texttt{single}, \texttt{i-ptr}_i = \bot, \texttt{m-ptr}_i = \bot$

$\texttt{invite} :: no\_invalid1\_neighbor(i) \wedge single(i) \wedge \exists j \in N(i)(\texttt{stage}_j = \texttt{single}\ or\ \texttt{proposing}) \mapsto \texttt{stage}_i = \texttt{proposing}, \texttt{i-ptr}_i = j$

Fig. 6. Algorithm MM1D

$\texttt{match} :: \textit{no\_invalid1\_neighbor(i)} \wedge \exists j \in N(i)($
$(\textit{single}(i) \wedge \texttt{i-ptr}_j = i \wedge \texttt{stage}_j = \texttt{proposing})$
$\vee (\textit{proposing}(i) \wedge \texttt{i-ptr}_j = i \wedge \exists k \in N(i)(\texttt{i-ptr}_i = k \wedge (j = k \vee (\texttt{stage}_k =$
$\texttt{proposing} \wedge i = \min(k,i,j)))) \wedge \texttt{stage}_j = \texttt{proposing})$
$\vee ((\textit{proposing}(i) \vee \textit{discouraged}(i)) \wedge \texttt{i-ptr}_i = j \wedge \texttt{m-ptr}_j = i \wedge \texttt{stage}_j =$
$\texttt{faithful})$
$\vee (\textit{approved}(i) \wedge \texttt{i-ptr}_i = j \wedge \texttt{i-ptr}_j = i \wedge \texttt{stage}_j = \texttt{ready}))$
$\mapsto \texttt{stage}_i = \texttt{faithful}, \texttt{i-ptr}_i = \perp, \texttt{m-ptr}_i = j$

$\texttt{get\_curious} :: \textit{no\_invalid1\_neighbor(i)} \wedge \textit{faithful}(i)$
$\wedge \exists j \in N(i)(\texttt{m-ptr}_i = j \wedge (\texttt{stage}_j = \texttt{faithful} \textit{ or } \texttt{curious}))$
$\wedge \exists k \in N(i)((\texttt{stage}_k = \texttt{single} \textit{ or } \texttt{proposing}) \wedge \texttt{i-ptr}_k \neq i)$
$\mapsto \texttt{stage}_i = \texttt{curious}, \texttt{i-ptr}_i = k$

$\texttt{open} :: \textit{no\_invalid1\_neighbor(i)} \wedge \textit{curious}(i) \wedge \exists j \in N(i)(\texttt{m-ptr}_i = j \wedge \texttt{i-ptr}_j \neq \perp$
$) \mapsto \texttt{stage}_i = \texttt{open}$

$\texttt{confirm} :: \textit{no\_invalid1\_neighbor(i)} \wedge (\textit{open}(i) \vee \textit{promise}(i)) \wedge \exists k \in N(i)(\texttt{i-ptr}_i =$
$k \wedge \texttt{i-ptr}_k = i \wedge \texttt{stage}_k = \texttt{approved}) \mapsto \texttt{stage}_i = \texttt{confirmed}$

$\texttt{promise} :: \textit{no\_invalid1\_neighbor(i)} \wedge \textit{open}(i) \wedge \exists j,k \in N(i)(\texttt{m-ptr}_i = j \wedge \texttt{i-ptr}_i =$
$k \wedge \texttt{stage}_j = \texttt{confirmed} \wedge \texttt{i-ptr}_k \neq i \wedge (\texttt{stage}_k = \texttt{proposing} \textit{ or } \texttt{approved})) \mapsto$
$\texttt{stage}_i = \texttt{promise}$

$\texttt{approve} :: \textit{no\_invalid1\_neighbor(i)}$
$\wedge ((\textit{single}(i) \wedge \exists x \in N(i)(\texttt{i-ptr}_x = i \wedge (\texttt{stage}_x = \texttt{open} \textit{ or } \texttt{promise})))$
$\vee (\textit{discouraged}(i) \wedge \exists j,x \in N(i)(\texttt{i-ptr}_i = j \wedge \neg(\texttt{stage}_j = \texttt{faithful} \wedge \texttt{m-ptr}_j =$
$i) \wedge \texttt{i-ptr}_x = i \wedge \texttt{stage}_x = \texttt{promise})))$
$\mapsto \texttt{stage}_i = \texttt{approved}, \texttt{i-ptr}_i = x$

$\texttt{discourage} :: \textit{no\_invalid1\_neighbor(i)} \wedge \textit{proposing}(i) \wedge \exists j,x \in N(i)(\texttt{i-ptr}_i =$
$j \wedge \texttt{i-ptr}_x = i \wedge (\texttt{stage}_j = \texttt{proposing} \textit{ or } \texttt{approved}) \wedge \texttt{stage}_x = \texttt{promise}) \mapsto$
$\texttt{stage}_i = \texttt{discouraged}$

$\texttt{get\_ready} :: \textit{no\_invalid1\_neighbor(i)} \wedge \textit{confirmed}(i) \wedge \exists j \in N(i)(\texttt{m-ptr}_i =$
$j \wedge (\texttt{stage}_j = \texttt{confirmed} \textit{ or } \texttt{ready})) \mapsto \texttt{stage}_i = \texttt{ready}$

$\texttt{migrate} :: \textit{no\_invalid1\_neighbor(i)} \wedge \textit{ready}(i) \wedge \exists j,k \in N(i)(\texttt{m-ptr}_i =$
$j \wedge \texttt{i-ptr}_i = k \wedge \texttt{stage}_k = \texttt{faithful} \wedge \texttt{m-ptr}_k = i \wedge (\texttt{stage}_j = \texttt{ready} \vee \texttt{m-ptr}_j \neq$
$i)) \mapsto \texttt{stage}_i = \texttt{faithful}, \texttt{i-ptr}_i = \perp, \texttt{m-ptr}_i = k$

$\texttt{cancel\_invitation} :: \textit{no\_invalid1\_neighbor(i)} \wedge \exists k \in N(i)(\texttt{i-ptr}_i = k \wedge$
$((\textit{proposing}(i) \wedge (\texttt{stage}_k = \texttt{discouraged} \vee (\texttt{stage}_k = \texttt{faithful} \wedge \texttt{m-ptr}_k \neq$
$i) \vee (\texttt{stage}_k = \texttt{curious}, \texttt{open}, \texttt{promise}, \texttt{confirmed} \textit{ or } \texttt{ready})))$
$\vee (\textit{approved}(i) \wedge ((\texttt{stage}_k = \texttt{faithful} \textit{ or } \texttt{curious}) \vee ((\texttt{stage}_k =$
$\texttt{open}, \texttt{promise}, \texttt{confirmed} \textit{ or } \texttt{ready}) \wedge \texttt{i-ptr}_k \neq i))))$
$\mapsto \texttt{stage}_i = \texttt{single}, \texttt{i-ptr}_i = \perp$

$\texttt{cancel\_migration} :: \textit{no\_invalid1\_neighbor(i)}$
$\wedge \exists j,k \in N(i)(\texttt{m-ptr}_i = j \wedge \texttt{i-ptr}_i = k$
$\wedge (((\textit{curious}(i) \vee \textit{open}(i) \vee \textit{promise}(i)) \wedge \texttt{m-ptr}_k \neq \perp)$
$\vee ((\textit{open}(i) \vee \textit{confirmed}(i)) \wedge \texttt{stage}_j = \texttt{faithful})))$
$\mapsto \texttt{stage}_i = \texttt{faithful}, \texttt{i-ptr}_i = \perp$

Fig. 7. Algorithm MM1D (cont.)

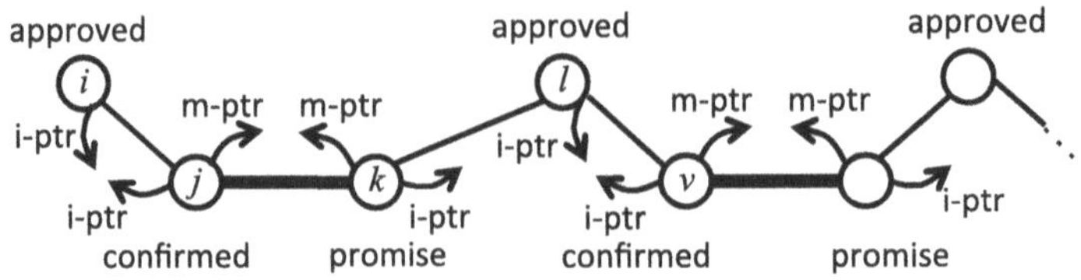

Fig. 8. Chain of nodes

execute `open` if k is `curious`, and j can execute `get_ready` if k is `confirmed`. Therefore, k is `open` or `promise`, and, from the validity of `open` and `promise`, there is a node $l \in N(k)$ such that $\texttt{i-ptr}_k = l$.

A node k can execute `cancel_migration` if $\texttt{m-ptr}_l \neq \perp$ that is l is `faithful`, `curious`, `open`, `promise`, `confirmed` (or `ready`). If l is `single`, l can execute `approve`. If l is `proposing` and $\texttt{i-ptr}_l = k$, l can execute `cancel_invitation`. If l is `proposing` and $\texttt{i-ptr}_l \neq k$, k can execute `promise` if k is `open`, and l can execute `discourage` if k is `promise`. From Lemma 2, l is `approved`. If $\texttt{i-ptr}_l = k$, k can execute `confirm`. Therefore, $\texttt{i-ptr}_l \neq k$, and if k is `open`, k can execute `promise`. This implies k is `promise`.

Let v be a node such that $\texttt{i-ptr}_l = v$. From validity *approved*(l), v is `faithful`, `curious`, `open`, `promise`, `confirmed` or `ready`. If v is `faithful` or `curious`, $\texttt{m-ptr}_v \neq l$ from Lemma 3 and v can execute `cancel_invitation`. If v is `open`, `promise` or `confirmed` and $\texttt{i-ptr}_v \neq l$, l can execute `cancel_invitation`.

Therefore, $\texttt{i-ptr}_v = l$ and v is `open`, `promise` or `confirmed`. If v is `open` or `promise`, v can execute `confirm`. Therefore, we can conclude v is `confirmed`.

Repeating the above observation, we can show there is an infinite sequence of nodes in stages `approved`, `confirmed`, `promise`, `approved`, `confirmed`, `promise`, `approved`, $\cdots$. However, there is no such a sequence since there is no cycle of length of a multiple of 3. A contradiction.

Lemma 5. *There is no* `approved` *node in any terminal configuration.*

Proof. By contradiction. Assume there is an `approved` node i in some terminal configuration. From validity *approved*(i), there is a node $j \in N(i)$ such that j is `faithful`, `curious`, `open`, `promise`, `confirmed`, or `ready`. From Lemma 1, j is not `ready`, and from Lemma 4, if j is `open`, `promise`, `confirmed`, $\texttt{i-ptr}_j \neq i$. Therefore, i can execute `cancel_invitation`. A contradiction.

Theorem 1. *A maximal matching is constructed in any terminal configuration of MM1D for any graphs without a cycle of length of a multiple of 3.*

Proof. By contradiction. Assume that a matching is not maximal in some terminal configuration. There are adjacent free nodes i and j in `single` or `proposing` by Lemmas 2 and 5. If one of the two node is `single`, it can invite the other. Therefore, both nodes are `proposing`.

Let k be a node such that $\texttt{i-ptr}_i = k$. If k is not free, k does not point to i by m-ptr by Lemma 3, and i can execute cancel_invitation. Therefore, i is pointing to a proposing node. If two proposing nodes point to each other, they can make a match. This implies that there is a cycle of proposing nodes where each node points to the next. In this case, the node with the minimum color can execute match. A contradiction.

Theorem 2. *A 1-maximal matching is constructed in any terminal configuration of MM1D for any graphs without a cycle of length of a multiple of 3.*

Proof. By contradiction. Assume that a matching is not 1-maximal in some terminal configuration. From Lemmas 1, 2 and 5, there is no discouraged, ready or approved node. Since it is terminal, a maximal matching is constructed by Theorem 1. Therefore, there are matched nodes i and j and both have free neighboring nodes.

Node i or j is not faithful since it can invite a free neighboring node if faithful. Node i is not curious since j is not faithful and it can become open. Therefore, i points to neighboring node k. Node k is not single since it can approve the invitation from i. Therefore, k is proposing.

From Theorem1, there is no adjacent free nodes, and therefore, k points to some non-free node x. From Lemma 3, $\texttt{m-ptr}_x \neq k$. In this case, k can execute cancel_invitation. A contradiction.

Now we show that MM1D always brings the network to a terminal configuration and evaluate the time complexity. In this part, the topology does not need to be restricted. That is, MM1D always brings the network to a terminal configuration with $O(e)$ moves even if the network includes a cycle of length of a multiple of 3.

Lemma 6. *If a single or proposing node i is valid, i is valid while it is single or proposing.*

Proof. Validities $single(i)$ and $proposing(i)$ check only the variables of a node i. That is the validity of a node is independent of its neighboring nodes. Since any move keeps the one node validity, a single or proposing valid node is valid while it is single or proposing.

Lemma 7. *Once a node executes match or migrate, the node never executes reset.*

Proof. By contradiction. Assume some nodes execute reset after executing match or migrate. Let i be a node that executes such a reset first. Let r be the move of such a reset, and m be the last match or migrate executed by i before r. The node i is faithful, curious, open, promise, confirmed or ready between m and r.

Let j be a node that i sets $\texttt{m-ptr}_i = j$ by m. Since i changes m-ptr by match, migrate and reset, $\texttt{m-ptr}_i = j$ until i executes r. When i executes m (i.e. immediately before i executes m), the node j is faithful and $\texttt{m-ptr}_j = i$, or

j is proposing or ready and $\texttt{i-ptr}_j = i$. The node j may become discouraged simultaneously with m.

Validity of i depends on i and j if i is faithful, curious, open or promise, depends on i, j and k if i is confirmed where $k = \texttt{i-ptr}_i$, and depends on i and k if i is ready. Validity is guaranteed if nodes follow the algorithm without reset. Therefore, no action except reset brings multi nodes invalidity. When i executes m, multi nodes validity holds for i and one node validity holds for any neighboring node of i, and this implies some neighboring nodes on which i's validity depends execute reset between m and r.

If j is proposing when i executes m, j is valid while it is proposing from Lemma 6 and will execute match to make a match with i. If j becomes discouraged simultaneously with m, validity of j holds while $\texttt{m-ptr}_i = j$ and i is faithful. Since i is faithful while j is discouraged, j is valid while it is discouraged and executes match to make a match with i. If j is ready when i executes m, validity of j also holds while $\texttt{m-ptr}_i = j$ and i is faithful, and j will execute match to make a match with i. Once i executes match after m, j does not execute reset before r from the assumption.

If j is faithful when i executes m, $\texttt{m-ptr}_j = i$ holds unless j executes match, migrate and reset. While j is faithful, curious, open or promise, $\texttt{m-ptr}_j = i$ and j's validity depends on only i and j. Therefore, j never executes reset unless i executes reset. Node j never resets before r once it executes match or migrate from the assumption.

A remaining case is that some node $k = \texttt{i-ptr}_i$ executes reset while i is confirmed or ready, or j resets while j is confirmed or ready and $\texttt{m-ptr}_j = i$. In the latter case, j's validity depends on i and some node $l = \texttt{i-ptr}_j$, and therefore, l executes reset and it causes j's reset.

That is, there is some node invited by i or j when it is confirmed or ready, and the invited node resets. A node becomes confirmed if it notices that the invited node approves its invitation. This implies the node invited by i or j became approved when it approved the invitation. While the node invited by i or j is approved, it remains valid because i or j is confirmed or ready. The invited node may become faithful by executing match. In this case, the node never executes reset after executing match before r from the assumption. A contradiction.

Lemma 8. *Total number of* reset *moves is $O(n)$.*

Proof. Once a node executes reset, it becomes *single*. The node never resets while it is single or proposing by Lemma 6. Once a node becomes faithful by executing match, it never resets by Lemma 7. A discouraged node i resets by violating one node validity in an initial configuration or violating multi nodes validity. The multi nodes invalidity means that there is no promise node k such as $\texttt{i-ptr}_k = i$ or there is no faithful node j such as $\texttt{m-ptr}_j = i$. Those happen if a promise or faithful node resets. That implies reset by a promise node may cause at most one more reset and reset by a faithful node may cause at most one more reset. Each node resets in promise or faithful at most once, and therefore, the total number of reset moves is $O(n)$.

Lemma 9. *Each node executes* `match` *at most once.*

Proof. A free node becomes non-free by `match`, and never executes `reset` once it executes `match` by Lemma 7. That is the node never goes back to free. Therefore, any node executes `match` at most once.

Lemma 10. *The total number of* `migrate` *moves is* $O(n)$.

Proof. Let m_1 and m_2 be two consecutive moves of `migrate` by a node i. The node i becomes `faithful` by m_1 and then invites some free neighboring node j. Then, node j executes `match` to make a match with i. That is, there is a move of `match` to make a match with i between two consecutive moves of `migrate` by i. Therefore, the total number of moves of `migrate` $\leq$ the total number of moves of `match` $+n$. From Lemma 9, it is bounded by $O(n)$.

Lemma 11. *The total number of* `cancel_invitation` *moves and* `cancel_migration` *moves is* $O(e)$.

Proof. A `proposing` node i executes `cancel_invitation` when it is initially possible or an invited node becomes `faithful`. A node i executes `cancel_migration` when it is initially possible or an invited node k = `i-ptr`$_i$ becomes non-free (`m-ptr`$_k$ $\neq\perp$) by `match` while i is `curious`, `open` or `promise`, or its partner j = `m-ptr`$_i$ becomes `faithful` by `cancel_migration` while i is `open` or `confirmed`.

Now we classify moves of `cancel_invitation` and `cancel_migration` with *direct cancels* and *indirect cancels*. The direct cancel is a move caused by `match` or its initial state. The indirect cancel is a cancel caused by `cancel_invitation` or `cancel_migration`.

To increase the number of matches, four nodes cooperatively work, and `cancel` by one of the four affects other three nodes. Therefore, one direct cancel causes at most three indirect cancels.

Each node executes a direct cancel caused by its initial state at most once. If a node i executes `match`, it causes at most δ_i direct cancels where δ_i is a degree of i. Since every node executes `match` at most once by Lemma 9, the total number of direct cancels caused by `match` is at most $\Sigma_{i\in V}\delta_i = e$. Therefore the total number of direct and indirect cancels is at most $4 \times (n + e) = O(e)$.

Lemma 12. *MM1D is silent and takes* $O(e)$ *moves to reach a terminal configuration.*

Proof. Let MOV_i denote the total number of moves of a node i, and R_i, C_i and M_i be the numbers of moves of `reset`, cancel (`cancel_invitation` or `cancel_migration`), and `migrate` by a node i. Figure 9 shows a stage transition in MM1D, where only `reset`, `cancel_invitation`, `cancel_migration` and `migrate` move to a left stage. A node executes at most 9 actions between these moves. From the observation and Lemmas 8, 10 and 11, the number of moves is bounded as follows.

$$MOV_i \leq 10(R_i + C_i + M_i + 1)$$

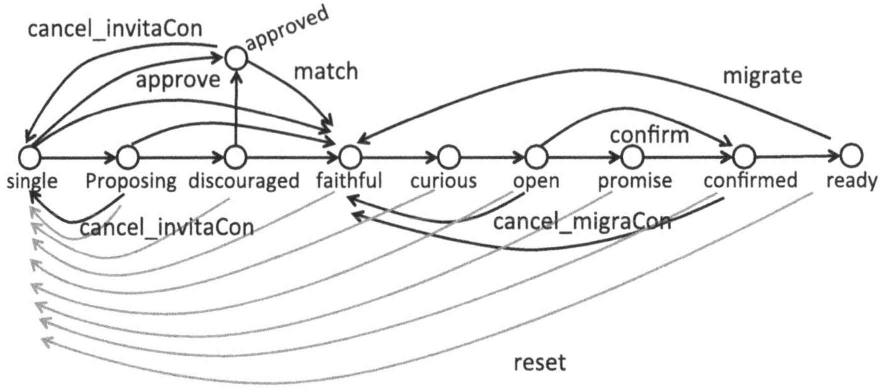

Fig. 9. Transitions of stages

$$\Sigma_{i \in V} R_i = O(n), \Sigma_{i \in V} C_i = O(e), \Sigma_{i \in V} M_i = O(n)$$

$$\Sigma_{i \in V} MOV_i \leq 10(\Sigma_{i \in V} R_i + \Sigma_{i \in V} C_i + \Sigma_{i \in V} M_i + \Sigma_{i \in V} 1) = O(e)$$

Since each node always takes a finite number of moves, MM1D always reaches a terminal configuration and this also implies MM1D is silent.

Theorem 3. *MM1D is silent and takes $O(e)$ moves to construct 1-maximal matching for any graphs without a cycle of length of a multiple of 3 under an unfair distributed daemon.*

Proof. Lemma 12 denotes that the system eventually reaches to a terminal configuration. In addition, Theorem 2 denotes a 1-maximal matching is constructed in any terminal configuration for any graphs without a cycle of length of a multiple of 3. Therefore, MM1D is silent and constructs a 1-maximal matching in $O(e)$ moves for any graphs without a cycle of length of a multiple of 3 under an unfair distributed daemon.

5 Conclusion

We proposed a 1-maximal matching algorithm MM1D that is silent and works for any arbitrarily shaped networks without a cycle whose length is a multiple of three under a distributed unfair daemon.

The time complexity of our algorithm matches the best known complexity for the central daemon, that is $O(e)$ moves, and significantly outperforms the best known complexity for the distributed daemon (that was exponential prior to this work). Using our approach, one does not have to trade efficiency (move complexity) for versatility (distributed unfair daemon).

Considering networks that do not contain cycles whose length is a multiple of three was mandated by impossibility results in the case without global structural information [10]. An intriguing open question remain, if one is to retain the best known time complexity (that is, $O(e)$ moves under the distributed unfair daemon), what is the minimal amount of global structural information that permits to handle arbitrary networks (including those with cycles whose size is a multiple of three)?

References

1. Asada, Y., Ooshita, F., Inoue, M.: An efficient silent self-stabilizing 1-maximal matching algorithm in anonymous networks. J. Graph Algorithms Appl. **20**(1), 59–78 (2016). http://dx.doi.org/10.7155/jgaa.00384
2. Blair, J.R., Manne, F.: Efficient self-stabilizing algorithms for tree networks. In: Proceedings of 23rd International Conference on Distributed Computing Systems, pp. 20–26. IEEE (2003)
3. Blair, J., Hedetniemi, S., Hedetniemi, S., Jacobs, D.: Self-stabilizing maximum matchings. Congressus Numerantium **153**, 151–160 (2001)
4. Chattopadhyay, S., Higham, L., Seyffarth, K.: Dynamic and self-stabilizing distributed matching. In: Proceedings of the Twenty-First Annual Symposium on Principles of Distributed Computing, pp. 290–297. ACM (2002)
5. Datta, A.K., Larmoreand, L.L., Masuzawa, T.: Maximum matching for anonymous trees with constant space per process. In: Proceedings of International Conference on Principles of Distributed Systems. pp. 1–16 (2015)
6. Devismes, S., Masuzawa, T., Tixeuil, S.: Communication efficiency in self-stabilizing silent protocols. In: Proceedings of 23rd International Conference on Distributed Computing Systems, pp. 474–481. IEEE (2009)
7. Dijkstra, E.W.: Self-stabilizing systems in spite of distributed control. Commun. ACM **17**(11), 643–644 (1974)
8. Dubois, S., Tixeuil, S.: A taxonomy of daemons in self-stabilization. CoRR abs/1110.0334 (2011). http://arxiv.org/abs/1110.0334
9. Dubois, S., Tixeuil, S., Zhu, N.: The byzantine brides problem. In: Kranakis, E., Krizanc, D., Luccio, F. (eds.) FUN 2012. LNCS, vol. 7288, pp. 107–118. Springer, Heidelberg (2012). doi:10.1007/978-3-642-30347-0_13
10. Goddard, W., Hedetniemi, S.T., Shi, Z., et al.: An anonymous self-stabilizing algorithm for 1-maximal matching in trees. In: Proceedings of International Conference on Parallel and Distributed Processing Techniques and Applications, pp. 797–803 (2006)
11. Guellati, N., Kheddouci, H.: A survey on self-stabilizing algorithms for independence, domination, coloring, and matching in graphs. J. Parallel Distrib. Comput. **70**(4), 406–415 (2010)
12. Hedetniemi, S.T., Jacobs, D.P., Srimani, P.K.: Maximal matching stabilizes in time $O(m)$. Inf. Process. Lett. **80**(5), 221–223 (2001)
13. Hsu, S.C., Huang, S.T.: A self-stabilizing algorithm for maximal matching. Inf. Process. Lett. **43**(2), 77–81 (1992)
14. Karaata, M.H., Saleh, K.A.: Distributed self-stabilizing algorithm for finding maximum matching. Comput. Syst. Sci. Eng. **15**(3), 175–180 (2000)
15. Kimoto, M., Tsuchiya, T., Kikuno, T.: The time complexity of Hsu and Huang's self-stabilizing maximal matching algorithm. IEICE Trans. Inf. Syst. E93-D **10**, 2850–2853 (2010)

16. Manne, F., Mjelde, M., Pilard, L., Tixeuil, S.: A new self-stabilizing maximal matching algorithm. Theor. Comput. Sci. **410**(14), 1336–1345 (2009)
17. Manne, F., Mjelde, M., Pilard, L., Tixeuil, S.: A self-stabilizing 2/3-approximation algorithm for the maximum matching problem. Theor. Comput. Sci. **412**(40), 5515–5526 (2011)
18. Tel, G.: Introduction to distributed algorithms. Cambridge University Press, New York (2000)

Self-stabilizing Byzantine Clock Synchronization with Optimal Precision

Pankaj Khanchandani[1(✉)] and Christoph Lenzen[2]

[1] Computer Engineering and Networks Laboratory (TIK), ETH Zurich, Zurich, Switzerland
kpankaj@ethz.ch
[2] Max Planck Institute for Informatics, Saarland Informatics Campus, Saarbrücken, Germany
clenzen@mpi-inf.mpg.de

Abstract. We revisit the approach to Byzantine fault-tolerant clock synchronization based on approximate agreement introduced by Lynch and Welch. Our contribution is threefold: (i) We provide a slightly refined variant of the algorithm yielding improved bounds on the skew that can be achieved and the sustainable frequency offsets. (ii) We show how to extend the technique to also synchronize clock rates. This permits less frequent communication without significant loss of precision, provided that clock rates change sufficiently slowly. (iii) We present a coupling scheme that allows to make these algorithms self-stabilizing while preserving their high precision. The scheme utilizes a low-precision, but self-stabilizing algorithm for the purpose of recovery.

1 Introduction

When designing synchronous distributed systems, the most fundamental question is how to generate and distribute the system clock. This task is mission critical, both in terms of performance and reliability. With ever-growing hardware complexity, reliable high-performance clocking becomes increasingly challenging; concurrently, the ramifications of clocking faults become harder to predict.

Against this background, it might be unsurprising that fault-tolerant distributed clock synchronization algorithms have found their way into real-world systems with high reliability demands: the Time-Triggered Protocol (TTP) [13] and FlexRay [9,10] tolerate *Byzantine* (i.e., worst-case) faults and are utilized in cars and airplanes. Both of these systems derive from the classic fault-tolerant synchronization algorithm by Lynch and Welch [18], which is based on repeatedly performing approximate agreement [7] on the time of the next clock pulse. Another application domain with even more stringent requirements is hardware for spacecraft and satellites. Here, a reliable system clock is in demand despite frequent transient faults due to radiation. In addition, quartz oscillators are prone to damage during launch, making the use of less accurate, electronic oscillators preferable.

Full paper available at arXiv.

B. Bonakdarpour and F. Petit (Eds.): SSS 2016, LNCS 10083, pp. 213–230, 2016.
DOI: 10.1007/978-3-319-49259-9_18

Unfortunately, existing implementations are not *self-stabilizing*, i.e., do not guarantee automatic recovery from transient faults. This is essential for the space domain, but also highly desirable in the systems utilizing TTP or FlexRay. This claim is supported by the presence of various mechanisms that monitor the nodes and perform resets in case of observed faulty behavior in both protocols. Thus, it is of interest to devise synchronization algorithms that stabilize on their own, instead of relying on monitoring techniques: these need to be highly reliable as well, or their failure may bring down the system due to erroneous detection of or response to faults.

Accordingly, in this work we set out to answer the following questions:

1. Can the guarantees of [18] be further improved? In particular, how does the approach perform if local clock sources are less precise than quartz oscillators?
2. Under which circumstances is it useful to apply the technique also to frequencies, i.e., algorithmically adjust clock rates?
3. Can the solution be made self-stabilizing?

Our Contribution. We obtain promising answers to the above questions, in the sense that conceptually simple (i.e., implementation-friendly!) variations on the Lynch-Welch approach achieve excellent performance guarantees. Specifically, we obtain the following main results.

1. We present a refined analysis of a variant of the Lynch-Welch algorithm. We show that the algorithm converges to a steady-state error $E \in \mathcal{O}((\vartheta - 1)T + U)$, where hardware clock rates are between 1 and ϑ, messages take between $d - U$ and d time to arrive at their destination, and $T \in \Omega(d)$ is the (nominal) time between consecutive clock pulses (i.e., the time required for a single approximate agreement step). This works even for very poor local clock sources: it suffices that $\vartheta \leq 1.1$, although the skew bound goes to infinity as ϑ approaches this critical value; for $\vartheta \leq 1.01$, the bound is fairly close to $2(\vartheta - 1)T + 4U$.[1]
2. We give a second algorithm that interleaves approximate agreement on clock *rates* with the phase (i.e., clock offset) correction scheme. If the clocks are sufficiently stable, i.e., the maximum rate of change ν of clock rates is sufficiently small, this enables to significantly extend T (and thus decrease the frequency of communication) without substantially affecting skews. Provided that ϑ is not too large and $\max\{(\vartheta - 1)^2 T, \nu T^2\} \ll U$, it is possible to achieve $\mathcal{O}(U)$ skew.
3. We introduce a generic approach that enables to couple either of these algorithms to FATAL [4,5]. FATAL is a self-stabilizing synchronization algorithm, but in comparison suffers from poor performance. The coupling scheme permits to combine the best of both worlds, namely the self-stabilization properties of FATAL with the small skew of the Lynch-Welch synchronization scheme.

[1] For comparison, the critical value in [18] is smaller than 1.025, i.e., we can handle a factor 4 weaker bound on $\vartheta - 1$. Non-quartz oscillators used in space applications, where temperatures vary widely, may have ϑ close to this value, cf. [1].

On the technical side, the first two results require little innovation compared to prior work. However, it proved challenging to obtain clean, easy-to-implement algorithms that are amenable to a tractable analysis and achieve tight skew bounds. This is worthwhile for two reasons: (1) there is strong indication that the approach has considerable practical merit,[2] and (2) no readily usable mathematical analysis of the frequency correction scheme exists in the literature.[3]

In contrast, the coupling scheme we use to combine our non-stabilizing algorithms with FATAL showcases a novel technique of independent interest. We leverage FATAL's clock "beats" to effectively (re-)initialize the synchronization algorithm we couple it to. Here, care has to be taken to avoid such resets from occurring during regular operation of the Lynch-Welch scheme, as this could result in large skews or spurious clock pulses. The solution is a feedback mechanism enabling the synchronization algorithm to actively trigger the next beat of FATAL at the appropriate time. FATAL stabilizes regardless of how these feedback signals behave, while actively triggering beats ensures that all nodes pass the checks which, if failed, trigger the respective node being reset.

Organization of the paper. After presenting related work and the model, we proceed in the order of the main results listed above: phase synchronization (Sect. 4), frequency synchronization (Sect. 5), and finally the coupling scheme adding self-stabilization (Sect. 6). Due to space constraints, all proofs are omitted from this extended abstract in favor of conceptual descriptions.

2 Related Work

TTP [13] and FlexRay [9,10] are both implemented in software (barring minor hardware components). This is sufficient for their application domains: the goal here is to enable synchronous communication between hardware components at frequencies in the megahertz range. Solutions fully implemented in hardware are of interest for two reasons. First, having to implement the full software abstraction dramatically increases the number of potential reasons for a node to fail – at least from the point of view of the synchronization algorithm. A slim hardware implementation is thus likely to result in a substantially higher degree of reliability of the clocking mechanism. Second, if higher precision of synchronization is required, the significantly smaller delays incurred by dedicated hardware make it possible to meet these demands.

Apart from these issues, the complexity of a software solution renders TTP and FlexRay unsuitable as fault-tolerant clocking schemes for VLSI circuits. The DARTS project [3,11] aimed at developing such a scheme, with the goal of coming up with a robust clocking method for space applications. Instead of being

[2] A prototype FPGA implementation achieves 182 ps skew [12], which is suitable for generating a system clock.

[3] The framework in [15,16] addresses frequency correction, but substantial specialization would be required to achieve good constants in the bounds.

based on the Lynch-Welch approach, it implements the fault-tolerant synchronization algorithm by Srikanth and Toueg [17]. Unfortunately, DARTS falls short of its design goals in two ways. On the one hand, the Srikanth-Toueg primitive achieves skews of $\Theta(d)$, which tend to be significantly larger than those attainable with the Lynch-Welch approach.[4] Accordingly, the operational frequency DARTS can sustain (without large communication buffers and communication delays of multiple logical rounds) is in the range of 100 MHz, i.e., about an order of magnitude smaller than typical system speeds. Moreover, DARTS is not self-stabilizing. This means that DARTS – just like TTP and FlexRay – is unlikely to successfully cope with high rates of transient faults. Worse, the rate of transient faults will scale with the number of nodes (and thus sustainable faults). For space environments, this implies that adding fault-tolerance without self-stabilization cannot be expected to increase the reliability of the system at all.

These concerns inspired follow-up work seeking to overcome these downsides of DARTS. From an abstract point of view, FATAL [4,5] can be interpreted as another incarnation of the Srikanth-Toueg approach. However, FATAL combines tolerance to Byzantine faults with self-stabilization in $\mathcal{O}(n)$ time with probability $1-2^{-\Omega(n)}$; after recovery is complete, the algorithm maintains correct operation deterministically. Like DARTS, FATAL and the substantial line of prior work on Byzantine self-stabilizing synchronization algorithms (e.g., [2,8]) cannot achieve better clock skews than $\Theta(d)$. The key motivation for the present paper is to combine the better precision achieved by the Lynch-Welch approach with the self-stabilization properties of FATAL.

Concerning frequency correction, little related work exists. A notable exception is the extension of the interval-based synchronization framework to rate synchronization [15,16]. In principle, it seems feasible to derive similar results by specialization and minor adaptions of this powerful machinery to our setting. Unfortunately, apart from the technical hurdles involved, this is very likely to result in worse constants and more involved algorithms, and it is unclear whether our approach to self-stabilization can be fitted to this framework. However, it is worth noting that the overall proof strategies for the (non-stabilizing) phase and frequency correction algorithms bear notable similarities to this generic framework: separately deriving bounds on the precision of measurements, plugging these into a generic convergence argument, and separating the analysis of frequency and phase corrections.

Coming to lower bounds and impossibility results, the following is known.

- In a system of n nodes, no algorithm can tolerate $\lceil n/3 \rceil$ Byzantine faults. All mentioned algorithms are optimal in that they tolerate $\lceil n/3 \rceil - 1$ Byzantine faults [6].
- To tolerate this number of faults, $\Omega(n^2)$ communication links are required.[5] All mentioned algorithms assume full connectivity and communicate by broad-

[4] d tends to be at least one or two orders of magnitude larger than U.

[5] If a node has fewer than $2f+1$ neighbors in a system tolerating f faults, it cannot distinguish whether it synchronizes to a group of f correct or f faulty neighbors.

casts (faulty nodes may not adhere to this). Less well-connected topologies are outside the scope of this work.

- The worst-case precision of an algorithm cannot be better than $(1-1/n)U$ in a network where communication delays may vary by U [14]. In the fault-free case and with $\vartheta - 1$ sufficiently small, this bound can be almost matched (cf. Sect. 4); all variants of the Lynch-Welch approach match this bound asymptotically granted sufficiently accurate local clocks.
- Trivially, the worst case precision of any algorithm is at least $(\vartheta-1)T$ if nodes exchange messages every T time units. In the fault-free case, this is essentially matched by our phase correction algorithm as well.
- With faults, the upper bound on the skew of the algorithm increases by factor $1/(1-\alpha)$, where $\alpha \approx 1/2$ if $\vartheta \approx 1$. It appears plausible that this is optimal under the constraint that the algorithm's resilience to Byzantine faults is optimal, due to a lower bound on the convergence rate of approximate agreement [7].

Overall, the resilience of the presented solution to faults is optimal, its precision asymptotically optimal, and it seems reasonable to assume that there is little room for improvement in this regard. In contrast, no non-trivial lower bounds on the stabilization time of self-stabilizing fault-tolerant synchronization algorithms are known. It remains an open question whether it is possible to achieve stabilization within $o(n)$ time.

3 Model

We assume a fully connected system of n nodes, up to $f := \lfloor (n-1)/3 \rfloor$ of which may be Byzantine faulty (i.e., arbitrarily deviate from the protocol). We denote by V the set of all nodes and by $C \subseteq V$ the subset of *correct* nodes, i.e., those that are not faulty.

Communication is by broadcast of "pulses," which are messages without content: the only information conveyed is when a node transmitted a pulse. Nodes can distinguish between senders; this is used to distinguish the case of multiple pulses being sent by a single (faulty) node from multiple nodes sending one pulse each. Note that faulty nodes are not bound by the broadcast restriction, i.e., may send a pulse to a subset of the nodes only. The system is semi-synchronous. A pulse sent by node $v \in C$ at (Newtonian) time $p_v \in \mathbb{R}_0^+$ is received by node $w \in C$ at time $t_{vw} \in [p_v + d - U, p_v + d]$; we refer to d as the *maximum message delay* (or, chiefly, delay) and to U as the *delay uncertainty* (or, chiefly, uncertainty).

For these timing guarantees to be useful to an algorithm, the nodes must have a means to measure the progress of time. Each node $v \in C$ is equipped with a hardware clock H_v, which is modeled as a strictly increasing function $H_v : \mathbb{R}_0^+ \to \mathbb{R}_0^+$. We require that there is a constant $\vartheta > 1$ such that for all times $t < t'$, it holds that $t' - t \leq H_v(t') - H_v(t) \leq \vartheta(t' - t)$, i.e., the hardware clocks have bounded drift. We remark that our results can be easily translated to the case of discrete and bounded clocks.[6] We refer to $H_v(t)$ as the *local time* of v at time t.

Executions are event-based, where an event at node v is the reception of a message, a previously computed (and stored) local time being reached, or the initialization of the algorithm. A node may then perform computations and possibly send a pulse. For simplicity, we assume that these operations take zero time; adapting our results to account for computation time is straightforward.

Problem. A clock synchronization algorithm generates distinguished events or *clock pulses* at times $p_v(r)$ for $r \in \mathbb{N}$ and $v \in C$ so that the following conditions are satisfied for all $r \in \mathbb{N}$.

1. $\forall v, w \in C: \ |p_v(r) - p_w(r)| \leq e(r)$
2. $\forall v \in C: \ A_{\min} \leq p_v(r+1) - p_v(r) \leq A_{\max}$

The first requirement is a bound on the synchronization error between the rth clock ticks; naturally, it is desired that $e(r)$ is as small as possible. The second requirement is a bound on the time between consecutive clock ticks, which can be translated to a bound on the frequency of the clocks; here, the goal is that $A_{\min}/A_{\max} \approx 1$. The *precision* of the algorithm is measured by the steady state error[7] $E := \lim_{r' \to \infty} \sup_{r \geq r'} \{e(r)\}$. Self-stabilization will be introduced and discussed in Sect. 6.

4 Phase Synchronization Algorithm

Our basic algorithm is a variant of the one by Lynch and Welch [18], which synchronizes clocks by simulating perpetual synchronous approximate agreement [7] on the times when clock pulses should be generated. We diverge only in terms of communication: instead of round numbers, nodes broadcast content-free pulses. Due to sufficient waiting times between pulses, during regular operation received messages from correct nodes can be correctly attributed to the respective round. In fact, the primary purpose of transmitting round numbers in the Lynch-Welch algorithm is to add recovery properties. Our technique for adding self-stabilization (presented in Sect. 6) leverages the pulse synchronization algorithm from [4,5] instead, which requires to broadcast constant-sized messages only.

Properties of Approximate Agreement Steps. Abstractly speaking, the synchronization performs approximate agreement steps in each (simulated synchronous) round. In approximate agreement, each node is given an input value and the goal is to let nodes determine values that are close to each other and within the interval spanned by the correct nodes' inputs.

[6] Discretization can be handled by re-interpreting the discretization error as part of the delay uncertainty. All our algorithms use the hardware clock exclusively to measure bounded time differences.

[7] Typically, $e(r)$ is a monotone sequence, implying that simply $E = \lim_{r \to \infty} e(r)$.

Algorithm 1. Approximate agreement step at node $v \in \mathbf{C}$ (with synchronous message exchange).

// node v is given input value x_v;
broadcast x_v to all nodes (including self);
// if $w \in C$, the received value $\hat{x}_{wv} \in [x_w - \delta, x_w + \delta]$;
receive first value $\hat{x}_{wv}$ from each node w ($\hat{x}_{wv} := x_v$ if no message from w received);
$S_v \leftarrow \{\hat{x}_{wv} \,|\, w \in V\}$;
denote by S_v^k the kth element of S_v w.r.t. ascending order;
$y_v \leftarrow \dfrac{S_v^{f+1} + S_v^{n-f}}{2}$;
return y_v;

In the clock synchronization setting, there is the additional obstacle that the communicated values are points in time. Due to delay uncertainty and drifting clocks, the communicated values are subject to a (worst-case) perturbation of at most some $\delta \in \mathbb{R}_0^+$. We will determine δ later in our analysis of the clock synchronization algorithms; we assume it to be given for now. The effect of these disturbances is straightforward: they may shift outputs by at most δ in each direction, increasing the range of the outputs by an additive 2δ in each step (in the worst case).

Algorithm 1 describes an approximate agreement step from the point of view of node $v \in C$. When implementing this later on, we need to make use of timing constraints to ensure that (i) correct nodes receive each other's messages in time to perform the associated computations and (ii) correct nodes' messages can be correctly attributed to the round to which they belong. Figure 1 depicts how a round unfolds assuming that these timing constraints are satisfied.

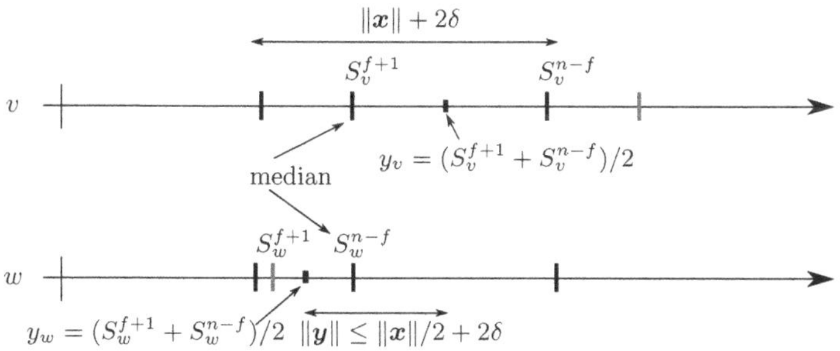

Fig. 1. An execution of Algorithm 1 at nodes v and w, where $n = 4$. There is a single faulty node, whose values are indicated in red. Note that the ranges spanned by the values received from non-faulty nodes are identical up to a perturbation of $\pm\delta$. (Color figure online)

Denote by $\boldsymbol{x}$ the $|C|$-dimensional vector of correct nodes' inputs, i.e., $(\boldsymbol{x})_v = x_v$ for $v \in C$. The *diameter* $\|\boldsymbol{x}\|$ of $\boldsymbol{x}$ is the difference between the maximum and minimum components of $\boldsymbol{x}$. Formally, $\|\boldsymbol{x}\| := \max_{v \in C}\{x_v\} - \min_{v \in C}\{x_v\}$. We will use the same notation for other values, e.g. $\boldsymbol{y}$ and $\|\boldsymbol{y}\|$. For simplicity, we assume that $|C| = n - f$ in the following; all statements can be adapted by replacing $n - f$ with $|C|$ where appropriate.

Consider the special case of $\delta = 0$. Intuitively, Algorithm 1 discards the smallest and largest f values each to ensure that values from faulty nodes cannot cause outputs to lie outside the range spanned by the correct nodes' values. Afterwards, y_v is determined as the midpoint of the interval spanned by the remaining values. Since $f < n/3$, i.e., $n - f \geq 2f + 1$, the median of correct nodes' values is part of all intervals computed by correct nodes. From this, it is easy to see that $\|\boldsymbol{y}\| \leq \|\boldsymbol{x}\|/2$, cf. Figure 1. For $\delta > 0$, we simply observe that the resulting values y_v, $v \in C$, are shifted by at most δ compared to the case where $\delta = 0$, resulting in $\|\boldsymbol{y}\| \leq \|\boldsymbol{x}\|/2 + 2\delta$.

Lemma 1. $\forall v \in C : \min_{w \in C}\{x_w\} - \delta \leq y_v \leq \max_{w \in C}\{x_w\} + \delta$.

Corollary 1. $\max_{v \in C}\{|y_v - x_v|\} \leq \|\boldsymbol{x}\| + \delta$.

Lemma 2. $\|\boldsymbol{y}\| \leq \|\boldsymbol{x}\|/2 + 2\delta$.

Algorithm. Algorithm 2 shows the pseudocode of the phase synchronization algorithm at node $v \in C$. It implements iterative approximate agreement steps on the times when to send pulses. The algorithm assumes that the nodes are initialized within a (local) time window of size F. In each round $r \in \mathbb{N}$, the nodes estimate the phase offset of their pulses[8] and then compute an according phase correction $\Delta_v(r)$. Figure 2 illustrates how a round of the algorithm plays out.

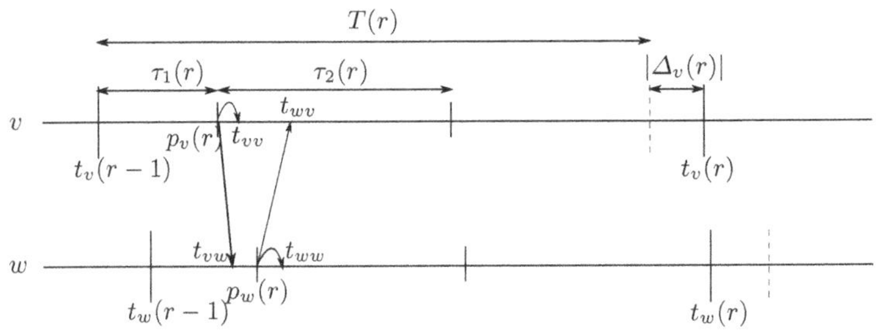

Fig. 2. A round of Algorithm 2 from the point of view of nodes v and w. Note that the durations marked on the horizontal axis are measured using the local hardware clock.

[8] Dividing the measured local time differences by $(\vartheta + 1)/2$ is an artifact of our "one-sided" definition of hardware clock rates from $[1, \vartheta]$; in an implementation, one simply reads the hardware clocks (which exhibit symmetric error) without any scaling.

Algorithm 2. Phase synchronization algorithm at $v \in C$. Round $r+1$, $r \in \mathbb{N}$, starts at time $t_v(r)$.

// $H_w(0) \in [0, F)$ for all $w \in V$
wait until time $t_v(0)$ with $H_v(t_v(0)) = F$;
foreach *round* $r \in \mathbb{N}$ **do**
    start listening for messages;
    wait until local time $H_v(t_v(r-1)) + \tau_1(r)$; // all nodes are in round r
    broadcast clock pulse to all nodes (including self);
    wait until local time $H_v(t_v(r-1)) + \tau_1(r) + \tau_2(r)$;// correct nodes' messages arrived
    for *each node* $w \in V$ **do**
        $\tau_{wv} := H_v(t_{wv})$, where first message from w received at t_{wv} ($\tau_{wv} := \infty$ if none received);
    $S_v \leftarrow \{2(\tau_{wv} - \tau_{vv})/(\vartheta + 1) \mid w \in V\}$ (as multiset);
    let S_v^k denote the kth smallest element of S_v;
    $\Delta_v(r) \leftarrow \dfrac{S_v^{f+1} + S_v^{n-f}}{2}$;
    // $T(r)$ denotes the nominal length of round r
    wait until time $t_v(r)$ with $H_v(t_v(r)) = H_v(t_v(r-1)) + T(r) - \Delta_v(r)$;

To fully specify the algorithm, we need to determine how long the waiting periods in each round are (in terms of local time), which will be given as $\tau_1(r)$, $\tau_2(r)$, and $T(r) - \Delta(r) - \tau_1(r) - \tau_2(r)$. Here, we must ensure for all $r \in \mathbb{N}$ that

1. for all $v, w \in C$, the message that v broadcasts at time $t_v(r-1) + \tau_1(r)$ is received by w at a local time from $[H_w(t_w(r-1)), H_w(t_w(r-1)) + \tau_1(r) + \tau_2(r)]$,
2. for all $v \in C$, $T(r) - \Delta_v(r) \geq \tau_1(r) + \tau_2(r)$, i.e., v computes $H_v(t_v(r))$ *before* time $t_v(r)$.

If these conditions are satisfied at all correct nodes, we say that *round r is executed correctly*, and we can interpret the round as an approximate agreement step. We will show in the next section that the following condition is sufficient for all rounds to be executed correctly.

Condition 1 *Define $e(1) := F + (1 - 1/\vartheta)\tau_1(1)$ and inductively for all $r \in \mathbb{N}$ that*

$$e(r+1) := \frac{2\vartheta^2 + 5\vartheta - 5}{2(\vartheta + 1)} e(r) + (3\vartheta - 1)U + \left(1 - \frac{1}{\vartheta}\right)(T(r) + \tau_1(r+1) - \tau_1(r)).$$

For $r \in \mathbb{N}$, we require $\tau_1(r) \geq \vartheta e(r)$, $\tau_2(r) \geq \vartheta(e(r) + d)$, and $T(r) \geq \tau_1(r) + \tau_2(r) + \vartheta(e(r) + U)$.

Here, $e(r)$ is a bound on the synchronization error in round r, i.e., we will show that $\|\boldsymbol{p}(r)\| \leq e(r)$ for all $r \in \mathbb{N}$, provided Condition 1 is satisfied.

Analysis. In this section, we prove that Condition 1 is indeed sufficient to ensure that $\|\boldsymbol{p}(r)\| \leq e(r)$ for all $r \in \mathbb{N}$. In the following, denote by $\boldsymbol{p}(r)$, $r \in \mathbb{N}_0$, the vector of times when nodes $v \in C$ broadcast their r^{th} pulse, i.e., $H_v(p_v(r)) = H_v(t_v(r-1)) + \tau_1(r)$. If $v \in C$ takes note of the pulse from $w \in C$ in round r, the corresponding value $\tau_{wv} - \tau_{vv}$ can be interpreted as inexact measurement of $p_w(r) - p_v(r)$. This is captured by the following lemma, which provides precise bounds on the incurred error.

Lemma 3. *Suppose $v \in C$ receives the pulses from both $w \in C$ and itself in round r at a time from $[H_v(t_v(r-1)), H_v(t_v(r-1)) + \tau_1(r) + \tau_2(r)]$. Then*

$$\left|\frac{2(\tau_{wv} - \tau_{vv})}{\vartheta + 1} - (p_w(r) - p_v(r))\right| < \vartheta U + \frac{\vartheta - 1}{\vartheta + 1}\|\boldsymbol{p}(r)\| .$$

Using Lemma 3, we can interpret the phase shifts $\Delta_v(r)$ as outcomes of an approximate agreement step with $\delta = \vartheta U + (\vartheta - 1)\|\boldsymbol{p}(r)\|/(\vartheta + 1)$, yielding the following corollary.

Corollary 2. *Suppose in round $r \in \mathbb{N}$, it holds for all $v, w \in C$ that v receives the pulse from $w \in C$ and itself in round r during $[H_v(t_v(r-1)), H_v(t_v(r-1)) + \tau_1(r) + \tau_2(r)]$. Then*

1. $|\Delta_v(r)| < \vartheta(\|\boldsymbol{p}(r)\| + U)$ *and*
2. $\max_{v,w \in C}\{p_v(r) - \Delta_v(r) - (p_w(r) - \Delta_w(r))\} \leq (5\vartheta - 3)\|\boldsymbol{p}(r)\|/(2(\vartheta + 1)) + 2\vartheta U$.

This readily yields a bound on $\|\boldsymbol{p}(r+1)\|$ – provided that all nodes can compute when to send the next pulse on time.

Corollary 3. *Assume that round $r \in \mathbb{N}$ is executed correctly. Then*

$$\|\boldsymbol{p}(r+1)\| \leq \frac{2\vartheta^2 + 5\vartheta - 5}{2(\vartheta + 1)}\|\boldsymbol{p}(r)\| + (3\vartheta - 1)U + \left(1 - \frac{1}{\vartheta}\right)T(r) .$$

This bound hinges on the assumption that the round is executed correctly. Calculations show that the bounds imposed by Condition 1 are sufficient.

Lemma 4. *Suppose that $\tau_1(r) \geq \vartheta(\|\boldsymbol{p}(r)\| - (d - U))$, $\tau_2(r) \geq \vartheta(\|\boldsymbol{p}(r)\| + d)$, and that $T(r) \geq \tau_1(r) + \tau_2(r) + \vartheta(\|\boldsymbol{p}(r)\| + U)$. Then round r is executed correctly.*

We have almost all pieces in place to inductively bound $\|\boldsymbol{p}(r)\|$ and determine suitable values for $\tau_1(r)$, $\tau_2(r)$, and $T(r)$. The last missing bit is an induction anchor, i.e., a bound on $\|\boldsymbol{p}(1)\|$. This follows from the assumption that all hardware clocks are initialized within F time units of each other.

Corollary 4. $\|\boldsymbol{p}(1)\| \leq F + (1 - 1/\vartheta)\tau_1(1) = e(1)$.

Theorem 1. *If Condition 1 is satisfied, for all $r \in \mathbb{N}$, it holds that $\|\boldsymbol{p}(r)\| \leq e(r)$. If $\alpha = (6\vartheta^2 + 5\vartheta - 9)/(2(\vartheta + 1)(2 - \vartheta)) < 1$ (which holds for $\vartheta \leq 1.1$), we can choose parameters so that this is true and Algorithm 2 has steady state error $E = \lim_{r \to \infty} e(r) \leq ((\vartheta - 1)d + (4\vartheta - 2)U)/((2 - \vartheta)\alpha)$.*

5 Phase and Frequency Synchronization Algorithm

In this section, we briefly summarize our results on extending the phase synchronization algorithm to also synchronize frequencies. The basic idea is to apply the approximate agreement not only to phase offsets, but also to frequency offsets. To this end, in each round the phase difference is measured twice, applying any phase correction only after the second measurement. This enables nodes to obtain an estimate of the relative clock speeds, which in turn is used to obtain an estimate of the differences in clock speeds.

Ensuring that this procedure is executed correctly is straightforward by limiting $|\mu_v(r) - 1|$ to be small, where $\mu_v(r)$ is the factor by which node v changes its clock rate during round r. However, constraining this multiplier means that approximate agreement steps cannot be performed correctly in case $\mu_v(r+1)$ would lie outside the valid range of multipliers. This is fixed by introducing a correction that "pulls" frequencies back to the default rate.

5.1 Additional Assumptions on the Clocks

We require that clock rates satisfy a Lipschitz condition as well. In the following, we assume that H_v is differentiable (for all $v \in C$) with derivative h_v, where h_v satisfies for $t, t \in \mathbb{R}_0^+$ that $|h_v(t') - h_v(t)| \leq \nu|t' - t|$ for some $\nu > 0$. Note that we maintain the model assumption that hardware clock rates are close to 1 at all times, i.e., $1 \leq h_v(t) \leq \vartheta$ for all $t \in \mathbb{R}_0^+$.

5.2 Algorithm

Algorithm 3 gives the pseudocode of our approach. Mostly, the algorithm can be seen as a variant of Algorithm 2 that allows for speeding up clocks by factors $\mu_v(r) \in [1, \vartheta^2]$, where $\vartheta h_v(t)$ is considered the nominal rate at time t.[9] For simplicity, we fix all local waiting times independently of the round length.

The main difference to Algorithm 2 is that a second pulse signal is sent before the phase correction is applied, enabling to determine the rate multipliers for the next round by an approximate agreement step as well. A frequency measurement is obtained by comparing the (observed) relative rate of the clock of node w during a local time interval of length $\tau_2 + \tau_3$ to the desired relative clock rate of 1. Since the clock of node v is considered to run at speed $\mu_v(r)h_v(t)$ during the measurement period, the former takes the form $\mu_v(r)\Delta_{wv}/(\tau_2 + \tau_3)$, where Δ_{wv} is the time difference between the arrival times of the two pulses from w measured with H_v. The approximate agreement step results in a new multiplier $\hat{\mu}_v(r+1)$ at node v; we then move this result by ε in direction of the nominal rate multiplier ϑ and ensure that we remain within the acceptable multiplier range $[1, \vartheta^2]$.

[9] Given that hardware clock speeds may differ by at most factor ϑ, nodes need to be able to increase or decrease their rates by factor ϑ: a single deviating node may be considered faulty by the algorithm, so each node must be able to bridge this speed difference on its own.

Algorithm 3. Phase and frequency synchronization algorithm, code for node $v \in C$. Time $t_v(r)$, $r \in \mathbb{N}_0$, is the time when round $r + 1$ starts.

1 // $H_w(0) \in [0, F)$ for all $w \in V$
2 wait until time $t_v(0)$ with $H_v(t_v(0)) = F$;
3 // initialize clock rate multiplier
4 $\mu_v(0) := \mu_v(1) := \vartheta$;
5 **foreach** *round* $r \in \mathbb{N}$ **do**
6 // phase correction step
7 start listening for messages;
8 wait until local time $H_v(t_v(r-1)) + \tau_1/\mu_v(r-1)$;
9 broadcast clock pulse to all nodes (including self);
10 wait until local time $H_v(t_v(r-1)) + (\tau_1 + \tau_2)/\mu_v(r)$;
11 **for** *each node* $w \in V$ **do**
12 $\tau_{wv} := H_v(t_{wv})$ (first message from w while listening at time t_{wv};
 $\tau_{wv} := \infty$ if none);
13 $S_v \leftarrow \{2(\tau_{wv} - \tau_{vv})/(\vartheta + 1) \mid w \in V\}$ (as multiset);
14 let S_v^k denote the kth smallest element of S_v;
15 $\Delta_v(r) \leftarrow \dfrac{S_v^{f+1} + S_v^{n-f}}{2}$;
16 // frequency correction step
17 start listening for messages;
18 wait until local time $H_v(t_v(r-1)) + (\tau_1 + \tau_2 + \tau_3)/\mu_v(r)$;
19 broadcast clock pulse to all nodes (including self);
20 wait until local time $H_v(t_v(r-1)) + (\tau_1 + \tau_2 + \tau_3 + \tau_4)/\mu_v(r)$;
21 **for** *each node* $w \in V$ **do**
22 $\tau'_{wv} := H_v(t'_{wv})$ (first message from w while listening at time t'_{wv};
 $\tau_{wv} := \infty$ if none);
23 $\Delta_{wv} := H_v(t'_{wv}) - H_v(t_{wv})$;
24 $S_v \leftarrow \{1 - \mu_v(r)\Delta_{wv}/(\tau_2 + \tau_3) \mid w \in V\}$ (as multiset);
25 let S_v^k denote the kth smallest element of S_v;
26 $\xi_v(r) \leftarrow \dfrac{S_v^{f+1} + S_v^{n-f}}{2}$;
27 $\hat{\mu}_v(r+1) \leftarrow \mu_v(r) + 2\xi_v(r)/(\vartheta + 1)$;
28 // pull back towards nominal frequency by ε, ensure minimum and maximum rate
29 **if** $\hat{\mu}_v(r+1) \leq \vartheta$ **then**
30 $\mu_v(r+1) \leftarrow \max\{\hat{\mu}_v(r+1) + \varepsilon, 1\}$;
31 **else**
32 $\mu_v(r+1) \leftarrow \min\{\hat{\mu}_v(r+1) - \varepsilon, \vartheta^2\}$;
33 wait until time $t_v(r)$ with $H_v(t_v(r)) + (T - \Delta_v(r))/\mu_v(r)$; // nominal round length is T

To fully specify the algorithm, we need to determine how long the waiting periods are (in terms of local time) and choose ε. These can be determined if we ensure that *round r was executed correctly* for all $r \in \mathbb{N}$, i.e.,

1. for all $v, w \in C$, the message v broadcasts at time $t_v(r-1) + \tau_1/\mu_v(r-1)$ is received by w at a local time from $[H_w(t_w(r-1)), H_w(t_w(r-1)) + \tau_1/\mu_v(r-1) + \tau_2/\mu_w(r)]$,
2. for all $v, w \in C$, the message v broadcasts at time $t_v(r-1) + \tau_1/\mu_v(r-1) + (\tau_2+\tau_3)/\mu_v(r)$ is received by w at a local time from $[H_w(t_w(r-1))+\tau_1/\mu_v(r-1) + \tau_2/\mu_w(r), H_w(t_w(r-1)) + \tau_1/\mu_v(r-1) + (\tau_2+\tau_3+\tau_4)/\mu_w(r)]$, and
3. for all $v \in C$, $T - \Delta_v(r) \geq \tau_1/\mu_v(r-1) + (\tau_2+\tau_3+\tau_4)/\mu_v(r)$, i.e., v computes $H_v(t_v(r))$ *before* time $t_v(r)$.

Main result. Due to space constraints, we omit the analysis, noting that the overall strategy is very similar to the one for Algorithm 2. In fact, we simply reuse the analysis from Sect. 4 to show that the modified algorithm executes rounds correctly. Then we analyze the convergence of frequencies and derive an improved skew bound by adapting Corollary 3 to yield a better bound if frequency deviations are small. This leads to the main result, which specializes to the following more readable corollary.

Corollary 5. *Suppose that $\vartheta \leq 1.01$ and $\alpha := (4\vartheta^6 + 5\vartheta^3 - 7)/(2(\vartheta^3+1)) \approx 1/2$. Then, for any nominal round length T satisfying $T \gg F + d$ and $\max\{(\vartheta-1)^2 T, \nu T^2\} \in \mathcal{O}(U)$, a steady state error of $\mathcal{O}(U)$ can be achieved.*

Corollary 5 basically states that increasing T is fine, as long as $\max\{(\vartheta - 1)^2 T, \nu T^2\} \in \mathcal{O}(U)$. This improves over Algorithm 2, where it is required that $(\vartheta-1)T \ll U$, as it permits to transmit pulses at significantly smaller frequencies (granted that ν is sufficiently small).

6 Self-stabilization

In this section, we propose a generic mechanism that can be used to transform our algorithms into *self-stabilizing* solutions; for simplicity, we assume that this algorithm is Algorithm 2 throughout this section. An algorithm is self-stabilizing, if it (re)establishes correct operation from arbitrary states in bounded time. If there is an upper bound on the time this takes in the worst case, we refer to it as the stabilization time. We stress that, while self-stabilizing solutions to the problem are known, all of them have skew $\Omega(d)$; augmenting the Lynch-Welch approach with self-stabilization capabilities thus enables to achieve an optimal skew bound of $\mathcal{O}((\vartheta-1)T+U)$ in Byzantine self-stabilizing manner for the first time.

Our approach can be summarized as follows. Nodes locally count their pulses modulo some $M \in \mathbb{N}$. We use a low-frequency, imprecise, but self-stabilizing synchronization algorithm (called FATAL) from earlier work [4,5] to generate a "heartbeat." On each such beat, nodes will locally check whether the next pulse with number 1 modulo M will occur within an expected time (local) window whose size is determined by the precision the algorithm would exhibit after M correctly executed pulses (in the non-stabilizing case). If this is not the case, the node is "reset" such that pulse 1 will occur within this time window.

This strategy ensures that a beat forces all nodes to generate a pulse with number 1 modulo M within a bounded time window. Assuming a value of F corresponding to its length in Algorithm 2 hence ensures that the algorithm will run as intended—at least up to the point when the next beat occurs. Inconveniently, if the beat is not synchronized with the next occurrence of a pulse 1 mod M, some or all nodes may be reset, breaking the guarantees established by the perpetual application of approximate agreement steps. This issue is resolved by leveraging a feedback mechanism provided by FATAL: FATAL offers a (configurable) time window during which a NEXT signal externally provided to each node may trigger the next beat. If this signal arrives at each correct node at roughly the same time, we can be sure that the corresponding beat is generated shortly thereafter. This allows for sufficient control on when the next beat occurs to prevent any node from ever being reset after the first (correct) beat. Since FATAL stabilizes regardless of how the externally provided signals behave, this suffices to achieve stabilization of the resulting compound algorithm.

FATAL. We sum up the properties of FATAL in the following corollary, where each node has the ability to trigger a local NEXT signal perceived by the local instance of FATAL at any time.

Corollary 6 (of [5]). *For suitable parameters $P, B_1, B_2, B_3, D \in \mathbb{R}^+$, FATAL stabilizes within $\mathcal{O}((B_1 + B_2 + B_3)n)$ time with probability $1 - 2^{-\Omega(n)}$. Once stabilized, nodes $v \in C$ generate beats $b_v(k)$, $k \in \mathbb{N}$, such that the following properties hold for all $k \in \mathbb{N}$.*

1. *For all $v, w \in C$, we have that $|b_v(k) - b_w(k)| \leq P$.*
2. *If no $v \in C$ triggers its NEXT signal during $[\min_{w\in C}\{b_w(k)\} + B_1, t]$ for some $t \leq \min_{w\in C}\{b_w(k)\} + B_1 + B_2 + B_3$, then $\min_{w\in C}\{b_w(k+1)\} \geq t$.*
3. *If all $v \in C$ trigger their NEXT signals during $[\min_{w\in C}\{b_w(k)\} + B_1 + B_2, t]$ for some $t \leq \min_{w\in C}\{b_w(k)\} + B_1 + B_2 + B_3$, then $\max_{w\in C}\{b_w(k+1)\} \leq t + P$.*

Algorithm. Our self-stabilizing solution utilizes both FATAL and the clock synchronization algorithm with very limited interaction (rendering the approach fairly generic). We already stressed that FATAL will stabilize regardless of the NEXT signals and note that it is not influenced by Algorithm 4 in any other way. Concerning the clock synchronization algorithm, we assume that a "careful" implementation is used that does not maintain state variables for a long time. Concretely, in Algorithm 2 this is achieved by clearing memory between loop iterations.

Algorithm 4 gives the interface code, which is basically an ongoing consistency check based on the beats that resets the clock synchronization algorithm if necessary. The feedback triggering the next beat in a timely fashion is implemented by simply triggering the NEXT signal on each Mth beat, with a small delay ensuring that all nodes arrive in the same round and have their counter variable i reading 0. The consistency checks then ask for $i = 0$ and the next pulse being triggered within a certain local time window; if either does not apply, the reset function is called, ensuring that both conditions are met. Figure 3 visualizes how FATAL and the clock synchronization algorithm interact. Naturally, the stabilization mechanism requires R^-, R^+, and M (the parameters of Algorithm 4) to satisfy certain constraints; we refer to the full version of the paper for the respective list.

Analysis. Our analysis starts with the first correct beat produced by FATAL, which is perceived at node $v \in C$ at time $b_v(1)$. We first establish that the first beat guarantees to "initialize" the synchronization algorithm such that it will run correctly from this point on. We use this do define the "first" pulse times $p_v(1)$, $v \in C$, as well.

Lemma 5. *Let $b := \min_{v \in C}\{b_v(1)\}$. We have that*

1. *Each $v \in C$ generates a pulse at time $p_v(1) \in [b + R^-/\vartheta, b + P + R^+ + \tau_1]$.*
2. *$\|\mathbf{p}(1)\| \leq e(1)$.*
3. *At time $p_v(1)$, $v \in C$ sets $i := 1$.*
4. *$w \in C$ receives the pulse sent by $v \in C$ at a local time from $[H_w(p_w(1)) - \tau_1, H_w(p_w(1)) + \tau_2]$.*
5. *This is the only pulse w receives from v at a local time from $[H_w(p_w(1)) - \tau_1, H_w(p_w(1)) + \tau_2]$.*
6. *Denoting by round 1 the execution of the for-loop in Algorithm 2 during which each $v \in C$ sends the pulse at time $p_v(1)$, this round is executed correctly.*

Up to the point in time where future beats interfere, we can conclude that the synchronization algorithm will be executed as intended.

Corollary 7. *Denote by N the infimum over all times $t \geq b+B_1$ at which some $v \in C$ triggers a NEXT signal. If $\min_{v \in C}\{p_v(M)+e(M)\} \leq \min\{N, b+B_1+B_2+B_3\}$, then all rounds $r \in \{1,\ldots,M\}$ are executed correctly and $\|\mathbf{p}(r)\| \leq e(r)$.*

This enables to show that the first time when node $v \in C$ triggers its NEXT signal after time $b+B_1$ falls within the window of opportunity for triggering the next beat provided by FATAL.

Lemma 6. *For $v \in C$, denote by $N_v(1)$ the infimum of times $t \geq b + B_1$ when it triggers its NEXT signal. We have $H_v(N_v(1)) = p_v(M)+\vartheta e(M)$ and $b+B_1+B_2 \leq N_v(1) \leq b + B_1 + B_2 + B_3$.*

This readily implies that the second beat occurs in response to the NEXT signals, which itself are aligned with pulse M. This yields that no correct node is reset by the second beat.

Corollary 8. *For all $v \in C$, $b_v(2) \in [p_v(M), p_v(M) + (\vartheta + 1)e(M) + P]$.*

Lemma 7. *Node $v \in C$ does not call the reset function of Algorithm 4 in response to beat $b_v(2)$.*

Algorithm 4. Interface algorithm, actions for node $v \in C$ in response to a local event at time t. Runs in parallel to local instances of FATAL and Algorithm 2.

1 // algorithm maintains local variable $i \in \{0, \ldots, M-1\}$
2 **if** v *generates a pulse at time t* **then**
3 $i := i + 1 \bmod M$;
4 **if** $i = 0$ **then**
5 wait for local time $H_v(t) + \vartheta e(M)$;
6 trigger NEXT signal;

7 **if** v *generates a beat at time t* **then**
8 **if** $i \neq 0$ **then**
9 // beats should align with every M^{th} pulse, hence reset
10 reset(R^+);

11 **else if** *next pulse would be sent before local time $H_v(t) + R^-$* **then**
12 // reset to avoid early pulse
13 reset$(R^+ - (H_v(t') - H_v(t)))$, where t' is the current time;

14 **else if** *next round has not started yet at local time $H_v(t) + R^+$* **then**
15 // reset to avoid late pulse and start listening for other nodes' pulses on time
16 reset(0);

17 **Function** reset(τ)
18 halt local instance of clock synchronization algorithm;
19 wait for τ local time;
20 $i := 0$;
21 $H_v(t_v(0)) := H_v(t')$, where t' is current time (i.e., $t_v(0) := t'$);
22 restart loop of clock synchronization algorithm (in round $r = 1$);

Repeating the above reasoning for all pairs of beats $\boldsymbol{b}(k)$, $\boldsymbol{b}(k+1)$, $k \in \mathbb{N}$, it follows that no correct node is reset by any beat other than the first. Thus, the clock synchronization algorithm is indeed (re-)initialized by the first beat to run without any further meddling from Algorithm 4.

Theorem 2. *Suppose that Algorithm 1 is executed with Algorithm 2 as synchronization algorithm. If $\vartheta \leq 1.03$, then all parameters can be chosen such that the compound algorithm self-stabilizes in $\mathcal{O}(n)$ time and has steady state error $E \leq ((\vartheta - 1)T + (3\vartheta - 1)U)/(1 - \beta)$, where $\beta = (2\vartheta^2 + 5\vartheta - 5)/(2(\vartheta + 1))$. Here, any nominal round length $T \geq T_0 \in \mathcal{O}(d_F + d)$ is possible.*

Observe that, in comparison to Theorem 1, the expression obtained for the steady state error replaces d by $\mathcal{O}(d_F + d)$, which is essentially the skew upon initialization by the first beat. Concerning stabilization, we remark that it takes $\mathcal{O}(n)$ time with probability $1 - 2^{-\Omega(n)}$, which is directly inherited from FATAL. The subsequent convergence to small skews is not affected by n, and will be much faster for realistic parameters, so we refrain from a more detailed statement.

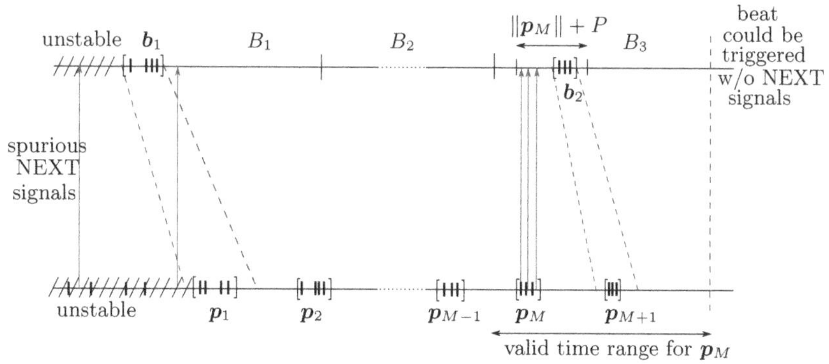

Fig. 3. Interaction of the beat generation and clock synchronization algorithms in the stabilization process, controlled by Algorithm 4. Beat b_1 forces pulse p_1 to be roughly synchronized. The approximate agreement steps then result in tightly synchronized pulses. By the time the nodes trigger beat b_2 by providing NEXT signals based on p_M, synchronization is tight enough to guarantee that the beat results in no resets.

References

1. Overview of Silicon Oscillators by Linear Technology (retrieved May 2016). http://cds.linear.com/docs/en/product-selector-card/2PB_osccalcfb.pdf
2. Daliot, A., Dolev, D.: Self-Stabilizing Byzantine Pulse Synchronization. Computing Research Repository abs/cs/0608092 (2006)
3. Distributed Algorithms for Robust Tick-Synchronization (2005–2008). http://ti.tuwien.ac.at/ecs/research/projects/darts. Accessed 5, 2014
4. Dolev, D., Függer, M., Lenzen, C., Posch, M., Schmid, U., Steininger, A.: Rigorously modeling self-stabilizing fault-tolerant circuits: an ultra-robust clocking scheme for systems-on-chip. J. Comput. Syst. Sci. **80**(4), 860–900 (2014)
5. Dolev, D., Függer, M., Lenzen, C., Schmid, U.: Fault-tolerant algorithms for tick-generation in asynchronous logic: robust pulse generation. J. ACM **61**(5), 1–74 (2014)
6. Dolev, D., Halpern, J.Y., Strong, H.R.: On the possibility and impossibility of achieving clock synchronization. J. Comput. Syst. Sci. **32**(2), 230–250 (1986)
7. Dolev, D., Lynch, N.A., Pinter, S.S., Stark, E.W., Weihl, W.E.: Reaching approximate agreement in the presence of faults. J. ACM **33**, 499–516 (1986)
8. Dolev, S., Welch, J.L.: Self-stabilizing clock synchronization in the presence of byzantine faults. J. ACM **51**(5), 780–799 (2004)
9. FlexRay Consortium, et al.: FlexRay communications system-protocol specification. Version **2**, 1 (2005)
10. Függer, M., Armengaud, E., Steininger, A.: Safely stimulating the clock synchronization algorithm in time-triggered systems - a combined formal & experimental approach. IEEE Trans. Ind. Inf. **5**(2), 132–146 (2009)
11. Függer, M., Schmid, U.: Reconciling fault-tolerant distributed computing and systems-on-chip. Distrib. Comput. **24**(6), 323–355 (2012)
12. Huemer, F., Kinali, A., Lenzen, C.: Fault-tolerant Clock Synchronization with High Precision. In: IEEE Symposium on VLSI (ISVLSI) (2016). to appear

13. Kopetz, H., Bauer, G.: The time-triggered architecture. Proc. IEEE **91**(1), 112–126 (2003)
14. Lundelius, J., Lynch, N.: An upper and lower bound for clock synchronization. Inf. Control **62**(2–3), 190–204 (1984)
15. Schossmaier, K.: Interval-based Clock State and Rate Synchronization. Ph.D. thesis, Technical University of Vienna (1998)
16. Schossmaier, K., Weiss, B.: An algorithm for fault-tolerant clock state and rate synchronization. In: 18th Symposium on Reliable Distributed Systems (SRDS), pp. 36–47 (1999)
17. Srikanth, T.K., Toueg, S.: Optimal clock synchronization. J. ACM **34**(3), 626–645 (1987)
18. Welch, J.L., Lynch, N.A.: A new fault-tolerant algorithm for clock synchronization. Inf. Comput. **77**(1), 1–36 (1988)

DecTDMA: A Decentralized-TDMA
With Link Quality Estimation for WSNs

Olaf Landsiedel, Thomas Petig(✉), and Elad M. Schiller

Chalmers University of Technology, Gothenburg, Sweden
{olafl,petig,elad}@chalmers.se

Abstract. In wireless sensor networks (WSNs), different motes may transmit packets concurrently, i.e., having overlapping transmission periods. As a result of this contention, there are no packet reception guarantees and significant bandwidth can be lost. This contention can have a strong impact on the performance together with other kinds of interference sources, e.g., ambient noise. As a result, WSN's connectivity tends to have a very dynamic nature.

In this paper, we devise DecTDMA (Decentralized-TDMA), a fully decentralized medium access controller (MAC) that significantly reduces contention. It is based on a self-stabilizing algorithm for time division multiple access (TDMA). This self-stabilizing TDMA algorithm uses no external assistance or external references, such as wireless access points (WAPs) and globally-synchronized clocks. We present the design and implementation of DecTDMA and report encouraging results: our Cooja simulations and Indriya testbed experiments show stable connectivity and high medium utilization in both single and multi-hop networks. Since DecTDMA has favorable characteristics with respect to connection stability, we show that common link quality estimation (LQE) techniques further improve the operation of DecTDMA in the dynamic environment of low-power wireless networks.

1 Introduction

Wireless sensor networks (WSNs) are self-organizing systems where computing devices, so called motes (or nodes), set up – by themselves – a networking infrastructure without relying on external assistance. In this paper, we focus on medium access control (MAC) in WSNs. We present DecTDMA (Decentralized-TDMA) — a fully-decentralized MAC protocol for WSNs. Our decentralized solution does not assume access to external references, such as wireless access points (WAPs), and individual nodes in DecTDMA do not have special tasks, such as acting as elected coordinators. In this work, we aim to mitigate one of the key sources of internal interference: concurrent transmissions by neighboring motes, which cause radio interferences. The event of concurrent transmissions refers to the occurrence of multiple transmissions, such that the periods of these transmissions overlap. Concurrent transmissions have a great impact on the throughput in WSNs. For example, they can reduce the packet reception ratio (PRR) [1]. DecTDMA uses a self-stabilizing algorithm [2] for time

B. Bonakdarpour and F. Petit (Eds.): SSS 2016, LNCS 10083, pp. 231–247, 2016.
DOI: 10.1007/978-3-319-49259-9_19

division multiple access (TDMA) that significantly reduces the occurrence of concurrent transmissions. In addition, we show that DecTDMA deals well with other causes of WSN dynamics, such as mote or link failure and wireless links of intermediate quality, i.e., links with a PRR between 10 % and 90 %. DecTDMA uses a link quality estimation (LQE) technique for estimating the PRR of both broadcasts and their respective acknowledgements. We use this elegant (light-weight) and software-based technique for masking short term link failures, i.e., sporadic (receiver-side) packet omissions. It allows DecTDMA to sift out both disconnected links and (many) intermediate quality links. We present a TinyOS implemention of DecTDMA and evaluate it via Cooja simulations and experiments in the Indriya testbed [3]. During these experiments, we observe rather stable PRR values. Moreover, during our experiments, DecTDMA achieves PRR values that approach the analytical bounds.

Challenges. In wireless communications, a single message may reach many receivers (due to the broadcast nature of radio transmissions). The success of message arrival depends on the distance between the transmitter and potential receivers as well as complex signal propagation patterns: wireless signals propagate unequally in different directions due to antenna characteristics, over many paths, and are subjected to interference. In WSNs, different (possibly neighboring) transmitters may send concurrently. In such cases, there are no guarantees for any receiver to get the packet and significant bandwidth can be lost. Thus, one of the key challenges in simplifying the use of WSNs is to limit the occurrence of such local contention factors. The studied question is whether one can device a MAC protocol that avoids contention, i.e., significantly reduces the occurrence of concurrent transmissions. We present DecTDMA and report encouraging results about the feasibility of TDMA protocols that require no external references, such as WAPs and global clocks.

Evaluation criteria. Medium access control with high throughput is essential for many WSN protocols, especially for routing protocols [4]. Using statistical characterization, methods for link quality estimation (LQE) provide insights for routing protocols on which links they should forward packets. By avoiding low and intermediate quality links, the MAC layer can limit its packet loss, reduce the number of re-transmissions, and provide better connectivity. This also impacts the higher layers, e.g., it reduces the need for selecting new routes at the network layer and reduce the end-to-end latency of the transport layer.

PRR is a common evaluation criterion in (wireless) communication networks [4]. For WSNs, PRR is often an elegant criterion that is easy to implement and according to which routing protocols can estimate link quality. In this work, we are interested both in the PRR values themselves and their stability over time. The motivation for the latter criterion is by the fact that stable PRR values are easier to work with (from the point of view of the higher layers).

The literature refers to PRR both as an evaluation criterion and as a basic mechanism for evaluating link quality. It is well-known that there are more advanced LQE mechanisms that provide more stable estimation than the average PRR mechanism [4]. We follow the common practice that often use average PRR mechanisms for simplicity and choose an LQE mechanism that considers the PRR values of both messages and their acknowledgements.

Design criteria. In this paper, we focus on MAC protocols for low-power wireless networks that autonomously set up their networking infrastructure. WSNs are subject to faults that occur due to temporal hardware or software malfunctions or the dynamic nature of low-power wireless communications.

Fault-tolerant systems that are self-stabilizing [5] can recover after the occurrence of transient faults. These faults can cause an arbitrary corruption of the system state (as long as the code of the program is still intact). Transient faults can also represent temporary violations of the assumptions according to which the communication links and the entire dynamic networks behaves during normal operation. In order to provide DecTDMA with properties of self-organization and self-recovery, we base the implementation of DecTDMA on an existing self-stabilizing TDMA algorithm [2]. This algorithm helps DecTDMA to significantly reduce the occurrence of concurrent transmissions. We note that the design of the TDMA algorithm in [2] focuses on packet loss due to concurrent transmissions and models all other kinds of packet loss as transient faults (after which a brief recovery period is needed). DecTDMA extends this, by utilizing an LQE technique for masking sporadic packet loss. Thus, DecTDMA considers fewer occurrences of sporadic packet loss as transient faults than the TDMA algorithm by Petig et al [2]. As a result, DecTDMA avoids unnecessary recovery periods. This increases the performance and the stability of the packet reception ratio (PRR) values.

Our design criteria of self-organization and self-recovery simplify the use of WSNs. It reduces the effect of local and low-level complications, such as contention management, that many systems leave to be handled by the higher layers. Consequently, we provide an important level of abstraction that allows the higher layers to focus on their tasks, such as routing table construction, packet forwarding, and end-to-end communications.

We do not claim that the studied implementation is self-stabilizing. Note that the implementation of a self-stabilizing system requires every system element to be self-stabilizing [6], rather than just a subset of the needed algorithms. This includes the use of compliers that preserve any invariant that is related to the corretness proof [7], as well as the use of self-stabilazing CPUs [8], self-stabilazing operating systems [9] to name a few.

Our Contribution. In this paper, we present DecTDMA — a decentralized TDMA that does not assume access to external references, such as wireless access points (WAPs) or a global clock. For DecTDMA, we (a) extend and (b) implement an existing self-stabilizing algorithm [2] and (c) evaluate our implementation both via WSN simulations and a real-world testbed. By that, we provide stable connectivity with high values of packet reception ratio (PRR). We also offer a masking technique as a way to further improve the channel stability by considering sporadic packet losses as normal faults rather than transient ones. The studied technique estimates the stability of every TDMA time slot and lets DecTDMA to keep only time slots that are above a predefined threshold. We evaluate our TinyOS implementation via Cooja simulations on both single and multiple hop networks as well as on Indriya Testbed at NUS (with 97 motes). The results validate that DecTDMA (and its LQE technique for masking sporadic packet loss) provides stable connectivity with high PRR values. For the studied cases of network simulations, DecTDMA achieves PRR values that are rather stable and approach the analytical bounds.

We believe that these findings demonstrate the feasibility of decentralized reference-free TDMAs that provide stable communication among the WSN motes without the need for an external coordinator nor access to a global time reference. The design and implementation of DecTDMA exposes the advantage of following the self-stabilization design criteria. DecTDMA is a multifaceted TDMA protocol that can deal with a number of failures. This fault model includes concurrent transmissions and sporadic packet loss, as well as different violations of the algorithm assumptions, which we model as transient faults.

Document Structure. As background knowledge (Sect. 2), we present the self-stabilazing TDMA algorithm by Petig et al. [2], which DecTDMA extends. We complete the description of DecTDMA by discussing the details of our LQE technique (Sect. 3). We present our evaluation of DecTDMA by studying the results of our experiments (Sect. 4). Finally, we discuss the related work (Sect. 5) and our concluding remarks (Sect. 6).

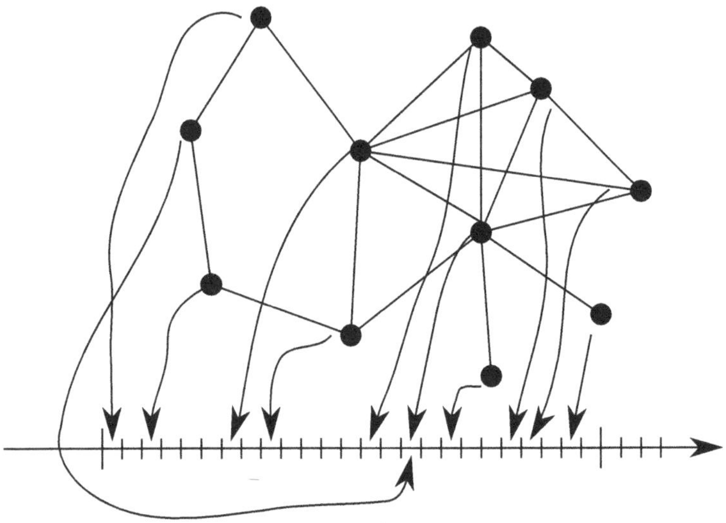

Fig. 1. Time slot assignment in multi-hop network graphs. Neighbours with a distance of at least 3 can share the same time slot without collision.

2 Background: Time Slot Alignment and Allocation

DecTDMA uses a TDMA algorithm by Petig et al. [2] for aligning the frame and letting each mote access a time slot that is unique within its 2-hop neighbourhood (Fig. 1). For the sake of self-containment of this paper, we describe the algorithm and how it works under the assumptions of Petig et al. [2]. In real-world WSNs, there are different sources for interferences that cause packet loss. The TDMA algorithm of Petig et al. [2] focuses on packet losses that are due to concurrent transmissions and models all other kinds of packet losses as transient faults (after which brief recovery periods are needed). Therefore, DecTDMA extends it and uses an LQE technique for masking sporadic packet loss (Sect. 3). We show that DecTDMA can perform well in real-world WSNs, which do not need to follow the assumptions made by Petig et al. (Sect. 4).

In the TDMA algorithm by Petig et al. [2], motes send both data and control packets. Also, the motes can play an active or a passive role according to their (local) status. When the mote p_i's status is active, it sends data packets during a time slot that is designated for p_i's data packets, which we call p_i's transmission time slot, s_i. When p_i's status is passive, it listens to the active motes, and it does not send any data packets. The motes send, regardless of their status, control packets which include the frame information (FI). The field FI includes data about the recently received data packets from direct neighbours. That information refers both to the sender identity and the packet sending time. The TDMA algorithm by Petig et al. aggregates the frame information it receives during the past frame. The algorithm relies on FI to acknowledge transmissions, resolve hidden terminal phenomena and avoid concurrent transmissions. The mote active-passive status changes according to the filed FI.

(1) **The passive mote p_i takes the following steps in order to become active.** It selects a random time slot, s_i, that no active mote within two hops uses according to p_i's FI. Mote p_i tests the use of time slot s_i by sending a control packet and waiting for acknowledgement from neighbouring motes. These acknowledgements are included in their data and control packets. Whenever that test works, mote p_i changes its status to active and uses s_i as its transmission time slot for data packets.

(2) **The active mote p_i can become passive due to the following.** An active mote p_i changes its status to passive after its FI field reports about another mote, p_j, that transmits during its time slot s_i, where p_j is at most two hops away from p_i. Recall that during the occurrence of hidden terminal phenomenon, mote p_i has a neighbour, p_j, and a distance two neighbour, p_ℓ, such that p_i and p_ℓ use time slots with overlapping periods. In this case, there is no grantee that p_i receives p_j's frame information (and acknowledgements) to p_i's packets. In order to deal with this issue, the TDMA algorithm by Petig et al. also considers the absence of p_j's acknowledgement as an implicit report on a possible occurrence of the hidden terminal phenomenon. Note that, unlike the TDMA algorithm by Petig et al., DecTDMA uses an LQE technique for mitigating the effect of sporadic packet loss, say,

due to ambient noise. Namely, DecTDMA lets p_i change its status from active to passive only according to LQE indication (Sect. 3).

Petig et al. [2] uses a random back-off mechanism for dealing with contention scenarios in which "too many" passive motes are testing random time slots concurrently, see case (1) above. This mechanism counts down (from a randomly selected backoff value) every time the node observes a time slot that for which it receives no message. The TDMA algorithm by Petig et al. also adopts a technique for clock synchronization according to which it aligns the TDMA time slots. Petig et al. [2] show that their self-stabilizing TDMA algorithm can provide, after a convergence period, guarantees that each active mote can transmit successfully once in every TDMA frame. The proof of self-stabilization by Petig et al. assumes that packet loss occurs only due to concurrent transmissions. However, in real-world WSNs the above assumption does not hold. This work proposes DecTDMA, which does not follow this assumption. Instead, it uses an LQE technique for avoiding a change in p_i status from active to passive due to the occurrence of sporadic packet losses (and does allow this change whenever p_i's time slot, s_i, losses packets repeatedly, see Sect. 3).

3 TDMA Protocol with Link Quality Estimation

In real-world WSNs, packet losses occur due to many reasons, such as external interference or concurrent transmissions, i.e., when neighboring nodes transmit during overlapping periods. DecTDMA addresses the challenge of sporadic packet losses via a Link Quality Estimation (LQE) procedure. Here, mote p_i does not stop sending a data packet in its transmission time slot s_i due to a sporadic packet loss. We use a software-based LQE technique that estimates p_i's LQE by accumulating the acknowledgments that p_i receives over a time window and comparing them to the number of transmitted packets. We use this lightweight LQE technique for deciding whether p_i shall keep its transmission time slot, s_i, or try to randomly select a new one after a random back-off period (Sect. 2).

Our LQE technique considers a time window of w TDMA frames. We use arrays of integers, $ack_i[]$ and $rx_i[]$ (each of w entries), which in the beginning of every time window, we initialize each entry with the zero value. During each time window, when p_i receives a data packet during time slot s_j, it increments $rx_i[j]$. Moreover, if that packet includes an acknowledgement for the packet p_i sent previously, it also increments $ack_i[j]$. At the end of each time window, p_i tests whether there is a time slot s_j for which $rx_i[j] \geq \mathcal{T}_{rx}$ (the reception threshold) and $ack_i[j] \leq \mathcal{T}_{ack}$ (the acknowledgement threshold). In case p_i finds such s_j, it stops using its transmission time slot, s_i. This process repeats in every time window during which p_i's status is active.

Note that we assume that the communication links have symmetrical packet loss behavior. We justify the packet reception and acknowledgement thresholds of $\mathcal{T}_{rx}$, and respectively, $\mathcal{T}_{ack}$ by considering a pair of neighbouring motes, p_i and p_j. Suppose that the successful transmission probability from p_i to p_j

(and visa verse) is p. In a given time window of w frames, the expected number of p_i's packets that p_j receives is wp and the expected amount of acknowledgements is wp^2. During our experiments, we have selected a window of $w = 20$ TDMA frames, the reception threshold $\mathcal{T}_{rx} = 0.8w = 16$ by taking $p = 0.8$ and considering a value that includes all reliable links, which are defined as the ones that have 90 % PRR [4]. We decided to consider $\mathcal{T}_{ack} = 0.4w = 8$ as the acknowledgement threshold since it presented a more stable behavior than $p^2 = 0.64$ during our experiments (Sect. 4).

4 Evaluation

We evaluate DecTDMA with respect to channel stability and throughput via the Cooja simulator and the Indriya Testbed at NUS with 97 motes. We implemented DecTDMA on top of TinyOS version 2.1.1. For the Cooja simulations, we select both single and multiple hop topologies whereas in the testbed experiments the focus is on the multiple hop case. Our results show a high throughput as well as acceptable channel stability performances of DecTDMA under real-world conditions. We also show that DecTDMA further improves the TDMA algorithm by Petig et al. [2] via the proposed mechanism for channel quality estimation.

Every WSN has a number of inherent uncertainties. In this dynamic environment, it is challenging for any node to maintain a stable rate of packet reception. This channel stability criterion is one of the important metrics, which we evaluate. Another important criterion is the throughput of DecTDMA, which considers the number of successful packet receptions. Note that for the simulation results, we normalize these numbers of successful packet receptions and compare them to an analytical maximum (which we tailor for each studied topology).

The TDMA frame setup. We use the notation below when presenting our results. DecTDMA considers the case in which every node uses at most one time slot per TDMA frame for data packets. Despite this assumption, DecTDMA is obviously extendable by simply allowing each mote to use more than one time slot. We use τ to denote the number of time slots per TDMA frame and ξ to refer to the length of each time slot in seconds. Node that each mote can transmit at most $((1\ \mathsf{s}/\xi)/\tau)$ packets per second. In our frame setup, $\varphi = ((1\ \mathsf{s}/\xi)/\tau) = 2$ is an upper bound on the number of frame per seconds that each node uses (after convergence) for data packets in every second.

Single hop WSNs: simulation results. Single hop WSNs represent the case in which every mote can communicate directly with any other mote. The complete graph topology of these networks is absent from multi-hop dynamics that are due to, for example, fading signal strength. Moreover, this setup has a clear analytical upper bound of the throughput, i.e., in a network of n transmitters at most $n - 1$ packets are received per transmission. In this basic setup, we are able to demonstrate that DecTDMA's throughput approaches the analytical upper bound. Note that even though this setup is simpler than all the others that we study, the presented performances are not straightforward, because our fully-decentralized implementation has no access to external assistance, such as access points, or external references, such as a global clock. Yet, we show that DecTDMA's performances are close to the analytical bounds.

We model a single-hop graph using the complete graph K_n. During the Cooja simulation, we use p as the transmission success probability when a packet is sent from a node to a neighboring one. We use these settings for evaluating how close can DecTDMA approach the analytical bounds, which depend on p. We normalize the number of received data packet per second using $\#pkts/T/(n-1)/(\varphi/n)$, where $\#pkts/T$ refers to the average number of received packets per second over a time period T and φ is the amount of data packets per node that we expect per second. Note that, $(n-1)/(\varphi/n)$ defines the expected number of received packets in K_n (if there is no packet loss). Therefore, $\#pkts/T/(n-1)/(\varphi/n)$ should approach p, when the packet reception probability is p.

The plot in Fig. 2 presents the (normalized) number of received packets for different numbers of nodes when considering K_n, where $n \in \{5, 6, \ldots, 40\}$. The chart shows that DecTDMA behaves well when the transmission (and reception) success probability is $p = 1$. Note that this is the case in which we are running DecTDMA as an implementation of Petig et al., because the settings are similar to the ones that Petig et al. considered in [2]. Since Petig et al. do not consider the

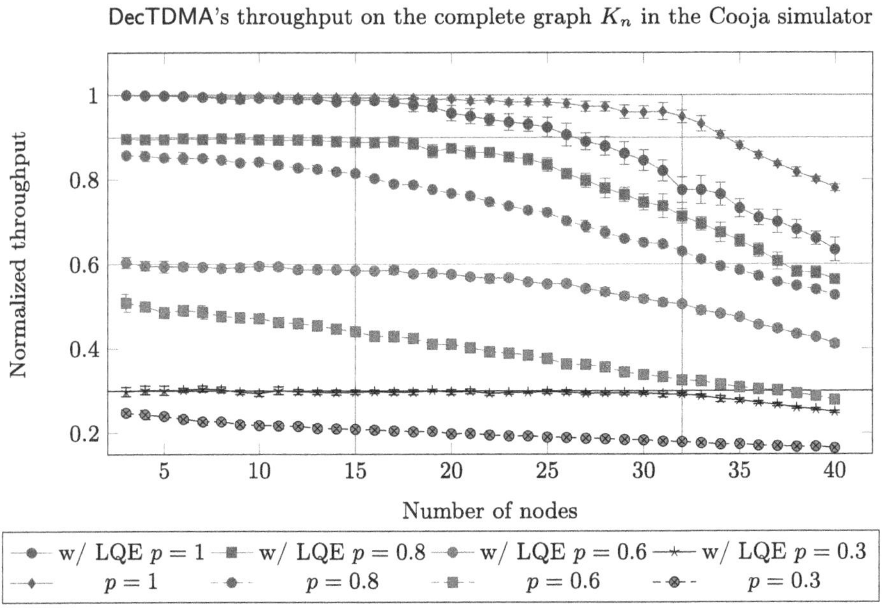

Fig. 2. DecTDMA without and with LQE on the complete graph K_n. The probability of a successful transmission is p. The throughput is normalized by $\#pkts/T/(n-1)/2/n$. The (colourful) horizontal lines represent the analytical bounds on the throughput. The (red) vertical lines stand for the bounds for guaranteed convergence, which is 15, and the frame size, which is 32. (Color figure online)

case of $p < 1$, DecTDMA version with LQE indeed out performs the one without. Thus, for the case of single hop networks, DecTDMA with LQE performs well for the case of $p < 1$ and for the case of $p = 1$, there is no need to use LQE as a masking technique (and the theoretical assumption that $p = 1$).

Multiple hop WSNs: simulation results. The phenomenon of hidden terminal consider the case in which mote p_1 can communicate directly with both p_0 and p_2 but p_0 and p_2 cannot communicate directly (Fig. 3). In this case, node p_0 is hidden from p_2 and thus the only way that it can identify that its transmissions occur concurrently with p_2 is via p_1 assistance. We consider a multiple hop setup, in which the hidden terminal phenomenon exists and yet we are able to compare between DecTDMA's throughput and an analytical upper bound that we tailor. Interestingly, these simulations show a behavior that is similar to the above single hop networks, which use the complete graph K_n.

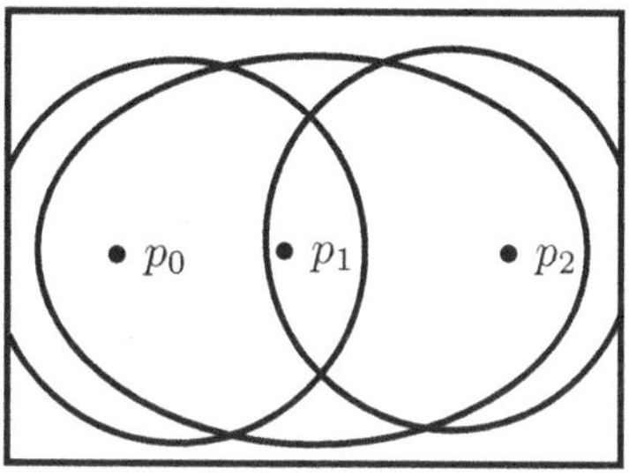

Fig. 3. The hidden terminal.

We also consider settings for the a 2-hop graph $G_2(n) := (V, E)(n)$ with n vertices. The set of vertices is partitioned in four sets S_0, S_1, S_2 and S_3, such that each set forms a clique in G_2 (Fig. 4). We define a cardinally constraint that requires these cliques to be of similar size: $|S_{i+1}| + 1 \geq |S_i| \geq |S_{i+1}|$ for $i \in \{0, 1, 2\}$ and $|S_3| + 1 \geq |S_0|$. In addition to the edges within every vertex to any other vertex in its clique, we define an edge between every vertex and any other vertex that is in a neighboring clique. We say that clique S_i is neighboring to clique $S_{i+1 \bmod 4}$ and $S_{i-1 \bmod 4}$. Note that for the case of $n \bmod 4 = 0$, G_2 is regular, i.e., all vertexes have the same degree. During the Cooja simulation, we use p and $q = 0.4p$ as the transmission success probabilities when a packet is sent from a node to a neighboring one that shares, and respectively, does not share the same clique. In this rather simple settings for multiple hop networks, we can still evaluate how DecTDMA is close to analytical bounds that depend on p and $q = 0.4p$. Note that we study DecTDMA behavior on multiple hop graph using testbed experiments.

We normalize the throughput (Fig. 5) by the expected throughput for the case there is no packet loss. The difference to the 1-hop case on the K_n is that from one clique, S_i, the opposite corner clique, $S_{i+2 \bmod 4}$, cannot be reached, thus the number of nodes we expect to received a packet is reduced by a quarter. This leads to $\#pkts/T/(\frac{3}{4}n - 1)/(\varphi/n)$. In Fig. 6, we use a different probability for successful reception for the neighboring cliques. Since they contain half of the nodes and packets are received with probability $q = 0.4$ in case $p = 1$, we get the bound $(0.5nq + 0.25n - 1)/(\varphi/n)$. Note that the rate q is linear in p. Thus, q scales down for smaller values of p. This leads to the fact that for a given transmission success rate of p (within the clique), we also expect p to be the normalized throughput.

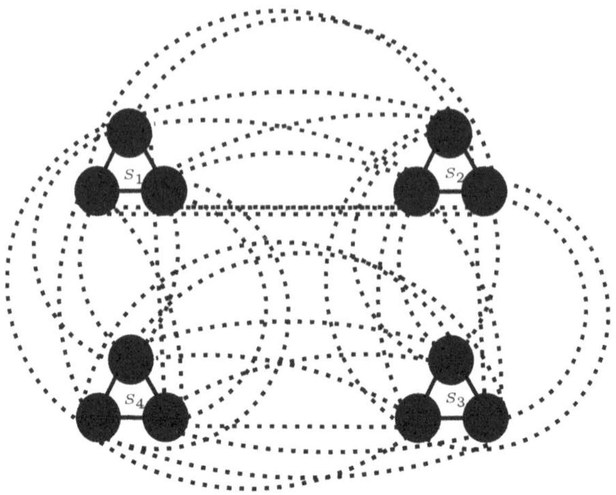

Fig. 4. The $G_2(12)$ graph. The solid lines represent communication link that their transmission success probability is p, whereas the dotted lines refers to linked with probability $q = p$ and $q = 0.4p$ as in Figs. 5, and respectively, Fig. 6.

The plots in Figs. 5 and 6 present the simulation results for the $G_2(n)$ topology and $n \in \{5, 6, \ldots, 40\}$ when considering the cases in which the successful transmission probability of links that connects nodes that are at different cliques is $q = 0.4p$ and within a clique p (cf. Figure 4). We note the similarly of the results that appear in Figs. 2 and 5 even though the latter set of experiments refer to a two hop communication graph, rather than one hop, as in the former set. Moreover, when running DecTDMA with LQE, we observe an acceptable degree of stability in the number of packets received for every transmission. Of course, the values in Fig. 6 are significantly less than the ones in Fig. 5 (due to higher packet loss rate between neighboring cliques).

Multiple hop WSNs: testbed experiments. We complete our evaluation of DecTDMA by running experiments in the Indriya Testbed at NUS [3]. This is a controllable environment and yet it is representative to real-world WSNs with respect to the actual interference that the deployed motes encounter, e.g., dynamic link behavior, say, with respect to PRR values [4]. Our experiments consider running DecTDMA over 97 motes that form a multipile hop network (Fig. 8). Such real-world networks are known to have different and dynamic transmission success rates. We compare between the cases in which DecTDMA includes and does not include our LQE technique. The plot in Fig. 8 shows the long term impact of ambient noise on DecTDMA with and without LQE. Whereas the former is able to improve over time by learning about the presence of links with low PRR values, the latter can spiral down due the fact the Petig et al. [2] do not consider sporadic packet omission.

Since this work considers experiments that run both on the Cooja simulator and the Indriya testbed, we also wanted to run in Cooja experiments on a

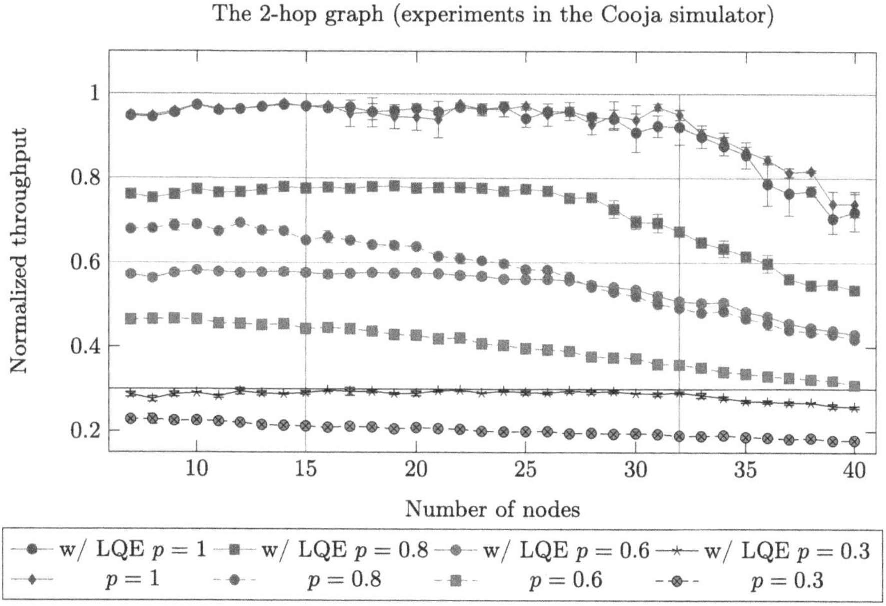

Fig. 5. DecTDMA with and without LQE on the 2-hop graph $G_2(n)$ and uniform probability, p, of successful transmissions, where $n \in \{6, 7, \ldots, 40\}$ and $p \in \{0.3, 0.5, 0.8, 1.0\}$ is the probability for successful transmission between any pair of motes that can communicate directly. The horizontal (colourful) lines represent the analytical bounds and the (red) vertical lines the bounds for convergence (15) and the frame size (32). The throughput is normalized by $\#pkts/T/(0.75n - 1)/2/n$. (Color figure online)

multiple hop graph that resembles the one that the Indriya testbed uses (Fig. 7). Broadly speaking, the two plots in Figs. 7 and 8 resembles. We note that there is no clear recipe for Cooja to consider in detail the dynamics of real-world WSNs, such as the Indriya testbed. Hence, differences between these plots are inevitable. Also, there is no straightforward way to compare our results on the Indriya testbed to an analytical bound, as we did in Figs. 2, 5 and 6.

Evaluation summary. DecTDMA with LQE presents high and stable throughput values in Cooja simulations (in single and multiple hop networks) that approach our analytical bounds. The Indriya testbed experiments show stability of the throughput values that resembles to the ones in the Cooja simulations.

5 Related Work

ALOHAnet and its many variances [10] are MAC protocols that schedule the medium access randomly. Time division multiple access (TDMA) follows a scheduled approach that divides the radio time into TDMA frames and then further divides these frames into time slots. We note that at high and stable PRR values, TDMA protocols offer inherently a greater degree of predictability than the

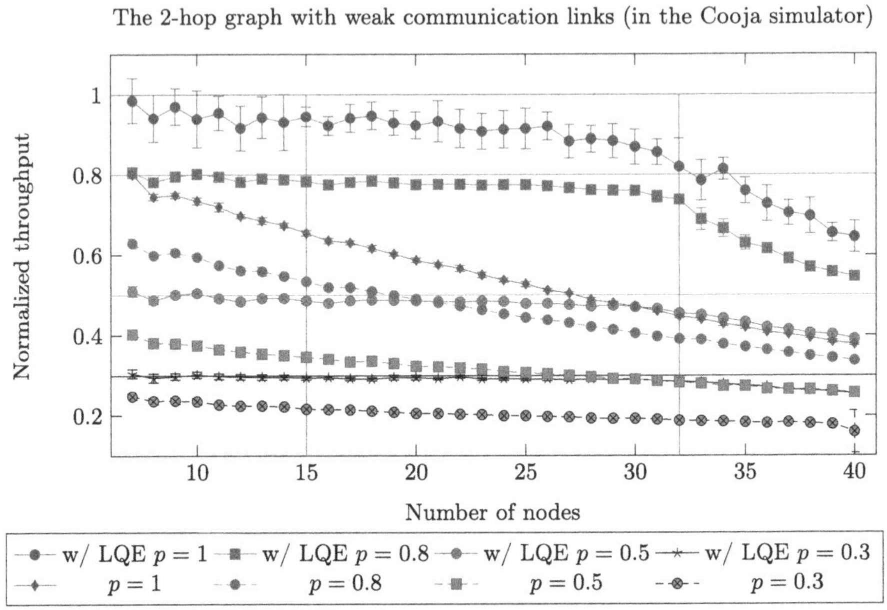

Fig. 6. DecTDMA with and without LQE on the 2-hop graph $G_2(n)$, where $n \in \{6, 7, \ldots, 40\}$. The probability of successful transmissions between any two motes that belong to the same clique is $p \in \{0.3, 0.5, 0.8, 1.0\}$. The ones that belong to neighboring cliques have the probability of $q = 0.4p$. The horizontal (colourful) lines represent the analytical bounds, which depends on p, and the (red) vertical lines the bounds for convergence (15) and the frame size (32). The throughput is normalized by $\#pkts/T/(0.75n - 1)/2/n$, as in Fig. 5. (Color figure online)

ones that access the medium randomly. The TDMA task that we consider in this work includes both the alignment of frames and time slots as well as the allocation of these time slots to the motes, rather than just the latter part of the task, as many existing TDMA protocols do.

Existing approaches for MAC-layer contention management consider priorities (for maintaining high bandwidth utilization while meeting the deadlines, such as [11]) or modifying the signal strength or carrier sense threshold [12]. We view both approaches as possible extensions to DecTDMA, which considers a single priority and does not adjust the radio settings dynamically. DecTDMA uses fixed size TDMA frames and it allocates TDMA time slots until saturation, i.e., no more time slots are left to allocate. Note that a number of techniques can prevent starvation in saturated situations, such as limiting the number of TDMA frames that the application can use consecutively without deferring further communication. Once, we apply such techniques, the (common) back-off mechanism of DecTDMA will prevent starvation.

The literature considers receiver-side collision detection [12,13], which requires hardware support for signal processing as well as receivers to notify

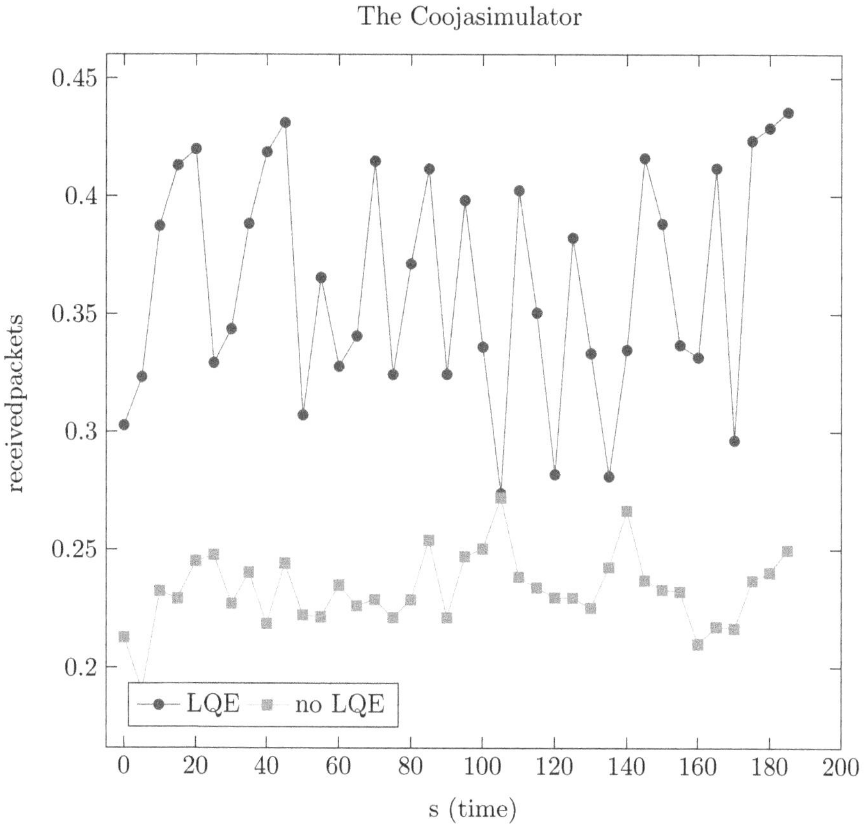

Fig. 7. Comparison between TDMA with and without link quality estimation on the Cooja simulator. This plot shows the number of received packets accumulated in intervals of 100 s in Cooja. The overall time of the experiment is 200 s on the 2-hop graph $G_2(40)$.

senders about the success or failure of transmissions. In this paper, we assume hardware that does not support collision detection (on the sending side or on the receiving side). In DecTDMA, however, the payload does include a short summary of the frame information (FI) [2]. We prefer not to assume access to external references and provide a fully-decentralized implementation since unbounded signal failure can occur, e.g., in underground tunnels. STDMA [14] is an example of a protocol that assumes the availability of an external reference (GNSS [15]). It allocates bandwidth according to the position of motes.

The (self-stabilization) literature on TDMA algorithms often does not answer the causality dilemma of "which came first, synchronization or communication." On one hand, existing clock synchronization algorithms often assume the existence of MAC algorithms that offer bounded communication delay. However, on the other hand, existing MAC algorithms that provide bounded communication

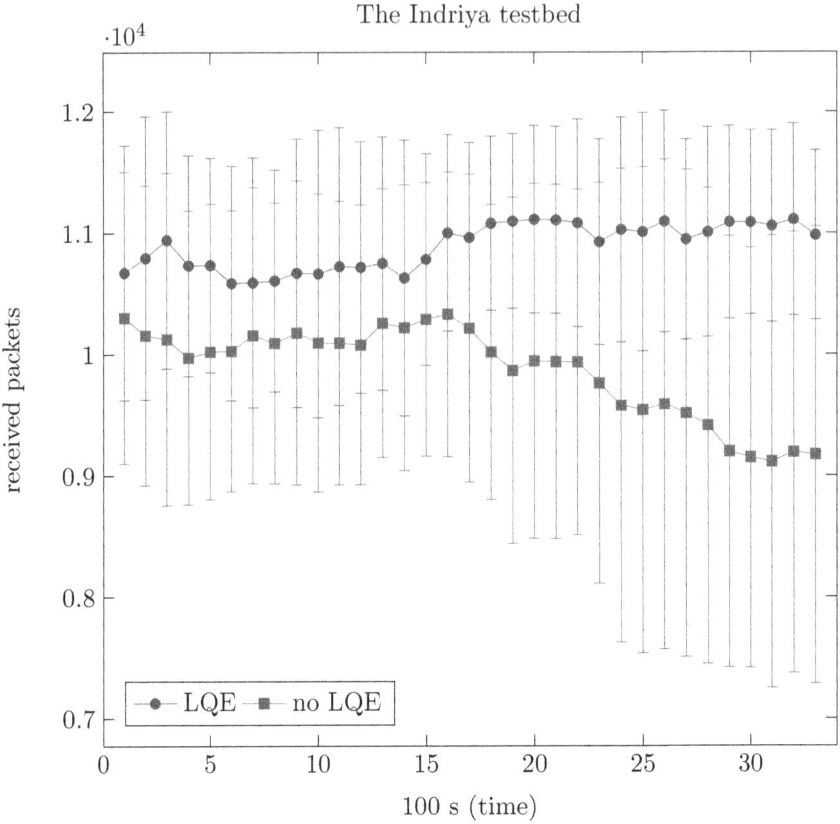

Fig. 8. Comparison between TDMA with and without link quality estimation on the INDRIYA testbed [3]. This plot shows the number of received packets accumulated in intervals of 100 s as an average over 10 run each. The total run time for each run is 3600 s. The error bars represent in both graphs the standard deviation.

delay, often assume access to synchronized clocks. For example, some TDMA protocols [16] assume the availability of a clock synchronization algorithm that can reach the needed clock synchrony bound before starting the allocation of time slots. Where there is no external reference or assistance, the implementation of TDMA protocol requires time slot alignment *during* the time slot allocation process. DecTDMA needs to address these tasks at the same time (without external reference). Busch et al. [17] and Petig et al. [2] propose TDMA algorithms that address the above challenge without assuming access to external references. Busch et al. [17] address this by assuming that the number of time slots in each frame is at least $2(\Delta+1)$, where Δ is an upper bound on the number of nodes with whom any node can communicate with using at most one intermediate node for relaying packets. Petig et al. [2] provides a solution that requires a frame size to could be $O(\sqrt{\Delta})$ times smaller. Moreover, they show that you cannot do much better than that. Schneider and Wattenhofer [18] present a local algorithm for vertex coloring that could be the basis a for self-organizing TDMA protocol. We chose to base DecTDMA on a TDMA algorithm [2] that considers self-stabilization explicitly. Other proposals for self-stabilizing MAC algorithms exist [19–21] as well as other algorithms cited by [2]. We choose the one that can deal with networks dynamics, assume no access to external reference, has a more attractive overhead (with respect to the frame information) and follows conventional TDMA practice, such as fix packet size.

We are not the first to consider the provision of improved link quality. One of the most notable examples is a line of research work that has started by Kuhn, Lynch and Newport [22], which presented the abstract MAC model. They propose a number of high-level communication primitives that use an (abstract) unreliable MAC layer, and yet provide guarantees with respect to the packet delivery to the application layer at the receiver-side, say, after a bounded number of retransmissions. We follow a complementary approach to the one of Kuhn, Lynch and Newport [22], because we are interested in possible guarantees with respect to the packet reception at the receiver-side without considering the possibility to retransmit a lost packet.

We note our previous work in the area, such as in [24,25]; none of which consider link quality estimation, dealing with sporadic packet loss and experiments in a real-world WSN testbed, such as Indriya [3].

6 Discussion

Designing and implementing a MAC protocol for WSNs is a non-trivial task. The challenges include a various source of interferences as well as the need to recover rapidly from the occurrence of failures that these interferences cause. Using DecTDMA, we were able to exemplify how to have the self-stabilization design criteria in mind while designing a MAC protocol that works well in a real-world WSN testbed, such as Indriya [3].

This design process started with the self-stabilizing TDMA algorithm by Petig et al. [2]. That algorithm modelled, for example, the communication graph and the manner in which the motes exchange messages. The focus of Petig et al. is on dealing with one of the most destructive interferences in WSNs, which is packet loss due to concurrent transmissions. Petig et al. consider a fault model that includes concurrent transmissions whereas sporadic packet losses, say, due to ambient noise, are considered as transient faults. This focus on concurrent transmissions allows, via a rigorous analysis, an exact design of their self-stabilizing TDMA algorithm. Our experiments validate that indeed, in the absence of transient faults, e.g., sporadic packet loss, the self-stabilizing TDMA algorithm Petig et al. addresses the challenge of avoiding concurrent transmissions (Figs. 2 and 5).

We present DecTDMA, which is a TDMA protocol that extends the fault model of Petig et al. and thus sporadic packet loss are no longer considered as transient faults. This paper shows that via an elegant LQE technique that masks the effect of sporadic packet loss, the PRR levels of DecTDMA are higher significantly than the ones of Petig el al. [2]. Moreover, we observe the stability of these PRR values also in a real-world testbeds, such as Indriya [3] (Fig. 8).

This work shows how to deal with failures and interferences in non-trivial real-world challenges, such as the design of fully-decentralized reference-free TDMA protocol. Our design process enhanced iteratively the fault model during the design of Petig el al. [2] and then in this work, we used an elegant masking technique to further enhance the fault model. DecTDMA is a successful example of the above design and development process that have the self-stabilization design criteria in mind. As future work, we offer the reader to study real-world problems and use the presented design and development process.

Acknowledgments. We knowledge the participation of Henning Phan in this work by assisting the protocol implementation [23]. This work has been partially supported by the Swedish Energy Agency under the program Energy, IT and Design.

References

1. Son, D., Krishnamachari, B., Heidemann, J.S.: Experimental study of concurrent transmission in wireless sensor networks. In: Proceedings of the 4th International Conference on Embedded Networked Sensor Systems, SenSys 2006, Boulder, Colorado, USA, October 31 - November 3, 2006, pp. 237–250 (2006)
2. Petig, T., Schiller, E., Tsigas, P.: Self-stabilizing TDMA algorithms for wireless ad-hoc networks without external reference. In: 13th Annual Mediterranean Ad Hoc Networking Workshop, MED-HOC-NET 2014, Piran, Slovenia, June 2–4, 2014, IEEE, pp. 87–94 (2014)
3. Doddavenkatappa, M., Chan, M.C., Ananda, A.L.: Indriya: a low-cost, 3D wireless sensor network testbed. In: Korakis, T., Li, H., Tran-Gia, P., Park, H.-S. (eds.) TridentCom 2011. LNICSSITE, vol. 90, pp. 302–316. Springer, Heidelberg (2012). doi:10.1007/978-3-642-29273-6_23
4. Baccour, N., Koubaa, A., Noda, C., Fotouhi, H., Alves, M., Youssef, H., Zuniga, M., Boano, C.A., Römer, K., Puccinelli, D., Voigt, T., Mottola, L.: Radio Link Quality Estimation in Low-Power Wireless Networks. Springer Briefs in Electrical and Computer Engineering. Springer, Heidelberg (2013)
5. Dolev, S.: Self-Stabilization. MIT Press, Cambridge (2000)
6. Brukman, O., Dolev, S., Haviv, Y.A., Lahiani, L., Kat, R.I., Schiller, E.M., Tzachar, N., Yagel, R.: Self-stabilization from theory to practice. Bull. EATCS **94**, 130–150 (2008)
7. Dolev, S., Haviv, Y.A., Sagiv, M.: Self-stabilization preserving compiler. ACM Trans. Program. Lang. Syst. **31**(6), 31–46 (2009)
8. Dolev, S., Haviv, Y.A.: Self-stabilizing microprocessor: Analyzing and overcoming soft errors. IEEE Trans. Comput. **55**(4), 385–399 (2006)
9. Dolev, S., Yagel, R.: Towards self-stabilizing operating systems. IEEE Trans. Softw. Eng. **34**(4), 564–576 (2008)
10. Abramson, N.M.: Development of the ALOHANET. IEEE Trans. Inf. Theor. **31**(2), 119–123 (1985)
11. Rom, R., Tobagi, F.A.: Message-based priority functions in local multiaccess communication systems. Comput. Netw. **5**, 273–286 (1981)

12. Scopigno, R., Cozzetti, H.A.: Mobile slotted aloha for vanets. In: Proceedings of the 70th IEEE Vehicular Technology Conference, VTC Fall 2009, 20–23, Anchorage, Alaska, USA, IEEE (2009) 1–5, September 2009
13. Demirbas, M., Soysal, O., Hussain, M.: A singlehop collaborative feedback primitive for wireless sensor networks. In: INFOCOM 2008 27th IEEE International Conference on Computer Communications, Joint Conference of the IEEE Computer and Communications Societies, 13–18, Phoenix, AZ, USA, pp. 2047–2055. IEEE, April 2008
14. Yu, F., Biswas, S.K.: Self-configuring TDMA protocols for enhancing vehicle safety with DSRC based vehicle-to-vehicle communications. IEEE J. Sel. Areas Commun. **25**(8), 1526–1537 (2007)
15. Scopigno, R., Cozzetti, H.A.: GNSS synchronization in vanets. In: NTMS 2009, 3rd International Conference on New Technologies, Mobility and Security, 20–23, Cairo, Egypt (2009). 1–5 December 2009
16. Rhee, I., Warrier, A., Min, J., Xu, L.: DRAND: distributed randomized TDMA scheduling for wireless ad hoc networks. IEEE Trans. Mob. Comput. **8**(10), 1384–1396 (2009)
17. Busch, C., Magdon-Ismail, M., Sivrikaya, F., Yener, B.: Contention-free MAC protocols for asynchronous wireless sensor networks. Distrib. Comput. **21**(1), 23–42 (2008)
18. Schneider, J., Wattenhofer, R.: Coloring unstructured wireless multi-hop networks. In: Proceedings of the 28th Annual ACM Symposium on Principles of Distributed Computing, PODC 2009, Calgary, Alberta, Canada, August 10–12, 2009, pp. 210–219 (2009)
19. Herman, T., Tixeuil, S.: A distributed TDMA slot assignment algorithm for wireless sensor networks. In: Nikoletseas, S.E., Rolim, J.D.P. (eds.) ALGOSENSORS 2004. LNCS, vol. 3121, pp. 45–58. Springer, Heidelberg (2004). doi:10.1007/978-3-540-27820-7_6
20. Jhumka, A., Kulkarni, S.: On the design of mobility-tolerant TDMA-based media access control (MAC) protocol for mobile sensor networks. In: Janowski, T., Mohanty, H. (eds.) ICDCIT 2007. LNCS, vol. 4882, pp. 42–53. Springer, Heidelberg (2007). doi:10.1007/978-3-540-77115-9_4
21. Lenzen, C., Suomela, J., Wattenhofer, R.: Local algorithms: self-stabilization on speed. In: Guerraoui, R., Petit, F. (eds.) SSS 2009. LNCS, vol. 5873, pp. 17–34. Springer, Heidelberg (2009). doi:10.1007/978-3-642-05118-0_2
22. Kuhn, F., Lynch, N.A., Newport, C.C.: The abstract MAC layer. Distrib. Comput. **24**(3–4), 187–206 (2011)
23. Phan, H.T.H.: Towards Wireless Communication with Bounded Delay. Master's thesis, Department of Computer science, Chalmers University of Technology, Gothenburg, Sweden (2016)
24. Leone, P., Papatriantafilou, M., Schiller, E.M., Zhu, G.: Chameleon-MAC: adaptive and self-* algorithms for media access control in mobile ad hoc networks. In: Dolev, S., Cobb, J., Fischer, M., Yung, M. (eds.) SSS 2010. LNCS, vol. 6366, pp. 468–488. Springer, Heidelberg (2010). doi:10.1007/978-3-642-16023-3_37
25. Leone, P., Schiller, E.: Self-Stabilizing TDMA algorithms for dynamic wireless ad hoc networks. IJDSN **2013** (2013). doi:10.1155/2013/639761, http://dblp.uni-trier.de/rec/bib/journals/ijdsn/LeoneS13

Self-stabilizing Metric Graphs

Robert Gmyr[1(✉)], Jonas Lefèvre[1,2], and Christian Scheideler[1]

[1] Department of Computer Science, Paderborn University, Paderborn, Germany
{gmyr,jlefevre,scheidel}@mail.upb.de

[2] IRIF, University Paris-Diderot – Paris 7, Paris, France
jlefevre@liafa.univ-paris-diderot.fr

Abstract. We present a self-stabilizing algorithm for overlay networks that, for an arbitrary metric given by a distance oracle, constructs the graph representing that metric. The graph representing a metric is the unique minimal undirected graph such that for any pair of nodes the length of a shortest path between the nodes corresponds to the distance between the nodes according to the metric. The algorithm works under both an asynchronous and a synchronous dæmon. In the synchronous case, the algorithm stablizes in time $O(n)$ and it is almost silent in that after stabilization a node sends and receives a constant number of messages per round.

Keywords: Overlay network · Self-stabilizing algorithms · Metric graph

1 Introduction

There is a plethora of work on the self-stabilizing construction of specific network topologies from simple structures like line graphs, rings, and spanning trees to more complex networks like De Bruijn graphs, Chord graphs, and Skip graphs. Next to these topology-specific results, there has been some work on generic approaches for the self-stabilizing construction of overlay networks like the Transitive Closure Framework by Berns *et al.* [2], which can construct any topology that is locally-checkable. In this work, we present a self-stabilizing algorithm for overlay networks that, for an arbitrary metric given by a distance oracle, constructs the graph representing that metric. Since every graph corresponds to a metric, our algorithm can be seen as a universal approach to self-stabilizing graph construction for situations in which the graph can be efficiently encoded as a metric. To the best of our knowledge, this is the first algorithm for constructing the graph of an arbitrary metric in a self-stabilizing manner. At the core of our algorithm lies a simple technique that uses a directed cycle covering all nodes to guide the construction of the metric graph. We think that this underlying technique could have applications beyond the construction of metric graphs and therefore should be of independent interest.

B. Bonakdarpour and F. Petit (Eds.): SSS 2016, LNCS 10083, pp. 248–262, 2016.
DOI: 10.1007/978-3-319-49259-9_20

1.1 Model

We represent an overlay network as a directed graph $G=(V,E)$ and define $n = |V|$. Each node u has a unique *identifier* $u.id \in [0,1[$. Identifiers are immutable and cannot be corrupted. We simply write u instead of $u.id$ when it is clear from the context that we refer to the identifier of u. The (directed) edge set E is given by $E = \{(u,v) \mid u \text{ knows } v\}$. We use a variant of the standard message-passing model that allows for a clean presentation of both our algorithm and the proofs. Our algorithm would work the same way in the standard message-passing model with FIFO message delivery. The computation proceeds in rounds. In every round each activated node can execute an arbitrary local computation and send a message to each node it knows. Messages are received at the end of a round. All nodes — including the nodes that are not activated — receive messages and update their local memories accordingly. In our protocol, received messages only cause simple changes on local variables; a message never triggers a complex calculation nor does it cause new messages to be sent immediately. Therefore, the assumption that even nodes that were not activated receive and process messages at the end of a round does not provide any additional power to the nodes. In their computation, the nodes can use the variables stored in their local memory and a *distance oracle* that provides access to a prescribed metric d. Given two identifiers u and v, the oracle returns the distance $d(u,v)$ between the corresponding nodes.

We consider both a synchronous and an asynchronous dæmon. For the synchronous dæmon, every node is activated in every round. With the asynchronous dæmon, in each round some non-empty subset of the nodes is activated. We assume that the activation under the asynchronous daemon is fair in that, starting at any step, each node is activated eventually. We formally specify an algorithm as a set of *actions* (or *rules*). A rule has the form

$$\langle\text{label}\rangle : \langle\text{guard}\rangle \to \langle\text{commands}\rangle.$$

A $\langle$label$\rangle$ constitutes the unique name of an action, a $\langle$guard$\rangle$ is a Boolean predicate over variables of the node, and $\langle$commands$\rangle$ consists of a sequence of instructions. Upon activation, a node sequentially checks the guards of the actions in the given order. If a guard is satisfied, the corresponding commands are executed.

The configuration of the network c_i in round i consists of the contents of the local memories of the nodes at the beginning of round i. Note that the messages sent during a round are received and processed at the end of that round. Therefore, there are no messages in transit between two rounds so we do not have to consider messages in our definition of a configuration. A computation is a sequence of configurations. Let C be the set of all configurations. An algorithm is *self-stabilizing* with respect to a set of *legal configurations* $L \subseteq C$ if starting from any configuration $c \in C$ the computation will eventually reach a configuration in L (*correctness*) and then stay in L (*closure*).

1.2 Related Work

There is a wealth of work on the self-stabilizing construction of specific network topologies: line graphs [10], rings [4,12], spanning trees [1,5], De Bruijn graphs [11], Chord graphs [9], and Skip graphs [3,6] are a few examples.

Besides these topology-specific approaches, Berns *et al.* [2] introduced a general approach for the self-stabilizing construction of locally-checkable topologies. However, the graph of an arbitrary metric is in general not locally-checkable and hence the approach of Berns *et al.* cannot be used. Still, there is an interesting connection between the work of Berns *et al.* and our work: As it turns out, with some minor modifications our algorithm can be used to construct arbitrary locally-checkable topologies in a way that is very similar to the approach by Berns *et al.* We elaborate on this in Sect. 5.

Most of the related work on metric graph construction algorithms considers very specific metrics like the two-dimensional Euclidean metric or its approximation using the Delaunay construction [7,8]. The Delaunay construction is a 2.42-approximation for the two-dimensional Euclidean metric [7] and has the advantage over the exact metric graph of being locally-checkable. In contrast, we aim to build the exact metric graph without imposing any restriction on the metric. To the best of our knowledge, we present the first algorithm for constructing the graph of an arbitrary metric in a self-stabilizing manner.

1.3 Our Contribution

We present a new algorithm in the domain of self-stabilizing graph construction. Our algorithm builds the graph associated with an arbitrary given metric. The input metric is provided to the nodes through a distance oracle. At the core of our algorithm lies a simple technique that uses a directed cycle covering all nodes to guide the construction of the metric graph. We think that this underlying technique could have applications beyond the construction of metric graphs and therefore should be of independent interest. Since every graph corresponds to a metric, our algorithm can be seen as a universal approach to self-stabilizing graph construction for situations in which the graph can be efficiently encoded as a metric. Our algorithm works both under a synchronous and under a (fair) asynchronous dæmon. Under a synchronous dæmon, the convergence time of our algorithm is linear and the overhead of our algorithm after stabilization is small: Every node sends and receives a constant number of messages per round and stores at most four identifiers of nodes that are not in its neighborhood as implied by the metric. To the best of our knowledge, this work presents the first algorithm for constructing the graph of an arbitrary metric in a self-stabilizing manner.

2 Problem Statement

We assume that the network contains a set of marked edges $D \subseteq E$. For simplicity, we consider D to be a set of undirected edges *i.e.* D contains an undirected edge $\{u, v\}$ whenever the network contains the corresponding directed marked edges (u, v) and (v, u). Let $d : V \times V \to \mathbb{R}^+$ be a finite metric and let $\overline{D}$ be the set of undirected edges of the graph corresponding to the metric d. Starting from any configuration in which $G = (V, E)$ is weakly connected, the network has to reorganize such that eventually $D = \overline{D}$.

To formally define $\overline{D}$, we introduce some notation. Let $(u_0, u_1, \ldots, u_k)$ be a sequence of nodes. We write $(u_0, u_1, \ldots, u_k) \in \overline{D}^*$ whenever the sequence of nodes forms a path with respect to $\overline{D}$, *i.e.* when $\{u_i, u_{i+1}\} \in \overline{D}$ for all $0 \leq i < k$. Furthermore, we define $d(u_0, u_1, \ldots, u_k) = \sum_{i=0}^{k} d(u_i, u_{i+1})$.

We formally require $\overline{D}$ to satisfy the following two conditions.

(Metric Graph) $\forall u, v \in V,$

$$\exists (u, u_1, \ldots, u_k, v)_{k \geq 0} \in \overline{D}^*, \ \left(d(u, u_1, \ldots, u_k, v) = d(u, v)\right)$$

(Minimality) $\forall u, v \in V,$

$$\left[\ \exists (u, u_1, \ldots, u_k, v)_{k \geq 1} \in \overline{D}^*, (d(u, u_1, \ldots, u_k, v) = d(u, v))\ \right] \Rightarrow \{u, v\} \notin \overline{D}$$

The first condition means that for any pair of nodes in the graph there exists an optimal path, i.e. a path whose length is the distance between those nodes according to the metric. The second condition implies that the graph has to be the smallest for the inclusion.

We define the set L of legal configurations as the set of configurations in which $D = \overline{D}$. Note that this corresponds to the classical definition of a metric graph where the weights of the edges of the graph are defined implicitly through the pairwise distances given by the metric. It is easy to prove that such a graph exists and is unique. Our goal is to construct the graph of a given metric quickly and with as little communication as possible while using only few extra edges, *i.e.* edges in $E \backslash \overline{D}$.

While the above definition is close to the intuition of what it means for a configuration to represent a metric, the equivalent condition given in Proposition 1 below will prove more useful throughout the paper. The equivalence follows via induction on the shortest paths and by considering only the first node of those paths.

Proposition 1. *The two following statements are equivalent:*

1. **(Metric Graph)** $\wedge$ **(Minimality)**
2. $\forall u, v \in V, \ \{u, v\} \notin \overline{D} \iff \left(\exists w \in V \backslash \{u, v\}, \{u, w\} \in \overline{D} \wedge d(u, w, v) = d(u, v)\right)$

3 Algorithm

Our algorithm consists of two parts. The first part reorganizes the nodes into a directed cycle in which the nodes are ordered by increasing identifier. This is achieved using the pure linearization algorithm presented in [10] to form a sorted list and the simple technique presented in [9] to close the sorted list by connecting the nodes with the lowest and highest identifier.

The second part then uses the cycle as a tool for constructing the metric graph $(V, \overline{D})$. The rules for this part are given in Algorithm 1. The remainder of this section is dedicated to the description of the second part of our algorithm. Keep in mind that since our algorithm is self-stabilizing, the two parts cannot be executed sequentially but have to be executed in parallel. Also note that the rules given in Algorithm 1 only cover the second part of the algorithm.

Algorithm 1. Arbitrary Metric Algorithm

The rules are applied by a node u.
Building the metric graph:

Delegate: $\exists v \neq w \in u.N,\ d(u,v,w) = d(u,w) \rightarrow u.N \leftarrow u.N \setminus \{w\}$
$v.N \leftarrow v.N \cup \{w\}$
$w.N \leftarrow w.N \cup \{v\}$

Add: $u.test \notin u.N \cup \{u\} \wedge$
$(\forall v \in u.N, d(u,v,u.test) > d(u,u.test)) \rightarrow u.N \leftarrow u.N \cup \{u.test\}$
$u.test.N \leftarrow u.test.N \cup \{u\}$

Moving the *test*-pointers:

Request: $True \rightarrow u.test.Req.enqueue(u)$
Reset: $u.last \neq \bot \rightarrow u.Req.remove(u.last)$
$u.last \leftarrow \bot$
Respond: $u.Req \neq \emptyset \rightarrow u.last \leftarrow u.Req.dequeue()$
$u.last.test \leftarrow u.succ$

Intuitively, the second part of our algorithm works as follows. Assume the construction of the cycle is complete. Every node u maintains a pointer (*i.e.* a variable containing an identifier) $u.test$ to some node in V. The *test*-pointers of the nodes traverse the cycle in a common direction. A node u uses the pointer $u.test$ to check whether the edge $\{u, u.test\}$ should be added to D. Additionally, every node checks for each of its outgoing edges whether it can be removed (or rather delegated) from the graph.

Formally, the algorithm consists of two groups of rules. The first group consists of the rules **Delegate** and **Add**. It manages the construction of the metric graph. The second group consists of the rules **Request**, **Reset**, and **Respond**. This group is responsible for moving the *test*-pointers along the cycle.

The algorithm associates the following variables with each individual node u: the identifier $u.id \in [0,1[$; a set $u.N$ of identifiers that represents the neighborhood of u in the current state of metric graph under construction; two pointers $u.pred$ and $u.succ$ that represent the predecessor and successor of u in the cycle; a pointer $u.test$ that specifies an outgoing edge that has to be tested in the metric graph construction; a queue $u.Req$ of nodes that requested the successor of u where we assume that a value is stored at most once (*i.e.* if a value is enqueued that is already present, the queue is not modified); and a pointer $u.last$ to remember the last node that u responded to. Note that the set of marked undirected edges D is stored distributively among all nodes, *i.e.* $D = \{\{u,v\} | u \in v.N \wedge v \in u.N\}$.

While the algorithm is essentially the same for both the synchronous and asynchronous dæmon, we make one distinction: For the synchronous dæmon we restrict the queues $u.Req$ to contain at most two elements. Whenever multiple elements compete to be enqueued, the queue is filled in an arbitrary way. For the asynchronous dæmon, the size of the queues is unbounded (however, since the elements of a queue must be distinct, the size of an individual queue is effectively bounded by n). Intuitively, we need the queues in the asynchronous case to avoid *test*-pointers being stuck at certain positions under unfortunate activation orders. The synchronous case suffers no such starvation problems and therefore only requires queues of constant size. We chose to restrict the queues to size two for technical reasons.

Note that while the notation in Algorithm 1 suggests that a node directly accesses a variable of another node, this is not the case. For instance, the instruction $u.test.N \leftarrow u.test.N \cup \{u\}$ in the **Add** rule simply means that u sends a message to $u.test$ containing u so that when the message is received at the end of the round, $u.test$ will add u to $u.test.N$. Finally, note that the **Reset** rule is necessary to correctly handle the case in which a node u sends a request to a node v in the same round as v responds to a previous request by u. In this case, the **Reset** rule causes v to ignore the superfluous request by u.

4 Analysis

It is easy to see that the second part of our algorithm as given in Algorithm 1 does not interfere with the formation of the directed cycle in the first part of our algorithm: the second part merely uses the result of the first part, i.e. it reads the pointers to the predecessors and successors along the cycle. Therefore, both the correctness and the stabilization time of the first part of our algorithm as shown in [9,10] are independent from the second part. Based on these results, we now analyse the second part of our algorithm.

We first show two basic properties concerning the rules for the construction of the metric graph.

Lemma 1. *The distance between two nodes as given by the current state of the metric graph* (V, D) *can only decrease.*

Proof. The only rules that can change the set D are the rules **Add** and **Delegate**. The addition of an edge by the **Add** rule can only create shorter path in the graph. The **Delegate** rule only removes an edge $\{u, v\}$ if there exists an alternative path of equal length between u and v. Therefore, the distance between two nodes given by the current state of the metric graph can only decrease.

We refer to an edge as a *final edge* if it is part of the metric graph corresponding to the given metric d, *i.e.* if it belongs to $\overline{D}$.

Lemma 2. *The following holds:*

1. *The* ***Delegate*** *rule never deletes a final edge.*
2. *The* ***Add*** *rule never adds an edge that was previously deleted by the* ***Delegate*** *rule.*

Proof. 1. Let $\{u, v\} \in D$ be a final edge. We assume that there is some node $w \in V$ such that $d(u, w, v) = d(u, v)$ and $\{w, u\} \in D$. Since $(V, \overline{D})$ is a metric graph, there is a node $w' \in V$ such that $\{w', u\} \in \overline{D}$ and $d(u, w) = d(u, w', w)$ (note that we may have $w = w'$). Therefore, we have

$$d(u, v) = d(u, w, v) = d(u, w', w, v) \geq d(u, w', v)$$

which implies $d(u, v) = d(u, w', v)$ and $\{w', u\} \in \overline{D}$. This is a contradiction to the assumption that $\{u, v\}$ is a final edge. It follows that there is no such edge $\{w, u\} \in D$. Therefore, the guard of the **Delegate** rule is never satisfied for this edge.

2. Assume that a node u has delegated the edge $\{u, w\}$ to a node v. Since u has applied the **Delegate** rule, we have $d(u, v, w) = d(u, w)$. Since $v \in u.N$ we know by Lemma 1 that there will always be a path between u and v of length at most $d(u, v)$. This means there will always be a node $t \in u.N$ (where we may have $t = v$) such that $d(u, t, v) = d(u, v)$. Therefore, we have

$$\begin{aligned} d(u, w) &= d(u, v) + d(v, w) \\ &= d(u, t) + d(t, v) + d(v, w) = d(u, t) + d(t, v, w) \\ &\geq d(u, t) + d(t, w) = d(u, t, w), \end{aligned}$$

and hence, $d(u, t, w) = d(u, w)$ by the triangle inequality. Accordingly, the following formula is always true: $\exists t \in u.N,\ d(u, t, w) = d(u, w)$. Therefore, the guard of the **Add** rule will never be satisfied for the edge $\{u, v\}$.

The remainder of this section is structured as follows. First, we show the algorithm to be correct in Sect. 4.1. We then analyse the runtime under the synchronous dæmon in Sect. 4.2 and argue about the behavior of the algorithm after stabilization in Sect. 4.3.

4.1 Correctness

In this section we show the correctness of our algorithm under both a synchronous and an asynchronous dæmon. All statements in this section hold for both cases. The only point where we have to distinguish between the two cases is the proof of Lemma 3; the remaining arguments are independent of whether we consider a synchronous and an asynchronous dæmon. We assume throughout this section that the cycle has already been constructed.

Lemma 3. *Let $u, v \in V$. Eventually, the node u is activated while $u.test = v$.*

Proof. We first consider the asynchronous case and then the synchronous case.

1. Let $u, v \in V$. We define the set $\theta(u)$ as the set of nodes w such that $u \in w.Req$ or $u.test = w$. This set is never empty because it contains at least $u.test$. The rule **Request** enqueues u in $u.test.Req$ and therefore does not increase $|\theta(u)|$. The rule **Reset** can only remove u from a queue and thus does not increase

$|\theta(u)|$. The rule **Respond** changes the value of $u.test$ and removes u from a queue and therefore does not increase $|\theta(u)|$. The other rules do not change the queues or the $test$-pointers. Therefore, the size of the set $\theta(u)$ can only decrease.
Assume that $|\theta(u)|$ does not decrease anymore (surely, this point will eventually be reached). Let be $w \in \theta(u)$. If $u \in w.Req$, then eventually w will be activated enough times to dequeue u and apply the rule **Respond**. Therefore, u eventually changes the value of its $test$-pointer to the node $w.succ$ and its value does not change before the next activation of u since otherwise $|\theta(u)|$ would decrease. So after the next activation of u, we have $u \in (w.succ).Req$. If $u \notin w.Req$, then $u.test = w$ and its value does not change before the next activation u since otherwise $|\theta(u)|$ would decrease. Eventually u is activated and, by applying the rule **Request**, is added to $w.Req$ so that we are back in the case above. So in any case, eventually $w.succ$ replaces the node w in $\theta(u)$. Since the cycle is finite, we get by induction that eventually the node u is activated while $u.test = v$.

2. For any $u \in V$, we define $T_i(u)$ to be the number of nodes pointing to u with their $test$-pointers in the i-th configuration, *i.e.*

$$T_i(u) = \#\{v \text{ such that } v.test = u \text{ at the beginning of round } i\}.$$

First note that a node responds to at most one request per round (see rule **Respond**). Therefore, after the first round (*i.e.* for $i > 1$), if $T_i(u) \geq 2$ for a node u then at least one of the nodes pointing at u in rounds i also pointed at u in round $i - 1$ and therefore the queue $u.Req$ contains at least one node in round i. In the following, we assume that we are in a round $i > 1$.
Let $u, v \in V$. It takes at least two rounds for a pointer to move from one node to its successor—one round to get in the queue and a second round to change the pointer. Additionally, every one or two rounds (depending on the content of the queue), a node u with $T_i(u) > 0$ forwards one pointer to its successor. Thus, the possible evolutions of $T(u)$ are as follows.
(a) If $T_i(u) = 0$ and $T_i(u.pred) = 0$, then $T_{i+2}(u) = 0$.
(b) If $T_i(u) = 1$ and $T_i(u.pred) = 0$, then $T_{i+2}(u) = 0$.
(c) If $T_i(u) \geq 2$ and $T_i(u.pred) = 0$, then $T_{i+2}(u) < T_i(u)$.
(d) If $T_i(u) = 0$ and $T_i(u.pred) \geq 1$, then $T_{i+2}(u) \leq 2$.
(e) If $T_i(u) = 1$ and $T_i(u.pred) \geq 1$, then $T_{i+2}(u) \leq 2$.
(f) If $T_i(u) \geq 2$ and $T_i(u.pred) \geq 1$, then $T_{i+2}(u) \leq T_i(u)$.
Furthermore, the sum of all the $T_i(u)$ is equal to n at any time i, because it is the number of $test$-pointers.

We look at the evolution of the values of T along the cycle over time from an intuitive perspective: From (a) and (b), we can deduce that the places where $T = 0$ move forward along the cycle every two rounds (they follow the pointers $succ$) as long as they do not meet a place where $T \geq 2$. According to (c), once a 0 meets a node u with $T(u) \geq 2$, the value of T at u strictly decreases. According to (f), the places where $T > 2$ might decrease in value but stay in place. Finally, when considering all cases together it is easy to observe that the value of T at a specific node is non-increasing as long as $T > 2$, and otherwise it cannot increase beyond 2.

Now consider the values of T along the cycle at the beginning of the second round. Since the sum over all $T(u)$ is n, we have that for each node with $T = 2 + k$ for some $k \geq 0$, there are $k+1$ positions where $T = 0$. Within $2(n-1)$ rounds, each of these initial 0's could completely traverse the cycle. However, according to (c) a 0 interacts with the first node where $T \geq 2$ and decreases the value of T at that position. Therefore, for all rounds $i \geq 2n$, we have that $\forall u \in V,\ T_i(u) \leq 2$.

We now show that after this point, a *test*-pointer moves from a node to its successor every second round. The proof involves many cases. For brevity, we only consider the most complex case and leave the remaining cases to the interested reader.

Consider a node u that points at a node v in round i but that did not point at v in round $i-1$. This means that in round $i-1$ we had $u.test = v.pred$ and $v.pred.Req = [u, \dots]$. We consider the case $T_{i-1}(v) = 2$ and $v.Req = [x, w]$ where x and w are two distinct nodes such that $x.test = v$ and $w.test = v$.

At the beginning of round i we have $u.test = v$, $v.Req = [w, x]$, $w.test = v$, $x.test = v.succ$ and $v.last = x$. After the application of the **Reset** rule, we have $v.Req = [w]$. Thus the application of the **Respond** rule sends $v.succ$ to w and removes w from the queue.

At the beginning of round $i+1$ we have $u.test = v$, $v.Req = [u, w]$ or $[w, u]$, $v.last = w$ and $w.test = v.succ$. After the application of the **Reset** rule, we have $v.Req = [u]$. Thus the application of the **Respond** rule sends $v.succ$ to u.

Finally, at the beginning of round $i+2$ we have then $u.test = v.succ$.

To conclude, once $\forall u \in V,\ T_i(u) \leq 2$ holds, a *test*-pointer moves from a node to its successor every second round. Thus, eventually (after at most $2(n-1)$ more rounds), we have $u.test = v$.

Lemma 4. *Eventually, D contains all final edges.*

Proof. Let $\{u, v\}$ be a final edge that is not in D. By the minimality condition given in Sect. 2 and the triangle inequality, we have that for all nodes $w \in V \setminus \{u, v\}$ it holds $d(u, w, v) > d(u, v)$. Furthermore, by Lemma 3 we have that eventually u is activated while $u.test = v$. Upon this activation, the guard of the rule **Add** is satisfied so that u adds $\{u, v\}$ to D. According to Lemma 2, a final edge is never removed.

Lemma 5. *Eventually, D does not change anymore.*

Proof. According to Lemma 4, the rule **Add** will eventually stop adding edges to the graph. It remains to show that the rule **Delegate** eventually stops delegating edges. According to Lemma 2, a final edge is never delegated. So consider a non-final edge in D. Upon delegation, the weight of such an edge according to the metric strictly decreases. Since the metric is finite, the edge can only be delegated a finite number of times.

We define the network to be *stable* if D does not change anymore. Hence, according to Lemma 5, the network will eventually stabilize. Note that even when stable, the *test*-pointers still move. We now turn to the main theorem of this section.

Theorem 1. *The Arbitrary Metric Algorithm is self-stabilizing with respect to the set L defined in the Sect. 2.*

Proof. We have to show that under the asynchronous dæmon, the algorithm reaches a configuration such that the current metric graph as defined by D satisfies the condition given in Proposition 1, and that this condition remains satisfied.

According to Lemma 5, eventually D does not change anymore. Together with Lemma 3 this means that the guards of the rules **Add** and **Delegate** are false for every node u in the network and for any $u.test = t$. Therefore, for all nodes $u, t \in V$ we have that

$$\neg (\exists v \neq w \in u.N, d(u, v, w) = d(u, w)) \tag{1}$$

and

$$\neg \big(t \notin u.N \ \wedge \big(\forall v \in u.N,\ d(u, v, t) > d(u, t)\big)\big). \tag{2}$$

Consider an edge $\{u, v\} \notin D$. Equation 2 gives us

$$\big(v \in u.N \vee \big(\exists w \in u.N.\ d(u, w, v) \leq d(u, v)\big)\big).$$

By the definition of D, we have $v \notin u.N$. Therefore, we can use the triangle inequality to deduce that

$$\exists w \in u.N,\ d(u, w, v) = d(u, v).$$

Hence, we have

$$\forall u, v \in V,\ \{u, v\} \notin D \Longrightarrow (\exists w \in u.N \setminus \{u, v\},\ d(u, w, v) = d(u, v)).$$

Now consider an edge $\{u, v\} \in D$ By the definition of D, we have $v \in u.N$. Therefore, Eq. 1 gives us

$$\neg (\exists w \in u.N,\ d(u, v, w) = d(u, w)).$$

Hence,

$$\forall u, v \in V,\ \neg (\{u, v\} \notin D) \Longrightarrow \neg (\exists w \in u.N \setminus \{v\},\ d(u, v, w) = d(u, w)).$$

In summary, eventually D satisfies the condition given in Proposition 1:

$$\forall u, v \in V,\ \{u, v\} \notin D \Longleftrightarrow \big(\exists w \in N(u) \setminus \{u, v\},\ d(u, w, v) = d(u, v)\big).$$

4.2 Runtime

We now analyse the runtime of the algorithm under a synchronous dæmon. According to [9,10] the first part of our algorithm takes $O(n)$ rounds to construct a cycle. We show that once the cycle construction is completed, the second part of our algorithm takes an additional $O(n)$ rounds to construct the final metric graph. Since the second part of our algorithm does not interfere with the first part, this gives us a linear runtime for the entire algorithm.

We first show that after $4n$ rounds, the *test*-pointer of each node pointed to every other node.

Lemma 6. *For all $u, v \in V$, there is a round $r \leq 4n$ such that $u.test = v$.*

Proof. The proof follows the exact same arguments as the proof of Lemma 3. After $2n$ rounds, it holds that $\forall u \in V,\ T_i(u) \leq 2$. After this point, a *test*-pointer moves from a node to its successor every second round. Thus, after at most $2n$ more rounds, we have $u.test = v$.

Now we can show that the algorithm constructs a supergraph of the final metric graph within $4n$ rounds. The proof of the following lemma is analogous to the proof of Lemma 4.

Lemma 7. *After $4n$ rounds, D contains all final edges.*

The previous lemmas lead to the following theorem.

Theorem 2. *Once the first part of our algorithm has successfully constructed a cycle, a stable configuration is reached in $5n$ rounds under the synchronous dæmon.*

Proof. After $4n$ rounds, D contains all the final edges. Only the **Delegate** rule can be applied and change the set D. A delegated edge can generate at most two new edges. Those edges can be delegated and generate new ones. Since all those delegations happen in parallel, we only have to determine the longest chain of delegations.

We consider the sequence of m edges: $(u_0, u_1), (u_1, u_2), \ldots, (u_{m-1}, u_m)$. For each $0 < i < m$, the edge (u_{i-1}, u_i) is delegated into (u_i, u_{i+1}) and (u_{m-1}, u_m) is a final edge.

Since each triple (u_i, u_{i+1}, u_{i+2}) consists of three different nodes, we have $u_0 \neq u_2$. The guard of the **Delegate** rule is satisfied each time and thus we have, for all $i = 1, .., m-1$ that $d(u_{i-1}, u_i) = d(u_{i-1}, u_{i+1}, u_i)$. From this, we deduce that:

$$\begin{aligned} d(u_0, u_1) &= d(u_0, u_2, u_1) \\ &= d(u_0, u_2, u_3, u_1) \\ &= d(u_0, u_2, u_4, u_3, u_1) \\ &\vdots \\ &= d(u_0, u_2, u_4, \ldots, u_{2k}, u_{2k+1}, \ldots, u_3, u_1) \end{aligned}$$

Assume, there exists j such that $u_0 = u_j$. Then we have:

$$d(u_0, u_1) = d(u_0, u_2, \ldots, u_j, \ldots, u_1)$$

and we obtain

$$d(u_0, u_1) = d(u_0, u_2, \ldots, u_j) + d(u_j, \ldots, u_1) \geq d(u_0, u_2, u_0) + d(u_0, u_1).$$

This is contradiction with the fact that d is a metric.

We just showed that all the nodes involved in a sequence of delegations are distinct. Therefore, we have $m < n$ which means that the longest chain of delegation requires at most $n - 1$ rounds.

To conclude, after $5n$ rounds, D contains all the final edges and has no more edges to delegated. Thus we have $D = \overline{D}$.

Since the construction of the cycle takes $O(n)$ rounds [9,10], we have the following corollary.

Corollary 1. *Under a synchronous dæmon, our algorithm builds the metric graph of a given arbitrary metric in a self-stabilizing manner in $O(n)$ rounds.*

4.3 After Stabilization

Our algorithm uses the construction of a cycle and the traversal of this cycle by the *test*-pointers as a tool for the construction of the metric graph. Under a synchronous dæmon, this tool allows our algorithm to check all $\Theta(n^2)$ possible edges in the network in linear time. In this section, we analyse the message complexity of the part of our algorithm that is responsible for the traversal of the cycle by the *test*-pointers. It is interesting to bound this message complexity because after stabilization the cycle construction only causes a constant number of messages to be sent and received per round at every node and the metric graph construction is silent (no more messages are sent). The traversal of the cycle by the *test*-pointers continues indefinitely, even after stabilization, and therefore causes some communication between the nodes.

Lemma 8. *Considering only the part of our algorithm responsible for moving the test-pointers, a node u sends at most 2 messages and receives at most $T(u)+1$ messages in any round.*

Proof. A node u sends 1 message to $u.test$ to ask for its successor and 1 message to one of the nodes asking for $u.succ$. A node receives $T(u)$ messages asking for its successor and at most 1 message as an answer to its own request concerning the successor of $u.test$.

Following Lemma 8 and the explanations above, we get the following theorem.

Theorem 3. *After stabilization, each node sends a constant number of messages per round.*

The above statements on the communication cost hold for both the synchronous and the asynchronous dæmon. When considering only the synchronous dæmon, we can also give a bound on the amount of memory required at each node. Let $\Delta(u)$ be the degree of a node u in the final metric graph. We have the following theorem.

Theorem 4. *After stabilization under a synchronous dæmon, a node u stores at most $\Delta(u) + 5$ identifiers in its memory.*

Proof. After stabilization, the memory of a node u contains the set $u.N$ consisting of $\Delta(u)$ identifiers, the identifiers $u.succ$, $u.prec$, and $u.test$, as well as at most two identifier in its queue $u.Req$.

5 Further Application

With some minor modifications, the algorithm can also be used to compute an α-approximation of the metric graph. We simply replace the rules **Delegate** and **Add** with the following rules.

Delegate: $\exists v, w \in u.N,\ d(u,v) + \alpha d(v,w) \leq \alpha d(u,w) \rightarrow u.N \leftarrow u.N \setminus \{w\}$
$v.N \leftarrow v.N \cup \{w\}$
$w.N \leftarrow w.N \cup \{v\}$

Add: $u.test \notin u.N \cup \{u\} \ \wedge\ \big(\forall v \in u.N,$
$d(u,v) + \alpha d(v, u.test) > \alpha d(u, u.test)\big) \rightarrow u.N \leftarrow u.N \cup \{u.test\}$
$u.test.N \leftarrow u.test.N \cup \{u\}$

These changes do not influence the correctness or the complexity of the algorithm. However, the constructed graph might be different in that it may have less edges. For example, a random Euclidean metric graph on a plane will have a quadratic number of edges with high probability, but the corresponding Delaunay graph — which is a 2.42-approximation (see [7,8] for more details on this topic) — has a linear number of edges. We cannot expect such results for the general case of arbitrary metrics but one can hope to obtain a sparser graph for the cost of a small approximation.

Another application of the general ideas of our algorithm is the construction of arbitrary locally-checkable topologies similarly to the Transitive Closure Framework of Berns *et al.* [2]. Assume that a node u can locally check whether it has to connect to a given node v to form the desired topology. By changing the rules of our algorithm that are responsible for the construction of the metric graph, we get an algorithm that can construct arbitrary locally-checkable topologies: First, we need to change the rule for adding edges so that it checks whether the edge $(u, u.test)$ is part of the network and, if so, adds it to the network. Second, we need to change the rule for delegating edges so that it checks for each outgoing edge whether it is part of the network and, if not, removes it. It is easy to see that once all test-pointers visited all nodes, the desired topology is reached.

6 Conclusion

We presented a self-stabilizing algorithm for overlay networks that, for an arbitrary metric given by a distance oracle, constructs the graph representing that metric. To the best of our knowledge, this is the first algorithm for constructing the graph of an arbitrary metric in a self-stabilizing manner. The algorithm works under both an asynchronous and a synchronous dæmon. For the synchronous case, the algorithm converges in time $O(n)$ and it is almost silent in that once it stabilizes, each node sends and receives at most a constant number of messages per round. Our algorithm is based around a simple technique that uses a directed cycle covering all nodes to guide the construction of the metric graph. We think that this underlying technique could have applications beyond the construction of metric graphs and therefore should be of independent interest.

Acknowledgments. This work was partially supported by the German Research Foundation (DFG) within the Collaborative Research Center "On-The-Fly Computing" (SFB 901) and by the EU within FET project MULTIPLEX under contract no. 317532.

References

1. Aggarwal, S., Kutten, S.: Time optimal self-stabilizing spanning tree algorithms. In: Shyamasundar, R.K. (ed.) FSTTCS 1993. LNCS, vol. 761, pp. 400–410. Springer, Heidelberg (1993). doi:10.1007/3-540-57529-4_72
2. Berns, A., Ghosh, S., Pemmaraju, S.V.: Building self-stabilizing overlay networks with the transitive closure framework. In: Défago, X., Petit, F., Villain, V. (eds.) SSS 2011. LNCS, vol. 6976, pp. 62–76. Springer, Heidelberg (2011). doi:10.1007/978-3-642-24550-3_7
3. Clouser, T., Nesterenko, M., Scheideler, C.: Tiara: a self-stabilizing deterministic skip list and skip graph. Theor. Comput. Sci. **428**, 18–35 (2012)
4. Cramer, C., Fuhrmann, T., Informatik, F.F.: Self-stabilizing ring networks on connected graphs. Technical report (2005)
5. Gärtner, F.C.: A survey of self-stabilizing spanning-tree construction algorithms. Technical report (2003)
6. Jacob, R., Richa, A., Scheideler, C., Schmid, S., Täubig, H.: A distributed polylogarithmic time algorithm for self-stabilizing skip graphs. In: Proceedings of the 28th ACM Symposium on Principles of Distributed Computing, pp. 131–140. ACM (2009)
7. Keil, J.M., Gutwin, C.A.: The Delaunay triangulation closely approximates the complete Euclidean graph. In: Dehne, F., Sack, J.-R., Santoro, N. (eds.) WADS 1989. LNCS, vol. 382, pp. 47–56. Springer, Heidelberg (1989). doi:10.1007/3-540-51542-9_6
8. Keil, J.M., Gutwin, C.A.: Classes of graphs which approximate the complete euclidean graph. Discrete Comput. Geom. **7**(1), 13–28 (1992)
9. Kniesburges, S., Koutsopoulos, A., Scheideler, C.: Re-chord: a self-stabilizing chord overlay network. Theory Comput. Syst. **55**(3), 591–612 (2014)

10. Onus, M., Richa, A.W., Scheideler, C.: Linearization: Locally self-stabilizing sorting in graphs. In: ALENEX (2007)
11. Richa, A., Scheideler, C., Stevens, P.: Self-stabilizing de bruijn networks. In: Défago, X., Petit, F., Villain, V. (eds.) SSS 2011. LNCS, vol. 6976, pp. 416–430. Springer, Heidelberg (2011). doi:10.1007/978-3-642-24550-3_31
12. Shaker, A., Reeves, D.S.: Self-stabilizing structured ring topology p2p systems. In: Fifth IEEE International Conference on Peer-to-Peer Computing, P2P, pp. 39–46 (2005)

Near-Optimal Self-stabilising Counting and Firing Squads

Christoph Lenzen[1] and Joel Rybicki[2(✉)]

[1] Department of Algorithms and Complexity, Max Planck Institute for Informatics, Saarland Informatics Campus, Saarbrücken, Germany
joel.rybicki@aalto.fi
[2] Helsinki Institute for Information Technology HIIT, Department of Computer Science, Aalto University, Espoo, Finland

Abstract. Consider a fully-connected synchronous distributed system of n nodes, where up to f nodes may be faulty and every node starts in an arbitrary initial state. In the *synchronous counting* problem, all nodes need to eventually agree on a counter that is increased by one modulo some C in each round. In the *self-stabilising firing squad* problem, the task is to eventually guarantee that all non-faulty nodes have simultaneous responses to external inputs: if a subset of the correct nodes receive an external "go" signal as input, then all correct nodes should agree on a round (in the not-too-distant future) in which to jointly output a "fire" signal. Moreover, no node should generate a "fire" signal without some correct node having previously received a "go" signal as input.

We present a framework reducing both tasks to binary consensus at very small cost while maintaining the resilience of the underlying consensus routine. Our results resolve various open questions on the two problems, most prominently whether (communication-efficient) self-stabilising Byzantine firing squads or sublinear-time solutions for either problem exist. For example, we obtain a deterministic algorithm for self-stabilising Byzantine firing squads with optimal resilience $f < n/3$, asymptotically optimal stabilisation and response time $O(f)$, and message size $O(\log f)$. As our framework does not restrict the type of consensus routines used, we can also obtain efficient randomised solutions, and it is straightforward to adapt our framework to allow $f < n/2$ omission or $f < n$ crash faults.

1 Introduction

The design of distributed systems faces several unique issues related to redundancy and fault-tolerance, timing and synchrony, and the efficient use of communication as a resource [17]. In this work, we give near-optimal solutions to two fundamental distributed synchronisation and coordination tasks: the synchronous counting and the firing squad problems. For both tasks, we devise fast self-stabilising algorithms [8] that are not only communication-efficient, but also tolerate the optimal number of permanently faulty nodes. That is, our algorithms efficiently recover from transient failures that may arbitrarily corrupt the state of the distributed system *and* permanently damage a large number of the nodes.

B. Bonakdarpour and F. Petit (Eds.): SSS 2016, LNCS 10083, pp. 263–280, 2016.
DOI: 10.1007/978-3-319-49259-9_21

Synchronous Counting and Firing Squads. We assume a synchronous message-passing model of distributed computation. The distributed system consists of a fully-connected network of n nodes, where up to f of the nodes may be faulty and the initial state of the system is arbitrary. To model the behaviour of faulty nodes, we consider three typical classes of permanent faults:

- crash (the faulty node stops sending information),
- omission (some or all of the messages sent by the faulty node are lost), and
- Byzantine faults (the faulty node exhibits arbitrary misbehaviour).

Note that even though the communication proceeds in a synchronous fashion, the nodes may have different notions of current time due to the arbitrary initial states. However, many typical distributed protocols assume that the system has either been properly initialised or that the nodes should collectively agree on the rounds in which to perform certain actions. Thus, we are essentially faced with the task of having to agree on a common time in a manner that is both self-stabilising and tolerates permanently faulty behaviour from some of the nodes. To address this issue, we study the synchronous counting and firing squad problems, which are among the most fundamental challenges in fault-tolerant distributed systems.

In the *synchronous counting* problem, all the nodes receive well-separated synchronous clock pulses that designate the start of a new round. The received clock pulses are anonymous, and hence, all correct nodes should eventually stabilise and agree on a round counter that increases consistently by one modulo C. The problem is also known as *digital clock synchronisation*, as all non-faulty nodes essentially have to agree on a shared logical clock. A stabilising execution of such a protocol for $n = 4$, $f = 1$, and $C = 3$ is given below:

Clock 

Node 1	1	1	2	1	0	1	2	0	1	2
Node 2	0	1	2	1	0	1	2	0	1	2
Node 3 (faulty)	*	*	*	*	*	*	*	*	*	*
Node 4	2	0	1	0	0	1	2	0	1	2
		stabilisation					counting			

In the *self-stabilising firing squad problem*, the task is to have all correct nodes eventually stabilise and respond to an external input simultaneously. That is, once stabilised, when a sufficiently large (depending on the type of permanent faults) subset of the correct nodes receive an external "go" signal, then all correct nodes should eventually generate a local "fire" event on the same round. The time taken to react to the "go" signal is called the response time. Note that before stabilisation the nodes may generate spurious firing signals, but after stabilisation no correct node should generate a "fire" event without some correct node having previously received a "go" signal as input. An execution of such a protocol with $n = 4$, $f = 1$, and response time $R = 5$ is illustrated below:

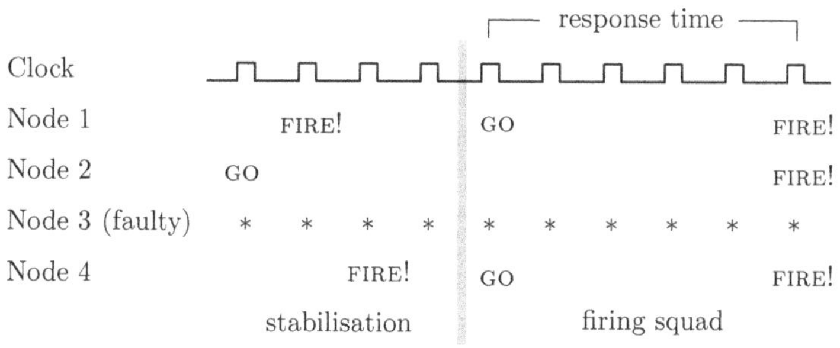

A firing squad protocol can be used, for example, to agree in a self-stabilising manner on when to initiate a new instance of a non-self-stabilising distributed protocol, as response to internal or external "go" inputs.

Connections to Fault-Tolerant Consensus. Reaching agreement is perhaps the most intrinsic problem in fault-tolerant distributed computing. It is known that both the synchronous counting [4] and the self-stabilising firing squad problem [7] are closely connected to the well-studied consensus problem [12,18], where each node is given an input bit and the task is to agree on a common output bit such that if every non-faulty node received the same value as input, then this value must also be the output value. Indeed, the connection is obvious on an intuitive level, as in each task the goal is to agree on a common decision (that is, the output bit, clock value, or whether to generate a firing event).

However, the key difference between the problems lies in self-stabilisation. Typically, the consensus problem is considered in a non-self-stabilising setting with only permanent faults (e.g. $f < n/3$ nodes with arbitrary behaviour), whereas synchronous counting copes with both transient and permanent faults. In fact, it is easy to see that synchronous counting is trivial in a non-self-stabilising setting: if all nodes are initialised with the same clock value, then they can simply locally increment their counters each round without any communication. Furthermore, in a properly initialised system, one can easily reduce the firing squad problem to repeatedly calling a consensus routine [3].

Interestingly, imposing the requirement of self-stabilisation – convergence to correct system behavior from arbitrary initial states – reverses the roles. Solving either the synchronous counting or firing squad problem in a self-stabilising manner also yields a solution to binary consensus, but the converse is not true. In fact, in order to internally or externally trigger a consistent execution of a consensus protocol (or any other non-self-stabilising protocol, for that matter), one first needs a self-stabilising counting or firing squad algorithm, respectively!

In light of this, the self-stabilising variants of both problems are important generalisations of consensus. While considerable research has been dedicated to both tasks [1,4–7,9,14,16], our understanding is significantly less developed than for the extensively studied consensus problem. Moreover, it is worth noting that all existing algorithms utilise consensus subroutines [6,14,16] or shared coins [1], the latter of which essentially solves consensus as well. Given that both tasks are at least as hard as consensus [4], this seems to be a natural approach. However, it raises the question how much of an overhead must be incurred by such a reduction. In this paper, we subsume and improve upon previous results by providing a generic reduction of synchronous counting and self-stabilising firing squad to binary consensus that incurs very small overheads.

Contributions. We develop a framework for efficiently transforming *non-self-stabilising* consensus algorithms into *self-stabilising* algorithms for synchronous counting and firing squad problems. In particular, the resulting self-stabilising algorithms have the same resilience as the original consensus algorithms, that is, the resulting algorithms tolerate the same number and type of permanent faults as the original consensus algorithm (e.g. crash, omission, or Byzantine faults).

The construction we give incurs a small overhead compared to time and bit complexity of the consensus routines: the stabilisation time and message size are, up to constant factors, given as the sum of the cost of the consensus routine for f faults and recursively applying our scheme to $f' < f/2$ faults. Finally, our construction can be used in conjunction with both deterministic and randomised consensus algorithms. This allows us to also obtain algorithms for randomised variants of the synchronous counting and firing squad problems.

Our novel framework enables us to address several open problems related to self-stabilising firing squads and synchronous counting. In the case of self-stabilising firing squads, Dolev et al. [7] posed the following two open problems:

1. Are there solutions that tolerate omission or Byzantine faults?
2. Are there algorithms using $o(n)$-bit messages only?

We answer both questions in the affirmative by giving algorithms that achieve both properties *simultaneously.* Concretely, our framework implies a deterministic solution for the self-stabilising Byzantine firing squad problem that (i) tolerates the optimal number of $f < n/3$ Byzantine faulty nodes, (ii) uses messages of $O(\log f)$ bits, and (iii) is guaranteed to stabilise and respond to inputs in linear-in-f communication rounds.

Thus, compared to prior state-of-the-art solutions [7], our algorithm tolerates a much stronger form of faulty behaviour and uses exponentially smaller messages, yet retains asymptotically optimal stabilisation and response time. Our framework is also applicable to different fault types: by using suitable consensus protocols, it is possible to obtain algorithms tolerating e.g. $f < n/2$ omission faults and $f < n$ crash faults while retaining a small message size of $O(\log f)$ bits.

Furthermore, we attain novel algorithms for synchronous counting, which is also known as self-stabilising Byzantine fault-tolerant *digital clock synchronisation* [1,9,10]. Our new algorithms resolve questions left open by our own prior work [16], namely, whether there exist

1. deterministic linear-time algorithms with optimal resilience and message size $o(\log^2 f)$ bits, or
2. randomised sublinear-time algorithms with small bit complexity.

We answer both questions positively using our framework developed in this paper. First, we give linear-time deterministic algorithms that have message size $O(\log f)$ bits. Second, our framework can utilise efficient randomised consensus algorithms to obtain probabilistic variants of the synchronous counting and firing squad problems. For example, in the full online version [15] we show that the result of King and Saia [11] implies algorithms that stabilise with high probability in polylog n rounds and use message size polylog n, assuming private communication links and an adaptive Byzantine adversary corrupting $f < n/(3+\varepsilon)$ nodes for an arbitrarily small constant $\varepsilon > 0$.

Outline of the Paper. This extended abstract is structured as follows. Due to lack of space, we confine the presentation to deterministic algorithms and Byzantine faults, omit proofs, and skip an in-depth discussion of related work; all these details are given in the full version [15]. In Sect. 2, we give formal definitions related to the model of computation, synchronous counting, and firing squads. In the sections following this, we show our main result in a top-down fashion by introducing a series of new problems and reductions between them:

- Section 3 shows how to obtain synchronous counting and firing squad algorithms that rely on binary consensus routines and *strong pulsers*,
- Section 4 devises strong pulsers with the help of *weak pulsers* and multivalued consensus,
- Section 5 constructs weak pulsers using *silent consensus* and less resilient strong pulsers.

2 Preliminaries

Notation. We use $\mathbb{N} = \{1, 2, \ldots\}$ to denote the set of positive integers and $\mathbb{N}_0 = \{0\} \cup \mathbb{N}$ to denote the set of all non-negative integers. For any $k \in \mathbb{N}$, we write $[k] = \{0, \ldots, k-1\}$ to be the set of first k non-negative integers.

Model of Computation. We consider a fully-connected synchronous network on node set V consisting of $n = |V|$ processors. We assume there exists a subset of $F \subseteq V$ faulty nodes that is (at least initially) unknown to all nodes, where the upper bound f on the size $|F| \leq f < n/3$ is known by the nodes. We say that nodes in $V \setminus F$ are correct and nodes in F are faulty.

All correct nodes in the system will follow a given algorithm **A** that is the same for all the nodes in the system. The execution proceeds in synchronous rounds, where in each round $t \in \mathbb{N}$ the nodes take the following actions in lock-step: (i) perform local computations, (ii) send messages to other nodes, and (iii) receive messages from other nodes. We assume nodes can distinguish the sender of incoming messages, e.g., by having a port numbering assigning distinct labels to the incoming links from each other node. In particular, our construction does not require any port numbering of the outgoing links or unique identifiers, unless the underlying consensus routine does. We say that an algorithm **A** has message size $M(\mathbf{A})$ if no node sends more than $M(\mathbf{A})$ bits to any other node during a single round.

The local computations of a node v determine the decision which messages to send to other nodes and what is the new state of the node v. As we are interested in self-stabilising algorithms, the initial state of a node is arbitrary; this is equivalent to assuming that transient faults have arbitrarily corrupted the state of each node, but the transient faults have ceased by the beginning of the first round. As mentioned above, we allow for additional (possibly permanent) *Byzantine* faults. A Byzantine faulty node $v \in F$ may deviate from the algorithm in an arbitrary way.

Synchronous Counting. In the *synchronous C-counting* problem, the task is to have each node $v \in V$ output a counter value $c(v,t) \in [C]$ on each round $t \in \mathbb{N}$ in a consistent manner. We say that an execution of an algorithm *stabilises in round* t if and only if all $t \leq t' \in \mathbb{N}$ and $v, w \in V \setminus F$ satisfy

- **Agreement:** $c(v,t') = c(w,t')$ and
- **Consistency:** $c(v,t'+1) = c(v,t') + 1 \bmod C$.

We say that $\mathbf{A}$ is an f-resilient C-counting algorithm that stabilises in time t if all executions with at most f faulty nodes stabilise by round t. The stabilisation time $T(\mathbf{A})$ of $\mathbf{A}$ is the maximum such t over all executions.

Self-stabilising Firing Squad. In the self-stabilising Byzantine firing squad problem, in each round $t \in \mathbb{N}$, each node $v \in V$ receives an external input $\mathrm{GO}(v,t) \in \{0,1\}$. Moreover, the algorithm determines an output $\mathrm{FIRE}(v,t) \in \{0,1\}$ at each node $v \in V$ in each round $t \in \mathbb{N}$. We say that an execution of an algorithm *stabilises in round* $t \in \mathbb{N}$ if the following three properties hold:

- **Agreement:** $\mathrm{FIRE}(v,t') = \mathrm{FIRE}(w,t')$ for all $v, w \in V \setminus F$ and $t \leq t' \in \mathbb{N}$.
- **Safety:** If $\mathrm{FIRE}(v,t_F) = 1$ for $v \in V \setminus F$ and $t \leq t_F \in \mathbb{N}$, then there is $t_F \geq t_G \in \mathbb{N}$ such that (i) $\mathrm{GO}(w,t_G) = 1$ for some $w \in V \setminus F$ and (ii) $\mathrm{FIRE}(v,t') = 0$ for all $t' \in \{t_G+1, \ldots, t_F-1\}$.
- **Liveness:** If $\mathrm{GO}(v,t_G) = 1$ for at least $f+1$ nodes $v \in V \setminus F$ and $t \leq t_G \in \mathbb{N}$, then $\mathrm{FIRE}(v,t_F) = 1$ for all nodes $v \in V \setminus F$ and some $t_G < t_F \in \mathbb{N}$.

Note that the liveness condition requires $f+1$ correct nodes to observe a GO input, as otherwise it would be impossible to guarantee that a correct node observed a GO input when firing; this corresponds to the definition of a strict Byzantine firing squad [3]. We say that an execution stabilised by round t has *response time R from round* t if

(i) when firing is required in response to (sufficiently many) GO inputs of 1 in round $t_G \geq t$, this happens no later than round $t_G + R$, and
(ii) when the squad fires in round $t_F \geq t$, there was sufficient support (in terms of GO inputs of 1) justifying this in a round t_G with $t_F > t_G \geq t_F - R$.

Finally, we say that an algorithm $\mathbf{F}$ is an f-resilient firing squad algorithm with stabilisation time $T(\mathbf{F})$ and response time $R(\mathbf{F})$ if in any execution of the system with at most f faulty nodes there is a round $t \leq T(\mathbf{F})$ such that the algorithm stabilised and has response time at most $R(\mathbf{F})$ from round t.

Consensus. Let us conclude this section by definining the *multivalued consensus problem*. Unlike the synchronous counting and self-stabilising firing squad problems, the standard definition of consensus does *not* require self-stabilisation: we assume that all nodes start from a fixed starting state and the algorithm terminates in finitely many communication rounds.

In the multivalued consensus problem for $L > 1$ values, each node $v \in V$ receives an input $x(v) \in [L]$ and the task is to have all correct nodes output the same $y \in [L]$. We say that an algorithm $\mathbf{C}$ is an f-resilient $T(\mathbf{C})$-round consensus algorithm if the following conditions hold when there are at most f faulty nodes:

- **Termination:** Each $v \in V \setminus F$ decides on an output $y(v) \in [L]$ by the end of round $T(\mathbf{C})$.
- **Agreement:** For all $v, w \in V \setminus F$, it holds that $y(v) = y(w)$.
- **Validity:** If there exists $x \in [L]$ such that for all $v \in V \setminus F$ it holds that $x(v) = x$, then each $v \in V \setminus F$ outputs the value $y(v) = x$.

We remark that one may ask for stronger validity conditions, but for our purposes this condition is sufficient. The *binary consensus* problem is the special case of $L = 2$ of the above multivalued consensus problem. In the case of binary consensus, the stated validity condition is equivalent to requiring that if $v \in V \setminus F$ outputs $y(v) = x \in \{0, 1\}$, then some $w \in V \setminus F$ has input value $x(w) = x$.

3 Synchronous Counting and Firing Squads

Our approach to the firing squad problem is to solve it by repeated consensus, which in turn is controlled by a joint counter. To minimise message size, however, we will not communicate counter values directly. Instead we make use of what we call a *strong pulser*.

Definition 1 (Strong pulser). *An algorithm* $\mathbf{P}$ *is an* f*-resilient strong* Ψ*-pulser that stabilises in* $T(\mathbf{P})$ *rounds if it satisfies the following conditions in the presence of at most* f *faulty nodes. Each node* $v \in V$ *produces an output bit* $p(v,t) \in \{0,1\}$ *on each round* $t \in \mathbb{N}$*. We say that* v *generates a pulse in round* t *if* $p(v,t) = 1$ *holds. We require that there is a round* $t_0 \leq T(\mathbf{P})$ *such that:*

S1. For any $v \in V \setminus F$ *and* $t = t_0 + k\Psi$*, where* $k \in \mathbb{N}_0$*, it holds that* $p(v,t) = 1$*.*
S2. For any $v \in V \setminus F$ *and* $t \geq t_0$ *satisfying* $t \neq t_0 + k\Psi$ *for* $k \in \mathbb{N}_0$*,* $p(v,t) = 0$*.*

Put otherwise, a strong Ψ-pulser generates pulses at all non-faulty nodes exactly every Ψ rounds. Figure 1 illustrates an execution of a strong 3-pulser. It is easy to see that strong pulsers and synchronous counting are almost equivalent.

Lemma 1. *Let* $C \in \mathbb{N}$ *and* $\Psi \in \mathbb{N}$*. If* C *divides* Ψ*, then a strong* Ψ*-pulser that stabilises in* T *rounds implies a synchronous* C*-counter that stabilises in at most* T *rounds. If* Ψ *divides* C*, then a synchronous* C*-counter that stabilises in* T *rounds implies a strong* Ψ*-pulser that stabilises in at most* $T + \Psi - 1$ *rounds.*

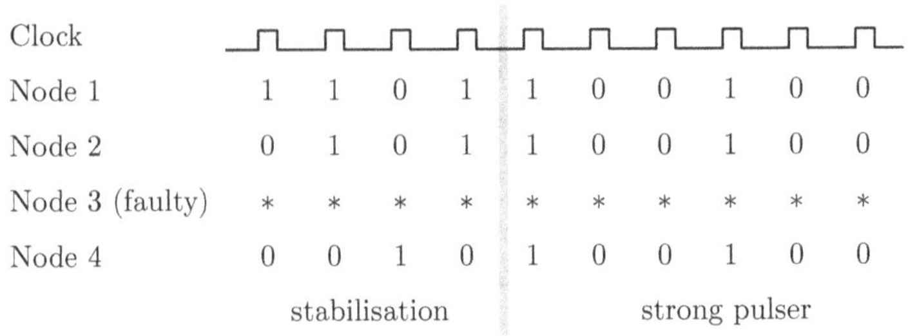

Fig. 1. An example execution of a strong 3-pulser on $n = 4$ nodes with $f = 1$ fault.

Firing Squads via Pulsers and Consensus. As a strong pulser can be used to control repeated execution of a non-self-stabilising algorithm, it enables us to run consensus on whether a firing event should be triggered or not repeatedly. As the firing squad problem is at least as hard as consensus, this maintains asymptotically optimal round complexity.

Recall that the liveness condition requires a firing event to be generated if at least $f+1$ non-faulty nodes $v \in V \setminus F$ recently saw $\mathrm{GO}(v,t) = 1$ on some round t. To ensure this, we have each node continuously inform all other nodes about its GO values. Whenever node $v \in V$ sees $f+1$ nodes $w \in V$ claim $\mathrm{GO}(w,t) = 1$, it will memorise this and use input $x(v) = 1$ for the next consensus instance. Otherwise, it will use the input value $x(v) = 0$; this ensures that at least one non-faulty node w had $\mathrm{GO}(w,t) = 1$ recently in case v uses input $x(v) = 1$. The validity condition of the (arbitrary) $T(\mathbf{C})$-round consensus routine $\mathbf{C}$ thus ensures both liveness and safety for the resulting firing squad algorithm. Apart from $\mathbf{C}$, the algorithm concurrently runs a strong Ψ-pulser $\mathbf{P}$ for some $\Psi > T(\mathbf{C})$.

Given a strong Ψ-pulser algorithm $\mathbf{P}$ and a binary consensus algorithm $\mathbf{C}$, each node v stores the following variables on every round t:

- $p(v,t) \in \{0,1\}$, the output variable of $\mathbf{P}$,
- $x(v,t) \in \{0,1\}$ and $y(v,t) \in \{0,1\}$, the input and output variables of $\mathbf{C}$, and
- $m(v,t) \in \{0,1\}$, an auxiliary variable used to memorise whether sufficiently many GO signals were received to warrant a firing event.

The algorithm lets node v execute the following operations in round $t \in \mathbb{N}$:

1. Broadcast $\mathrm{GO}(v,t)$.
2. If received at least $f+1$ times $\mathrm{GO}(w,t-1) = 1$, then set $x(v,t) = 1$ and $m(v,t) = 1$. Otherwise, set $x(v,t) = x(v,t-1)$ and $m(v,t) = m(v,t-1)$.
3. If $p(v,t) = 1$, start executing a new instance of $\mathbf{C}$ using the value $x(v,t-1)$ as input and set $m(v,t) = 0$ while aborting any previously running instance. More specifically, this entails the following:
   - Maintain a local round counter r, which is initialised to 1 in round t and increased by 1 after each round.
   - Maintain the local state variables related to the consensus routine $\mathbf{C}$.

 - On each round, execute round r of algorithm **C**; if the state variables indicate that **C** terminated at v, then do nothing.
 - At the end of the round when r becomes $T(\mathbf{C})$, stop the simulation (indicating this, e.g., by setting $r(v) = \perp$) and locally output the value of $y(v)$ computed by the simulation of **C**.

4. If **C** outputs $y(v,t) = 1$ in round t, then output $\text{FIRE}(v,t) = 1$ and set $x(v,t) = 0$. Otherwise, set $\text{FIRE}(v,t) = 0$.
5. If **C** outputs $y(v,t) = 0$ in round t and $m(v,t) = 0$, then set $x(v,t) = 0$.

In the above algorithm, in round t each correct node $v \in V \setminus F$ sends the bit $\text{GO}(v,t)$ and the message bits related to the strong pulser **P** and the consensus algorithm **C**.

Theorem 1. *Suppose there exists an f-resilient strong Ψ-pulser* **P** *and a consensus algorithm* **C**, *where $\Psi > T(\mathbf{C})$. Then there exists an f-resilient firing squad algorithm* **F** *that*

- *stabilises in time $T(\mathbf{F}) \leq T(\mathbf{P}) + T(\mathbf{C}) + 1$,*
- *has response time $R(\mathbf{F}) \leq \Psi + T(\mathbf{C})$, and*
- *uses messages of size $M(\mathbf{F}) \leq M(\mathbf{P}) + M(\mathbf{C}) + 1$ bits.*

4 From Weak Pulsers to Strong Pulsers

In the previous section, we established that it suffices to construct suitable strong pulsers to solve the synchronous counting and firing squad problems. We will now reduce the construction of strong pulsers to constructing *weak pulsers.*

Weak Pulsers. A weak Φ-pulser is similar to a strong pulser, but does not guarantee a fixed frequency of pulses. However, it guarantees to *eventually* generate a pulse followed by $\Phi - 1$ rounds of silence.

Definition 2 (Weak pulsers). *An algorithm* **W** *is an f-resilient weak Φ-pulser that stabilises in $T(\mathbf{W})$ rounds if the following holds. In each round $t \in \mathbb{N}$, each node $v \in V$ produces an output $a(v,t)$. Moreover, there exists a round $t_0 \leq T(\mathbf{W})$ such that*

W1. for all $v, w \in V \setminus F$ and all rounds $t \geq t_0$, $a(v,t) = a(w,t)$,
W2. $a(v,t_0) = 1$ for all $v \in V \setminus F$, and
W3. $a(v,t) = 0$ for all $v \in V \setminus F$ and $t \in \{t_0 + 1, \ldots, t_0 + \Phi - 1\}$.

We say that in round t_0 a good *pulse is generated by* **W**.

Figure 2 illustrates a weak 4-pulser. Note that while the definition formally only asks for one good pulse, the fact that the algorithm guarantees this property for any starting state implies that there is a good pulse at least every $T(\mathbf{W})$ rounds.

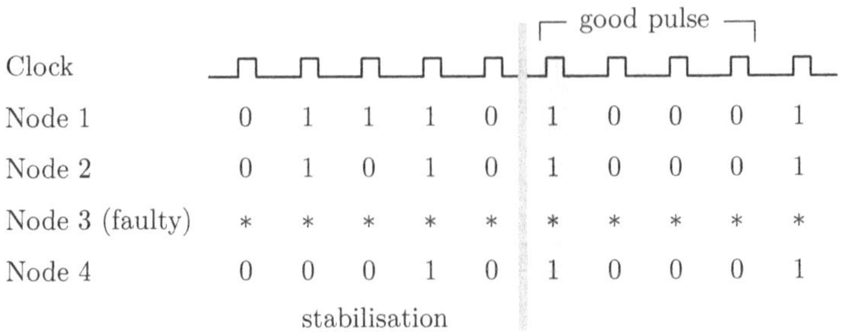

Fig. 2. An example execution of a weak 4-pulser on $n = 4$ nodes with $f = 1$ faulty node. Eventually, a good pulse is generated, which is highlighted. A good pulse is followed by three rounds in which no correct node generates pulse. In contrast, the pulse two rounds earlier is not good, as it is followed by only one round of silence.

Constructing Strong Pulsers from Weak Pulsers. Recall that a strong pulser can be obtained by having nodes locally count down the rounds until the next pulse, provided we have a way of ensuring that the local counters eventually agree. This can be achieved by using a weak pulser to control a suitable consensus routine, where we always have only a single instance running at any time. While some instances will be aborted before they can complete, this will not affect the counters, as we only adjust them when the consensus routine completes. On the other hand, the weak pulser guarantees that within $T(\mathbf{W})$ rounds, there will be a pulse followed by $\Phi - 1$ rounds of silence, enabling to complete a run of any consensus routine $\mathbf{C}$ satisfying $T(\mathbf{C}) \leq \Phi$. Thus, for constructing a strong Ψ-pulser, we assume that we have the following f-resilient algorithms available:

- a $T(\mathbf{C})$-round Ψ-value consensus algorithm $\mathbf{C}$ and
- a weak Φ-pulser $\mathbf{W}$ for $\Phi \geq T(\mathbf{C})$.

Beside the variables of the weak pulser $\mathbf{W}$ and (a single copy of) $\mathbf{C}$, our construction of a strong Ψ-pulser uses the following local variables:

- $a(v,t) \in \{0,1\}$ is the output variable of the weak Φ-pulser $\mathbf{W}$,
- $b(v,t) \in \{0,1\}$ is the output variable of the strong Ψ-pulser we construct,
- $c(v,t) \in [\Psi]$ is the local counter keeping track on when the next pulse occurs,
- $d(v,t) \in \{1,\ldots,T(\mathbf{C})\} \cup \{\bot\}$ keeps track of how many rounds an instance of $\mathbf{C}$ has been executed since the last pulse from the weak pulser $\mathbf{W}$. The value $\bot$ denotes that the consensus routine has stopped.

The strong pulser algorithm is as follows. Each node v executes the weak Φ-pulser algorithm $\mathbf{W}$ in addition to the following instructions on each round t:

1. If $c(v,t) = 0$, then set $b(v,t+1) = 1$ and otherwise $b(v,t+1) = 0$.
2. Set $c'(v,t) = c(v,t)$.
3. If $d(v,t) \neq \bot$, then
   (a) Execute the instructions of $\mathbf{C}$ for round $d(v,t)$.
   (b) If $d(v,t) \neq T(\mathbf{C})$, set $d(v,t+1) = d(v,t) + 1$.

   (c) If $d(v,t) = T(\mathbf{C})$, then
      i. Set $c'(v,t) = y(v,t) + T(\mathbf{C}) \bmod \Psi$, where $y(v,t)$ is the output value of $\mathbf{C}$.
      ii. Set $d(v,t+1) = \bot$.
4. Update $c(v,t+1) = c'(v,t) + 1 \bmod \Psi$.
5. If $a(v,t) = 1$, then
   (a) Start a new instance of $\mathbf{C}$ using $c'(v,t)$ as input (resetting all state variables of $\mathbf{C}$).
   (b) Set $d(v,t+1) = 1$.

In this algorithm, the first step simply translates the counter value to the output of the strong pulser. We then use a temporary variable $c'(v,t)$ to hold the counter value, which is overwritten by the output of $\mathbf{C}$ (increased by $T(\mathbf{C}) \bmod \Psi$) if it completes a run in this round. In either case, the counter needs to be increased by $1 \bmod \Psi$. The remaining code does the bookkeeping for running $\mathbf{C}$. Note that nodes send only the message bits related to the weak pulser $\mathbf{W}$ and the consensus algorithm $\mathbf{C}$; no additional message bits are needed.

Theorem 2. *The variables $c(v,t)$ in the above algorithm implement a synchronous Ψ-counter that stabilises in $T(\mathbf{W}) + T(\mathbf{C}) + 1$ rounds and uses messages of at most $M(\mathbf{W}) + M(\mathbf{C})$ bits.*

Corollary 1. *Let $\Psi > 1$. Suppose there exists an f-resilient Ψ-value consensus routine $\mathbf{C}$ and a weak Φ-pulser $\mathbf{W}$, where $\Phi \geq T(\mathbf{C})$. Then there exists an f-resilient strong Ψ-pulser $\mathbf{P}$ that*

- *stabilises in time $T(\mathbf{P}) \leq T(\mathbf{C}) + T(\mathbf{W}) + \Psi$, and*
- *uses message of size at most $M(\mathbf{P}) \leq M(\mathbf{C}) + M(\mathbf{W})$ bits.*

5 Weak Pulsers from Less Resilient Strong Pulsers

Having seen that we can construct strong pulsers from weak pulsers using a consensus algorithm, the only piece missing in our framework is the existence of efficient weak pulsers. In this section, we sketch a recursive construction of a weak pulser from strong pulsers of smaller resilience.

Our approach bears similarity to our constructions from earlier work [14,16], but attains better bit complexity and can be used with an arbitrary consensus routine. On a high level, we take the following approach:

1. Partition the network into two parts, each running a strong pulser. Our construction guarantees that at least one of the strong pulsers stabilises.
2. Consider the pulses generated by the strong pulsers as *potential* pulses.
3. Since one of the strong pulsers may not stabilise, it may generate *spurious* pulses, that is, pulses that only a subset of the correct nodes observe.
4. We first limit the frequency of the spurious pulses using a filtering mechanism based on threshold voting.

5. We then enforce any spurious pulse to be observed by all correct nodes by employing a *silent consensus* routine. In silent consensus, no message is sent (by correct nodes) if all correct nodes have input 0. Thus, if all nodes actually participating in an instance have input 0, non-participating nodes behave *as if they participated* with input 0. This avoids the chicken-and-egg problem of having to solve consensus on participation in the consensus routine.

The Filtering Construction. We partition V into two disjoint sets V_0 and V_1. For $i \in \{0,1\}$, let $\mathbf{P}_i$ be an f_i-resilient strong Ψ_i-pulser, which we run on V_i. Thus, $\mathbf{P}_i$ generates pulses every Ψ_i rounds once stabilised, granted that $|V_i \cap F| \le f_i$. Our construction tolerates $f = f_0 + f_1 + 1$ faulty nodes.

Let $a_i(v,t) \in \{0,1\}$ indicate the output bit of $\mathbf{P}_i$ for a node $v \in V_i$. Note that we might have a block $i \in \{0,1\}$ that contains more than f_i faulty nodes. Thus, it is possible that the algorithm $\mathbf{P}_i$ never stabilises. In particular, we might have the situation that some of the nodes in block i produce a pulse, but others do not. We say that a pulse generated by such a $\mathbf{P}_i$ is *spurious*. We proceed by showing how to filter out such spurious pulses if they occur too often.

We define five variables with the following semantics:

- $m_i(v,t+1)$ indicates whether at least $n_i - f_i$ nodes $u \in V_i$ sent $a_i(u,t) = 1$,
- $M_i(v,t+1)$ indicates whether at least $n - f$ nodes $u \in V$ sent $m_i(u,t) = 1$,
- $\ell_i(v,t)$ indicates when was the last time block i triggered a pulse,
- $w_i(v,t)$ indicates how long any firing events coming from block i are ignored,
- $b_i(v,t)$ indicates whether node v accepts a firing event from block i.

The first two of the above variables are set according to the following rules:

- $m_i(v,t+1) = 1$ if and only if $|\{u \in V_i : a_i(v,u,t) = 1|\} \ge n_i - f_i$,
- $M_i(v,t+1) = 1$ if and only if $|\{u \in V : m_i(v,u,t) = 1\} \ge n - f$.

We update the $\ell(\cdot,\cdot)$ variables using the rule

$$\ell_i(v,t+1) = \begin{cases} 0 & \text{if } |\{u \in V : m_i(u,t) = 1\}| \ge f+1, \\ \min\{\Psi_i, \ell_i(v,t)+1\} & \text{otherwise.} \end{cases}$$

In words, the counter is reset in round $t+1$ if v has proof that at least one correct node u had $m_i(u,t) = 1$, that is, some u observed $\mathbf{P}_i$ generating a pulse.

We reset the cooldown counter w_i whenever suspicious activity occurs, i.e., it is reset to its maximum value C by node v in the following two cases:

- some correct node $u \neq v$ observed block i generating a pulse, but v did not,
- block i generated a pulse, but this happened either too soon or too late.

To capture this behaviour, the cooldown counter is set with the rule

$$w_i(v,t+1) = \begin{cases} C & \text{if } M_i(v,t+1) = 0 \text{ and } \ell_i(v,t+1) = 0, \\ C & \text{if } M_i(v,t+1) = 1 \text{ and } \ell_i(v,t) \neq \Psi_i - 1, \\ \max\{w_i(v,t)-1, 0\} & \text{otherwise,} \end{cases}$$

where $C = \max\{\Psi_0, \Psi_1\} + \Phi + 2$. Finally, a node v accepts a pulse generated by block i if the node's cooldown counter is zero and it saw at least $n - f$ nodes supporting the pulse, indicated by the variable $b_i(v,t)$:

$$b_i(v,t) = \begin{cases} 1 & \text{if } w_i(v,t) = 0 \text{ and } M_i(v,t) = 1, \\ 0 & \text{otherwise.} \end{cases}$$

Observe that a node $v \in V_i$ sends the message bits related to the pulser algorithm $\mathbf{P}_i$ it is executing. In addition to this, each correct node only sends $O(1)$ bits every round to communicate the values of $m_i(\cdot)$ and $M_i(\cdot)$ in order to derive the output value $b_i(\cdot)$ for each $i \in \{0,1\}$.

We say that a block i is correct if it contains at most f_i faulty nodes. Note that since there are at most $f = f_0 + f_1 + 1$ faulty nodes, at least one block $i \in \{0,1\}$ is correct. Thus, eventually the algorithm $\mathbf{P}_i$ run by a correct block i will stabilise. We show that the pulses of the correct block are not filtered out and spurious pulses cannot occur too frequently.

Lemma 2. *If block i is correct, there is a round $t_0 \leq T(\mathbf{P}_i) + 2C$ so that for each $v \in V \setminus F$, $b_i(v,t) = 1$ for any $t \geq t_0$ if and only if $t = t_0 + k\Psi_i$ for $k \in \mathbb{N}_0$.*

Lemma 3. *Let $v, v' \in V \setminus F$ and $t > 2$. Suppose $b_i(v,t) = 1$ and suppose that $t' > t$ is minimal such that $b_i(v',t') = 1$. Then $t' = t + \Psi_i$ or $t' > t + C$.*

Introducing Silent Consensus. The above filtering mechanism prevents spurious pulses from occurring too often: if some node accepts a pulse from block i, then no node accepts a pulse from this block for at least Ψ_i rounds. We now strengthen the construction to enforce that *any* pulse generated by block i will be accepted by either all or no correct nodes. To achieve this, we employ *silent consensus*.

Definition 3 (Silent consensus). *A consensus protocol is* silent, *if in each execution in which all correct nodes have input* 0, *correct nodes send no messages.*

The idea is that this enables to have consistent executions even if not all correct nodes actually take part in an execution, provided we can ensure that in this case all participating correct nodes use input 0: the non-participating nodes send no messages either, which is the same behavior participating nodes exhibit. Silent consensus protocols can be obtained from non-silent ones at small overhead.

Theorem 3. *Any f-resilient consensus protocol $\mathbf{C}$ implies an f-resilient silent binary consensus protocol $\mathbf{C}'$ with $T(\mathbf{C}') = T(\mathbf{C}) + 2$ and $M(\mathbf{C}') = M(\mathbf{C})$.*

Using Silent Consensus to Prune Spurious Pulses. As the filtering construction bounds the frequency at which spurious pulses may occur from below, we can make sure that at each time, only one consensus instance can be executed for each block. However, we need to further preprocess the inputs to make sure that either (i) all correct nodes participate in an instance or (ii) no participating correct node has input 1; here, output 1 means agreement on a pulse being triggered.

Recall that $b_i(v,t) \in \{0,1\}$ indicates whether v observed a (filtered) pulse of the strong pulser $\mathbf{P}_i$ in round t. Moreover, assume that $\mathbf{C}$ is a silent consensus protocol running in $T(\mathbf{C})$ rounds. We use two copies $\mathbf{C}_i$, where $i \in \{0,1\}$, of $\mathbf{C}$. We require that $\Psi_i \geq T(\mathbf{C})$, which guarantees by Lemma 3 that (after stabilisation) every instance of $\mathbf{C}$ has sufficient time to complete.

Besides the local variables of $\mathbf{C}_i$, the pruning algorithm will use the following variables for each $v \in V$ and round $t \in \mathbb{N}$:

- $y_i(v,t) \in \{0,1\}$ denotes the output value of consensus routine $\mathbf{C}_i$,
- $r_i(v,t) \in \{1,\ldots,T(\mathbf{C})\} \cup \{\bot\}$ is a local round counter for controlling $\mathbf{C}_i$, and
- $B_i(v,t) \in \{0,1\}$ is the output of block i.

Now each node v executes the following in round t:

1. Broadcast $b_i(v,t)$.
2. If $b_i(w,t) = 1$ for $n - 2f$ nodes $w \in V$, then set $r_i(v,t+1) = 1$.
3. If $r_i(v,t) = 1$, then
   (a) start a new instance of $\mathbf{C}_i$, that is, re-initialise the variables of $\mathbf{C}_i$ correctly,
   (b) use input 1 if $b_i(w,t-1) = 1$ for $n - f$ nodes $w \in V$ and 0 otherwise.
4. If $r_i(v,t) = T(\mathbf{C})$, then
   (a) set $r_i(v,t+1) = \bot$,
   (b) set $B_i(v,t+1) = y_i(v,t)$, where $y_i(v,t)$ is the output variable of $\mathbf{C}_i$.
   Otherwise, set $B_i(v,t+1) = 0$.
5. If $r_i(v,t) \notin \{T(\mathbf{C}), \bot\}$, then
   (a) execute round $r_i(v,t)$ of $\mathbf{C}_i$, and
   (b) set $r_i(v,t+1) = r_i(v,t) + 1$.

Observe that in the above algorithm, in round t each node $v \in V \setminus F$ sends the bit $b_i(v,t)$ and any bits needed to compute $b_i(v,t)$. From previous discussion, we get that node $v \in V_i$ sends at most $O(1) + M(\mathbf{P}_i) + M(\mathbf{C}_0) + M(\mathbf{C}_1)$ bits in every round.

We say that $v \in V \setminus F$ *executes round* $r \in \{1,\ldots,T(\mathbf{C})\}$ of $\mathbf{C}_i$ in round t iff it executes the final step of the above algorithm in round t with $r_i(v,t) = r$. By Lemma 3, in rounds $t > T(\mathbf{C}) + 2$, there is always at most one instance of $\mathbf{C}_i$ being executed, and if so, consistently.

Corollary 2. *Suppose $v \in V \setminus F$ executes round 1 of $\mathbf{C}_i$ in some round $t > T(\mathbf{C})+2$. Then there is a subset $U \subseteq V \setminus F$ such that each $u \in U$ executes round $r \in \{1,\ldots,T(\mathbf{C})\}$ of $\mathbf{C}_i$ in round $t+r-1$ and no $u \in V \setminus (F \cup U)$ executes any round of $\mathbf{C}_i$ in round $t+r-1$.*

Exploiting silence of $\mathbf{C}_i$ and the choice of inputs, we can ensure that the case $U \neq V \setminus F$ causes no trouble.

Lemma 4. *Let $t > T(\mathbf{C}) + 2$ and U be as in Corollary 2. Then $U = V \setminus F$ or each $u \in U$ has input 0 for the respective instance of $\mathbf{C}_i$.*

Hence, if $U \neq V \setminus F$, all nodes executing the algorithm will compute output 0. Therefore, Corollary 2, Lemmas 3, and 4 imply the following corollary.

Corollary 3. *In rounds $t > T(\mathbf{C}) + 2$, $B_i(v,t) = B_i(w,t)$ for all $v, w \in V \setminus F$ and $i \in \{0,1\}$. Furthermore, if $B_i(v,t) = 1$ for $v \in V \setminus F$ and $t > T(\mathbf{C})+2$, then the minimal $t' > t$ so that $B_i(v,t') = 1$ (if it exists) satisfies either $t' = t + \Psi_i$ or $t' > t + C = t + \max\{\Psi_0, \Psi_1\} + \Phi + 2$.*

Finally, we observe that we do not filter out pulses from correct blocks.

Lemma 5. *If block i is correct, there is a round $t_0 \leq T(\mathbf{P}_i) + 2C + T(\mathbf{C}) + 1$ so that for any $t \geq t_0$, $B_i(v,t) = 1$ if and only if $t = t_0 + k\Psi_i$ for some $k \in \mathbb{N}_0$.*

Obtaining the Weak Pulser. We define the output variable of our weak pulser as

$$B(v, t+1) = \max\{B_0(v,t), B_1(v,t)\}.$$

That is, $B(v,t+1) = 1$ if either $B_0(v,t) = 1$ or $B_1(v,t+1) = 1$. As we have eliminated the possibility that $B_i(v,t) \neq B_i(w,t)$ for $v, w \in V \setminus F$ and $t > T(\mathbf{C})+2$, Property W1 in Definition 2 holds. Since there is at least one correct block i, Lemma 5 shows that there will be good pulses (satisfying Properties W2 and W3) regularly, unless block $1-i$ interferes by generating pulses violating Property W3 (i.e., in too short order after a pulse generated by block i). Here the filtering mechanism comes to the rescue: as we made sure that pulses are either generated at the chosen frequency Ψ_i or a long period of C rounds of generating no pulse is enforced (Corollary 3), it is sufficient to choose Ψ_0 and Ψ_1 as coprime multiples of Φ. Accordingly, we pick $\Psi_0 = 2\Phi$ and $\Psi_1 = 3\Phi$ and observe that this results in a good pulse within $O(\Phi)$ rounds after the B_i stabilised.

Lemma 6. *In the construction described in the previous two subsections, choose $\Psi_0 = 2\Phi$ and $\Psi_1 = 3\Phi$ for any $\Phi \geq T(\mathbf{C})$. Then $B(v,t)$ is the output variable of a weak Φ-pulser with stabilisation time $\max\{T(\mathbf{P}_0), T(\mathbf{P}_1)\} + O(\Phi)$.*

Proof. We have that $C = \max\{\Psi_0, \Psi_1\} + \Phi + 2 \in O(\Phi)$. By the above observations, there is a round $t \in \max\{T(\mathbf{P}_0), T(\mathbf{P}_1)\} + T(\mathbf{C}) + O(\Phi) = \max\{T(\mathbf{P}_0), T(\mathbf{P}_1)\} + O(\Phi)$ satisfying the following four properties. For either block $i \in \{0,1\}$, we have by Corollary 3 that

1. $B_i(v,t') = B_i(w,t')$ and $B(v,t') = B(w,t')$ for any $v, w \in V \setminus F$ and $t' \geq t$.

Moreover, for a correct block i and for all $v \in V \setminus F$ we have from Lemma 5 that

2. $B_i(v,t) = B_i(v, t + \Psi_i) = 1$,
3. $B_i(v,t') = 0$ for all $t' \in \{t+1, \dots, t+\Phi-1\} \cup \{t+\Psi_i+1, \dots, t+\Psi_i+\Phi-1\}$,

and for a (possibly faulty) block $1-i$ we have from Corollary 3 that

4. if $B_{1-i}(v,t') = 1$ for some $v \in V \setminus F$ and $t' \in \{t+1, \dots, t+\Psi_i+\Phi-1\}$, then $B_{1-i}(u,t'') = 0$ for all $u \in V \setminus F$ and $t'' \in \{t'+1, \dots, t'+C\}$ that do not satisfy $t'' = t' + k\Psi_{1-i}$ for some $k \in \mathbb{N}_0$.

Now it remains to argue that a good pulse is generated. As there are at most $f = f_0 + f_1 + 1$ faulty nodes, at least one block $i \in \{0, 1\}$ is correct. By the first property, it suffices to show that a good pulse occurs in round t or in round $t + \Psi_i$. From the second property, we get for all $v \in V \setminus F$ that $B(v, t) = 1$ and $B(v, t + \Psi_i) = 1$. If the pulse in round t is good, the claim holds. Hence, assume that there is a round $t' \in \{t + 1, \ldots, t + \Psi_i - 1\}$ in which another pulse occurs, that is, $B(v, t') = 1$ for some $v \in V \setminus F$. This entails that $B_{1-i}(v, t') = 1$ by the third property. We claim that in this case the pulse in round $t + \Psi_i$ is good. To show this, we exploit the fourth property. Recall that $C > \Psi_i + \Phi$, i.e., $t' + C > t + \Psi_i + \Phi$. We distinguish two cases:

- In the case $i = 0$, we have that $t' + \Psi_{1-i} = t' + 3\Phi = t' + \Psi_0 + \Psi > t + \Psi_0 + \Phi$, that is, the pulse in round $t + \Psi_0 = t + \Psi_i$ is good.
- In the case $i = 1$, we have that $t' + \Psi_{1-i} = t' + 2\Phi < t + 3\Phi \leq t + \Psi_0$ and $t' + 2\Psi_{1-i} = t' + 4\Phi = t' + \Psi_1 + \Phi > t + \Psi_1 + \Phi$, that is, the pulse in round $t + \Psi_1 = t + \Psi_i$ is good.

Either way, a good pulse occurs by round $t + \max\{\Psi_0, \Psi_1\} \in \max\{T(\mathbf{P}_0), T(\mathbf{P}_1)\} + O(\Phi)$.

This lemma and the constructions of this section yield the following theorem.

Theorem 4. *Let $n = n_0 + n_1$ and $f = f_0 + f_1 + 1$, where $n > 3f$. Suppose $\mathbf{C}$ is an f-resilient consensus algorithm on n nodes and $\mathbf{P}_i$, $i \in \{0, 1\}$, are f_i-resilient strong pulser algorithms on n_i nodes. Then, for any $\Phi \geq T(\mathbf{C}) + 2$, there exists an f-resilient weak Φ-pulser $\mathbf{W}$ on n nodes that satisfies*

- $T(\mathbf{W}) \in \max\{T(\mathbf{P}_0), T(\mathbf{P}_1)\} + O(\Phi)$,
- $M(\mathbf{W}) \in \max\{M(\mathbf{P}_0), M(\mathbf{P}_1)\} + O(M(\mathbf{C}))$.

Proof. By Theorem 3, we can transform $\mathbf{C}$ into a silent consensus protocol $\mathbf{C}'$, at the cost of increasing its round complexity by 2. Using $\mathbf{C}'$ in the construction, Lemma 6 shows that we obtain a weak Φ-pulser with the stated stabilisation time, which by construction tolerates f faults. Concerning the message size, note that we run $\mathbf{P}_0$ and $\mathbf{P}_1$ on disjoint node sets. Apart from sending $\max\{M(\mathbf{P}_0), M(\mathbf{P}_1)\}$ bits per round for its respective strong pulser, each node may send $M(\mathbf{C})$ bits each to every other node for the two copies $\mathbf{C}_i$ of $\mathbf{C}$ it runs in parallel, plus a constant number of additional bits for the filtering construction.

6 Main Results

We can now use the results of the previous sections to attain our main theorem.

Theorem 5. *Suppose that we are given a family of f-resilient deterministic consensus algorithms $\mathbf{C}(f)$ running on any number $n > 3f$ of nodes in $T(\mathbf{C}(f))$ rounds using $M(\mathbf{C}(f))$-bit messages, where $T(\mathbf{C}(f))$ and $M(\mathbf{C}(f))$ are increasing in f. Then, for any $\Psi, f \in \mathbb{N}$ and $n > 3f$, there exists a strong Ψ-pulser $\mathbf{P}$ on n nodes that*

- *stabilises in time* $T(\mathbf{P}) \in (1 + o(1))\Psi + O\left(\sum_{j=0}^{\lceil \log f \rceil} T(\mathbf{C}(2^j))\right)$ *and*
- *uses messages of size at most* $M(\mathbf{P}) \in O\left(1 + \sum_{j=0}^{\lceil \log f \rceil} M(\mathbf{C}(2^j))\right)$ *bits.*

Theorem 5 follows from showing by induction on k that for any $f < 2^k$ there exist f-resilient strong Ψ-pulsers $\mathbf{P}(f, \Psi)$ on $n > 3f$ nodes with the stated complexity, with the addition that the (bounds on) stabilisation time and message size of our pulsers are increasing in f. The base case of induction at $k = 0$, i.e., $f = 0$, follows readily from the fact that 0-resilient strong Ψ-pulsers for any $n \in \mathbb{N}$ trivially exist: it suffices that one node generates pulses locally and informs the other nodes when to generate a pulse as well. This requires 1-bit messages and stabilises in Ψ rounds. In the inductive step, we apply Theorem 4 to obtain weak pulsers which we can feed together with suitable multivalued consensus protocols [13] into Corollary 1. For a detailed proof, see the full online version [15].

Finally, we can plug in the phase king consensus protocol [2] into Theorem 5. The phase king protocol tolerates $f < n/3$ Byzantine faults, runs in $O(f)$ rounds, and uses messages of size $O(1)$. Thus, we can obtain the following results.

Corollary 4. *For any* $f \in \mathbb{N}$ *and* $n > 3f$*, an* f*-resilient firing squad on* n *nodes with stabilisation and response times of* $O(f)$ *and message size* $O(\log f)$ *exists.*

Corollary 5. *For any* $C, f \in \mathbb{N}$ *and* $n > 3f$*, an* f*-resilient* C*-counter on* n *nodes with stabilisation time* $O(f + \log C)$ *and message size* $O(\log f)$ *exists.*

Acknowledgements. We thank Danny Dolev for inspiring discussions and valuable comments, especially concerning silent consensus.

References

1. Ben-Or, M., Dolev, D., Hoch, E.N.: Fast self-stabilizing Byzantine tolerant digital clock synchronization. In: Proceedings of 27th Annual ACM Symposium on Principles of Distributed Computing (PODC 2008), pp. 385–394. ACM Press (2008). doi:10.1145/1400751.1400802
2. Berman, P., Garay, J.A., Perry, K.J.: Towards optimal distributed consensus. In: Proceedings of 30th Annual Symposium on Foundations of Computer Science (FOCS 1989), pp. 410–415. IEEE (1989). doi:10.1109/SFCS.1989.63511
3. Burns, J.E., Lynch, N.A.: The Byzantine firing squad problem. Adv. Comput. Res. **4**, 147–161 (1987)
4. Dolev, D., Függer, M., Lenzen, C., Schmid, U., Steininger, A.: Fault-tolerant distributed systems in hardware. Bull. EATCS (116) (2015). http://bulletin.eatcs.org/index.php/beatcs/issue/view/18
5. Dolev, D., Heljanko, K., Järvisalo, M., Korhonen, J.H., Lenzen, C., Rybicki, J., Suomela, J., Wieringa, S.: Synchronous counting and computational algorithm design. J. Comput. Syst. Sci. **82**(2), 310–332 (2016). doi:10.1016/j.jcss.2015.09.002
6. Dolev, D., Hoch, E.N.: On self-stabilizing synchronous actions despite byzantine attacks. In: Pelc, A. (ed.) DISC 2007. LNCS, vol. 4731, pp. 193–207. Springer, Heidelberg (2007). doi:10.1007/978-3-540-75142-7_17

7. Dolev, D., Hoch, E.N., Moses, Y.: An optimal self-stabilizing firing squad. SIAM J. Comput. **41**(2), 415–435 (2012). doi:10.1137/090776512
8. Dolev, S.: Self-Stabilization. The MIT Press, Cambridge (2000)
9. Dolev, S., Welch, J.L.: Self-stabilizing clock synchronization in the presence of Byzantine faults. J. ACM **51**(5), 780–799 (2004). doi:10.1145/1017460.1017463
10. Hoch, E.N., Dolev, D., Daliot, A.: Self-stabilizing Byzantine digital clock synchronization. In: Datta, A.K., Gradinariu, M. (eds.) SSS 2006. LNCS, vol. 4280, pp. 350–362. Springer, Heidelberg (2006). doi:10.1007/978-3-540-49823-0_25
11. King, V., Saia, J.: Breaking the $O(n^2)$ bit barrier. J. ACM **58**(4), 1–24 (2011). doi:10.1145/1989727.1989732
12. Lamport, L., Shostak, R., Pease, M.: The Byzantine generals problem. ACM Trans. Program. Lang. Syst. **4**(3), 382–401 (1982). doi:10.1145/357172.357176
13. Lenzen, C., Függer, M., Hofstätter, M., Schmid, U.: Efficient construction of global time in SoCs despite arbitrary faults. In: Proceedings of 16th Euromicro Conference on Digital System Design (DSD 2013), pp. 142–151 (2013). doi:10.1109/DSD.2013.97
14. Lenzen, C., Rybicki, J.: Efficient counting with optimal resilience. In: Moses, Y. (ed.) DISC 2015. LNCS, vol. 9363, pp. 16–30. Springer, Heidelberg (2015). doi:10.1007/978-3-662-48653-5_2
15. Lenzen, C., Rybicki, J.: Near-optimal self-stabilising counting and firing squads, manuscript, full version. arXiv:1608.00214 (2016)
16. Lenzen, C., Rybicki, J., Suomela, J.: Towards optimal synchronous counting. In: Proceedings of 34th ACM Symposium on Principles of Distributed Computing (PODC 2015), pp. 441–450. ACM (2015)
17. Lynch, N.A.: Distributed Algorithms. Morgan Kaufmann Publishers, San Francisco (1996)
18. Pease, M.C., Shostak, R.E., Lamport, L.: Reaching agreement in the presence of faults. J. ACM **27**(2), 228–234 (1980). doi:10.1145/322186.322188

Snap-Stabilizing PIF on Arbitrary Connected Networks in Message Passing Model

Florence Levé, Khaled Mohamed, and Vincent Villain(✉)

Laboratoire MIS, Université de Picardie Jules Verne,
33 Rue St Leu, 80039 Amiens Cedex 01, France
{florence.leve,khaled.mohamed,vincent.villain}@u-picardie.fr

Abstract. Starting from any configuration, a snap-stabilizing algorithm guarantees that the system always behaves according to its specification while a self-stabilizing algorithm only guarantees that the system will behave according to its specification in a finite time. So, a snap-stabilizing algorithm is a time optimal self-stabilizing algorithm (because it stabilizes in 0 rounds). That means that even the first attempt of using a snap-stabilizing algorithm by any user (human or algorithm) will produce a correct execution. This is a very desirable property, especially in the case of systems that are prone to transient faults. So the problem of the existence of snap-stabilizing solutions in the message passing model is a very crucial question from a practical point of view.

Snap-stabilization has been proven power equivalent to self-stabilization in the state model (a locally shared memory model) and for non-anonymous systems. That result is based on the existence of transformers built from a snap-stabilizing propagation of information with feedback (PIF) algorithm combined with some of its derivatives. In this paper, we present the first snap-stabilizing PIF algorithm for arbitrary connected networks in the message passing model. With a good setting of the timers, the time complexity of our algorithm is in $\theta(n \times k)$ rounds, where n and k are the number of processors and the maximal channel capacity, respectively. We then conclude that snap-stabilization is power equivalent to self-stabilization in the message passing model with bounded channels for non-anonymous systems.

1 Introduction

The concept of Propagation of Information with Feedback (PIF) has been introduced by Chang [5] and Segall [22]. The PIF scheme can be described as follows. A node, called root or initiator, initiates a wave by broadcasting a message m into the network (broadcast phase). Each non-root processor acknowledges to the root the receipt of m (feedback phase). The wave terminates when the root receives an acknowledgment from all other processors [14].

Self-stabilization has been introduced by Dijsktra in 1974 [19]. A distributed algorithm is self-stabilizing if, starting from any arbitrary global state, the system is able to recover itself in finite time. This property is crucial when considering systems after any faulty behavior (even any Byzantine behavior). In that case,

B. Bonakdarpour and F. Petit (Eds.): SSS 2016, LNCS 10083, pp. 281–297, 2016.
DOI: 10.1007/978-3-319-49259-9_22

the resulting configurations (unexpected messages and memory states) can be arbitrary and self stabilizing algorithms eventually recover without any external action. So, it is one of the most versatile techniques to handle transient faults occurring in distributed systems. There exist numerous approaches in the area of self-stabilization. Some of them try to overcome some drawbacks of self-stabilization, like high complexity [17]. Some try to make it stronger [18]. In 1999, snap-stabilization has been introduced by Bui *et al.* [3]. A distributed algorithm is snap-stabilizing if starting from any arbitrary global state the system always satisfies the specification. In other words, a snap-stabilizing algorithm is a self-stabilizing algorithm that stabilizes in 0 rounds, i.e., it is optimal in terms of the stabilization time. Snap-stabilization strongly enhances the safety of the system since the stabilization time is null. This very desirable theoretical property also has a great impact in practice. For example, after some transient faults, a self-stabilizing PIF algorithm is not guaranteed to receive the right feedback from all the processors in the first attempt, and it is generally the same for all the other attempts until the algorithm stabilizes. Moreover, the number of such attempts that fail cannot be bounded. On the contrary, for a snap-stabilizing algorithm, the very first attempt will produce a desirable/correct execution. To the best of our knowledge, snap-stabilization is the only variant of self-stabilization which has been proven power equivalent to self-stabilization in the context of the state model (a locally shared memory model) and for non-anonymous systems. That means that each problem admitting a self-stabilizing solution also admits a snap-stabilizing solution and vice versa [7,10]. So the existence of snap-stabilizing solutions in the message passing model is a very crucial problem from a practical point of view.

Related work. Several snap-stabilizing PIF algorithms have been proposed for oriented trees [3,4,20], for non-oriented trees [2,4,8,11,21], for fully connected networks [16], and for general networks [1,9,14]. In [10,13,15], snap-stabilizing PIF algorithms are the key tools for the transformation of algorithms into their snap-stabilizing versions. But, almost all the algorithms above are written in the state model. There exist only three snap-stabilizing algorithms that were written in the message passing model. A snap-stabilizing propagation of information with feedback (PIF) algorithm for full-connected networks has been presented in [16]. An idea for oriented trees has been presented in [20], but neither an algorithm nor its proof was provided. A snap-stabilizing PIF on un-oriented trees has been presented in [21]. All three algorithms work in networks with bounded capacity channels.

Contributions. In this paper, we present the first snap-stabilizing PIF algorithm for arbitrary connected networks in the message-passing model. Following the impossibility result in [16], we consider the capacity of the channels to be bounded. We then show that, with a good setting of the timers, the round complexity of our algorithm is in $\theta(n \times k)$, where n and k are the number of processors and the maximal channel capacity, respectively. Finally, we claim that snap-stabilization is power equivalent to self-stabilization in the context of the message passing model with bounded channels for non-anonymous systems.

Outline of the paper. The paper is organized as follows. In Sect. 2 we present the model assumed in this paper. We then present the snap-stabilizing PIF algorithm in Sect. 3, following by the proof and a short discussion about the complexities in Sect. 4. We conclude in the last section.

2 Preliminaries

Notations. We consider a network as an un-directed connected graph $G = (V, E)$ where V is a finite set of nodes (or *processors*) ($|V| = n$) and E is the set of *bidirectional asynchronous communication links.* A bidirectional communication link $\{p, q\}$ exists iff p and q are neighbors; in this case, p and q can communicate with each other by exchanging messages via the link. This link can be viewed as two *channels* (p, q) and (q, p), one by direction. The capacity of the channels is bounded, otherwise no deterministic snap-stabilizing solution is available [16]. To simplify the presentation, we assume that the bound is the same for every channel and is denoted as k. Channels are not reliable so messages can be lost. But, they are *fair*, i.e., if a processor infinitely often sends messages through a channel, then the channel will also deliver messages infinitely often. Messages can be lost when the channel has a faulty behavior or is full. When they are not lost, messages transmitted through a channel are received in a finite but not bounded time. Moreover, they arrive in the order they were sent (FIFO). Every processor p can distinguish and number all its adjacent channels from 0 to $\delta - 1$, where δ is the number of p's neighbors. For the sake of simplicity, we sometimes refer to a link $\{p, q\}$ (or a channel (p, q)) of a processor p by the label q instead of its local number. Our algorithm does not use any identity for the processors except the one called the *root* or r.

Programs. In our model, algorithms are *semi-uniform*, i.e., each processor executes the same program except r. We consider the message-passing model of computation. The message are sequentially received and processed by the processors, and the set of actions associated with a message reception is atomically executed. To compute the time complexity, we use the notion of *round.* Since in asynchronous systems, the local execution time is considered as null, the definition of a *round* captures the execution rate of the slowest message in any computation.

Definition 1 (Round). *Given an execution e of an algorithm A, the* first round *of e (let us call it e′) is the minimal prefix of e containing the reception or the loss of every message sent or already in a channel from the initial configuration. Let e″ be the suffix of e such that e = e′e″. The* second round *of e is the first round of e″, and so on.*

PIF. PIF is a well-known problem, so we simply specify the problem as follows:

Specification 1 (PIF). *An algorithm is a PIF algorithm if it satisfies the two following conditions:*

[PIF1] *r initiates a PIF by broadcasting a message m,*
[PIF2] *After the initialization, PIF terminates at r, and when that happens, all processors have acknowledged the receipt of m.*

3 Snap-Stabilizing PIF Algorithm

3.1 From Trees to Arbitrary Connected Networks

As in our work on trees [21], one of the problems to resolve is to detect the abnormal roots (processors $\neq r$ that are the source of a broadcast—see Definition 6 in Sect. 4.1 for a formal approach). emphParent pointers are used to follow the broadcast, so, from the source p of a broadcast to the end processors of the broadcast (called leaves), these pointers draw a tree $Tree_p$ (see Definition 9 in Sect. 4.1). But, the possible existence of cycles makes the abnormal configurations more complicated. We briefly present below the major differences with the case of a tree. The solution we propose is based on [12]. The idea of Point 3 below is taken from [12], and it is the fundamental mechanism to implement the snap stabilization.

1. *Parent* pointers can form a cycle of length greater than two, that are not locally detectable by using only *parent* pointers. In order to break these cycles, typically, the notion of level is used [6]. A processor p which forwards a broadcast message sent by one of its neighbors q has a level L_p equal to L_q+1. The growth of level values cannot be consistent in the cycle. There must exist at least two processors p_1 and p_2 such that p_1 is the parent of p_2 ($parent_{p_2} = p_1$) and $L_{p_2} \neq L_{p_1} + 1$.
2. An abnormal root p may have a neighbor q which belongs to $Tree_p$, but is not one of its children. If we allow p to leave $Tree_p$ without any constraint, it may attach to q and prevent the deletion of the abnormal tree previously rooted in p. To avoid this problem, we disable the processors of the abnormal tree [1] so that they cannot propagate the broadcast messages, and then allow new processors to join the tree when the abnormal root is removed.
3. The leaves of the broadcast tree $Tree_r$ may not have degree one. They may have neighbors other than their parents. To avoid a leaf from initializing a feedback when some of its neighbors have received a broadcast from an abnormal tree, we use a special mechanism, called a question phase, to get the authorization from the root to start the feedback.
4. We clean the links before sending a broadcast message to ensure that the neighbors receive the message. However this phase also has a complication in sending of the authorization by the root r. When a processor initializes the question phase, the processor along with its neighbors receive an authorization. We must make sure that these authorizations really come from the root and not from an initial message in the link or an extension of it. This is implemented by a special message sent by the leaves to the root preceded by link cleaning.

3.2 Algorithm Description

Algorithm 1 describes the data structures, the macros, and the predicates, Algorithm 2 describes the sub programs, and finally Algorithm 3 describes the PIF algorithm. The predicates and the sub-programs are sorted by alphabetic order. The predicates are evaluated as follows: In $(A \wedge B)$, if A is false then B is not evaluated and in $(A \vee B)$ if A is true then B is not evaluated. By this mechanism, we avoid the evaluation of part of predicates containing undefined variables. Variable PIF of a processor p indicates the step of the computation p is executing. During a normal execution, the sequence of the values of PIF is: $end \to cleanB \to B \to F \to end$. Values EB (Error Broadcast) and FB (Error Feedback) are only used by the processors but r to remove the abnormal trees. Variable Que is used to get the authorization from r to start the feedback phase when p is a leaf of a broadcast ($PIF = B$) only surrounded by processors with $PIF = B$. During a normal execution, the sequence of the values of Que for any processor but r is: $Q \to R \to cleanW \to W \to A \to Q$ and for r the sequence is only: $Q \to R \to A \to Q$. Variable $S[]$ contains what p knows about its neighbors: their PIF values, their levels, if they are children of p, stamp values of the link cleaning, and their Que values. Predicate $AbRoot$ holds if $p \neq r$ is the source of a broadcast. It is based on $GoodS$ that holds if the PIF value of p and that of its parent (through $S_p[parent].PIF$) are consistent and on $GoodL$ that holds if L value of p and that of its parent (through $S_p[parent].level$) are consistent. Predicate $Broadcast$ holds if $p \neq r$ is asleep ($PIF = end$) or ready to leave an abnormal tree (($PIF = EF$) $\wedge$ $AbRoot$) and a neighbor of p is in B through $S_p[i].PIF$ ($BAround$). In that case, p is ready to forward the broadcast. From now, we will simply omit to precise that p knowledge of the states of its neighbors is done through $S_p[]$. $BLeaf$ holds if p is in B and all its children are in F. $BFree$ holds if there exists no neighbor of p, that is not its child, in B, $EFree$ holds if no neighbor is in EB or EF state, and $EndFree$ holds if no neighbor is asleep. Predicate $Feedback$ holds if p satisfies $BLeaf$ and $EndFree$, meaning that p can no longer forward the broadcast, but p must satisfies $AnswerOk$ meaning that p and all its neighbors have received the authorization to feedback from r (in that case p can start the feedback phase). More precisely, Predicate $AnswerOk$ holds if the Que value of p is A, p is $EFree$, and the Que value of any child of p equals A. Predicates $Require$, $Wait$, and $Answer$ allow p to manage the question phase and eventually satisfy $AnswerOk$. Predicate $EndFeedback$ holds if p is in F and all its neighbors have taken that in account, p can set PIF to end. Predicates $EBroadcast$ and $EFeedback$ complete $AbRoot$ to deal with the propagation of the error messages EB-messages and EF-messages into the abnormal trees. Finally, Predicate $Error$ is only used to remove a locally inconsistent initialization of the variables of p.

We use two types of messages, instead of combining them in only one, to make the reading easier.

Algorithm 1. Environment

Constants :

k $\in \mathbb{N} \setminus \{0\}$ `// bound of the channel capacity`
M $= 2k + 1$ `// bound of the cleaning message stamp`
$\alpha \in \mathbb{N} \setminus \{0\}$ `// waiting time value of the timer`
$\delta \in \mathbb{N} \setminus \{0\}$ `// number of neighbors`
Neig $= \{0, \ldots, \delta - 1\}$ `// set of locally ordered neighbors`
parent $= NIL$ `// for r`

Messages :

(state,LV,isChild,isParent,question) where $state \in \{end, B, F, EB, EF\}, LV \in \mathbb{N}, isChild, isParent : boolean, question \in \{Q, R, W, A\}$
(state,X) where $state \in \{cleanB, cleanW, ack\}, X \in \{0, \ldots, M\}$

Variables :

parent $\in Neig \cup \{NIL\}$ `// for p ≠ r`
C, i $\in Neig \cup \{NIL\}$; L $\in \mathbb{N} \setminus \{0\}$
PIF $\in \{end, cleanB, B, F\}$; Que $\in \{Q, R, A\}$ `// for r`
PIF $\in \{end, cleanB, B, F, EB, EF\}$ `// for p ≠ r`
Que $\in \{Q, R, cleanW, W, A\}$ `// for p ≠ r`
S[0...$\delta - 1$]: array of structure $(PIF \in \{end, B, F, EB, EF\}, level \in \mathbb{N}, acceptChild : boolean, stamp \in \{0, \ldots, M\}, Que \in \{Q, R, W, A\})$

Macros :

- **Child** $= \{i \in Neig \mid (S[i].PIF \neq end) \wedge (S[i].acceptChild) \wedge (S[i].level = L + 1) \wedge [(PIF \neq S[i].PIF) \Rightarrow (((PIF = B) \wedge (S[i].PIF = F)) \vee (PIF = EB))]\}$

Predicates :

- **AbRoot** $\equiv (p \neq r) \wedge (\neg GoodS \vee \neg GoodL)$
- **Answer** $\equiv (PIF \in \{B, F\}) \wedge EFree \wedge ((PIF = B) \Rightarrow EndFree) \wedge (\forall i \in Child, S[i].Que \in \{W, A\}) \wedge (\forall i \in Neig, (S[i].PIF \neq end) \Rightarrow (S[i].Que \neq Q)) \wedge ((p = r) \Rightarrow (Que = R)) \wedge ((p \neq r) \Rightarrow ((Que = W) \wedge (S[parent].Que = A)))$
- **AnswerOk** $\equiv (Que = A) \wedge EFree \wedge (\forall i \in Neig, (S[i].PIF \neq end) \Rightarrow (S[i].Que = A))$
- **BAround** $\equiv \exists i \in Neig \setminus Child, S[i].PIF = B$
- **BFree** $\equiv \forall i \in Neig \setminus Child, S[i].PIF \neq B$
- **BLeaf** $\equiv (PIF = B) \wedge (\forall i \in Child, S[i].PIF = F)$
- **Broadcast** $\equiv (p \neq r) \wedge BAround \wedge ((PIF = end) \vee ((PIF = EF) \wedge AbRoot))$
- **EFree** $\equiv \forall i \in Neig, S[i].PIF \notin \{EB, EF\}$
- **EBroadcast** $\equiv (p \neq r) \wedge (AbRoot \vee (S[parent].PIF = EB)) \wedge (PIF \in \{cleanB, B, F\})$
- **EFeedback** $\equiv (PIF = EB) \wedge (\forall i \in Child, S[i].PIF = EF)$
- **EndFeedback** $\equiv (PIF = F) \wedge (Child = \emptyset) \wedge (\forall i \in Neig, S[i].PIF \in \{end, F\} \wedge ((p \neq r) \Rightarrow (S[parent].PIF = F)))$
- **EndFree** $\equiv \forall i \in Neig, S[i].PIF \neq end$
- **Error** $\equiv (p \neq r) \wedge (((PIF = cleanB) \wedge (Que = cleanW)) \vee (\forall i \in Neig, S[i].acceptChild) \vee (\exists i \in Neig, ((S[i].acceptChild \wedge (S[i].level \neq L + 1)))$
- **Feedback** $\equiv BLeaf \wedge EndFree \wedge AnswerOk$
- **GoodL** $\equiv (PIF \neq end) \Rightarrow (L = S[parent].level + 1)$
- **GoodS** $\equiv (PIF = end) \vee [((parent \neq NIL) \wedge (S.[parent].PIF \neq PIF)) \Rightarrow (((S[parent].PIF = B) \wedge (PIF \in \{cleanB, F\})) \vee (S[parent].PIF = EB))]$
- **PIFError** $\equiv AbRoot \vee EBroadcast \vee EFeedback$
- **Require** $\equiv (PIF \in \{B, F\}) \wedge EFree \wedge [(PIF = B) \Rightarrow EndFree] \wedge [[(Que = Q) \wedge (\forall i \in Neig, (S[i].PIF \neq end) \Rightarrow (S[i].Que \in \{Q, R\}))] \vee [(Que \in \{cleanW, W, A\}) \wedge (\exists i \in Neig, (S[i].PIF \neq end) \wedge ((S[i].Que = Q) \vee ((i \in Child) \wedge (S[i].Que = R))))]]$
- **Wait** $\equiv (p \neq r) \wedge (PIF \in \{B, F\}) \wedge EFree \wedge ((PIF = B) \Rightarrow EndFree) \wedge (Que = R) \wedge (S[parent].Que = R) \wedge (\forall i \in Child, S[i].Que \in \{W, A\}) \wedge (\forall i \in Neig, (S[i].PIF \neq end) \Rightarrow (S[i].Que \neq Q))$

Algorithm 2. Sub-programs

```
• AckManager(C)
  if ((PIF = cleanB) ∧ (C ≠ parent)) ∨ ((Que = cleanW) ∧ (C = parent)) then
  |  if X = S[C].stamp then
  |  |  if S[C].stamp < M then
  |  |  |  S[C].stamp ← S[C].stamp + 1;
  |  |  |  if PIF = cleanB then
  |  |  |  |  if (∀i ≠ parent, S[i].stamp = M) then PIF ← B; end
  |  |  |  else // Que = cleanW
  |  |  |  |  if (S[C].stamp = M) then Que ← W; end
  |  |  |  end
  |  |  |  ∀ i ∈ Neig, Timer[i] ← 0;
  |  |  end
  |  end
  end
• CleanManager(C)
  if (state = cleanB) ∧ (C = parent) then
  |  PIF ← EB; parent ← NIL; ∀ i ∈ Neig, Timer[i] ← 0;
  end
  Send (ack,X) to C;
• CleanUpdate(C)
  if (state = cleanB) ∧ (S[C].PIF ≠ end) then
  |  S[C].PIF ← end;
  else
  |  if (state = cleanW) ∧ (S[C].Que ≠ R) then S[C].Que ← R; end
  end
• ErrorManager()
  if AbRoot ∧ (parent ≠ NIL) then parent ← NIL; end
  if EBroadcast ∨ EFeedback then
  |  if EBroadcast then PIF ← EB; end
  |  if EFeedback then PIF ← EF; end
  end
  if AbRoot ∧ (PIF = EF) ∧ BFree then ExecEnd(); end
  if PIF ≠ end then ∀ i ∈ Neig, Timer[i] ← 0; end
• ExecEnd()
  PIF ← End; ∀ i ∈ Neig, S[i] ← (end,0,False,0,Q);
  if p ≠ r then parent ← NIL; end
• InitBroadcast()
  PIF ← cleanB;
  if p ≠ r then parent ← min{i ∈ Neig, S[i].PIF = B}; end
  ∀ i ∈ Neig \ {parent}, S[i] ← (end,0,False,0,Q); ∀ i ∈ Neig, Timer[i] ← 0;
• InitWait(C)
  Que ← cleanW; S[C].stamp ← 0; ∀ i ∈ Neig, Timer[i] ← 0;
• MessageManager(C)
  if (PIF = cleanB) ∨ (Que = cleanW) then
  |  if (PIF = cleanB) ∧ (C ≠ parent) ∧ (S[C].stamp ≤ M) then
  |  |  Send(PIF,S[C].stamp) to C;
  |  end
  |  if (Que = cleanW) ∧ (C = parent) ∧ (S[C].stamp ≤ M) then
  |  |  Send(Que,S[C].stamp) to C;
  |  end
  else
  |  Send(PIF,L,parent = C,C ∈ Child,Que) to C;
  end
• Update(C)
  if ((PIF ≠ end) ∨ (state = B)) ∧ ((PIF ≠ cleanB) ∨ (C = parent)) ∧ ((Que ≠ cleanW)
  ∨ (C ≠ parent) ∨ (state = EB)) then
  |  S[C].PIF ← state; S[C].level ← LV; S[C].acceptChild ← (isChild ∧ (LV = L + 1));
  |  S[C].Que ← question;
  |  if (C = parent) ∧ (¬ isParent) then parent ← NIL; end
  else
  |  if (PIF = end) ∧ (state ≠ end) then Send (end,0,False,False,Q) to C; end
  end
```

Algorithm 3. PIF

```
Program:
• Block 1: Spontaneously                                                  // for r
  if PIF = end then InitBroadcast(); end

• Block 2: At the reception of (state,LV,isChild,isParent,question) from C
  Update(C);
  if PIFError then ErrorManager(); end                                    // for p ≠ r
  if Broadcast then InitBroadcast(); end                                  // for p ≠ r
  if Require then
  |  Que ← R; ∀ i ∈ Neig, Timer[i] ← 0;
  end
  if Wait then InitWait(parent); end                                      // for p ≠ r
  if Answer then
  |  Que ← A; ∀ i ∈ Neig, Timer[i] ← 0;
  end
  if Feedback then
  |  PIF ← F; ∀ i ∈ Neig, Timer[i] ← 0;
  end
  if EndFeedback then ExecEnd(); end

• Block 3: At the reception of (state,X) from C
  CleanUpdate(C);
  if PIFError then ErrorManager(); end                                    // for p ≠ r
  if state = ack then
  |  AckManager(C);
  else // state ∈ {cleanB,cleanW}
  |  CleanManager(C);
  end

• Block 4: Timer[C]=0
  if PIF ≠ end then
  |  if Error then
  |  |  ExecEnd();
  |  else
  |  |  MessageManager(C);
  |  end
  |  Timer[C] ← α;
  end
```

4 Snap-Stabilization and Complexities

4.1 Definitions and Initial Results

Predicate *Error* is only used to remove a locally inconsistent initialization of the variables of a processor. Since after the first activation of its timer, no processor can satisfy *Error*, we will assume, in the rest of the paper, that every processor never satisfies *Error*, without any loss of generality.

Definition 2 (Residual Message). *A message which is already in a channel in the initial configuration is called a* residual *message.*

We will assume that the only residual messages a processor can take into account are those which match one of structures **Messages** defined in Algorithm 1. The system simply bypasses other messages.

Definition 3 (Active Message). *A message m is called an* active *message if the recipient changes the value of at least one of its variables upon receiving m.*

Definition 4 (Active Processor). *Processor p is called* active *during a round if it satisfies $PIF_p \neq end$ during at least one step of the round. A processor is said* infinitely active *if it is* active *during an infinite number of rounds. A processor is said* ultimately active *if it is* active *during an infinite number of successive rounds.*

Definition 5 (Passive Processor). *Processor p is said* passive *during a round if it always satisfies $PIF_p = end$ during the round. A processor is said* infinitely passive *if it is* passive *during an infinite number of rounds. A processor is said* ultimately passive *if it is* passive *during an infinite number of successive rounds.*

Remark 1 (Active-Passive Processor). Processor p can be both *infinitely active* and *infinitely passive* during an infinite execution, but it cannot be both *ultimately active* and *ultimately passive*.

Definition 6 (Abnormal Root). *Let p be a processor. We call p an* abnormal root *if p satisfies Predicate AbRoot of Algorithm 1.*

Definition 7 (PPath(p)). *Let p be a processor such that $PIF_p \neq end$, $PPath(p)$ is the unique path p_0, p_1, p_2, ..., $p_k = p$ satisfying the two following conditions:*
(i) $\forall i, 1 \leq i \leq k, (PIF_{p_i} \neq end) \wedge (parent_{p_i} = p_{i-1}) \wedge S_{p_{i-1}}[p_i].acceptChild \wedge \neg AbRoot_{p_i}$,
(ii) $(p_0 = r) \vee AbRoot_{p_0}$.

Definition 8 (PIF-trace). *Let S be a sequence of processors ($S = (p_0, p_1, ..., p_\alpha)$).* PIF-trace *of S is the sequence $PIF-trace(S) = (PIF_{p_0}, PIF_{p_1}, ..., PIF_{p_\alpha})$ of values of variable PIF in processors p_i with $i = 0...\alpha$.*

Definition 9 (Tree$_p$). *Let p be a processor such that $(p = r) \vee AbRoot_p$. We define $Tree_p$ as the set of processors such that: $\forall q \in V, q \in Arbre_p$ if and only if $PIF_q \neq end$ and p is the first processor in $PPath(q)$.*

We call normal *tree, the only tree rooted at r. Any tree rooted at a processor other than r is called an* abnormal *tree.*

Definition 10 (Alive and Dead Trees). *Tree T satisfies Predicate $Alive(T)$ (and is called* alive*) if and only if $\exists p \in T$ such that $PIF_p = B$. Tree T satisfies Predicate $Dead(T)$ (and is called* dead*) if and only if it satisfies $\neg Alive(T)$.*

Lemma 1 (Neighborhood Update). *Let p be an* infinitely active *processor. Then p receives messages from any of its neighbors infinitely often.*

Definition 11 (Sequence and cycle of values of Variables PIF and Que). *We call* state sequence *of Processor p the sequence of successive values of the ordered pair (PIF_p, Que_p) during an execution. When PIF_p is not in $\{B, F\}$, values of Que_p are not used by the algorithm (cf. Predicates Require, Wait, and Answer). So, we omit these values in the sequence. If this sequence begins and ends by end, we call it a* cycle*. We call* elementary *sequence any* *sequence containing at most one occurrence of each value and* elementary *cycle any cycle containing at most one occurrence of each value but end. So, for* r, $(B,Q) \to (B,R) \to (B,A) \to (F,A) \to end$ *is an elementary state sequence,* $end \to cleanB \to (B,Q) \to (B,R) \to (B,A) \to (F,A) \to end$ *is an elementary state cycle, and* $end \to cleanB \to (B,Q) \to (B,R) \to (B,A) \to (B,R) \to (B,A) \to (B,R) \to (B,A) \to (F,A) \to end$ *is a non-elementary cycle.*

Definition 12 (Sub-sequence). *Let* $A = a_1 \to a_2 \to ... \to a_x$ *(where* a_i *are values of* PIF *or* (PIF, Que) *with* $i = 1, ..., x$*) and* B *two state sequences of a processor. Then* A *is a* sub-sequence *of* B *if there exist sequences* B_0, B_1, ..., B_x *possibly empty such that* $B = B_0 \to a_1 \to B_1 \to a_2 \to ... \to B_{x-1} \to a_x \to B_x$.

By checking actions of Algorithm 3, we can claim the two following lemmas.

Lemma 2 (Elementary state cycles). *For any processor* p*, the elementary state cycles are the following ones:*

1. $p = r$. *The only possible elementary cycle is:* $end \to cleanB \to (B,Q) \to (B,R) \to (B,A) \to (F,A) \to end$.
2. $p \neq r$. *If the values* EB *and* EF *do not appear in the cycle, the only possible elementary cycle is:*
   $end \to cleanB \to (B,Q) \to (B,R) \to (B, cleanW) \to (B,W) \to (B,A) \to (F,A) \to end$
   if the values EB *and* EF *appear in the cycle, the only possible elementary cycles are:*
   $end \to cleanB \to EB \to EF \to end$
   $end \to cleanB \to (B,Q) \to EB \to EF \to end$
   $end \to cleanB \to (B,Q) \to (B,R) \to EB \to EF \to end$
   $end \to cleanB \to (B,Q) \to (B,R) \to (B, cleanW) \to EB \to EF \to end$
   $end \to cleanB \to (B,Q) \to (B,R) \to (B, cleanW) \to (B,W) \to EB \to EF \to end$
   $end \to cleanB \to (B,Q) \to (B,R) \to (B, cleanW) \to (B,W) \to (B,A) \to EB \to EF \to end$
   $end \to cleanB \to (B,Q) \to (B,R) \to (B, cleanW) \to (B,W) \to (B,A) \to (F,A) \to EB \to EF \to end$

Lemma 3 (Non-elementary sequences and cycles of PIF values). *Let* p *be a processor. A* non-elementary *sequence (respectively a* non-elementary *cycle) of* PIF_p *values is a sequence (respectively a cycle) containing:*

- *if* $p = r$, *occurrences of the sequence* $(B,R) \to (B,A)$ *after the value* (B,A),
- *if* $p \neq r$,
  - *occurrences of all or prefixe of the sequence* $(B,R) \to (B, cleanW) \to (B,W) \to (B,A) \to (F,A)$ *after the values* $(B, cleanW)$, (B,W), *or* (B,A),
  - *occurrences of all or prefixe of the sequence* $(F,R) \to (F, cleanW) \to (F,W) \to (F,A)$ *after the values* $(F, cleanW)$, (F,W), (F,A)
  - *occurrences of all or prefixe of the sequence* $cleanB \to (B,Q) \to (B,R) \to (B, cleanW) \to (B,W) \to (B,A) \to (F,A)$ *after the value* EF

Now we define the notion of consistency between the states of two neighboring processors. This definition reports on the gap between the state of a processor and the state of its parent due to the message transmission.

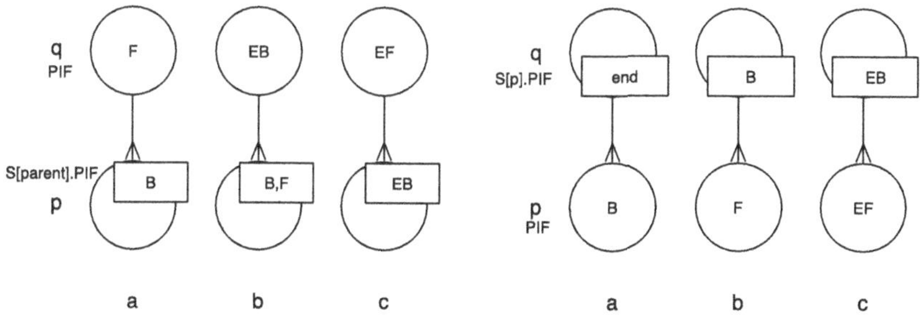

(a) PIF-consistency for the parent (b) PIF-consistency for the child

Fig. 1. PIF-consistency

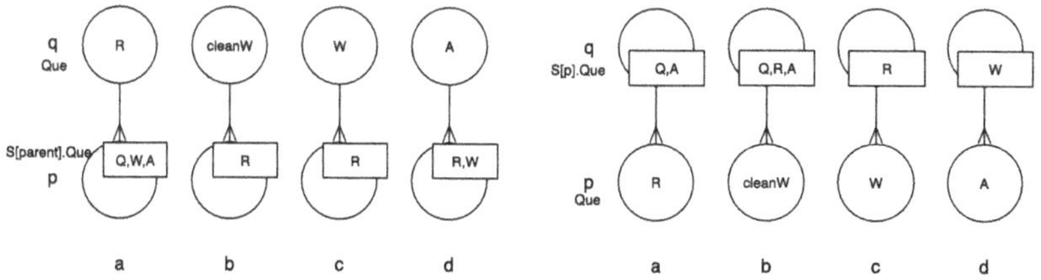

(a) Question-consistency for the parent (b) Question-consistency for the child

Fig. 2. Question-consistency

Definition 13 (Consistent processors). *Let p and q be two neighboring processors such that $parent_p = q$. We say that p and q are* PIF-consistent *if and only if values of PIF_p, PIF_q, $S_p[parent].PIF$, and $S_q[p].PIF$ are as described on Figs. 1(a) and (b). If it is not the case, p and q are said* PIF-inconsistent.

We say that p and q are question-consistent *if and only if values of Que_p, Que_q, $S_p[parent].Que$, and $S_q[p].Que$ are as described on Figs. 2(a) and (b). If it is not the case, p and q are said* question-inconsistent.

We say that p and q are consistent *if and only if the following predicate holds: (p and q are* PIF-consistent*) $\wedge$ (p and q are* question-consistent*).*
If it is not the case, p and q are said inconsistent.

Definition 14 (Consistent tree and configuration). *A normal or abnormal tree (resp. configuration) that contains no ordered pair of inconsistent processors is called a* consistent *tree (resp. configuration). In the contrary the tree or the configuration are said* inconsistent.

We can notice that if a tree is empty or contains a processor only, then it is consistent by default.

Any change of Variables PIF and Que of p and q by any action of Algorithm 3 follows the sequences of Definition 11. Since the only messages that p and q will receive by Link $\{p, q\}$ are really sent by p or q, we can deduce, from Lemmas 2 and 3, that the gap generated between Variables PIF and Que never generates any inconsistency between p and q. The same goes for the level values. So, we can claim the following lemma.

Lemma 4 (Inconsistent states generating). *Let p and q two neighboring processors. If p and q are consistent and $\{p, q\}$ contains no residual message then p and q will never be inconsistent.*

Clearly, if p and q are consistent and $\{p, q\}$ contains no residual message then p and q will never be inconsistent. So we can claim:

Lemma 5 (Consistent configurations in finite time). *Any execution only contains a finite prefix with inconsistent trees and/or configurations.*

Definition 15 (Normal configuration). *A consistent configuration which contains no abnormal tree is called a* normal *configuration. In the contrary the configuration is called* abnormal.

4.2 Proof of Snap Stabilisation

Because of the cleaning process by *({B,F},cleanW)*-messages, we can claim:

Lemma 6 (*({B,F},A)* -messages and abnormal trees). *Let q be a processor belonging to an* abnormal tree *such that $PIF_q \in \{B, F\}$ and $Que_q \in \{Q, R\}$, then q cannot receive any* active ({B,F},A)-*message while it belongs to the tree.*

Since a processor which joins a tree sets Variable PIF to B in finite time, we can deduce the following corollary from Lemma 6:

Corollary 1 (*({B,F},A)* -messages and abnormal trees 2). *A processor which joins an* abnormal tree *cannot receive any* active ({B,F},A)-*message while belonging to this tree.*

An immediate consequence of Corollary 1 is that any processeur p which joins an abnormal tree can never set PIF_p to F while belonging to this tree. So p will never be able to leave the tree because it satisfies Predicate $EndFeedback$. As the only ways to leave a tree are to satisfy $EndFeedback$ or $AbRoot \wedge (PIF = EF)$ (cf. Predicate $Broadcast$ and Sub-program $ErrorManager()$), we can deduce the following lemma:

Lemma 7 (Leaving an abnormal tree). *A processor cannot leave an* abnormal tree *more than once without satisfying $AbRoot$.*

Remark 2. The only time p may leave an abnormal tree while satisfying Predicate $EndFeedback$ is when the two following conditions hold:

1. p belongs to the abnormal tree at the initial configuration,
2. p already satisfies $EndFeedback$ or the reception of a residual message means that p will eventually satisfy $EndFeedback$.

Lemma 8 (Death of abnormal trees). *Any* abnormal tree *dies in finite time.*

Lemma 9 (Abnormal Root Life). *Let p be an* abnormal root *satisfying $PIF_p = EF$, then p cannot be an* abnormal root *forever.*

By Lemmas 8 and 9, we can easily deduce that all processors will eventually leave the abnormal tree and either become isolated ($PIF = end$) either hook on to another tree. So we can claim the following lemma:

Lemma 10 (Disappearance of abnormal trees). *Any processor in an* abnormal tree *will eventually execute $ExecEnd()$ or $InitBroadcast()$.*

By Lemma 5, configurations are eventually consistent, so, the only way for p to become an abnormal root is to belong to a dead abnormal tree, i.e., to satisfy $PIF_p = EB$ and to receive an *EF*-message from q. In this case, p becomes the abnormal root of a dead tree. So, generating an abnormal root of an alive abnormal tree can only occur during a finite prefix of the execution. The number of alive abnormal trees being finite and their life too (cf. Lemma 8), any abnormal tree is eventually dead. By Lemma 10, they eventually disappear and we can claim:

Theorem 1 (Normal Configuration). *Any execution eventually reaches a normal configuration and all the following configurations are normal.*

If r executes $InitBroadcast()$, the links to all its neighbors are cleaned by the sending of *cleanB*-messages. So, the following lemma is obvious.

Lemma 11 (Consistency of $Tree_r$). *If r executes $InitBroadcast()$ then $Tree_r$ is consistent forever.*

Lemma 12 (Persistence of $Tree_r$). *Assume that $Tree_r$ is consistent. Let p be a processeur which joins $Tree_r$. If p satisfies $Feedback$ then no neighbor of p belongs to an abnormal tree.*

Proof. When p joins $Tree_r$ by hooking on to q ($parent_p = q$), p cleans the links of all its neighbors but q (cf. $InitBroadcast()$). So there doest not exist residual messages any more between p and its neighbors. If p satisfies $Feedback$, then PIF_p values change according to a sequence which contains the sub-sequence $(B, Q) \rightarrow (B, R) \rightarrow (B, cleanW) \rightarrow (B, W) \rightarrow (B, A)$. When p satisfies $Require$ for the first time ($PIF_p = B$), then $\forall i \in Neig, (S_p[i].Que \in \{Q, R\})$ and Variable Que of all its neighbors got a value in $\{Q, R\}$). Before p satisfies $Feedback$, all its neighbors must previously have their state in $\{(B, A), (F, A)\}$. But by Lemma 6, no processor in an abnormal tree cannot get value (B, A) and then (F, A) as state value if this state previously got a value in $\{(B, Q), (B, R)\}$). So, when p satisfies $Feedback$, no neighbor belongs to an abnormal tree. □

Lemma 13 (PIF2). *If r executes $InitBroadcast()$ then Algorithm 3 terminates at r and when this happens, every processor has acknowledged the reception of the* B*-message generated by r.*

Proof. We first show that every processor eventually receives the message generated by r, i.e.,every processor joins $Tree_r$ and then a feedback of every processor goes back in $Tree_r$ to r.

Let us assume that there exist some processors which never join $Tree_r$. So at least one of them is a neighbor of a processor of $Tree_r$. Let p be one of these processors and let q be a neighbor of p in $Tree_r$. When q joined $Tree_r$, it cleaned its links and sent *(B,Q)*-messages to all its neighbors (but its parent if $q \neq r$). If p receives a B-message from q, either p is in an abnormal tree or $PIF_p = end$ but p has some neighbors i such that $S_p[i].PIF = B$ and, when p chooses a parent, q is not the $min\{i \in Neig_p, S_p[i].PIF = B\}$ (cf. $InitBroadcast()$). By Lemma 10, p will eventually leave its current abnormal tree. It can join another abnormal tree, but, from Theorem 1, it can do it only a finite number of times, after that PIF_p will equal *end* forever. By checking all the messages q may receive from p while p belongs to an abnormal tree, we can see that the value of (PIF_q, Que_q) and that of $(S_q[p].PIF, S_q[p].Que)$ never allow q to satisfy *Feedback*, what was already claimed in Lemma 12, but we also know that q remains in $Tree_r$ with $(PIF_q, Que_q) \in \{(B,Q),(B,R),(B,cleanW),(B,W),(B,A)\}$. So the question phase is not locked a priori (that would have been the case if one of the values R, *cleanB*, W, or A has became unattainable).

When p cannot join an abnormal tree any more, PIF_p is stuck to *end*. As we assumed that p never joins $Tree_r$, p never receive any B-message from q. By link fairness, q will eventually receive an *end*-message from p. Since $S_q[p].PIF$ equals *end* forever, PIF_q equals B forever and p eventually receives a B-message from q. So p joins $Tree_r$, a contradiction.

We just showed that every processor eventually joins $Tree_r$, now we must show that a feedback of every processor goes back in $Tree_r$ to r.

Obviously, the broadcast spreads step by step until some processors (the final leaves of $Tree_r$) satisfy $child = \emptyset$ et $EndFree$. If p is a final leaf, then p eventually satisfies *Require* because, while $Que_p = Q$, no neighbor of p can set PIF to a value not in $\{cleanB, B\}$ and when $PIF = B$, its state is necessarily in $\{(B,Q),(B,R)\}$. If p is not a final leaf, then by induction on the high of the sub-tree rooted in p in $Tree_r$, the children of p eventually get the state (B,R) and send *(B,R)*-messages to p which will eventually satisfy *Require* too, because the neighbors of p which are not its parent nor its children are:

1. isolated ($PIF = end$) and in this case they eventually join an abnormal tree or $Tree_r$,
2. in an abnormal tree and in this case, if p never receives a *({B,F},Q)*-message or a *({B,F},R)*-message from them, the abnormal trees will eventually disappear (cf. Theorem 1) and they will join $Tree_r$,
3. in $Tree_r$ (so their variable PIF has a value in $\{B,F\}$) and, in this case, their variable *Que* will eventually equals R. So they will send back *({B,F},R)*-messages to r.

So Processor p sets Que_p to R and *({B,F},R)*-messages go back to r. Similarly, the processors of $Tree_r$, whatever their variable PIF equals B or F, will set their variables *Que* to *cleanW* and W until r sets Que_r to A (r cannot satisfy

Predicate *Wait* but it directly satisfies Predicate *Answer*). The going down of *(*$\{B,F\}$*,A)*-messages to the leaves of $Tree_b$ may start. However, during the going back of *(*$\{B,F\}$*,cleanW)*-messages, the *(*$\{B,F\}$*, W)*-messages, and the going down of *(*$\{B,F\}$*,A)*-messages, a processor p can satisfy Predicate *Require* and set again Que_p to R because a p neighbor has joined $Tree_r$. The consequences are not local only, since the parent of p satisfies again *Require* when receiving a *(B,R)*-message from p and *(B,R)*-messages go back to r and can enforces the going back of *(*$\{B,F\}$*,R)*-messages in their neighboroud. These messages are then followed by new *(*$\{B,F\}$*,cleanW)*-messages and *(*$\{B,F\}$*, W)*-messages which also go back to r. During the going back of *(*$\{B,F\}$*,R)*-messages, the value of variables *Que* equals R again, but some *(*$\{B,F\}$*,A)*-messages can remain in the links in the opposite direction. The *(*$\{B,F\}$*,cleanW)*-messages ensure that these *(*$\{B,F\}$*,A)*-messages will not be active. When *(*$\{B,F\}$*, W)*-messages reach r again, the broadcast of *(*$\{B,F\}$*,A)*-messages can restart. This behavior can occur a finite number of times only, until the abnormal trees have disappeared. In this case, all the neighbors of p will eventually join $Tree_r$. So all the processors and of course the final leaves of $Tree_r$ eventually satisfy *AnswerOk*. The final leaves can set their variable PIF to F. Step by step, the processors p with $PIF_p = B$ satisfy *Feedback* when all their children have set their variable PIF to F and sent F-messages. Moreover they satisfy *EndFree* since their neighbors can satisfy *EndFeedback* (and so set their variable PIF to *end*) only if PIF_p is in $\{end, F\}$. Then Processeurs p satisfy *Feedback* and can set PIF_p to F. So every processors p in $Tree_r$ satisfying $PIF_p = B$ will eventually set PIF_p to F. □

Remark 3. It is obvious to check, when $Tree_r$ only contains processors with $PIF = F$, that these processors set their variable PIF to *end* from the leaves of $Tree_r$ back to r (cf. Predicate *EndFeedback*).

Lemma 14 (PIF1). *Starting from any configuration, if r has a message to send, it eventually executes InitBroadcast().*

Proof. Assume that r never executes *InitBroadcast*(). Then Theorem 1 ensures that the configurations will eventually be consistent and there exists no more abnormal trees. So the only way for r never executes *InitBroadcast*() is that $Tree_r$ is non-empty at the initial configuration and remains non-empty forever. A simplified read-trough of the proof, since there is no more abnormal trees, shows that in this case $Tree_r$ eventually disappears. So r can eventually execute *InitBroadcast*(). □

Remark 4 (Silent Algorithm). Since the timer is never activated when $PIF =$ *end* and the sending of an *end*-message only occurs at the reception of a message which is not an *end*-message, we can remark that Algorithm 3 is silent, i.e., when r has no message to broadcast the system eventually reaches a configuration from which no processor changes its variables and no message circulates.

The following theorem is a corollary of Lemmas 13 and 14 and Remark 4:

Theorem 2 (Snap Stabilizing PIF). *Algorithm 3 is snap stabilizing and silent.*

4.3 Complexities

Memory Requirement and Message Length. We can bound L and *level* (in array S) variables with N, an upper bound on the number of processors n. N is typically assumed to be in $\theta(n)$. Consider $S[0 \ldots \delta - 1]$ (where δ is the number of neighbors of the processor), which is an array of values in $(\{end, B, F, EB, EF\} \times \{0, ..., N\} \times \{true, false\} \times \{0, \ldots, M\} \times \{Q, R, W, A\})$. The size of this array is in $\theta(\delta \times (log(N) + log(M)))$ bits. Since M is proportional to k and N is in $\theta(n)$, the required space for every processor is in $\theta(\delta \times (log(n) + log(k)))$ bits. Obviously, the length of the messages is in $\theta(Max\{log(n), log(k)\})$ bits.

Time Complexity. We assume that the message losses are only due to full links in order to avoid mixing up the network performance with the algorithm performance. We also assume that timers are slow enough not to generate message congestions and we distinguish two types of timer—the *slow timers* (with a period of the order of k rounds), and the *fast timers* (with a period at most of the order of one round). We show that, starting from any arbitrary configuration, if Processor r has a message to broadcast, PIF is executed in $\theta(n \times k)$ and $\theta((n \times k) + k^2)$ rounds with slow timers and fast timers, respectively, where n and k are the number of processors and the maximum channel capacity, respectively.

5 Conclusion

In this paper, we have presented the first snap-stabilizing propagation of information with feedback (PIF) algorithm for arbitrary connected networks in the message passing model. One of the key features of snap-stabilization is its strong safety property—the stabilization time is null. Moreover, snap-stabilization has been shown to be power equivalent to self-stabilization in the state model and for non-anonymous systems [7,10]. The above result made the current work more compelling due to its practical impact. Using our snap-stabilizing PIF algorithm, we can easily design other snap-stabilizing algorithms, e.g., the leader election, reset, snapshot, and termination detection problems. As the transformers presented in [7,10] are compositions of those snap-stabilizing algorithms and the algorithm to snap-stabilize, the result of the power equivalence between snap-stabilization and self-stabilization for non-anonymous networks trivially holds in the message passing model as well.

References

1. Blin, L., Cournier, A., Villain, V.: An improved snap-stabilizing PIF algorithm. In: Proceedings SSS 2003, San Francisco, CA, USA, 24-25 June 2003, pp. 199–214 (2003)
2. Bui, A., Datta, A.K., Petit, F., Villain, V.: Snap-stabilizing PIF algorithm in the tree networks without sense of direction. In: SIROCCO 1999, Lacanau-Ocean, France, 1–3 July 1999, pp. 32–46. Carleton Scientific (1999)

3. Bui, A., Datta, A.K., Petit, F., Villain, V.: State-optimal snap-stabilizing PIF in tree networks. In: ICDCS Workshop on Self-stabilizing Systems, Proceedings, Austin, Texas, 5 June 1999, pp. 78–85 (1999)
4. Bui, A., Datta, A.K., Petit, F., Villain, V.: Snap-stabilization and PIF in tree networks. Distrib. Comput. **20**(1), 3–19 (2007)
5. Chang, E.J.H.: Echo algorithms: depth parallel operations on general graphs. IEEE Trans. Software Eng. **8**(4), 391–401 (1982)
6. Chen, N.-S., Yu, H.-P., Huang, S.-T.: A self-stabilizing algorithm for constructing spanning trees. Inf. Process. Lett. **39**(3), 147–151 (1991)
7. Cournier, A., Datta, A.K., Devismes, S., Petit, F., Villain, V.: The expressive power of snap-stabilization. Theor. Comput. Sci. **626**, 40–66 (2016)
8. Cournier, A., Datta, A.K., Petit, F., Villain, V.: Optimal snap-stabilizing PIF in un-oriented trees. In: Proceedings OPODIS, Manzanillo, Mexico, 10–12 December 2001, pp. 71–90 (2001)
9. Cournier, A., Datta, A.K., Petit, F., Villain, V.: Snap-stabilizing PIF algorithm in arbitrary networks. In: ICDCS, pp. 199–206 (2002)
10. Cournier, A., Datta, A.K., Petit, F., Villain, V.: Enabling snap-stabilization. In: ICDCS 2003, 19–22 May 2003, Providence, RI, USA, pp. 12–19. IEEE Computer Society (2003)
11. Cournier, A., Datta, A.K., Petit, F., Villain, V.: Optimal snap-stabilizing PIF algorithms in un-oriented trees. J. High Speed Netw. **14**(2), 185–200 (2005)
12. Cournier, A., Devismes, S., Petit, F., Villain, V.: Snap-stabilizing depth-first search on arbitrary networks. Comput. J. **49**(3), 268–280 (2006)
13. Cournier, A., Devismes, S., Villain, V.: From self- to snap- stabilization. In: Datta, A.K., Gradinariu, M. (eds.) SSS 2006. LNCS, vol. 4280, pp. 199–213. Springer, Heidelberg (2006). doi:10.1007/978-3-540-49823-0_14
14. Cournier, A., Devismes, S., Villain, V.: Snap-stabilizing PIF and useless computations. In: ICPADS, Minneapolis, Minnesota, USA, 12–15 July 2006, pp. 39–48 (2006)
15. Cournier, A., Devismes, S., Villain, V.: Light enabling snap-stabilization of fundamental protocols. TAAS **4**(1), 1–27 (2009)
16. Delaët, S., Devismes, S., Nesterenko, M., Tixeuil, S.: Snap-stabilization in message-passing systems. J. Parallel Distrib. Comput. **70**(12), 1220–1230 (2010)
17. Devismes, S., Petit, F., Villain, V.: Autour de l'autostabilisation 1. techniques généralisant l'approche. Technique et Science Informatiques **30**(7), 873–894 (2011)
18. Devismes, S., Petit, F., Villain, V.: Autour de l'autostabilisation 2. techniques spécialisant l'approche. Technique et Science Informatiques **30**(7), 895–922 (2011)
19. Dijkstra, E.W.: Self-stabilizing systems in spite of distributed control. Commun. ACM **17**(11), 643–644 (1974)
20. Dolev, S., Tzachar, N.: Empire of colonies: self-stabilizing and self-organizing distributed algorithm. Theor. Comput. Sci. **410**(6–7), 514–532 (2009)
21. Levé, F., Mohamed, K., Villain, V.: Snap-stabilizing PIF on non-oriented trees and message passing model. In: Proceedings SSS 2014, Paderborn, Germany, September 28–October 1 2014, pp. 299–313 (2014)
22. Segall, A.: Distributed network protocols. IEEE Trans. Inf. Theory **29**(1), 23–34 (1983)

Towards Efficient and Robust BFT Protocols with ER-BFT (Short Paper)

Lucas Perronne[1(✉)] and Sara Bouchenak[2(✉)]

[1] University Grenoble Alpes, LIG, Grenoble, France
Lucas.Perronne@imag.fr
[2] INSA Lyon, LIRIS, Lyon, France
Sara.Bouchenak@insa-lyon.fr

Abstract. Significant efforts have been made in designing Byzantine Fault-Tolerant (BFT) state machine replication. In addition to facing arbitrary types of faults, *efficient* BFT protocols aim at improving the performance in the absence of faults. This is usually obtained at the expense of higher cost when faults occur. Symmetrically, BFT protocols known as *robust* protocols tend to improve the performance when some types of faults occur. However, this usually implies a higher overhead in fault-free executions. ER-BFT associates efficiency *and* robustness to BFT protocols. The paper presents the design principles of ER-BFT, and its implementation through the ER-PBFT protocol. When compared to classical *robust* BFT protocols, ER-PBFT achieves better performance in fault-free cases, and in presence of faults.

Keywords: Byzantine fault tolerance · Attacks · Robustness · Performance

1 Introduction

With the expansion of cloud computing, concerns such as availability, liveness and security are attracting more interest. In such environments, hosted systems are replicated on different servers to prevent data loss and provide various guarantees to the customers. In order to provide an enhanced level of reliability, BFT protocols rely on State Machine Replication (SMR) to handle unpredictable events, termed as byzantine or arbitrary faults. By definition, these protocols assure (i) *liveness:* eventual execution of correct clients requests; and (ii) *safety:* consistency across replicas. The byzantine generals problem was first described by Lamport et al. [6], stating that a byzantine agreement requires $3f+1$ replicas to handle up to f byzantine faults under partial synchrony. We can broadly categorize most contributions of the area in two groups: protocols optimizing the performance under fault-free settings, referred as *efficient* BFT protocols [2,3], and protocols minimizing the performance degradation introduced by faulty components, refered as *robust* BFT protocols [1,5]. In this paper, we target both of

B. Bonakdarpour and F. Petit (Eds.): SSS 2016, LNCS 10083, pp. 298–303, 2016.
DOI: 10.1007/978-3-319-49259-9_23

these concerns, i.e., improving robustness to malicious components, while maintaining a high level of performance in fault-free settings. To do so, we first define the generic design principles of ER-BFT (*Efficient* and *Robust* BFT). Then, we apply these principles on the ER-PBFT protocol in order to show the efficiency of the proposed robustness policy in practice.

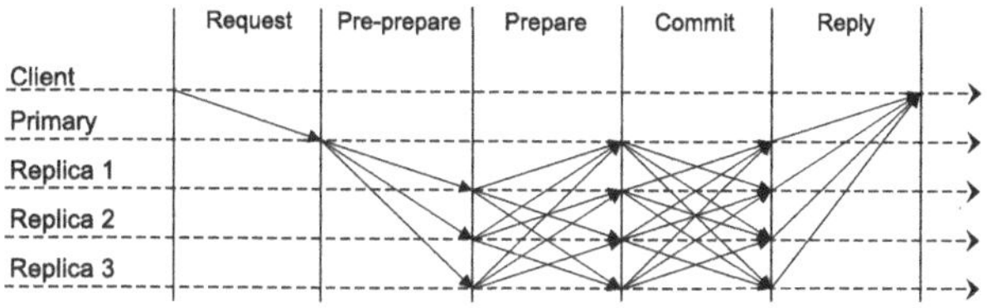

Fig. 1. Communication pattern of the PBFT protocol

2 Background

PBFT (cf. Fig. 1) was the first practical attempt to deal with the byzantine failure model using the state machine replication approach [4], and is nowadays considered as the baseline for practical byzantine fault tolerance. In order to handle contention (concurrent arrival of client requests), PBFT-like protocols rely on a dedicated replica called primary [1–5]. In such protocols, the primary first assigns sequence numbers to incoming requests (Pre-prepare). In a second round, a consensus involving all replicas is performed in order to reach an agreement on the proposed sequence numbers. This is practically achieved through the systematic exchange of the sequence numbers received from the primary (Prepare). Finally, if the exchanged sequence numbers are consistent, all replicas execute the same requests in the same order (Commit), thus ensuring the overall consistency of the system - *safety*. If no agreement is obtained in time, a *View-change* is triggered by correct backups (non-primary replicas) to replace the faulty primary and maintain the system ability to progress - *liveness*.

2.1 The Problem of MAC Attacks

In order to ensure the authenticity and the integrity of client requests, most BFT protocols rely on Messages Authentication Codes (MACs). The MAC used to authenticate a message is both generated and verified using a single secret key, shared between the sender and the receiver. Consequently, a vector of $3f + 1$ MACs (called *authenticator*) is computed by the clients, and appended to their requests. To ensure that a client is effectively the author of an incoming request, each replica authenticates that request by verifying its dedicated MAC among the $3f+1$ elements. *View-changes* can be intentionally triggered by faulty clients if these clients fill their *authenticators* with a corrupted MAC for the primary, and at least $f + 1$ corrects MACs among the $3f$ MACs dedicated to backups.

Respectively, as soon as a correct backup receives a request it can authenticate, it expects an agreement to be eventually obtained, since BFT protocols ensure the *liveness* property. However, the request which *appear correct* for the backup wont be successfully authenticated by the primary. The primary will discard that request, $f+1$ backups will eventually conclude that the primary is faulty, a *View-change* procedure will be triggered, and the primary will be replaced. Such denial-of-service attack can seriously tamper the performance of BFT protocols, especially if many clients compute a continuous load of corrupted *authenticators*.

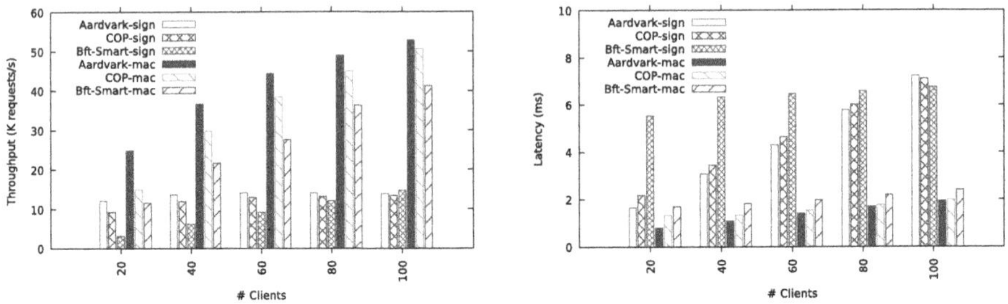

Fig. 2. Throughput and latency measured for various protocols.

In order to forbid malicious clients from triggering *View-changes*, the underlying authentication mechanism needs to provide the *non-repudiation* property, allowing *any* replica to confirm the authenticity and the integrity of *any* clients requests. *Robust* protocols, such as Aardvark and RBFT [1,5], systematically authenticate requests with digital signatures. A single signature is generated per request, and is consistently verified by all replicas. Replacing *Authenticators* with digital signatures however introduce an extra computational cost for both clients and replicas. To underpin this statement, we ran several experiments involving three BFT protocols, where requests authentication is performed both with MACs or digital signatures (cf. Fig. 2). We observe that the usage of signatures worsen both latency and throughput compared to MACs, without regards on the overlying protocol. We used the same cryptographic primitives than BFT-SMART's default ones for our experiments, being respectively Hmac:MD5 for MACs, and RSA:Sha1 for digital signatures [3].

3 Design Principles of ER-BFT

This section presents our contributions as three major recommandations regarding the design of *efficient* and *robust* BFT protocols. Respectively, we focus on requests management and *View-change* policies without modifying the core agreement itself, allowing our approach to be applied on most BFT protocols.

1. **Disabling Mac Attacks.** *View-changes* are not triggered on backups when an expected *MAC-authenticated* request does not commit.

reliability against MAC attacks, while avoiding the systematic usage of digital signatures for requests authentication. The experimental results through the ER-PBFT prototype demonstrate the efficiency of the proposed solution in practice.

References

1. Aublin, P.-L., Mokhtar, S.B., Quéma, V.: RBFT: Redundant Byzantine Fault Tolerance. In: ICDCS (2013)
2. Behl, J., Distler, T., Kapitza, R.: Consensus-oriented parallelization: how to earn your first million. In: Middleware (2015)
3. Bessani, A., Sousa, J., Alchieri, E.E.: State machine replication for the masses with BFT-SMaRt. In: DSN (2014)
4. Castro, M., Liskov, B.: Practical Byzantine fault tolerance. In: OSDI, pp. 173–186 (1999)
5. Clement, A., Wong, E.L., Alvisi, L., Dahlin, M., Marchetti, M.: Making Byzantine fault tolerant systems tolerate Byzantine faults. In: NSDI (2009)
6. Lamport, L., Shostak, R.E., Pease, M.C.: The Byzantine generals problem. ACM Trans. Program. Lang. Syst. **4**(3), 382–401 (1982)

Global Versus Local Computations: Fast Computing with Identifiers (Short Paper)

Mikaël Rabie(✉)

LIP, ENS de Lyon, Lyon, France
mikael.rabie@ens-lyon.org

Abstract. This paper studies what can be computed by using probabilistic local interactions between agents with a very restricted power in polylogarithmic parallel time.

If agents have a finite internal state (corresponding to the Population Protocol model by Angluin *et al.*), only semilinear predicates over the global input can be computed. If identifiers are added (corresponding to the Community Protocol model by Guerraoui and Ruppert), more global predicates over the input multiset can be computed. Local predicates over the input sorted according to the identifiers can also be computed, as long as the identifiers are ordered. The time of some of those predicates might require exponential parallel time.

In this paper, we consider what can be computed with Community Protocol in a polylogarithmic number of parallel interactions. We introduce the class $CPPL$ corresponding to protocols that use $O(n \log^k n)$, for some k, expected interactions to compute their predicates, or equivalently a polylogarithmic number of parallel expected interactions.

We provide some computable protocols, including one computing the size of the population. We also explore the limits of this model of computation by providing some arguments showing that local computations are no longer easy: the population does not have the time to compare a linear number of consecutive identifiers. The *Linearly Local* languages, such that the rational language $(ab)^*$, are not computable.

1 Introduction

Population Protocols, introduced by Angluin *et al.* in 2004 [2], are a model of finite states devices with a very restricted memory using pairwise interactions to communicate and compute a global result. Predicates computable by population protocols have been characterized as being precisely the semi-linear predicates; i.e. those definable in first-order Presburger arithmetic [1,2]. Semi-linearity was shown to be sufficient and necessary. Those predicates use the global multiset of the input.

The *community protocols* introduced by Guerraoui and Ruppert [6] assumes that agents are no longer anonymous: each agent has a unique identifier and

B. Bonakdarpour and F. Petit (Eds.): SSS 2016, LNCS 10083, pp. 304–309, 2016.
DOI: 10.1007/978-3-319-49259-9_24

can only remember $O(1)$ other agent identifiers. Guerraoui and Ruppert [6] using results about the so-called storage modification machines [7], characterized the expressive power of such protocols with a class of Turing machines: Predicates computed by this model with n agents are precisely the predicates in $NSPACE(n \log n)$. The sorted input symbols according to the identifiers can be analysed locally by the protocols to compute the right output.

Motivation

Angluin *et al.*, in [3], prove that any computable predicate by a Population Protocol can be computed in $O(n \log^5 n)$ expected interactions, as long as there is a unique leader at the beginning. This article suggests that there might be a protocol computing a leader election in $O(n \log n)$ expected interactions. Doty *et al.* proved in [5] that there cannot be a protocol computing a leader so fast. A protocol needs $\Omega(n^2)$ expected interactions to get to a configuration with a single leader, if every agent is a potential candidate at the beginning.

The exact characterization of what can be computed by populations having unique leaders lead naturally to look for what can be computed in $O(n \log^k n)$ expected interactions (for any $k > 0$), with the Community Protocols model [6]. We consider, as in [3], that each pair of agents (or identifiers) have the same probability to be chosen at each step of a computation. In [3], it is proved that dividing the number of expected interaction by n provides the expected number of parallel interactions.

Community protocols can be seen as interactions controlled by devices in a social group. For example, identifiers can correspond to phone numbers, and the devices can be applications on smartphones. In this vision, it seems intuitive to consider that a group of individuals does not want to stay too long together to compute some global information. Sorting a group of people depending on phone numbers to look for patterns does not seem intuitive, and hence useful.

This paper introduces the class *CPPL*, corresponding to what can be computed with Community Protocols in a polylogarithmic number of expected parallel interactions (i.e. a number of expected interactions bounded above by $n \log^k n$ for some k), or a polylogarithmic number of epidemics or broadcasts. We introduce a protocol proving that the size of the population (or some subset) can be computed in some sense to be explained.

We then show the limits of this model based on the fact that local computation cannot be performed over the whole input. More precisely, we prove that only a polylogarithmic number of agents can find the next or previous identifier to their own. We also introduce the class of linearly local languages, containing the rational language $(ab)^*$, and prove that none of its elements can be computed.

The paper is organized as follows: Sect. 2 describes the Community Protocol model introduced in [6] and recalls some known results. In Sect. 3 we describe some computable protocols, including a way to compute the size of the population. Section 4 brings our two impossibility results. It introduces the notion of Linearly Local languages and proves that these languages are not in $CPPL$.

Section 5 provides a lower bound of $CPPL$ in the form of a Turing Machine class.

2 Model

We use the protocols described by Guerraoui and Ruppert. The formal definition can be found in [6]. We will provide here just some key elements and the notion of complexity. This model has been proved in [6] to correspond to $NSPACE(n \log n)$, even if there are a fixed number of byzantine agents. We do not consider byzantine agents in this paper.

A *Community Protocol* is a protocol over agents. Each agent's state carries three elements: its identifier, its state, and d slots for identifiers. The set of possible identifiers is infinite, the number d of identifier slots is finite and depends on the protocol.

The transition function updates two agents' state depending on their previous state. This transition function has two restrictions: Agents cannot store identifiers that they never heard about and the transitions can only depend on the relative position of the identifiers.

An input is a word over Σ^*, where Σ is the input alphabet. The i-th letter will be given as input to the ith identifier of the population.

A protocol computes a set $L \subset \Sigma^*$ if, for any input word $w \in \Sigma^*$, the protocol provides an output, and the protocol accepts w if and only if $w \in L$. We then say that L is computable.

A language is computed in $f(n)$ expected interactions if, for any input w, the expected number of interactions to reach an output stable configuration is bounded above by $f(|w|)$.

The Community Protocols model has been fully characterized:

Theorem 1 ([6]). *The decisions problems computable by community protocols correspond exactly to the class $NSPACE(n \log n)$.*

Let us introduce now the class we will work with in this paper:

Definition 1. *We define the class* CPPL *as the sets of languages that can be recognized by a Community Protocol with $O(n \log^k n)$ expected interactions for some $k \in \mathbb{N}$, where each pair of agents has the same probability to interact at each moment.*

We say that a function f is n-polylog *if there exists some k such that we have $f(n) \leq n \log^k n$.*

Our protocols will use some tools introduced in [3]. We also use the main theorem of this paper about Population Protocols:

Theorem 2 ([3]). *For any predicate P definable in Presburger's Arithmetic, and for any $c > 0$, there is a probabilistic population protocol with a leader to compute P without error that converges in $O(n \log^5 n)$ interactions with probability at least $1 - n^{-c}$.*

3 Three Computable Protocols

We have the following main results about what can be computed in $CPPL$:

Theorem 3. *It is possible to compute a Leader Election, the leader being the agent with the smallest identifier, with $O(n \log n)$ expected interactions.*

Proof. Each agent starts as a potential leader. Each agent stores in an extra slot the smallest identifier it heard about. If an agents hears about a smaller identifier that its own, it abandons the idea to be a leader.

Once there remains a single leader, the computation is over.

Theorem 4. *Any predicate definable in Presburger's Arithmetic is in $CPPL$.*

Proof. The idea of the proof is to couple the fact that a leader can be computed in $O(n \log n)$ with the result of Theorem 2.

Theorem 5. *There exists a protocol that writes in binary on the first $\log n$ agents the size of the population, taking an expected number of $O(n \log^4 n)$ interactions.*

Proof. To build this protocol, we first create a protocol that finds the median identifier of a subset of agents. This first sub protocol works by updating bounds of this median identifier. It then chooses at random a candidate, and updates the bounds if the candidate is not the median identifier. We prove that this protocol expects $O(\log n)$ iterations to finally guess the correct identifier.

To know the smallest bit of the size of the population, we just need to compare the number of agents smaller and bigger than the median identifier (if it is equal, the bit is 1, else it is 0). We then compute the size of the first half of the population, and so on.

4 Two Impossibility Results

Let provide now two impossibility results about $CPPL$, the first being about finding a next identifier. An agent finds its Next when it hears about the smallest identifier bigger than its own.

Theorem 6. *Any population protocols needs at least $\Omega\left(n\sqrt{n}\right)$ expected interactions until each agent has found its $Next$.*

Here is our main impossibility result. We show that Community Protocols cannot link a linear number of consecutive identifiers in $CPPL$. To prove this, we introduce a new class of languages:

Definition 2. *Let $u = u_1 \dots u_N$ a word of size N and $i < N$. We call $\sigma_i(u)$ the word u where the ith letter is permuted with the next one. More formally, we have:*

$$\sigma_i(u) = u_1 \dots u_{i-1} u_{i+1} u_i u_{i+2} \dots u_N$$

We say that a language L is Linearly Local *if there exists some* $\alpha \in]0,1]$ *such that, for any n, there exists some* $u \in L$ *and some* $I \subset \mathbb{N}$ *such that:*

$u = u_1 \dots u_N$ *with* $N \geq n$, $\exists I \subset [1, N-1]$, $|I| \geq \alpha N$ *and for all* $i \in I$, $\sigma_i(u) \notin L$.

These languages are said linearly local as, for any size of input, we can find words that have a linear number of local regions where a small permutation of letter leads to a word not in the language.

Theorem 7. *There is no linearly local language in CPPL.*

Proof. The idea is to prove that for any protocol, and for any n, there exists some u in the language of length at least n and $i \in I$ such that there is a high enough probability that the protocol acts the same way on the inputs u and $\sigma_i(u)$.

Corollary 1. *The rational language* $(ab)^*$, *the rational language of words not containing the subword* (ab), *the well-formed parenthesis language and the palindrome language are not in CPPL.*

5 Turing Machine Lower Bound

We finally introduce a class of Turing Machines that computes everything we found to be computable yet. This class of machines is capable of computing global properties, through the ability to work on subsets of agents. It is capable to compute the size of sets of agents. It can perform any polylogarithmic number of steps of a regular Turing Machine.

Theorem 8. *Let* M_T *be a Turing Machine on alphabet* Γ *recognizing the language L having the following restrictions. There exists some* $k \in \mathbb{N}$ *such that*

- M_T *has 4 tapes. The first one is for the input* x.
- M_T *can only do at most* $\log^k |x|$ *unitary operations among the following ones:*
  1. *A regular Turing Machine step.*
  2. *Mark/Unmark the cells that have the symbol* γ *for any* $\gamma \in \Gamma$.
  3. *Write in binary on the 2nd tape the number of marked cells.*
  4. *Go to the cell of the number written on the 3rd tape if this number is smaller than* $|x|$.
  5. *Mark/Unmark all the cells left to the pointing head on the first tape.*
  6. *Turn into state* γ' *all the marked cells in state* γ *for any* $\gamma \in \Gamma$.

Then we have $L \in CPPL$.

References

1. Angluin, D., Aspnes, J., Eisenstat, D., Ruppert, E.: The computational power of population protocols. Distrib. Comput. **20**(4), 279–304 (2007)
2. Angluin, D., Aspnes, J., Diamadi, Z., Fischer, M.J., Peralta, R.: Computation in networks of passively mobile finite-state sensors. Principles Distrib. Comput. (PODC) **18**(4), 235–253 (2004)
3. Angluin, D., Aspnes, J., Eisenstat, D.: Fast computation by population protocols with a leader. Distrib. Comput. **21**, 183–199 (2008)
4. Bournez, O., Cohen, J., Rabie, M.: Homonym population protocols. In: Bouajjani, A., Fauconnier, H. (eds.) NETYS 2015. LNCS, vol. 9466, pp. 125–139. Springer, Heidelberg (2015)
5. Doty, D., Soloveichik, D.: Stable leader election in population protocols requires linear time. In: Moses, Y. (ed.) DISC 2015. LNCS, vol. 9363, pp. 602–616. Springer, Heidelberg (2015). doi:10.1007/978-3-662-48653-5_40
6. Guerraoui, R., Ruppert, E.: Names trump malice: tiny mobile agents can tolerate byzantine failures. In: Albers, S., Marchetti-Spaccamela, A., Matias, Y., Nikoletseas, S., Thomas, W. (eds.) ICALP 2009. LNCS, vol. 5556, pp. 484–495. Springer, Heidelberg (2009). doi:10.1007/978-3-642-02930-1_40
7. Schönhage, A.: Storage modification machines. SIAM J. Comput. **9**(3), 490–508 (1980)

Automatic Addition of Conflicting Properties

Mohammad Roohitavaf(✉) and Sandeep S. Kulkarni

Department of Computer Science and Engineering,
Michigan State University, East Lansing, MI 48824, USA
{roohitav,sandeep}@cse.msu.edu

Abstract. The problem of model/program repair focuses on revising an existing model/program to satisfy new properties. These properties can be safety, liveness, availability, or fault-tolerance requirements. Existing solutions focus on adding *compatible* properties, i.e., properties that can be satisfied while preserving the existing properties. In other words, they try to generate programs that satisfy the existing properties as well as the new desired properties. It follows that if one were to add a *conflicting* property, i.e., a property that cannot be satisfied while preserving existing properties, then the previous solutions declare failure to obtain the desired program. However, adding conflicting properties arises when one *replaces* an existing requirement with another– e.g., replacing fairness requirement with priority to some process. In this paper, we focus on the problem of adding conflicting properties. We present an algorithm for explicit addition of properties that adds new desired properties while preserving only an explicitly specified subset of existing properties. In turn, we use it to develop an algorithm for adding conflicting properties. We illustrate our algorithms with an example of job scheduling.

1 Introduction

In this paper, we focus on the problem of model repair in the context of conflicting properties. Model repair focuses on the problem of revising an existing program based on changing requirements and/or environment. In particular, model repair begins with an existing model/abstract program and a desired specification. The goal of the repair algorithm is to change the given program to one that satisfies the given specification. Model repair is also valuable when we utilize a model checker and find a counterexample. Manual revision of the given program has the potential to introduce new bugs, i.e., it can violate properties that were satisfied by the given program. In this case, model repair can be used to repair the given program to *fix* the bug while preserving the existing specification.

Previous algorithms for model repair assume that the new specification is *compatible* with the existing specification. In particular, if the given program satisfies specification Π, but does not satisfy another desired specification Γ, then the goal of the previous algorithms is to design a program that satisfies $\Pi \wedge \Gamma$.

Clearly, this approach declares failure if the new specification *conflicts* with the existing specification, i.e., if $\Pi \wedge \Gamma$ is unsatisfiable. Moreover, this failure

This work is supported by NSF CNS 1329807, NSF CNS 1318678, and XPS 1533802.

B. Bonakdarpour and F. Petit (Eds.): SSS 2016, LNCS 10083, pp. 310–326, 2016.
DOI: 10.1007/978-3-319-49259-9_25

is unavoidable, since, by definition, a program that satisfies $\Pi \wedge \Gamma$ does not exist. Our work in this paper focuses on developing algorithms for model repair when the new requirements conflict with existing requirements. One common occurrence for need of such repair is when we *replace* existing requirements.

Examples of model repair with conflicting new requirements. Consider a mutual exclusion protocol (e.g., Peterson's algorithm [12]) that guarantees that two processes $P1$ and $P2$ enter critical section in a round robin manner whenever both are requesting continuously. Suppose that we want to repair this protocol so that $P1$ has a higher priority than $P2$. This can be expressed as a requirement that $P2$ does not enter critical section when $P1$ is waiting for it. However, this new property (higher priority for $P1$) cannot be simultaneously satisfied with existing property (fairness among $P1$ and $P2$). Thus, we say the new property conflicts with the existing property.

In some cases, it is desirable to consider the existing and new properties to be conflicting even though they do not appear to be conflicting. As an illustration, consider the case where the existing program ensures that every request is satisfied in 5–10 s. Suppose we want to change the requirement to one that requires each request must be satisfied within 2–7 s. If we add this new requirement to the existing program as a new property while preserving existing properties, the resulting program would have to satisfy every request in 5–7 s which is unnecessarily stronger than what we want. In other words, in this example, adding the new property while preserving existing properties may reduce the design space substantially. This implies that even though these properties do not appear to be conflicting, we should treat them as conflicting properties so that the new program can potentially utilize the entire design space.

Hence, in this paper, we focus on model repair when we want to *remove* some existing properties from the given program so that the addition of the new property can be achieved.

First approach for adding conflicting properties. Since the existing specification Π, satisfied by the original program, conflicts with the new specification Γ, we cannot use existing algorithms for adding Γ. Instead, we can envision that we first introduce new behaviors in the original program. These new behaviors would then assist in satisfying Γ. When we add these new behaviors, the resulting program will no longer satisfy Π. Instead, it would satisfy a weaker version of Π. With this intuition, the first attempt to add conflicting properties is as follows:

- Begin with a program p that satisfies Π.
- Introduce new behaviors so that the resulting program satisfies the common (non-conflicting) requirements of Π and Γ. Let the resulting program be p''.
- Use existing approaches to add Γ. Since the conflicting properties in Π have been removed, we expect that adding Γ would now be feasible to obtain the desired program p'.

As an illustration, in the case where we want to add priority requirement to Peterson's algorithm we can introduce new behaviors that potentially allow one process to enter critical section even if another process is waiting. In the subsequent step, we will remove behaviors where $P2$ can enter critical section even when $P1$ wants to enter critical section.

We find that this approach, however, fails too often. In part, this is due to the fact that requiring the intermediate program to satisfy all common requirements of Π and Γ makes it impossible to design the desired program that satisfies Γ in the second step.

Our approach for adding conflicting properties. Since the first naïve approach fails to synthesize the desired program, we focus on an alternate version. One possibility is to design the intermediate program to be an arbitrary program. However, in this case, the new program and the existing program may have nothing in common. This is especially problematic since certain requirements (e.g., structure of the system, performance requirements etc.) are hard to characterize. Instead, it is desirable to *reuse* an existing program to the extent possible so that these properties will be preserved in the new program (assuming that they were satisfied by the original program).

Instead of using an arbitrary intermediate program, we focus on a two-step approach called *explicit addition* as follows:

- Begin with a program p that satisfies Φ.
- Introduce new behaviors so that the resulting program satisfies
  - the safety requirements in Φ, and
  - weakened version of liveness requirements in Φ.

  Let the resulting program be p''.
- Use existing approaches to add Γ and liveness properties in Φ so that the resulting program, say p', satisfies $\Phi \wedge \Gamma$.

Subsequently, we utilize this algorithm for explicit addition to add conflicting properties. In particular, we consider different subsets of requirements in Π. We instantiate the program for explicit addition where Φ is set to be this subset of requirements of Π. In turn, the algorithm to perform explicit addition introduces new behaviors that still preserve Φ. Subsequently, we add Γ to the program to obtain a program that satisfies $\Phi \wedge \Gamma$. By decreasing the size of the subset that is instantiated to be Φ, we can preserve as much behaviors as possible.

Contributions of the paper

- We present an algorithm for explicit addition of new properties to existing programs. While previous approaches focus on satisfying new properties by only removing behaviors that violate the new property, this algorithm is more general in that it allows addition of behaviors that satisfy the new requirements while preserving existing requirements that are specified explicitly as well.
- We utilize the algorithm for explicit addition of properties to develop an algorithm for adding conflicting properties while preserving compatible properties.
- We demonstrate our algorithm with a case study on scheduling to demonstrate how a *change in policy* can be incorporated to develop a new program from

an existing program. We also note that our approach can be used for several other case studies including those discussed earlier in this section.

Organization of the paper. The rest of the paper is organized as follows: In Sect. 2, we define the notion of programs and specifications. In Sect. 3, we identify the problem of *pruning addition* where the goal is to satisfy the new requirements by only removing behaviors that violate those new requirements. In Sect. 4, we introduce our new approach, *explicit addition*, that introduces new behaviors that may violate some properties not provided explicitly. This approach is used in Sect. 5 to add conflicting properties. We illustrate our algorithm with a case study in Sect. 6. Finally, we discuss related work in Sect. 7 and conclude in Sect. 8.

2 Programs and Specification

In this section, we define the notion of programs and specifications. We define a program in terms of its state space and its transitions. Intuitively, the state space of a program characterizes the set of all possible states that the program can be in. Transitions, on the other hand, identify how the program transitions from one state to another. A nonempty subset of states forms the initial states of the program. Hence, we define a program as follows:

Definition 1 (Program). *A program p is of the form $\langle S_p, I_p, \delta_p \rangle$ where S_p is the state space of p, $I_p \subseteq S_p$ is the set of initial states, and $\delta_p \subseteq S_p \times S_p$ is the set of transitions of p.*

A computation of a program is a sequence of states that begins in an initial state and then executes a program transition in every state. Furthermore, we require that if a computation is finite then the last state in the computation has no outgoing transition. Thus, we have

Definition 2 (Computation). *The sequence $\sigma = \langle s_0, s_1, s_2, ... \rangle$ is a computation of program $p = \langle S_p, I_p, \delta_p \rangle$ iff*

- *$s_0 \in I_p$, and*
- *$\forall i : i \geq 0 : s_i \in S_p$, and*
- *$\forall i : i \geq 0 : (s_i, s_{i+1}) \in \delta_p$, and*
- *σ is either infinite, or ends in state s_l such that $\nexists s' : s' \in S_p : (s_l, s') \in \delta_p$.*

Definition 3 (State Predicate). *A state predicate of p is any subset of S_p.*

The specifications we consider in this paper consist of a safety specification and a liveness specification. Our notion of safety and liveness is based on previous work by Alpern and Schneider [1]. The safety specification –that identifies bad things that the program should not do– is specified in terms of a set of (bad) transitions. Hence, a computation satisfies a safety specification if and only if it does not include any of transitions prohibited by the safety specification. Liveness specification –that identifies good things that the program should do–

is identified in terms of a set of leads-to properties. A leads-to property is of the form $R \rightarrow T$, where R and T are state predicates. It requires that if the program ever reaches a state in R then it eventually reaches a state in T. Formally, we have:

Definition 4 (Safety). *A safety property is specified in terms of a set of transitions, $\mathcal{B}$, that the program is not allowed to execute. We say that a sequence $\sigma = \langle s_0, s_1, \ldots \rangle$ satisfies the safety property $\mathcal{B}$ iff $\forall j : 0 < j < length(\sigma) : (s_j, s_{j+1}) \notin \mathcal{B}$.*

Definition 5 (Leads-to). *A leads-to property is specified in terms of $R \rightarrow T$, where R and T are state predicates. We say that a sequence $\sigma = \langle s_0, s_1, \ldots \rangle$ satisfies the leads-to property $R \rightarrow T$ iff $(\forall i : i \geq 0 : (s_i \in R) \Rightarrow (\exists j : j \geq i : s_j \in T))$. In other words, if R holds in s_i then there exists a state s_j where T eventually holds and $j \geq i$.*

Finally, a specification consists of a liveness specification (specified in terms of a set of leads-to properties) and a safety specification (specified in terms of a set of bad transitions). Thus, we have

Definition 6 (Specification). *The specification is specified in terms of $\langle \mathcal{L}, \mathcal{B} \rangle$ where $\mathcal{L}$ is a set of leads-to properties, and $\mathcal{B}$ is a safety property. We say that a sequence $\sigma = \langle s_0, s_1, \ldots \rangle$ satisfies specification $\langle \mathcal{L}, \mathcal{B} \rangle$ iff it satisfies all leads-to properties in $\mathcal{L}$ and safety property $\mathcal{B}$.*

Definition 7 (Program satisfies a specification). *We say program $p = \langle S_p, I_p, \delta_p \rangle$ satisfies specification $spec = \langle \mathcal{L}, \mathcal{B} \rangle$ iff every computation of p satisfies $spec$.*

We also introduce the notion of union of specifications. This notion is defined to concisely capture the requirement that both specifications $spec_1$ and $spec_2$ are satisfied.

Definition 8 (Union of Specifications). *The union of two specifications $spec_1 = \langle \mathcal{L}_1, \mathcal{B}_1 \rangle$ and $spec_2 = \langle \mathcal{L}_2, \mathcal{B}_2 \rangle$, denoted as $spec_1 \cup spec_2$ equals to $\langle \mathcal{L}_1 \cup \mathcal{L}_2, \mathcal{B}_1 \cup \mathcal{B}_2 \rangle$.*

Observe that in the above definition, we have combined the leads-to properties in liveness specification. Hence, if the program satisfies $spec_1 \cup spec_2$, it will satisfy liveness requirements in both. Likewise, it will disallow transitions ruled out by both $\mathcal{B}_1$ and $\mathcal{B}_2$. In other words, it will satisfy both $spec_1$ as well as $spec_2$.

3 Pruning Addition

In this section, we recall the problem of adding new properties (from [2]) to an existing program by pruning, i.e., by removing behaviors that violate the new requirements. We describe the problem statement in Sect. 3.1, and recall the sketch of an algorithm for the problem (from [2]) in Sect. 3.2. The algorithm in details is provided in the Appendix. We utilize this algorithm in our solution for adding conflicting properties. Hence, we also review the relevant properties of the algorithm.

3.1 Problem Statement

The problem of pruning addition begins with a program $p = \langle S_p, I_p, \delta_p \rangle$ and a specification $spec = \langle \mathcal{L}, \mathcal{B} \rangle$. The goal of the pruning addition is to revise p by removing some behaviors from p so that p satisfies the given specification *spec*. Since the pruning addition only removes behaviors, we require that the state space and initial state remain unchanged[1], and $\delta_{p'} \subseteq \delta_p$. Moreover, in the process of the pruning addition, we cannot add new deadlock states to the program. However, states that are deadlock in the original program may be deadlock in the revised program. Thus, the problem statement of the pruning addition is as follows:

Problem 3.1:Pruning Addition Problem.
Given program $p = \langle S_p, I_p, \delta_p \rangle$, and specification *spec*, identify $p' = \langle S_{p'}, I_{p'}, \delta_{p'} \rangle$ such that:

(P1) $S_{p'} = S_p$
(P2) $I_{p'} = I_p$
(P3) $\delta_{p'} \subseteq \delta_p$
(P4) p' satisfies *spec*
(P5) $\forall s : s \in S_{p'} \wedge s$ is reachable from a state in $I_{p'}$: (There is a transition in δ_p starting at $s \Rightarrow$ there is a transition in $\delta_{p'}$ starting at s)

Based on Problem 3.1, if p is the input program and p is the output program, then every behavior of p that starts from I_p is also a behavior of p. It follows that if p satisfies a specification $\langle \mathcal{L}, \mathcal{B} \rangle$ then p satisfies it as well. Thus, we have

Theorem 1 (Strong Property of Pruning Addition). *Let p and p' be two programs that satisfy all constraints of problem statement (Sect. 3.1). Also, let $\langle \mathcal{L}, \mathcal{B} \rangle$ be any specification such that p satisfies $\langle \mathcal{L}, \mathcal{B} \rangle$.*
Then p' satisfies $\langle \mathcal{L}, \mathcal{B} \rangle$.

The above theorem has several implications some good and some bad. One good implication is that even if we do not know the original specification of program p, we are guaranteed to preserve it. However, if the existing program has a property (that you may not have wanted in the first place), and this property is incompatible with the newly desired property then it is impossible to identify the desired program p'. For example, if the original program has the

[1] Another variation of this problem considered in the literature is one where $I_{p'} \subseteq I_p$ and $I_{p'} \neq \emptyset$. Our results can be extended for these cases as well. However, this issue is outside the scope of the paper.

property that processes enter critical section in a round-robin manner, and the new property is that one process needs to have a higher priority, then pruning addition would declare that the desired program does not exist.

3.2 Algorithm for Pruning Addition

For sake of space, we have provided the algorithm for pruning addition in the Appendix. The sketch of the algorithm is as follows:

First, we remove all transitions that violate the safety requirement. For each leads-to property of the form p leads to q, it removes states in p from where there is no path to a state in q. Then, it identifies the rank – the length of the shortest path from that node to a state in q– of each node. Subsequently, it removes transitions if it fails to decrease rank with respect to some leads-to property. This process is repeated until we reach a fixpoint where from every state in p that is still reachable, there is a path that reaches a state in q and on every transition on that path, the rank associated with all leads-to property decreases.

We reiterate the algorithm for pruning addition (from [2]) in the Appendix in algorithm *Pruning_addition*. The algorithms in the paper do not depend upon the *description* of this algorithm. They only depend upon the correctness of pruning addition which is characterized by the following theorem.

Theorem 2. *Algorithm Pruning_addition is sound, i.e., if it identifies a program then that program solves the constraints of the pruning addition problem. Also, time complexity of algorithm Pruning_addition is polynomial in the state space of the input program.*

4 Explicit Addition

In this section, we define the problem of explicit addition. This problem takes two specifications *spec* (old specification) and *spec'* (new specification) as input and constructs a program that satisfies both specifications. This problem differs from the pruning addition considered in previous section in two important aspects:

- The pruning addition ensures that any specification of the form $\langle \mathcal{L}, \mathcal{B} \rangle$ that is satisfied by the input program is also preserved by the new program. By contrast, explicit addition provides this guarantee only for the specifications *spec* and *spec'*, that are provided as input. Other specifications that may have been satisfied (accidentally or otherwise) by the original program may be violated by the revised program.
- The pruning addition only focuses on removing behaviors. By contrast, explicit addition also allows us to add new transitions/behaviors. These new transitions would be of help in adding new properties.

We proceed as follows: In Sect. 4.1, we define the problem statement. Then, in Sect. 4.2, we present our algorithm for this problem.

4.1 Problem Statement

In this section, we define the problem of explicit addition. The input to the problem consists of the original program, p, the original specification, *spec*, and the specification we want to add, *spec*$'$. The goal of the explicit addition problem is to identify program p' that satisfies both *spec* and *spec*$'$. Unlike the problem of pruning addition, explicit addition problem allows to introduce new behaviors. This implies that there is a possibility to identify program p' from scratch, i.e., without doing any reuse of program p. As mentioned before, we want to disallow that possibility and reuse the behavior of the given program as much as possible. We achieve this by requiring that we reuse behaviors of program p that already satisfy *spec* and *spec*$'$. Specifically, the problem of explicit addition is as follows:

Problem 4.1: Explicit Addition Problem.
Given program $p = \langle S_p, I_p, \delta_p \rangle$, and specifications $spec = \langle \mathcal{L}, \mathcal{B} \rangle$ and $spec' = \langle \mathcal{L}', \mathcal{B}' \rangle$ such that p satisfies *spec*, identify $p' = \langle S_{p'}, I_{p'}, \delta_{p'} \rangle$ such that:

(E1) $S_{p'} = S_p$
(E2) $I_{p'} = I_p$
(E3) p' satisfies $spec \cup spec'$
(E4) $\forall s : s \in S_p :$
$(\forall \sigma : \sigma$ is a computation of p starting at $s : \sigma$ satisfies $spec \cup spec')$
$\Rightarrow$
$(\forall \sigma : \sigma$ is a computation of $\langle S_p, I_p, \delta_p \cap \delta_{p'} \rangle$ starting at $s : \sigma$ satisfies $spec \cup spec')$

In the above problem, constraints $E1$ and $E2$ are identical to $P1$ and $P2$, respectively, in the pruning addition problem statement. Constraint $E3$ states that the output program p' satisfies *spec* and *spec*$'$. Finally, constraint $E4$ prevents one to design program from scratch. Instead, it requires the revised program to reuse some portion of p.

To illustrate constraint $E4$, we consider the example in Fig. 1. Assume that in Fig. 1(a), we want to add the liveness property $R \rightarrow T$ to the given program p, where $R = \{A, B, C\}$ and $T = \{D\}$. Thus, *spec*$'$ in the problem statement for this example is $\langle R \rightarrow T, \emptyset \rangle$. In other words, *spec*$'$ requires to add $R \rightarrow T$, but has a trivial safety specification. Let *spec* be $\langle \emptyset, \emptyset \rangle$. In other words, *spec* is a trivial specification that is satisfied by any program.[2]

Observe that all computations of p starting at A (i.e. $\langle A, B, D \rangle$) satisfy the specification $spec \cup spec'$. The revised program in Fig. 1(b) satisfies all first three constraints of the problem statement. However, it fails to satisfy the last constraint, because state A is a deadlock state in $\langle S_p, I_p, \delta_p \cap \delta_{p'} \rangle$.

[2] We have considered this trivial specification only to illustrate the constraint E4. A non-trivial specification is considered in Sect. 6.2.

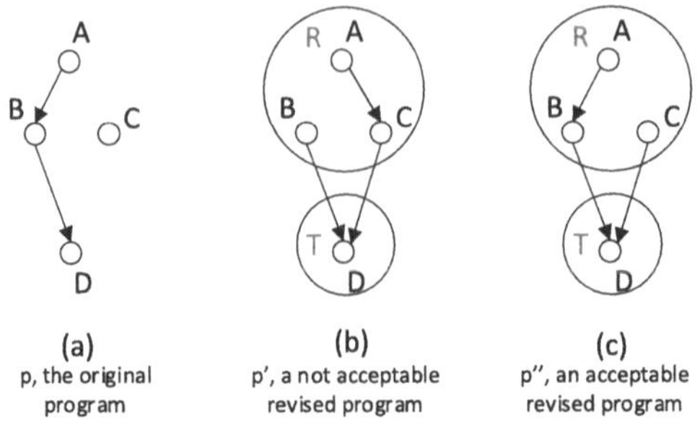

Fig. 1. Demonstration of the constraint E4 of the problem statement

By contrast, program in Fig. 1(c) satisfies all constraints of the problem statement. Observe that the program in Fig. 1(c) is reusing computations of the original program in Fig. 1(a). Condition $E4$ is intended to capture this requirement.

4.2 Algorithm for Explicit Addition

Our algorithm for explicit addition is provided in Algorithm 1. The input to Algorithm 1 consists of the original program $p = \langle S_p, I_p, \delta_p \rangle$, the specification $spec = \langle \mathcal{L}, \mathcal{B} \rangle$ which p already satisfies, and the new specification $spec' = \langle \mathcal{L}', \mathcal{B}' \rangle$ that we want to add to the p.

First, on Line 1 we remove any transition in $(\mathcal{B} \cup \mathcal{B}')$ from the set of program transitions, as any transition in $(\mathcal{B} \cup \mathcal{B}')$ violates safety properties. Next, we call *Behavior_addition*. This function focuses on adding more transitions to the program in such a way that from every state there exist computations that satisfy the desired leads-to property. Specifically, for a leads-to property of the form $R \rightarrow T$, it ensures that there is a computation from a state in R to a state in T. Furthermore, this function also avoids adding too many transitions. Thus, we add transitions only to states that have rank ∞ for a leads-to property. It adds transitions from such states to all other possible states as long as it is not disallowed by the safety specification $\mathcal{B} \cup \mathcal{B}'$.

After calling *Behavior_addition*, the safety specification is satisfied. However, a leads-to property may not be satisfied, as we may have created cycles when we added new transitions. We use the algorithm of pruning addition (provided in the Appendix) to ensure that these leads-to properties are satisfied. The result of the pruning addition algorithm identifies the program required by the explicit addition problem.

For Algorithm 1, we have the following theorem (proof is provided in the Appendix).

Theorem 3. *Algorithm 1 is sound, i.e., the program returned by it satisfies the constraints of Problem 4.1. Also, the time complexity of Algorithm 1 is polynomial in the state space of the input program.*

Algorithm 1. *Explicit_addition*

Input: program $p = \langle S_p, I_p, \delta_p \rangle$, specifications $spec = \langle \mathcal{L}, \mathcal{B} \rangle$ and $spec' = \langle \mathcal{L}', \mathcal{B}' \rangle$ such that p satisfies $spec$.

Output: $p' = \langle S_{p'}, I_{p'}, \delta_{p'} \rangle$.

$\delta_p = \delta_p - \mathcal{B}'$;
$\langle S_p, I_p, \delta_p \rangle = Behavior\_addition(\langle S_p, I_p, \delta_{p1} \rangle, \mathcal{L} \cup \mathcal{L}', \mathcal{B} \cup \mathcal{B}')$;
$\langle S_p, I_p, \delta_p \rangle = Pruning\_addition(\langle S_p, I_p, \delta_{p1} \rangle, \mathcal{L} \cup \mathcal{L}', \emptyset)$;
if $\langle S_p, I_p, \delta_p \rangle =$ failure **then**
    return failure
end if
return $\langle S_p, I_p, \delta_p \rangle$

$Behavior\_addition(\langle S_p, I_p, \delta_{p1} \rangle, \mathcal{L}, \mathcal{B})\{$
$\forall s, i : s \in S_p \wedge R_i \rightarrow T_i \in \mathcal{L} : Rank(s)[i]$ is the length of the shortest computation prefix of p that starts from s, and ends in a state in T_i; $Rank(s)[i] = \infty$ means T_i is not reachable from s.
while $\exists s_0, s_1$ such that $(\exists i : 0 \leq i \leq n : Rank(s_0)[i] = \infty) \wedge (s_0, s_1) \notin \mathcal{B} \wedge (\forall j : 0 \leq j \leq n : Rank(s_1)[j] < Rank(s_0)[j] \vee Rank(s_o)[j] = \infty)$ **do**
    $\delta_p = \delta_p \cup \{(s_0, s_1)\}$;
    update all *Ranks*;
end while
return $\langle S_p, I_p, \delta_p \rangle; \}$

5 Addition of Conflicting Properties

In this section, we utilize Algorithm 1 to design an algorithm for adding conflicting specifications. We say that two specifications $spec_1$ and $spec_2$ are conflicting if and only if there does not exist a program that satisfies both $spec_1$ and $spec_2$ simultaneously. Thus, if program p satisfies specification $spec_1$, and $spec_1$ is conflicting with specification $spec_2$, any attempt to add specification $spec_2$ to program p using pruning addition will result in a failure.

In this case, to add $spec_2$ to program p we have to *relax* $spec_1$. Specifically, instead of requiring the revised program to satisfy all specifications satisfied by p, we require the revised program to satisfy a subset of the original specifications satisfied by p. Moreover, in this addition, we may need to introduce new behaviors so that we can satisfy $spec_2$.

Therefore, when program p satisfies $spec_1$ and we want to add specification $spec_2$ that conflicts with $spec_1$, we need to select a subset $spec_1'$ of $spec_1$ which does not conflict with $spec_2$, and try to identify a program that satisfies $spec_1' \cup spec_2$ using Algorithm 1. To find a non-conflicting subset of $spec_1$, we try all possible subsets of $spec_1$. We consider these subsets in decreasing sizes so that we can try to satisfy $spec_1$ to the extent feasible. Thus, our solution is as shown in Algorithm 2.

Remark. Although we have written Algorithm 2 with the idea of arbitrary subsets of $\mathcal{L}$ and $\mathcal{B}$, we can only focus on the relevant subsets identified by the

Algorithm 2. *Conflicting_addition*

Input: program $p = \langle S_p, I_p, \delta_p \rangle$, specifications $spec = \langle \mathcal{L}, \mathcal{B} \rangle$ and $spec' = \langle \mathcal{L}', \mathcal{B}' \rangle$ such that p satisfies $spec$, and $spec$ and $spec'$ are conflicting.
Output: $p' = \langle S_{p'}, I_{p'}, \delta_{p'} \rangle$.

```
for i = |L| + |B| → 0 do
    for each spec'' = ⟨L'', B''⟩ where (L'' ⊆ L) ∧ (B'' ⊆ B) ∧ (|L''| + |B''| = i) do
        ⟨S_p, I_p, δ_p'⟩ = Explicit_addition(p, spec'', spec')
        if ⟨S_p, I_p, δ_p'⟩ ≠ failure then
            return ⟨S_p, I_p, δ_p'⟩
        end if
    end for
end for
return failure
```

designers. For example, if the designers can identify that satisfying fairness and priority together is impossible, they can avoid considering that subset. However, since this issue is very specific to a given problem, we do not discuss this further. We illustrate it with our example in Sect. 6. Also, instead of any arbitrary subset of $\mathcal{B}$, we select subsets of transitions such that either all transitions of a specific safety property are in the subset or none of them is in the subset. In this way, the number of subsets that the algorithm considers is not exponential in the number of transitions. For example, if one safety property is that the value of some variable never increases, then this property may correspond to several transitions in the state space. However, while considering subsets of $\mathcal{B}$ we consider only those subsets that either include all these transitions or none of these transitions. We illustrate this issue with an example in Sect. 6.

Assumption. Based on the above remark, we assume that the number of subsets considered in Algorithm 2 is much smaller than the size of state space of p. Under this assumption, we have the following theorem (proof is provided in the Appendix).

Theorem 4. *Algorithm 2 is sound, i.e., if it identifies a program then that program satisfies $spec'$. Also, under the assumption made above, time complexity of Algorithm 2 is polynomial in the state space of the input program.*

6 Case Study: Scheduler

In this section, we illustrate our algorithm for adding conflicting properties with an example of a scheduler. For sake of presentation, we consider the case where we have only two jobs, say job_1 and job_2, each of which takes one time unit to execute. We assume that both jobs arrive at time 0.

In our case study, we assume that the original specification requires sequential execution of jobs where at least one job should finish. It also requires that there should be a gap of 2 time units between jobs and no job should run after time 3. Thus, the original specification, $spec$, is captured by requirements $S1..S4$.

($S1$) No job should run after time unit 3.
($S2$) Concurrent execution of jobs is prohibited.
($S3$) There must be a gap of at least two time units between jobs.
($S4$) At least one job must be completed.

To illustrate the role of adding conflicting properties, suppose that we want to revise the specification so that both jobs must be done, and no job can start at time 0. Thus, the specification we want to add, $spec'$, is as follows:

($S5$) Both jobs must be completed.
($S6$) No job can start at time 0.

In this example, $S6$ requires that the earliest a job can start is at time 1. Since there is a gap of at least two time units between two jobs (from $S3$), it is impossible to finish both jobs before time 3. Thus, $spec$ and $spec'$ are conflicting, and cannot be satisfied simultaneously.

We demonstrate how $spec'$ can be added to a scheduler that satisfies $spec$ using Algorithm 2. Towards this end, in Sect. 6.1, we identify the scheduler that satisfies $S1..S4$. In Sect. 6.2, we show how we apply Algorithm 2 and identify a new scheduler that satisfies $spec'$ (and parts of $spec$).

6.1 Original Scheduler

Scheduler p described here satisfies all constraints of $spec$ namely S1 to S4. A state of the program is described by a tuple $\langle e_1, e_2, t\rangle$ where the meaning of e_1, e_2 and t is as follows:

e_1 : represents the status of job_1. Its domain is $D_e = \{-1, 0, 1, 2, 3, 4\}$ where -1 means job has not started, 0 means job is running, and $1 \leq i \leq 3$ means job is completed at time i, and 4 means that the job has not completed before time 4.

e_2 : represents the status of job_2, and its domain is the same as that of e_1.

t : represents the time. Its domain is $D_t = \{0, 1, 2, 3, \}$, where 4 represent any time unit greater than or equal to 4.

The original specification $spec$ is $\langle \mathcal{L}_1, \mathcal{B}_1\rangle$, where $\mathcal{B}_1$ is a safety property that capture $S1..S3$ and equals to equals $\delta_{b_1} \cup \delta_{b_2} \cup \delta_{b_3}$ where

- $\delta_{b_1} = \{(\langle i,j,t\rangle, \langle i',j',t'\rangle) | (i' = 0 \vee j' = 0) \wedge t \geq 3\} (S1)$
- $\delta_{b_2} = \{(\langle i,j,t\rangle, \langle i',j',t'\rangle) |\ i' = 0 \wedge j' = 0\} (S2)$
- $\delta_{b_3} = \{(\langle i,j,t\rangle, \langle i',j',t'\rangle) | (i > 0 \wedge j' = 0 \wedge t' - i < 2) \vee (j > 0 \wedge i' = 0 \wedge t' - j < 2)\} (S3)$

and $\mathcal{L}_1$ is a leads-to property that capture $S4$ and equals to $R \rightarrow T$ where

- $R = \{\langle i,j,t\rangle \ | i \leq 0 \wedge j \leq 0\}$
- $T = \{\langle i,j,t\rangle \ | i > 0 \vee j > 0\}$.

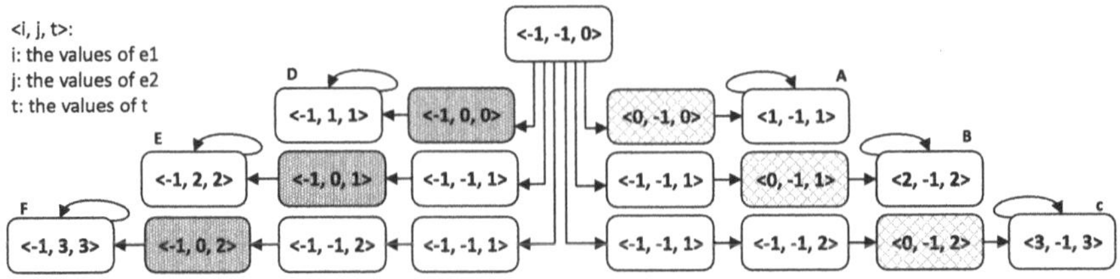

Fig. 2. Scheduler p that satisfies the original specification

In addition to *spec*, to have a useful scheduler, the scheduler should satisfies a set of sanity constraints that specify requirements such as time cannot go backward, a completed job cannot become incomplete and so on. The sanity specification is defined as safety specification with a set of bad transitions. For sake of space, the set of bad transitions for the sanity specification is provided in the Appendix.

Figure 2 shows the original scheduler p that satisfies $S1..S4$. Note that, the Fig. 2 shows only a subset of states that are relevant for our discussion.

6.2 Revised Scheduler

Observe that due to Theorem 1, if we apply pruning addition for addition of *spec'*, this will result in a failure since *spec* and *spec'* cannot be satisfied simultaneously. In this section, we apply Algorithm 2 to illustrate the addition of conflicting properties. Input p of Algorithm 2 is the scheduler program identified in Sect. 6.1. Input *spec* of Algorithm 2 consists of constraints $S1..S4$ whose formal representation is discussed in Sect. 6.1. Input *spec'* of Algorithm 2 captures $S5$ and $S6$ and is $\langle \mathcal{L}', \mathcal{B}' \rangle$ where $\mathcal{L}'$ is a leads-to property which captures $S5$ and equals $R' \rightarrow T'$ where

- $R' = \{\langle i, j, t \rangle \mid i \leq 0 \vee j \leq 0\}$
- $T' = \{\langle i, j, t \rangle \mid i > 0 \wedge j > 0\}$

and $\mathcal{B}'$ is a safety property that captures $S6$ and equals to

- $\{(\langle i, j, t \rangle, \langle i', j', t' \rangle) \mid (i' = 0 \vee j' = 0) \wedge t' = 0\}$.

Algorithm 2 considers the different subsets of *spec* to obtain a program that satisfies *spec'*. As discussed in the remark after the algorithm, we should only consider subsets that are relevant from the perspective of the designer. As an illustration, constraints $S5$ and $S6$ are compatible with the set of constraints $\{S1, S2, S4\}$ and the sanity constraints. They are also compatible with the set $\{S2, S3, S4\}$ and the sanity constraints. The exact subset that is selected by Algorithm 2 depends upon the importance given by the designer to these constraints. For sake of discussion, we assume that $S1$ is more important than $S3$. Hence, we discuss the application of Algorithm 2 when the set of constraints that are preserved is $\{S1, S2, S4\}$ and the sanity constraints. In this case, Algorithm 2 invokes Algorithm 1 where the constraints to be preserved are $S1$, $S2, S4$ and the sanity constraints.

In Line 1 of Algorithm 1, we removes any transition in δ_p that is in $\mathcal{B} \cup \mathcal{B}'$. Transitions that are removed by this line are shown with X in Fig. 3. Next, we call *Behavior_addition* function to add more behavior to the given scheduler. This function receives a program, a set of leads-to properties, and set of bad transition as a safety property. In the Loop of Lines 10–13, *Behavior_addition* tries to add transitions to states that have ranks infinity for some leads-to property. These transitions cannot be in the set of bad transitions $\mathcal{B} \cup \mathcal{B}'$, and must decrease the rank for all leads-to properties, unless the rank for a leads-to property is ∞. Once a new transition is added, the ranks are recomputed. The loop repeats, if there is more transition that can be added. The transitions added by *Behavior_addition* are shown by dashed arrows in Fig. 3.

After *Behavior_addition* added new transitions, we call the *Pruning_addition* algorithm provided in the Appendix. There is no need to pass the set of bad transitions to the *Pruning_addition*, as the program returned by the *Behavior_addition* already satisfies all safety properties. The *Pruning_addition* algorithm removes any transition to a state with rank infinity for some leads-to property. These transitions are marked with * in Fig. 3. This is all that the *Pruning_addition* needs to do, as in the *Behavior_addition* we avoided adding many transitions; we added transitions only to states that actually needed new transitions to satisfy leads-to properties. When *Pruning_addition* is done, Algorithm 1 returns the output of *Prunning_addition*. The final program is shown in Fig. 4.

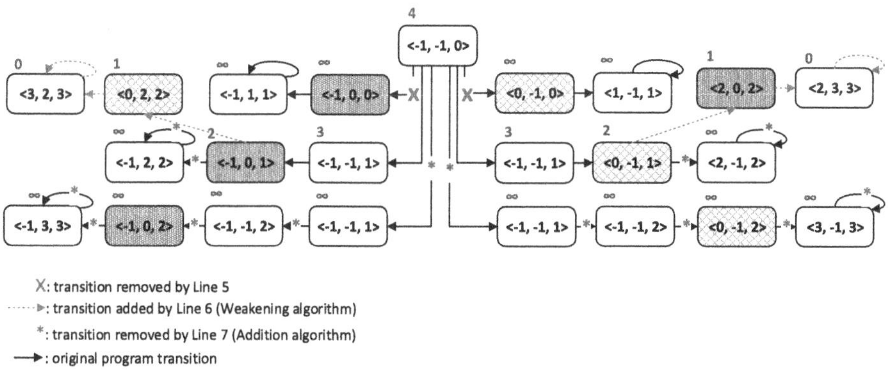

Fig. 3. Running Algorithm 2 on scheduler p shown in Fig. 2. Numbers above the states show the ranks.

7 Related Work

In this paper, we focused on the model repair problem where the existing program is repaired to satisfy a conflicting property. In [2], authors have considered

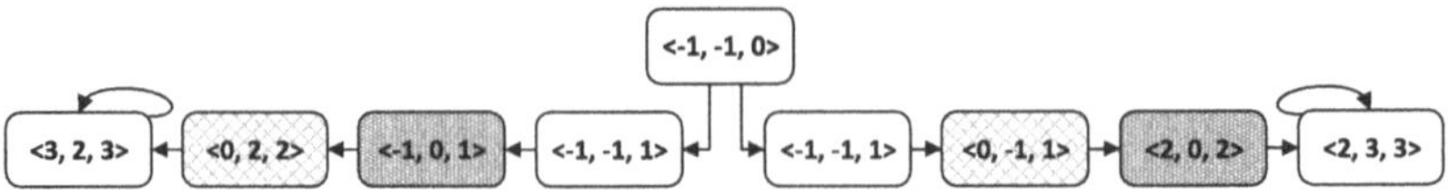

Fig. 4. The revised scheduler

the problem of revising an existing program to add UNITY properties [4]. In [3], authors considered the problem of adding fault-tolerance to an existing program. In [13], authors considered the problem of adding self-stabilization and fault-tolerance in presence of unchangeable environment actions. Model repair for distributed programs using a two phase lazy approach is proposed in [14]. Model repair has also been studied in the context of CTL properties in [5,9]. Model repair for probabilistic programs is considered in [15]. All of these are instances of pruning addition where no new behaviors can be added (in the absence of faults if applicable). Hence, all these approaches guarantee that safety and liveness properties satisfied by the original program are preserved in the repaired program. This implies that if the existing specification conflicts with the new requirements then they will declare failure to synthesize.

In the context of adding fault-tolerance [3,13], behaviors are added only in the states that are reached in the presence of faults. However, these new behaviors are only for a specific purpose, namely recovery to original legitimate states. Likewise, in [10], the problem of graceful degradation is considered. In this work, new behaviors are added outside legitimate states as well. By contrast, in the addition of conflicting properties, we need to introduce new behaviors that are essential to facilitate the satisfaction of the new specification.

Program repair differs from previous work on program synthesis [6–8] in that the latter begins with just a specification and tries to construct the program from scratch. By contrast, model repair focuses on reusing an existing program. Furthermore, due to reuse of an existing program, complexity of model repair is often much lower than that of model synthesis.

Program repair can also assist with traceability [11] that requires one to be able to trace code segments to corresponding properties in the program specification. Thus, newly added transitions in program repair can be traced back to the newly added property.

8 Conclusion

In this paper, we focused on the problem of adding a conflicting specification to an existing program. The need for adding a specification/property arises due to changes in program requirements/environment as well as by bugs identified in the program. The need for adding a *conflicting* specification arises when an existing requirement needs to be *replaced* with a new requirement.

Previous algorithms have focused on adding a new property while preserving all existing properties. This implies that if the new specification and the old specification cannot be satisfied simultaneously, previous approaches must declare a failure. In other words, existing approaches cannot be used when one needs to replace an existing property by another conflicting property.

Adding conflicting properties arises in several contexts. For example, we may want to replace a fairness property so as to permit high and low priority processes. Examples of this instance arise in problems such as mutual exclusion, resource assignment, and so on. It also arises in systems such as traffic control. For example, consider a protocol for traffic movement via signals at an intersection. Given a default protocol that treats every traffic in an identical manner, our approach could be used to design another protocol for night-time when traffic on one road is allowed move uninterrupted while the traffic on another road can move only when there is a gap between the opposite traffic. In general, the ability to replace properties of program allows us to begin with one program and generate a family of related programs (e.g., from a simple traffic light program to one for night-time traffic, one to rush-hour traffic and so on)

To develop an algorithm for adding conflicting properties, we introduced the problem of explicit addition. This problem focuses on preserving only an explicitly specified specification as well as adding more behaviors to satisfy new specification. We presented a sound algorithm that under the assumption made in the paper worked in polynomial time in the size of the state space of the input program.

We demonstrated our algorithm with an example on job scheduling. It illustrated how one can obtain a new scheduling algorithm from an existing scheduling algorithm when requirements change. We note that our solution is also applicable to the other problems discussed in the paper such as changing fairness to priority, changing timing requirements, and so on.

There are several future directions to this work. For one, we intend to combine this with the work on adding fault-tolerance. This would allow us to add fault-tolerance to a program while removing some existing properties that are not compatible with the desired fault-tolerance. We also intend to evaluate the tradeoff between the subset of specification that is satisfied during repair and the cost of repair. Additionally, we intend to evaluate how these algorithms can be applied in other contexts such as embedded and cyber-physical systems. The algorithm provided in this paper can be implemented symbolically, and it is another part of our future work.

References

1. Alpern, B., Schneider, F.B.: Defining liveness. Inf. Process. Lett. **21**, 181–185 (1985)
2. Bonakdarpour, B., Ebnenasir, A., Kulkarni, S.S.: Complexity results in revising UNITY programs. ACM Trans. Auton. Adapt. Syst. (TAAS) **4**(1), 1–28 (2009)
3. Bonakdarpour, B., Kulkarni, S.S., Abujarad, F.: Symbolic synthesis of masking fault-tolerant programs. Springer J. Distrib. Comput. (DC) **25**(1), 83–108 (2012)
4. Chandy, K.M., Misra, J.: Parallel Program Design: A Foundation. Addison-Wesley, Reading (1988)

5. Chatzieleftheriou, G., Bonakdarpour, B., Katsaros, P., Smolka, S.A.: Abstract model repair. Logical Methods in Computer Science 11(3) (2015)
6. Emerson, E.A., Clarke, E.M.: Using branching time temporal logic to synthesize synchronization skeletons. Sci. Comput. Program. **2**(3), 241–266 (1982)
7. Faghih, F., Bonakdarpour, B.: SMT-based synthesis of distributed self-stabilizing systems. TAAS **10**(3), 21 (2015)
8. Finkbeiner, B., Schewe, S.: Bounded synthesis. Int. J. Softw. Tools Technol. Transfer **15**(5), 519–539 (2012)
9. Jobstmann, B., Griesmayer, A., Bloem, R.: Program repair as a game. In: Etessami, K., Rajamani, S.K. (eds.) CAV 2005. LNCS, vol. 3576, pp. 226–238. Springer, Heidelberg (2005). doi:10.1007/11513988_23
10. Lin, Y., Kulkarni, S.S.: Automatic generation of graceful programs. In: IEEE 31st Symposium on Reliable Distributed Systems, SRDS, Irvine, CA, USA, pp. 225–230 (2012)
11. Murugesan, A., Whalen, M.W., Ghassabani, E., Heimdahl, M.P.E.: Complete traceability for requirements in satisfaction arguments. In: Proceedings of the International Conference on Requirements Engineering, Beijing, China September 2016
12. Peterson, G.L.: Myths about the mutual exclusion problem. Inf. Process. Lett. **12**(3), 115–116 (1981)
13. Roohitavaf, M., Kulkarni, S.: Stabilization and fault-tolerance in presence of unchangeable environment actions. In: Proceedings of the 17th International Conference on Distributed Computing, Networking (ICDCN 2016), New York, NY, USA, pp. 19:1–19:10 (2016)
14. Roohitavaf, M., Lin, Y., Kulkarni, S.S.: Lazy repair for addition of fault-tolerance to distributed programs. In: 2016 IEEE International Parallel and Distributed Processing Symposium (IPDPS), IL, USA, Chicago, pp. 1071–1080, May 2016
15. Samanta, R., Deshmukh, J.V., Emerson, E.A.: Automatic generation of local repairs for boolean programs. In: Formal Methods in Computer-Aided Design (FMCAD), pp. 1–10 (2008)

Complete Visibility for Robots with Lights in $O(1)$ Time

Gokarna Sharma[1(✉)], Ramachandran Vaidyanathan[2], Jerry L.Trahan[2], Costas Busch[2], and Suresh Rai[2]

[1] Department of Computer Science, Kent State University, Kent, OH 44242, USA
sharma@cs.kent.edu

[2] School of Electrical Engineering and Computer Science, Louisiana State University, Baton Rouge, LA 70803, USA
{vaidy,jtrahan,srai}@lsu.edu, busch@csc.lsu.edu

Abstract. We consider the problem of repositioning N autonomous robots on a plane so that each robot is visible to all others (the COMPLETE VISIBILITY problem); a robot cannot see another robot if its visibility is obstructed by a third robot positioned between them on a straight line. This problem is important since it provides a basis to solve many other problems under obstructed visibility. Robots operate following *Look-Compute-Move* (LCM) cycles and communicate with other robots using colored lights as in the recently proposed *robots with lights* model. The challenge posed by this model is that each robot has only a constant number of colors for its lights (symbols for communication) and no memory (except for the persistence of lights) between LCM cycles. Our goal is to minimize the number of rounds needed to solve COMPLETE VISIBILITY, where a round is measured as the time duration for all robots to execute at least one complete LCM cycle since the end of the previous round. The best previously known algorithm for COMPLETE VISIBILITY on this robot model has runtime of $O(\log N)$ rounds. That algorithm has the assumptions of full synchronicity, chirality, and robot paths may collide. In this paper we present the first algorithm for COMPLETE VISIBILITY with $O(1)$ runtime that runs on the semi-synchronous (and also the fully synchronous) model. The proposed algorithm is deterministic, does not have the chirality assumption, and is collision free.

1 Introduction

In the classical model of distributed computing by mobile robots, each robot is modeled as a point in the plane that is equipped with a local coordinate system and sensory capabilities to determine the positions of other robots [10]. The robots are *autonomous* (no external control), *anonymous* (no unique identifiers), *indistinguishable* (no external identifiers), and possibly *disoriented* (no agreement on local coordinate systems and units of distance measures). They execute the same algorithm. Each robot proceeds in *Look-Compute-Move* (LCM) cycles; that is, when a robot becomes active, it uses its sensory capabilities to get a

B. Bonakdarpour and F. Petit (Eds.): SSS 2016, LNCS 10083, pp. 327–345, 2016.
DOI: 10.1007/978-3-319-49259-9_26

snapshot of its surroundings (*Look*), then computes a destination point based on the snapshot (*Compute*), and finally moves towards the destination point (*Move*). Furthermore, the robots are assumed to be *oblivious* in the sense that in each cycle, each robot has no memory of its past LCM cycles [10].

Although the robots in the classical model have vision and mobility, they are *silent* because they do not communicate directly, and only vision and mobility enable the robots to coordinate their actions. While silence has advantages, for example in hostile environments, in many other situations direct communication is assumed. A model that incorporates direct communication is called *robots with lights* [7,10,15]. In this model, each robot is provided with a local externally visible light which can assume colors from a fixed constant size set; robots explicitly communicate with each other using these colors. The colors are persistent; i.e., the color is not erased at the end of a cycle. Except for the lights, the robots are oblivious as in the classical model.

Much of the work on both the classical model and the model of robots with lights assumes that visibility is *unobstructed*; that is, three collinear robots are assumed to be visible to each other. The notion of *obstructed visibility* is captured in the so-called *fat robot* model where robots are non-transparent unit discs [1,6]. However, the fat robot model does not assume the availability of lights.

Di Luna et al. [13] gave the first algorithm for robots with lights under obstructed visibility to solve the fundamental COMPLETE VISIBILITY problem: Given an arbitrary initial configuration of robots located in distinct points on a plane, reach a configuration in which each robot is in a distinct position from which it can see all other robots. This problem is important since it provides a basis to solve many other problems requiring complete visibility among robots under obstructed visibility. Moreover, robots cannot share positions during the execution of the algorithm to reach a complete visibility configuration, that is, sharing the same position by two or more robots constitutes a robot collision. Initially some robots may be obstructed from the view of other robots and the total number of robots, N, is not known to robots. The solution of Di Luna et al. [13] arranges robots on corners of a convex polygon, which naturally solves the COMPLETE VISIBILITY problem. They proved the correctness of their algorithm but gave no runtime analysis except a proof of its termination in finite time. Runtime is measured in terms of rounds. A *round* ends as soon as all robots have executed at least one complete LCM cycle since the end of the previous round [5].

Recently, Vaidyanathan et al. [17] presented an algorithm for this problem which has a running time of $O(\log N)$ rounds for any initial configuration of $N \geq 4$ robots in the fully synchronous setting (where all robots are active in all rounds). However, their solution allows the paths of robots to cross. Moreover, their solution assumes *chirality* [10] – robots agree on the orientation of the axes of their local coordinate system. The focus of other recent work is only on solvability, minimizing the number of colors and does not provide runtime. The goal of this work is to develop an optimal algorithm with constant runtime and constant number of colors for COMPLETE VISIBILITY on the robots with lights model.

Contributions. We consider the same robot model as in the work of Di Luna et al. [13], namely, robots are oblivious except for a persistent light that can assume a constant number of colors. Visibility could be obstructed by other robots in the line of sight. We assume that N is not known and the robots may be disoriented. We consider the fully synchronous and semi-synchronous models of computation (Sect. 2). Moreover, we assume that a robot in motion cannot be stopped (by an adversary). As in the model of Di Luna et al. [13], we assume that two robots cannot head to the same destination point (this would constitute a collision). In this paper, we present, to our knowledge, the first algorithm for COMPLETE VISIBILITY which has the running time of constant rounds and uses a constant number of colors. In particular, we prove the following theorem.

Theorem 1. *For any initial configuration of $N \geq 1$ robots with lights, there is a deterministic algorithm that solves* COMPLETE VISIBILITY *in $O(1)$ rounds with $O(1)$ colors and without collisions on the semi-synchronous model.*

Our algorithm is deterministic and has three phases: Phase 0 (*initialization*), that breaks up any initial linear arrangement of robots and places all robots within or on a convex polygon P (convex hull of points); Phase 1 (*interior depletion*), which places all robots on the corners or sides of a convex polygon P'; and Phase 2 (*edge depletion*), which moves each robot on a side of P' to a corner of a new convex polygon P''. Key to Phase 1 is a *corner moving* procedure that permits all interior robots to see all corners of the hull. Key to Phase 2 is a *corner insertion* procedure that moves robots to corners while retaining convexity. Both the corner moving and corner insertion procedures may have independent interest.

Previous Work. The problem of uniformly spreading robots in a line, studied by Cohen and Peleg [4], considers the case of obstructed visibility, but these robots have no lights. The work of Pagli et al. [14] considers a problem where collisions must be avoided between robots. However, they do not provide runtime analysis. Similarly, much work on the classical robot model (with no lights) [2,4,16,18] showed that GATHERING (robots come together to be in a not predefined point) is achieved in finite time without a full runtime analysis, except in a few cases [8,9,12]. Furthermore, Izumi et al. [11] considered the robot scattering problem (opposite of the gathering problem) in the semi-synchronous setting and provided a solution with an expected runtime of $O(\min\{N, D^2 + \log N\})$; here D is the diameter of the initial configuration.

Paper Organization. In Sect. 2 we provide details of our model and some preliminaries. For clarity, the COMPLETE VISILIBITY algorithm is first presented for the fully synchronous model in Sect. 3. The conversion of the algorithm to the semi-synchronous model is discussed in Sect. 4. We then conclude in Sect. 5. Many proofs, details, and pseudocodes are omitted due to space constraints.

2 Model and Preliminaries

This paper uses a distributed system of N robots (agents) with index from set $\mathcal{R} = \{0, 1, \cdots, N-1\}$. We will then use a variable, for example r, to indicate a robot on or the point on the plane it is positioned at. Each robot is a (dimensionless) point that can move in an infinite 2-dimensional real space $\mathbb{R}^2$. A robot i can see, and be visible to, another robot j iff there is no third robot k in the line segment joining i and j. Each robot has a light that can assume one of a constant number of colors.

Look-Compute-Move. Each robot i is either active or inactive. When a robot i becomes active, it performs the "Look-Compute-Move" cycle described below.

- *Look:* For each robot j that is visible to it, robot i can observe the position of j on the plane and the color of the light of j. Robot i can also observe its own color and position; that is, i is visible to itself. Each robot observes position on its own frame of reference. That is, two different robots observing the position of the same point may produce different coordinates. However a robot observes the positions of points accurately within its own reference frame.
- *Compute:* In any cycle, robot i may perform an arbitrary computation using only the colors and positions observed during the "look" portion of that cycle. This computation also includes determination of a (possibly) new position and light color for i for the start of next cycle. Robot i maintains this new color from the current cycle to the next cycle.
- *Move:* At the end of the cycle, robot i moves to its new position and changes its light to the new color.

In the fully synchronous model, every robot is active in every LCM cycle. In the semi-synchronous model, a subset of robots (zero to all) in $\mathcal{R}$ are active, and over an infinite number of LCM cycles, every robot is active infinitely often. In the fully synchronous model, one round is always one LCM cycle. In the semi-synchronous model, a round can take an arbitrary number of LCM cycles. Depending on the activation schedule, some robots may be active for many cycles in a round before every robot has been active at least once. Note that our time bounds for the semi-synchronous model hold regardless of the activation schedule.

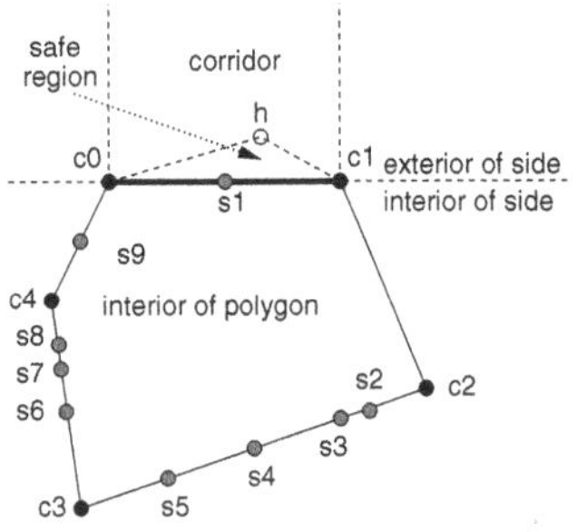

Convex Polygon. For $N \geq 3$, a *convex polygon* can be represented as a sequence $\mathbb{P} = (c_0, c_1, \cdots, c_{N-1})$ of *corner points* in a plane that enumerates the polygon vertices in clockwise order. A point s on the plane is a *side point* of $\mathbb{P}$ iff there exists $0 \leq i < N$ such that $c_i, s, c_{(i+1)(\text{mod } N)}$ are collinear; for the rest of the paper we will implicitly assume the above modulo operation and write $c_{(i+1)(\text{mod } N)} =$

c_{i+1}. A side $S = (c_i, s_1, s_2, \cdots, s_m, c_{i+1})$ is a sequence of collinear points whose beginning and end are adjacent corner points and whose remaining points are side points. We write $\overline{pq}$ for a line segment connecting two points p, q and denote by $\mathsf{length}(\overline{pq})$ its length. For a given polygon $\mathbb{P}$, the plane can be divided into the interior and exterior parts. For a given side S of $\mathbb{P}$, the infinite line obtained by extending side S divides the plane into the interior and exterior parts of the side. The interior part of S contains the interior of the polygon. The *corridor* of S is the infinite subregion on its exterior that is bounded by S and perpendicular lines through points c_i, c_{i+1} of S. The corridors of the sides of $\mathbb{P}$ are disjoint. The figure above illustrates these concepts.

Lines and Angles of View. For any robot r, let V_r be the set of robots (other than itself) visible to r. Let L_1, L_2 be lines through robot r, such that θ_1 is the smallest induced angle at r whose region accommodates all robots of V_r; call this the *region of view* of r. The line segments of L_1, L_2 that border the region of view of r are called the *lines of view* of r and the associated angle is called the *angle of view* of r. These ideas can also be used with a subset of the robots visible to r. The figure below illustrates these ideas: In the left part all elements of $V_r = \{r_2, r_3, r_4, r_6\}$ are considered; in the right part only r_3, r_4, r_6 are considered.

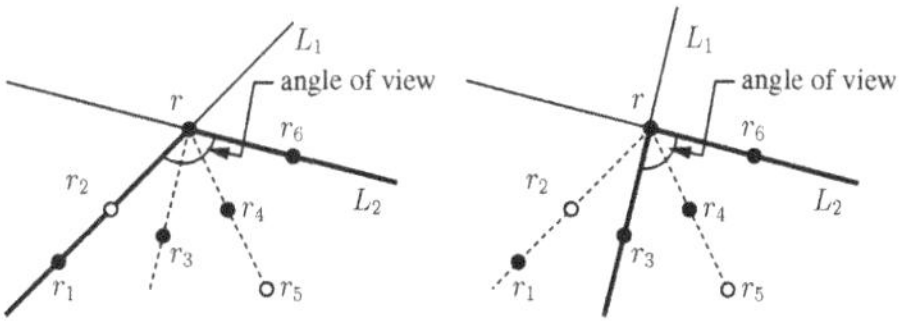

Configuration and Local Convex Polygon. A *configuration* $\mathbb{C} = \{(p_0, col_0), \ldots, (p_{N-1}, col_{N-1})\}$ defines the positions of the robots in $\mathcal{R}$ and their colors; here $p_i = (x_i, y_i)$ is the position of robot i and col_i is the color of its light. A configuration for a robot $i \in \mathcal{R}$, $\mathbb{C}(i)$, is a configuration that defines the positions of the robots in $\mathcal{R}$ that are visible to i (including i) and their colors, i.e., $\mathbb{C}(i) \subseteq \mathbb{C}$. The convex hull of points in $\mathbb{C}(i)$ is denoted by $\mathbb{P}(i)$. $\mathbb{P}(i)$ is *local* to i since $\mathbb{P}(i)$ depends only on the points that are visible to i. We sometime write $\mathbb{C}_t, \mathbb{P}_t, \mathbb{C}_t(i), \mathbb{P}_t(i)$ to denote $\mathbb{C}, \mathbb{P}, \mathbb{C}(i), \mathbb{P}(i)$, respectively, for any round $t \geq 0$. Moreover, we sometime write $\mathbb{C}(r_i), \mathbb{P}(r_i)$ instead of $\mathbb{C}(i), \mathbb{P}(i)$.

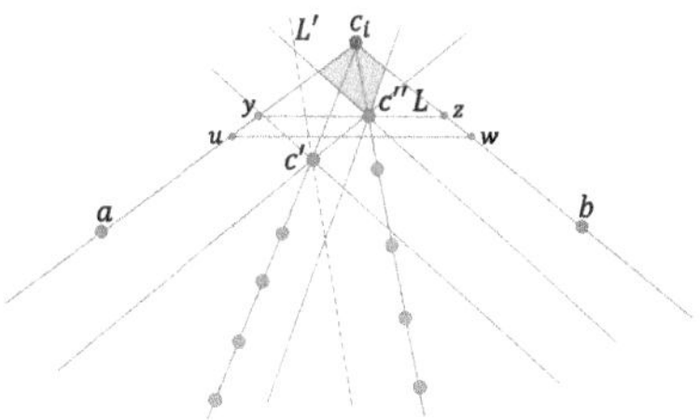

Eligible Area. Let $\mathcal{A}$ be a set of points and $\mathbb{P}$ be the convex polygon of the points in $\mathcal{A}$. Let R_c, R_s, R_i be the set of points at corners, sides, and the interior of $\mathbb{P}$. Moreover, let c_i be a corner point of $\mathbb{P}$ and a, b be the counterclockwise and clockwise neighbors of c_i in the perimeter of $\mathbb{P}$. The *eligible area* for c_i, denoted as $EA(c_i)$, is a polygonal subregion inside $\mathbb{P}$ within the triangle $c_i uw$, where u, w are the midpoints of edges $\overline{c_i a}, \overline{c_i b}$, respectively. It is easy to show that the eligible areas for any two corner points of $\mathbb{P}$ are disjoint. Due to obstructed visibility, $EA(c_i)$ is computed based on $\mathbb{C}(c_i)$ and the corresponding polygon $\mathbb{P}(c_i)$. One prominent property of the eligible area is that c_i remains a corner of $\mathbb{P}$ even after it moves to any point inside $EA(c_i)$ (except the points on the lines going through $EA(c_i)$). The other prominent property is that all the points in R_s, R_i are visible to c_i (and vice-versa), when c_i moves to any point inside $EA(c_i)$. This computation is used in Phase 1 of our algorithm.

We outline here how $EA(c_i)$ is computed for any corner point c_i of $\mathbb{P}$. The pseudocode is omitted due to space constraints. Initially, c_i sets the triangle c_iuw as its $EA(c_i)$. However, if c_i sees some point of $\mathcal{A}$ inside c_iuw, then it sets as $EA(c_i)$ the triangle c_iyz such that there is no point inside c_iyz. Note that $\overline{yz}$ is parallel to $\overline{ab}$. Let c' be a point in $\mathbb{C}(c_i)$. For every other point $c'' \in \mathbb{C}(c_i), c'' \neq c', c'' \neq c_i$, c_i computes a line, L', parallel to $\overline{c_ic''}$ passing through c'. Let HP be the half-plane divided by L' such that c_i is in HP. Corner c_i then updates its $EA(c_i)$ by keeping only the portion of $EA(c_i)$ that is in the half-plane HP. This process is repeated for all $c' \in \mathbb{C}(c_i)\backslash\{c_i\}$ and $EA(c_i)$ is updated in every iteration. Now from the area $EA(c_i)$ that remains, c_i removes the points that are in the perimeter of $EA(c_i)$ and also the points that are part of the lines $\overleftrightarrow{c_ix}, x \in \mathbb{C}(c_i)\backslash\{a, b, c_i\}$, passing from inside of $EA(c_i)$. This removal of points is crucial to guarantee that when c_i moves to a point in $EA(c_i)$, it does not become collinear with any robot in R_s, R_i. The figure above illustrates the computation of $EA(c_i)$; the shaded area is $EA(c_i)$ except the points on the lines inside it (e.g., the point of lines $\overline{c_ic'}$ and $\overline{c_ic''}$ inside $EA(c_i)$).

Lemma 1. *The eligible area $EA(c_i)$ for each corner robot c_i in $\mathbb{P}$ is non-empty. Moreover, when c_i moves to a point inside $EA(c_i)$, then c_i remains as a corner of $\mathbb{P}$ and all internal and side robots in $\mathbb{P}$ are visible to c_i (and vice-versa).*

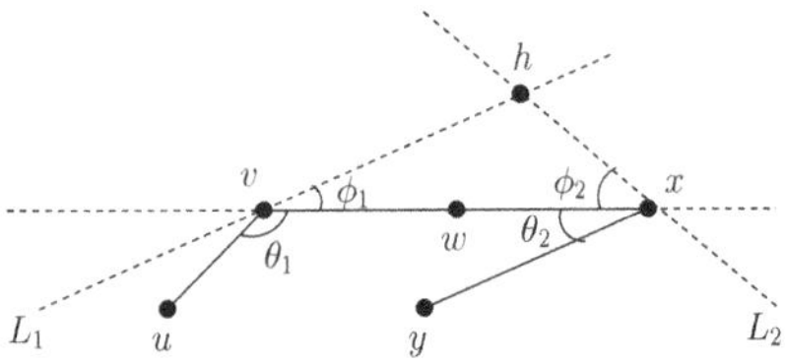

Safe Angle and Apex. Let u, v, w, x, y be points such that (a) v, w, x are collinear with w between v and x, (b) u, y are not collinear with line segment v, w, x, and (c) u, y lie on the same side of line v, w, x such that line segments $\overline{uv}$ and $\overline{xy}$ do not intersect. The figure below illustrates safe angles and apex. Define (non-reflex) angles $\theta_1, \theta_2 < 180°$ as $\theta_1 = \angle(u, v, w)$ and $\theta_2 = \angle(w, x, y)$. Let $\phi_1 = 45° - \frac{\theta_1}{4}$ and $\phi_2 = 45° - \frac{\theta_2}{4}$ be the "safe angles" for v and x, respectively. Let L_1 (resp., L_2) be the line traversing point v (resp., x) such that it forms an angle ϕ_1 (resp., ϕ_2) with line segment v, w, x as shown in the figure in the right. Since$\phi_1, \phi_2 < 45°$, lines L_1, L_2 will intersect on the side of line v, w, x, opposite to that of points u, y. Call this point of intersection h as the *safe apex* of w with respect to (or wrt)u, v, x, y.

Observe that if $\overline{vx}$ is a side S of $\mathbb{P}$ with v, x as corner points and w as a side point, and if u, y are adjacent corner points for side S, then define triangle v, x, h as the *safe area* for side S. The pseudocode outlining the technique of computing safe apex for a side robot s_i of $\mathbb{P}$ is omitted due to space constraints. This is used in Phase 2 of our algorithm.

3 Algorithm in the Fully Synchronous Model

We outline an $O(1)$ round algorithm for Complete Visibility in the fully synchronous model; we will then convert this algorithm for the semi-synchronous model in Sect. 4. Our algorithm consists of three phases converging toward a configuration where all the robots are in a convex hull (see Fig. 1). The goal of Phase 0 is to reposition robots (if needed) so that they are inside or on the corners and sides of a convex polygon $\mathbb{P}$. Phase 0 (initialization) is performed if a robot i sees only at most two other robots and the robots seen by i are in a line (this case happens only if $N \geq 2$ in $\mathcal{R}$ and all N robots are collinear). If i sees two other robots, it moves small distance δ directly perpendicular to the line joining $j, l \in \mathbb{C}(i)$. If $N \geq 3$, this action ensures that in the resulting configuration not all robots are collinear. Figure 1a depicts a worst case scenario where all robots are initially collinear.

Phase 1 (interior depletion) starts as soon as the robots in $\mathbb{C}_0$ reach a non-collinear configuration (robots on or in convex polygon $\mathbb{P}$). In Phase 1 the algorithm first identifies corner and side robots as follows (Fig. 1b). For robot i, if all other visible robots are within an angle of view of $< 180°$ (respectively, $= 180°$), then i is a corner (resp., side) robot of a convex polygon $\mathbb{P}$. The remaining robots (that lie in the interior of $\mathbb{P}$) are called "interior robots". Phase 1 moves all interior points of $\mathbb{P}$ to the sides of a slightly smaller convex polygon $\mathbb{P}'$ (Fig. 1e). It accomplishes this by first moving the corner robots of $\mathbb{P}$ to some point inside the eligible area in the interior of $\mathbb{P}$, where now all the corner robots are visible to the interior robots (Fig. 1b). The interior robots then move toward the closest corners of $\mathbb{P}'$ (Fig. 1c), and finally to the sides of $\mathbb{P}'$ (Fig. 1d). We show later that this phase runs in $O(1)$ rounds in any configuration of the robots.

Phase 2 (edge depletion) relocates side robots of $\mathbb{P}'$ to the corners of a slightly larger convex polygon $\mathbb{P}''$. It accomplishes this by moving only the side robots of $\mathbb{P}'$ into the safe area of the side they belong to. This proceeds by first moving two side robots that are neighbors of the corner robots of that side to the safe area (Fig. 1f), after that forming a circle segment using the information provided by three of (at most) four robots (two endpoints of the side, and one of the two robots that moved to the safe area, as shown in Fig. 1g), and then moving all other remaining side robots of that side perpendicularly to the points in the formed circle segment for the side. Figure 1h shows the resulting convex hull. This phase also runs in $O(1)$ rounds irrespective of the number of side robots in any side of $\mathbb{P}'$.

The pseudocode of the algorithm is omitted due to space constraints. Each robot i works autonomously having only the information about $\mathbb{C}(i)$. If $\mathbb{P}(i)$ is not a line segment for each $i \in \mathcal{R}$, then Phase 1 starts immediately. If $\mathbb{P}(i)$ is a line segment, then in one round, the robots in $\mathbb{C}_0$ result into a non-collinear configuration $\mathbb{C}_0$ and Phase 1 starts in the second round. Phase 1 proceeds autonomously until all (visible) robots are colored either `corner` or `side`. This acts as the starting configuration for Phase 2, which proceeds autonomously until all (visible) robots have color `corner`. The algorithm then terminates. The total number of colors used through Phases 0–2 is 9 and the algorithm runs for

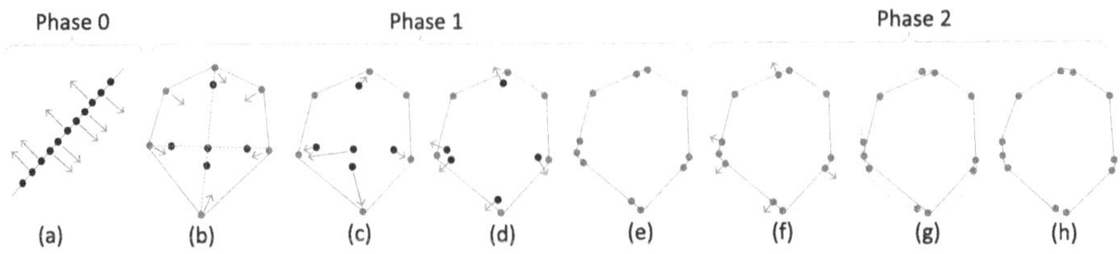

Fig. 1. The three phases of the algorithm.

(at most) 9 rounds. We provide details of Phases 0–2 separately below. The moves of each robot in Phases 0–2 can also be described as condition/action pairs (which we omit due to space constraints).

3.1 Phase 0 - Initialization

Initially, all $N \geq 1$ robots in $\mathcal{R}$ have color `start`. Assume that $\mathbb{C}_0$ is collinear (otherwise, this phase is not required). We have that $\mathbb{P}$ is a line segment. Let $r_j, \ldots, r_l$ be the robots in $\mathbb{P}$ (a line segment $\overline{r_j r_l}$) with r_j, r_l be the endpoints. Let x be a robot in $\overline{r_j r_l}$ between r_j, r_l and let y, z be two other robots it sees. Robot x moves perpendicular to line $\overline{yz}$ for a short distance δ keeping its color `start` in the first round. Robots r_j, r_l change their color to `ready` without moving, since they see only one other robot. At the end of the first round, it is impossible for robots in $\mathcal{R}$ to be in a straight line, if $N \geq 3$. Consequently, there exists polygonal $\mathbb{P}$ on or in which all robots lie. If $N = 2$, one robot sees the light of one other robot with color `ready` and figures out that there are only 2 robots in $\mathcal{R}$ and terminates. This happens at the second (and final) round. If a robot x sees no other robot, it can simply terminate.

3.2 Phase 1 - Interior Depletion

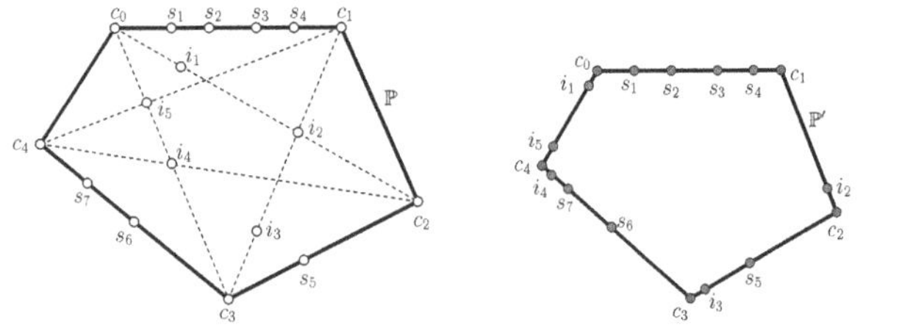

(a) Initial positions and colors (b) Final positions and colors

At the start of Phase 1, each robot is colored `start` or `ready`. All the robots in $\mathcal{R}$ are colored `start` if Phase 0 was not executed. A robot with color `ready` is located at a corner of $\mathbb{P}$ and a robot with color `start` is located at a corner or side or in the interior of $\mathbb{P}$. Let R_c, R_s, R_i be the sets of robots at corners, sides, and the interior of $\mathbb{P}$. Let $\mathbb{P}'$ be a convex hull formed by the robots in R_c after they moved to a point in their eligible areas, $EA(*)$, and have assumed color `corner`. Note that $\mathbb{P}'$ is completely contained inside $\mathbb{P}$. The goal of Phase 1 is to move the robots in sets R_s, R_i to make them side robots of $\mathbb{P}'$ with color `side`. Therefore, at the end of Phase 1, all the robots are in the corners and edges of $\mathbb{P}'$ with corner robots colored `corner` and side robots colored `side`. The figure above illustrates Phase 1.

Phase 1 has four rounds. In Round 1.1, all corners of $\mathbb{P}$ become corners of $\mathbb{P}'$ with color `corner` and the side robots of $\mathbb{P}$ change their color to `side1` without moving. In Round 1.2, all interior robots of $\mathbb{P}$ (also interior in $\mathbb{P}'$) assume color `transit` moving closer to their closest corners in $\mathbb{P}'$ and the robots with color `side1` move to the closest sides of $\mathbb{P}'$ assuming color `side`. In Round 1.3, some `transit` colored robots become side robots of $\mathbb{P}'$ and, by the end of Round 1.4, all `transit` colored robots become side robots of $\mathbb{P}'$.

We give details on each round separately below.

Round 1.1: Each corner r_c of $\mathbb{P}$ (the robot is in R_c) computes its eligible area $EA(r_c)$, moves to a point x in $EA(r_c)$, and assumes color `corner`. Since all the robots in R_c move simultaneously, they all become corners of $\mathbb{P}'$ by the end of Round 1.1 and do not move in any future rounds (Lemma 1). The side robots R_s of $\mathbb{P}$ also change their color to `side1` from `start` at Round 1.1 without moving. The interior robots of R_i do nothing. The figure on the right illustrates this round. We have the following results by the end of Round 1.1.

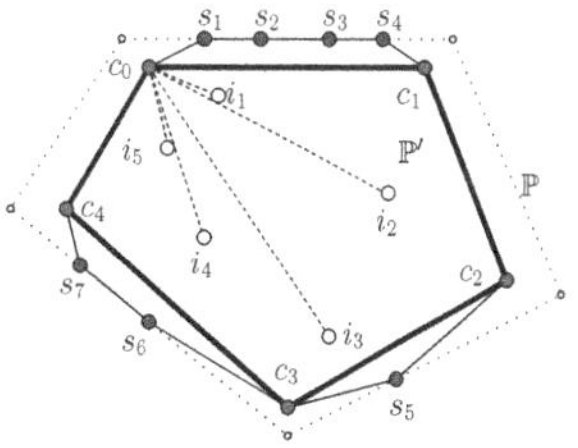

Lemma 2. *The set of robots R_i in the interior of $\mathbb{P}$ remain as interior robots of $\mathbb{P}'$.*

Observation 1. *Let r_c be a corner robot in $\mathbb{P}'$. Let r_{ccw}, r_{cw} be the neighbor corners of r_c in $\mathbb{P}'$ in the counterclockwise and clockwise directions of r_c, respectively, in its local coordinate system. Robot r_c sees both r_{ccw}, r_{cw}. (c_1 and c_4 for corner c_0 in the figure above.)*

Round 1.2: Since each $r_c \in R_c$ moved to $EA(r_c)$ and become a corner of $\mathbb{P}'$ in Round 1.1, all the robots in R_i, R_s see all corner robots of $\mathbb{P}'$ (Lemma 1) and each internal robot $r_i \in R_i$ can determine the closest corner robot r_c in $\mathbb{P}'$. Robot r_i can also see r_c's neighbors r_{ccw} and r_{cw} in $\mathbb{P}'$ (Lemma 1). Moreover, all robots in R_i are in the interior of $\mathbb{P}'$ (Lemma 2). We need the following definition.

Definition 1. Let r_c, r_{ccw}, r_{cw} be the robots defined in Observation 1. The line segment $\overline{xy}$ connects points x, y, where $x = \mathsf{length}(\overline{r_c r_{ccw}})/8$ from r_c in line $\overline{r_c r_{ccw}}$ and $y = \mathsf{length}(\overline{r_c r_{cw}})/8$ from r_c in line $\overline{r_c r_{cw}}$.

Interior robot r_i determines the line $\overline{xy}$, moves to the the intersection point z of $\overline{xy}$ and $\overleftrightarrow{r_i r_c}$, and assumes color `transit`. The robots in R_s (which were colored `side1` in Round 1.1) also see all the corner robots of $\mathbb{P}'$. Let S be a side of $\mathbb{P}'$ such that a robot $r_s \in R_s$ is in its corridor. Let $\hat{S} = \overline{x'y'}$ be the line segment connecting point x', y', where x' is

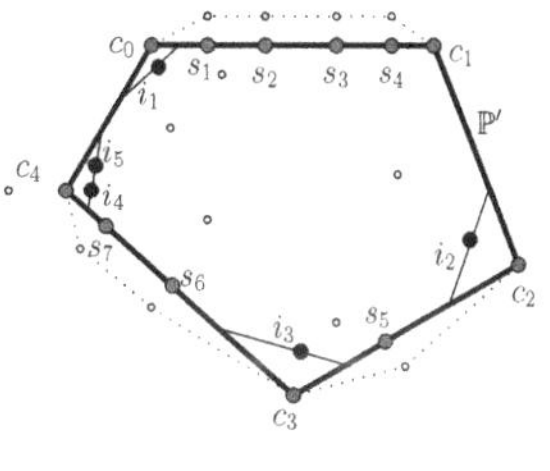

the point at S at distance $\mathsf{length}(S)/4$ from its one endpoint and y' is the point at distance $\mathsf{length}(S)/4$ from its other endpoint. Let p be the midpoint of $\hat{S}$ and $\alpha = \angle x'pr_s$. Robot r_s computes point $q = \frac{\alpha}{180°} \cdot \mathsf{length}(\hat{S})$ from x' on $\hat{S}$, moves to q, and assumes color `side`. This computation of q guarantees that each angle α is mapped to a different position q on $\hat{S}$ and q does not coincide with either x' or y' [17]. The figure above illustrates this round. We have the following observations at the end of Round 1.2.

Observation 2. *The internal robots R_i are in the lines $\overline{xy}$ of the corner robots of $\mathbb{P}'$ and the side robots R_s are in the sides of $\mathbb{P}'$.*

Observation 3. *Let S be a side in $\mathbb{P}'$. If there are robots on S, they are in the positions of S between points $x' = \mathsf{length}(S)/4$ from one endpoint of S and $y' = \mathsf{length}(S)/4$ from the other endpoint of S.*

Round 1.3: The robots in R_s do not move in the remaining rounds of Phase 1 since they already have become side robots of $\mathbb{P}'$ in Round 1.2. Therefore, we only deal with the internal robots in R_i (all are colored `transit`) in this and the next round. Using the same notation as in Round 1.2, each $r_i \in R_i$ sees r_c (the closest corner of $\mathbb{P}'$) even after it has moved to point z in $\overline{xy}$. If r_i sees both r_{ccw} and r_{cw} (as defined in Observation 1), it can move to become a side robot of $\mathbb{P}'$ as follows: r_i draws two lines L and L' parallel to line segments $\overline{r_c r_{ccw}}, \overline{r_c r_{cw}}$, respectively, passing through r_i, then moves to the intersection point of $L, \overline{r_c r_{cw}}$ or $L', \overline{r_c r_{ccw}}$ whichever is closest to r_i (with respect to the distance from r_i to the intersection points) and assumes color `side`.

There are situations where r_i may not see r_{ccw} and/or r_{cw}, for example, the moves of other internal robots in R_i with the closest corners r_{ccw}, r_{cw} may block the visibility of r_i to see r_{ccw}, r_{cw}. In this case, r_i tries to find whether it sees two robots, s_a, s_b, with color `side` as the adjacent robots of r_c in $\mathbb{P}'$, instead of r_{ccw}, r_{cw}.

Lemma 3. *Let r_c be the closest corner of $r_i \in R_i$. If $r_i \in \overline{xy}$ sees two robots s_a, s_b with color `side` adjacent to r_c in the counterclockwise and clockwise direction of r_c, respectively, then all the robots in $\overline{xy}$ see both s_a, s_b.*

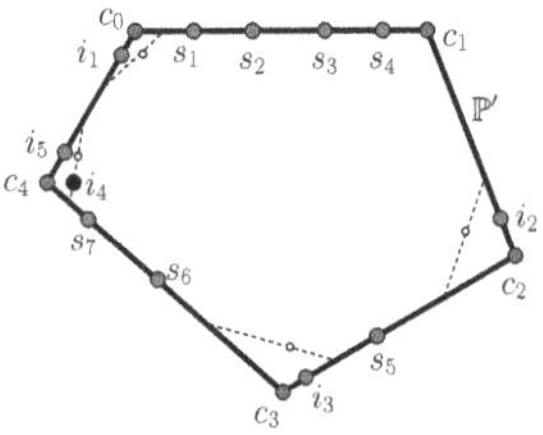

Robot r_i draws two lines L and L' parallel to line segments $\overline{r_c s_a}, \overline{r_c s_b}$, respectively (instead of $\overline{r_c r_{ccw}}, \overline{r_c r_{cw}}$), passing through r_i, and then moves to the intersection point of $L, \overline{r_c s_b}$ or $L', \overline{r_c s_a}$ whichever is closest to r_i (with respect to the distance from r_i to the intersection points) and assumes color `side`. The figure to the right illustrates this round. If each $r_i \in R_i$ sees either both s_a, s_b with color `side` or both r_{ccw}, r_{cw}, all the robots in R_i become side robots of $\mathbb{P}'$ in this round and Phase 1 finishes.

However, there are situations where all the robots in R_i may not even see both s_a, s_b. In this case, we have the following lemma.

Lemma 4. *Let $r_i \in R_i$ be the robot in line $\overline{xy}$ of corner r_c and $r_j \in R_i$ be the robot in line $\overline{xy}$ of corner r_{cw}. Suppose r_i, r_j are closest to the side $\overline{r_c r_{cw}}$ of $\mathbb{P}'$ among the robots in their lines $\overline{xy}$. At least one of r_i, r_j sees both r_c, r_{cw}.*

Proof. Robots r_i, r_c, r_{cw} form a triangle which is non-empty. Robot r_i sees r_c since there is no robot inside triangle $r_c xy$ and all robots closest to r_c are in line segment $\overline{xy}$. If r_i sees r_{cw}, we are done. Otherwise, r_j or some other robot in the line $\overline{xy}$ of r_{cw} must be collinear with side $\overline{r_i r_{cw}}$. Since r_j is the closest robot to side $\overline{r_c r_{cw}}$ and there is no robot in side $\overline{r_i r_c}$, r_j must see r_c. Moreover, r_j sees r_{cw} since r_{cw} is the closest corner to it. □

Therefore, either of r_i, r_j that sees both r_c, r_{cw} moves to the point at $\mathsf{length}(\overline{r_c r_{cw}})/4$ from its closest corner in $\mathbb{P}'$ in $\overline{r_c r_{cw}}$ and assumes color `side`.

Lemma 5. *Let $S = \overline{c_1 c_2}$ be a side of $\mathbb{P}'$. When a robot r' with light* `transit` *in a line $\overline{xy}$ of c_1 (or c_2) moves to a point at $\mathsf{length}(S)/4$ in S from c_1 (or c_2), then all the robots in lines xy of both c_1 and c_2 see r'.*

Proof. Let S' denote the other side incident on c_1 in $\mathbb{P}'$. Similar to Lemma 3, since the line $\overline{xy}$ of c_1 connects points $x = \mathsf{length}(S')/8$ from c_1 in S' and $x = \mathsf{length}(S)/8$ from c_1 in S and r' is in position $\mathsf{length}(S)/8$ from c_1 in S, the robots in $\overline{xy}$ can not be collinear with r'. Similarly, it holds for the robots in $\overline{xy}$ closest to c_2. □

Round 1.4: If Phase 1 did not finish in Round 1.3, each $r_i \in R_i$ sees r_c (the closest corner in $\mathbb{P}'$) and a robot each with light `side` as neighbors of r_c in both directions of r_c at the end of Round 1.3 (Lemma 5). The part b of the figure in the beginning of this section illustrates this round as i_4 moves to a side of $\mathbb{P}'$ and assumes color `side`. The move technique is similar to Round 1.3. We prove the following results for Phase 1.

Lemma 6. *At every round of Phase 1, each robot sees at least one robot with color from* {`start`, `ready`, `side1`, `transit`}.

Proof. Initially, all robots have color `start`. Some robot assume color `ready` if robots execute Phase 0. Therefore, at Round 1.1, each robot sees only `ready` or `start` colored robots. At Rounds 1.2 and 1.3 robots must see some robot with color in {`start`, `ready`, `side1`, `transit`}, otherwise there will be only `corner` and `side` colored robots in $\mathbb{P}'$ and Phase 1 execution is finished. □

Theorem 2. *Given a set of N robots placed on corners, sides, and interior of a convex polygon $\mathbb{P}$ such that all robots have color either* `start` *or* `ready`, *Phase 1 executes in at most four (fully synchronous) rounds avoiding collisions and uses 6 colors.*

Proof. We first prove that the rounds of Phase 1 follow in the order indicated by their names and if any round is skipped then all the robots are already colored either `corner` or `side` and they are in the perimeter of $\mathbb{P}'$.

Phase 1 begins when the set of colors visible to each robot is {start, ready}. This causes Round 1.1 to be executed by corner and side robots of $\mathbb{P}$. Since internal and side robots do not move until they see robots with light corner, Round 1.2 follows Round 1.1. All side robots of $\mathbb{P}$ become side robots of $\mathbb{P}'$ in Round 1.2 and do not move in future rounds. Similarly, Round 1.3 follows Round 1.2 since this is the first time internal robots have light transit. Similarly, Round 1.4 follows Round 1.3 since this is the first time the internal robots that did not see side robots as neighbors of their closest corner robot of $\mathbb{P}'$ will see such side robots.

Initially, all robots have color start. In Phase 0, only color ready is introduced. At Rounds 1.1, 1.2, and 1.3, colors {side1, transit, corner, side} are introduced. Therefore, there are total 6 colors.

We now show that the execution of Phase 1 is collision free. In Round 1.1, a corner robot r_c does not collide with any side or internal robot of $\mathbb{P}$ while moving to a point inside $EA(r_c)$ since there is no robot inside $EA(r_c)$. Robot r_c does not collide with any other corner robot r_d since eligible areas for any two corner robots of $\mathbb{P}$ do not overlap.

In Round 1.2, the robots with color side1 of $\mathbb{P}$ moving to become side robots of $\mathbb{P}'$ with color side do not collide, since the technique they use to find a point to move to in $\mathbb{P}$ guarantees that all robots moving to a side do not collide. The interior robots with color start moving to the positions of lines $\overline{xy}$ of their closest corners of $\mathbb{P}'$ also do not collide.

The argument is as follows. For another internal robot r_j moving to the same line segment $\overline{xy}$ as r_i, r_c is visible to both r_i and r_j (Lemma 1), so the path from r_i to r_c is unobstructed and so is the path from r_j to r_c. Robot r_i moves along line $\overleftrightarrow{r_i r_c}$ to the intersection with line segment $\overline{xy}$, while r_j moves along line $\overleftrightarrow{r_j r_c}$ to its intersection with line segment $\overline{xy}$, so the paths of r_i and r_j do not cross and they do not collide.

For another internal robot r_k closest to a corner robot r_d different from r_c, r_k moves along line $\overleftrightarrow{r_k r_d}$ to a point z'. Every point on the path from r_k to z' is closer to r_d than to any other corner. Likewise, every point on the path from r_i to z is closer to r_c than to any other corner. Therefore, the paths of r_i and r_k do not cross and hence r_i and r_k do not collide.

In Round 1.3, either all robots in line $\overline{xy}$ move to become side robots of $\mathbb{P}'$ or the two endpoint robots among the robots in $\overline{xy}$ move to become side robots. In the first case, the robots fall in the positions of sides $\overline{r_c x}$ and $\overline{r_c y}$ where there are no robots in those sides and there are no robots inside triangle $r_c xy$. Their paths to the positions in $\overline{r_c x}$ and $\overline{r_c y}$ do not cross since they go to the closest side between $\overline{r_c x}$ and $\overline{r_c y}$. The moves of endpoint robots also do not collide since all the other internal robots are in lines $\overline{xy}$ of the corner robots of $\mathbb{P}'$ and its destination on the side it is moving to is not occupied by any other robot and there is no robot in its path.

In Round 1.4, there is no collision using the similar argument as of Round 1.3. The theorem follows. □

3.3 Phase 2 - Edge Depletion

At the start of Phase 2, each robot is colored `corner` or `side` and is located at a corner or side of $\mathbb{P}'$. Let R_c, R_s be the set of robots at corners and sides, respectively of $\mathbb{P}'$. Phase 2 moves the robots of R_s to corners of an N-sided convex polygon $\mathbb{P}''$ that also has the robots of R_c as its corners. At the end of Phase 2, all robots have color `corner`.

Consider any side $S = \langle c_i, s_1, \cdots, s_m, c_{i+1}\rangle$, where c_i, c_{i+1} are corner points and $s_1, \cdots, s_m$ are side points. The other corner points of the side adjacent to S are c_{i-1} and c_{i+2}. For each side $S = \langle c_i, s_1, \cdots, s_m, c_{i+1}\rangle$, Phase 2 places all side points s_i on a circle segment traversing c_i and c_{i+1} and which has entirely within the safe area of S. To determine this circle, each robot needs to see three point on the circle. The figure to the right illustrates Phase 2 for a side with 5 side points (colored gray).

We will use this as a running example to illustrate this phase.

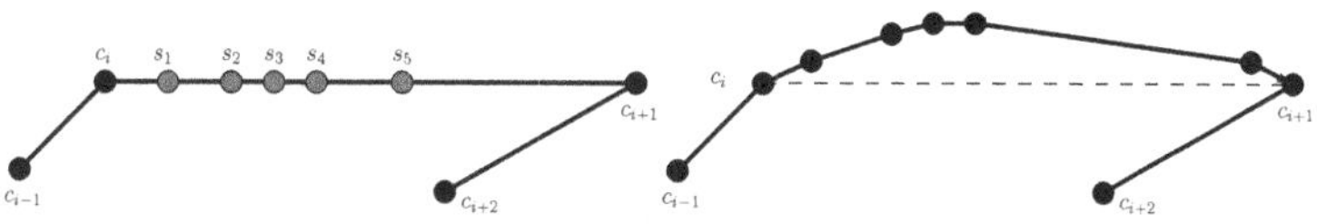

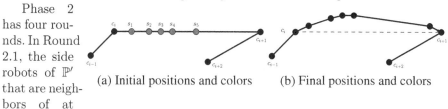

(a) Initial positions and colors (b) Final positions and colors

Phase 2 has four rounds. In Round 2.1, the side robots of $\mathbb{P}'$ that are neighbors of at least one corner of $\mathbb{P}'$ move to their safe apexes and assume color `scout1`. In Round 2.2, each scout for a particular side S of $\mathbb{P}'$ computes two circles (based on the two corners, itself, and the possibly another scout it sees), places itself on the circle with larger radius, and changes its color to `scout2`. If there is only one scout, the scout robot is already on a circle and can simply change its color to `scout`. In Round 2.3, two side robots in S that are now neighbors of their corners move to place themselves on the circle. This is simple since each of them can see a corner and two scouts on the circle. In Round 2.4, all remaining side robots of S move to the circle assuming color `corner` and the robots already in the circle change their color to `corner`.

We give details on each round separately below. For this discussion, we assume that $m \geq 5$. The case of $m < 5$ is explained later. Before we proceed, we develop a few results that will be useful later.

Round 2.1: Consider a robot s on side S that can see at least one of the two corners of S. Moreover, it cannot see any robot with color from $\{$`start`, `ready`, `side1`, `transit`$\}$.

The last sentence ensures that this condition is not met during Phase 1 (see Lemma 6). We assume this additional condition is added to each of the rounds of Phase 2 (although it is not needed, it will make the overall proof of correctness easier).

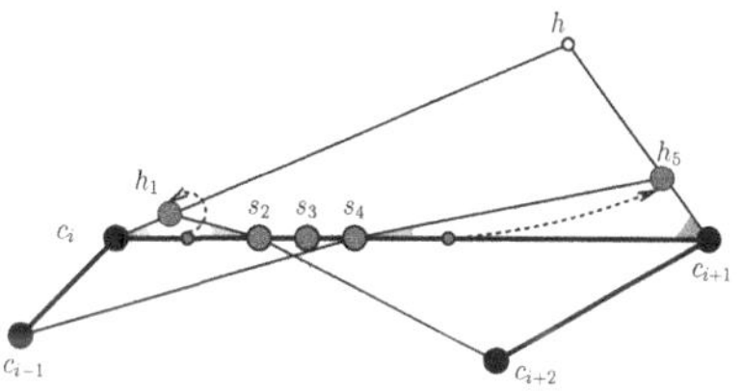

For our example, the two side points s_1, s_m bordering corner points, c_i, c_{i+1}, of S participate during this round; we will call these side points "extremal side points" of side S. Robot s_1 moves to its safe apex, h_1, wrt points $c_{i-1}, c_i, s_2, c_{i+2}$. Similarly, s_m moves to its safe apex, h_m, wrt $c_{i-1}, s_{m-1}, c_{i+1}, c_{i+2}$. Robots s_1, s_m assume color `scout1`.

The figure above illustrates Round 2.1. Color `scout1` is shown in red. Triangle c_i, c_{i+1}, h is the safe area for the entire side. For clarity, the safe angles for c_i, s_2 (due to point s_1) are shown in yellow and light blue, respectively. Similarly, the safe angles of s_4 and c_{i+1} are shown in pink and light green. Observe that s_1 easily determines its side S and that all of the points $c_{i-1}, c_i, s_2, c_{i+2}$ are visible to it.

Lemma 7. *At the end of Round 2.1, each scout of a side S can see the other scout (if any) of the side, as well as the corners c_i, c_{i+1} of side S.*

Round 2.2: It is well known (for example, [3, Sect. 7.2.3]) that for any three non-collinear points a, b, c, there is a unique circle that traverses a, b, c. Let $Circle(a, b, c)$ denote this circle. In this round, each scout for side S determines $Circle(c_i, h_1, c_{i+1})$ and $Circle(c_i, h_m, c_{i+1})$ and selects the one with the larger radius (flatter circle), denoted by $Circle(*)$ and called the *safe circle* of side S. From Lemma 7 each scout can see all the robots (including itself) to determine the circles $Circle(c_i, h_1, c_{i+1})$, $Circle(c_i, h_m, c_{i+1})$ and, hence, $Circle(*)$. The scout then moves (if needed) to position itself on the safe circle; this movement could, for example, be perpendicular to side S. It then changes its color to `scout2`.

The figure on the right illustrates these ideas. Color `scout2` is shown in purple; $Circle(c_i, h_1, c_{i+1}) = Circle(*)$ and $Circle(c_i, h_m, c_{i+1})$ are shown in blue and green, respectively. Observe that the arc of $Circle(*)$ between corners c_i, c_{i+1} lies entirely within the safe area of side S. Also note that placing corner points on $Circle(*)$ (over all sides S) will keep the polygon convex.

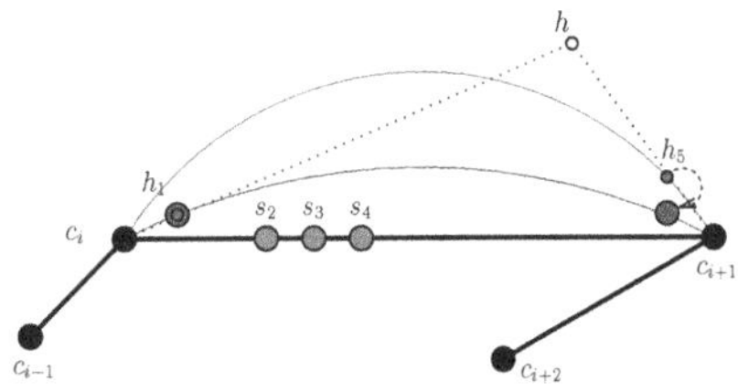

Round 2.3: Here the current extremal side points of S (s_2, s_4 in our example) move to the safe circle $Circle(*)$. This is straightforward as each extremal point can see a corner and two scouts (totally three non-collinear points) that are on $Circle(*)$.

We now explain this and the next round as condition/action pair (C,A). That is, each robot that satisfies a condition C performs a corresponding action A. The appendix gives all steps of the algorithm as condition/action pairs.

Condition 2.3.1: Robot s colored `side` is on side S and it can see at least one of the two corners of S and two points colored `scout2` in the exterior half-plane of S. Moreover, it cannot see any robot with color from {`anchor`, `start`, `ready`, `side1`, `transit`}.

Action 2.3.1: Robot s moves to the safe circle, *Circle*$(*)$, of S and colors itself `anchor`.

Figure on the right illustrates Round 2.3. Color `anchor` is shown in green. This round has another move needed for the case $m < 5$; this is explained later.

Condition 2.3.2: Robot s colored `scout2` corresponding to side S can see no points colored `side` in S. Moreover, it cannot see any robot with color from {`start`, `ready`, `side1`, `transit`}.

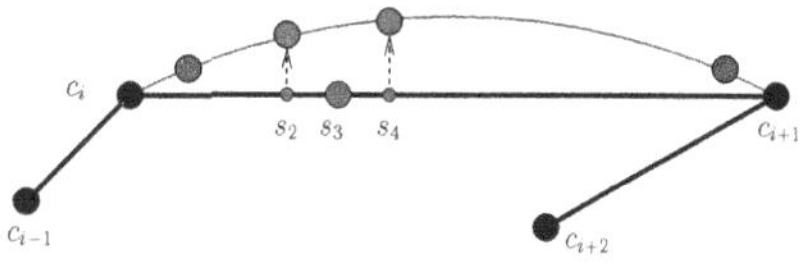

Action 2.3.2: Robot s colors itself `corner`.

Round 2.4: At this stage, every side robot on S can see at least four points on the safe circle *Circle*$(*)$. This allows the side point to determine *Circle*$(*)$ and position itself on the circle. All points are now placed on corners of a new convex polygon $\mathbb{P}''$.

Condition 2.4.1: Robot s colored `side` is on side S and it can see a point colored `anchor` in the exterior half-plane of S. Moreover, it cannot see any robot with color from {`start`, `ready`, `side1`, `transit`}.

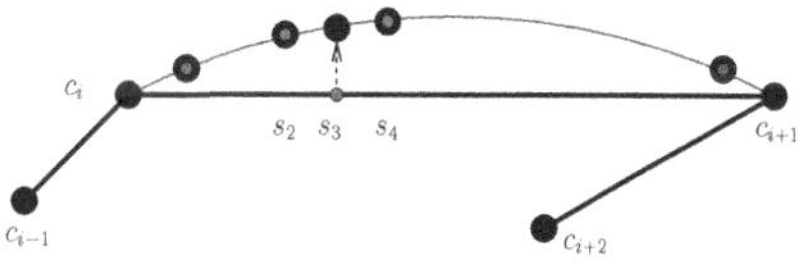

Action 2.4.1: Robot s moves perpendicular to S and places itself on *Circle*$(*)$. It changes its color to `corner`.

Robot s determines *Circle*$(*)$ as in Round 2.2. Observe that while our example shows only one robot, s_4, performing the above action, the above condition would be satisfied by all remaining side points on S and the action executed in parallel by all of them.

The following condition/action pair is to change the colors of robots already in *Circle*$(*)$ to `corner`.

Condition 2.4.2: Robot x has color from {`scout2`, `anchor`} and it can see a robot of color `anchor` (including possibly itself). Moreover, it cannot see any robot with color from {`start`, `ready`, `side1`, `transmit`}.

Action 2.4.2: Robot x changes its color to `corner`.

Here all that matters is that every anchor or scout will be able to see an anchor; whether the anchor is in its own corridor or not is not important. Figure on the right illustrates Round 2.4.

We have assumed that the number of side points m on side S is at least 5. If $m < 5$, then no robot satisfies Condition 2.4.1. For $m = 4$, four robots satisfy Condition 2.4.2 and the phase ends with these robots at corners of convex polygon $\mathbb{P}'$. If $m = 3$, then only one robot satisfies Condition 2.3.1 and three robots satisfy Condition 2.4.2. If $m = 2$, then the two scouts were the only side points on S. They change to color `corner` at Round 2.3 and terminate Phase 2 for the side. If $m = 1$, then there is only one scout and, again, Phase 2 terminates for side S after Round 2.3. If $m = 0$ (no side points), then the side does not execute Phase 2; notice that none of the conditions in the four rounds are satisfied by robots of color `corner`.

We have following theorem for the correctness of Phase 2 (a more systematic proof of overall correctness of the algorithm is omitted due to space constraints).

Theorem 3. *Given a set of N robots placed on corners and sides of a convex polygon $\mathbb{P}'$ with all corner robots colored* `corner` *and all side robots colored* `side`*, Phase 2 executes in at most 4 (fully synchronous) rounds avoiding collisions and uses 5 colors (out of which 2 colors are common with Phase 1).*

Proof. We first prove that the rounds of Phase 2 follow in the order indicated by their names and that if any side skips a round, then it has completed its side depletion with all robots, originally on that side, now colored `corner`. This does not affect the progress of other sides as corner robots of a side S are needed only by non-corner robots of side S to determine S itself and its exterior.

Initially, let us assume that the number of side points on a side S is $m \geq 5$. Phase 2 begins when the set of colors visible to each robot is $\{\texttt{corner}, \texttt{side}\}$. This causes Round 2.1 to be executed by robots satisfying Condition 2.1. Since S has a side point, all non-extremal elements of this side see a robot of color `scout1`. So Round 2.2 follows Round 2.1 as the color `scout1` appears only at the end of Round 2.1. Similarly, Rounds 2.3 follows Round 2.2 as this is the only time the color `scout2` is visible without color `anchor`. Now Round 2.4 follows Round 2.3 as this the only time `anchor` is visible.

It is easy to verify that when m (the number of side points in side S) is 4 or 3, then all four rounds are executed in the above order. If $m = 1, 2$, then after rounds 2.1, 2.2, and 2.3 the robots of side S are all colored `corner` and Round 2.4 is skipped. This does not impact other sides executing Round 2.4 as the color `corner` does not affect the conditions of this round.

We now show that the execution of Phase 2 is collision free. The robots in two different sides never collide since they do not go outside the corridor of the side they belong to at the end of Phase 1. In Round 2.1, according to the safe apex computation, the at most 2 robots moving to the safe apex for each do not collide. From Round 2.2 until Round 2.4 robots move perpendicularly to the side of $\mathbb{P}'$. □

We have the following theorem combining the results of Theorems 2 and 3.

Theorem 4. *For any initial configuration of $N \geq 1$ robots with lights, there is an algorithm that solves* Complete Visibility *avoiding collisions and has runtime of 9 rounds and uses 9 colors in the fully synchronous model of computation.*

4 Conversion to the Semi-synchronous Model

We now discuss how to convert the fully synchronous algorithm (Sect. 3) to the semi-synchronous model. The technique for Phase 0 converts similarly to Phase 0 for the semi-synchronous model and needs at most one (semi-synchronous) round. For Phases 1 and 2, we describe the difficulty in converting it to work in the semi-synchronous model, and then how we handle the difficulty. (The detailed description of each round of Phases 0–2 is omitted due to space constraints.)

Since not all corner robots are able to move to $EA(*)$ in the same cycle in the semi-synchronous model, an internal robot r_i may not see three corner robots (one closest corner and its two neighbor corners) necessary to make a move to become `transit` colored robot. Therefore, to be able to handle this situation for internal robots, we need at most 5 (semi-synchronous) rounds and two new colors `corner1`,`corner2` while converting Round 1.1 of the fully synchronous model to the semi-synchronous model.

In Round 1.1, instead of directly changing the color of corner and side robots of $\mathbb{P}$ from {`ready`, `start`} to `corner`, each corner robot r_c of $\mathbb{P}$ that moves to some point in $EA(r_c)$ changes its color to `corner1` and each side robot r_s of $\mathbb{P}$ changes its color to `side1` without moving. Therefore, by the end of Round 1.1, at least all corner robots of $\mathbb{P}$ have color `corner1` (and do not move in future rounds) and all side robots of $\mathbb{P}$ have color `side1`. In Round 1.2, side robots that are now corners and neighbor of r_c change their color to `corner1` after moving to $EA(*)$ if their color $\notin$ {`corner1`, `corner2`, `corner`}. After both the neighbors of any corner robot r_c have color $\in$ {`corner1`, `corner2`, `corner`}, then r_i sees three corner robots needed to become `transit` colored robot. However, if there are robots inside triangle r_cxy (points x, y are defined similarly as in Sect. 3), r_i's view of neighbor corner robots r_{ccw} and r_{cw} of r_c (Observation 1) may be blocked by other internal robots that have already moved to become `transit` colored robots, and therefore r_i might perceive a wrong view of r_{ccw} and r_{cw}. To avoid this situation, we use the technique in which if a corner r_c has color `corner1`, both of its neighbors in $\mathbb{P}$ have color $\in$ {`corner1`, `corner2`, `corner`}, and there are robots inside triangle r_cxy, then robot r_c changes its color to `corner2`. That means an internal robot r_i waits until r_c is colored `corner`. Using this technique, all corners r_c of $\mathbb{P}$ with robots inside triangle r_cxy will be colored `corner2` by the end of Round 1.3. By the end of Round 1.4, all the robots inside triangle r_cxy can move to line $\overline{xy}$ and assume color `transit`. Then, by the end of Round 1.5, all the corner robots of $\mathbb{P}$ assume color `corner`. This finishes the conversion of Round 1.1 of the fully synchronous model to the semi-synchronous model and the conversion makes sure that when an internal robot r_i sees r_c colored `corner`, it also sees its two neighbors r_{ccw} and r_{cw} that are in fact corners of $\mathbb{P}$.

Note also that by the end of Round 1.5, there is no internal robot in r_cxy of any corner r_c of $\mathbb{P}$. Therefore, similar to Round 1.2 of the fully synchronous model, by the end of Round 1.6, all internal robots of $\mathbb{P}$ move to lines $\overline{xy}$ and assume color `transit`. Furthermore, by the end of Round 1.8, all `transit` colored robots assume color `side`, all robots with color `side1` (if any) assume color `side`, and the robots with color `corner1`, `corner2` assume color `corner`. In other words, Rounds 1.2, 1.3, and 1.4 of the fully synchronous model convert to (semi-synchronous) Rounds 1.6, 1.7, and 1.8.

The conversion for Phase 2 is relatively simple and works for the semi-synchronous model with no change in the number of rounds. However, robots may face ambiguity about identifying the exterior direction of the side of $\mathbb{P}$ in Round 2.4 which is handled introducing one additional color `corner3`. We have the following theorem.

Theorem 5. *For any initial configuration of $N \geq 1$ robots with lights, there is an algorithm that solves* Complete Visibility *avoiding collisions and has runtime of 13 rounds and uses 12 colors in the semi-synchronous model of computation.*

We obtain Theorem 1 combining the results of Theorems 4 and 5.

5 Concluding Remarks

We have presented, to our knowledge, the first algorithm for Complete Visibility in the robots with lights model that has runtime of $O(1)$ rounds and uses $O(1)$ colors in the semi-synchronous (and also in the fully synchronous) model. This problem is fundamental with application in solving other problems, e.g., on the fully synchronous model, gathering robots to a point requires only one round beyondComplete Visibility.

Several questions remain open. Our solution assumes no intervention by an adversary.Can this be relaxed? Our solution assumes semi-synchrony.Is a similar algorithm possible for asynchronous robots?

References

1. Agathangelou, C., Georgiou, C., Mavronicolas, M.: A distributed algorithm for gathering many fat mobile robots in the plane. In: PODC, pp. 250–259 (2013)
2. Ando, H., Suzuki, I., Yamashita, M.: Formation and agreement problems for synchronous mobile robots with limited visibility. In: ISIC, pp. 453–460 (1995)
3. Barry, P.D.: Geometry with Trigonometry. Horwood Publishing Limited, Chichester (2001)
4. Cohen, R., Peleg, D.: Local spreading algorithms for autonomous robot systems. Theor. Comput. Sci. **399**(1–2), 71–82 (2008)
5. Cord-Landwehr, A., et al.: A new approach for analyzing convergence algorithms for mobile robots. In: Aceto, L., Henzinger, M., Sgall, J. (eds.) ICALP 2011. LNCS, vol. 6756, pp. 650–661. Springer, Heidelberg (2011). doi:10.1007/978-3-642-22012-8_52
6. Czyzowicz, J., Gasieniec, L., Pelc, A.: Gathering few fat mobile robots in the plane. Theor. Comput. Sci. **410**(6–7), 481–499 (2009)
7. Das, S., Flocchini, P., Prencipe, G., Santoro, N., Yamashita, M.: Autonomous mobile robots with lights. Theor. Comput. Sci. **609**, 171–184 (2016)
8. Degener, B., Kempkes, B., Langner, T., Meyer auf der Heide, F., Pietrzyk, P., Wattenhofer, R.: A tight runtime bound for synchronous gathering of autonomous robots with limited visibility. In: SPAA, pp. 139–148 (2011)

9. Degener, B., Kempkes, B., Meyer auf der Heide, F.: A local$o(n^2)$ gathering algorithm. In: SPAA, pp. 217–223 (2010)
10. Flocchini, P., Prencipe, G., Santoro, N.: Distributed computing by oblivious mobile robots. Synth. Lect. Distrib. Comput. Theor. **3**(2), 1–185 (2012)
11. Izumi, T., Potop-Butucaru, M.G., Tixeuil, S.: Connectivity-preserving scattering of mobile robots with limited visibility. In: Dolev, S., Cobb, J., Fischer, M., Yung, M. (eds.) SSS 2010. LNCS, vol. 6366, pp. 319–331. Springer, Heidelberg (2010). doi:10.1007/978-3-642-16023-3_27
12. Kempkes, B., Kling, P., Meyer auf der Heide, F.: Optimal and competitive runtime bounds for continuous, local gathering of mobile robots. In: SPAA, pp. 18–26 (2012)
13. Luna, G.A., Flocchini, P., Gan Chaudhuri, S., Santoro, N., Viglietta, G.: Robots with lights: overcoming obstructed visibility without colliding. In: Felber, P., Garg, V. (eds.) SSS 2014. LNCS, vol. 8756, pp. 150–164. Springer, Heidelberg (2014). doi:10.1007/978-3-319-11764-5_11
14. Pagli, L., Prencipe, G., Viglietta, G.: Getting close without touching. In: Even, G., Halldórsson, M.M. (eds.) SIROCCO 2012. LNCS, vol. 7355, pp. 315–326. Springer, Heidelberg (2012). doi:10.1007/978-3-642-31104-8_27
15. Peleg, D.: Distributed coordination algorithms for mobile robot swarms: new directions and challenges. In: Pal, A., Kshemkalyani, A.D., Kumar, R., Gupta, A. (eds.) IWDC 2005. LNCS, vol. 3741, pp. 1–12. Springer, Heidelberg (2005). doi:10.1007/11603771_1
16. Prencipe, G.: Autonomous mobile robots: a distributed computing perspective. In: Flocchini, P., Gao, J., Kranakis, E., Meyer auf der Heide, F. (eds.) ALGOSENSORS 2013. LNCS, vol. 8243, pp. 6–21. Springer, Heidelberg (2014). doi:10.1007/978-3-642-45346-5_2
17. Vaidyanathan, R., Busch, C., Trahan, J.L., Sharma, G., Rai, S.: Logarithmic-time complete visibility for robots with lights. In: IPDPS, pp. 375–384 (2015)
18. Yamashita, M., Suzuki, I.: Characterizing geometric patterns formable by oblivious anonymous mobile robots. Theor. Comput. Sci. **411**(26–28), 2433–2453 (2010)

$\mathcal{PSVR}$- Self-stabilizing Publish/Subscribe Communication for Ad-Hoc Networks (Short Paper)

G. Siegemund and V. Turau(✉)

Institute of Telematics, Hamburg University of Technology, Hamburg, Germany
{gerry.siegemund,turau}@tuhh.de

Abstract. $\mathcal{PSVR}$ is a novel routing algorithm for pub/sub systems in ad-hoc networks focusing on scenarios where communications links are unstable and nodes frequently change subscriptions. It is a compromise of size and maintenance effort for routing tables due to sub- and unsubscriptions and the length of routing paths. Designed in a self-stabilizing manner it scales well with network size. The evaluation with real world deployment reveals that $\mathcal{PSVR}$ only needs slightly more messages than a close to optimal routing structure for publication delivery, and creates shorter routing paths than an existing self-stabilizing algorithm.

1 Introduction

Industrial wireless sensor networks are an emerging field for process monitoring and control that require dynamic forms of the many-to-many communication paradigm for data dissemination. This communication style is best supported by publish/subscribe (pub/sub) systems instead of request-reply messaging. In channel-based pub/sub systems, publishers assign each message to one of several channels known by all nodes. Subscribers express interest in one or more channels (a.k.a. subscribing) and only receive messages assigned to these. The pub/sub paradigm guarantees disseminating all messages to nodes with a subscription for that channel. The advantage is the loose coupling, i.e., publishers are unaware of the subscribers that receive their messages. Nodes can at any time give up subscriptions and create new ones.

The efficiency of message dissemination in pub/sub systems depends on the used routing strategy. The goal is to deliver publications with a minimum number of messages to all subscribers. This number is minimal when publications are routed along the Steiner tree for the publishing node and all subscribers to the message's channel. Since Steiner trees are computationally too expensive many systems use a fixed spanning tree for routing. Publishers recursively forward messages into subtrees containing a subscriber for the message's channel. This does not always result in the shortest routing path. Other systems organize their nodes into a virtual ring. A publication is then simply forwarded once around this ring and thereby delivered to all subscribers. This does not require any routing

B. Bonakdarpour and F. Petit (Eds.): SSS 2016, LNCS 10083, pp. 346–351, 2016.
DOI: 10.1007/978-3-319-49259-9_27

tables and there is no need to distribute un-/subscriptions into the network. But it requires at least as many messages as nodes in the virtual ring.

Scenarios are considered where nodes frequently change their subscriptions, hence, an efficient update of the routing structure is required. Also delivery of publications must be guaranteed while subscriptions are changing. To meet this goal we propose the routing algorithm $\mathcal{PSVR}$, which is a significant extension of the algorithm in [2]. $\mathcal{PSVR}$ presents a compromise between the length of routing paths and the effort to maintain the routing tables. To increase robustness and to tolerate the failure and recovery of links and nodes the proposed algorithms are self-stabilizing. The full details are presented in [1].

2 $\mathcal{PSVR}$– Publication Handling

The architecture of $\mathcal{PSVR}$ is shown in Fig. 1. For details about the virtual ring, the spanning tree, and the TCA we refer to [2]. The spanning tree layer is slightly augmented to enhance the dissemination of subscriptions.

Routing structures in$\mathcal{PSVR}$ $RS(v)$ are stored in form of a $n_c \times n_p$ matrix, n_c denotes the number of channels and $n_p = |Pos(v)|$. RS stores tuples in the $\langle ns, t_s, nstmp \rangle$. When a message for the ${c_i}^{th}$ channel is received at the ${p_j}^{th}$ position, then $RS(v)[c_i, p_j].ns$ is the position of the subscriber for channel c_i which is counter clock wise (ccw) closest to p_j, i.e., the forwarding position.

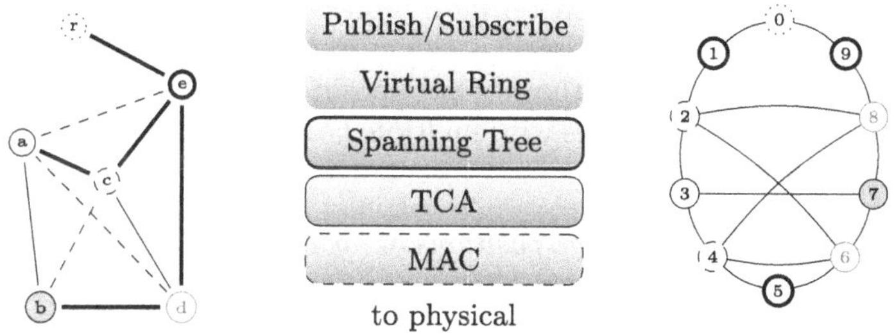

Fig. 1. Topology; layered system architecture; corresponding virtual ring graph.

Publications need to be routed to subscribers only. Hence, shortcuts can be used to skip non-subscribing nodes on the virtual ring. Furthermore, publications of nodes with multiple positions can be distributed concurrently over different paths. The following propositions are tied to the fact that the virtual ring is built upon a tree. Under a different scheme the routing still works, but some properties, e.g., that each subscriber receives a publication only once, are not guaranteed anymore.

Concurrent Routing. To explain publication routing on the virtual ring and the faced challenges when routing messages concurrently we recap tree-based routing. Each node maintains a routing table to identify branches where at least one subscriber is present. A publisher distributes messages into all such branches concurrently. The same reasoning is conducted by forwarding nodes, while avoiding to send messages back to previous senders. Trees are cycle free, hence, a publication is delivered once per subscriber. In the virtual ring, shortcuts introduce cycles. To avoid message duplication the concept of *routing into a branch* is transferred to the virtual ring. Therefore, the *end of a branch* is defined.

Nodes have multiple positions on the virtual ring, one for each neighbor in the tree. Hence, sending a message from every position in $Pos(v) = \langle p_1, \ldots, p_s \rangle$ to $p_1 + 1, \ldots, p_s + 1$, respectively is the equivalent of a tree node sending into all branches. In the routing structure RS the next subscriber for each position is stored, this reflects a node's understanding that a subscriber exists in a certain tree branch. Therefore, if a publisher knows that there is at least one subscriber in an interval $\mathcal{I} = [p_i, p_{i+1})$ for a given channel c then it sends a publication to a *goal* position in $\mathcal{I}$. The *goal* position is the ccw closest one-hop reachable position to the next subscriber in $\mathcal{I}$, i.e., *goal* is either the next position on the virtual ring or a position reachable by a shortcut.

Received publications are delivered to all nodes subscribing to the message's channel. Regardless of the delivery, publications are forwarded to ensure that all subscribers receive it. Forwarding of publications is restricted to the interval they are sent into. To avoid sending messages beyond interval borders the endpoint *ep* of each $\mathcal{I}$ is attached to publication messages: Pub $\langle goal, ep, c, data \rangle$. Where *ep* is the right endpoint of $\mathcal{I} = [p_i, p_{i+1})$, i.e., $ep = p_{i+1}$. A message is neither routed to *ep* nor to a position beyond it. Parameters *goal* and *ep* are updated at every forwarding node. Parameter *data* represents the payload.

The start position of an interval is the current position of a node and the endpoint position is defined by the ccw next position of the same node. Multiple delivery of a publication to nodes with multiple positions in an interval is avoided as shown in Lemma 1.

Lemma 1 (Proof see [1]). *The positions of nodes on the virtual ring are never interlaced. That is, a node v may have a position on the virtual ring which is followed by a node w's position, once another position of v appears there cannot be a further position of w.*

As Lemma 1 suggests, within a nodes's interval $\mathcal{I}$ may be further intervals of other nodes. For routing this means, that a node forwarding a publication applies the same reasoning as a publisher to determine how to forward messages. In the tree this corresponds to branching. Each branch containing a subscriber leads to an additional message sent concurrently. The analog in the virtual ring is as follows: Each subscriber in the interval $\mathcal{I}_f = [p_i, p_{i+1})$ with p_{i+1} ccw in between p_i and *ep* forwards the Pub message. That is, in the *subsection* of the virtual ring bounded by the current node position and the received endpoint position *ep*, independent concurrent routing is conducted. Therefore, the parameters of the Pub message are updated. The endpoint becomes p_{i+1} if p_{i+1} is ccw between p_i and *ep* otherwise it stays unchanged.

Algorithm 1. Handling and forwarding of publications

API provided by virtual ring layer (VR):	
getPosClosestTo(p, goal)	returns largest ccw position beyond p and prior (or equal to) *goal* within neighbor positions
sendOnRing(p, msg)	sends message *msg* to position p
isBetween(test, left, right)	checks if position *test* is in ccw ring segment bounded by positions *left* and *right* note: $isBetween(x, y, y) = true$ for arbitrary positions x and y
deliver(*data*)	delivers the *data* to the application

```
function publish(c, data)
  handlePub(P[0], P[0], c, data)
```

```
Upon reception of PUB⟨curPos, ep, c, data⟩
  if (c ∈ C_S)
    deliver(data)
  handlePub(curPos, ep, c, data)
```

```
function handlePub(curPos, ep, c, data)
  for all p ∈ P do
    nextS := RS[indexOf(c)][indexOf(p)]
    newEp := calcNewEP(p, ep)
    if (isBetween(nextS, curPos, newEp))
      goal := getPosClosestTo(p, nextS)
      sendOnRing(goal,
        PUB⟨goal, newEp, c, data⟩)
```

```
function calcNewEp(p, maxEp)
  i := indexOf(p)
  epIndex := i + 1 mod |P|
  if (isBetween(P[epIndex], p, maxEp))
    return P[epIndex]
  else
    return maxEp
```

Algorithm 1 shows the handling of publications and the calculation of associated endpoints. When a node generates a publication with content *data*, then the *handlePub()* function is called, i.e., message PUB$\langle P[0], P[0], c, data\rangle$ is sent.

Theorem 1 (Proof see [1]). *In error-free phases subscribers receive* PUB *messages exactly once.*

Resolving drawbacks of [2]. Firstly, *nodes receive publications multiple times* in [2]. For the example in Fig. 2 this means that the path a PUB message travels, starting at position 6 is: $\langle(6), 7, 8, 2, 3, 4\rangle$, i.e., $\langle(d), b, d, c, a, c\rangle$. Node d (positions 6 and 8) receives its previously published message in order to forward it. Additionally, node c receives the same publication twice. As can be examined in Fig. 2b, with $\mathcal{PSVR}$ two messages travel: $\langle(6), 7\rangle\langle(8), 2, 3\rangle$, i.e., $\langle(d), b\rangle\langle(d), c, a\rangle$.

Secondly, *publications travel further on the virtual ring as the last subscriber.* Consider an example where the next subscriber p_w lies beyond a publisher p_v. In [2] a publication from p_v is forwarded until a node at position p_u can determine that forwarding leads to routing the message past or to the original publisher p_v, then the node ceases forwarding. With $\mathcal{PSVR}$, due to the definition of the end position *ep* and the knowledge of the next subscriber p_w, such a situation is recognized by the ccw *last* subscriber p_t before publisher p_v. p_t checks if the next subscriber is between the current position and *ep*. If this is not the case, the message is not forwarded.

Self-stabilizing Properties: Self-stabilization is ensured by the leasing technique. Through the periodic renewal of subscriptions routing tables are

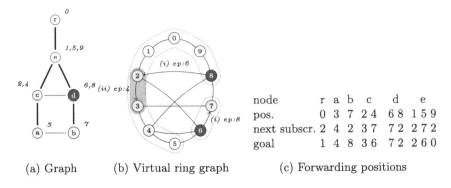

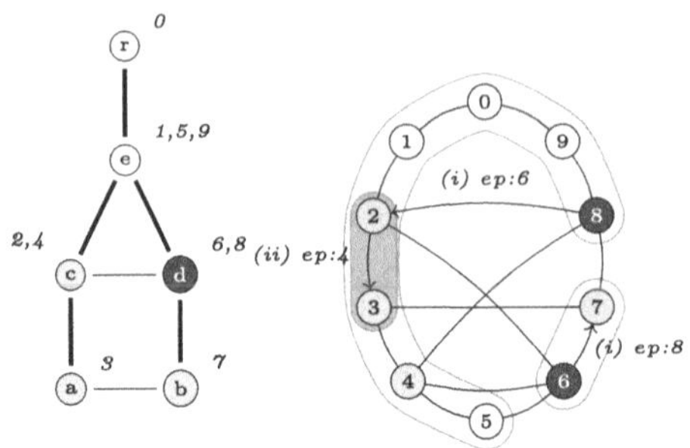

node	r	a	b	c	d	e
pos.	0	3	7	2 4	6 8	1 5 9
next subscr.	2	4	2	3 7	7 2	2 7 2
goal	1	4	8	3 6	7 2	2 6 0

(a) Graph (b) Virtual ring graph (c) Forwarding positions

Fig. 2. Illustration of the forwarding process (Subscribers: gray; publisher: black)

continually updated and errors are fixed. Storing a time-stamp of the last update t_s in the routing structure $RS(v)$ ensures that stale values can be recognized. Hence, inconsistencies due to message errors, loss, or obstruction are corrected. Proper publication routing is ensured by the correctness of $RS(v)$. Unsubscribing is self-stabilizing as well. To unsubscribe from a channel a node removes the channel identifier from C_S, this ceases sending Sub messages. The underlying structures, virtual ring and spanning tree are built using self-stabilizing algorithms. They are tied together using collateral composition where a layer does not influences a layer below.

Self-stabilizing algorithms inherently can not locally decide if the system is in a globally correct state. Thus, in a faulty case no guarantees can be given, but that eventually the system will recover. $\mathcal{PSVR}$ handles dynamic addition and removal of nodes, after addition to the virtual ring and the dispatch of the first Sub message it takes no longer than $O(n)$ rounds until Pub messages will be received.

3 Conclusion

The presented pub/sub system $\mathcal{PSVR}$ significantly enhances the algorithm of [2]. $\mathcal{PSVR}$ is optimized for scenarios where communications links are unstable and nodes frequently change subscriptions. It is a compromise of size and maintenance effort for routing tables due to sub- and unsubscriptions and the length of routing paths. Simulations and verification against theoretical, closer to optimal solutions revealed that our approach gives a fair trade-off between the scalability of the support structure and the message forwarding overhead. Real world tests confirmed its usability. The approach scales with the number of nodes and is suitable for wireless ad-hoc networks. A complete description and analysis as well as the results of the evaluation are contained in [1].

References

1. Siegemund, G., Turau, V.: PSVR - Self-stabilizing Publish/Subscribe Communication for Ad-Hoc Networks. CoRR, abs/1609.06841 (2016)
2. Siegemund, G., Turau, V., Maâmra, K.: A self-stabilizing publish/subscribe middleware for wireless sensor networks. In: Proceedings of the International Conference on Network System (2015)

Asynchronous Non-Bayesian Learning in the Presence of Crash Failures

Lili Su(✉) and Nitin H. Vaidya

Department of Electrical and Computer Engineering, University of Illinois at Urbana-Champaign, Urbana, USA
{lilisu3,nhv}@illinois.edu

Abstract. This paper addresses the problem of non-Bayesian learning in multi-agent networks, where agents repeatedly collect local observations about an *unknown* state of the world, and try to collaboratively detect the true state through information exchange. We focus on the impact of failures and asynchrony – two fundamental factors in distributed systems – on the performance of consensus-based non-Bayesian learning. In particular, we assume the networked agents may suffer crash faults, and messages delay can be *arbitrarily* long but finite.

1. We characterize the minimal global identifiability of the network for any consensus-based non-Bayesian learning to work.
2. Finite time convergence rate is obtained.
3. As part of our convergence analysis, we obtain a generalization of a celebrated result by Wolfowitz and Hajnal to submatrices, which might be of independent interest.

Keywords: Distributed learning · Crash failures · Asynchrony

1 Introduction

Decentralized hypothesis testing is an important component of many decision-making and learning algorithms for large-scale systems, and thus has received a significant amount of attention [1,3,5,18,19,21]. The traditional decentralized detection framework consists of a collection of spatially distributed sensors/agents and a fusion center [18,19]. The sensors/agents independently collect *noisy* observations of the environment state, and send only *summary* of the private observations to the fusion center, where a final decision is made. In the case when the sensors/agents directly send all the private observations, the detection problem can be solved using a centralized scheme. However, the above framework does not scale well, since each sensor needs to be connected to the fusion center and full reliability of the fusion center is assumed, which may not be practical as

This research is supported in part by National Science Foundation award NSF 1329681. Any opinions, findings, and conclusions or recommendations expressed here are those of the authors and do not necessarily reflect the views of the funding agencies or the U.S. government.

B. Bonakdarpour and F. Petit (Eds.): SSS 2016, LNCS 10083, pp. 352–367, 2016.
DOI: 10.1007/978-3-319-49259-9_28

the system scales. Distributed hypothesis testing in the absence of fusion center is introduced by Gale and Kariv [3] in the context of social learning, where fully Bayesian belief update rule is studied. Bayesian update rule is impractical in many applications due to memory and computation constraints of each agent, and the inter-agent coordination challenges.

Consensus-based Non-Bayesian learning rule is first proposed by Jadbabaie et al. [5] in the general setting where external signals are observed during each iteration of the algorithm execution. Specifically, the belief of each agent is repeatedly updated as the arithmetic mean of its local Bayesian update and the beliefs of its neighbors, combing iterative consensus algorithm with local Bayesian update. It is shown [5] that, under this learning rule, each agent learns the true state almost surely. Since the publication of [5], significant efforts have been devoted to designing and analyzing non-Bayesian learning rules with a particular focus on refining the fusion strategies and analyzing the (asymptotic and/or finite time) convergence rates of the refined algorithms [6,7,9–14].

Among the various proposed fusion rules, in this paper, we are particularly interested in the log-linear form of the update rule, in which, essentially, each agent updates its belief as the geometric average of the local Bayesian update and its neighbors' beliefs [11]. The log-linear form (geometric averaging) update rule is proposed in [11], and is shown to converge exponentially fast [6,12]. Taking an axiomatic approach, the geometric averaging fusion is shown to be optimal [9]. An optimization-based interpretation of this rule is presented in [12], using dual averaging method with properly chosen proximal functions. Finite-time convergence rates are investigated independently in [7,10,13]. Both [10] and [14] consider time-varying networks, with slightly different network models. Specifically, [10] assumes that the union of every consecutive B networks is strongly connected, while [14] considers random networks. In this paper, we assume that the network topology is static.

All the above work implicitly assumes synchronous systems and reliable agents. However, in the context of distributed learning, asynchrony (message asynchrony and/or computation asynchrony) and failures (link failures and/or agent failures) – two fundamental factors in practical distributed systems – have not been addressed yet except for [2] (with a different focus) and our companion paper [16] (where Byzantine faults are considered and synchrony is assumed). In this paper, we consider the scenario where some agents may suffer crash faults (i.e., cease operating), and messages delay can be *arbitrarily* long but finite [8]. The main challenge is that when an agent i does not receive messages from the incoming neighbor agent j within some timeout interval, from agent i's perspective, it is not possible to distinguish whether agent j has crashed, or the messages are delayed.

Contributions: Our contributions are three-fold:

1. We characterize the minimal global identifiability of the network for any consensus-based non-Bayesian learning to work.
2. Finite time convergence rate is obtained.

3. As part of our convergence analysis, we obtain a generalization of a celebrated result by Wolfowitz and Hajnal to submatrices, which might be of independent interest.

Organization: The rest of the paper is organized as follows. Section 2 presents the problem formulation and our learning rule. Section 3 introduces the notion of pseudo-belief vector, whose evolution captures the dynamics of the agents' beliefs, and admits a matrix representation. The limiting behavior of the update matrices product is investigated in Sect. 4, where we generalize a celebrated result by Wolfowitz and Hajnal. The minimal global identifiability condition is presented in Sect. 5. The convergence rate of our learning rule is obtained in Sect. 6. Section 7 concludes the paper.

2 Problem Formulation

Network Model: We consider an asynchronous system, where the message delay can be *arbitrarily* long but finite. A collection of n agents are connected by a *directed* network $G(\mathcal{V}, \mathcal{E})$, where $\mathcal{V} = \{1, \ldots, n\}$ and $\mathcal{E}$ is the collection of *directed* edges. Let $\mathcal{I}_i$ denote the set of incoming neighbors of agent $i \in \mathcal{V}$. In any execution, up to f agents suffer crash faults (i.e., cease operating). Let $\mathcal{N} \subseteq \mathcal{V}$ be the set of agents that operate correctly during a given execution. Note that $|\mathcal{V} - \mathcal{N}| \leq f$. As noted earlier, although we assume a static network topology, our results can be easily generalized to time-varying networks.

Throughout this paper, we use the terms agent and node interchangeably.

Observation Model: Let $\Theta = \{\theta_1, \ldots, \theta_m\}$ denote a finite set of m environmental states, which we call *hypotheses*. We consider asynchronous iterations. In the t-th iteration, each agent *independently* obtains private signal about the environmental state θ^*, which is initially unknown to every agent in the network. However, the private signals may not be sufficient for the agents to learn the true state θ^* individually. Thus, collaboration is needed for θ^* to be learned.

For ease of exposition, we assume that if multiple signals are observed, only one signal is used to update beliefs. Each agent i knows the structure of its private signal, which is represented by a collection of parameterized distributions $\mathcal{D}^i = \{\ell_i(w_i|\theta) | \theta \in \Theta, w_i \in \mathcal{S}_i\}$, where $\ell_i(\cdot|\theta)$ is a distribution with parameter $\theta \in \Theta$, and $\mathcal{S}_i$ is the finite private signal space. For each $\theta \in \Theta$, and each $i \in \mathcal{V}$, the support of $\ell_i(\cdot|\theta)$ is the whole signal space, i.e., $\ell_i(w_i|\theta) > 0$, $\forall\, w_i \in \mathcal{S}_i$ and $\forall\, \theta \in \Theta$. Let s_t^i be the private signal observed by agent i in iteration t, and let $\mathbf{s}_t = \{s_t^1, \ldots, s_t^n\}$ be the signal profile at time t (i.e., signals observed by all the agents in iteration t). The signal profile $\mathbf{s}_t$ is generated according to the joint distribution $\ell_1(\cdot|\theta^*) \times \cdots \times \ell_n(\cdot|\theta^*)$. The goal is to have all the non-faulty agents (agents in $\mathcal{N}$) collaboratively learn the environmental state θ^*.

Network Identifiability: In the absence of agent failures and messages asynchrony [5], for the networked agents to learn θ^*, it is enough to assume that $G(\mathcal{V}, \mathcal{E})$ is strongly connected, and that θ^* is globally identifiable, i.e.,

$$\sum_{i\in\mathcal{V}} D\left(\ell_i(\cdot|\theta^*)||\ell_i(\cdot|\theta)\right) \neq 0, \quad \forall\, \theta \in \Theta. \tag{1}$$

where $D\left(\ell_j(\cdot|\theta^*)||\ell_j(\cdot|\theta)\right) \triangleq \sum_{w_j\in\mathcal{S}_j} \ell_j(w_j|\theta^*) \log \frac{\ell_j(w_j|\theta^*)}{\ell_j(w_j|\theta)}$. Since θ^* may change from execution to execution, (1) is required to hold for any choice of θ and θ^* such that $\theta \neq \theta^*$. Intuitively, if any pair of states θ_1 and θ_2 (the two conditional distributions) can be distinguished by at least one agent in the network, then sufficient exchange of local beliefs over strongly connected network will enable every agent to distinguish θ_1 from θ_2.

However, in the presence of failures and asynchrony, the effective influence network may not be strongly connected, and a stronger global identifiability of the network is required (specified later).

Belief Update Rule: Each agent i keeps a belief μ^i, which is a distribution over the set Θ, with $\mu^i(\theta)$ being the probability with which the agent i *believes* that θ is the true environmental state. Since no signals are observed before the execution of an algorithm, the belief μ^i is often initially set to be uniform over the set Θ, i.e., $\left(\mu_0^i(\theta_1), \mu_0^i(\theta_1), \ldots, \mu_0^i(\theta_m)\right)^T = \left(\frac{1}{m}, \ldots, \frac{1}{m}\right)^T$.[1] In this work, we also adopt the above convention. (For our results to hold, it suffices to have $\mu_0^i(\theta) > 0$ for each $\theta \in \Theta$ and each $i \in \mathcal{V}$.)

In our algorithm, we will use a geometric averaging update rule that has been investigated in previous work [7,10,11,13]. Let $\mathcal{N}[t]$ be the set of agents that have not crashed *by the beginning* of iteration t, and let $\bar{\mathcal{N}}[t]$ be the set of agents that have not crashed *by the end* of iteration t. Note that $\mathcal{N}[t+1] \subseteq \mathcal{N}[t]$, $\mathcal{N}[t] - \bar{\mathcal{N}}[t]$ is the collection of agents that crash *during* iteration t, and that $\bar{\mathcal{N}}[t] = \mathcal{N}[t+1]$. In addition, $\lim_{t\to\infty} \mathcal{N}[t] = \mathcal{N} = \lim_{t\to\infty} \bar{\mathcal{N}}[t]$.

For $t \geq 1$, the steps to be performed by agent $i \in \mathcal{N}[t]$ are listed as follows, where messages are tagged with (asynchronous) iteration index.

1. *Transmit Step:* Transmit current belief vector μ_{t-1}^i on all outgoing edges.
2. *Receive Step:* Wait until a private signal s_t^i is observed and belief vectors are received from $|\mathcal{I}_i| - f$ incoming neighbors. Let $\mathcal{R}_i[t]$ be the set of incoming neighbors from whom agent i receives these belief vectors.
3. *Update Step:* For each $\theta \in \Theta$, update $\mu^i(\theta)$ as[2]

$$\mu_t^i(\theta) \triangleq \frac{\ell_i(s_t^i|\theta) \prod_{j\in\mathcal{R}_i[t]\cup\{i\}} \mu_{t-1}^j(\theta)^{\frac{1}{|\mathcal{I}_i|-f+1}}}{\sum_{p=1}^m \ell_i(s_t^i|\theta_p) \prod_{j\in\mathcal{R}_i[t]\cup\{i\}} \mu_{t-1}^j(\theta_p)^{\frac{1}{|\mathcal{I}_i|-f+1}}}. \tag{2}$$

Note that due to asynchrony and agent failures, $\mathcal{R}_i[t]$ may change over time and *is not* monotone. In contrast, in synchronous systems, $\mathcal{R}_i[t]$ is non-increasing, i.e., $\mathcal{R}_i[t+1] \subseteq \mathcal{R}_i[t]$ for any $t \geq 1$ and any $i \in \mathcal{V}$. In iteration t, if an agent crashes after performing the update step in (2) for all $\theta \in \Theta$, without loss of

[1] In this paper, every vector considered is column vector.

[2] In the notation μ_t^i, the superscript denotes agents and subscript denotes iterations.

generality, we say that this agent crashes in iteration $t+1$ (crash at right the beginning of iteration $t+1$, before it sends its belief vector). Note that each agent in $\mathcal{N}[t]-\bar{\mathcal{N}}[t]$ may crash at any time during iteration t. In particular, it may crash before performing (2) or while performing (2).

Our learning rule is different from the original geometric averaging learning rule [7,10,11,13] in the receive step, where each agent waits to receive messages from $|\mathcal{I}_i|-f$ incoming neighbors instead of waiting to hear from all of its incoming neighbors. Recall that θ^* is the true state. We say the networked agents collaboratively detect θ^* if for each non-faulty agent $i \in \mathcal{N}$,

$$\lim_{t\to\infty} \mu_t^i(\theta^*) = 1. \tag{3}$$

3 Matrix Representation

In this section, we define a matrix representation of the agents' belief update. In synchronous and reliable networks, the update matrix $\mathbf{A}[t]$ is often chosen to be the weighted adjacency matrix of the network [7,10,13]. However, the above matrix representation is improper in the presence of message asynchrony and agent failure, observing that transmitted messages may not be used due to message delay, and agents *not* in $\bar{\mathcal{N}}[t]$ may not perform (2) for all $\theta \in \Theta$ (and may not even observe new private signals). To resolve the above complication, we introduce pseudo-belief vector $\tilde{\mu}^i$ for each $i \in \mathcal{V}$. The evolution of the pseudo-belief vectors admits a simple matrix representation, and captures the update of μ^i for each non-faulty agent $i \in \mathcal{N}$. For each $i \in \bar{\mathcal{N}}[t]$, define

$$\mathbf{A}_{ij}[t] \triangleq \begin{cases} \frac{1}{|\mathcal{I}_i|-f+1}, & j \in \mathcal{R}_i[t] \cup \{i\} \\ 0, & \text{otherwise}, \end{cases} \tag{4}$$

and for each $i \notin \bar{\mathcal{N}}[t]$,

$$\mathbf{A}_{ii}[t] \triangleq 1, \text{ and } \mathbf{A}_{ij}[t] \triangleq 0, \forall j \neq i. \tag{5}$$

Note that in iteration t, an agent can only receive messages tagged with (asynchronous) iteration index t from agents that have not crashed by the beginning of iteration t. Thus, $\mathbf{A}_{ij}[t]=0$, $\forall j \notin \mathcal{N}[t]$, and $1=\sum_{j=1}^n \mathbf{A}_{ij}[t]=\sum_{j\in\mathcal{N}[t]}\mathbf{A}_{ij}[t]$.

The pseudo-belief is defined as follows: For all $i \in \mathcal{V}$, $\tilde{\mu}_0^i(\theta)=\mu_0^i(\theta)=\frac{1}{m}$; and when $t \geq 1$,

$$\tilde{\mu}_t^i(\theta) \triangleq \frac{\ell_i(s_t^i|\theta)\prod_{j=1}^n \tilde{\mu}_{t-1}^j(\theta)^{\mathbf{A}_{ij}[t]}}{\sum_{p=1}^m \ell_i(s_t^i|\theta_p)\prod_{j=1}^n \tilde{\mu}_{t-1}^j(\theta_p)^{\mathbf{A}_{ij}[t]}}, \quad \forall i \in \bar{\mathcal{N}}[t], \forall \theta \in \Theta \tag{6}$$

$$\tilde{\mu}_t^i(\theta) \triangleq \frac{\prod_{j=1}^n \tilde{\mu}_{t-1}^j(\theta)^{\mathbf{A}_{ij}[t]}}{\sum_{p=1}^m \prod_{j=1}^n \tilde{\mu}_{t-1}^j(\theta_p)^{\mathbf{A}_{ij}[t]}} = \tilde{\mu}_{t-1}^i(\theta), \quad \forall i \notin \bar{\mathcal{N}}[t], \forall \theta \in \Theta. \tag{7}$$

Note that, in contrast to (6), no private signal is involved in (7). In addition, (7) is equivalent to defining $\tilde{\mu}_t^i(\theta)=\tilde{\mu}_{t-1}^i(\theta)$ It is easy to see (by induction) that

$$\tilde{\mu}_t^i(\theta)=\mu_t^i(\theta), \forall i \in \bar{\mathcal{N}}[t].$$

Note that $\tilde{\mu}^i(\theta)$ only captures the evolution of $\mu^i(\theta)$ for $i \in \bar{\mathcal{N}}[t]$, i.e., each agent that has not crashed *at the end* of iteration t. Since an agent $i \in \mathcal{N}[t] - \bar{\mathcal{N}}[t]$ may crash during the update step (2), $\tilde{\mu}^i(\theta)$ may not capture the real update performed by nodes in $\mathcal{N}[t] - \bar{\mathcal{N}}[t]$ for some subset of Θ. This inconsistency does not affect the accuracy of our analysis. Intuitively, since the nodes in $\mathcal{N}[t] - \bar{\mathcal{N}}[t]$ are crashing away, they will not affect further system evolution.

For any $\theta \in \Theta$, and any $i \in \mathcal{V}$, let

$$\psi_t^i(\theta) \triangleq \log \frac{\tilde{\mu}_t^i(\theta)}{\tilde{\mu}_t^i(\theta^*)}. \tag{8}$$

Note that for each $i \in \mathcal{N}$, $\mu_t^i(\theta^*) \xrightarrow{\text{a.s.}} 1$ (as $t \to \infty$) if and only if $\psi_t^i(\theta) \xrightarrow{\text{a.s.}} -\infty$ (as $t \to \infty$) for $\theta \neq \theta^*$. In addition, let $\mathcal{L}_t(\theta) \in \mathbb{R}^n$ such that

$$\mathcal{L}_t^i(\theta) \triangleq \begin{cases} \log \frac{\ell_i(s_t^i|\theta)}{\ell_i(s_t^i|\theta^*)}, & \forall\, i \in \bar{\mathcal{N}}[t], \\ 0, & \text{otherwise.} \end{cases} \tag{9}$$

Then, for each $i \in \bar{\mathcal{N}}[t]$, we have

$$\begin{aligned} \psi_t^i(\theta) = \log \frac{\tilde{\mu}_t^i(\theta)}{\tilde{\mu}_t^i(\theta^*)} &= \sum_{j=1}^n \mathbf{A}_{ij}[t] \log \frac{\tilde{\mu}_{t-1}^j(\theta)}{\tilde{\mu}_{t-1}^j(\theta^*)} + \log \frac{\ell_i(s_t^i|\theta)}{\ell_i(s_t^i|\theta^*)} \\ &= \sum_{j=1}^n \mathbf{A}_{ij}[t] \psi_{t-1}^j(\theta) + \mathcal{L}_t^i(\theta) \quad \text{by (9)} \end{aligned} \tag{10}$$

and for each $i \notin \bar{\mathcal{N}}[t]$, we have

$$\begin{aligned} \psi_t^i(\theta) = \log \frac{\tilde{\mu}_t^i(\theta)}{\tilde{\mu}_t^i(\theta^*)} &= \sum_{j=1}^n \mathbf{A}_{ij}[t] \log \frac{\tilde{\mu}_{t-1}^j(\theta)}{\tilde{\mu}_{t-1}^j(\theta^*)} \\ &= \sum_{j=1}^n \mathbf{A}_{ij}[t] \psi_{t-1}^j(\theta) + \mathcal{L}_t^i(\theta) \quad \text{by (9)} \end{aligned} \tag{11}$$

Let $\psi_t(\theta) \in \mathbb{R}^n$ be the vector that stacks $\psi_t^i(\theta)$, with the i–th entry being $\psi_t^i(\theta)$ for all $i \in \mathcal{V}$. The evolution of $\psi(\theta)$ can be compactly written as

$$\psi_t(\theta) = \mathbf{A}[t]\psi_{t-1}(\theta) + \mathcal{L}_t(\theta). \tag{12}$$

Expanding (12), we get

$$\begin{aligned} \psi_t(\theta) &= \mathbf{A}[t]\mathbf{A}[t-1] \cdots \mathbf{A}[1]\psi_0(\theta) + \sum_{r=1}^{t-1} \mathbf{A}[t]\mathbf{A}[t-1] \cdots \mathbf{A}[r+1]\mathcal{L}_r(\theta) + \mathcal{L}_t(\theta) \\ &= \mathbf{\Phi}(t,1)\psi_0(\theta) + \sum_{r=1}^{t} \mathbf{\Phi}(t,r+1)\mathcal{L}_r(\theta) = \sum_{r=1}^{t} \mathbf{\Phi}(t,r+1)\mathcal{L}_r(\theta), \end{aligned} \tag{13}$$

where $\mathbf{\Phi}(t,r) = \mathbf{A}[t] \cdots \mathbf{A}[r]$ for $r \leq t+1$. By convention, $\mathbf{\Phi}(t,t+1) = \mathbf{I}$. Since μ_0^i is uniform, $\psi_0^i(\theta) = 0$ – the last equality in (13) holds.

4 Convergence of $\Phi(t, r)$: Information Mixing

To show the correctness of our learning rule, we first characterize the tight topological condition on $G(\mathcal{V}, \mathcal{E})$ so that information can be sufficiently propagated over the network.

In this section, we present the tight condition on $G(\mathcal{V}, \mathcal{E})$ such that for all $r \le t+1$ and all $k \in \mathcal{V}$

$$\lim_{t \to \infty} |\mathbf{\Phi}_{ik}(t, r) - \mathbf{\Phi}_{jk}(t, r)| = 0 \quad \text{for}\, i, j \in \mathcal{N}. \tag{14}$$

Note that (14) is weaker than requiring $\mathbf{\Phi}(t, r)$ to be weakly ergodic, where (14) needs to hold for any $i, j \in \mathcal{V}$. If the infinite backward product $\lim_{t \to \infty} \mathbf{\Phi}(t, r)$ satisfies (14), we say the product is weakly ergodic restricted to indices in $\mathcal{N}$.

Definition 1. *A reduced graph $\mathcal{H}$ of $G(\mathcal{V}, \mathcal{E})$ is obtained by*

(i) removing up to f incoming links for each $i \in \mathcal{V}$;
(ii) in the obtained graph, removing up to f sinks, if any.[3]

Let $\mathcal{C}$ be the set of all reduced graph of $G(\mathcal{V}, \mathcal{E})$. Note that $\chi = |\mathcal{C}| < \infty$.

Definition 2. *Given a graph, a source component is a strongly connected component that does not have an incoming link from outside the component.*

The following condition is both necessary and sufficient for (14) to hold.

Condition 1 *Each reduced graph of $G(\mathcal{V}, \mathcal{E})$ has a unique source component.*

Note that if (14) holds, asynchronous crash consensus is achieved [8]. Thus the necessary condition for asynchronous consensus is also necessary for (14). The following tight condition of asynchronous crash consensus is found in [17].

Condition 2 *For any node partition L, R, C such that $L \neq \varnothing$ and $R \neq \varnothing$, at least one of the following holds:*

(1) there exists $i \in L$ such that $|\mathcal{I}_i \cap (R \cup C)| \ge f+1$; or
(2) there exists $j \in R$ such that $|\mathcal{I}_j \cap (L \cup C)| \ge f+1$.

Theorem 1. *Conditions 1 and 2 are equivalent.*

Theorem 1 is proved in our full version [15].

Remark 1. Let $\mathcal{H}'$ be the subgraph of $G(\mathcal{V}, \mathcal{E})$ obtained by removing up to f incoming links for each $i \in \mathcal{V}$. Indeed, we are able to show that Condition 2 holds if and only if $\mathcal{H}'$ contains a single source component. That is the removal of sink nodes does not matter for the convergence of consensus because it does not affect the uniqueness of source component and the only state evolution of the non-faulty nodes matter in the consensus problem.

[3] For a given graph, a node s is called a sink if it has no outgoing links.

Recall that $\chi = |\mathcal{C}|$ is the total number of reduced graphs of $G(\mathcal{V}, \mathcal{E})$. We can show that $|\mathbf{\Phi}_{ik}(t,r) - \mathbf{\Phi}_{jk}(t,r)|$, where $i,j \in \mathcal{N}$, decays exponentially fast.

Theorem 2. *Let $\xi \triangleq \frac{1}{1+\max_{i\in\mathcal{V}}|\mathcal{I}_i|}$. Suppose $r \le t$. For any $i,j \in \bar{\mathcal{N}}[t]$ and for any $k \in \mathcal{V}$, it holds that*

$$|\mathbf{\Phi}_{ik}(t,r) - \mathbf{\Phi}_{jk}(t,r)| \le \min\{1, (1-\xi^{n\chi})^{\lfloor \frac{t-r+1}{n\chi} \rfloor - f}\}.$$

Theorem 2 is proved in our full version [15]. The proof of Theorem 2 relies on a couple of intermediate results, which are generalizations of the well-known results obtained by Wolfowitz [20] and Hajnal [4].

We first briefly review the corresponding results obtained by Wolfowitz [20] and Hajnal [4]. Two coefficients that measure the ergodicity of a stochastic matrix are defined in [4,20] as follows. For $t \ge 1$, $t' \ge t$ and $r \ge 1$,

$$\hat{\delta}_r(\mathbf{\Phi}(t',t)) \triangleq \max_{j\in\mathcal{V}} \max_{i,i'\in\mathcal{V}} |\mathbf{\Phi}_{ij}(t',t) - \mathbf{\Phi}_{i'j}(t',t)|.$$

$$\hat{\eta}_r(\mathbf{\Phi}(t',t)) \triangleq \min_{i,i'\in\mathcal{V}} \sum_{j\in\mathcal{V}} \min\{\mathbf{\Phi}_{ij}(t',t), \mathbf{\Phi}_{i'j}(t',t)\}$$

The following lemmas were proved in [4,20].

Lemma 1. *For each $t \ge 0$ and $t' \ge t$, we have $\hat{\delta}_t(\mathbf{\Phi}(t',t)) \le 1 - \hat{\eta}_t(\mathbf{\Phi}(t',t))$.*

Lemma 2. *For $t_2 > t_1 \ge t_0 \ge 1$, define $\mathbf{P} = \mathbf{\Phi}(t_2, t_1+1)$, $\mathbf{G} = \mathbf{\Phi}(t_1, t_0)$, and $\mathbf{F} = \mathbf{\Phi}(t_2, t_0)$. Then it holds that $\hat{\delta}_{t_1+1}(\mathbf{F}) \le (1 - \hat{\eta}_{t_1+1}(\mathbf{P}))\, \hat{\delta}_{t_1+1}(\mathbf{G})$.*

This set of results are not applicable to our problem, since both $\hat{\delta}(\cdot)$ and $\hat{\eta}(\cdot)$ measure the ergodicity of the whole matrix. However, in our problem, since some agents may crash, the rows in $\mathbf{\Phi}(r,t)$ corresponding to the crashed agents will stop updating when crash occurs. Thus, the mixing property of the whole $\mathbf{\Phi}(r,t)$ may be irrelevant to us – we only care about whether the rows associated with the non-faulty agents will asymptotically be identical.

Thus, we generalize the above results as follows.

Specifically, for $t \ge 1$, $t' \ge t$ and $r \ge 1$,

$$\delta_r(\mathbf{\Phi}(t',t)) \triangleq \max_{j\in\mathcal{V}} \max_{i,i'\in\mathcal{N}[r]} |\mathbf{\Phi}_{ij}(t',t) - \mathbf{\Phi}_{i'j}(t',t)|. \tag{15}$$

$$\eta_r(\mathbf{\Phi}(t',t)) \triangleq \min_{i,i'\in\mathcal{N}[r]} \sum_{j\in\mathcal{V}} \min\{\mathbf{\Phi}_{ij}(t',t), \mathbf{\Phi}_{i'j}(t',t)\}. \tag{16}$$

The following lemmas hold.

Lemma 3. *For each $t \ge 0$ and $t' \ge t$, we have $\delta_t(\mathbf{\Phi}(t',t)) \le 1 - \eta_t(\mathbf{\Phi}(t',t))$.*

Lemma 4. *For $t_2 > t_1 \ge t_0 \ge 1$, define $\mathbf{P} = \mathbf{\Phi}(t_2, t_1+1)$, $\mathbf{G} = \mathbf{\Phi}(t_1, t_0)$, and $\mathbf{F} = \mathbf{\Phi}(t_2, t_0)$. Then it holds that $\delta_{t_1+1}(\mathbf{F}) \le (1 - \eta_{t_1+1}(\mathbf{P}))\, \delta_{t_1+1}(\mathbf{G})$.*

The proofs of Lemmas 3 and 4 can be found in our full version [15].

An immediate consequence of Theorem 2 is that (14) holds, proving Condition 2 is also sufficient for (14) to hold.

The following results are useful for our convergence analysis in Sect. 5.

Lemma 5. *For all $i \in \mathcal{N}$, the i-th row of $\mathbf{\Phi}(t,r)$, denoted by $\mathbf{\Phi}_{i\cdot}(t,r)$ converges to a stochastic vector $\boldsymbol{\pi}^T(r)$, i.e., $\mathbf{\Phi}_{i\cdot}(t,r) \to \boldsymbol{\pi}^T(r), \forall r$.*

That is, the rows of $\mathbf{\Phi}(t,r)$ with indices in $\mathcal{N}$ have a common limit. Indeed, for each $i \in \mathcal{N}$, the row $\mathbf{\Phi}_{i\cdot}(t,r)$ converges to $\boldsymbol{\pi}(r)$ exponentially fast.

Proposition 1. *Suppose $r \le t$. For any $i \in \mathcal{N}$ and for any $k \in \mathcal{V}$, it holds that*

$$|\mathbf{\Phi}_{ik}(t,r) - \pi_k(r)| \le \min\{1, (1-\xi^{n\chi})^{\lfloor \frac{t-r+1}{n\chi} \rfloor - f}\}.$$

Let $\mathcal{H}$ be an arbitrary reduced of $G(\mathcal{V},\mathcal{E})$ with source component $\mathcal{S}_{\mathcal{H}}$. Define

$$\gamma \triangleq \min_{\mathcal{H} \in C} |\mathcal{S}_{\mathcal{H}}|, \tag{17}$$

i.e., γ is the minimum source component size in all reduced graphs. Note that $\gamma \ge 1$. The limit vector $\boldsymbol{\pi}(r)$ has the following property.

Lemma 6. *For any r, there exists a reduced graph $\tilde{\mathcal{H}}[r]$ with source component S_r such that $\pi_j(r) \ge \xi^{n\chi}$, for each $j \in S_r$. In addition, $|S_r| \ge \gamma$.*

The proofs of Lemmas 5 and 6, and Proposition 1 can be found in our full version [15].

5 Convergence of Non-Bayesian Learning

We assume the following network identifiability, which builds upon Condition 1.

Condition 3. *Suppose $G(\mathcal{V},\mathcal{E})$ satisfies Condition 1. For any $\theta \neq \theta^*$, and for any reduced graph $\mathcal{H}$ of $G(\mathcal{V},\mathcal{E})$ with $\mathcal{S}_{\mathcal{H}}$ denoting the unique source component, the source component should be able to learn θ^*, i.e.,*

$$\sum_{i \in \mathcal{S}_{\mathcal{H}}} D\left(\ell_i(\cdot|\theta^*) || \ell_i(\cdot|\theta)\right) \neq 0. \tag{18}$$

In contrast to (1), where the summation is taken over all the agents in the network, the summation in (18) is taken over the source component of an arbitrary reduced graph. Condition 3 is necessary for (3) to be achievable: if Condition 3 is violated, no information outside the source component is available to the agents in the component to distinguish two hypotheses, and θ^* cannot be learned. In addition, Condition 3 is also sufficient for θ^* to be learned, shown next.

Our convergence analysis has a similar structure to that in [10,13].

Recall that $\mathcal{C}$ is the collection of all reduced graphs of $G(\mathcal{V}, \mathcal{E})$. Let $\mathcal{H} \in \mathcal{C}$ with source component $\mathcal{S}_{\mathcal{H}}$. Define C_0 and C_1 as

$$-C_0 \triangleq \min_{i\in\mathcal{V}} \min_{\theta_1,\theta_2\in\Theta;\theta_1\neq\theta_2} \min_{w_i\in\mathcal{S}_i} \left(\log \frac{\ell_i(w_i|\theta_1)}{\ell_i(w_i|\theta_2)}\right), \tag{19}$$

$$C_1 \triangleq \min_{\mathcal{H}\in\mathcal{C}} \min_{\theta_1,\theta_2\in\Theta;\theta_1\neq\theta_2} \sum_{i\in\mathcal{S}_{\mathcal{H}}} D\left(\ell_i(\cdot|\theta_1)||\ell_i(\cdot|\theta_2)\right). \tag{20}$$

Since $|\Theta| = m < \infty$ and the finiteness of $|\mathcal{S}_i|$ for each $i \in \mathcal{V}$, we know that $-C_0 > -\infty$. In addition, it is easy to see that $-C_0 \leq 0$ (thus, $C_0 \geq 0$). From Condition 3 and the fact that $|\mathcal{C}| = \chi < \infty$, we get $C_1 > 0$.

Theorem 3. *Suppose Condition 3 holds. Then each non-faulty agent $i \in \mathcal{N}$ learns the true hypothesis θ^* almost surely, i.e., $\mu_t^i(\theta^*) \xrightarrow{\text{a.s.}} 1, \forall i \in \mathcal{N}$.*

Proof. Our proof parallels the structure of a proof in [10,13], but with some key differences to take into account our update rule for the belief vector.

Define $H(\theta) \in \mathbb{R}^n$ such that

$$H_i(\theta) \triangleq \sum_{w_i\in\mathcal{S}_i} \ell_i(w_i|\theta^*) \log \frac{\ell_i(w_i|\theta)}{\ell_i(w_i|\theta^*)} = -D\left(\ell_i(\cdot|\theta^*)||\ell_i(\cdot|\theta)\right). \tag{21}$$

Since $D\left(\ell_i(\cdot|\theta^*)||\ell_i(\cdot|\theta)\right) \geq 0$, it follows that $H_i(\theta) \leq 0$. Note that, for each $t \geq 1$ and for each $i \in \bar{\mathcal{N}}[t]$, it holds that

$$H_i(\theta) = \mathbb{E}^*[\mathcal{L}_t^i(\theta)], \tag{22}$$

where the expectation $\mathbb{E}^*[\cdot]$ is taken over $\ell_i(\cdot|\theta^*)$. Since the support of $\ell_i(\cdot|\theta)$ is the whole signal space $\mathcal{S}_i$ for each agent $i \in \mathcal{V}$, it holds that $\left|\frac{\ell_i(w_i|\theta)}{\ell_i(w_i|\theta^*)}\right| < \infty$ for each $w_i \in \mathcal{S}_i$, and $H_i(\theta) \geq= -C_0 > -\infty$. Recall that $\boldsymbol{\pi}(r+1) \in \mathbb{R}^n$ is the limit of $[\boldsymbol{\Phi}(t, r+1)]_{i\cdot}$ for each $i \in \mathcal{N}$. Thus, $-\infty < -C_0 \leq \boldsymbol{\pi}^T(r+1)H(\theta) \leq 0$. Due to the finiteness of $\boldsymbol{\pi}^T(r+1)H(\theta)$, we are able to add $\sum_{r=1}^t \mathbf{1}_n\boldsymbol{\pi}^T(r+1)H(\theta)$ to and subtract $\sum_{r=1}^t \mathbf{1}_n\boldsymbol{\pi}^T(r+1)H(\theta)$ from (13), where $\mathbf{1}_n \in \mathbb{R}^n$. So we get

$$\begin{aligned}\psi_t(\theta) &= \sum_{r=1}^t \left(\boldsymbol{\Phi}(t, r+1)\mathcal{L}_r(\theta) - \mathbf{1}_n\boldsymbol{\pi}^T(r+1)H(\theta)\right) \\ &\quad + \sum_{r=1}^t \mathbf{1}_n\boldsymbol{\pi}^T(r+1)H(\theta).\end{aligned} \tag{23}$$

For each $i \in \mathcal{N}$, we have

$$\begin{aligned}\psi_t^i(\theta) &= \sum_{r=1}^t \left(\sum_{k=1}^n \boldsymbol{\Phi}_{ik}(t, r+1)\mathcal{L}_r^k(\theta) - \sum_{k=1}^n \pi_k(r+1)H_k(\theta)\right) \\ &\quad + \sum_{r=1}^t \sum_{k=1}^n \pi_k(r+1)H_k(\theta).\end{aligned} \tag{24}$$

To show $\lim_{t\to\infty} \mu_t^i(\theta^*) \xrightarrow{\text{a.s.}} 1$, it is enough to show $\psi_t^i(\theta) \xrightarrow{\text{a.s.}} -\infty$ for $\theta \neq \theta^*$.

We first bound the second term of the RHS of (24). For each $r \le t$, let S_r be the set of agents that has the property stated in Lemma 6. Then, we have

$$
\begin{aligned}
\sum_{r=1}^{t}\sum_{k=1}^{n} \pi_k(r+1)H_k(\theta) &\le \sum_{r=1}^{t}\sum_{k\in S_{r+1}} \pi_k(r+1)H_k(\theta) \quad \text{since } H_k(\theta)\le 0 \\
&= -\sum_{r=1}^{t}\sum_{k\in S_{r+1}} \pi_k(r+1)D(\ell_k(\cdot|\theta^*)||\ell_k(\cdot|\theta)) \quad \text{by (21)} \\
&\le -\sum_{r=1}^{t}\xi^{n\chi}\sum_{k\in S_{r+1}} D(\ell_k(\cdot|\theta^*)||\ell_k(\cdot|\theta)) \quad \text{by Lemma 6} \\
&\le -t\xi^{n\chi}C_1 \quad \text{by (20)}
\end{aligned} \tag{25}
$$

Now we show that $\frac{1}{t}\sum_{r=1}^{t}\left(\sum_{k=1}^{n}\mathbf{\Phi}_{ik}(t,r)\mathcal{L}_r^k(\theta) - \sum_{k=1}^{n}\pi_k(r+1)H_k(\theta)\right)$ goes to 0 almost surely. Specifically,

$$
\begin{aligned}
&\frac{1}{t}\sum_{r=1}^{t}\left(\sum_{k=1}^{n}\mathbf{\Phi}_{ik}(t,r+1)\mathcal{L}_r^k(\theta) - \sum_{k=1}^{n}\pi_k(r+1)H_k(\theta)\right) \\
&= \frac{1}{t}\sum_{r=1}^{t}\sum_{k=1}^{n}\left(\mathbf{\Phi}_{ik}(t,r+1) - \pi_k(r+1)\right)\mathcal{L}_r^k(\theta) \\
&\quad + \frac{1}{t}\sum_{r=1}^{t}\left(\sum_{k=1}^{n}\pi_k(r+1)\mathcal{L}_r^k(\theta) - \sum_{k=1}^{n}\pi_k(r+1)H_k(\theta)\right).
\end{aligned} \tag{26}
$$

By (9), we have

$$
\left|\mathcal{L}_r^k(\theta)\right| \le \left|\log\frac{\ell_i(s_t^i|\theta)}{\ell_i(s_t^i|\theta^*)}\right| \le \max_{i\in\mathcal{V}}\ \max_{\theta_1,\theta_2\in\Theta;\theta_1\neq\theta_2}\ \max_{w_i\in\mathcal{S}_i}\left|\log\frac{\ell_i(w_i|\theta_1)}{\ell_i(w_i|\theta_2)}\right| \le C_0. \tag{27}
$$

Note that $\sum_{r=1}^{t}\min\{1,(1-\xi^{n\chi})^{\lfloor\frac{t-r}{n\chi}\rfloor - f}\}$ is a geometric series for sufficient large t, and is convergent. In particular,

$$
\sum_{r=1}^{\infty}\min\{1,(1-\xi^{n\chi})^{\lfloor\frac{t-r}{n\chi}\rfloor - f}\} \triangleq C < \infty. \tag{28}
$$

For each $i\in\mathcal{N}$, the absolute value of the first term in the right hand side of (26) can be bounded as follows.

$$
\begin{aligned}
&\frac{1}{t}\left|\sum_{r=1}^{t}\sum_{k=1}^{n}\left(\mathbf{\Phi}_{ik}(t,r+1)-\pi_k(r+1)\right)\mathcal{L}_r^k(\theta)\right| \\
&\le \frac{1}{t}\sum_{r=1}^{t}\sum_{k=1}^{n}\left|\mathbf{\Phi}_{ik}(t,r+1)-\pi_k(r+1)\right| C_0 \text{ by (27)} \\
&\overset{(a)}{\le} \frac{1}{t}\left(\sum_{r=1}^{t-1}\sum_{k=1}^{n}\left|\mathbf{\Phi}_{ik}(t,r+1)-\pi_k(r+1)\right| C_0 + nC_0\right) \\
&\le \frac{1}{t}\left(\sum_{r=1}^{t-1} n\cdot \min\{1,\ (1-\xi^{n\chi})^{\lfloor\frac{t-r}{n\chi}\rfloor - f}\}C_0 + nC_0\right) \quad \text{by Proposition 1} \\
&\overset{(b)}{\le} \frac{1}{t}\sum_{r=1}^{t} n\cdot \min\{1,\ (1-\xi^{n\chi})^{\lfloor\frac{t-r}{n\chi}\rfloor - f}\}C_0 \\
&\le \frac{1}{t}nCC_0 \quad \text{by (28)}
\end{aligned}
\tag{29}
$$

The inequality (a) is true since $|\mathbf{\Phi}_{ik}(t,r+1)-\pi_k(r+1)|\le 1$; and inequality (b) follows from the fact that $\min\{1,(1-\xi^{n\chi})^{\lfloor\frac{t-t}{n\chi}\rfloor - f}\} = 1$. Thus, for every sample path, the following holds.

$$
\lim_{t\to\infty}\frac{1}{t}\sum_{r=1}^{t}\sum_{k=1}^{n}\left(\mathbf{\Phi}_{ik}(t,r+1)-\pi_k(r+1)\right)\mathcal{L}_r^k(\theta) = 0. \tag{30}
$$

Kolmogorov's strong law of large number states that if $\{X_r\}_{r=1}^{\infty}$ is a sequence of *independent* random variables such that $\sum_{r=1}^{\infty}\frac{Var(X_r)}{r^2}<\infty$, then $\frac{1}{t}\sum_{r=1}^{t}X_k - \frac{1}{t}\sum_{r=1}^{t}\mathbb{E}[X_r] \xrightarrow{\text{a.s.}} 0$.

Now we bound the second term in the right hand side of (26) using Kolmogorov's strong law of large number. For each r, let

$$
X_r \triangleq \sum_{k=1}^{n}\pi_k(r+1)\mathcal{L}_r^k(\theta). \tag{31}
$$

Since the private signals s_r^i's are i.i.d. across iterations, X_r's are independent. In addition, since

$$
\mathbb{E}\left[X_r^2\right] = \mathbb{E}\left[\left(\sum_{k=1}^{n}\pi_k(r+1)\mathcal{L}_r^k(\theta)\right)^2\right] \le \mathbb{E}\left[\max_{k\in\mathcal{V}}|\mathcal{L}_r^k(\theta)|^2\right] \le C_0^2,
$$

where the last inequality follows from (27), we get

$$
\sum_{r=1}^{\infty}\frac{Var\left(X_r\right)}{r^2} \le \sum_{r=1}^{\infty}\frac{\mathbb{E}\left[X_r^2\right]}{r^2} \le \sum_{r=1}^{\infty}\frac{1}{r^2}C_0^2 < \infty.
$$

For each $i \in \mathcal{N}$ and each $k \in \mathcal{V}$, by Lemma 5, it holds that $\pi_k(r+1) = \lim_{t\to\infty} \mathbf{\Phi}_{ik}(t, r+1)$. In addition, for each $k \notin \mathcal{N}[t+1]$, we have

$$\pi_k(r+1) = \lim_{t\to\infty} \mathbf{\Phi}_{ik}(t, r+1) = 0. \tag{32}$$

Thus, we get

$$X_r = \sum_{k=1}^{n} \pi_k(r+1)\mathcal{L}_r^k(\theta) = \sum_{k\in\mathcal{N}[t+1]} \pi_k(r+1)\mathcal{L}_r^k(\theta). \tag{33}$$

Thus, we have, for each $i \in \mathcal{N}$

$$\begin{aligned}
&\frac{1}{t}\sum_{r=1}^{t}\left(\sum_{k=1}^{n} \pi_k(r+1)\mathcal{L}_r^k(\theta) - \sum_{k=1}^{n} \pi_k(r+1)H_k(\theta)\right) \\
&= \frac{1}{t}\sum_{r=1}^{t}\left(X_r - \sum_{k=1}^{n} \pi_k(r+1)H_k(\theta)\right) = \frac{1}{t}\sum_{r=1}^{t}\left(X_r - \sum_{k\in\mathcal{N}[r+1]} \pi_k(r+1)H_k(\theta)\right) \\
&= \frac{1}{t}\sum_{r=1}^{t}\left(X_r - \sum_{k\in\mathcal{N}[r+1]} \pi_k(r+1)\mathbb{E}^*[\mathcal{L}_r^k(\theta)]\right) \quad \text{by (22)} \\
&= \frac{1}{t}\sum_{r=1}^{t}(X_r - \mathbb{E}^*[X_r]) \xrightarrow{\text{a.s.}} 0 \quad \text{by Kolmogorov's SLLN}
\end{aligned} \tag{34}$$

By (30), (34) and (26), we obtain that

$$\frac{1}{t}\sum_{r=1}^{t}\left(\sum_{k=1}^{n} \mathbf{\Phi}_{ik}(t,r)L_r^k(\theta) - \sum_{k=1}^{n} \pi_k(r+1)H_k(\theta)\right) \xrightarrow{\text{a.s.}} 0. \tag{35}$$

From (24) and (35), we know $\limsup_{t\to\infty} \frac{1}{t}\psi_t^i(\theta) \le -\xi^{n\chi}C_1$ holds almost surely for each $i \in \mathcal{N}$ and $\theta \neq \theta^*$. Consequently, for each $i \in \mathcal{N}$ and each $\theta \neq \theta^*$,

$$\psi_t^i(\theta) \xrightarrow{\text{a.s.}} -\infty, \quad \text{and} \quad \lim_{t\to\infty} \mu_t^i(\theta) \xrightarrow{\text{a.s.}} 0.$$

Due to (8) and the fact that $\tilde{\mu}_t^i(\theta) = \mu_t^i(\theta), \forall i \in \mathcal{N}$, we get $\lim_{t\to\infty} \mu_t^i(\theta) \xrightarrow{\text{a.s.}} 0$ for all $\theta \neq \theta^*$. Equivalently, for each $i \in \mathcal{N}$,

$$\lim_{t\to\infty} \mu_t^i(\theta^*) \xrightarrow{\text{a.s.}} 1,$$

proving the theorem.

6 Non-Asymptotic Rate of Convergence

Following the analysis in [10,13], finite time convergence rate can be derived using similar argument as the almost surely argument, using McDiarmid's inequality.

Let λ be a constant defined as

$$\lambda \triangleq \sum_{r=0}^{\infty} \min\{1, (1-\xi^{n\chi})^{\lfloor \frac{r}{n\chi} \rfloor} - f\}. \tag{36}$$

Lemma 7. *For any $\theta \neq \theta^*$ and $i \in \mathcal{N}$, we have*

$$\mathbb{E}^* \left[\psi_t^i(\theta, \theta^*)\right] \leq n\lambda C_0 - \xi^{n\chi} C_1 t,$$

where C_0 and C_1 are defined in (19) *and* (20)*, respectively.*

Lemma 7 is proved in our full version [15].

Similar to [10,13], McDiarmid's Inequality is used.

Theorem 4 (McDiarmid's Inequality). *Let $X_1, \cdots, X_t$ be independent random variables and consider the mapping $H : \mathcal{X}^t \to \mathbb{R}$. If for $r = 1, \cdots, t$, and every sample $x_1, \cdots, x_t$, and $x_r' \in \mathcal{X}$, the function H satisfies*

$$|H(x_1, \cdots, x_r, \cdots, x_t) - H(x_1, \cdots, x_r', \cdots, x_t)| \leq c_r,$$

then for all $\epsilon > 0$, it holds that

$$\mathbb{P}\left[|H(x_1, \cdots, x_t) - \mathbb{E}[H(x_1, \cdots, x_t)]| \geq \epsilon\right] \leq \exp\left(\frac{-2\epsilon^2}{\sum_{r=1}^t c_r^2}\right).$$

Theorem 5. *Under Condition 3, for any $\rho \in (0,1)$, there exists an integer $T(\rho)$ such that with probability $1-\rho$, for all $t \geq T(\rho)$ and all $\theta \neq \theta^*$, we have*

$$\mu_t^i(\theta) \leq \exp\left(n\lambda C_0 - \frac{\xi^{n\chi} C_1}{2} t\right),$$

where C_0, C_1 and λ are defined in (19), (20) *and* (36)*, respectively.*

Proof. Since $\mu_t^i(\theta^*) \in (0,1]$, we have

$$\mu_t^i(\theta) \leq \frac{\mu_t^i(\theta)}{\mu_t^i(\theta^*)} = \exp\left(\psi_t^i(\theta, \theta^*)\right).$$

Thus, we have

$$\begin{aligned}\mathbb{P}\left(\mu_t^i(\theta) \geq \exp\left(n\lambda C_0 - \frac{\xi^{n\chi} C_1}{2} t\right)\right) &\leq \mathbb{P}\left(\psi_t^i(\theta) \geq n\lambda C_0 - \frac{\xi^{n\chi} C_1}{2} t\right) \\ &\leq \mathbb{P}\left(\psi_t^i(\theta) - \mathbb{E}^*\left[\psi_t^i(\theta)\right] \geq \frac{\xi^{n\chi} C_1}{2} t\right).\end{aligned}$$

Note that $\psi_t^i(\theta, \theta^*)$ is a function of the random vector $\mathbf{s}_1, \cdots, \mathbf{s}_t$. For a given sample path $\mathbf{s}_1, \cdots, \mathbf{s}_t$, and for all $p \in \{1, \cdots, t\}$, it is easy to see that

$$\max_{\mathbf{s}_p \in \mathcal{S}_1 \times \cdots \times \mathcal{S}_t} \psi_t^i(\theta) - \min_{\mathbf{s}_p \in \mathcal{S}_1 \times \cdots \times \mathcal{S}_t} \psi_t^i(\theta) \leq 2C_0.$$

By McDiarmid's inequality (Theorem 4), we obtain that

$$\mathbb{P}\left(\psi_t^i(\theta) - \mathbb{E}^*\left[\psi_t^i(\theta)\right] \geq \frac{\xi^{n\chi}C_1}{2}t\right) \leq \exp\left(-\frac{2\left(\frac{\xi^{n\chi}C_1}{2}t\right)^2}{\sum_{p=1}^t (2C_0)^2}\right)$$
$$\leq \exp\left(-\frac{\xi^{2n\chi}C_1^2 t}{8C_0^2}\right).$$

Therefore, for a given confidence level ρ, in order to have

$$\mathbb{P}\left(\mu_t^i(\theta) \geq \exp\left(n\lambda C_0 - \frac{\xi^{n\chi}C_1}{2}t\right)\right) \leq \rho,$$

we require that $t \geq T(\rho) = \frac{8C_0^2}{\xi^{2n\chi}C_1^2}\log\frac{1}{\rho}$.

7 Conclusions

This paper addresses the problem of consensus-based non-Bayesian learning over multi-agent networks when an unknown subset of agents may crease unexpectedly, and the message delay can be arbitrarily long but finite. Under minimal assumptions on the underlying network structure and the global identifiability of the network, we show that all the non-faulty agents asymptotically agree on the true state almost surely. In addition, a finite time learning rate is derived. As part of our analysis, we obtain a generalization of a celebrated result by Wolfowitz and Hajnal to submatrices, which might be of independent interest.

References

1. Chamberland, J.-F., Veeravalli, V.V.: Decentralized detection in sensor networks. IEEE Trans. Signal Process. **51**(2), 407–416 (2003)
2. Feldman, M., Immorlica, N., Lucier, B., Weinberg, S.M.: Reaching consensus via non-Bayesian asynchronous learning in social networks. CoRR, abs/1408.5192 (2014)
3. Gale, D., Kariv, S.: Bayesian learning in social networks. Games Econ. Behav. **45**(2), 329–346 (2003)
4. Hajnal, J., Bartlett, M.: Weak ergodicity in non-homogeneous Markov chains. In: Mathematical Proceedings of the Cambridge Philosophical Society, vol. 54, pp. 233–246. Cambridge Univ Press (1958)
5. Jadbabaie, A., Molavi, P., Sandroni, A., Tahbaz-Salehi, A.: Non-Bayesian social learning. Games Econ. Behav. **76**(1), 210–225 (2012)
6. Jadbabaie, A., Molavi, P., Tahbaz-Salehi, A.: Information heterogeneity and the speed of learning in social networks. Columbia Business School Research Paper, (13–28) (2013)
7. Lalitha, A., Sarwate, A., Javidi, T.: Social learning and distributed hypothesis testing. In: IEEE International Symposium on Information Theory, pp. 551–555. IEEE (2014)

8. Lynch, N.A.: Distributed Algorithms. Morgan Kaufmann, San Francisco (1996)
9. Molavi, P., Tahbaz-Salehi, A., Jadbabaie, A.: Foundations of non-Bayesian social learning. Columbia Business School Research Paper (2015)
10. Nedić, A., Olshevsky, A., Uribe, C.A.: Nonasymptotic convergence rates for cooperative learning over time-varying directed graphs. In: American Control Conference (ACC), pp. 5884–5889. IEEE (2015)
11. Rad, K.R., Tahbaz-Salehi, A.: Distributed parameter estimation in networks. In: 49th IEEE Conference on Decision and Control (CDC), pp. 5050–5055. IEEE (2010)
12. Shahrampour, S., Jadbabaie, A.: Exponentially fast parameter estimation in networks using distributed dual averaging. In: 52nd IEEE Conference on Decision and Control, pp. 6196–6201. IEEE (2013)
13. Shahrampour, S., Rakhlin, A., Jadbabaie, A.: Distributed detection: finite-time analysis and impact of network topology (2014)
14. Shahrampour, S., Rakhlin, A., Jadbabaie, A.: Finite-time analysis of the distributed detection problem. CoRR, abs/1512.09311 (2015)
15. Su, L., Vaidya, N.H.: Asynchronous distributed hypothesis testing in the presence of crash failures. University of Illinois at Urbana-Champaign, Technical report (2016)
16. Su, L., Vaidya, N.H.: Non-Bayesian learning in the presence of Byzantine agents. In: Gavoille, C., Ilcinkas, D. (eds.) DISC 2016. LNCS, vol. 9888, pp. 414–427. Springer, Heidelberg (2016). doi:10.1007/978-3-662-53426-7_30
17. Tseng, L.: Fault-tolerant consensus and shared memory consistency model. Ph.D dissertation University of Illinois at Urbana-Champaign (2015)
18. Tsitsiklis, J.N.: Decentralized detection. In: Advances in Statistical Signal Processing, pp. 297–344. JAI Press (1993)
19. Varshney, P.K.: Distributed Bayesian detection: parallel fusion network. Distributed Detection and Data Fusion, pp. 36–118. Springer, New York (1997)
20. Wolfowitz, J.: Products of indecomposable, aperiodic, stochastic matrices. Proc. Am. Math. Soc. **14**(5), 733–737 (1963)
21. Wong, E., Hajek, B.: Stochastic Processes in Engineering Systems. Springer Science & Business Media, New York (2012)

Robust Multi-agent Optimization: Coping with Byzantine Agents with Input Redundancy

Lili Su(✉) and Nitin H. Vaidya

Department of Electrical and Computer Engineering,
University of Illinois at Urbana-Champaign, Urbana, USA
{lilisu3,nhv}@illinois.edu

Abstract. This paper addresses the multi-agent optimization problem in which the agents try to collaboratively minimize $\frac{1}{k}\sum_{i=1}^{k} h_i$ for a given choice of k input functions $h_1, \ldots, h_k$. This problem finds its application in distributed machine learning, where the data set is too large to be processed and stored by a single machine. It has been shown that when the networked agents may suffer Byzantine faults, it is impossible to minimize $\frac{1}{k}\sum_{i=1}^{k} h_i$ with no redundancy in the local cost functions.

We are interested in the impact of the local cost functions redundancy on the solvability of $\frac{1}{k}\sum_{i=1}^{k} h_i$. In particular, we assume that the local cost function of each agent is formed as a *convex combination* of the k input functions $h_1, \ldots, h_k$. Depending on the availability of side information at each agent, two slightly different variants are considered. We show that for a given graph, the problem can indeed be solved despite the presence of faulty agents. In particular, even in the absence of side information at each agent, when adequate *redundancy* is available in the optima of input functions, a distributed algorithm is proposed in which each agent carries minimal state across iterations.

Keywords: Distributed optimization · Multi-agent network · Coding theory · Byzantine faults · Redundancy · Security

1 Introduction

Fault-tolerant consensus [15] is closely related to the optimization problem considered in this paper. There is a significant body of work on fault-tolerant consensus, including [4,5,7–10,23]. Two variants that are most relevant to the algorithms in this paper are *iterative approximate Byzantine consensus* [7,9,23] and *condition-based consensus* [4,8,11]. Iterative approximate consensus requires that the agents agree with each other only approximately, using local communication

This research is supported in part by National Science Foundation awards NSF 1329681 and 1421918. Any opinions, findings, and conclusions or recommendations expressed here are those of the authors and do not necessarily reflect the views of the funding agencies or the U.S. government.

B. Bonakdarpour and F. Petit (Eds.): SSS 2016, LNCS 10083, pp. 368–382, 2016.
DOI: 10.1007/978-3-319-49259-9_29

and maintaining *minimal* state across iterations. Condition-based consensus [11] restricts the inputs of the agents to be within some acceptable set. [4] showed that if a condition (the set of allowable system inputs) is f*-acceptable*, then consensus can be achieved in the presence of up to f crash failures over complete graphs. A connection between asynchronous consensus and error-correcting codes (ECC) was established in [8], observing that crash failures and Byzantine failures correspond to erasures and substitution errors, respectively, in ECCs. Condition-based approach can also be used in synchronous system to speed up the agreement [11,12].

There has been significant research on the distributed optimization problem of the form [6,13,14,21], in which the global objective $h(x)$ is a summation of n convex functions, i.e., $h(x) = \sum_{j=1}^{n} h_j(x)$, with function $h_j(x)$ being known to the j-th agent. The need for robustness for distributed optimization problems has received some attentions recently [6,13]. In particular, Duchi et al. [6] and Nedic et al. [13] investigated the impact of random communication link failures and time-varying communication topology. Duchi et al. [6] assumed that each realizable link failure pattern considered in [6] is assumed to admit a doubly-stochastic matrix which governs the evolution dynamics of local estimates of the optimum. The doubly-stochastic requirement is relaxed in [13], using the push-sum technique. In contrast, we consider the system in which up to f agents may be Byzantine, i.e., up to f agents may be adversarial and try to mislead the system to function improperly. Byzantine faults are considered in [19,20], where the fundamental limits are characterized in [20] and an optimal distributed algorithm with simple communication is proposed in [19]. We are not aware of existing work on Byzantine agents with input redundancy.

2 System Model and Problem Formulation

The system under consideration is synchronous, and consists of n agents connected by an arbitrary directed communication network $G(\mathcal{V}, \mathcal{E})$, where $\mathcal{V} = \{1, \ldots, n\}$ is the set of n agents, and $\mathcal{E}$ is the set of directed edges between the agents in $\mathcal{V}$. Up to f of the n agents may be Byzantine faulty. We assume $n > 3f$. Let $\mathcal{F}$ denote the set of faulty agents in a given execution. Agent i can reliably transmit messages to agent j if and only if the directed edge (i,j) is in $\mathcal{E}$. Each agent can send messages to itself as well, however, for convenience, we *exclude self-loops* from set $\mathcal{E}$. That is, $(i,i) \notin \mathcal{E}$ for $i \in \mathcal{V}$. With a slight abuse of terminology, we will use the terms *edge* and *link* interchangeably, and use the terms *nodes* and *agents* interchangeably in our presentation.

For each agent i, let N_i^- be the set of agents from which i has incoming edges. That is, $N_i^- = \{\, j \mid (j,i) \in \mathcal{E} \,\}$. Similarly, define N_i^+ as the set of agents to which agent i has outgoing edges. That is, $N_i^+ = \{\, j \mid (i,j) \in \mathcal{E} \,\}$. Since we exclude self-loops from $\mathcal{E}$, $i \notin N_i^-$ and $i \notin N_i^+$.

We say that a function $h : \mathbb{R} \to \mathbb{R}$ is *admissible* if (i) $h(\cdot)$ is convex and L-Lipschitz continuous for some positive constant L, and (ii) the set $\operatorname{argmin} h(x)$ containing the optima of $h(\cdot)$ is non-empty and compact (i.e., bounded and closed). Given k admissible input functions $h_1(\cdot), \ldots, h_k(\cdot)$, each agent $i \in \mathcal{V}$ is initially provided with a local cost function $g_i(\cdot)$ of the form

$$g_i(x) = \mathbf{A}_{1i}h_1(x) + \mathbf{A}_{2i}h_2(x) + \ldots + \mathbf{A}_{ki}h_k(x), \forall x \in \mathbb{R}$$

where $\mathbf{A}_{ji} \geq 0$ and $\mathbf{A}_{ji} \geq 0$ and $\sum_{j=1}^{k} \mathbf{A}_{ji} = 1$ for all $i \in \mathcal{V}$ and all $j = 1, \ldots, k$. Compactly, we have $\mathbf{g}(x) = \mathbf{h}(x)\mathbf{A}$, where $\mathbf{h}(x) = [h_1(x), h_2(x), \ldots, h_k(x)]$, $\mathbf{g}(x) = [g_1(x), g_2(x), \ldots, g_n(x)]$ and $\mathbf{A} \in \mathbb{R}^{k \times n}$. Our problem formulation is motivated by the work on condition-based consensus [4,8,11], where the inputs of the agents are restricted to be within some acceptable set.

Each agent i maintains state x_i, with $x_i(t)$ denoting the local estimate of the optimal x, computed by node i at the *end* of the t-th iteration of the algorithm, with $x_i(0)$ denoting its initial local estimate. At the *start* of the t-th iteration ($t > 0$), the local estimate of agent i is $x_i(t-1)$. The algorithms of interest will require each agent i to perform the following three steps in iteration t, where $t > 0$. Note that the faulty agents may deviate from this specification. Since each $h_j(\cdot)$ is convex and L-Lipschitz continuous, and $\sum_{j=1}^{k} \mathbf{A}_{ji} = 1$, it follows that each $g_i(\cdot)$ is also convex and L-Lipschitz continuous. Note that the formulation allows $n < k$ as well as $n \geq k$. The matrix $\mathbf{A}$ is termed as a *job assignment matrix*. The goal here is to develop algorithms that output $x_i = \widetilde{x}$ at each non-faulty agent i such that

$$\widetilde{x} \in \text{argmin } h(x) = \frac{1}{k}\sum_{j=1}^{k} h_j(x). \tag{1}$$

That is, we are interested in developing algorithms in which the local estimate of each non-faulty agent will eventually reach consensus, and the consensus value is an optimum of function $h(\cdot)$.

Let $X_j = \text{argmin } h_j(x)$ for all $j = 1, \ldots, k$, and let $X = \text{argmin } h(x)$. For ease of future reference, we refer to the above optimization problem 1 as Problem (1). Problem 1 is said to be solvable if there exists an algorithm that outputs $\widetilde{x} \in \text{argmin } h(x)$ at each non-faulty agent i for any collection of k admissible functions. Problem 1 can be further formulated differently depending on whether each non-faulty agent i knows the assignment matrix $\mathbf{A}$ or not. We refer to the formulation where the agents know matrix $\mathbf{A}$ as condition-based Byzantine multi-agent optimization **with** side information; otherwise the problem is called condition-based Byzantine multi-agent optimization **without** side information.

Our formulation is more general than the common formulation adopted in [6,13,14,21], in which $f = 0$ and the assignment matrix $\mathbf{A} = \mathbf{I}_k$ (identity matrix) is considered. Despite the elegance of the algorithms proposed in [6,13,14,21], none of these algorithms work in the presence of Byzantine agents when $f \geq 1$ and $\mathbf{A} = \mathbf{I}_k$. Informally speaking, this is because under $\mathbf{g}(\cdot) = \mathbf{h}(\cdot)\mathbf{I}_k = \mathbf{h}(\cdot)$ assignment, the information about the input function $h_i(\cdot)$ is exclusively known to agent i in the system. If agent i is faulty and misbehaves, or crashes at the beginning of an execution, then the information about $h_i(\cdot)$ is not accessible to the non-faulty agents. When $\sum_{j=1}^{k} h_j(\cdot)$ and $\sum_{j=1, j\neq i}^{k} h_j(\cdot)$ do not have common optima, there does not exist a correct algorithm. A stronger impossibility result is presented next, which is proved in Part I of our work [17].

Theorem 1. [17] *Problem 1 is not solvable when* $f \geq 1$ *and* $\mathbf{A} = \mathbf{I}_k$.

In contrast, function redundancy can be added to the system by applying a properly chosen job assignment matrix $\mathbf{A}$ to $\mathbf{h}(x)$. For example, suppose $k = 2$, $f = 1$ and the optimal sets of functions $h_1(x)$ and $h_2(x)$ are $[-1, 0]$ and $[0, 1]$, respectively. Let $\mathbf{g}(x) = \mathbf{h}(x)\mathbf{G}$, where $\mathbf{G}$ is a generator matrix of a repetition code with $d = 2f + 1 = 3$. Informally speaking, by applying linear code $\mathbf{G}$ on input functions $\mathbf{h}(x)$, i.e., $\mathbf{g}(x) = \mathbf{h}(x)\mathbf{G}$, the Byzantine agents' ability in hiding information about input functions can be weakened. This observation and Theorem 1 together justify our problem formulation.

Contributions: We introduce a condition-based approach to Byzantine multi-agent optimization problem. Two slightly different variants are considered: with side information and without side information. For the former, when side information is available at each agent, a decoding-based algorithm is proposed, assuming that each input function is differentiable. This algorithm combines the gradient method with the decoding procedure introduced in [2] (namely matrix $\mathbf{A}$). With such a decoding subroutine, our algorithm essentially performs the gradient method, where gradient computation is performed distributedly over the multi-agent system. When side information is not available at each agent, we propose a simple consensus-based algorithm in which each agent carries minimal state across iterations. This consensus-based algorithm solves Problem 1 under the additional assumption over input functions that all input functions share at least one common optimum.

3 With Side Information

In this section we consider condition-based Byzantine multi-agent optimization with side information, where each agent knows the assignment matrix $\mathbf{A}$. Let $\{\alpha(t)\}_{t=0}^{\infty}$ be a sequence of step sizes. A simple decoding-based algorithm, Algorithm 1, formally presented below, works in an iterative fashion. Recall that $x_i(0)$ is the initial state of local estimate for each non-faulty agent $i \in \mathcal{V} - \mathcal{F}$, and $G(\mathcal{V}, \mathcal{E})$ is the underlying communication graph. Without loss of generality, we assume that $x_i(0) = x_0$ for $i \in \mathcal{V} - \mathcal{F}$ and some arbitrary but fixed $x_0 \in \mathbb{R}$. Otherwise, we can add an additional initialization step to guarantee identical "initial state" using an arbitrary exact consensus algorithm. Let $x_i(t)$ be the local estimate of an optimum in X, computed by node i at the *end* of the t-th iteration of the algorithm. At the *start* of the t-th iteration ($t > 0$), the local estimate of agent i is $x_i(t-1)$.

For Algorithm 1 to work, we assume that each input function $h_i(\cdot)$ is differentiable. Consequently, the local objective $g_i(\cdot)$ is also differentiable for each $i \in \mathcal{V}$. Let $\mathbf{A} \in \mathbb{R}^{k \times n}$ be a matrix that can corrects up to f arbitrary entry-wise errors in [2]. At iteration t, each non-faulty agent i computes the gradient of $g_i(t)$

at $x_i(t-1)$. Let $\mathbf{d}(t)$ be the k-dimensional vector of the gradients of the k input functions at $x_i(t-1)$, where $i \in \mathcal{V} - \mathcal{F}$. For the j–th entry in $\mathbf{d}(t)$, i.e., $\mathbf{d}_j(t)$, it holds that $\mathbf{d}_j(t) = h'_j(x_i(t-1))$. Later we will show that $x_i(t-1) = x_j(t-1)$ for all $i, j \in \mathcal{V} - \mathcal{F}$. Thus $\mathbf{d}(t)$ is well-defined. In addition, we assume the structure of the underlying graph $G(\mathcal{V}, \mathcal{E})$ admits Byzantine broadcast. For instance, when $G(\mathcal{V}, \mathcal{E})$ is undirected, for a correct Byzantine broadcast algorithm to exist, node connectivity of $G(\mathcal{V}, \mathcal{E})$ is at least $2f+1$.

Algorithm 1. Steps to be performed by agent $i \in \mathcal{V}$ in iteration $t \geq 0$

Initialization: $x_i(0) \leftarrow x_0$;
Compute $g'_i(x_i(t-1))$, the gradient of $g_i(\cdot)$ at $x_i(t-1)$, and perform Byzantine broadcast of $g'_i(x_i(t-1))$ to all agents;
Receive gradients from all other agents. Let $\mathbf{y}^i(t)$ be a n–dimensional vector of received gradients, with $\mathbf{y}^i_j(t)$ being the value received from agent j. If $j \in \mathcal{V} - \mathcal{F}$, then $\mathbf{y}^i_j(t) = g'_j(x_j(t-1))$;
Perform the decoding procedure in [2] to recover $\mathbf{d}(t) = [h'_1(x_i(t-1)), \cdots, h'_k(x_i(t-1))]^T$;
$x_i(t) \leftarrow x_i(t-1) - \alpha(t-1)\sum_{j=1}^{k} h'_j(x_i(t-1))$.

At iteration $t = 1$, each non-faulty agent i computes $g'_i(x_i(0))$–the gradient of $g_i(\cdot)$ at the current estimate $x_i(0) = x_0$, and performs Byzantine broadcast of $g'_i(x_0)$. Note that a faulty agent p, instead of $g'_p(x_0)$, may perform Byzantine broadcast of some arbitrary value to other agents. Recall that $\mathbf{y}^i(1) \in \mathbb{R}^n$ is a n–dimensional real vector, with $\mathbf{y}^i_j(1)$ be the value received from agent j at iteration 1. Since $\mathbf{g}(\cdot) = \mathbf{h}(\cdot)\mathbf{A}$, then we can write $\mathbf{y}^i(1)$ as $\mathbf{y}^i(1) = \mathbf{d}(1)\mathbf{A} + \mathbf{e}^i(1)$, where $\mathbf{e}^i(1)$ corresponds to the errors induced by the faulty agents. Let p be a nonzero entry in $\mathbf{e}^i(1)$, it should be noted that $\mathbf{e}^i_p(1)$ can be arbitrarily away from 0. Since messages/values are transmitted via Byzantine broadcast, it holds that $\mathbf{e}^i(1) = \mathbf{e}^{i'}(1)$ for all $i, i' \in \mathcal{V} - \mathcal{F}$. Consequently, we have $\mathbf{y}^i(1) = \mathbf{y}^{i'}(1)$ for all $i, i' \in \mathcal{V} - \mathcal{F}$. For each $i \in \mathcal{V} - \mathcal{F}$, $\mathbf{d}(1)$ can be recovered using the decoding procedure in [2]. By the updating function in Step 5, we know $x_i(1) = x_j(1)$ for all $i, j \in \mathcal{V} - \mathcal{F}$. Inductively, it can be shown that $x_i(t) = x_j(t)$ for all $i, j \in \mathcal{V} - \mathcal{F}$, and for all $t \geq 0$. Thus, $\mathbf{d}(t)$ is well-defined for each $t \geq 0$. The remaining correctness proof of Algorithm 1 follows directly from the standard gradient method convergence analysis for convex objective.

Due to the use of Byzantine broadcast, the communication load in Algorithm 1 is high. The communication cost can be reduced by using a matrix $\mathbf{A}$ that has stronger error-correction ability. In general, there is some trade-off among the communication cost, the graph structure and the error-correcting capability of $\mathbf{A}$. Our main focus of this paper is the case when no side-information is available at each agent, thus we do not pursue this tradeoff further.

4 Without Side Information

In this section, we consider the scenario when side information about the assignment matrix $\mathbf{A}$ is not known to each agent. We will classify the collection of input functions into three classes depending on the level of redundancy in the input function solutions. For functions with adequate redundancy in their optima, a simple consensus-based algorithm, named Algorithm 2, is proposed. Although Algorithm 2, at least in its current form, only works for a restricted class of input functions, it is more efficient in terms of both memory and local computation, compared to Algorithm 1. We leave the adaptation of Algorithm 2 to the general input functions as future work.

The job assignment matrices used in this section are characterized by *sparsity parameter*–a new property (introduced in this paper) over matrices.

4.1 Classification of Input Functions Collections

Recall that protective function redundancy is added to the system by applying a proper matrix $\mathbf{A}$ to $\mathbf{h}(\cdot)$, i.e., $\mathbf{g}(\cdot) = \mathbf{h}(\cdot)\mathbf{A}$. In Algorithm 1 sufficient redundancy is added to the system such that Algorithm 1 works for any collection of input functions. However, for some collection of input functions, such function redundancy may not be necessary. Consider the case when all k input functions are strictly convex and have the same optimum, i.e., $X_i = \{x^*\}$ for some x^* and for all $i = 1, \dots, k$. In addition, the agents know that $X_i = X_j$ and $|X_i| = 1$ for all $i, j \in \mathcal{V}$. It can be checked that $h(x) = \frac{1}{k}\sum_{j=1}^{k} h_j(x)$ is also strictly convex and $X = \{x^*\}$. Even if there is no redundant agents in the system and no redundancy added when applying $\mathbf{A}$, i.e., $\mathbf{A} = \mathbf{I}_k$, Problem 1 can be solved trivially by requiring each non-faulty agent to minimize its own local objective $h_i(x)$ individually without exchanging any information with other agents.

Informally speaking, as suggested by the above example, the optimal sets of the given input functions may themselves have redundancy. For ease of further reference, we term this redundancy as *solution redundancy.* Closer examination reveals that the collections of input functions can be categorized into three classes according to solution redundancy.

Case 1: The k input functions are strictly convex and $X_i = \{x^*\}$ for all $i = 1, \dots, k$, and the agents know that $X_i = X_j$ and $|X_i| = 1$ for all $i, j \in \mathcal{V}$;
Case 2: The k input functions share at least one common optimum, i.e., $\cap_{i=1}^{k} X_i \neq \emptyset$, and the agents know that $\cap_{i=1}^{k} X_i \neq \emptyset$;
Case 3: The k input functions share no optima, i.e., $\cap_{i=1}^{k} X_i = \emptyset$.

If the collection of k input functions belongs to Cases 1 or 2, we refer to this scenario as *solution-redundant* functions; similarly, we refer to the collection of k functions that falls within Case 3 as *solution-independent* functions. When the given collection of input functions fits Cases 2 or 3 (but not Case 1), information exchange among agents is in general required in order to achieve asymptotic consensus over local estimates of non-faulty agents.

4.2 Algorithm Structure

In this section, we are particularly interested in the family of algorithms of the following structure.

Recall that each agent i maintains state x_i, with $x_i(t)$ denoting the local estimate of an optimum in X, computed by node i at the *end* of the t-th iteration of the algorithm, with $x_i(0)$ denoting its initial local estimate. At the *start* of the t-th iteration ($t > 0$), the local estimate of agent i is $x_i(t-1)$. The algorithms of interest will require each agent i to perform the following three steps in iteration t, where $t > 0$. Note that the faulty agents may deviate from this specification.

1. Transmit message $m_i(t)$ on all outgoing edges (to agents in N_i^+).
2. Receive messages on all incoming edges (from agents in N_i^-). Denote by $r_i(t)$ the vector of messages received from its neighbors.
3. Agent i updates its local estimate using a transition function Z_i,

$$x_i(t) = Z_i\left(r_i(t), x_i(t-1), g_i(\cdot)\right), \tag{2}$$

   where Z_i is a part of the specification of the algorithm.

Note that $x_i(t)$ only depends on $g_i(\cdot)$, $x_i(t-1)$ and $r_i(t)$. No other information collected in any previous iteration will affect the update step in iteration t. Intuitively, non-faulty agent i is assumed to have no memory across iterations except x_i. Note that the information available at each non-faulty node $i \in \mathcal{V} - \mathcal{F}$ is the local estimate $x_i(t-1)$ and the local objective $g_i(\cdot)$. Thus, $m_i = F_i(x_i(t-1), g_i(\cdot))$, i.e., the message $m_i(t)$ is a function of $x_i(t-1)$ and $g_i(\cdot)$ only.

An algorithm is said to be correct (1) if $\lim_{t\to\infty} |x_i(t) - x_j(t)| = 0$ and $\lim_{t\to\infty} x_j(t) \in X$, for all initial states $x_j(0)$ and for all $i, j \in \mathcal{V} - \mathcal{F}$, and (2) if there exists a finite t_0 such that $x_i(t_0) = x_j(t_0)$ and $x_i(t_0) \in X$ for all $i, j \in \mathcal{V} - \mathcal{F}$, then $x_i(t) = x_i(t_0)$ for all $i \in \mathcal{V} - \mathcal{F}$ and for all $t \geq t_0$.

Case 1 above is a special form of Case 2. For Case 1, where $h_j(\cdot)$'s are strictly convex and have the same optimum, the problem can be solved trivially. However, for Case 2, the redundancy that is necessary may depend on the underlying graph structure. Henceforth, we consider the scenario when the input functions falls in Case 2. Note that Theorem 1 still holds when restricting to Case 2 input functions. Next, we introduce the notion of sparsity parameter of a job assignment matrix, and characterize the tradeoff between the sparsity parameter and the necessary and sufficient condition, for a correct algorithm to exist.

Definition 1. *Given a job assignment matrix* $\mathbf{A}$*, the sparsity parameter of* $\mathbf{A}$*, denoted by* $sp(\mathbf{A})$*, is the smallest integer such that the sum vector of any* $sp(\mathbf{A})$ *columns of* $\mathbf{A}$ *is component-wise positive, i.e., every coordinate of the sum vector is positive. In particular, if the sum vector of all columns of* $\mathbf{A}$ *is not component-wise positive, then* $sp(\mathbf{A}) \triangleq n+1$ *by convention.*

Recall that $\mathbf{A} \geq \mathbf{0}$ is a nonnegative matrix, $sp(\mathbf{A}) \triangleq n+1$ implies that there exists a row in $\mathbf{A}$ that contains only zeros. The following lemma presents a lower bound on the number of nonzero elements in a row of $\mathbf{A}$, given that $sp(\mathbf{A}) = k'$.

Lemma 1. *Given an assignment matrix* $\mathbf{A}$*, its sparsity parameter* $sp(\mathbf{A}) = k'$ *if and only if there are at most* $k' - 1$ *zero entries in each row of* $\mathbf{A}$ *and there exists one row that contains exactly* $k' - 1$ *zero entries.*

Lemma 1 is proved in our full version [18].

The sparsest assignment matrix $\mathbf{A}$ with $sp(\mathbf{A}) = k'$ can be constructed by choosing arbitrary $k' - 1$ entries in each row to be zero. By the proof of Lemma 1, it can be checked that the sparsity parameter of the obtained matrix $\mathbf{A}$ is k'. In addition, the total number of non-zero entries in $\mathbf{A}$ is $(n - k' + 1)\,k$.

4.3 Terminology of Consensus

Our condition is based on characterizing a special of subgraphs of $G(\mathcal{V}, \mathcal{E})$, termed by reduced graph [23], formally defined below.

Definition 2. [23] *Given a graph* $G(\mathcal{V}, \mathcal{E})$*, a reduced graph* $\mathcal{H}$ *is obtained by (i) removing all the faulty agents from* $\mathcal{V}$ *along with their edges; (ii) removing any additional up to* f *incoming edges at each non-faulty agent.*

Denote the collection of all the reduced graphs for a given $G(\mathcal{V}, \mathcal{E})$ by $R_{\mathcal{F}}$. Thus, $\mathcal{V} - \mathcal{F}$ is the set of agents in each element in $R_{\mathcal{F}}$. Let $\tau = |R_{\mathcal{F}}|$. It is easy to see that τ depends on $\mathcal{F}$ as well as the underlying network $G(\mathcal{V}, \mathcal{E})$, and it is finite.

Definition 3. *A source component* S *of a given graph* $G(\mathcal{V}, \mathcal{E})$ *is the collection of agents each of which has a directed path to every other agent in* $G(\mathcal{V}, \mathcal{E})$*.*

It can be easily checked that the source component S, if any, is a strongly connected component in $G(\mathcal{V}, \mathcal{E})$.

4.4 Necessary Condition

We now present a necessary condition on the underlying communication graph $G(\mathcal{V}, \mathcal{E})$ for solving Problem 1. Our necessary condition is based on characterizing the connectivity of each reduced graph of $G(\mathcal{V}, \mathcal{E})$.

Theorem 2. *Given a graph* $G(\mathcal{V}, \mathcal{E})$*, if there exists a correct algorithm that can solve Problem 1 when the agents do not have knowledge of the matrix, under any assignment matrix* $\mathbf{A}$ *for any* k *solution-redundant input functions, then a source component must exist containing at least* $\max\{f + 1, sp(\mathbf{A})\}$ *nodes.*

The proof of Theorem 2 can be found in our full version [18]. For future reference, we term the necessary condition in Theorem 2 as Condition 1.

Condition 1 implies a lower bound on n, stated below.

Corollary 1. *For a given graph* $G(\mathcal{V}, \mathcal{E})$*, if Condition 1 is true, then* $n \geq \max\{sp(\mathbf{A}) + 2f, 3f + 1\}$.

This lower bound is indeed tight. Consider the complete graph of size $sp(\mathbf{A}) + 2f$, denoted by $K_{sp(\mathbf{A})+2f}$. It can be easily proved by contradiction that $K_{sp(\mathbf{A})+2f}$ satisfies Condition 1. The proof of Corollary 1 is presented in our full version [18].

4.5 Sufficiency of Condition 1

Let $\{\alpha(t)\}_{t=0}^{\infty}$ be a sequence of stepsizes such that $\alpha(t) \leq \alpha(t+1)$ for all $t \geq 0$, $\sum_{t=0}^{\infty} \alpha(t) = \infty$, and $\sum_{t=0}^{\infty} \alpha^2(t) < \infty$. We show that Condition 1 is also sufficient. Let $\phi = |\mathcal{F}|$. Thus $\phi \leq f$. Without loss of generality, let us assume that the non-faulty agents are indexed as 1 to $n - \phi$. Recall that the system is synchronous. If a non-faulty agent does not receive an expected message from an incoming neighbor (in the *Receive step* below), then that message is assumed to have some default value. With the exception of the update step (3) below, the algorithm is similar to the consensus algorithms in [14,22,23].

Algorithm 2. Steps to be performed by agent $i \in \mathcal{V}$ in the t-th iteration:

1. Transmit current state $x_i(t-1)$ on all outgoing edges;
2. Receive values on all incoming edges. These values form multiset $r_i(t)$ of size $|N_i^-|$;
3. Sort the values in $r_i(t)$ in an increasing order, and eliminate the smallest f values, and the largest f values (breaking ties arbitrarily). Let $N_i^*(t)$ denote the identifiers of agents from whom the remaining $|N_i^-| - 2f$ values were received, and let w_j denote the value received from agent $j \in N_i^*(t)$. For convenience, define $w_i = x_i(t-1)$;
4. Update its state as follows.

$$x_i(t) = \sum_{j \in \{i\} \cup N_i^*(t)} a_i \, w_j - \alpha(t-1) \, d_i(t-1), \tag{3}$$

where $a_i = \frac{1}{|N_i^*(t)|+1}$ and $d_i(t-1)$ is a gradient of agent i's objective function $g_i(\cdot)$ at $x = x_i(t-1)$.

Recall that $i \notin N_i^*(t)$ because $(i,i) \notin \mathcal{E}$. The "weight" of each term on the right-hand side of (3) is a_i, and these weights add to 1. Observe that $0 < a_i \leq 1$. Let $\mathbf{x} \in \mathbb{R}^{n \times \phi}$, be a real vector of dimension $n - \phi$, with x_i being the local estimate of agent $i, \forall i \in \mathcal{V} - \mathcal{F}$. Thus, $\mathbf{x}(t)$ is a vector of the local estimates of non-faulty agents at iteration t.

Since $G(\mathcal{V}, \mathcal{E})$ satisfies Condition 1, as shown in [22], the updates of $\mathbf{x} \in \mathbb{R}^{n-\phi}$ in each iteration can be written compactly in a matrix form.

$$\mathbf{x}(t+1) = \mathbf{M}(t)\mathbf{x}(t) - \alpha(t)\mathbf{d}(t). \tag{4}$$

The construction of $\mathbf{M}(t)$ and relevant properties are given in [22] and are also presented in our full version [18] for completeness. Let $\mathcal{H} \in R_{\mathcal{F}}$ be a reduced graph of the given graph $G(\mathcal{V}, \mathcal{E})$ with $\mathbf{H}$ as adjacency matrix. It is shown that in every iteration t, and for every $\mathbf{M}(t)$, there exists a reduced graph $\mathcal{H}(t) \in R_{\mathcal{F}}$ with adjacency matrix $\mathbf{H}(t)$ such that

$$\mathbf{M}(t) \geq \beta \mathbf{H}(t), \tag{5}$$

where $0 < \beta < 1$ is a constant. The definition of β can be found in [22]. Equation (4) can be further expanded out as

$$\mathbf{x}(t+1) = \mathbf{\Phi}(t,0)\mathbf{x}(0) - \sum_{r=1}^{t+1} \alpha(r-1)\mathbf{\Phi}(t,r)\mathbf{d}(r-1), \tag{6}$$

where $\mathbf{\Phi}(t,r) = \mathbf{M}(t)\mathbf{M}(t-1)\ldots\mathbf{M}(r)$ and by convention $\mathbf{\Phi}(t,t) = \mathbf{M}(t)$ and $\mathbf{\Phi}(t,t+1) = \mathbf{I}_{n-\phi}$, the identity matrix. Note that $\mathbf{\Phi}(t,r)$ is a backward product (i.e., therein index decrease from left to right in the product).

Convergence of the Transition Matrices $\mathbf{\Phi}(t,r)$. It can be seen from (6) that the evolution of estimates of non-faulty agents $\mathbf{x}(t)$ is determined by the backward product $\mathbf{\Phi}(t,r)$. Thus, we first characterize the evolutional properties and limiting behaviors of the backward product $\mathbf{\Phi}(t,r)$, assuming that the given $G(\mathcal{V},\mathcal{E})$ satisfies Condition 1.

Let $k' = sp(\mathbf{A})$. The following lemma describes the structural property of $\mathbf{\Phi}(t,r)$ for sufficient large t. For a given r, Lemma 2 states that all non-faulty agents will be influenced by at least $\max\{k', f+1\}$ common non-faulty agents, and this set of influencing agents may depend on r. Proof of Lemma 2 can be found in our full version [18].

Lemma 2. *Let $\nu = \tau(n-\phi)$. There are at least $\max\{sp(\mathbf{A}), f+1\}$ columns in $\mathbf{\Phi}(r+\nu-1,r)$ that are lower bounded by $\beta^\nu\mathbf{1}$ component-wise for all r, where $\mathbf{1} \in \mathbb{R}^{n-\phi}$ is an all one column vector of dimension $n-\phi$.*

Using coefficients of ergodicity theorem, it is showed in [22] that if the given graph $G(\mathcal{V},\mathcal{E})$ satisfies Condition 1, then $\mathbf{\Phi}(t,r)$ is weak-ergodic. Moreover, because weak-ergodicity is equivalent to strong-ergodicity for backward product of stochastic matrices [3], as $t \to \infty$ the limit of $\mathbf{\Phi}(t,r)$ exists

$$\lim_{t\ge r,\ t\to\infty} \mathbf{\Phi}(t,r) = \mathbf{1}\pi(r), \tag{7}$$

where $\pi(r) \in \mathbb{R}^{n-\phi}$ is a row stochastic vector (may depend on r). It is shown, using ergodic coefficients, in [1] that the rate of the convergence in (7) is exponential, as formally stated in Theorem 3. Recall that $\tau = |R_{\mathcal{F}}|$, $n-\phi$ is the total number of non-faulty agents, and $0 < \beta < 1$ is a constant for which (5) holds.

Theorem 3. [1] *Let $\nu = \tau(n-\phi)$ and $\gamma = 1-\beta^\nu$. For any sequence $\mathbf{\Phi}(t,r)$,*

$$|\mathbf{\Phi}_{ij}(t,r) - \pi_j(r)| \le \gamma^{\lceil \frac{t-r+1}{\nu} \rceil}, \forall t \ge r. \tag{8}$$

Our next lemma is an immediate consequence of Lemma 2 and the convergence of $\mathbf{\Phi}(t,r)$, stated in (7).

Lemma 3. *For any fixed r, there exists a subset $\mathcal{I}_r \subseteq \mathcal{V}-\mathcal{F}$ such that $|\mathcal{I}_r| \ge \max\{sp(\mathbf{A}), f+1\}$ and for each $i \in \mathcal{I}_r$, $\pi_i(r) \ge \beta^\nu$.*

The proof of Lemma 3 can be found in our full version [18].

Convergence Analysis of Algorithm 2. Here, we study the convergence behavior of Algorithm 2. The structure of our convergence proof is rather standard, which is also adopted in [6,14,21]. We have shown that the evolution dynamics of $\mathbf{x}(t)$ is captured by (4) and (6). Suppose that all agents, both non-faulty agents and faulty agents cease computing $d_i(t)$ after some time $\bar{t}$, i.e., after $\bar{t}$ subgradient is replaced by 0.

Let $\{\bar{\mathbf{x}}(t)\}$ be the sequences of local estimates generated by the non-faulty agents in this case. From (6) we get $\bar{\mathbf{x}}(t) = \mathbf{x}(t)$, for all $t \le \bar{t}$. From (4) and (6), we have for all $s \ge 0$, it holds that

$$\bar{\mathbf{x}}(\bar{t}+s+1) = \mathbf{\Phi}(t,0)\mathbf{x}(0) - \sum_{r=1}^{\bar{t}} \alpha(r-1)\mathbf{\Phi}(\bar{t}+s,r)\mathbf{d}(r-1). \tag{9}$$

Note that the summation in RHS of (9) is over $\bar{t}$ terms since all agents cease computing $d_j(t)$ starting from iteration $\bar{t}$. As $s \to \infty$, we have

$$\lim_{s\to\infty} \bar{\mathbf{x}}(\bar{t}+s+1) = \left(\langle \pi(0), \mathbf{x}(0)\rangle - \sum_{r=1}^{\bar{t}} \alpha(r-1) \langle \pi(r), \mathbf{d}(r-1)\rangle \right) \mathbf{1}, \tag{10}$$

where $\langle \cdot, \cdot \rangle$ is used to denote the inner product of two vectors of proper dimension. Let $\mathbf{y}(\bar{t})$ denote the limiting vector of $\bar{\mathbf{x}}(\bar{t}+s+1)$ as $s+1 \to \infty$. Since all entries in the limiting vector are identical we denote the identical value by $y(\bar{t})$. Thus, $\mathbf{y}(\bar{t}) = [y(\bar{t}), \ldots, y(\bar{t})]'$.

From (10) we have

$$y(\bar{t}) = \langle \pi(0), \mathbf{x}(0)\rangle - \sum_{r=1}^{\bar{t}} \alpha(r-1) \langle \pi(r), \mathbf{d}(r-1)\rangle . \tag{11}$$

If, instead, all agents cease computing $d_i(t)$ after iteration $\bar{t}+1$, then the identical value, denoted by $y(\bar{t}+1)$, equals

$$y(\bar{t}+1) = y(\bar{t}) - \alpha(\bar{t}) \langle \pi(\bar{t}+1), \mathbf{d}(\bar{t})\rangle , \tag{12}$$

where each entry $d_i(\bar{t})$ in $\mathbf{d}(\bar{t})$ denotes the subgradient of $g_i(\cdot)$ computed by agent i at $x_i(\bar{t})$. With a little abuse of notation, henceforth we use t to replace $\bar{t}$. The actual reference of t should be clear from the context.

In our convergence analysis, we use the well-know "almost supermartingale" convergence theorem in [16]. We present a simpler deterministic version of the theorem in the next lemma.

Lemma 4. [16] *Let $\{a_t\}_{t=0}^{\infty}, \{b_t\}_{t=0}^{\infty}$, and $\{c_t\}_{t=0}^{\infty}$ be non-negative sequences. Suppose that $a_{t+1} \le a_t - b_t + c_t$ for all $t \ge 0$, and $\sum_{t=0}^{\infty} c_t < \infty$. Then $\sum_{t=0}^{\infty} b_t < \infty$ and the sequence $\{a_t\}_{t=0}^{\infty}$ converges to a non-negative value.*

The basic iterative relation of the consensus value $y(t)$ is stated as follows.

Lemma 5. *Let $\{y(t)\}_{t=0}^{\infty}$ be the sequence of limiting consensus value defined by (11), and $\{x_i(t)\}_{t=0}^{\infty}$ be the sequence for $i \in \mathcal{V} - \mathcal{F}$ generated by (6). Let $\{\delta_i(t)\}_{t=0}^{\infty}$ be a sequence of subgradients of g_i at $y(t)$ for all $i \in \mathcal{V} - \mathcal{F}$. Then the following basic relations hold. For any $x \in \mathbb{R}$ and any $t \geq 0$,*

$$|y(t+1) - x|^2 \leq |y(t) - x|^2 + 4L\alpha(t) \sum_{j=1}^{n-\phi} \pi_j(t+1)\, |y(t) - x_j(t)|$$
$$- 2\alpha(t) \sum_{j=1}^{n-\phi} \pi_j(t+1)\left(g_j\left(y(t)\right) - g_j(x)\right) + \alpha^2(t)(n-\phi)L^2$$

The proof of Lemma 5 can be found in [14]. We present the proof in the full version [18]. For each t and each $i \in \mathcal{V} - \mathcal{F}$, the distance between the consensus value $y(t)$ and the local estimate $x_i(t)$ is bounded from above.

Lemma 6. *Let $U = \max_{i \in \mathcal{V}-\mathcal{F}} x_i(0)$, and $u = \min_{i \in \mathcal{V}-\mathcal{F}} x_i(0)$. For every $i \in \mathcal{V} - \mathcal{F}$, a uniform bound on $|y(t) - x_i(t)|$ for $t \geq 1$ is given by:*

$$|y(t) - x_i(t)| \leq (n-\phi) \max\{|u|, |U|\} \gamma^{\lceil \frac{t}{\nu} \rceil}$$
$$+ (n-\phi)\, L \sum_{r=1}^{t-1} \alpha(r-1) \gamma^{\lceil \frac{t-r}{\nu} \rceil} + 2\alpha(t-1)L. \qquad (13)$$

When $t = 1$, $\sum_{r=1}^{t-1} \alpha(r-1)\gamma^{\lceil \frac{t-r}{\nu} \rceil} = 0$ by convention.

Note that the upper bound on $|y(t) - x_i(t)|$ in (13) depends on t. In fact, this upper bound will diminish over time, as formally stated below.

Lemma 7. *For each $i \in \mathcal{V} - \mathcal{F}$, $\lim_{t \to \infty} |y(t) - x_i(t)| = 0$.*

Our main convergence result is stated below.

Theorem 4 (Convergence). *For each $i \in \mathcal{V} - \mathcal{F}$, $\{x_i(t)\}_{t=0}^{\infty}$ converges to the same optimum in X, i.e., $\lim_{t \to \infty} |x_i(t) - x^*| = 0$, where $x^* \in X$.*

We provide a proof sketch below. Formal proof can be found in our full version [18].

Recall that each $g_i(\cdot)$ is defined as $g_i(\cdot) = \mathbf{A}_{1i}h_1(\cdot) + \ldots + \mathbf{A}_{ki}h_k(\cdot)$, for $i \in \mathcal{V}$, where $\mathbf{A}_{ji} \geq 0$ and $\sum_{j=1}^{k} \mathbf{A}_{ji} = 1$. Let $Y^i = \text{argmin } g_i(x)$ and $Y_j^i = \text{argmin } \mathbf{A}_{ji}h_j(x)$ for $j = 1, \ldots, k$. Since for each $j \in \{1, \ldots, k\}$ such that $\mathbf{A}_{ji} = 0$, argmin $\mathbf{A}_{ji}h_j(x) = 0$ is a constant function over the whole real line, it holds that $Y_j^i = \mathbb{R}$. Since positive constant scaling does not affect the optimal set of a function, for each $j \in \{1, \ldots, k\}$ such that $\mathbf{A}_{ji} > 0$, it holds that $Y_j^i = X_j$. In addition, because $h_1(x), \ldots, h_k(x)$ are solution redundant functions, i.e., $\cap_{j=1}^{k} X_j \neq \emptyset$, functions $\mathbf{A}_{1i}h_1(x), \ldots, \mathbf{A}_{ki}h_k(x)$ are also solution redundant. It can be shown (formally proved in our full version [18]) that

$$Y^i = \cap_{j:\mathbf{A}_{ji}>0} X_j \supseteq \cap_{j=1}^{k} X_j = X, \text{ for all } i \in \mathcal{V}.$$

Let $x' \in X$. Define g_j^* as the optimal value of function $g_j(\cdot)$ for each $j \in \mathcal{V}$. Then

$$|y(t+1) - x'|^2 = |y(t) - x'|^2 + 4L\alpha(t) \sum_{j=1}^{n-\phi} \pi_j(t+1)\, |y(t) - x_j(t)| \tag{14}$$

$$- 2\alpha(t) \sum_{j=1}^{n-\phi} \pi_j(t+1) \left(g_j\left(y(t)\right) - g_j^*\right) + \alpha^2(t)(n-\phi)L^2, \tag{15}$$

which follows from Lemma 5 and because of $x' \in X \subseteq Y^j$ for each $j \in \mathcal{V}$, then $g_j(x') = g_j^*$. For each $t \geq 0$, define

$$a_t = |y(t) - x'|^2, \;\; b_t = 2\alpha(t) \sum_{j=1}^{n-\phi} \pi_j(t+1) \left(g_j(y(t)) - g_j^*\right),$$

$$c_t = 4L\alpha(t) \sum_{j=1}^{n-\phi} \pi_j(t+1)|y(t) - x_j(t)| + \alpha^2(t)(n-\phi)L^2.$$

It is easy to see that $a_t \geq 0$ and $c_t \geq 0$ for each t. Since g_j^* is the optimal value of function $g_j(\cdot)$, it holds that $b_t \geq 0$ for each t. Thus, $\{a_t\}_{t=0}^{\infty}$, $\{b_t\}_{t=0}^{\infty}$ and $\{c_t\}_{t=0}^{\infty}$ are three non-negative sequences. By (14), it holds that $a_{t+1} \leq a_t - b_t + c_t \, \forall \, t \geq 0$.

To apply Lemma 4, we need to show that $\sum_{t=0}^{\infty} c_t < \infty$. In fact, the following lemma holds.

Lemma 8. $\sum_{t=0}^{\infty} \alpha(t) \sum_{j=1}^{n-\phi} \pi_j(t+1)|y(t) - x_j(t)| < \infty$.

The proof of Lemma 8 is presented in our full version [18]. In addition, since $\sum_{t=0}^{\infty} \alpha^2(t) < \infty$, it holds that $(n-\phi)L^2 \sum_{t=0}^{\infty} \alpha^2(t) < \infty$. Thus, we get

$$\begin{aligned}\sum_{t=0}^{\infty} c_t &= \sum_{t=0}^{\infty} \left(4L\alpha(t) \sum_{j=1}^{n-\phi} \pi_j(t+1)|y(t) - x_j(t)| + \alpha^2(t)(n-\phi)L^2 \right) \\ &= 4L \sum_{t=0}^{\infty} \left(\alpha(t) \sum_{j=1}^{n-\phi} \pi_j(t+1)|y(t) - x_j(t)| \right) + (n-\phi)L^2 \sum_{t=0}^{\infty} \alpha^2(t) \; < \infty.\end{aligned}$$

Therefore, applying Lemma 4 to the sequences $\{a_t\}_{t=0}^{\infty}$, $\{b_t\}_{t=0}^{\infty}$ and $\{c_t\}_{t=0}^{\infty}$, we have that for any $x' \in X$, $a_t = |y(t) - x'|$ converges, and

$$\sum_{t=0}^{\infty} b_t = \sum_{t=0}^{\infty} \alpha(t) \sum_{j=1}^{n-\phi} \pi_j(t+1) \left(g_j(y(t)) - g_j^*\right) < \infty.$$

Since $|y(t) - x'|$ converges for any fixed $x' \in X$, by definition of sequence convergence and the dynamic of $y(t)$ in (11), it is easy to see that $y(t)$ also converges. Let $\lim_{t \to \infty} y(t) = y$. Next we show that $y \in X$.

Let $\mathcal{I}_{t+1} \subseteq \mathcal{V} - \mathcal{F}$ such that $\pi_j(t+1) \geq \beta^\nu$, $\forall j \in \mathcal{I}_{t+1}$. As $G(\mathcal{V}, \mathcal{E})$ satisfies Condition 1, $|\mathcal{I}_{t+1}| \geq \max\{k', f+1\}$. Since $g_j(y(t)) - g_j^* \geq 0$ for all j, then

$$\sum_{j=1}^{n-\phi} \pi_j(t+1)\left(g_j(y(t)) - g_j^*\right) \geq \sum_{j\in\mathcal{I}_{t+1}} \pi_j(t+1)\left(g_j(y(t)) - g_j^*\right)$$

$$\geq \beta^\nu \sum_{j\in\mathcal{I}_{t+1}} \left(g_j(y(t)) - g_j^*\right) \;=\; \beta^\nu \sum_{j\in\mathcal{I}_{t+1}} \sum_{i=1}^{k} \mathbf{A}_{ij}\left(h_i(y(t)) - h_i^*\right)$$

$$= \beta^\nu \sum_{i=1}^{k} \left(\sum_{j\in\mathcal{I}_{t+1}} \mathbf{A}_{ij}\right)\left(h_i(y(t)) - h_i^*\right) \;\geq\; k\beta^\nu C_2\left(h(y(t)) - h^*\right),$$

where $C_2 = \min_{\mathcal{I}\subseteq\mathcal{V}:\,|\mathcal{I}|\geq\max\{k',f+1\}} \sum_{i\in\mathcal{I}} \mathbf{A}_{ij}$, and the last inequality follows from the fact that $h_i(y(t)) - h_i^* \geq 0$. In addition, as $sp(\mathbf{A}) = k'$, then $\sum_{i\in\mathcal{I}} \mathbf{A}_{ij} > 0$ for every $\mathcal{I} \subseteq \mathcal{V}: |\mathcal{I}| \geq \max\{k', f+1\}$. Since $\mathbf{A}$ is finite, C_2 is well-defined and $C_2 > 0$. If $y \notin X$, it can be shown that $k\beta^\nu C_2\left(h(y(t)) - h^*\right) = \infty$, contradicting the fact that $\sum_{t=0}^{\infty} b_t < \infty$. Thus, $y \in X$.

Therefore, we conclude that limit of $|x_i(t) - y|$ exists and $\lim_{t\to\infty} |x_i(t) - y| = 0$, proving Theorem 4.

5 Summary and Conclusion

In this paper, we introduce the condition-based approach to Byzantine multi-agent optimization. We have shown that when there is enough redundancy in the local cost functions, or in the local optima, Problem 1 can be solved iteratively. Although the consensus-based algorithm can only solve Problem 1 for a restricted class of input functions, nevertheless, as each non-faulty agent does not need to store the job matrix $\mathbf{A}$ throughout execution and does not need to perform the decoding procedure at each iteration, the requirements on memory and computation are less stringent comparing to the decoding-based algorithm. In addition, in contrast to the decoding-based algorithm, the consensus-based algorithm also works for nonsmooth input functions. Thus, the consensus-based algorithm may be more practical in some applications.

References

1. Anthonisse, J., Tijms, H.: Exponential convergence of products of stochastic matrices. J. Math. Anal. Appl. **59**(2), 360–364 (1977)
2. Candes, E.J., Tao, T.: Decoding by linear programming. IEEE Trans. Inf. Theory **51**(12), 4203–4215 (2005)
3. Chatterjee, S., Seneta, E.: Towards consensus: some convergence theorems on repeated averaging. J. Appl. Probab. **14**(1), 89–97 (1977)
4. Chaudhuri, S.: More choices allow more faults: set consensus problems in totally asynchronous systems. Inf. Comput. **105**, 132–158 (1992)

5. Dolev, D., Lynch, N.A., Pinter, S.S., Stark, E.W., Weihl, W.E.: Reaching approximate agreement in the presence of faults. J. ACM **33**(3), 499–516 (1986)
6. Duchi, J., Agarwal, A., Wainwright, M. Dual averaging for distributed optimization: convergence analysis and network scaling. IEEE Trans. Autom. Control (2012)
7. Fekete, A.D.: Asymptotically optimal algorithms for approximate agreement. Distrib. Comput. **4**(1), 9–29 (1990)
8. Friedman, R., Mostefaoui, A., Rajsbaum, S., Raynal, M.: Asynchronous agreement and its relation with error-correcting codes. IEEE Trans. Comput. **56**(7), 865–875 (2007)
9. LeBlanc, H.J., Zhang, H., Sundaram, S., Koutsoukos, X.: Consensus of multi-agent networks in the presence of adversaries using only local information. In: Proceedings of the 1st International Conference on High Confidence Networked Systems, HiCoNS 2012, pp. 1–10. ACM, New York (2012)
10. Mostefaoui, A., Rajsbaum, S., Raynal, M.: Conditions on input vectors for consensus solvability in asynchronous distributed systems. J. ACM (JACM) **50**(6), 922–954 (2003)
11. Mostefaoui, A., Rajsbaum, S., Raynal, M.: Using conditions to expedite consensus in synchronous distributed systems. In: Fich, F.E. (ed.) DISC 2003. LNCS, vol. 2848, pp. 249–263. Springer, Heidelberg (2003). doi:10.1007/978-3-540-39989-6_18
12. Mostefaoui, A., Rajsbaum, S., Raynal, M.: Synchronous condition-based consensus. Distrib. Comput. **18**(5), 325–343 (2006)
13. Nedic, A., Olshevsky, A.: Distributed optimization over time-varying directed graphs. IEEE Trans. Autom. Control **60**(3), 601–615 (2015)
14. Nedic, A., Ozdaglar, A.: Distributed subgradient methods for multi-agent optimization. IEEE Trans. Autom. Control **54**(1), 48–61 (2009)
15. Pease, M., Shostak, R., Lamport, L.: Reaching agreement in the presence of faults. J. ACM **27**(2), 228–234 (1980)
16. Robbins, H., Siegmund, D.: A convergence theorem for non negative almost supermartingales and some applications. In: Lai, T., Siegmund, D. (eds.) Herbert Robbins Selected Papers, pp. 111–135. Springer, New York (1985)
17. Su, L., Vaidya, N.: Byzantine multi-agent optimization: Part i. arXiv,abs/1506.04681 (2015)
18. Su, L., Vaidya, N.: Byzantine Multi-agent optimization: part II (2015)
19. Su, L., Vaidya, N.H.: Fault-tolerant multi-agent optimization: optimal iterative distributed algorithms. In: Proceedings of the ACM Symposium on Principles of Distributed Computing, pp. 425–434. ACM (2016)
20. Su, L., Vaidya, N.H.: Multi-agent optimization in the presence of byzantine adversaries: fundamental limits. In: Proceedings of IEEE American Control Conference (ACC), July 2016
21. Tsitsiklis, J.N., Bertsekas, D.P., Athans, M., et al.: Distributed asynchronous deterministic and stochastic gradient optimization algorithms. IEEE Trans. Autom. Control **31**(9), 803–812 (1986)
22. Vaidya, N.H.: Matrix representation of iterative approximate Byzantine consensus in directed graphs. CoRR, abs/1203.1888 (2012)
23. Vaidya, N.H., Tseng, L., Liang, G.: Iterative approximate byzantine consensus in arbitrary directed graphs. In: Proceedings of ACM Symposium on Principles of Distributed Computing (PODC) (2012)

Plane Formation by Semi-synchronous Robots in the Three Dimensional Euclidean Space

Taichi Uehara(✉), Yukiko Yamauchi, Shuji Kijima, and Masafumi Yamashita

Kyushu University, Fukuoka, Japan
{taichi.uehara,yamauchi,kijima,mak}@inf.kyushu-u.ac.jp

Abstract. We consider the *plane formation problem* that requires a set of autonomous mobile robots initially placed in the three-dimensional space to land on a common plane that is not defined a priori. The problem was first introduced for *fully-synchronous (FSYNC)* robots with *rigid movement* (i.e., the robots always reach the next position) and solvable instances are characterized in terms of the symmetry among the robots, i.e., the rotation group of the initial configuration of robots (Yamauchi et al. DISC 2015). We consider the plane formation problem for *semi-synchronous (SSYNC)* robots with non-rigid movement. We present a plane formation algorithm for oblivious SSYNC robots, and show that the SSYNC robots with non-rigid movement have the same plane formation power as the FSYNC robots with rigid movement.

Keywords: Mobile robots · The plane formation problem · Semi-synchronous model · Non-rigid movement · Symmetry breaking

1 Introduction

Self-organization of autonomous computing entities attracts much attention because of its wide applications for mobile robots, drones, molecular robots, biological systems, and so on. A variety of problems have been proposed as fundamental techniques, for example shape formation, gathering, coating, and exploration. In this paper, we consider *autonomous mobile robots* moving in the three-dimensional space (3D-space). Formation problems have been investigated for mobile robots moving in the two-dimensional space (2D-space); the point formation problem requires the robots to gather at a point [2,8,9], the circle formation problem requires the robots to form a circle (i.e., a regular polygon) [5], and the pattern formation problem requires the robots to form a specified target pattern [7–9]. The *plane formation problem* requires the robots in 3D-space to land on a common plane [10] so that these existing results in 2D-space are used in higher dimensions.

This work was supported by JSPS KAKENHI Grant Numbers JP15H00821, JP15K15938, JP25700002, JP15K11987, JP15H02666, and a Grant-in-Aid for Scientific Research on Innovative Areas "Molecular Robotics" (No. 24104003) of MEXT, Japan.

B. Bonakdarpour and F. Petit (Eds.): SSS 2016, LNCS 10083, pp. 383–398, 2016.
DOI: 10.1007/978-3-319-49259-9_30

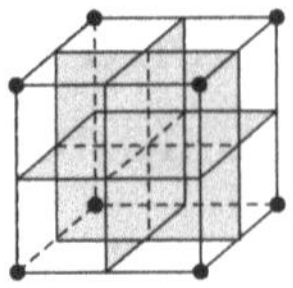

Fig. 1. Cubic initial configuration and an example of proposed symmetric planes.

The conventional robot model assumes robots with very weak capabilities. Each robot is an *anonymous* (indistinguishable) point and they follow a common algorithm, i.e., they are *uniform*. The robots have neither any access to the global coordinate system nor any explicit communication medium. They cooperate with each other by just observing the positions of other robots, though their observation obtained in their own *local coordinate systems* may be inconsistent. Each robot repeats a *Look-Compute-Move cycle*, where it observes the positions of other robots in its local coordinate system (Look), computes its next position and the route to there by the common algorithm (Compute), and moves to the next position (Move). The local coordinate system of a robot is a right-handed x-y-z coordinate system, whose origin is the current position of the robot and whose coordinate axes and unit distance are arbitrary. The robots are *oblivious* in the sense that it does not remember past cycles. The input to Compute is the observation obtained in the Look of the current cycle. In Move, each robot may stop en route after moving an unknown minimum moving distance along the computed route. Such movement is called *non-rigid*, while rigid movement guarantees that each robot reaches its next position in any Move. Regarding the synchrony among robots, the first seminal paper proposed two models [8]. In the *fully-synchronous (FSYNC)* model, the robots execute the i-th cycle synchronously for any $i = 1, 2, \cdots$. In other words, all robots are activated at each time step to execute a cycle. In the *semi-synchronous (SSYNC)* model, non-empty subset of robots are activated at each time step to execute a cycle. Later the *asynchronous (ASYNC)* model is introduced that imposes no assumptions on the executions of cycles [6].

The plane formation problem was first introduced for FSYNC robots with rigid movement [10]. Consider an initial configuration of eight robots forming a cube. Because the eight robots do not agree even on the vertical direction, the planes that they propose cannot be unique (Fig. 1). The authors measured the symmetry among the robots by using the rotation groups in 3D-space, each of which is recognized as a set of rotation axes and their arrangement. There are five types of rotation groups in 3D-space; the *cyclic groups*, the *dihedral groups*, the *tetrahedral group*, the *octahedral group*, and the *icosahedral group*. The former two groups are called 2D rotation groups since they can act on a set of points on a plane, while the latter three groups are called 3D rotation groups since they cannot. Surprisingly, it has been shown that even when the robots form a regular polyhedron (except a regular icosahedron), they can break the symmetry and accomplish the plane formation task [10]. The trick is the fact that the symmetry

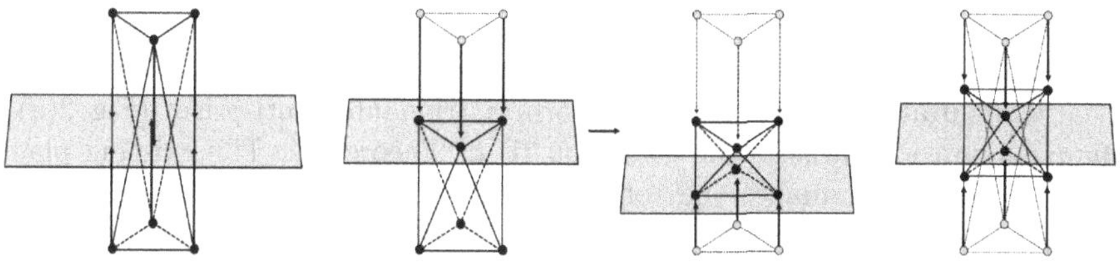

Fig. 2. Worst case executions of the plane formation algorithm [10] in the SSYNC model with non-rigid movement. The existing algorithm lands the robots to the target plane shown in (a). There exists an SSYNC schedule that allows convergence to a plane (b), and non-rigid movement allows regular octahedron (c).

among the robots is not the symmetry of their positions, but symmetry of their local coordinate systems which is usually equal to or lower than the symmetry of their positions. This notion is later formalized as *symmetricity* in 3D-space [11]. Let P be a set of points. The rotation group $\gamma(P)$ of P is the rotation group that acts on P and none of its proper supergroup in the five kinds of rotation groups acts on P. Then P is decomposed into orbits by the group action of $\gamma(P)$. This decomposition is called the $\gamma(P)$-*decomposition* of P. The following theorem is shown in [10].

Theorem 1 ([10]). *Let P and $\{P_1, P_2, \ldots, P_m\}$ be an initial configuration and the $\gamma(P)$-decomposition of P, respectively. Then oblivious FSYNC robots with rigid movement can form a plane from P if and only if (i) $\gamma(P)$ is a 2D rotation group, or (ii) $\gamma(P)$ is a 3D rotation group and there exists an element P_i such that $|P_i| \not\in \{12, 24, 60\}$.*

These two papers show that the robots can show their symmetricity by deterministic rigid movement in the FSYNC model. That is, in a configuration P satisfying condition (ii), there are robots on some rotation axes of $\gamma(P)$ and by these robots leaving their positions, the robots can translate P to another configuration P' satisfying the condition (i). The algorithm is called "go-to-center" algorithm since these robots on rotation axes form a uniform polyhedron, and the algorithm makes each of them select a face of the polyhedron and move toward the center of the selected face.

In this paper, we show that the oblivious SSYNC robots with non-rigid movement have the same plane formation ability as the oblivious FSYNC robots with rigid movement. The impossibility is clear because the SSYNC model with non-rigid movement allows the worst case executions in the FSYNC model with rigid movement. To show the solvability, we present a novel plane formation algorithm for the SSYNC robots with non-rigid movement, because the existing plane formation algorithm [10] relies heavily on the FSYNC schedule and rigid movement.

We start with an example that shows the effect of semi-synchrony and non-rigid movement on the existing plane formation algorithm in [10]. Consider an initial configuration where six robots form a triangular anti-prism (Fig. 2(a)). This configuration satisfies the condition (i) of Theorem 1. The existing plane formation algorithm makes the robots agree on the plane that is parallel to the bases and contains the center of the triangular anti-prism, and sends each robot to the plane along the perpendicular to the plane. Consider an SSYNC schedule of the robots (with rigid movement) where in an odd time step the robots forming the top base execute a cycle, and at an even time step, the robots forming the bottom base execute a cycle. Then the robots converge to a plane, but they never land on one plane (Fig. 2(b)). Consider non-rigid movement in the FSYNC model, for example, the robots stop at the points where each side face of their anti-prism forms a regular triangle. Thus they form a regular octahedron (Fig. 2(c)). Though the algorithm of [10] guarantees that the robots can form a plane from a regular octahedron, during the formation, the algorithm allows the robots to form a triangular anti-prism. Thus the robots may fall into a loop between a regular octahedron and a triangular anti-prism.[1]

Additionally, the correctness proof of the go-to-center algorithm in [10] heavily relies on the rigid movement. The authors consider all possible next positions, that form a uniform polyhedron. Because the robots cannot select all the vertices of the uniform polyhedron, the go-to-center algorithm succeeds in symmetry breaking. However, when SSYNC robots with non-rigid movement execute the go-to-center algorithm, the new positions of the robots are not always on the vertices of the uniform polyhedron. The go-to-center algorithm does not work correctly in our model.

We present a new plane formation algorithm ψ_{PLF} that consists of a landing algorithm ψ_{LND} and a symmetry breaking algorithm ψ_{SB}. Algorithm ψ_{LND} is executed when the current configuration satisfies the condition (i) of Theorem 1. To overcome the difficulties in the SSYNC model with non-rigid movement, we introduce two new movements, *twist* and *shrink*. Algorithm ψ_{LND} slightly twists a prism (or an anti-prism) so that the robots never increase their symmetry, and it lands the robots to a plane with shrinking to the center of the smallest enclosing ball of themselves so that the robots can recognize the SSYNC schedule and avoid convergence to a plane. Algorithm ψ_{SB} is executed when the current configuration satisfies the condition (ii) of Theorem 1 and breaks an element satisfying condition (ii) so that any resulting configuration satisfies the condition (i) of Theorem 1. We will show that by repeating the go-to-center algorithm, the robots can break the initial 3D rotation group in finite time. Then the entire algorithm shows that the condition of Theorem 1 is a sufficient condition for the oblivious SSYNC robots with non-rigid movement to form a plane. Consequently, we show the oblivious SSYNC robots with non-rigid movement have the same plane formation power as the oblivious FSYNC robots with rigid movement.

[1] We note that the effect of this non-rigid movement is rather moderate because the robots can get out of this loop when their moving distance becomes smaller than the minimum moving distance.

Related work. The FSYNC robots with rigid movement determines the limit of the ability of the robots, since SSYNC (thus ASYNC) robot with non-rigid movement allows FSYNC schedule and rigid movement of the robots. In other words, if the FSYNC robots with rigid movement cannot achieve a task, then the SSYNC (thus ASYNC) robots with non-rigid movement cannot achieve the task. On the other hand, if the ASYNC robots with non-rigid movement can achieve a task with an algorithm, the SSYNC (thus FSYNC) robots with non-rigid movement can also achieve the task with the algorithm. However as we will briefly show in the following part, there are many difficulties to overcome when we design an algorithm for the ASYNC robots with non-rigid movement.

The *pattern formation problem* requires the robots to form a target pattern from a given initial configuration. The pattern formation ability of the robots in 2D-space was first discussed for the FSYNC and the SSYNC model [8,9], and then for the ASYNC model [7]. The result is summarized as follows: The *symmetricity* $\rho(P)$ of a set of points P in 2D-space is the number of angles θ such that the rotation of P by θ produces P itself. The symmetricity in 2D-space is basically the order of the cyclic group that acts on P. However when the center of the smallest enclosing circle of P is in P, $\rho(P)$ is defined to be 1. Then irrespective of obliviousness and asynchrony, the robots can form a target pattern F from an initial configuration P if and only if $\rho(P)$ divides $\rho(F)$ except the case where F is a point of multiplicity 2. The exception is called the *rendezvous problem*. Consider two FSYNC robots in 2D-space (thus they cannot move vertically). They succeed in rendezvous by a simple algorithm: Each robot goes to the midpoint. Even when their movement is non-rigid, because the distance of the two robots monotonically decreases, they finish the rendezvous in a finite time. However this algorithm does not allow rendezvous of two SSYNC robots while it allows *convergence* to a point. It has been shown that two SSYNC robots cannot solve the rendezvous problem in 2D-space [8,9]. Thus the rendezvous problem separates the FSYNC model from the SSYNC (thus ASYNC) model.

When the impossibility of some task for the robots is caused by the symmetry among themselves, obliviousness limits the power of the non-oblivious robots (equipped with memory), since the local memory contents of symmetric robots keep on symmetric forever. On the other hand, oblivious solutions promises *self-stabilization* [3], i.e., tolerance to transient faults and self-organization ability.

The ASYNC model involves the difficulty caused by non-rigid movement because a robot may perform Look while some other robots are in Move. Thus non-rigid movement is an important step to design an algorithm for ASYNC robots. Of course, asynchrony imposes more complicated situations because each robot cannot recognize whether another robot is moving. To overcome these difficulties, existing formation problems use a variety of geometric fixed properties. The point formation algorithm for the oblivious ASYNC robots adopts a fixed gathering point that does not change because of the movement of the robots [2]. The pattern formation algorithm for the oblivious ASYNC robots adopts the *clockwise matching* that keeps a one-to-one correspondence between the robots and the (embedded) target pattern [7].

The application of the plane formation problem is somewhat restricted although the first motivation in [10] was to reuse existing algorithms for robots in 2D-space in the 3D-space. Consider two robots with right-handed x-y-z coordinate system that are put on one plane. If their z-axis are perpendicular to the plane and are opposite to each other, these two robots cannot agree on the clockwise direction on the plane. In other words, these two robots lack *chirality*. In 2D-space, the formation power of the oblivious ASYNC robots without chirality has been investigated to reveal the weakest assumption for the robots to accomplish a given task. Cieliebak et al. showed that more than three such robots can form a point [2], and Flocchini et al. showed that more than four such robots can form a circle [5]. Only these two tasks are known to be solvable without additional assumption on the robots.

See the book by Flocchini et al. that provides most of the existing results for the robots in 2D-space [4].

Organization. Section 2 shows the system model and necessary notions related to the rotational symmetry in 3D-space. We present our main result with a plane formation algorithm for the oblivious SSYNC robots in Sect. 3. We conclude this paper with Sect. 4.

2 Robot Model and Preparation

2.1 Robot Model

Let $R = \{r_1, r_2, \ldots, r_n\}$ be a set of n anonymous robots. We use r_i just for description. Each robot is a point in a 3D-space. We consider discrete time $t = 0, 1, 2, \cdots$ and let $p_i(t) = (x_i(t), y_i(t), z_i(t)) \in \mathbb{R}^3$ be the position of r_i at time t in the global coordinate system Z_0, where $\mathbb{R}$ is the set of real numbers. The configuration of R at time t is $P(t) = \{p_i(t) \mid 1 \leq i \leq n\}$. We denote the set of all possible configurations of R by $\mathcal{P}^n$. We assume that the initial positions of robots are distinct, i.e., $p_i(0) \neq p_j(0)$ for $r_i \neq r_j$ and $|P(0)| = n$. We assume that $n \geq 4$ since any three robots are on one plane. Each robot r_i has no access to the global coordinate system, and it uses its local coordinate system Z_i. Each Z_i is a right-handed x-y-z coordinate system and its origin is the current position of r_i. The unit distance, the directions, and the orientations of the x, y, and z axes of Z_i are arbitrary and never change. We denote the coordinates of a point p in Z_i by $Z_i(p)$.

In this paper, we consider the *semi-synchronous (SSYNC)* model. At each time step t ($t = 0, 1, 2, \ldots$), a robot is either *active* or *inactive*. We assume that at least one robot is active at each time t. The active robots execute a *Look-Compute-Move cycle* with each of Look (observation of other robots), Compute (computation of the next position), and Move (move to the next position) completely synchronized. At time t, each active robot r_i obtains a set $Z_i(P(t)) = \{Z_i(p_1(t)), Z_i(p_2(t)), \ldots, Z_i(p_n(t))\}$ in the Look. Then r_i computes its next position and the route to reach there by using a common algorithm ψ in the Compute. Each robot is *oblivious* in the sense that it does not remember past observations and computation. Thus the input to ψ is $Z_i(P(t))$. Finally, r_i moves to the next point in the Move. Each robot moves at least an unknown minimum moving distance δ along the computed route, but after moving δ, it may stop en route, i.e., we consider *non-rigid movement.*

An execution of an algorithm ψ from an initial configuration $P(0)$ is a sequence of configurations $P(0), P(1), P(2), \cdots$. There is more than one execution from $P(0)$ depending on the SSYNC schedule (activation of the robots) and non-rigid movement.

The *plane formation problem* requires that the robots land on a plane, which is not predefined, without making any multiplicity. Hence point formation is not a solution for the plane formation problem. We say that an algorithm ψ *forms a plane* from an initial configuration $P(0)$, if, regardless of the choice of initial local coordinate systems Z_i for each $r_i \in R$, any execution $P(0), P(1), \cdots$ eventually reaches a configuration $P(t)$ $(t \geq 0)$ that satisfies the following three conditions:

(i) $P(t)$ is contained in a plane,
(ii) $|P(t)| = n$, i.e., all robots occupy distinct positions, and
(iii) once the system reaches $P(t)$, the robots do not move anymore.

For a set of points P, we denote the smallest enclosing ball (SEB) of P by $B(P)$ and its center by $b(P)$. A point on the sphere of a ball is said to be on the ball, and we assume that the interior or the exterior of a ball does not include its sphere. The innermost empty ball $I(P)$ is the ball whose center is $b(P)$, that contains no point of P in its interior, and that contains at least one point of P on its sphere.

2.2 Rotational Symmetry in 3D-space

We consider symmetry among the robots which is caused by not only the symmetric positions of the robots but also the symmetric local coordinate systems of the robots. Because any local coordinate system is obtained by a uniform scaling, a translation, a rotation, or a combination of them on the global coordinate system, we focus on symmetry operations by rotations. A k-fold rotation axis admits rotations by $2\pi/k, 4\pi/k, \cdots, 2\pi$. These k operations form the *cyclic group* C_k. When there is more than one rotation axis, they form a group, and there are five kinds of rotation groups, each of which is determined by the types of rotation axes and the arrangement of the rotation axes [1]. Clearly, these multiple rotation axes intersect at one point. The *dihedral group* D_ℓ consists of a single ℓ-fold axis called the *principal axis* and ℓ 2-fold axes perpendicular to the principal axis. We can recognize D_ℓ by the rotations on a prism with regular ℓ-gon bases. The remaining three rotation groups are the *tetrahedral group*, the *octahedral group*, and the *icosahedral group*, and we can recognize them by the rotations on the corresponding regular polyhedra. The *tetrahedral group* T consists of three 2-fold axes and four 3-fold axes, and its order is 12. The *octahedral group* O consists of six 2-fold axes, four 3-fold axes, and three 4-fold axes, and its order is 24. The *icosahedral group* I consists of fifteen 2-fold axes, ten 3-fold axes, and six 5-fold axes, and its order is 60. Let $\mathbb{S} = \{C_k, D_\ell, T, O, I \mid k = 1, 2, \cdots, \ell = 2, 3, \cdots\}$ where C_1 consists of only the identity element. We call the cyclic groups and the dihedral groups *2D rotation groups*, and we call remaining three rotation groups T, O, and I *3D rotation groups*.

Let $P \in \mathcal{P}^n$ be a set of n points. The *rotation group* $\gamma(P)$ of P is the rotation group that acts on P and none of its proper supergroup in $\mathbb{S}$ acts on P. Clearly, $\gamma(P)$ is uniquely determined. Then P is decomposed into disjoint subsets according to the group action of $\gamma(P)$. Let $Orb(p) = \{g * p \mid g \in \gamma(P)\}$ be the orbit of $p \in P$ and the orbit space $\{Orb(p) \mid p \in P\} = \{P_1, P_2, \ldots, P_m\}$ is called the $\gamma(P)$-decomposition of P. Each element P_i is *transitive* because it is one orbit regarding $\gamma(P)$.

Yamauchi et al. showed that in configuration P without any multiplicity, the robots can agree on the $\gamma(P)$-decomposition $\{P_1, P_2, \ldots, P_m\}$ of P and a total ordering among the elements so that (i) P_1 is on $I(P)$, (ii) P_m is on $B(P)$, and (iii) P_{i+1} is not in the interior of the ball centered at $b(P)$ and containing P_i on its sphere [10]. In the following, we assume that $\{P_1, P_2, \ldots, P_m\}$ is sorted by this ordering.

3 Plane Formation Algorithm for Oblivious SSYNC Robots

In this section, we show the following necessary and sufficient condition for the oblivious SSYNC robots with non-rigid movement to form a plane.

Theorem 2. *Let P and $\{P_1, P_2, \ldots, P_m\}$ be an initial configuration and the $\gamma(P)$-decomposition of P, respectively. Then oblivious SSYNC robots with non-rigid movement can form a plane from P if and only if (i) $\gamma(P)$ is a 2D rotation group, or (ii) $\gamma(P)$ is a 3D rotation group and there exists an element P_i such that $|P_i| \not\in \{12, 24, 60\}$.*

The necessity of Theorem 2 is clear because the condition is also a necessary condition for the oblivious FSYNC robots with rigid movement. As addressed in Sect. 1, the existing plane formation algorithm [10] does not guarantee correctness for our robots, because SSYNC model allows convergence to a plane and non-rigid movement may increase the symmetry among the robots. We present a new plane formation algorithm and prove the sufficiency of Theorem 2.

The suggestions from the existing result [10] are the following two points: First, when P satisfies the first condition of Theorem 2, the robots can agree on the plane that is perpendicular to the single (or the principal) rotation axis and that contains $b(P)$. Second, when P satisfies the second condition of Theorem 2, there is a possibility that the robots reduce their rotation group to a 2D rotation group by a deterministic algorithm. The proposed algorithm ψ_{PLF} accepts these two suggestions. Section 3.1 focuses on the first suggestion and shows that the robots can land on this plane. Section 3.2 focuses on the second suggestion and shows that there exists a deterministic symmetry breaking algorithm for the oblivious SSYNC robots with non-rigid movement. We show the entire plane formation algorithm in Sect. 3.3. Due to space limitation, we show the sketch of the correctness proofs together with the algorithm description.

3.1 Landing Algorithm ψ_{LND}

We show a landing algorithm ψ_{LND} for an initial configurations P that satisfies condition (i) of Theorem 2. We assume that $b(P) \notin P$ because the robots can translate any such configuration to another configuration P' by the robot on $b(P)$ leaving its current position so that $\gamma(P') = C_1$ and $b(P') \notin P'$ hold. In the same way, when $\gamma(P)$ is a cyclic group and there exists a robot on the single rotation axis, this robot can translate P to another configuration P'' with $\gamma(P'') = C_1$ by leaving the single rotation axis. We consider the following three types of initial configurations: (A) $\gamma(P) = C_1$, (B) $\gamma(P) = C_k$ ($k = 2, 3, \cdots$) and no robot is on the single rotation axis, and (C) $\gamma(P) = D_\ell$ ($\ell = 2, 3, \cdots$).

The key points of ψ_{LND} are the agreement on a plane (called *the target plane*) and how the robots land on the target plane without increasing their rotation group. In the following, we describe ψ_{LND} for a current configuration P because the robots are oblivious. We note that no configuration that appears in an execution of ψ_{LND} contains multiplicity.

Landing Algorithm for Cyclic Groups. We start with ψ_{LND} for Case (A) and Case (B).

Case A. Consider a current configuration P that satisfies $\gamma(P) = C_1$. The robots can agree on the total ordering among themselves as shown in Sect. 2 since each element of the $\gamma(P)$-decomposition of P is a singleton. We assume $\{r_1, r_2, \ldots, r_n\}$ is ordered in this total ordering. Thus r_n is on $B(P)$. Algorithm ψ_{LND} keeps asymmetric positions of robots by keeping $B(P)$ during the landing phase. The choice of the target plane depends on the number of robots that determines $B(P)$, i.e., 2, 3, or 4. Algorithm ψ_{LND} first checks the set of robots $Q(P) \subseteq P$ that determines $B(P)$. When $Q(P)$ is not uniquely fixed, ψ_{LND} selects the minimum size among such sets. When there are multiple candidates for $Q(P)$ with the minimum size, for each candidate set, ψ_{LND} sorts the indexes of its robots in the decreasing order. This is the label of this candidate and the candidates are sorted by the lexicographic ordering of this labeling. Then ψ_{LND} selects the last candidate as $Q(P)$. When $Q(P)$ consists of three robots, they form a large circle of $B(P)$ and the target plane is the plane containing $Q(P)$. When $Q(P)$ consists of two robots, ψ_{LND} keeps another robot on $B(P)$ so that these three robots fix a large circle of $B(P)$. When $Q(P)$ consists of four robots, ψ_{LND} translates it to an asymmetric tetrahedron to avoid a regular tetrahedron and a sphenoid by moving the robot with maximum index among $Q(P)$. The target plane is the face of this tetrahedron with the maximum face.

To keep $Q(P)$ during the landing, ψ_{LND} sends the robots not in $Q(P)$ to the interior of $B(P)$ one by one. When $r_i \in R \setminus Q(P)$ moves, its destination is the intersection of the line $\overline{r_i b(P)}$ and the ball $B_i(P)$ that is centered at $b(P)$ and contains all robots in the interior of $B(P)$ in its interior. This choice of

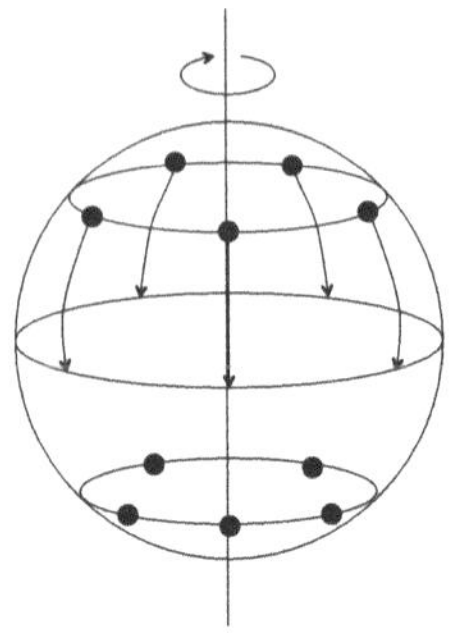

Fig. 3. The track of the robots in P_f when $\gamma(P) = C_5$.

destination keeps the rotation group of the robots and the ordering among the robots even when the robot stops en route.

Let P' be a resulting configuration where $B(P')$ contains only $Q(P')$. (Thus $\gamma(P') = C_1$.) When $Q(P')$ forms a regular tetrahedron, r_n moves slightly on the sphere of $B(P)$ to break the symmetry of $Q(P')$. When $Q(P')$ consists of two robots, ψ_{LND} sends r_{n-2} to $B(P')$.

Next ψ_{LND} sends the robots $r_1, r_2, \ldots$ one by one to the target plane. If the intersection of the target plane and $B(P')$ forms a large circle of $B(P')$, robot r_i moves to the target plane when $\{r_1, r_2, \ldots, r_{i-1}\}$ are on the target plane. ψ_{LND} at r_i outputs a position that keeps the rotation group and the ordering of the robots, and avoids multiplicity. Such point and a route to reach there always exist. By repeating this, the robots finish the landing phase. If the target plane is fixed by the four robots on $B(P')$, the robots follow almost the same procedure, but the order of robots is determined by the distance from the target plane.

Case B. Consider a current configuration P with $\gamma(P) = C_k$ ($k = 1, 2, \cdots$) that has no robot on the single rotation axis of $\gamma(P)$. The $\gamma(P)$-decomposition of P consists of at least two elements each of which forms a regular k-gon, since otherwise P is on a plane. Let $P_1, P_2, \ldots, P_m$ be the $\gamma(P)$-decomposition of P. The target plane F is the plane perpendicular to the single rotation axis and containing $b(P)$. Algorithm ψ_{LND} first fixes the intersection of F and $B(P)$ i.e., a large circle $C(P)$ of $B(P)$ by sending some element P_i to $C(P)$. Then ψ_{LND} sends other robots to F. During the execution, the rotation group of the robots may drop to C_1. Then the robots start ψ_{LND} for case (A) from the next configuration. As we will show in the following, in any execution of ψ_{LND}, the rotation group of the robots remains an subgroup of $\gamma(P)$.

Algorithm ψ_{LND} selects the element that forms the largest regular k-gon and sends the robots forming the element to $C(P)$. The tie is broken first by the distance from F to the polygon, then by the index of the element. Let P_f and R_f be this element and the set of the robots forming P_f, respectively. When P_f is not on $B(P)$, ψ_{LND} first sends R_f to $B(P)$. Then ψ_{LND} twists the regular k-gon if $\gamma(P \setminus P_f)$ is (a supergroup of) a dihedral group; each robot of R_f is ordered to slightly circulate on the smallest enclosing circle of P_f by the "right-screw rule" with the positive direction being the direction from $b(P)$ to the center of P_f. This movement keeps the rotation group a cyclic group in the succeeding landing movement. Then R_f moves to the nearest point on $C(P)$ along the track with the minimum length on the sphere of $B(P)$ (Fig. 3). Because of the choice of P_f (and the twist), there is no other robot on the tracks and the robots do not make multiplicities during the movement. The rotation group of the robots also does not increase: First, the SEB of the robots does not change during this movement. Assume for contradiction that $B(P') \neq B(P)$ for some configuration P' that appears during this movement. Clearly, $B(P')$ is in the interior or on $B(P)$. Because $\gamma(P) = C_k$ and no other element is on $C(P)$, there is another element P'_f ($|P'_f| = k$) on $B(P)$. Because $B(P') \neq B(P)$, the intersection of $B(P')$ and $B(P)$ is the smallest enclosing circle of P'_f. Then such $B(P')$ does not contain any point of the tracks of the robots of R_f. Second, because the robots of P'_f do not move during the transition from P to P', P'_f forms a regular k-gon face of P'. Thus when $k \geq 5$, a k-fold rotation axis of $\gamma(P')$ passes the center of this k-gon, thus the only possible case is $\gamma(P') = \gamma(P)$. We can easily show the same property for $k = 2, 3, 4$.

After P_f reaches the target plane, the other robots leave the SEB. Let P'' be the configuration where these robots are in the interior of $B(P'')(= B(P))$. Then ψ_{LND} sends the elements of the $\gamma(P'')$-decomposition of P'' to F one by one with avoiding multiplicities. During this movement, the rotation group of the robots does not change because there are (twisted) k robots on their SEB. Thus we have the following lemma.

Lemma 1. *Let P be an arbitrary initial configuration with $\gamma(P) = C_k$ ($k = 1, 2, \cdots$). The above algorithm ψ_{LND} makes the robots land on a common plane and accomplishes the plane formation.*

Landing Algorithm for Dihedral Groups. We show ψ_{LND} for Case (C). Consider a current configuration P with $\gamma(P) = D_\ell$ ($\ell = 2, 3, \cdots$). In this case, the target plane F is the plane that contains the 2-fold axes of $\gamma(P)$, i.e., the plane perpendicular to the principal axis of $\gamma(P)$ and containing $b(P)$. We note that the target plane is determined by the current configuration, and it changes during the execution because of SSYNC schedule and non-rigid movement. We also note that during an execution of ψ_{LND}, the rotation group of the robots may drop to a cyclic group. In this case, the robots start executing ψ_{LND} for Case (A) or (B).

When P forms a sphenoid ($|P| = 4$), a triangular anti-prism ($|P| = 6$), or a square prism ($|P| = 8$), the landing algorithm ψ_{LND} avoids a regular tetrahedron, a regular octahedron, or a cube, respectively, by the following two steps; ψ_{LND} first "twists" the polyhedron, then sends the robots to F. When the distance between the top and the bottom base becomes small enough (here we adopt the length of the edge of the bases as a threshold), ψ_{LND} changes the tracks of the robots to avoid convergence to a plane. They move to F with slightly

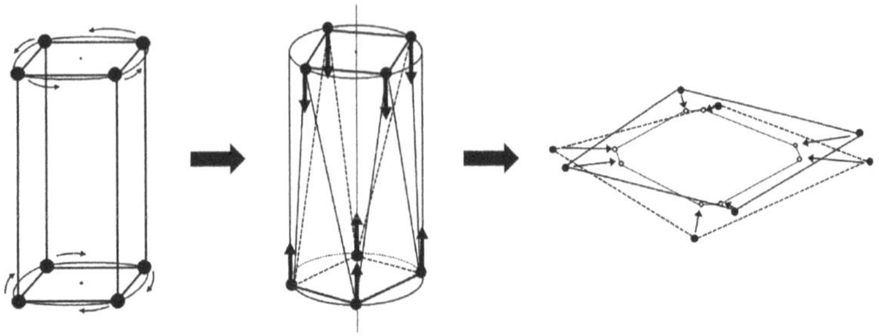

Fig. 4. Robots move on the cylinder until the top and the bottom bases close enough.

shrinking to the center of F. This movement allows the robots to recognize the SSYNC schedule since SSYNC schedule breaks the 2D rotation group (Fig. 4).

Depending on the number of elements of the $\gamma(P)$-decomposition of P, we have the following two cases.

Case C (i). Let $\{P_1, P_2, \ldots, P_m\}$ $(m \geq 2)$ be the $\gamma(P)$-decomposition of P. Algorithm ψ_{LND} makes these elements land on the target plane one by one. Element P_i moves when $P_1, P_2, \ldots, P_{i-1}$ are on the target plane. When P_i forms a prism, ψ_{LND} first twists P_i by ordering the robots of P_i circulate on the smallest enclosing circle of each base with the right-screw rule so that the robots avoid multiplicities. Then the robots move along a perpendicular to the target plane. Note that irrespective of non-rigid movement in the SSYNC model, during this movement, the rotation group of the robots remains $\gamma(P)$ since any rotation applicable to intermediate configuration P' is also applicable to $P \setminus P_i$. By repeating this procedure, each element of the $\gamma(P)$-decomposition of P land on the target plane.

Case C (ii). Consider an initial configuration P whose $\gamma(P)$-decomposition consists of one element. In this case, ψ_{LND} first slightly twists P, then sends the robots to the target plane until the two bases become close enough, and after that the robots move to the target plane by slightly shrinking to the center of the target plane. We show the detail of each phase. In the first phase, when P forms a sphenoid (D_2), a regular triangular anti-prism (D_3), or a regular prism, ψ_{LND} makes the robots circulate along the smallest enclosing circle of the bases with the right-screw rule by $2\pi/4\ell$. Clearly, this movement does not increase the rotation group of the robots. In the second phase, the robots move along the perpendicular from their current positions to the target plane until the distance between the two bases (i.e., regular ℓ-gon) becomes smaller than the length of the edge of the bases.

When $|P| \neq \{4, 6, 8\}$, this movement does not increase the rotation group of the robots to a 3D rotation group. Because P is transitive regarding a dihedral group, the tracks of the robots are on a sphere of a cylinder. If the rotation group of the robots becomes a 3D rotation group, the robots form a transitive set(s) of points regarding T, O, or I that are also on the sphere of the cylinder. However we can show the following lemma. (We omit the proof due to page limitation.)

Lemma 2. *Let P be a transitive set of points that satisfies $|P| \notin \{4,6,8\}$ and $\gamma(P) \in \{T, O, I\}$. The orthogonal projection of P onto any plane F is not on any circle on F.*

Thus the robots can converge to a plane without increasing their rotation group to a 3D rotation group.

Finally, in the third phase, the robots move to the target plane by shrinking to the center of the target plane. When one of the robots of one base move along this track, the rotation group of the resulting configuration is no more a dihedral group. Then the robots start the landing for cyclic groups as shown in Sect. 3.1. In the same way, non-rigid movement results in a configuration with the same dihedral group or a configuration with a cyclic group. Thus robots can show the result of non-rigid movement in the SSYNC model by their tracks and eventually finishes the plane formation. Thus we have the following lemma.

Lemma 3. *Let P be an arbitrary initial configuration with $\gamma(P) = D_\ell$ ($\ell = 2, 3, \ldots$). The above algorithm ψ_{LND} makes the robots land on a common plane and accomplishes the plane formation.*

3.2 Symmetry Breaking Algorithm ψ_{SB}

To prove the sufficiency of Theorem 2, we show that when a current configuration P satisfies the second condition of Theorem 2, the robots can translate P into another configuration P' that satisfies the first condition of Theorem 2. For the oblivious FSYNC robots, Yamauchi et al. showed that the robots can accomplish this symmetry breaking task with the go-to-center algorithm [10]. Let $\{P_1, P_2, \ldots, P_m\}$ be the $\gamma(P)$-decomposition of P. The go-to-center algorithm first selects an element $|P_i|$ that satisfies $|P_i| \notin \{12, 24, 60\}$. If there is more than one such element, it selects the element with the minimum index, say P_s. Hence P_s is the inner most element satisfying this condition. Because $|\gamma(P)| = 12, 24$, or 60, the robots forming P_s are on some rotation axes of $\gamma(P)$ and P_s forms a uniform polyhedra, i.e., a regular tetrahedron, a regular octahedron, a cube, a regular dodecahedron, or a icosidodecahedron. Then the algorithm makes these robots leave the rotation axes; The robots of P_s select an adjacent face and move to the center of the face, but it stops ϵ before the center. The correctness proof of [10] relies on the FSYNC model and the rigid movement of the robots.

We modify the go-to-center algorithm for the oblivious SSYNC robots with non-rigid movement. The robots repeat the go-to-center algorithm until the robots succeed in the symmetry breaking. Algorithm 3.1 shows the pseudo code of ψ_{SB}. Consider the case where the $\gamma(P)$-decomposition of P consists of more than one element. As we will show, we can assume that $P_s = P_1$. Thus $B(P)$ does not change during the execution of the modified algorithm. Then consider an execution $P(0)(= P), P(1), \cdots$. When not all robots of P_1 move at time 0, then P_1 is divided into more than one element in the $\gamma(P(1))$-decomposition

Algorithm 3.1. Symmetry breaking algorithm ψ_{SB} for robot $r_i \in R$

Notation

P: The positions of robots with $\gamma(P) \in \{T, O, I\}$ observed in Z_i.
$\{P_1, P_2, \ldots, P_m\}$: the $\gamma(P)$-decomposition of P.
p: Current position of r_i.
P_s: The element of the $\gamma(P)$-decomposition of P with $|P_s| \neq |\gamma(P)|$.
ϵ: $\ell/100$ where ℓ is the length of an edge of the polyhedron that P_s forms.

Algorithm

```
If P_s ≠ P_1 then
    If p ∈ P_s then
        Move to b(P) along the line pb(P).
        Destination d is the intersection of the line and the ball with radius
        rad(I(P))/2 and centered at b(P).
    endif
else
    If p ∈ P_s then
        Switch (P_s) do
            Case cuboctahedron: Select an adjacent triangle face of P_s.
            Case icosidodecahedron: Select an adjacent pentagon face of P_s.
            Default: Select an adjacent face of P_s.
        enddo
        Destination d is the point ε before the center of the selected face
        on the line from p to the center.
    endif
endif
```

of $P(1)$. Thus $\gamma(P(1)) \prec \gamma(P(0))$. In the same way, when some robots stop en route, P_1 is divided into more than one element in $P(1)$. The remaining case is when the $\gamma(P)$-decomposition of P is a singleton. If all robots execute an action in $P(0)$ and move by the same distance, the correctness is clear from the existing result. We consider SSYNC execution and non-rigid movement. We first consider the effect of the SSYNC movement. Because $P \in \{4, 6, 8, 20, 30\}$, when not all the robots move in $P(0)$, $P(1)$ consists of transitive sets of points regarding $\gamma(P(1)) \in \{T, O, I\}$. Because the size of a transitive set of points regarding a 3D rotation group is $4, 6, 8, 12, 20, 24, 30, 60$, the possible cases are $|P| = 8, 20$, or 30. However, in these cases the $\gamma(P(1))$-decomposition of $P(1)$ contains an element of size $4, 6, 8, 20$, or 30. Thus, the robots execute the go-to-center algorithm again. Because the size of the robots forming a new P_s is smaller than the initial one, the number of repetition is finite, and the symmetry breaking is accomplished in finite time.

3.3 Overview of ψ_{PLF}

The proposed algorithm ψ_{PLF} consists of two phases; the symmetry breaking phase (Sect. 3.2) and the landing phase (Sect. 3.1). In a configuration P, each robot checks which of the two conditions of Theorem 2 is satisfied. When condition (i) is satisfied, the robots execute ψ_{LND} and when condition (ii) is satisfied, the robots execute the algorithm ψ_{SB}. The robots can agree on the algorithm because the conditions of Theorem 2 does not depend on the local coordinate system to observe P. When the robots are on one plane, they do not execute ψ_{PLF} anymore.

We show the sketch of the proof for the sufficiency of Theorem 2. Starting from an initial configuration $P(0)$ that satisfies the condition of Theorem 2, any execution $P(0), P(1), P(2), \cdots$ reaches a configuration $P(t)$ $(t \geq 0)$ where $P(t)$ is contained in one plane. The progress is guaranteed by the existence of the unknown minimum moving distance δ and the two algorithms shown in Sects. 3.1 and 3.2.

We finally note that the robots can agree on the termination of ψ_{LND}, ψ_{SB}, and ψ_{PLF}. By observing the current configuration P in their local coordinate systems, the robots can determine whether they execute ψ_{LND} (ψ_{SB}, ψ_{PLF}, respectively) thereafter.

4 Conclusion

We showed a necessary and sufficient condition for the SSYNC robots with non-rigid movement to solve the plane formation problem together with a novel plane formation algorithm. Our results show that the oblivious SSYNC robots with non-rigid movement have the same formation power as the oblivious FSYNC robots with rigid movement. In [11], the authors introduce the notion of *symmetricity* that captures the symmetry that the robots can never break. For a set of points P, we say a rotation axis of $\gamma(P)$ is *occupied* if it contains some point of P, otherwise *unoccupied*. The *symmetricity* $\varrho(P)$ of P is the set of rotation groups in $\mathbb{S}$ that is formed by the unoccupied rotation axes of $\gamma(P)$. Our characterization is rephrased as follows by using symmetricity: Oblivious SSYNC (thus FSYNC) robots with non-rigid movement can form a plane from an initial configuration P if and only if $\varrho(P)$ consists of 2D rotation groups.

One of the most important future works is a plane formation algorithm for ASYNC model, where non-rigidity is essentially unavoidable. The proposed algorithm provides an important bridge between the SSYNC model and the ASYNC model.

References

1. Cromwell, P.: Polyhedra. University Press, Cambridge (1997)
2. Cieliebak, M., Flocchini, P., Prencipe, G., Santoro, N.: Distributed computing by mobile robots: gathering. SIAM J. of Comput. **41**(4), 829–879 (2012)
3. Dijkstra, E.W.: Self stabilizing systems in spite of distributed control. Comm. ACM **17**, 643–644 (1974)
4. Flocchini, P., Prencipe, G., Santoro, N.: Distributed Computing by Oblivious Mobile Robots. Morgan & Claypool, San Rafeal (2012)

5. Flocchini, P., Prencipe, G., Santoro, N., Viglietta, G.: Distributed computing by mobile robots: Solving the uniform circle formation problem. In: Proceedings OPODIS 2014, pp. 217–232 (2014)
6. Flocchini, P., Prencipe, G., Santoro, N., Widmayer, P.: Arbitrary pattern formation by asynchronous, anonymous, oblivious robots. Theor. Comput. Sci **407**, 412–447 (2008)
7. Fujinaga, N., Yamauchi, Y., Ono, H., Kijima, S., Yamashita, M.: Pattern formation by oblivious asynchronous mobile robots. SIAM J. Comput. **44**(3), 740–785 (2015)
8. Suzuki, I., Yamashita, M.: Distributed anonymous mobile robots: Formation of geometric patterns. SIAM J. on Comput. **28**(4), 1347–1363 (1999)
9. Yamashita, M., Suzuki, I.: Characterizing geometric patterns formable by oblivious anonymous mobile robots. Theor. Comput. Sci. **411**, 2433–2453 (2010)
10. Yamauchi, Y., Uehara, T., Kijima, S., Yamashita, M.: Plane formation by synchronous mobile robots in the three dimensional euclidean space. In: Moses, Y. (ed.) DISC 2015. LNCS, vol. 9363, pp. 92–106. Springer, Heidelberg (2015). doi:10.1007/978-3-662-48653-5_7
11. Yamauchi, Y., Uehara, T., Yamashita, M.: Brief announcement: pattern formation problem for synchronous mobile robots in the three dimensional euclidean space. In: Proceedings of PODC 2016, pp. 447–449 (2016)

Searching for an Evader in an Unknown Graph by an Optimal Number of Searchers

Takahiro Yakami(✉), Yukiko Yamauchi,
Shuji Kijima, and Masafumi Yamashita

Graduate School of Information Science and Electrical Engineering,
Kyushu University, Fukuoka, Japan
{takahiro.yakami,yamauchi,kijima,mak}@inf.kyushu-u.ac.jp

Abstract. The graph search problem is the problem of searching a graph G for a mobile evader by mobile searchers. The edge search is an offline and centralized version, and $es(G)$ denotes the number of searchers necessary and sufficient to edge search G. An online and distributed setting assumes a port numbering of G, a distinct homebase and a whiteboard in each node. Search algorithms typically respect the monotone and connected search strategy to protect the information on whiteboards; however, $\Omega(\frac{n}{\log n} es(G))$ searchers are necessary even for trees, where n is the order of G. We investigate the problem under a new online and distributed setting: We assume that searchers can exchange information wherever they meet, instead of assuming a port numbering, a homebase and whiteboards. Under this setting, we propose a search algorithm for $es(G)$ searchers, which is optimal.

Keywords: Anonymous graph · Asynchronous searcher · Graph search problem · Online and distributed setting · Pursuit and evasion in graph

1 Introduction

Offline and Centralized Graph Search. The *graph search problem* is a problem of finding an evader in a dark cave by a group of searchers. Parsons [15] models a cave by a finite undirected connected graph $G = (V, E)$. Let $\mathcal{L}$ be a straight line representation of G in $\mathbb{R}^3$, i.e., an embedding of G in $\mathbb{R}^3$ such that every edge in E is embedded as a line segment. A schedule for a searcher i is a continuous function s_i from $[0, \infty)$ to $\mathcal{L}$, where $s_i(t)$ denotes the position of i at time t. A set $S = \{s_1, \ldots, s_k\}$ is said to be a *search schedule* on $\mathcal{L}$ for k searchers, if for any continuous function ε from $[0, \infty)$ to $\mathcal{L}$ (which represents

This work was supported in part by Grant-in-Aids for Scientific Research on Innovative Areas "Molecular Robotics" (24104003 and 15H00821) of the Ministry of Education, Culture, Sports, Science, and Technology, Japan, Grant-in-Aid for Scientific Research on Innovative Areas MEXT Japan "Exploring the Limits of Computation (ELC)" (24106005), and JSPS KAKENHI Grants JP15H02666, JP15K11987 and JP15K15938.

B. Bonakdarpour and F. Petit (Eds.): SSS 2016, LNCS 10083, pp. 399–414, 2016.
DOI: 10.1007/978-3-319-49259-9_31

the move of the evader), there are an i and a t such that $\varepsilon(t) = s_i(t)$. The minimum k sufficient to construct a search schedule S on $\mathcal{L}$ for k searchers is the *search number*. This is an *offline and centralized setting*: We can design a search schedule S using the whole $\mathcal{L}$, and the k searchers synchronously execute S, i.e. they are simultaneously at positions $s_1(t), s_2(t), \dots, s_k(t)$ at time t.

The *edge search game*, which is a discrete version of this graph search problem under the offline and centralized setting, is formulated in a form of pebble game, whose goal is to simultaneously clear all edges of a given $G = (V, E)$, where an edge is said to be *clear* if the evader cannot be hidden in the edge. Initially all edges are *contaminated* (i.e., not clear). The player can (1) place a pebble at a node, (2) remove a pebble, or (3) slide a pebble along the edge from a node to another. We can clear an edge $e = (u, v) \in E$ by placing two pebbles at u, and then sliding one pebble to v along e. A clear edge e remains clear as long as every path connecting e and a contaminated edge e' contains a pebble. On the contrary, a clear edge e is *recontaminated* as soon as a path connecting e and a contaminated edge e' that contains no pebbles emerges. When all edges incident on u except an edge $e = (u, v)$ are clear and there is a pebble at u, we can thus clear e and expand the set of clear edges by sliding the pebble from u to v along e, regardless of whether or not there is a second pebble at u. The minimum number of pebbles sufficient to clear the whole E, denoted $es(G)$, is called the *edge search number* of G. As is pointed out by Parsons, $es(G)$ is equivalent to the search number of $\mathcal{L}$, for any straight line representation $\mathcal{L}$ of G.

Online and Distributed Graph Search. The graph search problem has been investigated roughly under the following *online and distributed setting* [3,6,7,9][1]. Consider a set of autonomous and asynchronous searchers (robots or mobile agents) in a graph $G = (V, E)$. Searchers have distinct identifiers, but the graph is anonymous and the nodes are not labeled, except the homebase $v_0 \in V$ from which the searchers start searching.[2] For the searchers to specify to which edge they proceed, the edges incident to any node $u \in V$ are labeled from 1 to its degree $deg(u)$. These labels are called *port numbers*. Each node has a local memory called *whiteboard*, in which the searchers can read, erase and write symbols in a mutually exclusive manner. There are no other communication tools. The searchers obey the same search algorithm and are asked to clear a given graph G, (typically) using very limited a priori knowledge of G.

The papers which investigate the graph search problem under this online and distributed setting respect the monotone and connected search strategy, since it ensures secure communication between searchers. Here a search is said to be *monotone* if no edges are recontaminated during the search, and is said to be *connected* if the set of clear edges always introduces a connected subgraph of G. Let $mcs(G, v_0)$ be the minimum number k of searchers sufficient to edge search G from v_0 in a monotone and connected way (under the offline and centralized setting). Obviously $mcs(G, v_0) \geq es(G)$. The algorithm in [3] enables

[1] Actually, the settings that these paper adapt are slightly different each other.

[2] Formally, the nodes are defined to be anonymous. The searchers however can mark the node as the homebase in its whiteboard introduced below.

$mcs(G, v_0) + 1$ searchers to clear G in a connected way (which however may not be monotone). Ilcinkas et al. [9] proposed a monotone and connected search algorithm that requires $O(\frac{n}{\log n} mcs(G, v_0))$ searchers to search any graph G of order n from any node v_0, and showed its optimality, provided a monotone and connected search. See also [2,6,7] for other search algorithms, which assume some a priori information about G, based on the monotone and connected graph search.

New Setting of Online and Distributed Graph Search. We introduce a new online and distributed setting that directly models the Parsons's original motivation of searching an evader in a dark cave. Roughly, under this setting, the cave is not equipped with any artificial facilities such as whiteboards or port numbers, and communication is possible only when searchers meet. All searchers do not necessarily start from the same node.

1. Like the original online and distributed setting, we consider a set of autonomous and asynchronous searchers having unique identifiers in a graph.
2. The graph does not have a distinguished node and the nodes are completely anonymous. Also, it does not have the homebase from which all searchers start searching. The searchers start from arbitrary nodes, but they cannot mark these nodes as their homebases.
3. We imagine that a node is a round room with doors (i.e., ports) aligned on the wall, each of which is "open" to one of the edges incident to the node. The doors are anonymous and indistinguishable. In particular, they do not have port numbers. Instead, we assume that each searcher in a room can select a door, can specify the door from which it enters the room as long as it stays in the room, and has the common sense of clockwise direction so that it can specify the h-th door in clockwise from the door from which it entered the room. Note that the graph is dark; a searcher cannot perceive which door another searcher uses to arrive or leave the node.
4. Each node does not have a local memory. In particular, it does not have a whiteboard to support communication between searchers. Instead, each searcher has a local memory of sufficient size, and searchers exchange information with identifier tag wherever they meet, even in an edge, which implies that a searcher is always aware of the identifier and the contents of local memory of each of the searchers occupying the same place.

Our Contribution. Let $s(G)$ be the number of searchers necessary and sufficient to search G under this new online and distributed setting. Obviously $es(G) \leq s(G)$. We show the following theorem.

Theorem 1. *For any graph G, $es(G) = s(G)$.*

To show $es(G) \geq s(G)$, we present a search algorithm OLSEARCH for $es(G)$ searchers, which is obviously optimal in terms of the number of searchers. It is worth emphasizing that OLSEARCH does *not* require any global information on G such as an upper bound b on the order n of G as initial information.

Related Works. There is huge volume of literature on graph search and related topics, a part of which we have touched in this section. However, returning to the original problem of Parson, the cave is more naturally modeled by a polygon possibly with holes. Under this geometric setting, an evader is caught by a searcher when he is in the visibility range of the searcher. This *polygon search problem* was first introduced in [17] and has been extensively studied [8,14]. An interesting difference between the graph formalization and the geometric formalization is that, unlike the former [12], recontamination *does* help in the latter [8,17]. The impact of the visibility range of a searcher to its search power is a typical research topic. One flashlight is strictly less powerful [17], but two flashlights are already as powerful as full visibility [10,14]. These resutls however are for a single searcher.

Polygon search by a group of searchers has also been investigated [5,13,19]. In [5,13], searching a polygonal region by a chain of searchers is considered; the searchers form a polygonal chain such that neighboring searchers are mutually visible, and the chain is swept across the region. It is shown that searchers with one flashlight have the same search power as ones with full visibility, as long as this strategy is adopted [13]. To search a polygon with bushiness b[3], $1 + \lfloor \log_3(2b + 1) \rfloor$ searchers with one flashlight are sometimes necessary and always sufficient [19]. See e.g., [18] for more information.

Organization. In Sect. 2, after introducing our model and defining the online search problem, we prepare some notions necessary to construct and analyze our online search algorithm OLSEARCH. Section 3 describes OLSEARCH, and shows that $es(G)$ searchers are sufficient to search G by OLSEARCH. Finally concluding remarks and open problems are given in Sect. 4.

2 Preliminaries

2.1 Model and Graph Search Problem

Our Model. Consider a set of k searchers $1, 2, \ldots, k$ in a finite undirected connected graph $G = (V, E)$. G is anonymous and neither the nodes nor the edges are labeled. A node u with degree $deg(u)$ is a tiny round room with $deg(u)$ ports (i.e., doors to incident edges) aligned on the wall, among which a clockwise direction is defined and is available to any searcher in u. However, these ports are anonymous, and port numbers are not attached to them. Node u does not support local memory (or whiteboard).

Each searcher i has a unique identifier $id(i) \in \mathbf{N}$, where $\mathbf{N}$ is the set of natural numbers, and has sufficiently large local memory. Initially, i is placed at a node $u \in V$ sometimes called the "homebase." Searcher i does not have a marking device like pebbles, so that i cannot mark u as its homebase to distinguish it

[3] The bushiness b of a polygon P is the minimum number of triangles that share no edges with P over all triangulations of P.

from the other nodes. The homebases of searchers may not be distinct. i catches the evader when they meet, and to meet is the only way to catch the evader.

Each searcher i in $u \in V$ can traverse any edge $e = (u, v)$ incident to u by "choosing" the port p corresponding to e. Recall however that the ports are anonymous. The algorithm specifies p in one of the following two ways:

1. The algorithm can instruct i to choose an arbitrary port. Then i non-deterministically chooses a port, which is assumed to be the worst port for the algorithm. That is, the selection is governed by an adversary.
2. When i arrived u from another node, the algorithm can use the port q from which i entered u and the clockwise direction among the ports to specify p. We assume that i remembers q as long as it stays in u. Then the algorithm can specify a port by stating e.g., the h-th port from q clockwise, where the 0-th port from q is q itself. Note that i forgets q if it leaves u.

We assume that edge $e = (u, v)$ is a kind of corridor, and searcher i who enters e from u remembers the forward direction from u to v (as long as it stays in e), and monotonically moves towards v. It then reaches (and enters) v within a finite time, unless it meets the evader (and ends the search) or another searcher. Next paragraph explains what happens when searchers meet.

Recall that a node does not have a whiteboard to support communication between searchers. Instead, two searchers can communicate with each other when they meet, even in an edge. That is, when searchers meet, each of them immediately terminates the action it is executing and starts a communication and computation operation: If ℓ searchers $i_1, i_2, \ldots, i_\ell$ meet at time t, every searcher i_j automatically receives information $I = \{(id(i_h), c(i_h)) : h = 1, 2, \ldots, \ell\}$, where $c(i_h)$ is the contents of local memory of i_h at time t, and then examines I to decide the next action based on a given algorithm. This communication and computation operation is assumed to be instantaneous.

Finally, the searchers are fully asynchronous.

Graph Search Problem under Online and Distributed Setting. We are interested in designing a graph search algorithm A given to every searcher. An instance of the problem is a triple $\mathcal{I}$ of a graph $G = (V, E)$, the identifiers $ID = \langle id(1), id(2), \ldots, id(k) \rangle$ and the homebases $HB = \langle hb(1), hb(2), \ldots, hb(k) \rangle$ of k searchers $1, 2, \ldots, k$. A searcher i does not have any a priori knowledge of $\mathcal{I}$ besides $id(i)$. The set of full trajectories of the searchers executing A for $\mathcal{I}$, which is simply called the (global) *behavior*, is by no means deterministic, as A may instruct a searcher to choose an arbitrary port, and the searchers' motions are not synchronized. Let $\mathcal{B}$ be the set of all possible behaviors. We say that A solves the graph search problem for $\mathcal{I}$ when the following conditions hold:

1. If there is an evader in G, then a searcher eventually meets the evader, in any behavior in $\mathcal{B}$.
2. If there is no evader in G, then every searcher eventually terminates A reporting that it did not meet an evader, in any behavior in $\mathcal{B}$.

We say that A solves the graph search problem on G by k searchers, if A solves the graph search problem for any instance $\mathcal{I} = \langle G, ID, HB \rangle$, where ID and HB are a list of k distinct natural numbers and a list of k nodes in V, respectively. If there is an algorithm A that solves the graph search problem on G by k searchers, G is *searchable* by k searchers. The search number of G, denoted $s(G)$, is the minimum number k of searchers sufficient to search G.

Proposition 1. *Let G be any graph. Then $es(G) \leq s(G)$.*

Proof. Suppose that G is searchable by k searchers. We show that there is an edge search schedule on G for k pebbles. Let A be an algorithm that solves the graph search problem for G by k searchers. Then for any instance $\mathcal{I} = \langle G, ID, HB \rangle$, A solves the graph search problem for $\mathcal{I}$, where ID and HB are the identifiers and the homebases of the k searchers. Since the searchers are asynchronous, there is a behavior that satisfies the following condition: No two searchers move simultaneously, and once a searcher i in some node u enters an edge $e = (u, v)$, then the other searchers do not move until i reaches v. That is, in B, at most one searcher traverses an edge, and it never meets another searcher in an edge. It is now easy to construct an edge search schedule on G for k pebbles, by simulating the trajectory of searcher i by the i-th pebble. □

2.2 Meeting Problem

The meeting problem for a set of $k(\geq 2)$ searchers in a graph G asks that at least one pair of searchers meet in G. Notice that the rendezvous problem is the meeting problem for $k = 2$. Let n be the order of G. Then the meeting problem in G is trivially solvable when $k \geq n + 1$. The meeting number $\mu(G)$ of G is the minimum number k of searchers for which the meeting problem in G is solvable; more formally, $\mu(G)$ is the smallest number of searchers such that there is an algorithm A which solves the meeting problem on any instance $\mathcal{I} = \langle G, ID, HB \rangle$.

Lemma 1. *Suppose that $es(G) \geq 2$. Then there is no search algorithm for k searchers in G, if there is no meeting algorithm for k searchers in G. That is, $\mu(G) \leq s(G)$.*

Proof. Observe that G is not a path graph since $es(G) \geq 2$. To derive a contradiction, suppose that there is a search algorithm A for k searchers in G, but there is no meeting algorithm for k searchers in G. Since A is not a meeting algorithm in G, there is a global behavior $B \in \mathcal{B}$ of the searchers executing A such that no two searchers meet in G during B.

For B, define a trajectory $\varepsilon(t)$ of evader ε such that any searcher cannot catch ε in B. To describe $\varepsilon(t)$, we draw G in the 3-dimensional Euclidean space, where every edge is represented by a line segment. Let ℓ and ℓ' denote the minimum length of any edge and the minimum distance between any pair of searchers in B, respectively. That is, $d(s(t), s'(t)) \geq \ell'$ for any two searchers s and s' and for any time t, where $d(u, v)$ is the Euclidean distance between u and v. Since A is not a meeting algorithm, $\ell' > 0$. Let $\delta = \min\{\ell, \ell'\}$.

Arbitrarily choose a searcher s and fix it. We construct $\varepsilon(t)$ so that $d(s(t), \varepsilon(t)) = \delta/2$ holds for all t, which is sufficient to show the lemma, since no searcher s' (including s) can catch ε because $d(s'(t), \varepsilon(t)) \geq \delta/2$ holds for all t. It is worth emphasizing that we can use the behavior of s in B in the construction of $\varepsilon(t)$.

The basic move of ε is the following: If s leaves, then ε follows s, keeping $d(s(t), \varepsilon(t)) = \delta/2$. If s approaches, then ε leaves s, keeping $d(s(t), \varepsilon(t)) = \delta/2$. All what we need to explain is that ε is never driven into a leaf, i.e., ε is *safe* forever. Observe that ε is not safe only when (1) there is exactly one path between ε and the leaf, (2) the path does not contain a node with degree more than two, and (3) s is approaching ε to go to the leaf.

We first show that there is a safe point $\varepsilon(0)$ at time $t = 0$. By definition $s(0)$ is a node $u \in V$. Suppose first that the degree of $s(0)$ is at least three. Then there is a node v adjacent to u such that s does not enter (u, v) when s starts moving. Then we take $\varepsilon(0)$ in (u, v) with distance $\delta/2$ from u. Suppose otherwise that the degree of $s(0)$ is less than three. Then there is a shortest path connecting u and a node w with degree at least three since G is not a path graph. Let v be the node in the path adjacent to u. Then again we take $\varepsilon(0)$ in (u, v) with distance $\delta/2$ from u. Obviously $\varepsilon(0)$ is safe in both cases.

We next show that ε can be kept safe forever. Suppose that ε is safe at t and s is approaching. If s does not reach a point within distance $\delta/2$ from a leaf, obviously the basic move mentioned above can avoid a near miss forever. If s reaches a point within distance $\delta/2$ from a leaf, let $u_0, u_1, \ldots, u_f$ be the sequence of nodes that s visits to reach a point near leaf u_L, where u_L is the leaf that s approaches next. Since ε is safe at t, there is a node u_i with degree at least three. Then there is a node v adjacent to u_i besides u_{i-1} and u_{i+1}, and s does not enter edge (u_i, v). Now, evader ε can enter (u_i, v) when ε reaches u_i, and follow s after s passes u_i to u_{i+1}, to keep its situation safe. □

2.3 Gathering Problem

The gathering problem for a set of $k(\geq 2)$ searchers in a graph G asks all searchers to gather in a node. The gathering number $\gamma(G)$ of G is the minimum number $k(\geq 2)$ of searchers for which the gathering problem in G is solvable; more formally, $\gamma(G)$ is the smallest number $k(\geq 2)$ of searchers such that there is an algorithm A which solves the gathering problem on any instance $\mathcal{I} = \langle G, ID, HB \rangle$. Obviously $\mu(G) \leq \gamma(G)$. Later in Sect. 3 we will show $\mu(G) = \gamma(G) = 2$ for any G.

The gathering problem plays a key role in our search algorithm. Once all searchers have gathered, they can elect a leader. The leader then recognizes the topology G with an assistant searcher that it appoints, constructs a monotone edge search schedule π for G (if $k \geq es(G)$), and distributes π to each of the searchers. Finally, they simulate π to search G.

2.4 Exploration Problem

In order to solve the meeting or the gathering problem, searchers try to traverse all nodes and edges in G, which is completely unknown initially. Universal exploration sequences we introduce below help them.

Let $\mathcal{G}(N, D)$ be the set of all undirected connected graphs with the order at most N and the maximum degree at most D. A *universal traversal sequence* (UTS) for $\mathcal{G}(N, D)$ is a sequence $Q = (q_1, q_2, ..., q_f)$ of non-negative integers less than D satisfying the following condition: For any graph $G = (V, E) \in \mathcal{G}(N, D)$, any (global) port numbering function λ for G and any node $u_0 \in V$, define $u_i \in V$ for $i = 1, 2, \dots, f$ by $u_i = \lambda_{u_{i-1}} q_i$, where λ is a function from V to a (local) port numbering function, i.e., for each $u \in V$, λ_u is a one-to-one function from $\{0, 1, \dots, deg_G(u) - 1\}$ to the set $N_G(u)$ of nodes adjacent to u. Here $deg_G(u) = |N_G(u)|$ is the degree of u in G. In other words, $(u_1, u_2, \dots, u_f)$ is the trajectory of a searcher when it follows port numbers $q_1, q_2, ..., q_f$ in this order starting from u_0. Then $\{u_0, u_1, \dots, u_f\} = V$, i.e., the searcher can visit all nodes in G. For any N and D, there is a UTS of length $O(N^3 D^2 \log N)$ [1].

Koucky [11] showed that a universal sequence with the same property as UTS is also given as a sequence $O = (o_1, o_2, ..., o_f)$ of offsets, where if a searcher arrives u_{i-1} via a port (number) q_{i-1}, then it leaves u_{i-1} via the port (number) $(q_{i-1} + o_i) \mod deg_G(u_{i-1})$. The proof in [1] shows that the same upper bound $O(N^3 D^2 \log N)$ holds. This sequence O is called a *universal exploration sequence* (UXS). A UXS $O = (o_1, o_2, ..., o_f)$ can also define a universal sequence under our model, under which the port numbers are not attached; if a searcher is in u_{i-1} then it enters the edge (u_{i-1}, u_i) corresponding to the o_i-th port clockwise from the port from which it arrives u_{i-1}, where the searcher selects an arbitrarily port when $i = 0$. It is because the behavior of UXS under our setting is the same as the one under the Koucky's setting, provided that the ports are numbered in a clockwise order in each node.

2.5 Sharing Port Numbers and Related Problem

Cooperative search by a group of searchers are done based on sharing their trajectories, each of which could be described as a sequence of port numbers if there were. Since port numbers are not attached under our setting, we propose a way to describe a trajectory and a method to share it with another searcher. Suppose that a searcher s at a node u_0 in $G = (V, E)$ traverses a path $X : u_0, u_1, \dots, u_f$, where $e_i = (u_{i-1}, u_i) \in E$ for $i = 1, 2, \dots, f$. Then s can memorize $P : p_1, p_2, \dots, p_{f-1}$, where the port leading to e_{i+1} in u_i is the p_i-th port clockwise from the port from which it arrives u_i (through e_i) for $i = 1, \dots, f-1$. Searcher s also remembers the port p_f[4] from which it enters u_f as long as it stays in u_f, but cannot specify which port in u_0 it used to start traversing X. Nevertheless, s can traverse X in reverse direction and can return to u_0 using

[4] Note that p_i for all $i = 1, \dots, f - 1$ are integers representing offsets from the 0-th port. However, p_f is neither an integer nor an offset. It is an (anonymous) door from which it enters u_f.

information P; we use the port p_f to reach u_{f-1}, and use the p_i-th port *counter-clockwise* to reach u_{i-1} from u_i. Thus another searcher s' in u_f can also traverse X (in reverse direction), if it can recognize the port p_f of s.

The following algorithm PORT-INFO solves this problem: First s moves to u_{f-1} through port p_f. (Recall that s' cannot perceive from which port s leaves.) Then for each $p = 0, 1, \ldots, deg(u_f)-1$, s' chooses the p-th port clockwise starting from its 0-th port, and examines if this choice is successful. That is, it moves to the adjacent node u through the p-th port, and checks if it meets s in u. If it meets s, it returns to u_f and remember p as the port p_f of s.

Searchers s and s' meeting in an edge $e = (u, v)$ may also need to exchange information from which node they each arrive, the problem which is however easy to solve.

3 Searching Unknown Graph by Optimal Number of Searchers

This section presents an online graph search algorithm OLSEARCH, which verifies $s(G) = es(G)$. For the convenience of description, we first present another graph search algorithm OLS. OLSEARCH is obtained as a modification of OLS. OLS is an online graph search algorithm for $\max\{es(G), \gamma(G)\}$ searchers, provided that G is *not* a path graph. Obviously $es(G) = 1$ if and only if G is a path graph. Then OLS requires $es(G)$ searchers to search G, unless G is a path graph, since we will show $\gamma(G) = 2$ in this section. OLSEARCH is an extension of OLS so that it can search a path graph by one searcher.

Let us present algorithm OLS that searches any graph $G = (V, E)$ by $\max\{es(G), \gamma(G)\}$ searchers, provided that G is not a path graph. OLS consists of the following five phases (sub-algorithms):

(MEET) Solve the meeting problem.
(UPBOUND) Find an upper bound b on the order n of G.
(GATHER) Solve the gathering problem.
(TOPOLOGY) Recognize G.
(SEARCH) Simulate an edge search.

Among the five algorithms, we borrow algorithms MEET and GATHER from [4] and use them after modifying them to correctly work under our model. More accurately, the gathering algorithm called SGL[5] in [4] uses two subroutines RV-asynch-poly and ESST to solve the meeting problem and to estimate an upper bound on the order of G, respectively. Except ESST, the modification of SGL is easy. In fact, as MEET, we use RV-asynch-poly as it is; however, its correctness proof under our setting, whose outline is given in the following subsection, is extremely involved. Algorithm ESST, on the other hand, heavily makes use of

[5] Algorithm SGL is originally proposed as an algorithm to gather some information, e.g., all identifiers, exploring an unknown graph [4]. In this paper, we modify and use it as a gathering algorithm, modification of which is simple.

the port numbering. We thus newly design UPBOUND that estimates an upper bound on the order of G under our model. Algorithm TOPOLOGY is based on the breadth first search and is conventional. Finally SEARCH simulates an edge search schedule for G and needs some tricks.

3.1 MEET

Algorithm OLS first solves the meeting problem by MEET. Here we use RV-asynch-poly as MEET. It correctly solves the meeting problem under the setting in [4]. In order to justify MEET, we show that RV-asynch-poly also solves the meeting problem under our setting, by observing that the behavior of RV-asynch-poly under our setting is essentially the same.

A summary of the model used in [4] is as follows: There are two searchers with distinct identifiers in an unknown graph $G = (V, E)$. The graph G has a port numbering. The searchers' moves are asynchronous, and they do not even know an upper bound b on the order $n = |V|$. Two searchers must meet regardless of their homebases. Note that the meeting algorithm RV-asynch-poly, which is based on a UXS, depends on the identifier of the searcher executing it.

The searchers dynamically produce a UXS whenever it becomes necessary by using the Reingold's algorithm [16]. More accurately, they use a modification of the Reingold's UXS O so that a searcher s can traverse all edges not only all nodes. When s reaches a node u following O, before moving to the next node v specified by O, s takes a round trip to each of u's neighbors $v_1, v_2, \dots v_{deg(u)}$ (including v) in this order, where v_i is the i-th neighbor. When s follows O under our setting, although the trajectory may be different, s visits all nodes as explained in Subsect. 2.4, and s can take the same round-trip travels to neighbors whenever it reaches a new node. Thus O produces an *integral* trajectory under both settings, where a trajectory is said to be integral, if it traverses all edges (and hence visits all nodes). We assume that a trajectory means an integral trajectory after modification mentioned above.

Let $R(b, v)$ be the trajectory produced by the Reingold's UXS $O(b)$, where b is an (estimation of) upper bound on n and v is the initial node. Provided that $q_0 = 0$,[6] where q_0 is defined in Subsect. 2.4, $R(b, v)$ is determined uniquely. In [4], let $X(b, v) = R(b, v)\overline{R(b, v)}$ and $Q(b, v) = X(1, v)X(2, v) \dots X(b, v)$, where $\overline{R}$ denotes the reversal of R. Here $Q(b, v)$ is well-defined since $X(b, v)$ always returns to v.

In RV-asynch-poly, each searcher s estimates an upper bound b on n. If s finishes the algorithm in vain without meeting with another searcher perhaps because its guess b is wrong, it re-invokes RV-asynch-poly for a larger b, which eventually reaches a correct $b \geq n$. Suppose that s at u (resp. s' at u') estimates a correct upper bound b (resp. b'), where $b \geq b'$ and $b \geq n$. A key trick of RV-asynch-poly is that s is forced to traverse $X(b', u')$ at least once, before s' finishes traversing $X(b', u')$ a given (large number of) times. Specifically, s traverses

[6] This assumption is not explicit in [4]. However, in order to define the trajectory $R(b, v)$ from parameter b and v, a constant q_0 must be given.

$R(b,u)$, but it initiates $Q(b,v)$ whenever it reaches a new node v in $R(b,u)$. Then s traverses $X(b',v')$ at least once, since $v' \in R(b,u)$ and $b' \leq b$. (Although the trick also forces s' to traverse $X(b',u')$ many times, we can show that the trick works correctly under our setting.) Since $X(b',u') = R(b',u')\overline{R(b',u')}$, they can successfully meet.

However, under our setting, the trajectory generated by $O(b)$ also depends on q_0, which is not a constant. To reflect q_0, by $R(b,v,e)$, we denote the trajectory, where e is the edge from which it enters v (or an arbitrarily selected edge if s has never moved.) As above, let $X(b,v,e) = R(b,v,e)\overline{R(b,v,e)}$.

Suppose that s' repeats executing $X(b',u',e')$. Then s (executing RV-asynch-poly) starts traversing $R(b,u,e)$, and reaches node u'. Here as mentioned, s takes round-trip travels to all neighbors, in particular, to a node connected by e'. When s finishes this travel, it traverses $Q(b,u',e')$, where $Q(b,u',e') = X(1,u',e')X(2,u',e')\ldots X(b,u',e')$. (Observe that s can specify the port corresponding to e' when it returns from $X(1,u',e')$ to continue $X(2,u',e')$.) Then s traverses $X(b',u',e')$ at least once since $b' \leq b$. Now, s successfully meets s'.

3.2 GATHER

We use SGL to present algorithm GATHER. Observe first that a searcher s who runs RV-asynch-poly eventually meets all the other searchers s' if it does not terminate the algorithm when it meets a searcher, since RV-asynch-poly correctly solves the meeting problem, i.e., s can meet another searcher s', no matter where s' is initially located. Each searcher s who runs RV-asynch-poly can collect the identifiers of all searchers and thus count the number k of searchers. Then the leader s_0, the searcher who has the minimum identifier among the searchers, can call the other searchers together to its homebase u_0. Here it is worth emphasizing that this incremental feature of RV-asynch-poly is not sufficient to convince that a searcher s has already met all the searchers, and that s needs to convince that a b currently examining is a correct upper bound. To implement this idea by using RV-asynch-poly, after RV-asynch-poly solves the meeting problem and s meets another searcher s', SGL estimates an upper bound b of n by using an algorithm called ESST.

Unfortunately however, it is difficult to modify ESST so that it can correctly run under our model unlike the rest of SGL. We thus propose an algorithm UPBOUND to estimate an upper bound b in the next subsection. For the time being, assuming that b is available, we explain that SGL can be modified so that it can correctly work under our model.

An outline of GATHER, which is a modification of SGL and solves the gathering problem under our model, is as follows: We have observed that RV-asynch-poly solves the meeting problem under our model and we can use it as MEET. Each searcher s executes RV-asynch-poly and meets another searcher s'. Without loss of generality, we assume that s has a smaller identifier than s'. Suppose that they meet at a node u. (If they meet in an edge $e = (u,v)$, they regard the place in e as an imaginary node.) Then s and s' suspend the execution of RV-asynch-poly and start executing UPBOUND to calculate b.

Then s resumes RV-asynch-poly from the position at which it was interrupted, until RV-asynch-poly ends for $2(b+\ell)+1$ and guarantees s to have met all the searchers, where $\ell = 2m+2$ and m is the length of the smallest identifier. When s meets another searcher s'' with a smaller identifier, s terminates RV-asynch-poly and waits for the leader s_0 arriving to teach the way leading to its homebase u_0, at which the searchers will gather.

If s is the leader s_0, s_0 terminates RV-asynch-poly when RV-asynch-poly guarantees s_0 to have met all the searchers. Then it goes back the way it has come in RV-asynch-poly to meet again all the other searchers s' waiting for its arrival. When s_0 meets s', it teaches s' the way to u_0 by using algorithm PORT-INFO given in Subsect. 2.5, and s' goes to u_0 to solve the gathering problem.

3.3 UPBOUND

We present algorithm UPBOUND to calculate an upper bound b on n, assuming that two searchers s and s' at a node v_0 start executing UPBOUND. Here n is the number of nodes, including the imaginary ones we explained in Subsect. 3.2. Without loss of generality, we assume that s has a smaller identifier than s'. One important restriction here is that at least one of them must stay at v_0 during the execution of UPBOUND to guarantee the correctness of RV-asynch-poly (which is executed by other searchers including s and s'). In UPBOUND, s' always stays at v_0 and only s moves to calculate b.

UPBOUND is an implementation of the breadth first search (BFS), but s and s' cannot count the exact order n unlike usual BFS, because of the restriction mentioned above. It makes use of a queue Q that contains nodes v which have been *discovered* but not yet have been *visited* to examine their neighbors. It also uses a set U that contains the nodes which have been visited. Since nodes are anonymous, in Q and U, each node v is identified by a shortest path X_v from v_0, and Q keeps v in the increasing order of its length $|X_v|$. What we need to emphasize here is that in Q or U, a node v may occur more than once, since v may have two (or more) shortest paths X_v and Y_v representing v, and in general, s and s' cannot determine whether or not two nodes represented by X_v and Y_v are equivalent. For the sake of accuracy, we define Q and U as follows: Q contains the set of paths X_v such that v has been discovered but not yet has been visited, while U contains the set of paths X_v such that v has been visited.

Like the standard BFS, initially Q contains v_0, or an empty sequence λ that represents v_0, and U is empty. In what follows, a node v frequently means a path representing v. In each round, s picks the first node v from Q and visits v to examine each neighbor v' of v as follows: Let $X_{v'}$ be the path representing v'. That is, $X_{v'} = X_v p$, where v' is reachable from v by taking the p-th port. Let $h = |X_{v'}|$. We test if h is the distance of v' from v_0, or in other words, if $X_{v'}$ is a shortest path of v' from v_0. To this end, starting from v', s executes (another) BFS to test if s encounters s' (at v_0) in distance less than h from v'. If v' (i.e., $X_{v'}$) is a shortest path, s puts v' at the end of Q. Then s puts v to U when it ends the test for each neighbor v' of v, and it terminates the round.

UPBOUND terminates when Q becomes empty. Let $\mathcal{X}$ be the set of shortest paths between v_0 and nodes v, whose size is finite. By the nature of BFS, s inserts each path in $\mathcal{X}$ to Q at least once and the same path is not inserted to Q twice, which implies $U = \mathcal{X}$ when UPBOUND terminates. Then $b = |U|$ is a correct upper bound on n.

Recall the definition of gathering number $\gamma(G)$ of G, which is the minimum number k of searchers greater than 1 such that the gathering is solvable in G. We have first shown that the meeting problem is solvable in G for any $k > 1$ searchers. We have also shown that if two searchers s and s' meet, then they can calculate upper bound b on the order n of G, and if s can calculate b, then all the searchers can gather. Thus the following lemma holds:

Lemma 2. *For any G, $\mu(G) = \gamma(G) = 2$.*

3.4 TOPOLOGY

We present algorithm TOPOLOGY to construct G by using queue Q and set U in UPBOUND. Suppose that the gathering problem has been solved in u_0, where u_0 is the homebase of the leader s_0. Let s_1 be the searcher with the smallest identifier but s_0. Then s_0 and s_1 execute TOPOLOGY to construct G. Unlike UPBOUND, they can leave u_0 simultaneously in TOPOLOGY, and hence can execute a standard BFS to decide G and n. Although Q and U play roles similar to UPBOUND, Q and U contain at most one representation of a node v unlike UPBOUND, and hence $|U| = n$ when TOPOLOGY terminates.

Specifically, s_0 and s_1 can test whether or not v' occurs in $Q \cup U$, when the BFS is at v and is exploring a neighbor v' of v. To this end, s_1 first moves to v'. Then s_0 visits each node in $Q \cup U$ to check if s_1 is there. If s_0 finds s_1 when it visits v'', then they find an edge (v, v''). Otherwise, v' does not occur in $Q \cup U$. It is easy to observe that s_0 can construct G when TOPOLOGY terminates by using this test.

3.5 SEARCH

When SEARCH is invoked, we assume the following without loss of generality: All the searchers are in the homebase u_0 of the leader s_0, and s_0 knows the number k of the searchers and graph $G = (V, E)$. Since they can communicate with each other, they have the same representation of G, i.e., for each node $v \in V$, they share the same representation, and for each edge $(u, v) \in E$, they share the port information leading to (u, v) from each of its end nodes u and v. Furthermore, by using PORT-INFO, they share the 0-th port of s_0 at u_0.

In SEARCH, s_0 first computes an edge search schedule π for $es(G)$ searchers, and then modifies it to an online search schedule for each searcher s, if $k \geq es(G)$. Otherwise if $k < es(k)$, s_0 declares that they give up searching G. Without loss of generality, we can assume that π is monotone.

Suppose that $k \geq es(G)$. Then the move of the i-th pebble for $i = 0, 1, \ldots, es(G) - 1$ is simulated by the searcher s_i, which has the i-th smallest identifier among the k searchers. Note that we can arrange the edge search schedule so that each pebble initially stays at u_0 and is not removed from G.[7] Let π_i be the schedule for pebble i. Then π_i can be a repetition of the following types of steps:

(SYNCHRONIZE) Stay at the node until it simultaneously meets a group of pebbles $i_1, i_2, \ldots, i_h$, where i_j is a pebble that has just traversed a path X_{i_j} for $j = 1, 2, \ldots, h$.
(MOVE) Move to the next node (or stay unmoved).

Obviously, SYNCHRONIZE is feasible among the group of searchers $s_i, s_{i_1}, s_{i_2}, \ldots, s_{i_h}$, since these searchers exchange all information whenever they meet. Also the next node in MOVE is easily given to searcher s_i, since all searchers share the representation of G as mentioned. In SEARCH, for $i = 0, 1, \ldots, es(G) - 1$, s_0 constructs an online search schedule for s_i, which simulates π_i, and gives it to s_i. (Note that searcher s_j for $j \geq es(G)$ is instructed to stay at u_0 forever.) Finally, each searcher s_i executes its schedule. Then the next lemma holds:

Lemma 3. *Let G be any graph and assume that G is not a path graph. Then OLS is a search schedule for $es(G)$ searchers on G.*

Proof. As observed, OLS is a search schedule for $\max\{es(G), \gamma(G)\}$ searchers. Since $es(G) \geq 2$ because G is not a path graph and $\gamma(G) = 2$ by Lemma 2, $\max\{es(G), \gamma(G)\} = es(G)$. □

3.6 OLSEARCH

If G is a path graph and $es(G) = 1$, a single searcher on G executing OLS cannot successfully search G, since MEET never terminates. Here we present an algorithm MEET*, which is a modification of MEET. MEET* is exactly the same as MEET, except that it successfully searches G by a single searcher, if G is a path graph. OLSEARCH invokes MEET* instead of MEET.

MEET* and MEET are exactly the same, unless the following situation occurs: Searcher s executing MEET* reaches two different leaves ℓ and ℓ' before reaching a node with degree at least three. If it occurs, then G is a path graph, and G has been searched; s declares the end of search, terminating MEET* (and OLSEARCH). Otherwise, it eventually reaches a node with degree at least three, i.e., G is not a path graph; OLSEARCH and OLS are the same in this case.

Finally we observe that s can detect the second leaf $\ell'(\neq \ell)$. After s reaches the first leaf ℓ, whenever it reaches a node v, it calculates its distance from ℓ, which is indeed possible since it never reaches a node with degree more than two. When s reaches a leaf with a positive distance, it declares that s finds the second leaf ℓ'.

[7] This simulation of π may not be monotone, since searcher s_i needs to travel inside G violating the monotonicity, when the i-th pebble is picked up from a node and placed at a different node.

Corollary 1. *For any graph G, OLSEARCH is an online graph search algorithm for $es(G)$ searchers on G.*

Now, we can conclude that Theorem 1 holds by Corollary 1.

4 Conclusions

We have investigated the problem of searching an unknown graph for a mobile evader by a group of mobile searchers under a new online and distributed setting, which directly models the Parsons's dark cave. The graph, which models the cave, is completely anonymous and ports are not labeled. Furthermore, nodes have no whiteboards for communication. Instead, we assume that searchers can exchange information wherever they meet. Our algorithm OLSEARCH searches any graph G by $es(G)$ searchers without requiring any a priori information on G, where $es(G)$ is the edge search number of G, and hence is optimal, since $es(G) \leq s(G)$.

A problem left unsolved is the graph search problem by anonymous searchers under our online and distributed setting. Provided unique identifiers, we have shown that the graph search problem is solvable if the meeting problem is solvable. It seems to be interesting if this theorem holds for anonymous searchers.

In this paper, we have not discussed the time complexity. As usual, the trade-off between the time and space complexities is another interesting research topic.

References

1. Aleliunas, R., Karp, R.M., Lipton, R.J., Lovasz, L., Rackoff, C.: Random walks, universal traversal sequences, and the complexity of maze problems. In: Proceedings of the IEEE Symposium on Foundations of Computer Science (FOCS), pp. 218–223 (1979)
2. Barrière, L., Flocchini, P., Fraigniaud, P., Santoro, N.: Capture of an intruder by mobile agents. In: Proceedings of the Symposium on Parallel Algorithms and Architectures (SPAA), pp. 200–209 (2002)
3. Blin, L., Fraigniaud, P., Nisse, N., Vial, S.: Distributed chasing of network intruders. In: Flocchini, P., Gasieniec, L. (eds.) SIROCCO 2006. LNCS, vol. 4056, pp. 70–84. Springer, Heidelberg (2006). doi:10.1007/11780823_7
4. Dieudonné, Y., Pelc, A., Villain, V.: How to meet asynchronously at polynomial cost. SIAM J. Comput. **44**(3), 844–867 (2015)
5. Efrat, A., Guibas, L.J., Har-Peled, S., Lin, D., Mitchell, J., Murali, T.: Sweeping simple polygon with a chain of guards. In: Proceedings of the Symposium on Discrete Algorithms (SODA), pp. 927–936 (2000)
6. Flocchini, P., Huang, M.J., Luccio, F.L.: Decontaminating chordal rings and tori using mobile agents. Int. J. Found. Comput. Sci. **18**(3), 547–563 (2007)
7. Flocchini, P., Huang, M.J., Luccio, F.L.: Decontamination of hypercubes by mobile agents. Networks **53**(3), 167–178 (2008)
8. Guibas, L., Latombe, J., LaValle, S., Lin, D., Motwani, R.: A visibility-based pursuit-evasion problem. Int. J. Comput. Geom. Appl. **9**(5), 471–494 (1999)

9. Ilcinkas, D., Nisse, N., Soguet, D.: The cost of monotonicity in distributed graph searching. Distrib. Comput. **22**, 117–127 (2009)
10. Kameda, T., Suzuki, I., Yamashita, M.: An alternative proof for the equivalence of ∞-searcher and 2-searcher. Theor. Comput. Sci. **634**, 108–119 (2016)
11. Koucký, M.: Universal traversal sequences with backtracking. J. Comput. Syst. Sci. **65**(4), 717–726 (2002)
12. LaPaugh, A.S.: Recontamination does not help to search a graph. J. ACM **40**(2), 224–245 (1993)
13. Lee, J.-H., Park, S.-M., Chwa, K.-Y.: Equivalence of search capability among mobile guards with various visibilities. In: Albers, S., Radzik, T. (eds.) ESA 2004. LNCS, vol. 3221, pp. 484–495. Springer, Heidelberg (2004). doi:10.1007/978-3-540-30140-0_44
14. Park, S.-M., Lee, J.-H., Chwa, K.-Y.: Visibility-based pursuit-evasion in a polygonal region by a searcher. In: Orejas, F., Spirakis, P.G., Leeuwen, J. (eds.) ICALP 2001. LNCS, vol. 2076, pp. 456–468. Springer, Heidelberg (2001). doi:10.1007/3-540-48224-5_38
15. Parsons, T.D.: Pursuit-evasion in a graph. In: Alavi, Y., Lick, D.R. (eds.) Theory and Applications of Graphs. Lecture Notes in Mathematics, vol. 642, pp. 426–441. Springer, Heidelberg (1976)
16. Reingold, O.: Undirected connectivity in log-space. J. ACM **55**(4), 17 (2008)
17. Suzuki, I., Yamashita, M.: Searching for a mobile intruder in a polygonal region. SIAM J. Comput. **21**(5), 863–888 (1992)
18. Urrutia, J.: Art gallery and illumination problems. In: Handbook of Computational Geometry, pp. 973–1022. Elsevier (2000)
19. Yamashita, M., Umemoto, H., Suzuki, I., Kameda, T.: Searching for mobile intruders in a polygonal region by a group of mobile searchers. Algorithmica **31**, 208–236 (2001)

Wait-Free Solvability of Colorless Tasks in Anonymous Shared-Memory Model

Nayuta Yanagisawa(✉)

Department of Mathematics, Graduate School of Science, Kyoto University, Kyoto 606-8502, Japan
nayuta87@math.kyoto-u.ac.jp

Abstract. We investigate the capability of distributed systems in the *anonymous asynchronous shared-memory model*, in which processes have no identifiers and communicate through multi-writer/multi-reader atomic registers. The present paper assumes that an arbitrary number of processes may fail by crashing.

We propose a *full-information protocol* for colorless tasks and give a topological characterization of colorless tasks that are wait-free solvable in the anonymous model. The characterization implies, as long as colorless tasks are concerned, that the anonymity does not reduce the computational power of the asynchronous shared-memory model.

Keywords: Anonymous system · Shared-memory · Wait-free solvability · Full-information protocol · Colorless task · Combinatorial topology

1 Introduction

In most of the studies on the theoretical distributed computing, it is routinely assumed that a distributed system is *non-anonymous*, i.e., processes have unique identifiers and are capable of using them. However, there are certain distributed systems, in which processes cannot make use of their identifiers. For example, peer-to-peer file sharing systems sometimes require anonymization for the reason of privacy [7]. In some sensor network, sensors do not even have identifiers [3]. In addition to the practical viewpoint, it is theoretically interesting to investigate whether the existence of unique identifiers is intrinsically needed for the design of distributed algorithms.

We investigate the capability of the *anonymous asynchronous shared-memory model*, in which processes with no identifier execute the identical code. We assume that an arbitrary number of processes may fail by crashing. Processes communicate via multi-writer/multi-reader (MWMR) atomic registers, which are initialized to some default value. We are not allowed to use single-writer shared registers, because they allow processes to identify themselves, conflicting with the notion of anonymity.

In the past few decades, the topological nature of distributed computing [22] has been extensively studied in the context of the (non-anonymous) fault-tolerant

B. Bonakdarpour and F. Petit (Eds.): SSS 2016, LNCS 10083, pp. 415–429, 2016.
DOI: 10.1007/978-3-319-49259-9_32

shared-memory computing. Most significantly, the asynchronous computability theorem [24], which gives a necessary and sufficient condition for decision tasks to be wait-free solvable, and impossibility results [13] for various decision tasks (e.g., renaming task and k-set agreement task) have been devised. The fundamental algorithmic tool in the topological theory of distributed computing is the *full-information protocol* [17], which is the most generic form of protocol that can instantiate any implementable protocol. This universality of the full-information protocol much simplifies the arguments on the computability issues.

We extend the topological theory of distributed computing to encompass the anonymous asynchronous shared-memory model. Specifically, we investigate the wait-free solvability of *colorless tasks* in the anonymous model. A colorless task is a specification that relates each input assignment to a set of possible output assignments without referring to which process has which value. In other words, a colorless task only concerns the set of values held in the system. Throughout this paper, we assume that the set of possible input values to each colorless task is finite. Colorless tasks cover a significant class of decision tasks such as consensus, set agreement, and loop agreement [14], [6], [19] and is extensively studied in the context of the non-anonymous shared-memory computing [20,21,23,28].

The primary obstacle to the topological theory of anonymous shared-memory computing is the lack of a full-information protocol. We propose a full-information protocol for colorless tasks, which we call the *anonymous full-information protocol*. In the protocol, different processes may write to an identical component of shared objects, though in which case they are forced to write an identical value. This prevents the value in a component from being overwritten by a different value, making the protocol full-informative. The protocol makes use of much more registers, in exchange for full-informativeness, compared with the corresponding non-anonymous protocol, which has the same computational power as the anonymous one.

We also give a topological characterization of colorless tasks that are wait-free solvable in the anonymous asynchronous shared-memory model. The characterization implies that the anonymity does not reduce the computational power of the asynchronous shared-memory model, as long as colorless tasks are concerned. That is, a colorless task is wait-free solvable in the non-anonymous model if and only if it is wait-free solvable in the anonymous one.

This computational equality indicates that topological arguments [17,19] for colorless tasks in the non-anonymous asynchronous shared-memory model would be applicable to the anonymous one. As an example, we show that it is undecidable whether a given decision task, which is not necessarily colorless, is wait-free solvable in the anonymous model. It is also implied that the classification of loop agreement tasks [19] is also possible in the anonymous model.

Herlihy and Shavit [24] have studied the shared-memory model with a sort of anonymity, in which processes have unique identifiers but are allowed to use them in a very restricted way. They have established the *anonymous computability theorem*, which gives a necessary and sufficient condition for a given decision task to be wait-free solvable in the model. The crucial difference between their work and the present paper is that they have assumed traditional single-writer/multi-reader (SWMR) registers. Thus, their results are not immediately applicable to our setting, where processes are not allowed to use identifiers at all and assume MWMR registers.

To summarize, the major contributions of the present paper are:

Full-information protocol We propose the anonymous full-information protocol for colorless tasks;

Characterization We give a topological characterization of colorless tasks that are wait-free solvable in the model;

Computational equality We show that the computational power of the anonymous model is essentially the same as that of the non-anonymous one, as long as colorless tasks are concerned. This leads to the undecidability of the wait-free solvability of decision tasks in the anonymous model.

This paper is organized as follows. Section 2 provides some basic definitions and elementary facts in combinatorial topology. Section 3 describes the anonymous asynchronous shared-memory model and the colorless task. In Sect. 4, we give a formal and detailed description of the anonymous full-information protocol and study its space complexity. Section 5 presents our main results, a characterization of colorless tasks that are wait-free solvable in the anonymous model and the computational equality between the anonymous model and the non-anonymous one. Section 6 concludes the paper and presents directions for further research.

Related Work

Colorless tasks have been firstly introduced by Herlihy and Rajsbaum [18], under the name of convergence tasks, to analyze decidability of distributed decision tasks. Herlihy and Rajsbaum [20] have given a characterization of colorless tasks that are solvable in the non-anonymous asynchronous shared-memory model with adversarial schedulers characterized by core and survivor set [26]. Mendes et al. [28] have given a necessary and a sufficient condition for colorless tasks to have a t-resilient protocol in asynchronous Byzantine systems. Herlihy et al. [23] have given a topological characterization of colorless tasks that are solvable with n processes in the d-solo model.

Herlihy et al. [17] have discussed (non-anonymous) colorless protocols, in which each process only uses process identifiers for accessing shared objects. In other words, the local computation of each process is ignorant of process identifiers. Our anonymous full-information protocol can be seen as a totally anonymous variant of the colorless layered immediate snapshot protocol, found in Chap. 4 of [17].

Gafni and Koutsoupias [15] have firstly shown that the wait-free solvability for three or more processes is undecidable in the non-anonymous asynchronous shared-memory model. This undecidability result has been extended to encompass other models by Herlihy and Rajsbaum [18].

Guerraoui and Ruppert [16] have studied, for the first time, which object can be implemented in the anonymous asynchronous shared-memory model prone to crash failures. Especially, they propose an anonymous wait-free implementation of the atomic snapshot object. Ruppert [29] has been investigated the wait-free solvability of consensus and naming in anonymous systems with shared objects of various types. To the best of author's knowledge, the nature of the failure-prone anonymous model has not been well-studied, not only from the topological viewpoint but also from the operational one.

Several papers have investigated computability issues over the failure-free anonymous asynchronous shared-memory model with MWMR atomic registers. Attiya et al. [5] have shown that consensus is solvable in the model, in which shared registers are initialized to some default value, and the number of processes is not known. They have also given a characterization of the class of consensus-like decision tasks, called agreement tasks, that are solvable in the model. Besides, Jayanti and Toueg [25] have shown that consensus is not solvable if shared registers are not initialized to any known state.

There have been many papers, starting from [2], that have investigated the computability and complexity of the anonymous message-passing model.

There has been a series of works, starting from [8], that have investigated the homonymous message-passing model, in which ℓ distinct identifiers are assigned to n processes ($1 \leq \ell \leq n$) and several processes may be assigned the same identifier. The anonymous model and the non-anonymous model can be seen as the two extreme cases of the homonymous model, i.e., $\ell = 1$ and $\ell = n$. Delporte-Gallet et al. have studied necessary and sufficient conditions for the Byzantine agreement problem to be solvable in both the asynchronous model [8,9] and the synchronous model [10].

2 Topological Preliminaries

In this section, we briefly present some topological notions that are commonly used in the topological theory of distributed computing. See [17] or [30] for more detailed discussions.

2.1 Abstract Simplicial Complex

A *finite abstract simplicial complex* K on a finite set $V(K)$ of *vertices* is a family of nonempty subsets of $V(K)$, called *abstract simplices*, such that

1. $\{v\} \in K$ for every $v \in V(K)$.
2. $s \in K$ and $s' \subseteq s$ imply $s' \in K$.

If there is no ambiguity, we occasionally write *simplex* and *complex*, dropping the prefix 'abstract'. A subset of a simplex s is called a *face* of s. A *subcomplex* L of a complex K is a subset of K that is also a complex. The *closure* of $S \subseteq K$, denoted by $\operatorname{Cl} S$, is the smallest subcomplex of K that contains S.

A simplex $s \in K$ is said to be of *dimension* $\#s - 1$, denoted by $\dim s$, where $\#s$ represents the cardinality of s. The dimension of a complex K, denoted by $\dim K$, is defined to be the maximum dimension of simplices contained in K. The *k-skeleton* $\mathrm{skel}^k K$ of a complex K is a subcomplex of K such that $\mathrm{skel}^k K = \{s \in K \mid \dim s \leq k\}$.

Let K_1 and K_2 be complexes. A *simplicial map* $\phi : K_1 \to K_2$ is a function from $V(K_1)$ to $V(K_2)$ such that $s \in K_1$ implies $\phi(s) \in K_2$, where $\phi(s)$ is the image of s. It is easy to see that the composition of any two simplicial maps is also a simplicial map.

A *carrier map* Φ from K_1 to K_2 is a mapping $\Phi : K_1 \to 2^{K_2}$ such that

1. $\Phi(s)$ is a subcomplex of K_2 for every $s \in K_1$.
2. $s \in K_1$ and $s' \subseteq s$ imply $\Phi(s') \subseteq \Phi(s)$.

We write $\Phi(L_1) = \cup_{s \in L_1} \Phi(s)$ for a subcomplex L_1 of K_1. Any pair of carrier maps are composed to a carrier map in a trivial way.

2.2 Geometric Realization

Given an abstract simplicial complex K, we associate a corresponding topological space $|K| \subseteq \mathbb{R}^d$, called the *geometric realization* of K, for a sufficiently large positive integer d. For a simplex $s = \{v_0, \ldots, v_n\} \in K$, $|s|$ denotes the convex hull of $v_0, \ldots, v_n$ that are placed in $\mathbb{R}^d$ in affinely independent positions. Let $|K| = \cup_{s \in K} |s|$, the union of all convex hulls of simplices in K so that every set of common faces of simplices are identified. This construction is unique up to homeomorphism.

Let K_1 and K_2 be complexes, and $\phi : K_1 \to K_2$ be a simplicial map. The map ϕ induces a continuous map $|\phi| : |K_1| \to |K_2|$ such that $|\phi|$ maps $|v| \in |\mathrm{skel}^0 K_1|$ to $|\phi(v)| \in |\mathrm{skel}^0 K_2|$, and is extended linearly to other points in $|K_1|$.

Let $f : |K_1| \to |K_2|$ be a continuous map and $\Delta : K_1 \to K_2$ be a carrier map. The map f is said to be *carried by* Δ if $f(|s|) \subseteq |\Delta(s)|$ for every $s \in K_1$. A simplicial map $\phi : K_1 \to K_2$ is called a *simplicial approximation* to f if $f(x) \in |s_2|$ implies $|\phi|(x) \in |s_2|$ for every $x \in |K_1|$ and $s_2 \in K_2$.

Lemma 1 ([30, Corollary 3.4.4]). *Let $f : |K_1| \to |K_2|$ be a continuous map such that $f(|L_1|) \subseteq |L_2|$ for $L_1 \subseteq K_1$ and $L_2 \subseteq K_2$ and let $\phi : K_1 \to K_2$ be a simplicial approximation to f. Then $\phi|_{L_1}$ maps L_1 to L_2 and is a simplicial approximation to $f|_{|L_1|}$.*

2.3 Barycentric Subdivision

A complex K_1 is said to be a *subdivision* of a complex K_2 if $|K_1| = |K_2|$, and furthermore, for each simplex $s_2 \in K_2$, there is a subcomplex L_1 of K_1 such that $|s_2| = |L_1|$.

Let K be a complex. Its *barycentric subdivision*, denoted by $\mathrm{Bary} K$, is defined to be a complex whose every vertex is a simplex of K. A simplex of $\mathrm{Bary} K$ is a

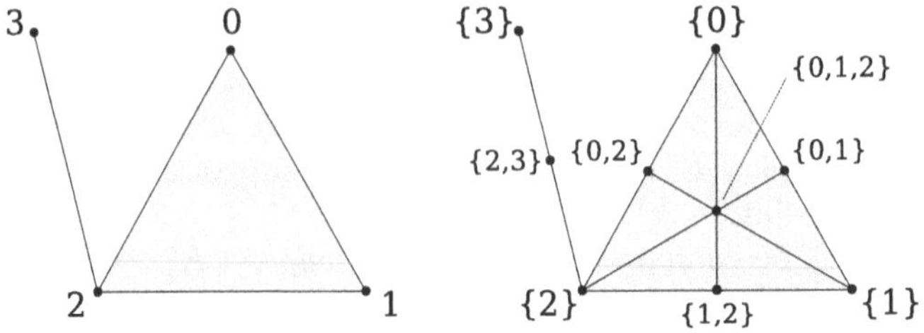

Fig. 1. A complex K and its barycentric subdivision Bary$K$

set $\{s_0, \ldots, s_k\}$ such that $s_0 \subsetneq \cdots \subsetneq s_k$. To see that the barycentric subdivision is actually a subdivision, see the example Fig. 1.

Bary s denotes Bary Cl $\{s\}$ for $s \in K$. The barycentric subdivision induces a carrier map from K to Bary$K$, by which $s \in K$ is mapped to Bary s. The carrier map is denoted by Bary : $K \to$ Bary$K$ for an abuse of notation.

We write Bary$^b K$ for the *b-iterated barycentric subdivision* of K, that is, Bary$^b K$ = Bary(Bary$^{b-1} K$) with Bary$^0 K = K$.

Lemma 2 ([17, Theorem 3.7.5]). *Let K_1 and K_2 be simplicial complexes. Given a continuous map $f : |K_1| \to |K_2|$, there is a non-negative integer b such that f has a simplicial approximation ϕ :* Bary$^b K_1 \to K_2$.

3 Anonymous Model and Colorless Tasks

In this section, we briefly describe the anonymous asynchronous shared-memory model and the colorless tasks.

3.1 Anonymous Asynchronous Shared-Memory Model

In the *anonymous asynchronous shared-memory model* [5], a distributed system consists of $n + 1$ sequential processes that have no identifiers. The processes are programmed identically and communicate through reliable MWMR *atomic registers*, which are initialized to some default value. A register is said to be *bounded* (resp., *unbounded*) if the set of values that can be stored in the register is finite (resp., infinite).

We assume that an arbitrary number of processes may fail by *crashing*, in which case they simply halt and remain silent. Moreover, we assume that the number of processes is known in advance.

In this paper, we are solely concerned with *wait-free protocols*, in which every non-faulty process terminates in a finite number of steps regardless of other processes' behavior. We call a protocol that works in the anonymous model an *anonymous protocol*. We sometimes refer to the processes by unique identifiers $p_0, \ldots, p_n$ for the convenience of exposition, but processes themselves have no means to access these identifiers.

Without loss of generality, we may assume that, in addition to the ordinary atomic registers, processes can communicate through MWMR *atomic snapshot objects* [16], which have an anonymous wait-free implementation from atomic registers. An atomic snapshot object consists of m-component ($1 < m < \infty$), and supports two types of operations $\texttt{update}_i$ and $\texttt{scan}$. Each $\texttt{update}_i$ operation atomically writes a value into the i-th component, and each $\texttt{scan}$ operation atomically reads the contents of all the components.

The traditional asynchronous shared-memory model [27], in which processes have unique identifiers and are capable of using them, is referred to as the *non-anonymous* asynchronous shared-memory model. A protocol for the non-anonymous model is called a *non-anonymous protocol.*

3.2 Colorless Tasks

Throughout this paper, we are solely concerned with a class of decision tasks called *colorless tasks* [17].

Definition 3. *A* colorless task *is a triple* $T = (I, O, \Delta)$, *where* I *and* O *are simplicial complexes and* $\Delta : I \to 2^O$ *is a carrier map. We assume that* $\dim I < n+1$ *and* $\dim O < n+1$.

I and O are called input complex and output complex, respectively. The set of vertices $V(I)$ (resp., $V(O)$) consists of possible input (resp., output) values for the system. Each simplex in I (resp., O) represents a possible set of inputs (resp., output) values of the task. Being colorless, values in $V(I)$ nor $V(O)$ contains no information on processes' identifiers.

A colorless task specifies protocols in the following way: Each process starts with its own input value $v \in V(I)$, where distinct processes can have the same input value. In each execution path, if the set of all input values s is in I, then the set of all output values must be in $\Delta(s)$.

If there is an anonymous (resp., non-anonymous) wait-free protocol that realizes such executions, we say that the colorless task is *anonymously* (resp., *non-anonymously*) *wait-free solvable.*

The following observation holds because every anonymous protocol trivially works as a non-anonymous one.

Lemma 4. *If a colorless task* T *is anonymously wait-free solvable,* T *is also non-anonymously wait-free solvable.*

Colorless tasks cover a significant class of decision tasks, e.g., consensus, k-set agreement, and loop agreement tasks [14], [6], [19], [17]. On the other hand, they do not cover decision tasks concerning process identifiers (e.g., renaming task [4]) and ones with unbounded input values (e.g., approximate agreement task [11]).

Let us see some examples of colorless tasks. We define

$$D^2 = \{\{0\}, \{1\}, \{2\}, \{0,1\}, \{1,2\}, \{2,0\}, \{0,1,2\}\}.$$

Example 5. Let b be a positive integer. The *b-iterated barycentric agreement task* with an input complex I is a colorless task $T_b = (I, \mathrm{Bary}^b I, \mathrm{Bary}^b)$. We will see later that T_b is anonymously wait-free solvable for any input complex I.

Example 6. The *k-set agreement task* with an input complex I is a colorless task $T = (I, \mathrm{skel}^k I, \mathrm{skel}^k)$, where $\mathrm{skel}^k s$ is defined to be $\mathrm{skel}^k(\mathrm{Cl}\{s\})$ for $s \in I$. It is known that T is not non-anonymously wait-free solvable for $k < n+1$ [17,24].

Example 7. Assume that K is a 2-dimensional complex, and ℓ is a simple edge loop in K, which is divided into three distinct edge path $\ell_{0,1}$, $\ell_{1,2}$, $\ell_{0,2}$ by points v_0, v_1, v_2 (see Fig. 2).

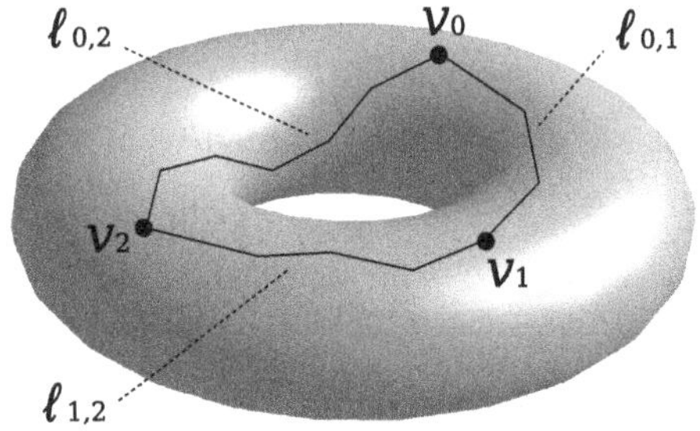

Fig. 2. A 2-dim. complex K and a simple edge loop ℓ

The *loop agreement task* with a triangle loop ℓ is a colorless task $T_{K,\ell} = (D^2, K, \Delta)$, where the carrier map Δ is defined by

$$\Delta(s) = \begin{cases} v_i & \text{if } s = \{i\}, \\ \ell_{i,j} & \text{if } s = \{i,j\}, 0 \le i < j \le 2, \\ K & \text{if } s = \{0,1,2\}. \end{cases}$$

See [19] or [17] for more detailed treatments of the loop agreement task.

The followings are the fundamental theorems about the non-anonymous wait-free solvability of colorless tasks.

Theorem 8 ([20, Theorem 4.3]). *A colorless task $T = (I, O, \Delta)$ is non-anonymously wait-free solvable if and only if there is a continuous map $f : |I| \to |O|$ carried by Δ.*

Theorem 9 ([18, Theorems 1 and 2]). *It is undecidable whether a given loop agreement task is non-anonymously wait-free solvable, where $n \ge 2$.*

Theorem 8 characterize the non-anonymous wait-free solvability of colorless tasks in a purely topological manner and Theorem 9 implies the undecidability of general decision tasks for three or more processes. In Sect. 5, we will establish counterparts to these theorems for the anonymous systems.

4 Full-Information Protocol and Space Complexity

In this section, we introduce a full-information protocol for anonymous systems and study its space complexity.

4.1 Anonymous Full-Information Protocol

We propose an *anonymous full-information protocol*, a generic form of protocol that can instantiate any implementable protocol for colorless tasks. The protocol makes use of multiple atomic snapshot objects and is a variant of the (non-anonymous) *colorless layered immediate snapshot protocol* [17], which makes use of SWMR immediate snapshot objects. This universality of our protocol will be shown in Sect. 5.

The fundamental idea that makes the protocol full-informative, even in the anonymous setting, is to let processes write the same value to the same component of an atomic snapshot object. This implies that once a value written to a component, the value is never overwritten by a different value. To achieve this, we index components by possible values to be written, in place of process identifiers, and permit each process to write a value v only to a register indexed by the very value v.

Figure 3 presents the anonymous full-information protocol for a colorless task $T = (I, O, \Delta)$. The protocol, denoted by $P_{(b,\delta)}$, is characterized by two parameters, i.e., a non-negative integer b and a simplicial map $\delta : \mathrm{Bary}^b I \to O$, called a *decision map*. The protocol uses b distinct atomic snapshot object $\mathtt{SM}_0, \ldots, \mathtt{SM}_{b-1}$, where each $\mathtt{SM}_\ell$ is an m_ℓ-component atomic snapshot object with m_ℓ being the cardinality of $V(\mathrm{Bary}^\ell I)$. Let $f_\ell : V(\mathrm{Bary}^\ell I) \to [\#\mathrm{Bary}^\ell I]$ be an injective map for $\ell = 0, \ldots, b-1$, where $[\#\mathrm{Bary}^\ell I]$ denotes the set of natural numbers less than $\#\mathrm{Bary}^\ell I$.

```
1 P_(b,δ)(input)
2     view:=input
3     for ℓ:=0 to b−1 do
4         SM_ℓ.update_{f_ℓ(view)}(view)
5         snap:=SM_ℓ.scan
6         view:= set of values in snap
7     return δ(view)
```

Fig. 3. An anonymous full-information protocol $P_{(b,\delta)}$

In the protocol $P_{(b,\delta)}$, each process starts with its private input value (line 1) and assigns the value to a local variable `view` (line 2). Next, the process iterates b-times, writing its `view` to the component indexed by $f_\ell(\mathtt{view})$, taking a snapshot and updating its `view` (line 3–6). Then the process determines its output value by applying the map δ to the value of `view` (line 7).

Example 10. Figure 4 represents an execution path of the protocol $P(2, \delta)$. In the figure, the process q starts with value 0, writes its view to the component of $\mathtt{SM}_0$ indexed by $f_0(0)$, and takes a snapshot, updating the view by the result $\{0, 1\}$ of the snapshot, whilst the other processes p and r interleave their updates and scans. The protocol execution finishes with process q's write of its view to the component of $\mathtt{SM}_1$ indexed by $f_1(\{0, 1\})$ and a snapshot, updating the view by the result $\{\{0\}, \{0, 1\}\}$ of the most recent snapshot. Finally, the process q halts with its output $\delta(\{\{0\}, \{0, 1\}\})$.

p	q	r
Update$_{f_0(0)}$(0)		
scan		
		Update$_{f_0(1)}$(1)
	Update$_{f_0(0)}$(0)	
		scan
	scan	
Update$_{f_1(\{0\})}$({0})		
scan		
		Update$_{f_1(\{0,1\})}$({0,1})
		scan
	Update$_{f_1(\{0,1\})}$({0,1})	
	scan	

Fig. 4. An execution of $P_{(2,\delta)}$

It might look redundant to hold a value v at each component indexed by the very same value v. As a matter of fact, it is enough to write a constant value, say 1, to each component, which is initially 0, as presented in Fig. 5. However, we stick to the presentation in Fig. 3 because it corresponds fairly well to the colorless layered immediate snapshot protocol [17] and is easier to understand.

Theorem 11. *The full-information protocol* $P(b, \mathrm{id})$ *solves the* b*-iterated barycentric subdivision task* $T_b = (I, \mathrm{Bary}^b I, \mathrm{Bary}^b)$ *for any input complex* I*, where* $\mathrm{id} : \mathrm{Bary}^b I \to \mathrm{Bary}^b I$ *denotes an identity map.*

Proof. We prove the theorem by induction on b. The base case basically follows the structure of the proof of Theorem 4.2.8 in [17].

For the base case $b = 1$, assume that the set of all inputs to $P(1, \mathrm{id})$ is $s \in I$, and s_i is the output value of the process p_i. It holds that $s_i \subseteq s$ for any i, and either $s_i \subseteq s_j$ or $s_j \subseteq s_i$ for any i and j by the atomicity of the atomic snapshot object. Thus, the set of all outputs of $P(1, \mathrm{id})$ must be $t = \{s_{i_0}, \ldots, s_{i_k}\}$ for some chain $s_{i_0} \subseteq \cdots \subseteq s_{i_k}$. t is a simplex of $\mathrm{Bary}\, s$ by the definition, and this shows that $P(1, \mathrm{id})$ solves T_1.

```
P'_(b,δ)(input)
    view:=input
    for ℓ:=0 to b−1 do
        SM_ℓ.update_{f_ℓ(view)}(1)
        snap:=SM_ℓ.scan
        view:={f_ℓ^{-1}(i) | SM_ℓ[i] = 1}
    return δ(view)
```

Fig. 5. A variant of $P(b, \delta)$ that writes only 1-bit

For the induction step, we prove that the protocol $P(b, \mathrm{id})$ solves the task $T_b = (I, \mathrm{Bary}^b I, \mathrm{Bary}^b)$. The protocol $P(b, \mathrm{id})$ can be seen as a successive execution of protocols $P(b-1, \mathrm{id})$ and $P(1, \mathrm{id})$ as shown in Fig. 6, where input complexes for $P(b-1, \mathrm{id})$ and $P(1, \mathrm{id})$ are I and $\mathrm{Bary}^{b-1} I$ respectively. Note that $P(b-1, \mathrm{id})$ and $P(1, \mathrm{id})$ use distinct atomic snapshot objects.

```
Protocol(input)
    view:=input
    view:=P(b−1,id)(view)
    view:=P(1,id)(view)
    return id(view)
```

Fig. 6. Protocol $P(b, \mathrm{id})$, unwound

If the set of all inputs to $P(b, \mathrm{id})$ is $s \in I$, the set of all inputs to the subprotocol $P(b-1, \mathrm{id})$ is s or its face. In that case, the set t of all outputs of $P(b-1, \mathrm{id})$ is in $\mathrm{Bary}^{b-1} s$ by induction hypothesis. Then, the set of all inputs to the subprotocol $P(1, \mathrm{id})$ is t or its face, and the set of all outputs of $P(1, \mathrm{id})$ is in $\mathrm{Bary}\, t$, which is a subcomplex of $\mathrm{Bary}^b s$, by the case of $b = 1$. This implies that $P(b, \mathrm{id})$ solves $T_b = (I, \mathrm{Bary}^b I, \mathrm{Bary}^b)$. □

4.2 Space Complexity of Anonymous Protocols

The *anonymous* protocol $P(b, \delta)$ makes use of a considerably larger number of registers compared to the corresponding *non-anonymous* protocol that has the same computational power as $P(b, \delta)$.

The protocol $P(b, \delta)$ uses b distinct $(\#\mathrm{Bary}^\ell I)$-component atomic snapshot object for $\ell = 0, \ldots, b-1$, where I is the input complex. Currently, only a few anonymous wait-free implementation of the atomic snapshot object are known. Here we make use of the one proposed by Guerraoui and Ruppert [16] and Ellen et al. [12], which uses $m + (n+1)$ unbounded registers for the m-component snapshot. Thus, the number of registers used in the protocol is

$$\sum_{\ell=0,\ldots,b-1} \left(\#\mathrm{Bary}^\ell I + (n+1)\right) = \sum_{\ell=0,\ldots,b-1} \#\mathrm{Bary}^\ell I + b(n+1).$$

An m-component atomic snapshot object needs $m+(n+1)$ unbounded registers, even if each update operation only writes 1-bit.

Let k be $\dim I$. It is easy to see that $\#\mathrm{Bary}^b I > (k!)^b$ by counting k-dimensional faces of $\mathrm{Bary}^b I$. Thus, the protocol makes use of more than $(k!)^b + b(n+1)$ unbounded registers.

On the other hand, the non-anonymous protocol, presented in Fig. 7, only makes use of b distinct single-writer $(n+1)$-component snapshot objects, and wait-free solves the class of colorless tasks solved by $P(b, \delta)$ precisely. It is known that $n+1$ unbounded registers are enough for non-anonymous wait-free implementation of the single-writer $(n+1)$-component snapshot object [1]. Thus, the protocol uses only $b(n+1)$ unbounded registers.

```
Protocol(input_i)
    view:=input_i
    for ℓ:=0 to b−1 do
        SM_ℓ.update_i(view)
        snap:=SM_ℓ.scan
        view:= set of values in snap
    return δ(view)
```

Fig. 7. A non-anonymous full-information protocol for p_i

The above observation implies that the protocol $P(b, \delta)$ requires much more registers compared to the corresponding non-anonymous one, especially when the dimension of the input complex I and the number of iteration b are large.

5 Characterization of Wait-Free Solvability

We give a topological characterization of colorless tasks that are anonymously wait-free solvable. The characterization is formally stated as follows.

Theorem 12. *A colorless task $T = (I, O, \Delta)$ is anonymously wait-free solvable if and only if there is a continuous map $f : |I| \to |O|$ carried by Δ.*

Proof. The only if part immediately follows from Lemma 4 and Theorem 8.

For the if part, let $f : |I| \to |O|$ be a continuous map carried by Δ and $\delta : \mathrm{Bary}^b I \to O$ be its simplicial approximation. Lemma 1 implies that δ satisfies $\delta(\mathrm{Bary}^b s) \subseteq \Delta(s)$ for every $s \in I$. We now prove that the full-information protocol $P(b, \delta)$ solves the task T for the above b and δ. The protocol $P(b, \delta)$ can be seen as an operation, in which each process executes the protocol $P(b, \mathrm{id})$ as a subprotocol, and then the process determines its output according to the decision map δ. If the set of all inputs to $P(b, \delta)$ is $s \in I$, the set of all outputs of the subprotocol $P(b, \mathrm{id})$ must be in $t \in \mathrm{Bary}^b s$ by Theorem 11, and it is mapped into $\Delta(s)$ by $\delta : \mathrm{Bary}^b I \to O$. This completes the proof. □

The theorem shows that the anonymous wait-free solvability of colorless tasks can be characterized in a purely topological manner with no explicit mention to a concrete protocol or its executions. A colorless task $T = (I, O, \Delta)$ is anonymously wait-free solvable if and only if there is a continuous map $f : |I| \to |O|$, which is consistent with the carrier map Δ.

The proof of Theorem 12 also implies that the anonymous full-information protocol is universal for colorless tasks, i.e., every anonymously wait-free solvable colorless task is solved by the anonymous full-information protocol.

Interestingly, the solvability condition of Theorem 12 is superficially the same as one for the non-anonymous model. Theorems 8 and 12 establish the following computational equality.

Theorem 13. *A colorless task is anonymously wait-free solvable if and only if it is non-anonymously wait-free solvable.*

As a consequence of Theorem 13, the following undecidability results hold.

Proposition 14. *It is undecidable whether a loop agreement task is anonymously wait-free solvable, where $n \geq 2$.*

Proof. The proposition is clear from Theorems 9 and 13. □

Proposition 15. *It is undecidable whether a decision task, which is not necessarily colorless, is wait-free solvable in the anonymous asynchronous shared-memory model, where $n \geq 2$.*

Proof. The proposition immediately follows from Proposition 14 because general decision tasks include colorless tasks. □

We can also show that the classification of loop agreement tasks [19] is possible in the anonymous asynchronous shared-memory model. This means that there is an infinite hierarchy based on the mutually implementability of colorless tasks in the anonymous model as so is in the non-anonymous one. The proof is similar to the non-anonymous case [17,19].

6 Conclusion and Further Research

We have extended the topological theory of distributed computing to encompass the anonymous asynchronous shared-memory model, in which the number of processes is a priori known. Specifically, we have proposed the anonymous full-information protocol and given a topological characterization of colorless tasks that are wait-free solvable in the model. Our characterization implies that the anonymity does not reduce, as long as colorless tasks are concerned, the computational power of the asynchronous shared-memory model. We have also proved that the wait-free solvability of general decision tasks is undecidable in the anonymous model.

It is easy to see that the very same results would hold for the homonymous asynchronous shared-memory model prone to crash failures, because the homonymous model [8] is at least as powerful as the anonymous model. On the other hand, we cannot immediately extend our results to anonymous system with unbounded number of processes, because existing anonymous wait-free implementations of atomic snapshot object inherently use the information about the number of processes in the system [16].

A promising research direction would be to extend our characterization to the case of general decision tasks, giving a *totally anonymous version* of the asynchronous computability theorem [24]. To do this, our anonymous full-information protocol is insufficient because the protocol is ignorant of the initial values given to the processes. We would need to devise a new full-information protocol, which conveys richer information including initial values of processes.

It would also be interesting to investigate solvability of colorless tasks in the anonymous model with adversarial schedulers that are characterized by core and survivor set [26]. The situation would be harder than the non-anonymous case [20] because physically different processes with the same local state are indistinguishable, and thus each process cannot simply wait for other processes in the anonymous model, even if only a few processes would fail.

Acknowledgement. I would like to express my gratitude to Prof. Susumu Nishimura for enlightening discussion and helpful advice on writing this paper.

References

1. Afek, Y., Attiya, H., Dolev, D., Gafni, E., Merritt, M., Shavit, N.: Atomic snapshots of shared memory. J. ACM **40**(4), 873–890 (1993)
2. Angluin, D.: Local and global properties in networks of processors. In: Proceedings of 12th ACM Symposium on Theory of Computing, pp. 82–93. ACM, New York (1980)
3. Angluin, D., Aspnes, J., Diamadi, Z., Fischer, M.J., Peralta, R.: Computation in networks of passively mobile finite-state sensors. Distrib. Comput. **18**(4), 235–253 (2006)
4. Attiya, H., Bar-Noy, A., Dolev, D., Peleg, D., Reischuk, R.: Renaming in an asynchronous environment. J. ACM **37**(3), 524–548 (1990)
5. Attiya, H., Gorbach, A., Moran, S.: Computing in totally anonymous asynchronous shared memory systems. Inf. Comput. **173**(2), 162–183 (2002)
6. Chaudhuri, S.: More choices allow more faults: set consensus problems in totally asynchronous systems. Inf. Comput. **105**(1), 132–158 (1993)
7. Chothia, T., Chatzikokolakis, K.: A survey of anonymous peer-to-peer file-sharing. In: Enokido, T., Yan, L., Xiao, B., Kim, D., Dai, Y., Yang, L.T. (eds.) EUC 2005. LNCS, vol. 3823, pp. 744–755. Springer, Heidelberg (2005). doi:10.1007/11596042_77
8. Delporte-Gallet, C., Fauconnier, H., Guerraoui, R., Kermarrec, A.M., Ruppert, E., et al.: Byzantine agreement with homonyms. In: Proceedings of 30th ACM SIGACT-SIGOPS Symposium on Principles of Distributed Computing, pp. 21–30. ACM, New York (2011)
9. Delporte-Gallet, C., Fauconnier, H., Guerraoui, R., Kermarrec, A.M., Ruppert, E., et al.: Byzantine agreement with homonyms. Distrib. Comput. **26**(5–6), 321–340 (2013)

10. Delporte-Gallet, C., Fauconnier, H., Tran-The, H.: Byzantine agreement with homonyms in synchronous systems. In: Bononi, L., Datta, A.K., Devismes, S., Misra, A. (eds.) ICDCN 2012. LNCS, vol. 7129, pp. 76–90. Springer, Heidelberg (2012). doi:10.1007/978-3-642-25959-3_6
11. Dolev, D., Lynch, N.A., Pinter, S.S., Stark, E.W., Weihl, W.E.: Reaching approximate agreement in the presence of faults. J. ACM **33**(3), 499–516 (1986)
12. Ellen, F., Fatourou, P., Ruppert, E.: The space complexity of unbounded timestamps. Distrib. Comput. **21**(2), 103–115 (2008)
13. Fich, F., Ruppert, E.: Hundreds of impossibility results for distributed computing. Distrib. Comput. **16**(2–3), 121–163 (2003)
14. Fischer, M.J., Lynch, N.A., Paterson, M.S.: Impossibility of distributed consensus with one faulty process. J. ACM **32**(2), 374–382 (1985)
15. Gafni, E., Koutsoupias, E.: Three-processor tasks are undecidable. SIAM J. Comput. **28**(3), 970–983 (1999)
16. Guerraoui, R., Ruppert, E.: Anonymous and fault-tolerant shared-memory computing. Distrib. Comput. **20**(3), 165–177 (2007)
17. Herlihy, M., Kozlov, D., Rajsbaum, S.: Distributed Computing Through Combinatorial Topology. Morgan Kaufmann, San Francisco (2013)
18. Herlihy, M., Rajsbaum, S.: The decidability of distributed decision tasks. In: Proceedings of Symposium on Theory of Computing, pp. 589–598. ACM, New York (1997)
19. Herlihy, M., Rajsbaum, S.: A classification of wait-free loop agreement tasks. Theor. Comput. Sci. **291**(1), 55–77 (2003)
20. Herlihy, M., Rajsbaum, S.: The topology of shared-memory adversaries. In: Proceedings of 29th ACM SIGACT-SIGOPS Symposium on Principles of Distributed Computing, pp. 105–113. ACM, New York (2010)
21. Herlihy, M., Rajsbaum, S.: Simulations and reductions for colorless tasks. In: Proceedings of 2012 ACM Symposium on Principles of Distributed Computing, pp. 253–260. ACM, New York (2012)
22. Herlihy, M., Rajsbaum, S., Raynal, M.: Power and limits of distributed computing shared memory models. Theor. Comput. Sci. **509**, 3–24 (2013)
23. Herlihy, M., Rajsbaum, S., Raynal, M., Stainer, J.: Computing in the presence of concurrent solo executions. In: Pardo, A., Viola, A. (eds.) LATIN 2014. LNCS, vol. 8392, pp. 214–225. Springer, Heidelberg (2014). doi:10.1007/978-3-642-54423-1_19
24. Herlihy, M., Shavit, N.: The topological structure of asynchronous computability. J. ACM **46**(6), 858–923 (1999)
25. Jayanti, P., Toueg, S.: Wakeup under read/write atomicity. In: Leeuwen, J., Santoro, N. (eds.) WDAG 1990. LNCS, vol. 486, pp. 277–288. Springer, Heidelberg (1991). doi:10.1007/3-540-54099-7_19
26. Junqueira, F.P., Marzullo, K.: Synchronous consensus for dependent process failures. In: Proceedings of 23rd International Conference on Distributed Computing Systems, pp. 274–283. IEEE (2003)
27. Lynch, N.A.: Distributed Algorithms. Morgan Kaufmann, San Francisco (1996)
28. Mendes, H., Tasson, C., Herlihy, M.: Distributed computability in Byzantine asynchronous systems. In: Proceedings of 46th ACM Symposium on Theory of Computing, pp. 704–713. ACM, New York (2014)
29. Ruppert, E.: The anonymous consensus hierarchy and naming problems. In: Tovar, E., Tsigas, P., Fouchal, H. (eds.) OPODIS 2007. LNCS, vol. 4878, pp. 386–400. Springer, Heidelberg (2007). doi:10.1007/978-3-540-77096-1_28
30. Spanier, E.: Algebraic Topology, vol. 55. McGraw-Hill, New York (1966). (reprinted by Springer-Verlag)

Author Index